Dynamic Modeling of Monetary and Fiscal Cooperation Among Nations

Dynamic Modeling and Econometrics in Economics and Finance

VOLUME 8

Aims and Scope

The series will place particular focus on monographs, surveys, edited volumes, conference proceedings and handbooks on:

- Nonlinear dynamic phenomena in economics and finance, including equilibrium, disequilibrium, optimizing and adaptive evolutionary points of view; nonlinear and complex dynamics in microeconomics, finance, macroeconomics and applied fields of economics.

- Econometric and statistical methods for analysis of nonlinear processes in economics and finance, including computational methods, numerical tools and software to study nonlinear dependence, asymmetries, persistence of fluctuations, multiple equilibria, chaotic and bifurcation phenomena.

- Applications linking theory and empirical analysis in areas such as macrodynamics, microdynamics, asset pricing, financial analysis and portfolio analysis, international economics, resource dynamics and environment, industrial organization and dynamics of technical change, labor economics, demographics, population dynamics, and game theory.

The target audience of this series includes researchers at universities and research and policy institutions, students at graduate institutions, and practitioners in economics, finance and international economics in private or government institutions.

Dynamic Modeling of Monetary and Fiscal Cooperation Among Nations

by

Joseph Plasmans
University of Antwerp, Belgium and Tilburg University, The Netherlands

Jacob Engwerda
Tilburg University, The Netherlands

Bas van Aarle
University of Maastricht, The Netherlands

Giovanni Di Bartolomeo
University of Rome "La Sapienza", Rome, Italy

and

Tomasz Michalak
University of Antwerp, Belgium

Springer

A C.I.P. Catalogue record for this book is available from the Library of Congress.

ISBN-10 0-387-27931-8 (e-book)
ISBN-13: 978-1-4419-3910-4
ISBN-13 978-0-387-27931-2 (e-book)

Published by Springer,
P.O. Box 17, 3300 AA Dordrecht, The Netherlands.

www.springer.com

Printed on acid-free paper

Printed in the Netherlands.

Contents

Preface ix
Acknowledgement xi
List of abbreviations xiii
List of symbols xv

1 International Policy Coordination **1**
1.1 Introduction 1
1.2 The textbook approach 3
1.3 A more general view 7
1.3.1 Can cooperation be counterproductive? 7
1.3.2 Cooperation, commitment and credibility 9
1.3.3 The rule of uncertainty 10
1.4 Monetary and fiscal coordination in an MU 11
1.4.1 Principles of a monetary union 11
1.4.2 A textbook illustration of the OCA problem 13
1.4.3 Monetary and fiscal policy in an MU 14
1.5 Coordination at work - the EMU 16
1.5.1 European monetary integration processes 16
1.5.2 Design of monetary and fiscal policies 19
1.5.3 Asymmetries in macroeconomic shocks, policy preferences, sizes and structures 21
1.5.4 Macroeconomic policy coordination 21
1.5.5 A textbook example of policy coordination in the EMU . 24
1.5.6 Brief general literature overview 28
1.6 Coordination at work - other international arrangements 30
1.6.1 The G-7 process 30
1.6.2 Financial crises in emerging markets - the need for international coordination 33
1.6.3 Some general observations on coordination experiences . . 36
1.7 A look ahead 36

2 Mathematical Background **41**
2.1 Linear algebra 41
2.2 The basic mathematical model 51

2.3 The one-player case 54
2.4 The cooperative game 60
2.5 The non-cooperative game 67
2.6 The game with coalitions 77

3 The Basic Symmetric Two-Country Model 85
3.1 Introduction 85
3.2 A dynamic stabilization game in an MU 86
3.3 Non-cooperative and cooperative fiscal policies 89
3.3.1 The non-cooperative case 89
3.3.2 The cooperative case 91
3.3.3 The effect of fiscal stringency conditions on adjustment speed λ 93
3.3.4 Consequences of a European federal transfer system . . . 95
3.4 Numerical simulations with the model 97
3.5 Conclusions 103

4 An MU Model with Active Monetary Policy 111
4.1 Introduction 111
4.2 An MU model with active monetary policy 112
4.3 Monetary policy management in an MU 113
4.4 Macroeconomic policy design in the MU 116
4.4.1 The non-cooperative case 117
4.4.2 The cooperative case 118
4.4.3 Cases with policymakers' coalitions 118
4.4.4 Some coalition formation terminology 119
4.5 The symmetric case 119
4.5.1 The various equilibrium strategies 120
4.5.2 First findings 121
4.6 A simulation study 122
4.6.1 Baseline: A symmetric MU 123
4.6.2 Asymmetric fiscal policy preferences 126
4.6.3 Asymmetric monetary policy transmission 128
4.6.4 Asymmetric bargaining powers 130
4.6.5 Asymmetric degree of competitiveness 132

5 Endogenous Coalition Formation Concepts 145
5.1 Introduction 145
5.2 General setting and definitions 146
5.3 Single-agreement games 154
5.3.1 External and internal stability 154
5.4 Multiple-agreement games 156
5.4.1 Simultaneous games - classic setting 156
5.4.2 Simultaneous games - MU setting 163
5.4.3 Alternative way to find stable coalition structures in simultaneous games 170

5.4.4 Sequential negotiation game . . . 180
5.5 Institutional design and equilibrium concepts . . . 185
5.6 Social optimum and indices . . . 189
5.7 Appendix . . . 191

6 A Multi-Country Closed-Economy MU Model 197
6.1 Introduction . . . 197
6.2 Model . . . 198
6.3 Numerical solutions of the model . . . 200
6.3.1 Symmetric baseline model . . . 200
6.3.2 The role of spillovers . . . 212
6.3.3 Structural asymmetric setting . . . 215
6.3.4 Structural asymmetric setting with asymmetric bargaining power . . . 219
6.4 Concluding remarks . . . 222
6.5 Appendix . . . 224

7 Accession to a Monetary Union 229
7.1 Introduction . . . 229
7.2 The basic economic framework . . . 232
7.3 International economic interdependencies . . . 235
7.4 General aspects of accession . . . 236
7.5 Numerical solutions of the model . . . 238
7.5.1 General setup . . . 238
7.5.2 Pre-accession stage, symmetric model . . . 241
7.5.3 Post-accession stage, symmetric model . . . 247
7.5.4 Asymmetry in the model . . . 251
7.5.5 Stable coalition structures . . . 253
7.5.6 Effects of accession . . . 258
7.6 Conclusion . . . 262
7.7 Appendix A . . . 264
7.8 Appendix B . . . 269
7.9 Appendix C . . . 270

8 World-wide Regional Policy Coordination 273
8.1 Introduction . . . 273
8.2 Model of international economy . . . 275
8.2.1 A setting for two MUs . . . 276
8.2.2 Parameterization . . . 277
8.2.3 Shocks . . . 278
8.3 Results of numerical simulations . . . 279
8.3.1 Symmetric scenario sc_1 . . . 279
8.3.2 Asymmetric scenario sc_2 . . . 288
8.3.3 Asymmetric scenario sc_3 . . . 289
8.3.4 Normative analysis - social optima . . . 289

8.3.5 Positive analysis - stable coalition structures in the EMG$^*(\Gamma)$ 292
8.4 Conclusion 294
8.5 Appendix 296

9 Concluding Remarks **303**

10 References **309**

Preface

This book analyzes the conduct of monetary and fiscal stabilization policies and cooperation among monetary and fiscal policymakers using a dynamic game framework. The volume presents in a concise manner the results obtained from an extensive research project on monetary and fiscal policy design in the (European) Economic and Monetary Union (EMU). In addition, techniques and conclusions of this research on EMU are used to construct a more general theory of macroeconomic cooperation between nations in a world-wide setting, mainly in the later chapters of the book. In this way, the book provides more insights into recent initiatives aiming to create monetary unions or other possible forms of macroeconomic cooperation. In fact, such initiatives are recently considered in all major regions of the world.

The analysis of stabilization policies in a monetary union is carried out using a simplified version of (New-) Keynesian dynamic open-economy macroeconomic models, in which economic linkages between countries form a kernel part. Such linkages give rise to many spillovers and economic externalities connected with macroeconomic policies of nation-based agents (governments and/or central banks). This implies that the evolution of the economies over time is important, and, therefore, dynamic modelling shall be used. Indeed, dynamic models have the characteristic that the state vector, describing the current state of the economy at a certain point of time, is affected by actions of different policymakers. Hence, economic externalities arising from individual policies and their propagation over time are explicitly taken into account. In its most extensive setting, an n-countries, m-central banks dynamic model of (possible) multiple monetary unions results.

Since every policymaker is primarily interested in solving the policy issues of her own country, the induced economic spillovers and externalities may be important. Hence, the natural question of possible gains from cooperation arises. If these gains are present, the presence of institutional settings that support desired cooperation becomes an important issue. To model potential cooperation of individually optimizing players, the approach in this book combines the recent literature on dynamic games among monetary and fiscal policymakers (e.g. Engwerda (1998a) and Engwerda *et al.* (1999, 2002)) with that on endogenous coalition formation (e.g. Bloch (1996), Ray and Vohra (1997, 1999) and Yi (1997)).

The book is as much as possible self-contained and written in a manner well understandable for graduate university students. Together with scholars and researchers at universities and international institutions, they constitute the most important readership of the book. The contents and form of the volume are designed in a way that enables it to be used as a textbook for a specialized course in the area of policymaking in the presence of (a) monetary union(s).

We hope that our general perspective and potential to apply the model with its results to different regions of the world make the book interesting for less academic-oriented readers, such as policymakers and policy advisors throughout. Therefore, the book may constitute a valuable contribution to the ongoing discussions on gains from and desirability of tightening fiscal and monetary cooperation in different parts of the world.

Acknowledgements

This book is the result of our research project on monetary unions and their effects that started in 1997 when the euro area was close to its start but many fundamental aspects of it remained unclear (to us). The EMU project became the focus of our academic interests. These interests are theoretical rather than empirical: on empirical issues the reader will not find much material in this book, as there are other sources that deal with empirical questions. Over time, we extended our theoretical analysis further and further, finding answers to some of our questions but at the same time often touching upon more new issues. This book is essentially an account of our theoretical voyage in Euroland and its surroundings. While travelling, we met many colleagues at numerous conferences, seminars and through correspondences that have helped very much shaping our thoughts with their questions and remarks. We express our sincere gratitude to all of them. Further, Arie Weeren provided crucial help on a number of issues that were finally kept out of this book, but are published as van Aarle *et al.* (2001). Maurice Peek elaborated the analysis in Section 3.3.4, while Jorge Fornero contributed to Chapter 8 and helped formatting the book at several places. Working on similar topics, Reinhard Neck provided on several occasions very insightful remarks and suggestions. To all these named persons we owe a lot and are especially thankful.

Giovanni Di Bartolomeo acknowledges the financial support from the University of Rome 'La Sapienza' (MURST 2000) and the University of Antwerp (Special Research Fund). Bas van Aarle and Tomasz Michalak acknowledge the financial support from FWO (Fonds voor Wetenschappelijk Onderzoek - Vlaanderen).

The authors also thank the editors of the international journals, in which our previous papers appeared, for their allowance to reproduce a large part of the main results contained in the papers cited. Finally, we would like to thank the editor of the series, Prof. W. Semmler, for scientific editorial advice and also Herma Drees for administrative editorial assistance.

May 2005.

Joseph PLASMANS, Jacob ENGWERDA, Bas van AARLE, Giovanni DI BARTOLOMEO, Tomasz MICHALAK.

Acknowledgments

List of abbreviations

AD(S)	aggregate demand (supply)
AFTA	ASEAN Free Trade Area
ARE	algebraic Riccati equation
ASEAN	Association of South East Asian Nations
ASEAN+3	ASEAN and People's Republic of China, Japan and South Korea
cA	aggregate cooperative
CB	central bank
cN	national cooperative
CS	coalition structure
CSDS	coalition-structure deviation set
$CSDS^F$	coalition-structure full deviation set
CSSS	coalition-structure strategy set
EC	European Commission
ECB	European Central Bank
ECOFIN	Council of Economics and Finance Ministers of the EU countries
EEC	European Economic Community
EFTS	European fiscal transfer system
EMG(Δ)	exclusive-membership game (Δ-version)
$EMG^C(\Delta)$	class of exclusive-membership games (Δ-version)
$EMG^{ST}(\Delta)$	set of stable CSs in the exclusive-membership game (Δ-version)
EMG(Γ)	exclusive-membership game (Γ-version)
$EMG^*(\Gamma)$	restricted EMG (Γ) that contains a subset of feasible CSs
$EMG^C(\Gamma)$	class of exclusive-membership games (Γ-version)
$EMG^{ST}(\Gamma)$	set of stable CSs in the exclusive-membership game (Γ-version)
EMI	European Monetary Institute
EMS	European Monetary System
EMU	(European) Economic and Monetary Union
ERM	Exchange Rate Mechanism (in the EU)
EU	European Union
Euro-12	subgroup of the ECOFIN, specific to the EMU
FOC	first order condition
G-3	Euroland, USA, Japan
G-5	G-7 except for Canada and Italy
G-7	Group of seven (most developed countries)
G-8	G-7 and Russia
GATT	General Agreement of Trade and Tariff
GDP	gross domestic product
IMF	International Monetary Fund
IS curve	locus of points where goods markets are in equilibrium (S=I)
LM curve	locus of points where money market is in equilibrium (L=M)
LQ	linear-quadratic
MERCOSUR	Mercado Común del Sur (Common Market of the South)
MU	monetary union
NAFTA	North American Free Trade Area
NKE	New-Keynesian Economics

NNS	New-Neoclassical Synthesis
OCA	optimal currency area
OECD	Organization of Economic Cooperation and Development
OMG	open-membership game
OMG^C	class of open-membership games
OMG^{ST}	set of stable CSs in the open-membership games
PPP	purchasing parity power
PRC	People's Republic of China
R&D	research and development
ROMG	restricted open-membership game
$ROMG^C$	class of restricted open-membership games
ROW	rest of the world
SGP	Stability and Growth Pact
SNG	sequential negotiation game
SNGE	sequential negotiation game equilibrium
SNG^{ST}	stable coalition in the sequential negotiation game
SVAR	structural VAR
s.t.	subject to
UIP	uncovered interest rate parity
US(A)	United States (of America)
UK	United Kingdom
VAR	vector autoregressive or vector autoregression
viz.	respectively
vs.	versus
w.r.t.	with respect to
WTO	World Trade Organization

List of symbols

$\leq (\geq)$	not greater (not less) than for a vector
$\leqq (\geqq)$	not greater (not less) than for a scalar
$\simeq$	approximation up to first order
$\cong$	good approximation (at least up to second order)
$:=$	defined as
$\neq$	different from
$\Rightarrow$	leads to
$\Longleftrightarrow$	if and only if
$\forall$	all
$\exists$	there exists at least one
$\in$	set inclusion
iid	identically and independently distributed
$\varepsilon_t \overset{iid}{\sim} (0, \sigma_\varepsilon^2)$	all ε_ts are iid with mean 0 and variance σ_ε^2
$(-)\infty$	(minus) infinity
arg max(min)	argument that maximizes (minimizes)
A_{cl}	closed-system matrix
$BJS(b)$	bank jurisdictional set of bank b
$\mathbb{C}$	the set of complex numbers
$\mathbb{C}^+(\mathbb{C}^-)$	right (left) half complex plane
C	full coalition of players in a game
$CFI(.)$	coalition formation index
Cj	country j
C_k	coalition k
δ_{ij}	Kronecker's delta, $\delta_{ij} = 1$ for $i = j$ and $= 0$ elsewhere
$\dim(S)$	dimension of subspace S
E_λ	eigenspace of λ
$E(\cdot)$	(unconditional) expected value
$E_{t-1}(\cdot)$	expected value conditional on $t-1$ information set
i	imaginary unit (squared root of -1)
F	set of fiscal players in a game
Γ_i	strategy space of player i in LQ game
h^V	history of the SNG at stage V
$\mathrm{Im}(x)$	imaginary part of variable x in $\mathbb{C}$
$\mathrm{Im}\ A$	image or range of matrix A
I_n	$n \times n$ identity matrix
$\Im_t$	information set at time t
J	Jordan matrix
$\ker A$	kernel of matrix A
λ	eigenvalue
$\max_x(\min_x)$	maximize (minimize) as a function of x
$\mathbb{N} := \{0, 1, 2, 3, ...\}$	the set of natural numbers
NC	non-cooperative regime
NE	Nash equilibrium
$N(A)$	null space of matrix A

Pi	player i
$p(\lambda)$	characteristic polynomial in λ
Π	set of feasible coalition structures
Π^F	full set of feasible coalition structures
Π^R	reduced set of feasible coalition structures
Π^{MU}	MU set of feasible coalition structures
$\mathbb{R}$	the set of real numbers
$\mathbb{R}^n$	the set of vectors with n entries
$\mathbb{R}^{n\times m}$	the set of matrices with $n \times m$ entries
$R(A)$	range of matrix A, $R(A) = \text{Im } A$
$\text{rank}(A)$	rank of matrix A
$\sigma(A)$	spectrum of matrix A
span $\{\}$	set of vectors which are linearly independent
$S^{\perp}$	orthogonal complement of a subspace S
τ	asymmetric bargaining power matrix
U	(monetary) union or set of (monetary) unions
$WIX(.)$	welfare index
$\overline{WIX}$	expected $WIX(.)$
$\|x\|$	modulus of x, absolute value
$\dot{x}$	derivative of x w.r.t. time
$\overline{x}$	average of x
$\|X\|$ or $\det(X)$	determinant of matrix X (also cardinality of a set X)
$\\|x\\|_2$	(Euclidean) length of vector x, where $\\|x\\|_2 = \sqrt{x_1^2 + \cdots + x_n^2}$
X^T	transpose of matrix X
X^*	adjoint of matrix X
X^{-1}	inverse of matrix X

Chapter 1

International Policy Coordination

"*Coordination of macroeconomic policies is certainly not easy; maybe it is impossible. But in its absence, I suspect nationalistic solutions will be sought – trade barriers, capital controls and dual exchange-rate systems. Wars among nations with these weapons are likely to be mutually destructive. Eventually, they, too, would evoke agitations for international coordination.*" James Tobin.

1.1 Introduction

In the aftermath of the Bretton-Woods agreement, the general perception was that a flexible exchange rate was a way of insulating domestic employment from foreign economic disturbances, including foreign monetary policy. Thus, there was no need for central banks to intervene in foreign exchange markets or to coordinate their monetary policies for stabilizing the economy. All that was needed were flexible exchange rates.

Twenty years after Bretton Woods, the Chicago School view of the alleged superiority of flexible exchange rates has been challenged by a number of economists, who provided a theoretical rationale for policy coordination by introducing a first generation of game-theoretic models that predict positive effects of monetary policy coordination in stabilizing the economy. The main shortcoming of these models was that -notwithstanding that they did provide a theoretical rationale for policy coordination- the gains from coordination were quantitatively small. These non-convincing empirical results would explain the decreasing interest in international policy coordination after the golden ages of the 1970s and 1980s (McKibbin(1997)). However, more recently a renovating interest has been resorted to two different respects: a) the introduction of the New-Keynesian macroeconomic paradigm and b) the creation of the euro area.

A new generation of models of policy coordination have been introduced by

Obstfeld and Rogoff (2002) and Corsetti and Pesenti (2001) and others. All these New-Keynesian models incorporate micro-foundations (optimizing households and firms), an intertemporal approach, monopolistic competition, and some form of nominal inertia.[1] The need for policy coordination in second-generation models is still an open question: Obstfeld and Rogoff's (2002) paper concluded that, under plausible assumptions, the stabilization gains from having separate currencies are not largely deteriorated in the absence of effective international monetary policy coordination. In contrast, Canzoneri *et al.* (2004) develop a two-industry, two-country model and find that the gains can be non-trivial. This result arises, basically, because they relax the assumption of perfect correlation of technological shocks in previous works and also allowing a non-unitary correlation between industrial technological shocks.

Regarding the (European) Economic and Monetary Union (EMU), its creation has also changed the way macroeconomic policy has been conducted within and outside Europe. The euro area is in fact unique in the sense that it consists of many sovereign states with a single currency. Economic policymaking powers at the euro area level differ significantly from those in fully-fledged federations. In particular, while fiscal policy is formulated in the context of the Stability and Growth Pact (SGP), virtually all fiscal competencies remain at the national level according to the principle of subsidiarity. By contrast, the European Central Bank (ECB) sets monetary policy for the area as a whole and bases its decisions on average macroeconomic conditions.

This new framework, on the one hand, raises the issue of coordination of macroeconomic policies at the euro area level, specifically the coordination among fiscal authorities and between them and the ECB. On the other hand, it raises issues regarding the relations of the EMU with outside countries. In particular, the establishment of a common currency has created a major rival to the dollar and yen in the international financial markets. One question of crucial importance for developments in the world economy is whether the central banks of the United States, Japan and Europe should cooperate or not in pursuing stabilization policies and on the management of exchange rates.

This chapter provides a basic overview of the literature on international cooperation and is organized as follows. The next section discusses international policy coordination in a textbook form as a prisoners' dilemma and highlights the importance of economic spillovers and externalities in the evaluation of international coordination. Section 1.3 analyzes the international coordination in more general terms, highlighting the possible counterproductive effects of partial cooperation and the need of institutional or discretional commitment to support cooperative solutions. Section 1.4 introduces the issue of coordination in a monetary union (MU) context and discusses the issue of symmetric and asymmetric shocks. Section 1.5 discusses various aspects of monetary and fiscal policy coordination in the EMU. Section 1.6 describes the implementation of international macroeconomic policy coordination. It begins by considering the Group-of-Seven (G-7) process, afterwards the European monetary integration

[1] See VanHoose (2004) for an overview on the New-Keynesian literature.

process is analyzed. It finally considers the more recent developments of international policy coordination in emerging markets. Section 1.7 gives a look ahead to the book.

1.2 The textbook approach

In an integrated international economy, macroeconomic conditions in one country affect economic conditions in other countries; that is, they induce spillovers on other countries. Economic externalities are the effects of the decisions of one agent on other agents' preferences or welfare.[2] In the context of integrated economies, spillovers between countries lead to economic externalities since they result in the transmission of the effects of policies in one country to other countries. The key insight of the literature is that coordination of policies among economies, that takes into account these externalities, may lead to higher welfare for all of them. Starting with this key insight, the modelling of international policy coordination has moved in different directions. The literature considered among others:

- the methods to enforce international agreements,
- the roles that uncertainty and information sharing play in the coordination process, and
- the measurement of the gains from policy coordination.

In general, the need for coordination arises if the following two circumstances occur: (i) there is interdependence between the different economies and (ii) the non-coordinated action of the various countries would produce suboptimal outcomes.

Let us begin with the first point. Economic interdependence among different economies implies that shocks in one country, including those induced by government actions, have repercussions in other countries. These repercussions, called economic externalities, can be positive or negative.

The need for coordination clearly emerges from the existence of spillovers and economic externalities. Policy conflicts that create an incentive for policy coordination are of two main types:

1. *Ongoing conflicts are permanent*; they occur even if markets are perfectly flexible. Ongoing conflicts arise when countries have inconsistent objectives such as different desired values for the bilateral current account or different desired values for the real exchange rate between two currencies.

2. *Stabilization conflicts are temporary*; they occur because of inertia of nominal variables and eventually disappear as these nominal variables adjust;

[2] In Chapter 5 we define the concept of externalities from coalition formation, which are a direct consequence of economic externalities.

stabilization conflicts can arise as a result of either exogenous shocks or policy changes.

This book mainly deals with the latter type of spillovers and economic externalities since our interest is in macroeconomic stabilization policies. The main source of stabilization conflicts are exogenous shocks. We devote attention to three basic configurations of shocks that hit economies at the same time:

1. *Symmetric shocks* are shocks that hit all countries at the same time and manner;
2. *Asymmetric shocks* (also referred to as *idiosyncratic or country-specific shocks*) hit only a specific country (or block of countries) and not the other countries;
3. *Anti-symmetric shocks* (or perfectly asymmetric shocks) hit specific countries in an equal but opposite manner.

Following Meyer *et al.* (2002), oil price shocks can be seen as examples of symmetric shocks for most industrial countries in the 70s. The simultaneous fiscal expansion in the United States and contraction in Europe and Japan in the early 1980s can be viewed as an asymmetric shock for monetary authorities. The early 1985 appreciation of the dollar can be interpreted as an anti-symmetric shock that raised the demand for dollar assets and lowered the demand for assets denominated in the other major currencies. Finally, the German reunification in the early 1990s and the crisis of the Japanese (fixed) assets in the beginning of the 21st century are good examples of country-specific shocks.

Stabilization conflicts on monetary policy can arise because of initial conditions that one or more countries regard as suboptimal and changes in fiscal policy that are driven by political or other non-stabilization considerations such that they effectively become exogenous. Suboptimal initial conditions and exogenous changes in fiscal policy can be divided into symmetric, asymmetric and anti-symmetric initial conditions. E.g. inflation rates in Western European countries in the early 1980s can be thought of as symmetric suboptimal initial conditions.

Regarding the suboptimal outcomes, how can they emerge in the presence of economic externalities? As any case of strategic interdependence, the effects of international economic externalities can be interpreted in terms of the tools provided by game theory. Table 1.1 illustrates a simple example, where two countries (Europe and United States) have two targets (balance of payments in equilibrium and full employment) and two strategies (expansion and contraction). It describes a traditional prisoners' dilemma problem.

Table 1.1 Policy cooperation as prisoners' dilemma[3]

	US	
EU	*Expansion*	*Contraction*
Expansion	I(-9,-9)	III(-11,-8)
Contraction	II(-8,-11)	IV(-10,-10)

Let us analyze in more detail the optimal choices for both (blocks of) countries. If the policy of the United States (US) is contraction, Europe will also adopt contraction to prevent the balance of payments to deteriorate. If the US policy is expansion, Europe will again adopt contraction to increase the balance of payments. Thus, Europe will always play contraction irrespective of the US choice. Since the game is symmetric the US will also find it optimal to play contraction. Therefore, both countries will finally play the contraction strategy. This solution is clearly suboptimal: if both countries would play expansion, both can achieve a better outcome. The reason this does not occur is the lack of coordination: if each country fears that the other will not expand its economy enough, the outcome may be that none of them expands. In theory, it is thus possible to increase the welfare of both countries by employing some form of policy coordination, thereby achieving a Pareto-optimal outcome,

Our example describes a situation of pure discretionary coordination: the various countries decide on a case-by-case basis to internalize the economic externalities resulting from macroeconomic interdependence and each country may gain without giving up anything of its sovereignty. However, even the partial fulfilment of a target has a value, i.e. there is a trade-off between target variables. Then, there are cases of discretionary coordination through compromise, in which each country gains with reference to one objective but loses with respect to another, while still achieving a net gain.

The discretionary coordination through compromise is related to the policy-optimization approach to economic policy (flexible-target approach). In such an analysis, the agents are the same national governments with well-defined, exogenous preferences (or loss functions) to be maximized under interdependent constraints, describing the way in which policies and shocks originating in one country affect other countries (i.e. the interactions among national economies). In these policy games, each national government acts in a strategic way according to its interests which are biased towards domestic welfare. The decisions of national governments are interpreted as optimal solutions of cooperative or non-cooperative games.

In a non-cooperative game structure, policymakers maximize their own national welfare. Unilateral national behaviour is often modelled as Nash or Stackelberg non-cooperative behaviour. This behaviour will be contrasted with cooperative approaches and the incentives to deviate from cooperative outcomes can be studied. In a cooperative game the national governments will jointly maximize a weighted average of their individual welfare, i.e. a joint welfare function. Cooperative games will generate Pareto-optimal outcomes.[4]

---

[3] Smaller absolute values are preferred to larger absolute values.

[4] Canzoneri *et al.* (2004) distinguish between constrained and unconstrained Pareto optimality. If there is deadweight loss due to monopolistic competition and the government does not subsidize the production to reach the competitive outcome, then even with coordination,

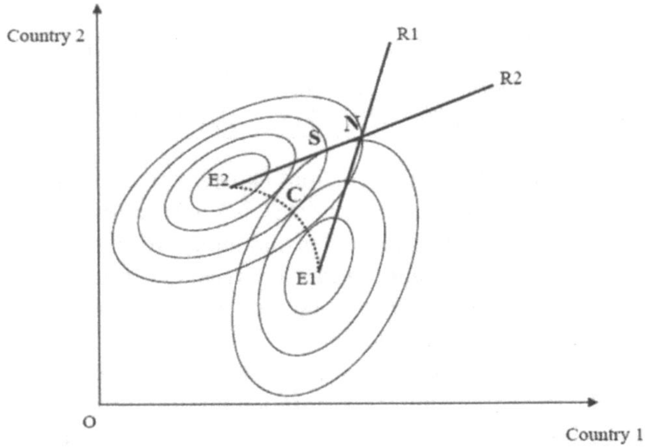

Figure 1.1: Hamada's diagram

An example is provided by international economic externalities from monetary policy in a symmetric two-country world. In such a model, one country's attempt to improve its output-inflation trade-off by running a beggar-thy-neighbour policy is frustrated by the reaction of the other country. The non-cooperative outcome is a deflationary bias with both countries worse off relative to a cooperative situation in which each country takes care of domestic inflation without attempting to affect the exchange rate (Cooper (1985)).

The discretionary coordination through compromise is displayed in graphic form in Figure 1.1.

On the axes we represent the policies of the two countries; the policy of country 1 (2) is shown on the horizontal (vertical) axis. Thus, each point represents a policy combination (and corresponding economic result). The losses of the two policymakers are represented by iso-loss (indifference) curves centered in E1 and E2 (first bests or "bliss points"). A curve further away from the origin indicates a higher loss.

The non-cooperative equilibrium of the game is represented by point N, where the two policymakers' reaction functions intersect (point S is the Stackelberg equilibrium). The reaction function is a policymaker's best response given the opponent's policy. If the economy is in a point on a policymaker's reaction function, it has not the incentive to change its policy. Of course, in N both policymakers have no incentive to deviate from their policy. Thus, it represents a game equilibrium (Nash equilibrium).

---

the outcome will be a constrained Pareto-optimal outcome (a second-best). The first-best outcome is the solution in a perfectly competitive setting.

Point N is clearly suboptimal, moving south-west it is, in fact, possible to reduce both policymakers' losses. Pareto-efficient equilibria, as point C, are represented along the (contract) curve *E1-E2* and can be implemented as the results of a cooperative agreement. Of course, the agreement should be binding since points as C are out of the reaction functions, so they imply an *ex-post* incentive for both policymakers to deviate from their reaction function. We will come back on the issue of commitment later on.

Summarizing, in the presence of international economic externalities, game-theoretic analysis demonstrates that a failure to coordinate monetary policy internationally could result in non-cooperative solutions that are Pareto inferior to the cooperative solution that is achieved by coordinating policies. However, this cooperative solution may not yield a permanent equilibrium as there is an incentive for countries to renege or cheat in the absence of a binding commitment.

1.3 A more general view

1.3.1 Can cooperation be counterproductive?

Several analysts have questioned the prisoners' dilemma approach to international monetary policy coordination. For example, Rogoff (1985) suggests that cooperation may be counterproductive if a third (non-cooperative) player is introduced into the game; these results thus turn the prisoners' dilemma into a deadlock game.

In his influential paper, Rogoff (1985) considers a symmetric two-country economy, where monetary authorities have an inflationary bias problem because desired outputs are above natural outputs. Even though inflation is costly, the equilibrium rate of inflation must be high enough that the incentive to increase the money supply in order to raise output is just offset by the extra cost of additional consumer price inflation. In a non-cooperative policy regime, an increase in the money supply in one country increases its inflation both by increasing its output price inflation and by causing its currency to depreciate in real terms, making imports more expensive. By contrast, in a cooperative policy regime (joint maximization between monetary authorities) and non-cooperative play against the private sector, when one country expands its money supply the additional real depreciation of its currency helps the other country by lowering consumer price inflation there. Thus, the extra cost of consumer price inflation for the two countries taken together is lower and the equilibrium rate of inflation must be higher if the incentive to try to raise output is to be matched by additional joint costs of consumer price index inflation. The inflation bias in both countries is finally higher.

A different view is explored by Carraro and Giavazzi (1991), who provide a counterexample to Rogoff's (1985) paper by showing how coordinated strategies may be dominant even in the presence of a third, non-cooperative player, if coordination is not embodied in an institutional arrangement, but it is rather seen as a contingent (feedback) policy decision. In their model, the prisoners' dilemma approach is turned into a *game of harmony.* More generally, recent literature on the non-cooperative formation of environmental coalitions argues that, when an n-country game is analyzed, the likely non-cooperative equilibrium of the game in which countries first decide whether or not to cooperate, and then set their policies, is cooperation among a subset of the n countries, whereas the remaining ones find it optimal to free-ride. In this case, it can be shown that the appropriate framework to describe the policy coordination problem is a *chicken game.*[5] The same argument could be applied even to a monetary policy coordination game, whenever the (negative) slope of all countries' reaction functions is sufficiently low in absolute value (see Carraro (1999)).

These examples indicate that the same international policy game can be described by different game-theoretic structures: the prisoners' dilemma is just one of them, but chicken, deadlock, *Stag-hunt* and *harmony* games[6] should also be considered as possible adequate representations of the interactions among central banks. Which theoretical structure best describes countries' interactions in an international policy game is therefore an open question. It depends, among other things, on economic structures and on policymakers' preferences, and especially on the possibility of partial coordination with the formation of coalitions. It is worth noticing that in the examples designed to show that coordination can be counterproductive, it is assumed that the participants in the policy game cannot credibly make all the commitments necessary for achieving the efficient equilibrium but that some participants can commit to jointly maximize and play Nash against others. This type of commitment can be counterproductive for those who engage in it. Thus, a relevant feature to determine the nature of the strategic interactions is the number of players involved in the game and their relations, in particular, the possibility of the formation of partial cooperation (coalitions).

---

[5] A *chicken game* can be described as follows. Two tough guys sit in their idling cars at opposite ends of a single-lane road. Upon a signal their cars hurtle towards each other. Each driver can either swerve out of the way or stay the course and risk death. The driver who swerves becomes the chicken, while the other gets the girl and is the most popular boy in town. Formally, two strategies are to swerve (S) or to hold (H), the preference ordering is as follows: $HS \succ SS \succ SH \succ HH$. As a result there is no dominant strategy and two deficient equilibria emerge: HS and SH. The Pareto-optimal outcome (SS) is unstable.

[6] *Stag-hunt* and *harmony* games are well-known games. The situation described in the stag-hunt game derives from the French philosopher J.J. Rousseau. Two men go to hunt a stag. If they catch the stag they will both eat well. They can catch the stag only if they hunt together (cooperate). If one of them abandons the hunt for the stag (defects) to catch a passing hare, he eats reasonably well, the stag escapes and the other player eats nothing. If both abandon the stag-hunt to catch hares, they both eat reasonably well, after competing to catch the hares. Formally, the two strategies are to cooperate in the hunt of the stag (C) or to chase a passing rabbit (N), thus letting the stag escape. The preference ordering is $CC \succ NC \succ NN \succ CN$. There is no dominant strategy and two equilibria are possible: CC (Pareto-optimal) and NN (deficient).

By contrast, in the case of a harmony game, players prefer cooperation since self-interest leads to mutual gains. Formally, in such a game the preference ordering is $CC \succ NC$, $CN \succ NN$. Since C is the dominant strategy for both players, there is a Pareto-optimal equilibrium: CC.

1.3.2 Cooperation, commitment and credibility

Full (or partial) cooperation will become non-sustainable if policymakers do not stick to their commitment and cheat by deviating in their policies from the agreed policy stance. Cooperation, in fact, implies a solution on the Pareto frontier outside of the reaction functions. The problem is closely related to the reputation issue and the international institutional design like e.g. the existence of a supranational authority that enforces international cooperation agreements.

If countries face the same international coordination problem in the future, i.e. the game is repeated each period, it must be possible to achieve efficient outcomes by a reputation mechanism. If a country comes to a decision node where there is an incentive to renege on the cooperative outcome, such a cooperative agreement will clearly lack credibility and rational policymakers will not enter into such an agreement and, by symmetry, no cooperation is the outcome. The *folk theorem* of repeated games stresses that even if policymakers have an incentive to renege they will not do so because they fear to lose payoffs when other players can punish them in the subsequent periods. The reason why trigger strategies can support repeated games, consistent with efficient policies, is that for each country the value of deviating from the efficient policy in each period is outweighed by the discounted value of having efficient policies played in the future. Therefore, for trigger strategies to work, payoffs in the future must not be discounted too heavily.

Another way to restore sustainability is to develop an incentive mechanism through sanctions against reneging. If there are supranational institutions that can legally enforce the coordinated solution, then policies will be credible. Such an institution will reduce the likelihood that policymakers renege upon their commitments. The supranational enforcement implies a loss of sovereignty (see Canzoneri and Henderson (1991)) in comparison with a sovereign policymaking process, whereby countries coordinate on an agreed outcome and employ a trigger mechanism to enforce it.

Recently, the idea of *issue linkage* has been introduced as a device supporting cooperation; this is basically an agreement designed where participants do not negotiate on only one issue, but on two or more issues. The intuition is that by adopting cooperative behaviour, some agents gain in a given issue, whereas other agents gain in another. By linking the two issues, the agreement in which agents decide to cooperate on both issues may become profitable to all of them. Issue linkage is a way to increase cooperation on issues where the incentives to free-ride are particularly strong with the goal of determining under which conditions players actually prefer to link the negotiations on two different issues rather than negotiating on the two issues separately in the context of endogenous coalition formation (see Carraro and Marchiori (2003)). An example of issue linkage is represented by the negotiations of macroeconomic policy coordination during the Bonn Summit of G-7 in July 1978. Together with the oil price control and fiscal policies to support growth, a formula to conclude the Tokyo Round of trade negotiations was added to conclude the bargain.[7]

[7] However, trade negotiations have rarely played a role in macroeconomic policy coordina-

In practice, coordination can be implemented through *ad hoc* discretional agreements or through the adoption of rules that give rise to institutionalized cooperation. The latter normally involves creating rules or regimes that enable the countries to avoid at least part of the inefficiencies derived from unilateral solutions, thus providing a certain and lasting form of cooperation. The gold standard, the Bretton-Woods system, the EMS and the rules laid down at Maastricht for participation in Stage 3 of EMU, the SGP and the EMU itself are examples of this type of coordination. Some of them offer precise policy prescriptions, others adopted a shared intermediate target (exchange rate stability), which was expected to have beneficial consequences for the operation of the different economies (e.g., in order to avoid beggar-thy-neighbour policies).

There are reasons *pro* and *con* to prefer institutionalized rule-based cooperation over discretionary (*ad hoc*) solutions.

1. The need to repeat *ad hoc* negotiations before each concerted action makes this approach inefficient, all the more so if there are problems of political instability in the negotiating countries, with the related turnover of negotiators.

2. Discretionary solutions are more vulnerable to pressure from various interest groups.

3. Rules established within the framework of institutionalized cooperation are difficult to renegotiate (in theory, rules should be complied with for an indefinite, or at least lengthy, period). Fixed rules may thus accentuate the difficulties of this type of coordination.

4. Discretionary intervention may be required whenever the system has to cope with events that are not provided for in the rules of institutionalized cooperation or specific circumstances force policymakers to take actions different from those contemplated by the rules.

5. Finally, rules require regular review, which cannot be ignored simply to avoid slow and difficult negotiations. Without such a revision, the discretion and flexibility needed to adapt to the evolution of the historical context would be provided by the technocrats of the institutions themselves, which could produce distortions.

Finally, it is worth noticing here that both rules and discretionary agreements must be supported by a credible commitment.

1.3.3 The role of uncertainty

In the late 80s the literature on international coordination moved on to analyze also the implications of the choice of model uncertainty, which means the technical reference to uncertainty about the true model. It was explicitly introduced

tion despite the potential existence of policy tradeoffs. This is probably due to the slow and complicated nature of trade discussions and the low speed with which they are implemented.

in the theoretical analysis by Ghosh and Masson (1987, 1991, 1994), Masson (1992), Frankel (1988, 1990), and Frankel and Rockett (1988).

Feldstein (1988) and Frankel and Rockett (1988) first pointed out that nations might lose by working together under uncertainty *ex-post*. In particular, Frankel and Rockett (1988) provided a static framework for evaluating uncertainty on the true model of the economy. Their analysis is based on ten large multi-country models with the assumptions that each country uses its own model to measure the gains of a coordination solution and that governments do not exchange information but that they agree to coordinate when their own calculation of welfare effects shows that it will be beneficial for them.

In contrast, a number of studies have reversed the above negative result. The presence of model uncertainty may provide an additional incentive to coordinate policies, provided that policymakers recognize that they cannot know the true model. Ghosh and Masson (1991, 1994) show that uncertainty is likely to increase the potential gains *ex-ante*. Indeed, countries may have different information sets that they can share, and by doing so, get better expected outcomes. In models where policymakers must set their policies before uncertainty is resolved, the expected gain from coordination is greater whenever there is multiplicative or parameter uncertainty. In addition, Ghosh and Masson argue that uncertainty provides a rationale for episodic efforts at coordination, since crises generate large uncertainties, and hence potential gains, and are also, fortunately, infrequent.

1.4 Monetary and fiscal coordination in an MU

1.4.1 Principles of a monetary union

Monetary unions (MUs) form the most far-reaching monetary policy arrangement that states or nations can choose: sharing a common currency and joint responsibility of a common monetary policy and common central bank is typically only to be expected for federal states (e.g. the US) or countries that have achieved a very high degree of economic and political integration (e.g. the euro area).

For participating countries, membership of an MU implies a number of losses and benefits. The theory of Optimal Currency Areas (OCAs), developed by Mundell (1961) and McKinnon (1963), studies MUs and their consequences. With the introduction of the EMU, this theory has seen a very strong interest and revival as a large number of new theoretical and empirical studies witnesses.

The main potential cost of joining an MU concerns the loss of sovereign monetary policy, in particular the interest rate and exchange rate as monetary policy instruments/shock absorbers for the participating countries. How big this cost is depends on the frequency and nature of the shocks that will hit the MU and their transmission. The cost is highest if situations arise where substantially disparate monetary conditions would be called for in different countries, due to economic disturbances that have uneven impacts across the area (i.e. asymmetric shocks) or even opposite impacts (anti-symmetric shocks). In the case of shocks that affect all countries more or less equally (i.e. symmetric shocks), the loss of monetary autonomy is in principle of less concern, because the area-wide policy would likewise tend to deliver monetary conditions that are appropriate for each country. However, this need not be strictly the case if the transmission mechanism for monetary policy operates significantly different across countries, because even a uniform policy response would not yield uniform impacts in that case. Such differences in transmission mechanisms may weaken over time as an MU takes form, an idea worked out in the so-called 'endogenous' OCA (Frankel and Rose (1997)): countries that may not form an OCA *ex-ante* may do so *ex-post,* as the MU fosters economic integration and convergence of economic structures and institutions.

In the case of asymmetric shocks, with monetary conditions constrained to respond to the average conditions in the area as a whole, fiscal instruments can be applied at national levels to promote macroeconomic stabilization. However, in the case of supply shocks, changes in relative prices and production patterns are generally needed. While macroeconomic policies can buffer the income effects of such shocks and buy time for the adjustment needed to take place, they cannot by themselves assure the necessary structural changes. Policy reforms in individual countries are the most important instruments for improving adaptability. From this perspective, a crucial question is whether an MU provides a more or less favourable environment for the supply side adjustments that are required to occur.

The introduction of a common currency also delivers a number of economic benefits. These include reduced transaction costs associated with trade and financial flows between MU countries, the absence of *intra*-MU exchange rate risk, greater overall price stability and higher price transparency. The absence of exchange rate risk implies that interest rate risk premiums should be small (Uncovered Interest-rate Parity hypothesis) and, therefore, lower borrowing costs in many countries. An MU is also likely to generate endogenous consequences such as more transparent prices contributing to stronger competitive forces, possibly fewer policy-induced shocks compared with the past as a result of the stability-oriented macroeconomic policy framework and it may serve as a catalyst to speed-up structural changes. These indirect and dynamic benefits are difficult to quantify, but could be more important than the static gains.

Moreover, there remain a number of shock-absorbing mechanisms which can limit the potential cost of giving up national monetary policy autonomy. In particular, more flexible factor and product markets and fiscal policy flexibility can act as shock absorbers. Greater integration of capital and credit markets may contribute to consumption smoothing in the MU, as agents can diversify idiosyncratic risks by holding financial assets of other countries. In other words, the traditional OCA theory emphasizes the flexibility of production factors, especially labour, to absorb shocks. Greater overall labour market flexibility would support job mobility and accelerate the pace of wage and price changes at the regional or country level in order to achieve real exchange rate corrections following an adverse shock. Fiscal and structural policies provide instruments that facilitate macroeconomic adjustments in an MU and influence the adjustment channels. If these mechanisms are weak or slow, the necessary adjustments would fall more on employment.

The OCA theory provides explanations why countries form MUs: as long as their benefits (are perceived to) exceed their costs, countries will have an interest in participating in an MU; conversely, MUs are likely to break up when the (perceived) benefits no longer cover the (perceived) costs. History learns that break-ups are often taking place in a broader context of secession and collapses of economic unions and federal states (think e.g. of the recent demise of the Soviet Union and the rouble zone and the disintegration of the Federal Republic of Yugoslavia).[8] Indeed, MUs among major sovereign nations have never been observed to last in the long run without strong political integration.

1.4.2 A textbook illustration of the OCA problem

A textbook example taken from De Grauwe (2003) is insightful to illustrate the OCA problem in a graphical analysis. Figure 1.2 provides the aggregate demand and supply relations in countries 1 and 2 that form an MU.

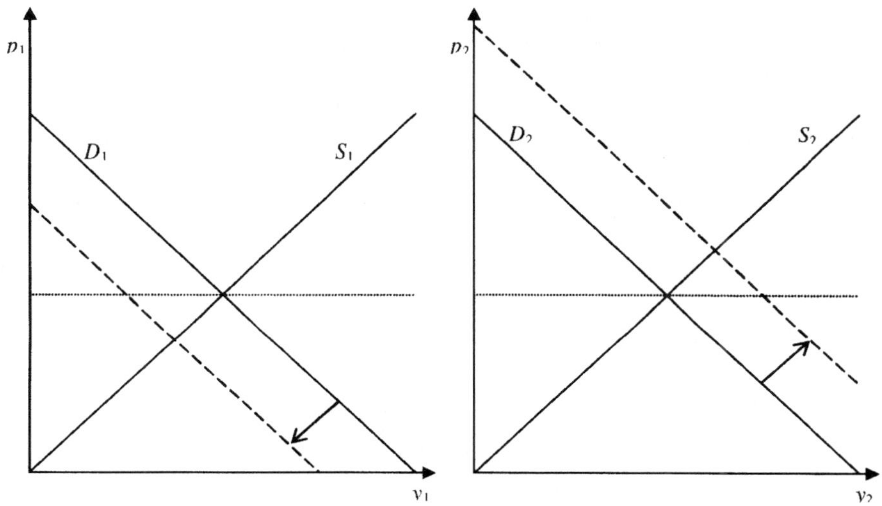

Figure 1.2. A relative preference shock in an MU

It is assumed that a shock to preferences shifts away demand for goods produced in country 1 to demand for goods of country 2. This shock leads to lower output and higher unemployment in country 1 and higher output/ lower unemployment in country 2. In the absence of an MU, a devaluation of country 1's currency could be used to improve the competitiveness of its

[8] Bordo and Jonung (2003) analyze the history of MUs and the possible lessons from it that can be relevant for the EMU.

goods by reducing their relative price. That would shift up the demand curve of country 1 and shift down the one of country 2, restoring the initial equilibrium in a straightforward manner. In an MU this possibility is no longer present and alternative adjustment mechanisms are sought for.

Three alternative adjustment mechanisms in an MU exist to alleviate the adjustment burden from shocks like in Figure 1.2: (i) wage flexibility, (ii) labour mobility and (iii) fiscal flexibility. Flexible wages will entail a downward pressure on wages in country 1 and an upward pressure on wages in country 2. This restores competitiveness of country 1 shifting up the demand for its goods, whereas the demand for country 2's products shifts downward as the wage pressures erodes its competitiveness. Labour mobility is an alternative shock absorber in this MU: the unemployed workers of country 1 could move to country 2, where there is an excess demand for labour due to the shock. This movement of labour implies that it is no longer necessary to adjust relative wages and prices to restore equilibrium and the unemployment in country 1 disappears, and so, the inflationary pressure on wages in country 2. Finally, also fiscal policies can act as shock absorbers in the MU. First, a flexible fiscal policy in country 1 would allow it to undertake a discretionary fiscal impulse to stimulate demand in country 1 after the negative shock. But the flexibility of fiscal policy is subject to constraints: (a) it is necessary that long-run fiscal sustainability is not endangered, (b) an MU may come with constraints on the use of national fiscal policies in order to safeguard fiscal discipline and not to endanger the stability of the common monetary policy. Second, a federal budget or fiscal transfer mechanisms may effectively act as shock absorbers by their redistribution of spending power away from prosperous regions towards stagnating parts.

This simple two-country OCA example is useful to introduce in a clear way the mechanisms that will reappear several times and in more complicated forms in various chapters of the book. In particular, the relative preference/relative price shock will be the focus of interest of chapters 3 and 4, that deal with such a two-country MU model. In chapters 6-8, we study an MU of more countries and will also look at different types of shocks.

1.4.3 Monetary and fiscal policy in an MU

Of crucial importance for the well-functioning of MUs is not only the question whether the participating countries are (close to) an OCA, also the design of monetary and fiscal policies in an MU is essential. A well-designed institutional framework in which decisions about monetary and fiscal policies in an MU are taken and implemented, will contribute strongly to its efficiency and has therefore significant welfare implications. Conversely, an MU with an inadequate institutional design of its macroeconomic policies, may contribute strongly to its actual collapse even if otherwise the countries may constitute an OCA. Not only the institutional framework concerning fiscal policies of the participating countries and the monetary policy of the common central bank (CB) are important in this respect, but also the interaction between monetary and fiscal policies. In the presence of economic externalities, there is scope for policy coordination as uncoordinated policies will lead to inefficient and ineffective outcomes.

In particular, the following spillovers seem relevant in an MU context:

(i) *output spillovers*: changes in output in one country will influence through its imports also the output in other countries via the 'trade channel';

(ii) *price spillovers*: inflation in one country can influence inflation in other countries via its imports according to the 'pass-through' hypothesis;

(iii) *competitiveness spillovers*: price changes are also likely to lead to relative price changes in the MU, resulting in spillovers via the 'competitiveness channel'; this effect is similar to the beggar-thy-neighbour effect of competitive devaluations in the case of independent monetary policy;

(iv) *interest rate spillovers*: in an MU fiscal policies can induce changes in the short-run interest rate set by the CB; this will affect output via the 'interest rate channel' of monetary policy;

(v) *spillovers via the external exchange rate*: interest rate changes will also induce effects on the external exchange rate of the MU, affecting the external competitiveness of countries and pass-through of inflation from external countries via the 'exchange rate channel';

(vi) *government debt spillovers*: in an MU, government debt is likely to affect long-term real interest rates; spillovers will occur only if financial markets do not price the risk of government debt of individual countries appropriately, e.g. due to the possibility that no-bail out clauses are imperfectly credible; in that case, excessive fiscal debt in individual countries leads to higher real interest rates in all countries of the MU.

Spillovers of the types(ii)-(vi) are related to the standard beggar-thy-neighbour arguments for policy coordination: policy coordination enables to internalize/attenuate the negative economic externalities produced from these channels. In general, the stronger the degree of integration between the participating countries, the stronger the economic externalities start to operate and, therefore, the stronger in principle the potential benefits from appropriately designed policy coordination.

The academic literature has focussed on two important interactions between monetary and fiscal policies in an MU.

(a) The links between fiscal deficits, government debt, inflation, and interest rates via the dynamic government budget constraints. The interactions between monetary and fiscal policies in the MU result from the joint influence on the government debt dynamics. E.g. in the absence of sufficient fiscal discipline, countries may run excessive deficits and accumulate non-sustainable debt that will eventually spillover to other, more prudent countries in the form of higher interest rates or even forced bail-outs in the form of monetization by the common CB (monetary bail-out) or fiscal transfers (fiscal bail-out). These interactions are more situated in a medium- to long-run perspective; hence, the emphasis lies on long-run fiscal sustainability when dealing with these interactions. Policy coordination may already partly take out the strongest economic externalities as individual countries will be confronted with the consequences of individual policies on other participants. The basic ideas go back to the famous Sargent and Wallace (1981) analysis of the interaction of monetary and fiscal policy and their 'unpleasant monetarist arithmetic' and recently revived in the *Fiscal Theory of the Price Level* (see e.g. Canzoneri and Diba (1999) for a euro area analysis).

(b) The links between monetary and fiscal policies in a short-run macroeconomic stabilization perspective. Here, both the fiscal policies of member states and the common monetary policy affect macroeconomic conditions in the individual countries and the aggregate MU. These interactions are also related to the analysis of the OCA: e.g. if countries are facing an asymmetric shock, national fiscal flexibility is likely to be beneficial but may be partly counteracted by fiscal policies in other countries and/or the monetary policy of the common CB. In addition, fiscal policy constraints may limit the flexibility of the fiscal policymaker. Also here, one sees that if the spillovers and resulting economic externalities are strong, there is a need and scope for macroeconomic policy coordination.

This book entirely focuses on the interactions of monetary and fiscal policies in an MU from the perspective of aspect (b). It was also constructed having in mind the context of European monetary integration. For that reason, the next section takes a more detailed look at the EMU.

1.5 Coordination at work - the EMU

After a short historical introduction to European monetary integration processes, in this section we analyze three interdependent issues that play a crucial role in the EMU.

1.5.1 European monetary integration processes

In the aftermath of the Bretton-Woods agreement the general perception was that a flexible exchange rate was a way of insulating domestic employment from foreign economic disturbances. All that was needed were flexible exchange rates. Thus, in the early 1960s, exchange rate policy was not a major concern in the European integration process, which mainly concentrated on trade integration (within the European Economic Community, EEC).

The international monetary situation however changed in the late 1960s, when the US began to run an expansionary monetary policy to finance the Vietnam War. The American monetary policy consisted of printing an excessive amount of money and, therefore, increasing the inflation rate. The Bretton-Woods link between the major currencies and the dollar transmitted the inflation to the rest of the world. These imported inflationary tensions started to stimulate the EEC to investigate the possibility of increasing monetary integration.

In 1970, after the The Hague declarations, the European Leaders began to work on their MU project. The Council requested to a special committee to prepare a report on the possibility of an MU. The committee was chaired by the Luxembourg Premier Pierre Werner. Drawing on studies taken in the early

1960s, the Werner Committee laid out a visionary step-by-step road to an MU. The realization of the MU was planned for 1980 and it should have realized in three steps through a gradual harmonization.

The harmonization criteria were the major crux of discussions. Two major views emerged (the opposite German and French perspectives).

1. West Germany supported an economic harmonization, i.e. the creation of an MU should have required the preliminary convergence of economic domestic indicators (e.g. inflation rates, interest rates, balance of payments, public debts) to the values of the strongest European currencies to avoid the risk of destabilization of such currencies.

2. By contrast, France supported a monetary harmonization. In the French view, the stability of the mark and guilder should have been the tool to stabilize the other currencies.

These two opposite visions differently distributed the cost of the monetary integration. In the German proposal the major costs were associated to the destabilized economies, which should have followed restrictive policies to make order in the domestic accounts with high cost in terms of employment. By contrast, according to the French proposal, the major burden was let to West Germany that in the transition step to the MU should have supported the unstable economies by supporting monetary policy (mark depreciations) and, therefore, by accepting a higher domestic inflation rate. The two proposals were the mirror of the European economic situations of West Germany and France.

The distance between the two points of view was too large and, in 1971, the Council, in a very optimistic perspective, was only able to propose a form of monetary coordination among the EEC members as the first step of the plan of the Werner Committee.

The failure of the Werner plan, however, was not due to the opposition of the German and French interests but mainly because of the changes in the international context. In October 1973, some months after the monetary project started, the Yom Kippur War broke out in the Middle East. The war triggered an Arab oil boycott to the Western World. Oil price quadruplicated in a few months. The sharp rise in oil prices had limited effects on oil producers, but it dramatically affected Western Europe and the Bretton-Woods system, which gradually collapsed between 1971 and 1973. The second oil shock in 1979 eliminated any hope of its recovery. The latent inflationary tendency created by the American policies exploded under the pressure of the oil prices. In addition, attempts of compensating the inflationary effects with expansionary fiscal and monetary policies worsened the situation and Europe faced stagflation, i.e. high inflation and low employment.

Oil shocks, general stagnation and the differences in inflation rates among European countries[9] made the monetary integration project unfeasible and, consequently, different and less ambitious forms of coordination were implemented

[9] E.g. in Italy and the UK the average inflation rate rose to 15%. By contrast, West Germany was able to constrain the inflationary pressure (the average West-German inflation

until 1991: the snake in 1972 and the Exchange Rate Mechanism (ERM) in 1979.

As in 1971, the weakness of the dollar between 1977 and 1978 gave a new opportunity to the EEC countries for the birth of a new European project and for reinforcing European cohesion. The weakness of the dollar again corresponded with an appreciation of the D-mark, highlighting a reverse relationship between the two currencies. In order to smooth the effects of the variability of US monetary policy on German exports, the Social-Democrat Chancellor Helmut Schmidt started to think of a plan to coordinate European monetary policy and, therefore, to stabilize European exchange rates. The German proposal found the support of France, where the Liberal President Giscard d'Estaing had a priority in escaping the inflation-depreciation spiral. In 1976 d'Estaing appointed Barre as head of the government and France was driven to a rigorous public debt consolidation and restrictive monetary policies. In such a context the support to the German proposal should have two important effects for the French policy. It constituted: 1) a remark of the robustness of French intentions and 2) a solid external constraint to follow an unpopular rigorous policy. Both effects supported French policy credibility.

After long national discussions, the proposal also found the adhesions of Italy, Ireland and the other EEC countries with the exception of the UK, where Labour Premier James Callaghan was convinced that pegging the sterling to the D-mark was a brake for the British growth because of the implied restrictive fiscal policy. The European Monetary System (EMS) became a reality in March 1979 after the agreement in December 1978. The EMS governed exchange rates in Europe until 31 December 1999. The European snake and the EMS marked an increase in international macroeconomic policy coordination. The novelty of this coordination was the direct realization through contacts between governments beyond the action of supranational institutions.

The EMS worked well until the 1990s, but in 1992-93, the abolition of capital controls by the Single European Act allowed the full force of the impossible trinity to bear on the ERM, which then became progressively inconsistent. When, as a result of German unification, the D-mark strengthened further as a response to high German interest rates and the now open capital account, the strain became too heavy in 1992-1993 and the hard EMS collapsed. Italy and the UK were forced out of the EMS in 1992. German unification and its monetary management (i.e. the one-to-one exchange between the D-mark and the Ostmark) forced a fundamental fiscal imbalance that could not be accommodated within the zone that the initial parities adopted in EMS.[10] The collapse of the (hard) EMS paved the way for a soft EMS, a weaker agreement.

In the early 1990s, just before the European currency crises, the Maastricht Treaty of the EU constituted a turning point in the European integration

between 1974 and 1979 was 4.7%). Moreover, after the failure of any attempt to formulate a common reaction to the shocks, the different performances within European countries led Italy and Denmark to unilaterally apply import restrictions to redress their balance of payments.

[10]The German Bundesbank under Otto Pohl opposed the one-to-one exchange as incompatible with the Bundesbank's role of anchor currency issuer (Yergin and Stanislaw (1998)).

process. By modifying the previous treaties (i.e. Paris, Rome and Single European Act), the initial economic objective of the Community, building a common market, was outstripped and, for the first time, a distinctive vocation of political union was claimed. The Treaty of Maastricht had a structure based on three pillars, according to the artificial parlance created by those who devised and edited it.[11] For our scope the most important pillar is the first one, which involved the EMU project. The introduction of a European currency, the euro, was decided. It would take place following a three phase scheme: i) From 1990 to 31 December 1993: its objective would be a completely free circulation of capital. ii) From 1 January 1994 to 1 January 1999: the member countries must coordinate their economic policies in order to achieve some objectives, fixed quantitatively and known as convergence criteria: reduction of inflation and interest rates, control of government deficit and debt and respect of normal fluctuation margins provided for by the exchange rate mechanism of the EMS, the countries that reached those objectives could pass on to the third phase. iii) From 1 January 1999 to 1 January 2002: establishment of the European Central Bank (ECB), fixing of exchange rates and introduction of a single currency.

Thus, Werner's dream became finally true in December 1991 with the signing of the Maastricht Treaty. The Maastricht Treaty succeeded in forcing major fiscal consolidations in all EU countries by the middle to late 1990s. The Stability and Growth Pact (SGP) of 1997 aimed to cement fiscal gains going forward by establishing goals and incentives for fiscal deficits once the MU would be introduced. In May 1998, eleven countries were ratified as initial members of the MU based on their fulfilment of the convergence criteria during 1997. By irrevocably fixing the exchange rates between their currencies, the countries effectively introduced an MU between them. On 1 January 1999, the euro was introduced as legal tender in the 11 countries comprising the European single-currency area.[12] Until 1 January 2002, the euro and national currencies coexisted where the euro could only be used in book transactions since the printing and minting of notes and coins was still under way. The ECB took over exclusive monetary policy for the Euroland from 1 January 1999 onwards, headed by its first President, Dr. Wim Duisenberg from the Netherlands. The ECB built upon the preparatory work done by the European Monetary Institute (EMI), that was established with the Maastricht Treaty to work out the European System of Central Banks (ESCB). By 1 July 2002, national currencies ceased to exist and the euro became the single official currency for the 12 EMU member countries. After a difficult start, the ECB over time established itself as a stable institution and an important macroeconomic policymaker.

1.5.2 Design of monetary and fiscal policies

The introduction of the euro on January 1, 1999 completed the economic policy architecture designed by the Maastricht Treaty on the EMU. The single mon-

[11] The metaphor used refers to the Treaty of the EU, made up as a Greek temple sustained by three pillars.

[12] Greece joined in 2001.

etary policy has been delegated to a supra-national authority, the ECB with a complex framework of objectives, policy instruments and decision-making procedures. According to the Maastricht Treaty, the ECB should safeguard price stability in the EMU and - subject to the condition that it does not interfere with price stability - promote economic growth in the EMU. Its policies are therefore directed at controlling economic developments of the EMU economy: price stability is now to be maintained in the euro area as a whole, which does not necessarily imply it at any time in each and every country composing the euro area.

The Governing Council of the ECB is charged with the formulation of the single monetary policy and for setting the guidelines for policy implementation; its responsibilities include decisions related to intermediate monetary objectives, key interest rates and the supply of reserves in the eurosystem. Each member of the Governing Council has one vote and monetary policy decisions require only a simple majority. The Governing Council is composed of the governors of the national CBs of the countries that fully participate in the EMU, and the members of the Executive Board. The Executive Board, in turn, is composed of the President, the Vice-President and four other members and is mainly responsible for the implementation of monetary policy. In this role it provides instructions to the twelve national CBs. The interaction between the Governing Council and the Executive Board and various other aspects of the decision-making framework of the ECB have received a strong interest, see e.g. Alesina and Grilli (1992), von Hagen and Suppel (1994), and De Haan (1997) for the most important results.

Responsibility for national budgetary policy and structural policies remains with the Member States, subject to their obligations stemming from the Treaty or from secondary legislation such as the SGP. Also wages continue to be negotiated nationally, according to the prevailing wage-bargaining arrangements. The design of the EMU with a highly independent monetary authority and decentralized fiscal authorities that are subject to fiscal restrictions in the form of the SGP, reflects the opinion that monetary and fiscal policies need to be clearly laid down and constrained to avoid a danger of fiscal profligacy and an ECB that is governed by political and/or national interests of politicians.

Fiscal and structural policies remain delegated to the national level in the EMU, reflecting the subsidiarity principle of the EU Treaty. The design of fiscal policies in the EMU is complicated by the set of constraints on national fiscal policy imposed by the SGP, according to which excessive deficits are to be avoided and subject to sanctions. The SGP stipulates that Member States adhere to the medium-term objective of budgetary positions 'close to balance or in surplus'. This should allow them to keep the general government deficit below 3 per cent of GDP in the face of 'normal' cyclical fluctuations without resorting to pro-cyclical fiscal tightening. Subject to certain provisions, including a waiver in the event of exceptionally severe recessions, pecuniary sanctions can be applied if the deficit threshold is crossed. Multilateral surveillance is exercised through the annual submission to the European Commission of programs containing macroeconomic and fiscal projections, showing how the countries plan to achieve their medium-term objectives.

1.5.3 Asymmetries in macroeconomic shocks, policy preferences, sizes and structures

One of the most important discussions in the EMU concerns the consequences of a common monetary policy in a setting with possible asymmetries in policy preferences and structural characteristics and when the EMU is hit by symmetric and asymmetric shocks in divergent macroeconomic conditions.

Empirical research initiated by the work of Bayoumi and Eichengreen (1993) on shock (a)symmetry in the EMU and by Artis and Zhang (1997) on the common business cycle components in the euro area suggest that in the euro area both symmetric and asymmetric shocks are important and also that the observed business cycles contain both a component that could be labelled 'the common euro area business cycle' and a component that reflects country-specific business cycle fluctuations.

Asymmetries in structural characteristics will lead to differences in the transmission of monetary and fiscal policies between different EMU countries. The transmission mechanisms of monetary policy for the area as a whole and the individual constituents are, moreover, quite uncertain and not uniform; see e.g. Ehrmann (2000). In fact, the euro area economy is not yet a well-known economic entity and past behavioural regularities may have changed with the advent of the euro. There are several potential sources of different regional responses to a common monetary policy. These include differences in the composition of output, the degree of openness, the level of development and structure of financial markets, industry balance sheet positions, and the flexibility and institutional features of labour and product markets. This aspect is likely to complicate macroeconomic policy design and coordination in the EMU to a significant extent.

Another concern is the possibility that regional conditions could have an unwarranted influence on policy. Even in the US, despite the high degree of centralization of decision making, there is some evidence that local conditions have an influence on the votes of regional presidents. The eurosystem is even more vulnerable in this regard. The composition of the Governing Council may carry the risk that heterogeneity of preferences about the output-inflation trade-off could result in an undue weight being placed on regional conditions. This, in turn, could lead to inefficient choices in ECB policies. Such pressures may intensify if the transmission mechanisms significantly differ across the euro area.

1.5.4 Macroeconomic policy coordination

With the move to the EMU, participating Member States will take an increased mutual interest in their economic performance: a high degree of economic interdependence exists throughout the EMU as a result of the completion of the Single Market. In addition, countries in the euro area now face the same monetary policy conditions. Economic trends in any part of the currency area can have a bearing on these conditions and can, therefore, have an impact on other parts of the currency area via various direct and indirect spillovers. Under EMU, consequently, there is a strong case for improved policy coordination because spillover channels lead to a high degree of externalities. Policy coordination can contribute to achieving an appropriate economic policy mix for the euro area as a whole as well as for its constituents. This includes taking into account possible negative economic externalities that could occur under non-coordinated decision making. Also, to avoid free-rider behaviour where policymakers renege on their own responsibilities and adopt a wait-and-see approach in an attempt to benefit from the efforts of others. In general, the outcome of policy coordination depends on the nature of the interactions as well as the type of macroeconomic shock. The EMU is supported by an extensive and sophisticated institutional framework; coordination of economic policies has been strengthened and there are long-standing initiatives to promote economic integration.

The annual Broad Economic Policy Guidelines of the Member States and the Community are the central element in this system. They give guidance to the policymakers at the national and Community levels with regard to macroeconomic and structural conditions. These guidelines seek to ensure consistency in the policy stance across policy instruments and across countries and the full use of available policy tools. General guidelines apply to the EU and the euro area as a whole and country-specific guidelines address issues of particular relevance for individual countries. In the EMU, the dimension of policy coordination can be decomposed into two elements. First, the possibility of fiscal policy coordination arises. As noted earlier, the EMU leaves fiscal policy design principally to the individual countries but setting a framework of fiscal constraints. It does not foresee the move to a fiscal federation either. In an integrated area like the EMU, individual fiscal policies have important effects on the other countries through a variety of spillover channels in goods, labour and financial markets in the EMU. Coordination of national fiscal policies enables to internalize the resulting externalities and by that to improve macroeconomic performance compared to non-cooperative fiscal policy design in the EU. This makes the possibility of fiscal coordination such an important aspect of macroeconomic policy design in the EMU.

Coordination of fiscal policy has considerably been strengthened since the early 1990s, as the Maastricht Treaty sets deficit and debt criteria to be respected before a country could join the euro area, and the SGP made these more stringent. The institutional side of coordination has also been enhanced with the Broad Economic Policy Guidelines, the SGP and the high-level EU policy groups such as ECOFIN (Economics and Finance Ministers), the Economic and Financial Committee and the Euro-12 Group (a subgroup of the ECOFIN specific to the EMU). The instrument of multilateral surveillance is used to reinforce the excessive deficit procedure and coordination of fiscal policies in the euro area. The ECB also plays a role in this procedure: it expresses its opinions about the stability programmes and the Broad Economic Policy Guidelines and in the discussions about the achievement of objectives and possible corrective measures that need to be taken.

Second, the possibility exists of monetary and fiscal policy coordination at the aggregate EMU level to stabilize output and inflation fluctuations in the EMU economy and to limit regional divergences. This issue has received less attention than the fiscal policy coordination issue. Nevertheless, the coordination of national fiscal policies with the common monetary policy of the ECB could be an important aspect of EMU, given the existence of interdependencies. At an empirical level, studies like Mélitz (2000) have tried to determine whether monetary and fiscal policies act as complements or substitutes in the EU. In the first case, both policies are mutually reinforcing and conflicts may only arise on how much of the adjustment burden is borne by which policy. In the second case, both policies are counteracting each other and there are likely to arise conflicts not only about the sharing of adjustment burdens but also about the optimal directions of monetary and fiscal policies in the EU.

A second important issue concerns the imposed fiscal stringency requirements by the 'Excessive Deficits Procedure' of the Maastricht Treaty and its detailed elaboration convened in the SGP, that was signed at the June 1997 Amsterdam summit of the Council of EU Ministers. It imposes a set of restrictions on fiscal flexibility under EMU. The SGP has a double role: (i) a preventive role of early warning against excessive budget deficits (budget surveillance), and (ii) a penalizing role for sustained budget shortages. The medium-term goal is approximate budget equilibrium or budget surplus. It was motivated by the fear that undisciplined fiscal behaviour is likely to put at risk the low inflation commitment of the ECB, since it will be difficult to rule out a monetary bail-out by the ECB under all circumstances. Undisciplined fiscal behaviour may also result in fiscal bail-outs through fiscal transfers in the EU. Finally, excessive deficits could induce upward pressure on interest rates and an appreciation of the euro. In both cases, pressure on the ECB could arise to ease its monetary policy. In all cases, the burdens associated with individual fiscal indiscipline will partly be transmitted to the other EU countries.

The SGP seeks to address longer-term economic externalities related to persistent biases toward excessive deficits and to foster monetary policy credibility. The SGP does, however, not address the issue of whether macroeconomic externalities in EMU are important enough to necessitate additional coordination of policies. In part, it will depend on the nature of the shock encountered. Large symmetric shocks are likely to require strong coordination of policies -including monetary policy- in the EMU. If the shock is country-specific, temporary and does not impinge much on the euro area aggregate, the appropriate instrument is national fiscal policy, and there may be less need for coordination. If the shock has implications for euro area wide inflation, the primary instrument should be monetary policy. Monetary policy should also take into account the implications of the fiscal policy stance for prospective price developments, especially if economic externalities between monetary and fiscal policies are considerable. This is more likely to be the case if large euro area economies, or a number of small economies simultaneously adjust fiscal policy, since their actions may have an impact on euro area-wide activity and inflation prospects to prompt a monetary policy response. Situations, however, may arise where the need for fiscal flexibility and the need for fiscal stringency will create a conflict and sub-optimal macroeconomic policies will be pursued. Buti *et al.* (2003) review the debate on changing the SGP because of its alleged lack of effectiveness in ensuring fiscal discipline and at the same time providing fiscal flexibility. Dismissing proposals of grand re-design of the SGP, they propose to improve the current rules by allowing a certain country-specificity, rebalancing 'sticks and carrots' and enhancing enforcement mechanisms.

The EMU, finally, also raises more general questions concerning a political and fiscal union in the EU. While the EU is currently far from a federal state, it can be useful to study some of the issues of policy coordination from a fiscal federalism perspective. In a longer-term perspective, one may imagine that, following the principles of fiscal federalism (see Oates (1972)), it will be decided to transfer certain types of fiscal decisions and instruments to the centralized EU level rather than relying on discretionary and *ad-hoc* fiscal coordination. Others will remain deliberately decentralized to the lower governments. Transfer mechanisms could be designed that compensate those agents who may lose by joining (leaving) the coalition (e.g. side-payments).

1.5.5 A textbook example of policy coordination in the EMU

A textbook example of the coordination of monetary and fiscal policies in the EMU is provided by a static aggregate demand (AD)-aggregate supply (AS) model of two symmetric countries that form an MU.[13] The model is described by the following equations:

$$y_1^d = -\gamma(i - \pi_1^e) - \delta(\pi_1 - \pi_2) + \eta f_1 + \rho y_2 + e_1 \tag{1.1}$$

$$y_1^s = \xi(\pi_1 - \pi_1^e) + u_1 \tag{1.2}$$

$$f_1 = f_1^s - \alpha y_1 \tag{1.3}$$

$$y_2^d = -\gamma(i - \pi_2^e) + \delta(\pi_1 - \pi_2) + \eta f_2 + \rho y_1 + e_2 \tag{1.4}$$

$$y_2^s = \xi(\pi_2 - \pi_2^e) + u_2 \tag{1.5}$$

$$f_2 = f_2^s - \alpha y_2 \tag{1.6}$$

Equations (1.1) and (1.4) show aggregate demand y^d for both countries as a function of the real interest rate, defined as the nominal interest rate i minus

[13]See Buti *et al.* (2001) and extensions of that analysis by Beetsma *et al.* (2001). See also Buti and Guidice (2002) and Lambertini and Rovelli (2003). In Buti *et al.* (2001) and Buti and Guidice (2002) the two countries are lumped together to one aggregate country, but otherwise the analysis is the same.

expected inflation π^e, the real exchange rate, approximated by the inflation differential, the fiscal deficit f, output in the other country and a demand shock e. Equations (1.2) and (1.5) are the individual country's aggregate supply as a function of (surprise) inflation and a supply shock u. Assume that demand and supply shocks in a country are non-correlated. The fiscal deficit consists according to (1.3) (and (1.6)) of the structural deficit and the automatic stabilizers which imply that the deficit is lowered by an increase in output and *vice versa*. If the correlation of demand shocks (supply shocks, respectively) in both countries is equal to one, symmetric shocks are faced, if it is minus one there are anti-symmetric shocks (see also Section 1.4). Finally if the correlation is equal to zero, the shocks are independently distributed or asymmetric.

The preference functions of the fiscal authorities and the CB are given by:

$$L_1 = \frac{1}{2}\left[\alpha(\pi_1 - \bar{\pi}_1)^2 + \beta(y_1 - \bar{y}_1)^2 + \chi(f_1 - \bar{f}_1)^2\right] \qquad (1.7)$$

$$L_2 = \frac{1}{2}\left[\alpha(\pi_2 - \bar{\pi}_2)^2 + \beta(y_2 - \bar{y}_2)^2 + \chi(f_2 - \bar{f}_2)^2\right] \qquad (1.8)$$

$$L_{CB} = \frac{1}{2}\left[\alpha_{CB}(\pi_U - \bar{\pi}_U)^2 + \beta_{CB}(y_U - \bar{y}_U)^2 + \chi_{CB}(i - \bar{\imath})^2\right], \qquad (1.9)$$

where $\pi_U := \omega\pi_1 + (1-\omega)\pi_2$ and $y_U := \omega y_1 + (1-\omega)y_2$ are average inflation and output in the MU. Reflecting e.g. ideological or electoral considerations, fiscal players are concerned with a mix of price stability, output stability and deficit stability. The target values of these variables are denoted with a bar and may for simplicity also be put to zero. The fiscal deficit target could be the result of the SGP, which implies that non-compliance leads to sanctions in pecuniary and non-pecuniary form entailing costs for the policymaker. Similarly, the ECB weighs the costs from (euro area) inflation, output and interest rate variability.

Three different policy regimes can be analyzed. In regime 1, authorities do not coordinate leading to the Nash equilibrium. In regime 2, there is *ex-ante* full coordination of the fiscal authorities who then play non-cooperatively against the CB. Regime 3, implies full cooperation of monetary and fiscal policies in the MU.

Solving the respective optimization problems subject to the structure of the economies and the constraints imposed by the policy regimes, yields the players' reaction functions which can be given an interpretation of policy rules. By substituting out further, one can write the monetary and fiscal policies as linear functions of (i) the macroeconomic shocks, (ii) the other players' instruments; the reaction of policies to shocks and the other instruments varies across the different regimes.

In this way, one can also determine under which conditions policy instruments act as complements or as substitutes. This will strongly depend on the type of shock, the sign and strength of policy spillovers and the policy regime including the strength of the CB, i.e. the degree of commitment of the CB. E.g.

in the case of supply shocks, output and inflation move in opposite directions and fiscal and monetary policies are likely to be substitutes if the fiscal policymakers are strongly output-oriented and the CB is very anti-inflationary. As argued by Buti *et al.* (2001), this setting is in particular susceptible to gains from policy coordination: under coordination, the fiscal authorities keep deficits low as they consider that the CB will keep inflation under control. Conversely, under coordination the CB will not restrict interest rates by more than strictly needed to absorb the higher rate of inflation. Instead, under non-coordination, each player strongly moves in the opposite direction optimal for the other player, leading to excessively lose fiscal policies and an excessively restrictive monetary policy.

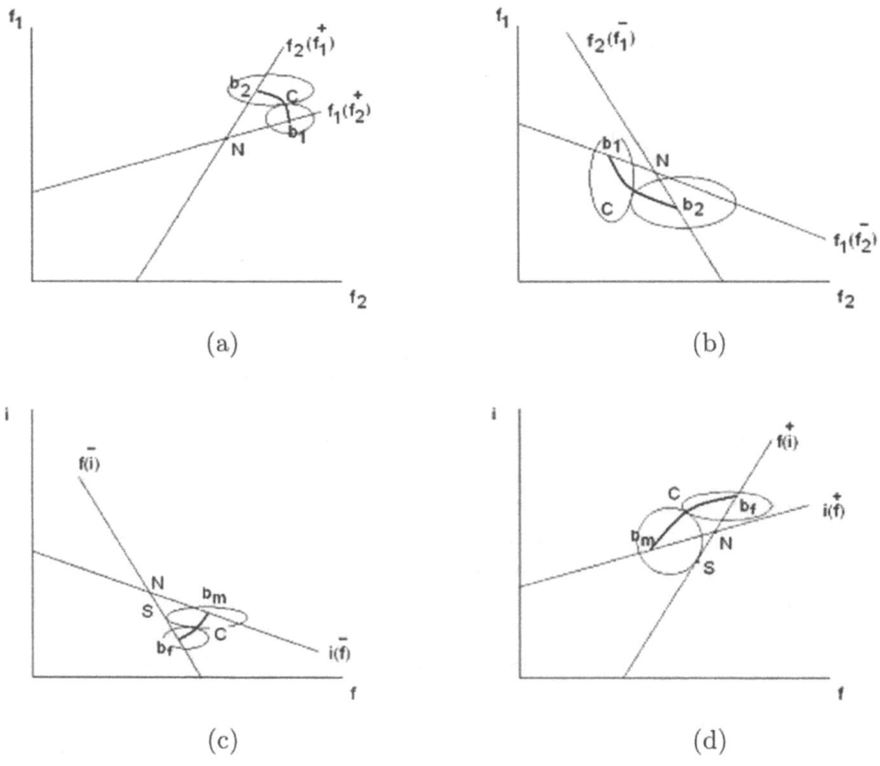

Figure 1.3
Policy complementarity ((a) and (c)) vs. policy substitutability ((b) and (d)).

Buti *et al.* (2001) argue that gains from coordination are likely to be smaller in case of demand shocks. In Buti and Guidice (2002), the model is focussed on the functioning of the SGP: it is shown that if fiscal authorities want to stabilize output by letting automatic stabilizers work while maintaining fiscal discipline, they have to focus on structural rather than actual deficits. Only then the necessary room for manoeuvre can be created to allow the full working of automatic stabilizers. Lambertini and Rovelli (2003) add Stackelberg equilibria to the game outlined above. In the case of Stackelberg leadership of the fiscal players, they can impose their preferred point of the reaction curve of the monetary authorities; vice versa in the case of Stackelberg leadership of the monetary player who can impose on the fiscal players that fiscal strategy on the fiscal reaction curve that minimizes the CB's welfare losses.

Figure 1.3 illustrates cases where fiscal policies of countries 1 and 2 are (a) strategic complements and (b) strategic substitutes. Similarly, in (c) fiscal policies and the monetary policy of the ECB are complements and in (d) they act as strategic substitutes.

Depicted are in all cases the Nash equilibrium (N), the benchmark for non-cooperative policymaking and the locus of cooperative (C) equilibria. In the case of monetary and fiscal policy interaction we also indicate the Stackelberg equilibria with Stackelberg leadership of the monetary player. The players' 'bliss-points' are indicated by a b. In the case policies are complements, non-cooperative policies are generally too restrictive: policy coordination will provide more fiscal activism in both countries (panel (a)) and a more expansionary monetary-fiscal policy mix (panel (c)). Conversely, if policy instruments are substitutes, non-cooperation leads to too lax policies: policy coordination will induce fiscal tightening (panel (b)) and a more restrictive monetary-fiscal policy mix (panel (d)).

Positive economic externalities can explain why policies are set as complements: e.g. if an expansionary fiscal policy in country 1 is accompanied by also an expansionary fiscal policy in country 2, the positive output spillover of the latter via the import channel will reinforce in country 1 the initial expansionary fiscal policy creating the externality. If negative spillovers dominate, policies are likely to be set as substitutes: e.g. if an expansionary fiscal policy in country 1 is accompanied by a restrictive monetary policy of the CB to counteract inflation; this will reduce the expansionary effects of the initial fiscal policy of country 1 not only in country 1 but also in country 2. In the case policies act as substitutes there is scope for conflicts between players on both the directions and sizes of the adjustments, in case of complements players agree on the directions of policies and can only disagree on the size of preferred adjustments. This clearly matters for the design, implementation and outcomes of policy coordination: the gains of coordination are potentially larger if negative economic externalities dominate, but in that case it is also more difficult to implement and enforce. This can also explain why in some circumstances, namely where the negative economic externalities of fiscal policy dominate, restrictions on national fiscal policy may be welfare improving, whereas they become welfare reducing in the case where positive economic externalities dominate and a lack of flexibility at the national level is inefficient from a welfare perspective. In addition, if the differences in preferences between players get larger, the scope for strong conflicts rises. This becomes clear from a combination of a very conservative monetary player that is strongly biased towards price stability and governments that are mainly output concerned. The divergence of preferences heightens the conflicts between monetary and fiscal policies and increases the gains from policy coordination.

The incentives for coordination depend on the welfare gains and losses in response to shocks. The welfare effects on their turn also depend on the structural characteristics of the economies as summarized by the various model parameters that determine various positive and negative spillovers, the policymakers' preferences and restrictions on policies in the form of the SGP. Using numerical examples, one can analyze how monetary and fiscal instruments interact, the resulting output and inflation and the fiscal and monetary players' losses in different coordination regimes and under different types of shocks. Policy instruments act as substitutes, complements or do not affect each other depending on the structural parameters, type of shock and the type of policy coordination. Beetsma *et al.* (2001) find that in the case of symmetric shocks, fiscal coordination is likely to worsen outcomes as it worsens the conflict with the ECB, suggesting that fiscal cooperation is likely to be counterproductive. On the other hand, if shocks are anti-symmetric, monetary policy remains passive and fiscal coordination becomes desirable, since, in that case, fiscal authorities internalize the fact that their actions are partially offsetting and there is no adverse reaction from the monetary policymaker.

This stylized analysis based on this textbook example of a static two-country EMU is therefore very useful to analyze the main implications of policy coordination in the EMU. Another important benefit is that its setup and spirit is strongly related to the framework in Chapters 3 and 4, where we will analyze similar issues in a dynamic framework finding that several insights carry over to a dynamic setting, where in addition, a number of interesting additional insights appear.

1.5.6 Brief general literature overview

Although the textbook case is relevant, many additional issues about monetary and fiscal policy interactions in the EMU have been raised in the literature. This subsection briefly summarizes the main results. We focus both on theoretical and empirical contributions.[14]

Including the studies mentioned in the subsection above, a significant theoretical literature on the interaction of monetary and fiscal policies in the EMU has been developed. Most analyses of the interaction of monetary and fiscal policies in the EMU take a static or quasi-static approach in the spirit of the well-known Barro-Gordon or the Alesina-Tabellini model.[15] Despite that many of the insights of these studies are important, it is not always obvious that they can be transformed to the analysis in this book, which is set in a dynamic framework, where issues of dynamic interactions and dynamic propagations of shocks

[14] The institutional framework in which policy coordination between the ECB and the ECOFIN is situated is reviewed in detail by Italianer (1999), Bini Smaghi and Casini (2000), and Alesina and Perotti (2004).

[15] See, e.g., Dixit (2003) or Acocella and Di Bartolomeo (2004) for the former model; Beetsma and Bovenberg (1998), Beetsma and Uhlig (1999), von Hagen and Suppel (1994) for the latter model.

and policies are the crucial focus, rather than their static effects. Moreover, in these static models, the effects of monetary and fiscal policies are often set to work only on the supply side of the economy. Such a focus may seem rather narrow and risks to attach too much value to the supply-side effects of monetary and fiscal policies, which in practice may actually be of limited relevance/take a very long time to materialize. In our approach the workings are situated at the demand side of the economy and supply is essentially held fixed throughout.

There are a few theoretical works that also analyze monetary and fiscal policies in an MU using a dynamic framework. Krichel *et al.* (1996) analyze the effects of fiscal coordination and full coordination in a dynamic two-country EMU model that is very different from the model used in our analysis, making direct comparisons of conclusions very difficult. Hughes Hallett and Ma (1996) have suggested that this form of policy coordination is indeed relevant in the EMU context. Neck *et al.* (2002a and 2002b) analyze the interactions of monetary and fiscal policies in the EMU using simulations of a large-scale dynamic and empirically-estimated model, studying various policy regimes and various types of shocks. It is found that cooperation among fiscal policymakers in the EMU is nearly always superior to non-cooperative equilibrium solutions. A similar approach is undertaken by Breuss and Weber (2001), who find that the SGP may significantly limit the potential benefits from cooperation in the EMU as optimal fiscal policies often require breaching the SGP.

There are also a number of empirical studies. Contributions in this area are mainly based on panel data techniques and VAR analyses. Cross-sectional or panel data examine the relationship between fiscal and monetary policies over the cycle. Mélitz (2000) and Wyplosz (1999) broadly support the view that the two policies have acted as strategic substitutes over the last decades. Von Hagen *et al.* (2001) find an asymmetric interdependence, i.e. looser fiscal stances match monetary contractions, whereas monetary policies broadly accommodate fiscal expansions. Peersman (2004) includes growth of industrial output, inflation, the German interest rate and the domestic interest rate in the estimated VAR of the UK, France, the Netherlands, Belgium, Austria, Italy and Spain. Muscatelli *et al.* (2002) examine the interaction between fiscal and monetary policy instruments using conventional VAR and Bayesian VAR models for several G-7 economies (Germany, France, Italy, the UK and the US), and show that the fiscal shocks, identified in the VAR, have a significant impact. They find that the result of strategic substitutability does not hold uniformly for all countries and report strong evidence that the linkages between fiscal and monetary policies has shifted *post*-1980, when fiscal and monetary policies became much more complementary.

The main problem with this empirical literature is however that, without a structural model, it is difficult to interpret the empirical correlations between the two policy variables. In addition, although in the estimated VARs the focus is on the reaction of policy instruments to other policy shocks, it is notoriously difficult to interpret implicit policy reaction functions in VARs, especially if the true underlying structural model is forward-looking.

Monticelli and Tristani (1999) use a structural VAR (SVAR) model of the aggregate EMU economy to study the transmission of aggregate demand shocks, aggregate supply shocks and innovations to monetary policy. Ehrmann (2000) and Wehinger (2000) compare monetary policy transmission across EU countries using the SVAR approach, finding evidence for considerable heterogeneity across countries. Garcia and Verdelhan (2001) study the fiscal and monetary policy transmission mechanisms in the aggregate euro area economy. Supply shocks, nominal shocks, fiscal policy shocks and monetary policy shocks are identified and their impacts on the euro area economy are assessed. Dalsgaard and de Serres (2000) estimate an SVAR model for eleven individual EMU countries. The four-variable VAR contains real output growth, inflation, change of private sector savings and the change in the ratio of government net lending to GDP. Van Aarle *et al.* (2003) analyze the transmission of monetary and fiscal policies in the aggregate euro area and in individual euro area countries using SVAR models.

1.6 Coordination at work - other international arrangements

Since the breakdown of the Bretton-Woods system, the most important 'place' for policy coordination was without doubts the Group of Seven (G-7). However, more recently the primate of the G-7 Summit has been challenged by other institutions. The relevance of the European institutions has, e.g., increased over time, especially with the creation of the euro. The recent globalization process has enforced centralization processes and the rule of the international institutions (as the WTO, IMF, OECD and the World Bank), also by the creation of trade unions as MERCOSUR, NAFTA, ASEAN and so on.

This section discusses the most relevant cases of macroeconomic and currency coordination starting from the G-7 Summits and the European experience to the most recent developments related to emerging economies and currency crises. The current debate about the possibility of creating an MU in South East Asia and South America will also be discussed.

1.6.1 The G-7 process

The now-called G-7 was created in March 1973 when US Treasury Secretary George Shultz invited the German, French and British Finance Ministers to an informal meeting in the ground floor library of the White House.[16] Discussions were centred around the international monetary system. The result of the meeting was an agreement to abandon attempts to re-establish fixed parities between the dollar and European currencies, thereby helping to usher in the floating-rate era. The G-7 operations had begun.

In the fall of the same year, the Japanese Finance Minister was invited to join the Library Group. Afterwards, the informal meetings were augmented

[16] For this reason the group was initially called the 'Library Group'.

by annual economic summits at the country leaders' level and CB Governors were also involved. In November 1975 Italy was invited to participate to the Rambouillet (France) summit and in 1976 the Group of Seven was completed by Canada's participation at the 1976 summit in Puerto Rico. The Presidents of the European Commission and the European Council have also regularly attended the Leaders' summits since 1977 and 1986, respectively. Although invited, however, Italy and Canada were on the border of the ministerial process as cooperation remained largely limited to the original countries of the Library Group until the early 1980s. The group officially became the G-7 with the entrance of Italy and Canada only in 1986. Since then the G-7 finance ministers and CB governors have met regularly every year. The President of Russia was invited to meet with the G-7 Leaders for the first time in 1991. After the end of the Soviet regime, in fact, Russia's participation has increased over time such that the summit is now called the G-8 Summit.[17]

The first attempt at policy coordination of G-5 occurred in the wake of the oil price shock of December 1973. After the oil price shock, as each country began to experience higher inflation and a deteriorating balance of payments, the world faced the danger of excessive monetary and fiscal contraction as each country's tighter policies tended to raise inflation and reduce net exports of its neighbours. This scenario is the classical textbook example to describe the potential gains from international coordination by internalizing economic externalities. In such a circumstance, G-5 countries attempted to coordinate their policy. Rather than agree on specific macro policies, however, the G-5 decided a different institutional alternative based on two pillars. First, the G-5 Leaders agreed to establish the International Energy Agency, affiliated with the OECD, as a forum for oil-importing nations to discuss energy strategies. Second, the G-5 attempted to give countries an alternative to fiscal tightening by pushing a new oil-adjustment facility in the IMF.

In 1977, industrialized countries again attempt to coordinate their macroeconomic policy during the G-7 London Summit. Objectives of the coordinated policy were unspecified, but broadly-accepted, growth targets. The failure in achieving the targets was the main reason to support formal promises in the subsequent Summit held in Bonn. On the one hand, France, Germany and Japan pledged specific fiscal expansions and, on the other hand, the US promised to decontrol domestic oil prices. Even if all the participants essentially carried through with the agreements reached in Bonn, some economists have underlined that the agreement was a failure because it promoted misguided policies, i.e. the time-coordinated policies were agreed upon economic problems that had already shifted. According to this view, which, however, is not indisputable,[18] the Bonn agreement determined the burst of global inflation and subsequent recession in 1979-81.

The Plaza Agreement of September 1985 and the Louvre Accord of February 1987 are two of the most-known interventions of the G-7. These agreements are

[17] However, during the summit, the leaders arrange some time to meet without Russia to discuss macroeconomic policies and certain other IMF-centred issues, such as debt relief.

[18] See Meyer *et al.* (2002).

relevant on both the macroeconomic policy and currency coordination. As results of the agreements, all the Leaders promised to undertake a list of specified policy actions in terms of macroeconomic policy and to cooperate in currency intervention. Differently from the previous debate, where the central themes were inflation and growth, the primary area of concern of the 1985 and 1987 agreements were the large external imbalances between the major regions, which were raising protectionist pressures that the Leaders feared they could not resist. The agreements were based on commitments to reduce deficits and implement tax cuts, institutional reforms designed to increase economic efficiency, resistance to protectionist policies. Japan promised to liberalize its financial markets to ease consumer credit, to facilitate the internationalization and strengthening of the yen, to conduct monetary policy 'with due attention to the yen rate' and to cut the discount rate. Despite that the monetary commitments were fulfilled, at least for a short while, the fiscal ones largely were not achieved, particularly French promises to reduce taxes, Japanese promises on fiscal stimulus, and US promises on deficit reduction were not met.

The Plaza and Louvre accords were also relevant for coordination in the currency policies.[19] The Plaza agreement in fact called for dollar depreciation whereas the Louvre agreement declared that dollar depreciation had gone far enough. Both announcements described participants as being ready for concerted intervention to encourage the desired exchange rate adjustment whenever it was appropriate.

The Leaders of the G-7 have informally engaged in concerted intervention on occasion ever since the first Library Group meeting. After the announcements of 1985 and 1987, in 1989 the G-7 decided for an intervention trying to limit the appreciation of the dollar. In the 1990s, there was a change of route by the virtual abandonment of coordinated intervention with few exceptions. However, G-7 statements regularly repeat the threat of possible future coordinated intervention if warranted by the circumstances.

The decreasing relevance of currency coordination in the most recent years could also be due to the position of the Bank of Japan, which attributes to the Louvre Accord some responsibility for the Japanese bubble, and to the development of the European monetary integration process culminated with the creation of the ECB.

[19] "The motivation for currency intervention is to avoid large swings in exchange rates that bring about unsustainable current account imbalances and impose large adjustment costs on the economy. To the extent that these swings are induced by the fundamental macroeconomic policy mix, currency intervention is ineffective at best and harmful at worst. However, when financial markets overshoot the exchange rates consistent with fundamental policies, intervention may be able to help restore equilibrium, although such a presumption is not universally accepted." (Meyer *et al.* (2002), p. 21).

1.6.2 Financial crises in emerging markets - the need for international coordination

The creation of the euro zone has stimulated a large debate about the possibility of exporting this model to different areas and to consider the consequences of an international scenario where only a few trade and monetary blocks ultimately will remain. Such a scenario may become increasingly relevant in the coming decades.

The recent strengthening of the globalization process has in fact supported the creation of trade and monetary integration in all the world. The number of trade blocks and currency unions has considerably risen in the last decades. Apart from the European case discussed above, the most prominent examples are the North American Free Trade Area (NAFTA), the Association of South East Asian Nations (ASEAN), the Common Market of the South or *Mercado Común del Sur* (MERCOSUR), the Eastern Caribbean Currency Union, the Western Africa Economic and Monetary Union, the Central Africa Economic and Monetary Community and recent initiatives by states of he former Soviet Union. Compared to the euro area all these unions are clearly in a rather infantile state.[20]

Globalization should have positive effects by increasing the international competitiveness, but it also increases the needs and scopes for international policy coordination by increasing economic externalities among nations. The frequent emergence of international currency crises seems to support this point of view. The effects of the EMU project are thus particularly relevant for two geographic areas: South East Asia and South America, where strong processes of integration and international coordination are already in act and a high financial fragility has been highlighted by recent turbulences.

This section briefly surveys the attempts of international policy coordination in these areas. In particular, we focus on the Asian area, where cooperation needs were associated with the financial crisis. We also discuss the attempts to cooperate in South America.

In the last decades, the entire East Asian region was experiencing miraculous economic growth, the so-called East Asian miracle. From the 1960s to 1996, East Asia's economic growth averaged about 8% a year, which was higher than the growth experienced by most industrial, well-developed countries during that period.

Integration among Asian countries has mainly been developed within the ASEAN,[21] which was created as an anti-communist, political organization in 1967. The ASEAN economies are very different[22] and until the 1990s were

[20] However, apart from the EMU, existing currency unions are remnants of a common colonial heritage with a single currency.

[21] ASEAN includes ten countries (Indonesia, Malaysia, Philippines, and Singapore since 1967; Thailand and Brunei since 1984; Vietnam since 1995; Laos and Myanmar since 1997; and Cambodia since 1999). It covers a population of about 500 million, and a total area of 4.5 million square kilometers. Its total GDP in 2003 was US$737 billion.

[22] Some of them have very open financial markets as Singapore, which is one of the most advanced countries in the world. By contrast, other countries are not advanced and are still

mostly closed economies. However, in January 1992 the fourth ASEAN Summit created the ASEAN Free Trade Area (AFTA). The main objective of AFTA was to increase ASEAN's competitive edge as a producer and to promote greater economic efficiency and competitiveness of the manufacturing sector by eliminating intra-ASEAN tariffs and non-tariff barriers.[23] The AFTA agreement has shown some significant results by increasing trade among the countries of ASEAN.

Trade integration calls for monetary integration. In 1994, Eichengreen (1994) started the debate on the possibility of monetary cooperation in East Asia.[24] It was, however, the 1997 East Asian currency crisis that gave it urgency, especially the observation that the drastic appreciation of the dominant anchor currency, the US dollar, was partly to blame for the crisis.

The dynamic economic progress in fact collapsed with the 1997 crisis that exposed the fragile nature of the financial and banking systems of East Asia. Through the contagion effect, the currency crisis spread from Thailand to Indonesia, to Malaysia and to the Philippines. Other Asian and ASEAN countries were also affected negatively.

In order to face and prevent further crises, economic integration has become a necessity in the ASEAN area. Regional financial cooperation in East Asia has so far focussed on three major initiatives: creation of a regional liquidity support facility through the so-called *Chiang Mai Initiative*,[25] which involved a currency swap network among the ASEAN and the People's Republic of China (PRC), Japan and the Republic of Korea (ASEAN+3).

In May 2004 the ASEAN+3 countries have begun to review the *Chiang Mai Initiative* starting, including the amount, modality and IMF linkages. This review involves not only the *Chiang Mai Initiative* issues but also wider issues pertinent to regional financial cooperation, even including exchange rate policy coordination.

Summarizing, the Asian crisis has radically changed the view to exchange-rate management in the area and stimulated a debate among economists and policymakers. Before 1997, most East Asian countries had pegged their curren-

---

struggling to survive. For example, Vietnam is still at the beginning stages of establishing itself in the world economy.

[23] AFTA presented a programme of regional tariff reduction called, 'the Agreement on the Common Effective Preferential Tariff Scheme'. This scheme commenced in 1993 and had as a goal the reduction of import tariffs levied on a wide range of products to at least five percent. It also seeks to eliminate other non-tariff barriers in the region. Indonesia, Malaysia, Philippines, Singapore and Thailand had to meet the requirements of the agreement by 2003. Vietnam is supposed to meet the AFTA requirements by 2006, Laos and Myanmar by 2008, and Cambodia by 2010.

[24] Dornbusch and Park (1998) propose the yen block. Before the collapse of the Japanese bubble economy in the late 1990s, the yen block proposal would have been the most natural for East Asia. The fate of the yen block has however dimmed away with the persistent problems of the Japanese economy.

[25] Participants facing capital outflow can quickly borrow foreign exchange for currency defense, from either the *Expanded ASEAN Swap Arrangement* (to provide liquidity in dollar, yen, or euro) or a network of bilateral swap arrangements or repurchase (sale and buy-back of appropriate securities) agreements among the ASEAN countries, PRC, Japan, and Korea. The ASEAN Swap Arrangement facility is now worth $1.0 billion.

cies to the dollar or yen, but during the crisis they were forced to float their currencies. Since then, a lively debate is seen concerning the perfect exchange rate regime for the East-Asian countries. Floating the currency, pegging the currency to the dollar, yen or euro, forming an internal basket peg, and even forming an ASEAN MU are the many options that economists and policymakers are considering.

On the other side of the Pacific Ocean, macroeconomic turmoils (Brazilian currency devaluation and the Argentinean crisis) have also recently characterized the South American experience. These turbulences, the fear of contagion, and existing externalities have raised new questions about the future of MERCOSUR. The debate is mainly focussed upon two opposite alternatives: i) limiting the South American experience to the minimal project of a free trade agreement by joining the NAFTA; or ii) create a new framework for economic management to change the style of fiscal policies and modify the financial and monetary system in the EMU fashion.

The MERCOSUR agreement (Treaty of Asuncion in 1991)[26] was in fact initially signed by the presidents of Argentina, Brazil, Paraguay, and Uruguay with the purpose of creating a customs union and a common market with a common external tariff by 1994. However, MERCOSUR had among its objectives the coordination of macroeconomic and industry policies in addition to the free movement of goods, services and productive factors between member countries, and the adoption of a common trade policy. The medium-term goal of harmonization of macroeconomic policies, often interpreted as working toward the introduction of a single currency, was made explicit in the treaty.

Argentina's President Carlos Menem suggested the creation of a common currency for MERCOSUR countries at the MERCOSUR President's meeting in April 1997.[27] The need and the possibility of having a common currency has then been discussed in policy circles for some time.

Fratianni and Hausknecht (2002) argue that MERCOSUR needs a long-term monetary strategy. MERCOSUR countries have to pursue monetary integration if they intend to save their custom's union and further deepen economic integration. These countries have two options: a decentralized monetary union, whereby each member country either pegs to the US dollar or dollarizes outright; or a centralized MU with its own currency, its own CB, and the adoption of common minimum financial standards in an EMU style. Eichengreen (1998) and Eichengreen and Taylor (2003) also address the question of whether MERCOSUR needs a single currency and what the monetary consequences of a Free Trade Area of the Americas would be by using cross-country panel-data techniques. In their view, to assess the conditions for monetary cooperation, it is necessary to investigate the determinants of bilateral exchange rate volatility. Their main conclusion on MERCOSUR is that no important economic imped-

[26] Argentina and Brazil embarked on a process of economic integration already in the mid-1980s, with the establishment of the bilateral 'Programa de Integracion y Cooperation Argentino-Brasileño'.

[27] After the devaluation of the Real, President Menem had also suggested the adoption of the US dollar as legal tender.

iments exist for monetary cooperation and that the lack of political consensus might be the most important obstacle.[28] However, monetary integration in the MERCOSUR area faces even more practical problems[29] than in the Asian one and can be seen only as a very long-term project.

Regarding the NAFTA agreements, it does not include provisions for macroeconomic policy coordination of any kind. Indeed, debates about the advantages and disadvantages of exchange rate regimes have taken place, however, but without clear conclusions. There are two more probable reasons for the lack of macroeconomic policy coordination: (i) there is no political consensus to increase integration if any loss of sovereignty of the member countries would be required and (ii) the macroeconomic environment has been stable and very conducive to promoting trade during the span of the NAFTA agreement, which has led to a lack of urgency for policy coordination.[30]

1.6.3 Some general observations on coordination experiences

There are several conclusions to draw from the above discussion. The most striking aspect of the foregoing historical outline are probably the very different directions taken by policy coordination within Europe compared to those within the G-7. The G-7 has moved away from specific policy pledges to a more general sense of the desired direction of policy. By contrast, the core of Europe has moved toward ever tighter monetary and fiscal policy coordination (Meyer *et al.* (2002)).

More in general, macroeconomic policy coordination can take many shapes and forms, and as the review of experience around the world shows, the type of policy coordination chosen usually depends on the economic and political specificities of the region at hand. In the two regions, which have experienced macroeconomic instability in recent years, namely the MERCOSUR and ASEAN regions, regional trade integration has fallen.

1.7 A look ahead

After having briefly introduced the main general subjects of the research in this book, we outline the rough contents of the next chapters, which (almost) all are based on papers published in international scientific journals.

The next three chapters of the book will introduce the reader to the dynamic modelling of fiscal and monetary policy cooperation. The functioning of the model will be shown for a number of issues, which are discussed in the OCA/MU

[28] "The failure to engage in monetary cooperation in Mercosur is not obviously a function of economic variables. The countries do not have unusual size, trade, composition, or other economic characteristics that militate against monetary cooperation; in this respect they are reasonably similar to the EU. Rather, the sources of the cooperation deficit lie elsewhere" (Eichengreen and Taylor (2003), p. 25).

[29] In particular, in terms of fiscal convergence, credibility and political economy.

[30] There have been no devaluations since the peso was devalued in 1995.

literature, such as fiscal coordination, fiscal stringency requirements, structural asymmetries between countries, bargaining powers, fiscal transfer systems and the design of monetary and fiscal policymaking in an MU. In the final three chapters we will introduce a multiple-player setting and we will study aspects of fiscal and/or monetary coordination using endogenous coalition formation approaches. The analysis will be focussed on shock and model asymmetries and issues of multi-country coordination in the presence of (possibly many) MUs.

More in detail, Chapter 2 sets out mathematical tools necessary to solve the models formulated as a dynamic optimization problem. The theory is presented in a general form so as to enable the reader to solve modified models from the book or to apply it to own research problems. Subsequent chapters are going to be examples in the application of the toolkit presented in this chapter and this in an ever increasing advanced form. This mathematical chapter is based on Engwerda (2005a). The consideration of a dynamic framework in a multi-agent context requires a precise definition of the information the agents have in the model. In this book we deal with the so-called *open-loop* information structure. That is, the case where every player knows at time $t \in [0, \infty)$ just the initial state x_0, and the model structure. This scenario can be interpreted as that the players simultaneously determine their actions, next submit their actions to some authority who then enforces these plans as binding commitments. An analysis about the interaction of monetary and fiscal policies with a *feedback* information structure may be found in van Aarle *et al.* (2001).

Chapter 3 focuses on the design of fiscal policy in a closed and symmetric MU. The (New-) Keynesian dynamic open-economy macroeconomic model that underlies the approach is introduced to the reader and the basics of the approach presented. In its basic form it entails a dynamic two-country continuous-time model with a passive central bank. The adjustment dynamics resulting from initial shocks are examined, both when countries coordinate and do not coordinate their fiscal instruments, and the resulting gains of cooperation are studied. The effects of fiscal coordination are analyzed in detail. It is shown how the effects of fiscal coordination are influenced by (i) fiscal stringency requirements that restrict the flexibility of fiscal policy, (ii) asymmetric bargaining weights, (iii) the introduction of a fiscal transfer system. The chapter is based on Engwerda *et al.* (2002).

In Chapter 4, a common central bank is added to the focus of attention. It enables us to study the common monetary policy and its interactions with national fiscal policies. It introduces active monetary policy (and asymmetry) to the symmetric two-country MU model outlined in Chapter 3. Clearly, it raises a whole array of new issues. The focus of the analysis is on the interaction of national fiscal policies and the common monetary policy in the MU. It is shown how the institutional design of monetary and fiscal policies will be crucial in the outcomes produced by an MU. Here, not only fiscal coordination is analyzed again but also the coordination of monetary and fiscal policies. Fiscal coordination becomes in this setting a form of 'partial coordination': the coordinated fiscal policy is interacting with the common monetary policy. A comparison with Chapter 3's passive monetary policy shows that outcomes are markedly affected by relaxing this assumption. In addition, the possibility of partial coalitions between one fiscal player and the common central bank are allowed and it is shown that such coalitions are only likely in rather specific conditions. In Chapter 4, we also study the effects of a number of asymmetries: (i) asymmetry in fiscal players' preferences, (ii) structural asymmetries (asymmetries in monetary policy transmission and asymmetry of competitiveness effects), (iii) asymmetry of bargaining power. Regarding the last issue, we compare the obtained results with those of Chapter 3. The basis for this chapter is formed by van Aarle *et al.* (2002a, 2002b, 2004).

In Chapter 5 basic ideas of coalition formation theory are studied. A few different equilibrium concepts are presented, starting from the simplest myopic open-membership approach, through restricted and exclusive-membership rules, to most sophisticated sequential games characterized by farsightedness. The algorithms to obtain solutions of the different equilibrium concepts in a simple way are listed in an appendix of the chapter, which is based on Michalak *et al.* (2005).

Chapter 6 extends the basic two-country MU model to an n-country closed-economy model of an MU to analyze monetary and fiscal policy in an MU of several countries. Numerical analysis of a three-country MU is used to illustrate a number of important insights. Results of macroeconomic stabilization policies are compared with the results of Chapters 3 and 4. The conceptual framework of endogenous coalition formation is applied in this chapter as well. The basis for this chapter forms Di Bartolomeo *et al.* (2003, 2004).

A next step is taken in Chapter 7, where the closed-economy model of the MU used so far is extended by opening up the MU introducing a multi-country open-economy MU model. In this setting, possibly more than one MU is operating and the MU(s) is (are) interacting with non-members. Exchange rates are introduced as novel channels of macroeconomic policy transmissions, implying additional economic spillovers. The possibility of accessions/secessions to/from MU(s) is analyzed by considering the costs and benefits of accession of new members and this from the perspective of the acceding country, the current member states and even the non-acceding non-member states. This analysis, based on Engwerda *et al.* (2005), is therefore very relevant for the current issue of enlargement of the euro area. In the numerical simulation part, we consider five countries (the current EMU consisting of two (blocks of) countries, a previously existing EU non-EMU country (as e.g. the UK) or block of countries (Denmark, Sweden, UK), a new EU non-EMU country (as e.g. Poland) or block of countries (as the 10 EU-accession countries), and the ROW (represented e.g. by the USA)).

Chapter 8 further extends the previous chapter by considering an n-country world economy with regional blocks that can choose various degrees of monetary and fiscal policy coordination. In this general form, several new interesting aspects of macroeconomic policy coordination are present and analyzed. We consider the possibility of multiple MUs or blocks of countries cooperating in their fiscal policies and we analyze the effects of such settings. In particular, these settings involve questions on international monetary and fiscal policy coordination and interactions between them. Such aspects played an important role e.g. in recent G-7 meetings, where the need for policy coordination was stressed.

Chapter 9 collects the most important (economic) insights obtained in the book.

Chapter 2

Mathematical Background

This chapter provides the mathematical material that is used throughout this book. In particular it describes the standard general framework of the differential games and the numerical algorithms that will be used in the coming chapters to solve the policy coordination problems.

It is assumed that the reader has some knowledge on linear algebra and differential equations. Basic elements of linear algebra that are essential for the understanding of the rest of this chapter will be recalled in Section 2.1. Readers interested in more details on these subjects are referred to standard books on linear algebra, like e.g. Lay (2003), Lancaster and Tismenetsky (1985) or Horn and Johnson (1985). Section 2.2 introduces the general dynamic framework that will be considered throughout this book. As a preliminary to the multi-player game sections, Section 2.3 deals with the one-player 'game'. This section presents results on the linear quadratic dynamic optimization problem, that are used in the subsequent sections. In Section 2.4 the case that policymakers decide to cooperate in realizing their objectives is dealt with, whereas Section 2.5 treats the case that the policymakers decide not to cooperate. Intermediate situations, where some policymakers decide to cooperate and others not, are of course in actual decision making also possible. This case is dealt with in Section 2.6.

Most of the theory of this chapter is presented more extensively and in a mathematical more rigorous way in Engwerda (2005a). Therefore, readers interested in more (mathematical) details on the linear-quadratic framework that will be pursued here are referred to this work. More information (and references) on dynamic games can e.g. be found in Başar and Olsder (1999) and on game theory in general e.g. in Tijs (2004).

2.1 Linear algebra

Throughout this book $\mathbb{R}$ will denote the set of real numbers and $\mathbb{C}$ the set of complex numbers. Furthermore, $\mathbb{R}^n$ will denote the set of vectors with n entries, where each entry is an element of $\mathbb{R}$. Now, let $x_1, \cdots, x_k \in \mathbb{R}^n$. An element of the form $\alpha_1 x_1 + \cdots + \alpha_k x_k$ with $\alpha_i \in \mathbb{R}$ is a *linear combination* of $x_1, \cdots, x_k$. The set of all linear combinations of $x_1, x_2, \cdots, x_k \in \mathbb{R}^n$, called the *span* of $x_1, x_2, \cdots, x_k$, constitutes a *linear subspace* of $\mathbb{R}^n$. That is, with any two elements in this set also the sum and any scalar multiple of an element belong to this set. We denote this set by $\text{Span}\{x_1, x_2, \cdots, x_k\}$.

A set of vectors $x_1, x_2, \cdots, x_k \in \mathbb{R}^n$ are called *linearly dependent* if there exists $\alpha_1, \cdots, \alpha_k \in \mathbb{R}$, not all zero, such that $\alpha_1 x_1 + \cdots + \alpha_k x_k = 0$; otherwise they are said to be *linearly independent.*

Let S be a subspace of $\mathbb{R}^n$, then a set of vectors $\{b_1, b_2 \cdots, b_k\}$ is called a *basis* for S if this set of vectors are linearly independent and $S = \text{Span}\{b_1, b_2, \cdots, b_k\}$.

A basis for a subspace S is not unique. However, all bases for S have the same number of elements. This number is called the *dimension* of S and is denoted by $\dim(S)$.

Next, we consider the problem under which conditions two vectors are perpendicular. To that end the *(Euclidean) length* of a vector x is introduced which will be denoted by $\|x\|_2$. If $x = \begin{bmatrix} x_1 \\ x_2 \end{bmatrix}$ then, using the theorem of Pythagoras, the length of x is $\|x\|_2 = \sqrt{x_1^2 + x_2^2}$. Using induction it is easily verified that the length of a vector $x = \begin{bmatrix} x_1 \\ \vdots \\ x_n \end{bmatrix} \in \mathbb{R}^n$ is $\|x\|_2 = \sqrt{x_1^2 + \cdots + x_n^2}$. Introducing the superscript T for *transposition* of a vector, i.e. $x^T = [x_1, \cdots, x_n]$, we can rewrite this result in shorthand as $\|x\|_2 = \sqrt{x^T x}$. Now, two vectors x and y are perpendicular if they constitute an angle of 90°. Using again this same theorem of Pythagoras, we conclude that two vectors x and y are perpendicular if and only if the length of the hypothenusa $\|x - y\|^2 = \|x\|^2 + \|y\|^2$. Or, rephrased in our previous terminology: $(x - y)^T(x - y) = x^T x + y^T y$. Using the elementary vector calculation rules and the fact that the transpose of a scalar is the same scalar (i.e. $x^T y = y^T x$), straightforward calculation shows that the next theorem holds.

Theorem 2.1 *Two vectors $x, y \in \mathbb{R}^n$ are perpendicular (or orthogonal) if and only if $x^T y = 0$.* □

Based on this result we introduce next the concept of orthogonal subspaces. A set of vectors $\{x_1, \cdots, x_n\}$ are mutually *orthogonal* if $x_i^T x_j = 0$ for all $i \neq j$ and *orthonormal* if $x_i^T x_j = \delta_{ij}$. Here, δ_{ij} is the *Kronecker delta function* with $\delta_{ij} = 1$ for $i = j$ and $\delta_{ij} = 0$ for $i \neq j$. More generally, a collection of subspaces $S_1, \cdots, S_k$ are called mutually orthogonal if $x^T y = 0$ whenever $x \in S_i$ and $y \in S_j$, for $i \neq j$.

The *orthogonal complement* of a subspace S is defined by

$$S^\perp := \{y \in \mathbb{R}^n | y^T x = 0 \; for \; all \; x \in S\}.$$

The set of all $n \times m$ matrices with entries in $\mathbb{R}$ will be denoted by $\mathbb{R}^{n\times m}$. If $m = n$, A is called a *square matrix*. With matrix $A \in \mathbb{R}^{n\times m}$ one can associate the linear map $v \to Av$ from $\mathbb{R}^m \to \mathbb{R}^n$. The *kernel* or *null space* of A is defined by

$$\ker A = N(A) := \{v \in \mathbb{R}^m | Av = 0\},$$

and the *image* or *range* of A is

$$\operatorname{Im} A = R(A) := \{y \in \mathbb{R}^n | y = Av, v \in \mathbb{R}^m\}.$$

One can easily verify that $\ker A$ is a subspace of $\mathbb{R}^m$ and $\operatorname{Im} A$ is a subspace of $\mathbb{R}^n$. Let a_i, $i = 1, \cdots, m$, denote the columns of matrix $A \in \mathbb{R}^{n\times m}$, then

$$\operatorname{Im} A = \operatorname{Span}\{a_1, \cdots, a_m\}.$$

The *rank* of a matrix A is defined by $\operatorname{rank}(A) = \dim(\operatorname{Im} A)$, and thus the rank of a matrix is just the number of independent columns in A. One can show that $\operatorname{rank}(A) = \operatorname{rank}(A^T)$. Consequently, the rank of a matrix also coincides with the number of independent rows in A. A matrix $A \in \mathbb{R}^{n\times m}$ is said to have *full row rank* if $n \leqq m$ and $\operatorname{rank}(A) = n$. Dually, it is said to have full column rank if $m \leqq n$ and $\operatorname{rank}(A) = m$. A full-rank square matrix is called a *non-singular* or *invertible matrix*, otherwise it is called singular. If a matrix A is invertible one can show that the matrix equation $AX = I$ has a unique solution $X \in \mathbb{R}^{n\times n}$. Here I is the $n \times n$ *identity matrix* with entries $e_{ij} := \delta_{ij}$, $i, j = 1, \cdots, n$, and δ_{ij} is the Kronecker delta. Moreover, this matrix X also satisfies the matrix equation $XA = I$. Matrix X is called the *inverse* of matrix A and the notation A^{-1} is used to denote this inverse.

A notion that is useful to see whether a square $n \times n$ matrix A is singular is the *determinant* of A, denoted by $\det(A)$. The next theorem lists some properties of determinants.

Theorem 2.2 *Let $A, B \in \mathbb{R}^{n\times n}$; $C \in \mathbb{R}^{n\times m}$; $D \in \mathbb{R}^{m\times m}$; and $0 \in \mathbb{R}^{m\times n}$ be the matrix with all entries zero. Then,*

1. $\det(AB) = \det(A)\det(B)$;
2. *A is invertible if and only if* $\det(A) \neq 0$;
3. *If A is invertible,* $\det(A^{-1}) = \frac{1}{\det(A)}$;
4. $\det(A) = \det(A^T)$;
5. $\det\left(\begin{bmatrix} A & C \\ 0 & D \end{bmatrix}\right) = \det(A)\det(D)$. □

Let $A \in \mathbb{R}^{n\times n}$, then $\lambda \in \mathbb{R}$ is called an *eigenvalue* of A if there exists a vector $x \in \mathbb{R}^n$, different from zero, such that $Ax = \lambda x$. If such a scalar λ and corresponding vector x exist, the vector x is called an *eigenvector*. If A has an eigenvalue λ, it follows that there exists a nonzero vector x such that $(A-\lambda I)x = 0$. Stated differently, matrix $A-\lambda I$ is singular. So, according to Theorem 2.2, λ is an eigenvalue of matrix A if and only if $\det(A-\lambda I)=0$. All vectors x in the null space of $A-\lambda I$ are then the with λ corresponding eigenvectors. As a consequence we have that the set of eigenvectors corresponding with an eigenvalue λ form a subspace. This subspace is called the *eigenspace* of λ and we denote this subspace by E_λ. So, to find the eigenvalues of a matrix A we have to find those values λ for which $\det(A-\lambda I)=0$. Since $p(\lambda) := \det(A-\lambda I)$ is a polynomial of degree n, $p(\lambda)$ is called the *characteristic polynomial* of A. The set of roots of this polynomial is called the *spectrum* of A and is denoted by $\sigma(A)$.

An important property of eigenvectors corresponding to different eigenvalues is that they are always independent.

Theorem 2.3 *Let $A \in \mathbb{R}^{n\times n}$ and λ_1, λ_2 be two different eigenvalues of A with corresponding eigenvectors x_1 and x_2, respectively. Then $\{x_1, x_2\}$ are linearly independent.* □

Example 2.1

1. Consider matrix $A_1 = \begin{bmatrix} 3 & -2 \\ 1 & 0 \end{bmatrix}$. The characteristic polynomial of A_1 is

$$p(\lambda) = \det(A_1 - \lambda I) = (\lambda-1)(\lambda-2).$$

So, $\sigma(A_1) = \{1,2\}$. Furthermore, $E_1 = N(A_1 - I) = \{\alpha \begin{bmatrix} 1 \\ 1 \end{bmatrix}, \alpha \in \mathbb{R}\}$ and $E_2 = N(A_1 - 2I) = \{\alpha \begin{bmatrix} 2 \\ 1 \end{bmatrix}, \alpha \in \mathbb{R}\}$.

2. Consider matrix $A_2 = \begin{bmatrix} 4 & 1 \\ -1 & 2 \end{bmatrix}$. The characteristic polynomial of A_2 is $(\lambda-3)^2$. So, $\sigma(A_2) = \{3\}$. Furthermore, $E_3 = N(A_2 - 3I) = \{\alpha \begin{bmatrix} 1 \\ -1 \end{bmatrix}, \alpha \in \mathbb{R}\}$.

3. Consider matrix $A_3 = \begin{bmatrix} -1 & 0 \\ 0 & -1 \end{bmatrix}$. The characteristic polynomial of A_3 is $(\lambda+1)^2$. So, $\sigma(A_3) = \{-1\}$. Furthermore, $E_{-1} = N(A_3 + I) = \mathbb{R}^2$.

4. Consider matrix $A_4 = \begin{bmatrix} 7 & 4 \\ -10 & -5 \end{bmatrix}$. The characteristic polynomial of A_4 is $\lambda^2 - 2\lambda + 5$. This polynomial has no real roots. So, matrix A_4 has no real eigenvalues. □

The above example illustrates a number of properties that hold in the general setting too (see e.g. Lancaster and Tismenetsky (1985)).

Theorem 2.4 *Any polynomial $p(\lambda)$ can be factorized as the product of different linear and quadratic terms, i.e. there exist nonnegative integers n_i, $i = 1, \cdots, r$ (with possibly $n_i = 0$ for $i \geqq k$) such that*

$$p(\lambda) = c(\lambda-\lambda_1)^{n_1}(\lambda-\lambda_2)^{n_2}\ldots(\lambda-\lambda_k)^{n_k}(\lambda^2+b_{k+1}\lambda+c_{k+1})^{n_{k+1}}\ldots(\lambda^2+b_r\lambda+c_r)^{n_r},$$

for some scalars c, λ_i, b_i *and* c_i. *Here, for* $i \neq j$, $\lambda_i \neq \lambda_j$ *and* $\begin{bmatrix} b_i \\ c_i \end{bmatrix} \neq \begin{bmatrix} b_j \\ c_j \end{bmatrix}$ *and the quadratic terms do not have real roots. Furthermore,* $\sum_{i=1}^{k} n_i + 2\sum_{i=k+1}^{r} n_i = n$. □

The power index n_i, appearing in the factorization with factor $\lambda - \lambda_i$, is called the *algebraic multiplicity* of the eigenvalue λ_i. Closely related to this number is the so-called *geometric multiplicity* of the eigenvalue λ_i, which is the dimension of the corresponding eigenspace E_{λ_i}. In Example 2.1 we see that for every eigenvalue the geometric multiplicity is smaller than or equal to its algebraic multiplicity. For instance, for A_1 both multiplicities are 1 for both eigenvalues, whereas for A_2 the geometric multiplicity of the eigenvalue 3 is 1 and its algebraic multiplicity is 2. This property holds in general.

Theorem 2.5 *Let* λ_i *be an eigenvalue of* A. *Then its geometric multiplicity is always smaller than (or equal to) its algebraic multiplicity.* □

Theorem 2.4 shows that the characteristic polynomial of an $n \times n$ matrix involves a polynomial of degree n that can be factorized as the product of different linear and quadratic terms. Furthermore, it is not possible to factorize any of these quadratic terms as the product of two linear terms. Without loss of generality, such a quadratic term can be written as

$$p(\lambda) = \lambda^2 - 2a\lambda + b^2 + a^2.$$

Next introduce the symbol i to denote the square root of -1. So, by definition

$$i := \sqrt{-1}.$$

Using this notation, the equation $p(\lambda) = 0$ has the two, so-called complex, solutions

$$\lambda_j = \frac{2a \pm \sqrt{4a^2 - 4(a^2 + b^2)}}{2} = a \pm \sqrt{i^2 b^2} = a \pm bi.$$

If a non-real number $\lambda \in \mathbb{C}$ satisfies $\det(A - \lambda I) = 0$, then λ is called a *complex eigenvalue* of A. Moreover, all $x \in \mathbb{C}^n (\neq 0)$ satisfying $(A - \lambda I)x = 0$ are (complex) eigenvectors corresponding to λ.

Example 2.2 *Let* $A_4 = \begin{bmatrix} 7 & 4 \\ -10 & -5 \end{bmatrix}$. *Its characteristic polynomial is* $\det(A_4 - \lambda I) = \lambda^2 - 2\lambda + 5$. *The complex roots of this equation are* $\lambda_1 = 1 + 2i$ *and* $\lambda_2 = 1 - 2i$. *The with* λ_1 *corresponding eigenvectors are* $N(A_4 - (1+2i)I) = \{\alpha \begin{bmatrix} 2 \\ -3+i \end{bmatrix}, \alpha \in \mathbb{C}\}$. *The with* λ_2 *corresponding eigenvectors are* $N(A_4 - (1-2i)I) = \{\alpha \begin{bmatrix} 2 \\ -3-i \end{bmatrix}, \alpha \in \mathbb{C}\}$. □

From Example 2.2, we see that with $\lambda_1 = 1 + 2i$ being an eigenvalue of A_4, also its so-called conjugate, $1 - 2i$, is an eigenvalue of A_4. This is a property that holds in general.

Theorem 2.6 *Let $A \in \mathbb{R}^{n\times n}$. If $\lambda = a + bi \in \mathbb{C}$ is an eigenvalue of A and $z = x + iy$ $(x, y \in \mathbb{R}^n)$ a corresponding eigenvector, then also its conjugate $\bar{\lambda} := a - bi$ is an eigenvalue of A and $\bar{z} := x - iy$ a corresponding eigenvector.* □

Theorem 2.7, below, shows that whenever $A \in \mathbb{R}^{n\times n}$ has a complex eigenvalue, then A has a so-called two-dimensional invariant subspace.

Theorem 2.7 *Let $A \in \mathbb{R}^{n\times n}$. If $\lambda = a + bi$ $(a, b \in \mathbb{R}, b \neq 0)$ is a complex eigenvalue of A and $z = x+iy$, with $x, y \in \mathbb{R}^n$, a corresponding eigenvector, then A has a two-dimensional invariant subspace $S = \text{Im}\,[x\ y]$. More in particular:*

$$AS = S \begin{bmatrix} a & b \\ -b & a \end{bmatrix}.$$

□

Example 2.3

1. (see also Example 2.2) Let $A = \begin{bmatrix} 2 & 0 & 0 \\ 0 & 7 & 4 \\ 0 & -10 & -5 \end{bmatrix}$. *The characteristic polynomial of A is $(2 - \lambda)(\lambda^2 - 2\lambda + 5)$. So, A has one real root $\lambda_1 = 2$ and two complex roots. The complex roots of this equation are $\lambda_2 = 1 + 2i$ and $\lambda_3 = 1 - 2i$. The with λ_2 corresponding eigenvectors are* $N(A - (1 + 2i)I) = \{\alpha \begin{bmatrix} 0 \\ 2 \\ -3 + i \end{bmatrix}, \alpha \in \mathbb{C}\}$. *The real part of this eigenvector is* $x := \begin{bmatrix} 0 \\ 2 \\ -3 \end{bmatrix}$ *and the imaginary part of this eigenvector is* $y := \begin{bmatrix} 0 \\ 0 \\ 1 \end{bmatrix}$. *Therefore, A has a two-dimensional invariant subspace consisting of* $S = \text{Im} \begin{bmatrix} 0 & 0 \\ 2 & 0 \\ -3 & 1 \end{bmatrix}$. *Indeed, with $1 + 2i =: a + bi$ we have (see Theorem 2.7)*

$$AS = \begin{bmatrix} 0 & 0 \\ 2 & 4 \\ -5 & -5 \end{bmatrix} = \begin{bmatrix} 0 & 0 \\ 2 & 0 \\ -3 & 1 \end{bmatrix} \begin{bmatrix} 1 & 2 \\ -2 & 1 \end{bmatrix} = S \begin{bmatrix} a & b \\ -b & a \end{bmatrix}.$$

2. Let $A = \begin{bmatrix} -2 & 2 & 1 \\ 0 & -2 & 0 \\ -1 & 1 & -2 \end{bmatrix}$. *The characteristic polynomial of A is*

$p(\lambda) = (\lambda^2 + 4\lambda + 5)(\lambda + 2)$. So, A has one real root $\lambda_1 = -2$ and two complex roots. The complex roots of this equation are $\lambda_2 = -2 + i$ and $\lambda_3 = -2 - i$.

The with λ_2 corresponding eigenvectors are $N(A-(-2+i)I) = \{\alpha \begin{bmatrix} 1 \\ 0 \\ i \end{bmatrix}, \alpha \in \mathbb{C}\}$. *Therefore, A has a two-dimensional invariant subspace consisting of* $S = \text{Im} \begin{bmatrix} 1 & 0 \\ 0 & 0 \\ 0 & 1 \end{bmatrix}$. *Verification shows that indeed with $a = -2$ and $b = 1$,* $AS = S \begin{bmatrix} a & b \\ -b & a \end{bmatrix}$. □

Let λ be an eigenvalue of $A \in \mathbb{R}^{n\times n}$ and x be a corresponding eigenvector. Then $Ax = \lambda x$ and $A(\alpha x) = \lambda(\alpha x)$ for any $\alpha \in \mathbb{R}$. Clearly, the eigenvector x defines an one-dimensional subspace that is invariant with respect to pre-multiplication by A since $A^k x = \lambda^k x, \forall k$. In general, a subspace $S \subset \mathbb{R}^n$ is called *A-invariant* if $Ax \in S$ for every $x \in S$. In other words: S is A-invariant means that the image of S under A is contained in S, i.e. $\text{Im } AS \subset S$. Examples of A-invariant subspaces are for instance the trivial subspace $\{0\}$, $\mathbb{R}^n$, $\ker A$ and $\text{Im } A$.

A-invariant subspaces play an important role in calculating solutions of the so-called algebraic Riccati equations. These solutions constitute the basis for determining various equilibria in our dynamic games as we will see later on. A-invariant subspaces are intimately related to the (generalized) eigenspaces of matrix A. A complete picture of all A-invariant subspaces is in fact provided by considering the so-called *Jordan canonical form* of matrix A. It is a well known (but nontrivial) result in linear algebra that any square matrix $A \in \mathbb{R}^{n\times n}$ admits a *Jordan canonical representation*.

To grasp the idea of the Jordan form, first consider the case that A has n different eigenvalues λ_i, $i = 1, \cdots, n$. Let x_i, $i = 1, \cdots, n$, be the corresponding eigenvectors. From Theorem 2.3 it follows then straightforwardly that $\{x_1, x_2, \cdots, x_n\}$ are linearly independent and in fact constitute a basis for $\mathbb{R}^n$. Now, let matrix $S := [x_1\ x_2\ \cdots\ x_n]$. Since this matrix is of full rank its inverse exists. Then $AS = [Ax_1\ Ax_2\ \cdots\ Ax_n] = [\lambda_1 x_1\ \lambda_2 x_2\ \cdots\ \lambda_n x_n] = SJ_1$, where J_1 is the diagonal matrix $J_1 = \begin{bmatrix} \lambda_1 & & & \\ & \lambda_2 & & \\ & & \ddots & \\ & & & \lambda_n \end{bmatrix}$. So, if matrix A has n different eigenvalues it can be factorized as $A = SJ_1S^{-1}$. Notice that this same procedure can be used to factorize matrix A as long as matrix A has n independent eigenvectors. The fact that the eigenvalues are all different from each other is not crucial for this construction. For the general case the theorem reads as follows.

Theorem 2.8 *(Jordan canonical form)*[1]
For any square matrix $A \in \mathbb{R}^{n\times n}$ there exists a non-singular matrix T such that

$$A = TJT^{-1}$$

[1] Jordan was a famous French engineer/mathematician, who lived from 1838 till 1922.

where $J = diag\{J_1, J_2, \cdots, J_r\}$ and J_i either has one of the following (upper bi)diagonal real ($\mathbb{R}$), real-extended ($\mathbb{R}E$), complex ($\mathbb{C}$) or complex-extended ($\mathbb{C}E$) forms

$$i)\ J_{\mathbb{R}} = \begin{bmatrix} \lambda_j & & & & \\ & \lambda_j & & & \\ & & \ddots & & \\ & & & \lambda_j & \\ & & & & \lambda_j \end{bmatrix};\ ii)\ J_{\mathbb{R}E} = \begin{bmatrix} \lambda_j & 1 & & & \\ & \lambda_j & \ddots & & \\ & & \ddots & \ddots & \\ & & & \lambda_j & 1 \\ & & & & \lambda_j \end{bmatrix}$$

$$iii)\ J_{\mathbb{C}} = \begin{bmatrix} C_j & & & & \\ & C_j & & & \\ & & \ddots & & \\ & & & C_j & \\ & & & & C_j \end{bmatrix};\ iv)\ J_{\mathbb{C}E} = \begin{bmatrix} C_j & I & & & \\ & C_j & \ddots & & \\ & & \ddots & \ddots & \\ & & & C_j & I \\ & & & & C_j \end{bmatrix}$$

Here, $\{\lambda_j,\ j = 1, \cdots, r\}$ are the distinct real eigenvalues of A, $C_j = \begin{bmatrix} a_j & b_j \\ -b_j & a_j \end{bmatrix}$, $j = k+1, \cdots, r$, and I is the 2×2 identity matrix. The matrix T consists of sets of basis vectors, where each set corresponds with a basis for the (generalized) eigenspace of λ_j.[2] □

In the above theorem the numbers a_j and b_j in the boxes $C_j = \begin{bmatrix} a_j & b_j \\ -b_j & a_j \end{bmatrix}$ come from the complex roots $a_j + b_j i$, $j = k+1, \cdots, r$, of matrix A. Note that the characteristic polynomial of C_j is $\lambda^2 + 2a_j\lambda + a_j^2 + b_j^2$.

An immediate consequence of this theorem is the following

Corollary 2.1 *Let $A \in \mathbb{R}^{n \times n}$. Then,*

1. *All A-invariant subspaces can be constructed from the Jordan canonical form.*
2. *Matrix A has a finite number of invariant subspaces if and only if all geometric multiplicities of the (possibly complex) eigenvalues are one.* □

From the above corollary it is clear that with each A-invariant subspace V one can associate a part of the spectrum of matrix A. We will denote this part of the spectrum by $\sigma(A|_V)$.

Now, generically, a polynomial of degree n will have n distinct (possibly complex) roots. Therefore, if one considers an arbitrary matrix $A \in \mathbb{R}^{n \times n}$, its Jordan form is most of the times a combination of the first, $J_{\mathbb{R}}$, and third, $J_{\mathbb{C}}$, Jordan form. That is

[2] For the moment it suffices to recall that a basis for the with λ_i corresponding generalized eigenspace is obtained by constructing a basis for $N((A - \lambda_j)^n)$, if $A \in \mathbb{R}^{n \times n}$

Example 2.4 *(Generic Jordan canonical form)*
If $A \in \mathbb{R}^{n \times n}$ has n distinct (possibly complex) eigenvalues then its Jordan form is

$$J = \begin{bmatrix} \lambda_1 & & & & & & & & & \\ & \lambda_2 & & & & & & & & \\ & & \ddots & & & & & & & \\ & & & \lambda_{k-1} & & & & & & \\ & & & & \lambda_k & & & & & \\ & & & & & a_{k+1} & b_{k+1} & & & \\ & & & & & -b_{k+1} & a_{k+1} & & & \\ & & & & & & & \ddots & & \\ & & & & & & & & a_r & b_r \\ & & & & & & & & -b_r & a_r \end{bmatrix},$$

where all numbers appearing in this matrix differ. If A has only real roots the numbers a_i, b_i disappear and $k = n$. □

Example 2.5 *Consider matrix* $A = \begin{bmatrix} -7 & -15 & 0 \\ 6 & 11 & 0 \\ -4 & 1 & 2 \end{bmatrix}$. *The characteristic polynomial of A is $(2-\lambda)(\lambda^2-4\lambda+13)$. Therefore, it has one real eigenvalue, 2, and two complex eigenvalues, $2+3i$ and $2-3i$. Consequently, the Jordan canonical form of A is* $J = \begin{bmatrix} 2 & 0 & 0 \\ 0 & 2 & 3 \\ 0 & -3 & 2 \end{bmatrix}$. □

In our analysis symmetric positive definite matrices will frequently occur. Formally, a square symmetric matrix A is said to be *positive definite (semi-definite)*, denoted by $A > 0$ ($A \geq 0$), if $x^T Ax > 0$ ($\geqq 0$) for all $x \neq 0$. A is called *negative definite (semi-definite)*, denoted by $A < 0$ ($A \leq 0$), if $x^T Ax < 0$ ($\leqq 0$) for all $x \neq 0$. There is a nice characterization of these matrices in terms of their eigenvalues.

Theorem 2.9 *Let $A \in \mathbb{R}^{n \times n}$. Then, $A > 0$ (≥ 0) if and only if all eigenvalues λ_i of A satisfy $\lambda_i > 0$ ($\geqq 0$).* □

Let A_i, Q, and R be real $n \times n$ matrices with Q symmetric and $R > 0$ (and thus symmetric). Then an *algebraic Riccati equation*[3] (ARE) in the $n \times n$ matrix X is the following quadratic matrix equation:

$$A_1^T X + XA_2 - XRX + Q = 0. \tag{2.1}$$

[3] Count Jacopo Francesco Riccati (1676-1754) studied in Riccati (1724) the differential equation $\dot{x}(t) + t^{-n}x^2(t) - nt^{m+n-1} = 0$, where m and n are constants. Since then, this kind of equations have been extensively studied in the literature. See Bittanti (1991) and Bittanti *et al.* (1991) for a (historic) overview of the main issues revolving around the Riccati equation.

This matrix equation plays a crucial role in solving our differential games later on. The above equation can be rewritten as

$$[I\ X]\begin{bmatrix} Q & A_1^T \\ A_2 & -R \end{bmatrix}\begin{bmatrix} I \\ X \end{bmatrix} = 0.$$

From this we infer that the image of matrix $[I\ X]$ is orthogonal to the image of $\begin{bmatrix} Q & A_1^T \\ A_2 & -R \end{bmatrix}\begin{bmatrix} I \\ X \end{bmatrix}$. Or, stated differently, the image of $\begin{bmatrix} Q & A_1^T \\ A_2 & -R \end{bmatrix}\begin{bmatrix} I \\ X \end{bmatrix}$ belongs to the orthogonal complement of the image of matrix $[I\ X]$. It is easily verified that the orthogonal complement of the image of matrix $[I\ X]$ is given by the image of $\begin{bmatrix} -X \\ I \end{bmatrix}$. Therefore, the ARE (2.1) has a solution if and only if there exists a matrix $\Lambda \in \mathbb{R}^{n\times n}$ such that

$$\begin{bmatrix} Q & A_1^T \\ A_2 & -R \end{bmatrix}\begin{bmatrix} I \\ X \end{bmatrix} = \begin{bmatrix} -X \\ I \end{bmatrix}\Lambda.$$

Pre-multiplication of both sides from the above equality with the matrix $\begin{bmatrix} 0 & I \\ -I & 0 \end{bmatrix}$ yields then

$$\begin{bmatrix} A_2 & -R \\ -Q & -A_1^T \end{bmatrix}\begin{bmatrix} I \\ X \end{bmatrix} = \begin{bmatrix} I \\ X \end{bmatrix}\Lambda.$$

Or, stated differently, the solutions X of the ARE (2.1) can be obtained by considering the invariant subspaces of matrix

$$H := \begin{bmatrix} A_2 & -R \\ -Q & -A_1^T \end{bmatrix}. \tag{2.2}$$

Theorem 2.10 gives a precise formulation of this observation.

Theorem 2.10 *Let $V \subset \mathbb{R}^{2n}$ be an n-dimensional invariant subspace of H, and let $X_1, X_2 \in \mathbb{R}^{n\times n}$ be two real matrices such that*

$$V = \mathrm{Im}\begin{bmatrix} X_1 \\ X_2 \end{bmatrix}.$$

If X_1 is invertible, then $X := X_2X_1^{-1}$ is a solution to the Riccati equation (2.1) and $\sigma(A - RX) = \sigma(H|_V)$. Furthermore, the solution X is independent of the specific choice of the basis of V. □

The converse of Theorem 2.10 also holds.

Theorem 2.11 *If $X \in \mathbb{R}^{n\times n}$ is a solution to the Riccati equation (2.1), then there exist matrices $X_1, X_2 \in \mathbb{R}^{n\times n}$, with X_1 invertible, such that $X = X_2X_1^{-1}$ and the columns of $\begin{bmatrix} X_1 \\ X_2 \end{bmatrix}$ form a basis of an n-dimensional invariant subspace of H.* □

Matrix H is called a *Hamiltonian matrix*. If $A_2 = A_1$ it has a number of nice properties. One of them is that whenever $\lambda \in \sigma(H)$, then also $-\lambda \in \sigma(H)$. That is, if $A_2 = A_1$, the spectrum of a Hamiltonian matrix is symmetric with respect to the imaginary axis.

From Theorems 2.10 and 2.11 it will be clear why the Jordan canonical form is so important in this context. As we saw in the previous section, the Jordan canonical form of a matrix H can be used to construct all invariant subspaces of H. So, all solutions of (2.1) can be obtained by considering all n-dimensional invariant subspaces $V = \text{Im}\begin{bmatrix} X_1 \\ X_2 \end{bmatrix}$ of (2.2), with $X_i \in \mathbb{R}^{n\times n}$, that have the additional property that X_1 is invertible. A subspace V that satisfies this property is called a *graph subspace* (since it can be 'visualized' as the graph of the map: $v \rightarrow X_2X_1^{-1}v$).

From this relationship it will be clear that in general the ARE (2.1) will not have a unique solution. In fact there are examples where there are none, one, a finite number or even an infinite number of solutions.

However, as we will see in the next sections, we will be just interested in the solutions of this ARE that have an additional property. Only solutions for which $\sigma(A_2 - RX) \subset \mathbb{C}^-$ (the so-called *stabilizing solutions*) will interest us. Since this stabilizing property plays such an important role, it is formalized in the next definition.

Definition 2.1 *A solution X of the ARE (2.1) is called*

a. *stabilizing, if $\sigma(A_2 - RX) \subset \mathbb{C}^-$;* [4]

b. *strongly stabilizing if both*

i. it is a stabilizing solution, and

ii. $\sigma(A_1^T - XR) \subset \mathbb{C}^-$; □

From, e.g. Engwerda (2005a), we have then the next result

Theorem 2.12

1. *If the ARE (2.1) has a strongly stabilizing solution, then it is unique.*

2. *Assume $A_1 = A_2$. Then, the ARE (2.1) has at most one stabilizing solution. This solution is symmetric.* □

2.2 The basic mathematical model

In this section we describe the basic mathematical model that will be used throughout this book. For both didactical and notational convenience we will restrict the presentation to the two-player case. The general case will be clear from this.

[4] $\mathbb{C}^- = \{\lambda \in \mathbb{C} \mid Re(\lambda) < 0\}$; $\mathbb{C}_0^+ = \{\lambda \in \mathbb{C} \mid Re(\lambda) \geqq 0\}$.

We will assume that the performance criterion player $i = 1,2$ likes to minimize is:

$$J_i(u_1,u_2) := \int_0^\infty [x^T(t),\ u_1^T(t),\ u_2^T(t)]M_i \begin{bmatrix} x(t) \\ u_1(t) \\ u_2(t) \end{bmatrix} dt, \tag{2.3}$$

where $M_i = \begin{bmatrix} Q_i & P_i & L_i \\ P_i^T & R_{1i} & N_i \\ L_i^T & N_i^T & R_{2i} \end{bmatrix} \geq 0,\ R_{ii} > 0,\ i = 1,2$, and $x(t)$ is the solution from the linear differential equation

$$\dot{x}(t) = Ax(t) + B_1u_1(t) + B_2u_2(t),\ x(0) = x_0. \tag{2.4}$$

Differential equation (2.4) models the evaluation of the state of the system over time. This development is assumed to depend on the controls u_i the players use. The state of the system usually consists of a number of variables the players are interested in and which they like to manipulate. In principle each player i wants to manipulate this state vector such that her cost functional (2.3) is minimized. The cost functional models in particular the fact that the players dislike the use of control $u_i(.)$ and that they like to steer the state towards zero. For that reason, one can best think of the system as modelling a set of variables that are temporarily out of equilibrium, whereas the goal of the players is to control these variables back to equilibrium, subject to the fact that they are restricted in their control possibilities.

In trying to minimize their cost functional (2.3), the players can either decide to cooperate or not. This gives rise to different control problems, that will be discussed in the next three sections.

Remark 2.1 *Often, a discount factor is included in the above cost functions with M_i to express the idea that future costs are less important than current costs. Assume that (2.3) is replaced by*

$$J_i(u_1,u_2) := \int_0^\infty e^{-\theta t}[x^T(t),\ u_1^T(t),\ u_2^T(t)]M_i \begin{bmatrix} x(t) \\ u_1(t) \\ u_2(t) \end{bmatrix} dt.$$

Now introduce $\tilde{x}(t) := e^{-\frac{1}{2}\theta t}x(t)$ and $\tilde{u}_i(t) := e^{-\frac{1}{2}\theta t}u_i(t)$. Then it is straightforwardly verified that the minimization of this discounted cost functional w.r.t. system (2.4) can be rewritten as the minimization of

$$J_i(\tilde{u}_1,\tilde{u}_2) := \int_0^\infty [\tilde{x}^T(t),\ \tilde{u}_1^T(t),\ \tilde{u}_2^T(t)]M_i \begin{bmatrix} \tilde{x}(t) \\ \tilde{u}_1(t) \\ \tilde{u}_2(t) \end{bmatrix} dt$$

subject to the system

$$\dot{\tilde{x}}(t) = (A - \frac{1}{2}\theta I)\tilde{x}(t) + B_1\tilde{u}_1(t) + B_2\tilde{u}_2(t),\ \tilde{x}(0) = \tilde{x}_0.$$

Also the case that both players use a different discount factor can be solved within this framework. For details on this we refer to, e.g., Engwerda (2005a).

So, the only change in the model that takes place by taking into account a discount factor θ is that matrix A in system equation (2.4) is replaced by $A - \frac{1}{2}\theta I$. □

However, before we can introduce the formal optimization problems we first have to introduce some important concepts in *linear system theory*. To introduce these concepts we consider system (2.4) with the number of players equal to 1, that is $N = 1$, and we drop the subscript i. So, consider

$$\dot{x} = Ax + Bu. \tag{2.5}$$

Stability plays an important role in (robust) control theory. We recall the next definition.

Definition 2.2 *The dynamic system $\dot{x} = Ax$ is said to be stable if all the (possibly complex) eigenvalues of A are in the open left-half of the complex plane, i.e., the real part of every eigenvalue of A is strictly smaller than zero. A matrix A with such a property is said to be stable.* □

Next, we consider the notion of *stabilizability*. Informally speaking, the system is called stabilizable if it is possible to ultimately regulate the state from any initial position towards zero.

Definition 2.3 *The dynamic system described by equation (2.5) or the pair (A, B) is said to be stabilizable if, for any initial state x_0, there exists a (piecewise continuous) input $u(.)$ such that the solution of (2.5) converges to zero.* □

From e.g. Zhou *et al.* (1996) we recall the next well-known properties that give several characterizations for the stabilizability of a system.

Theorem 2.13 *The following properties are equivalent:*

1. *(A, B) is stabilizable.*
2. *The matrix $[A - \lambda I,\ B]$ has full row rank for all $\lambda \in \mathbb{C}_0^+$.*
3. *There exists a matrix F such that the eigenvalues of $A + BF$ are all located in the left-half of the complex plane, $\mathbb{C}^-$.* □

Example 2.6 *Consider* $A = \begin{bmatrix} 1 & 0 & 5 \\ 2 & 3 & 4 \\ 0 & 0 & -1 \end{bmatrix}$ *and* $B = \begin{bmatrix} 1 & 1 \\ 1 & 0 \\ 0 & 0 \end{bmatrix}$. *Then*

$$[A - \lambda I,\ B] = \begin{bmatrix} 1-\lambda & 0 & 5 & 1 & 1 \\ 2 & 3-\lambda & 4 & 1 & 0 \\ 0 & 0 & -1-\lambda & 0 & 0 \end{bmatrix}.$$

Obviously, for $\lambda \in \mathbb{C}_0^+$ which are not an eigenvalue of A, matrix A is invertible and consequently the above matrix has full row rank. The eigenvalues of A are $\{1,\ 3,\ -1\}$. So the only two cases that require a further inspection are $\lambda = 1$ and $\lambda = 3$. For $\lambda = 1$, this matrix equals $\begin{bmatrix} 0 & 0 & 5 & 1 & 1 \\ 2 & 2 & 4 & 1 & 0 \\ 0 & 0 & -2 & 0 & 0 \end{bmatrix}$. *It is easily verified that this matrix has full row rank too. In a similar way one verifies that also for $\lambda = 3$ the matrix has full row rank. So, (A, B) is stabilizable.*

□

2.3 The one-player case

In this section, we consider the problem of finding a control function $u(.) \in U_s$ for each $x_0 \in \mathbb{R}^n$ that minimizes the cost functional

$$J(x_0, u) := \int_0^\infty \{x^T(t)Qx(t) + 2x^T(t)Pu(t) + u^T(t)Ru(t)\}dt. \tag{2.6}$$

Here, Q is a symmetric matrix and $R > 0$, and the state variable x is the solution of

$$\dot{x}(t) = Ax(t) + Bu(t),\ x(0) = x_0. \tag{2.7}$$

The set of admissible control functions consists of the set of functions

$$\mathcal{U}_s = \left\{u \in L_{2,loc} \mid J_i(x_0, u) \text{ exists in } \mathbb{R} \cup \{-\infty, \infty\}, \lim_{t\to\infty} x(t) = 0\right\},$$

where $L_{2,loc}$ is the set of locally square-integrable functions, i.e.,

$$L_{2,loc} = \{u[0,\infty) \mid \forall T > 0, \int_0^T u^T(s)u(s)ds < \infty\}.$$

In the policy problems that will be studied in the next chapters, usually Q will be assumed to be positive (semi-)definite. Since the formulation of the next theorem does not require this assumption, we will not make this assumption here, yet.
By Theorem 2.13, the imposed stabilization constraint is equivalent with the requirement that the system is stabilizable. Therefore, throughout this section, the assumption is made that the pair (A, B) is stabilizable. For convenience, the notation $S := BR^{-1}B^T$ is used.

The next ARE plays a crucial role in solving the optimization problem (2.6)-(2.7)

$$A^TX + XA - (XB + P)R^{-1}(B^TX + P^T) + Q = 0.$$

Notice that this equation can also be rewritten as

$$(A - BR^{-1}P^T)^TX + X(A - BR^{-1}P^T) - XSX + Q - PR^{-1}P^T = 0. \tag{2.8}$$

Recall from Section 2.1 that a solution X_s of this equation is called stabilizing if the matrix $A - BR^{-1}P^T - SX_s$ is stable and, furthermore, from Theorem 2.12, that such a solution, if it exists, is unique. A proof of the next result can e.g. be found in Engwerda (2005b).

Theorem 2.14 *(Infinite horizon linear-quadratic control problem)*
Assume that (A, B) is stabilizable. The linear-quadratic control problem (2.6)-(2.7) has a minimum $u^*(.) \in U_s$ for $J(x_0, u)$ for each x_0 if and only if the ARE (2.8) has a symmetric stabilizing solution X_s.
If the linear-quadratic control problem has a solution, then the unique optimal control in feedback form is given by

$$u^*(t) = -R^{-1}(B^T X_s + P^T)x^*(t). \tag{2.9}$$

Here, $x^*(t)$ is the solution of the differential equation $\dot{x}^*(t) = A_{cl}x^*(t)$ with $x^*(0) = x_0$, where $A_{cl} := A - BR^{-1}P^T - SX_s$. In open-loop form, the optimal control is

$$u^*(t) = -R^{-1}(B^T X_s + P^T)\Phi(t, 0)x_0 \tag{2.10}$$

where Φ is the transition matrix of

$$\dot{\Phi}(t) = A_{cl}\Phi(t), \ \Phi(0) = I.$$

The resulting closed-loop state trajectory is given by $x^*(.)$.
Moreover, $J(x_0, u^*) = x_0^T M x_0$, where M is the unique solution of the Lyapunov equation

$$A_{cl}^T M + MA_{cl} = -[I, \ -(X_sB + P)R^{-1}] \begin{bmatrix} Q & P \\ P^T & R \end{bmatrix} \begin{bmatrix} I \\ -R^{-1}(B^T X_s + P^T) \end{bmatrix}. \tag{2.11}$$

□

Remark 2.2 *Recall from Section 3.1 that the unique stabilizing solution X_s of the ARE (2.8) can be calculated by determining the graph subspace $Im\begin{bmatrix} X_1 \\ X_2 \end{bmatrix}$ of the Hamiltonian matrix*

$$\begin{bmatrix} A - BR^{-1}P^T & -S \\ -Q + PR^{-1}P^T & -(A - BR^{-1}P^T)^T \end{bmatrix}$$

that has the property that all eigenvalues of the matrix $A - BR^{-1}P^T - SX_2X_1^{-1}$ have a strictly negative real part. As we already noticed in Section 2.1, this graph subspace is uniquely determined if it exists and $X_s = X_2X_1^{-1}$. □

This approach has been elaborated in the literature in more detail. Lancaster and Rodman (1995, Theorem 22.4.1)(see also Laub (1991), p.175) have shown that the existence of the stabilizing solution of the ARE can for instance be verified by checking whether the above Hamiltonian matrix has no purely imaginary eigenvalues, and whether a rank condition on the matrix sign of a certain matrix is satisfied. An extensive literature on algorithms for accurately computing the matrix sign exists, and one finds a comprehensive list of references in the review paper of Laub (1991).

Example 2.7 *Consider the minimization of*

$$J := \int_0^\infty \{3x^T(t)x(t) + u^2(t)\}dt,$$

subject to the system

$$\dot{x}(t) = \begin{bmatrix} 1 & 0 \\ 0 & -2 \end{bmatrix} x(t) + \begin{bmatrix} 1 \\ 0 \end{bmatrix} u(t),\ x(0) = [1,\ 1]^T.$$

This system is stabilizable. So, according to Theorem 2.14, the problem has a solution $u^* \in U_s$ if and only if the next ARE has a stabilizing solution

$$\begin{bmatrix} 1 & 0 \\ 0 & -2 \end{bmatrix} X + X \begin{bmatrix} 1 & 0 \\ 0 & -2 \end{bmatrix} - X \begin{bmatrix} 1 & 0 \\ 0 & 0 \end{bmatrix} X + \begin{bmatrix} 3 & 0 \\ 0 & 3 \end{bmatrix} = 0.$$

By, e.g., straightforward substitution, one verifies that

$$X = \begin{bmatrix} 3 & 0 \\ 0 & \frac{3}{4} \end{bmatrix}$$

is the stabilizing solution of this Riccati equation. The resulting optimal control and cost are

$$u^*(t) = -[3,\ 0]x(t) \text{ and } J^* = 3\frac{3}{4},$$

respectively.

The optimal policy is in this case to control the system in such a way that the controllable part of the system converges at the same speed towards zero as the uncontrollable part. □

Example 2.8 *Consider the minimization of*

$$J := \int_0^\infty \{3x^T(t)x(t) + u^2(t)\}dt,$$

subject to the system

$$\dot{x}(t) = \begin{bmatrix} \sqrt{6} & 1 \\ 0 & -2 \end{bmatrix} x(t) + \begin{bmatrix} 1 \\ 0 \end{bmatrix} u(t),\ x(0) = [1,\ 1]^T.$$

This system is stabilizable. So, according to Theorem 2.14, the problem has an optimal solution $u^* \in U_s$ if and only if the next ARE has a stabilizing solution

$$\begin{bmatrix} \sqrt{6} & 0 \\ 1 & -2 \end{bmatrix} X + X \begin{bmatrix} \sqrt{6} & 1 \\ 0 & -2 \end{bmatrix} - X \begin{bmatrix} 1 & 0 \\ 0 & 0 \end{bmatrix} X + \begin{bmatrix} 3 & 0 \\ 0 & 3 \end{bmatrix} = 0.$$

To solve this problem, consider the with this problem corresponding Hamiltonian matrix

$$H := \begin{bmatrix} A & -S \\ -Q & -A^T \end{bmatrix} = \begin{bmatrix} \sqrt{6} & 1 & -1 & 0 \\ 0 & -2 & 0 & 0 \\ -3 & 0 & -\sqrt{6} & 0 \\ 0 & -3 & -1 & 2 \end{bmatrix}.$$

The eigenvalues of H are $\{-3,-2,2,3\}$. Eigenvectors corresponding with the eigenvalues -3 and -2 are

$$\begin{bmatrix} \frac{5}{\sqrt{6}+3} \\ 0 \\ 5 \\ 1 \end{bmatrix} \text{ and } \begin{bmatrix} 2-\sqrt{6} \\ 5 \\ 3 \\ 4\frac{1}{2} \end{bmatrix}, \text{ respectively.}$$

Therefore, the invariant subspace corresponding with the eigenvalues $\{-3,-2\}$ is

$$Span\{\left\{\begin{bmatrix} \frac{5}{\sqrt{6}+3} \\ 0 \\ 5 \\ 1 \end{bmatrix}, \begin{bmatrix} 2-\sqrt{6} \\ 5 \\ 3 \\ 4\frac{1}{2} \end{bmatrix}\right\}.$$

So, the stabilizing solution of the ARE is

$$\begin{aligned} X &:= \begin{bmatrix} 5 & 3 \\ 1 & 4\frac{1}{2} \end{bmatrix} \begin{bmatrix} \frac{5}{\sqrt{6}+3} & 2-\sqrt{6} \\ 0 & 5 \end{bmatrix}^{-1} \\ &= \frac{3+\sqrt{6}}{25} \begin{bmatrix} 25 & 5 \\ 5 & \frac{41}{2} - \frac{13}{2}\sqrt{6} \end{bmatrix}. \end{aligned}$$

The resulting optimal control and cost are

$$u^*(t) = -\frac{3+\sqrt{6}}{25}[25,\ 5]x(t) \text{ and } J^* = \frac{3+\sqrt{6}}{25}\left(\frac{111}{2} - \frac{13}{2}\sqrt{6}\right),$$

respectively.

Compared to Example 2.7, the optimal response of coping with the constant 'disturbance' by the second state variable of the first state variable seems to be to control the first state variable faster to zero. □

Example 2.9 *Consider the minimization of*

$$J := \int_0^\infty \{3x^T(t)x(t) + u^2(t)\}dt,$$

subject to the system

$$\dot{x}(t) = \begin{bmatrix} 1 & 1 \\ 0 & -2 \end{bmatrix} x(t) + \begin{bmatrix} 1 \\ 1 \end{bmatrix} u(t),\ x(0) = [1,\ 1]^T.$$

This system is stabilizable. By Theorem 2.14, the problem has an optimal solution $u^* \in U_s$ if and only if the next ARE has a stabilizing solution

$$\begin{bmatrix} 1 & 0 \\ 1 & -2 \end{bmatrix} X + X \begin{bmatrix} 1 & 1 \\ 0 & -2 \end{bmatrix} - X \begin{bmatrix} 1 & 1 \\ 1 & 1 \end{bmatrix} X + \begin{bmatrix} 3 & 0 \\ 0 & 3 \end{bmatrix} = 0.$$

To solve this problem, consider the with this problem corresponding Hamiltonian matrix

$$H := \begin{bmatrix} A & -S \\ -Q & -A^T \end{bmatrix} = \begin{bmatrix} 1 & 1 & -1 & -1 \\ 0 & -2 & -1 & -1 \\ -3 & 0 & -1 & 0 \\ 0 & -3 & -1 & 2 \end{bmatrix}.$$

Using the computer software package MATLAB, we find that the eigenvalues of H are $\{-2.3802 \pm 0.4068i, 2.3802 \pm 0.4068i\}$. Notice that H has two eigenvalues with a negative real part. So, to find out whether the ARE has a stabilizing solution, we just have to verify whether the with these eigenvalues corresponding invariant subspace is a graph subspace.
An eigenvector corresponding with the eigenvalue $-2.3802 + 0.4068i$ is

$$\begin{bmatrix} 0.1205 + 0.1191i \\ -0.7757 - 0.0614i \\ 0.1708 + 0.3092i \\ -0.4907 - 0.0170i \end{bmatrix}.$$

Therefore, the invariant subspace corresponding with the eigenvalues $\{-2.3802 \pm 0.4068i\}$ is

$$Span \left\{ \begin{bmatrix} 0.1205 \\ -0.7757 \\ 0.1708 \\ -0.4907 \end{bmatrix}, \begin{bmatrix} 0.1191 \\ -0.0614 \\ 0.3092 \\ -0.0170 \end{bmatrix} \right\}.$$

Since the by-these-two-vectors-implied matrix $\begin{bmatrix} 0.1205 & 0.1191 \\ -0.7757 & -0.0614 \end{bmatrix}$ is invertible, the above subspace is a graph subspace. So, the stabilizing solution of the ARE is

$$\begin{aligned} X \quad : &= \begin{bmatrix} 0.1708 & 0.3092 \\ -0.4907 & -0.0170 \end{bmatrix} \begin{bmatrix} 0.1205 & 0.1191 \\ -0.7757 & -0.0614 \end{bmatrix}^{-1} \\ &= \begin{bmatrix} 2.6988 & 0.1991 \\ 0.1991 & 0.6635 \end{bmatrix}. \end{aligned}$$

The resulting optimal control and cost are

$$u^*(t) = -[2.8979,\ 0.8626]x(t) \text{ and } J^* = 3.7605,$$

respectively. □

Example 2.10 *Consider the minimization of*

$$J := \int_0^\infty \{3x^T(t)x(t) + u^2(t)\}dt,$$

subject to the system

$$\dot{x}(t) = \begin{bmatrix} 1 & 1 \\ 0 & -2 \end{bmatrix} x(t) + \begin{bmatrix} 1 \\ 0 \end{bmatrix} u(t),\ x(0) = [1,\ 1]^T.$$

This system is stabilizable. Therefore, again by Theorem 2.14, the problem has a solution $u^* \in U_s$ if and only if the next ARE has a stabilizing solution

$$\begin{bmatrix} 1 & 0 \\ 1 & -2 \end{bmatrix} X + X \begin{bmatrix} 1 & 1 \\ 0 & -2 \end{bmatrix} - X \begin{bmatrix} 1 & 0 \\ 0 & 0 \end{bmatrix} X + \begin{bmatrix} 3 & 0 \\ 0 & 3 \end{bmatrix} = 0.$$

To solve this problem, consider the with this problem corresponding Hamiltonian matrix

$$H := \begin{bmatrix} A & -S \\ -Q & -A^T \end{bmatrix} = \begin{bmatrix} 1 & 1 & -1 & 0 \\ 0 & -2 & 0 & 0 \\ -3 & 0 & -1 & 0 \\ 0 & -3 & -1 & 2 \end{bmatrix}.$$

The eigenvalues of H are $\{-2, -2, 2, 2\}$. Furthermore, the generalized eigenspace corresponding with the eigenvalues -2 is

$$N((H+2I)^2) = N\left(\begin{bmatrix} 12 & 3 & -4 & 0 \\ 0 & 0 & 0 & 0 \\ -12 & -3 & 4 & 0 \\ 3 & -12 & -5 & 16 \end{bmatrix}\right) = Span\left\{\begin{bmatrix} -48 \\ 192 \\ 0 \\ 153 \end{bmatrix}, \begin{bmatrix} 4 \\ 0 \\ 12 \\ 3 \end{bmatrix}\right\}.$$

It is obvious that this subspace is a graph subspace. Therefore,

$$\begin{aligned} X \ &: = \begin{bmatrix} 0 & 12 \\ 153 & 3 \end{bmatrix} \begin{bmatrix} -48 & 4 \\ 192 & 0 \end{bmatrix}^{-1} \\ &= \frac{1}{776} \begin{bmatrix} 3 & \frac{3}{4} \\ \frac{3}{4} & \frac{63}{64} \end{bmatrix}, \end{aligned}$$

is the stabilizing solution of the ARE. The resulting optimal control and cost are

$$u^*(t) = -[3,\ \frac{3}{4}]x(t) \text{ and } J^* = 5\frac{31}{64},$$

respectively. The eigenvalues of the closed-loop system are -2.

Notice that, compared to Example 2.8, a less active control policy is used and that the involved costs are smaller. A quite intuitive result: the more unstable the system is, the more active control policy is needed to stabilize the system.

Furthermore, compared to Example 2.7, we see that the effect of the fact that the second state variable now continuously disturbs the first state variable also implies a more active control policy (and consequently higher cost). Notice that in this case the eigenvalues of both closed-loop systems coincide. □

2.4 The cooperative game

In this section we consider the model outlined in Section 2.2. That is, we consider the minimization of

$$J_i(u_1, u_2) := \int_0^{\infty} [x^T(t),\ u_1^T(t),\ u_2^T(t)] M_i \begin{bmatrix} x(t) \\ u_1(t) \\ u_2(t) \end{bmatrix} dt, \tag{2.12}$$

where

$$M_i = \begin{bmatrix} Q_i & P_i & L_i \\ P_i^T & R_{1i} & N_i \\ L_i^T & N_i^T & R_{2i} \end{bmatrix},$$

with $M_i \geq 0,\ R_{ii} > 0,\ i = 1, 2$, subject to the dynamic constraint

$$\dot{x}(t) = Ax(t) + B_1 u_1(t) + B_2 u_2(t),\ x(0) = x_0. \tag{2.13}$$

For notational convenience, let $B := [B_1,\ B_2]$. Assume that (A, B) is stabilizable.

Since, now, two players are involved in the optimization problem, we have to specify the problem more accurately. The first thing that needs clarification is whether both players will pull together in order to realize their goals or not. In this section we assume that both players agree to cooperate.

Note that due to the fact that both players influence the underlying state of the system, in general, the cost one specific player incurs depends on the actions of her opponent. In particular, this cost is not uniquely determined anymore. If both players decide, e.g., to use their control variables to reduce player 1's cost as much as possible, a different minimum is attained for player 1 from that in the case that both players agree to collectively help player 2 in minimizing her cost. So, depending on how the players choose to 'divide' their control efforts, a player incurs different 'minima'. So, in general, each player is confronted with a whole set of possible outcomes from which somehow one outcome (which usually does not coincide with a player's overall lowest cost) is cooperatively selected. Now, if there are two strategies γ_1 and γ_2 such that both players have a lower cost if strategy γ_1 is played, then it seems reasonable to assume that both players will prefer this strategy. We say that the solution induced by strategy γ_1 *dominates* in that case the solution induced by strategy γ_2. So, dominance means that the outcome is better for all players. Proceeding in this line of thinking, it seems reasonable to consider only those cooperative outcomes which have the property that, if a strategy different from the one corresponding with this cooperative outcome is chosen, then at least one of the players has higher costs. Or, stated differently, to consider only solutions that are such that they cannot be improved upon by all players simultaneously. This motivates the concept of Pareto efficiency.[5]

[5]The Italian economist/sociologist Vilfredo Pareto, who studied classics and engineering in Turin, lived from 1848 to 1923.

Definition 2.4 *Let Γ_i be the strategy space of player i, $\Gamma := \Gamma_1 \times \Gamma_2$ and $\gamma_i \in \Gamma_i$. A set of strategies $(\hat{\gamma}_1, \hat{\gamma}_2) \in \Gamma$ is called Pareto efficient if the set of inequalities*

$$J_i(\gamma_1, \gamma_2) \leqq J_i(\hat{\gamma}_1, \hat{\gamma}_2), \; i = 1, 2,$$

where at least one of the inequalities is strict, does not allow for any solution (γ_1, γ_2) in the strategy space Γ. The corresponding point $(J_1(\hat{\gamma}_1, \hat{\gamma}_2), J_2(\hat{\gamma}_1, \hat{\gamma}_2)) \in \mathbb{R}^2$ is called a Pareto solution. The set of all Pareto solutions is called the Pareto frontier. □

A Pareto solution is therefore never dominated, and is for that reason also called an *non-dominated solution.* Typically, there is always more than one Pareto solution, because dominance is a property which generally does not provide a total ordering.

It turns out that there is a nice way to determine all Pareto-efficient outcomes for our cooperative game, defined by the equations (2.12) and (2.13). To that end we introduce the notation

$$\mathcal{A} := \{\alpha = (\alpha_1, \alpha_2) \mid \alpha_i \geqq 0 \text{ and } \alpha_1 + \alpha_2 = 1\}.$$

and recall from Engwerda (2005a) the following theorem.

Theorem 2.15 *Let $\alpha_i > 0$, $i = 1, 2$, satisfy $\sum_{i=1}^{2} \alpha_i = 1$. If $\hat{\gamma} \in \Gamma$ is such that*

$$\hat{\gamma} \in \arg\min_{\gamma \in \Gamma} \{\sum_{i=1}^{2} \alpha_i J_i(\gamma)\},$$

then $\hat{\gamma}$ is Pareto efficient.
Moreover, if Γ_i is convex and J_i is convex for all $i = 1, 2$, then for all Pareto efficient $\hat{\gamma}$ there exist $\alpha \in A$, such that

$$\hat{\gamma} \in \arg\min_{\gamma \in \Gamma} \{\sum_{i=1}^{2} \alpha_i J_i(\gamma)\}.$$

□

Next, consider, as a particular case, our linear-quadratic differential game (2.12)-(2.13). Similar to Engwerda (2005a), Section 6.1, it can be shown that the cost functionals (2.12) are convex if $M_i \geq 0$. An immediate corollary from Theorem 2.15 is then

Corollary 2.2 *Consider the optimization problem (2.12)-(2.13). Under the assumption that $M_i \geq 0$, $i = 1, 2$, $J_i(u)$ are convex.*
Cooperative Pareto solutions are obtained for all $\alpha \in A$, with $\alpha_i > 0$, for which

$$u^*(\alpha) = \arg\min_{u \in \mathcal{U}_s} \alpha_1 J_1 + \alpha_2 J_2, \; \textit{subject to } (2.13) \textit{ exists.} \qquad (2.14)$$

The corresponding Pareto solutions are

$$(J_1(u^*(\alpha)),\ J_2(u^*(\alpha))). \tag{2.15}$$

Moreover, the only additional Pareto solutions that may exist are obtained by considering the strategies that satisfy (2.14) for $\alpha \in A$ with $\alpha_i = 1$ for some i. □

Theorem 2.15 and Corollary 2.2 show that to find all cooperative solutions for the linear-quadratic game one has to solve a linear-quadratic optimal control problem, which depends on a parameter α. Using Theorem 2.14 we have then the next result.

Theorem 2.16 *(Solution of cooperative game)*
Assume that (A, B) is stabilizable and J_i is given by (2.12) with $(u_1, u_2) \in U_s$. For $\alpha \in A$, let

$$M(\alpha) := \alpha_1 M_1 + \alpha_2 M_2 =: \begin{bmatrix} \tilde{Q} & \tilde{P} \\ \tilde{P}^T & \tilde{R} \end{bmatrix},$$

where

$$\begin{aligned} \tilde{Q} &= \alpha_1 Q_1 + \alpha_2 Q_2,\ \tilde{P} = [\alpha_1 P_1 + \alpha_2 P_2,\ \alpha_1 L_1 + \alpha_2 L_2], \\ \text{and } \tilde{R} &= \alpha_1 \begin{bmatrix} R_{11} & N_1 \\ N_1^T & R_{21} \end{bmatrix} + \alpha_2 \begin{bmatrix} R_{12} & N_2 \\ N_2^T & R_{22} \end{bmatrix}. \end{aligned}$$

With $\tilde{S} := B\tilde{R}^{-1}B^T$, let A_0 denote all $\alpha \in A$ (with $\alpha_i > 0$) for which the ARE

$$(A - B\tilde{R}^{-1}\tilde{P}^T)^T X + X(A - B\tilde{R}^{-1}\tilde{P}^T) - X\tilde{S}X + \tilde{Q} - \tilde{P}\tilde{R}^{-1}\tilde{P}^T = 0 \tag{2.16}$$

has a symmetric stabilizing solution X_s (i.e. $\sigma(A - B\tilde{R}^{-1}\tilde{P}^T - \tilde{S}X_s) \subset \mathbb{C}^-$).
Then

$$(J_1(u^*(\alpha)), J_2(u^*(\alpha)),\ \text{where } \alpha\ \in \mathcal{A}_0,$$

are Pareto solutions. Here

$$u^*(t) = -\tilde{R}^{-1}(B^T X_s + \tilde{P}^T)x(t) \tag{2.17}$$

and, with $A_{cl} := A - B\tilde{R}^{-1}\tilde{P}^T - \tilde{S}X_s$, the closed-loop system is $\dot{x}(t) = A_{cl}x(t)$, $x(0) = x_0$ and $J_i(x_0, u^*) = x_0^T\tilde{M}_i x_0$, where $\tilde{M}_i$ is the unique solution of the Lyapunov equation

$$A_{cl}^T\tilde{M}_i + \tilde{M}_i A_{cl} = -[I,\ -(X_sB + \tilde{P})\tilde{R}^{-1}]M_i \begin{bmatrix} I \\ -\tilde{R}^{-1}(B^T X_s + \tilde{P}^T) \end{bmatrix}. \tag{2.18}$$

All other potential Pareto-efficient strategies are obtained as the solution of the optimization problem (2.14) with either $(\alpha_1, \alpha_2) = (1, 0)$ or $(\alpha_1, \alpha_2) = (0, 1)$. □

Using the relationship between solutions of (2.16) and invariant subspaces of the with this ARE corresponding Hamiltonian matrix (see Section 3.1) the next numerical algorithm yields then (apart from the potential solutions that may arise at the boundaries of the set A) the Pareto frontier of the cooperative game. In this algorithm we use the notation introduced in Theorem 2.16.

Algorithm 2.1

Start with $\alpha_1 = 0.01$.

Step1: $\alpha_2 := 1 - \alpha_1$.

Calculate the eigenstructure of $H(\alpha) := \begin{bmatrix} A - B\tilde{R}^{-1}\tilde{P}^T & -\tilde{S} \\ -\tilde{Q} + \tilde{P}\tilde{R}^{-1}\tilde{P}^T & -(A - B\tilde{R}^{-1}\tilde{P}^T)^T \end{bmatrix}$.

If H has an n-dimensional stable graph subspace, then proceed. Otherwise, go to Step 3.

Step2: Determine the n-dimensional stable graph subspace V.

Calculate $n \times n$ matrices X and Y such that $\text{Im}\begin{bmatrix} X \\ Y \end{bmatrix} = V$.

Denote $X_s := YX^{-1}$. Then

$$u^*(t) := -\tilde{R}^{-1}(B^T X_s + \tilde{P}^T)x(t)$$

yields a Pareto strategy. The spectrum of the corresponding closed-loop matrix A_{cl} equals $\sigma(H|_V)$. The involved cost for player i is $J_i(x_0, u^*(\alpha)) = x_0^T \tilde{M}_i x_0$, where $\tilde{M}_i$ is the unique solution of the Lyapunov equation (2.18).

Step3: If $\alpha_1 < .99$, then $\alpha_1 := \alpha_1 + 0.01$, and return to Step 1. Otherwise, terminate the algorithm. □

Remark 2.3

1. *Obviously, the number .01 in the above algorithm is arbitrary and may be replaced by any other number that better suits the user of the algorithm.*

2. *For either $\alpha_1 = 1$ or $\alpha_2 = 1$ matrix $\tilde{R}$ is often not positive definite, but just positive semi-definite. This case does not fit into the general theory we presented here. For that reason we will usually skip a detailed analysis of these cases. Since it only may concern two boundary points of the Pareto frontier, in general this does not seem to be a severe restriction.*

3. *In the computer package MATLAB, there are standard routines to calculate the stabilizing solution of an ARE as well as standard routines to calculate the solution of a Lyapunov equation. Obviously, using these routines, the implementation of the above numerical algorithm can be shortened tremendously.* □

In Lancaster and Rodman (1995, Section 11.3), it is shown that if the parameters appearing in an ARE are, e.g., differentiable functions of some parameter α (or, more general, depend analytically on a parameter α), and the maximal solution exists for all α in some open set W, then this maximal solution of the Riccati equation will be a differentiable function of this parameter α too on W (depend analytically on this parameter α too). Since in the linear-quadratic case, the parameters depend linearly on α, this implies that the Pareto frontier will be a smooth function of α (provided that the maximal solution exists for all α).

Example 2.11 *Consider the minimization of*

$$J_1 := \int_0^\infty \{3x^T(t)x(t) + u_1^2(t)\}dt \text{ and } J_2 := \int_0^\infty \{x^T(t)x(t) + 3u_2^2(t)\}dt,$$

subject to the system

$$\dot{x}(t) = \begin{bmatrix} 1 & 0 \\ 0 & -2 \end{bmatrix} x(t) + \begin{bmatrix} 1 \\ 0 \end{bmatrix} u_1(t) + \begin{bmatrix} 1 \\ 0 \end{bmatrix} u_2(t),\ x(0) = [\bar{x},\ \bar{y}]^T,$$

where $\bar{x}$ and $\bar{y}$ are some arbitrary numbers. The system $\left(\begin{bmatrix} 1 & 0 \\ 0 & -2 \end{bmatrix}, \begin{bmatrix} 1 & 1 \\ 0 & 0 \end{bmatrix}\right)$ is stabilizable. Now, let $\alpha \in (0,1)$ be an arbitrary number. Then, according to Theorem 2.16, $(u_1(\alpha), u_2(\alpha))^* \in U_s$ is a Pareto solution if the ARE

$$A^TX + XA - XSX + Q = 0,$$

with

$$Q = \alpha \begin{bmatrix} 3 & 0 \\ 0 & 3 \end{bmatrix} + (1-\alpha) \begin{bmatrix} 1 & 0 \\ 0 & 1 \end{bmatrix} = \begin{bmatrix} 1+2\alpha & 0 \\ 0 & 1+2\alpha \end{bmatrix},\ A = \begin{bmatrix} 1 & 0 \\ 0 & -2 \end{bmatrix},$$

$$\text{and} \quad S = \begin{bmatrix} 1 & 1 \\ 0 & 0 \end{bmatrix} \begin{bmatrix} \frac{1}{\alpha} & 0 \\ 0 & \frac{1}{3(1-\alpha)} \end{bmatrix} \begin{bmatrix} 1 & 0 \\ 1 & 0 \end{bmatrix} = \frac{3-2\alpha}{3\alpha(1-\alpha)} \begin{bmatrix} 1 & 0 \\ 0 & 0 \end{bmatrix},$$

has a stabilizing solution.

Straightforward calculations show that with $\beta := 1 + \sqrt{1 + \frac{(3-2\alpha)(1+2\alpha)}{3\alpha(1-\alpha)}}$ and $x_s := \frac{3\alpha(1-\alpha)}{3-2\alpha}\beta$, the ARE has the stabilizing solution

$$X := \begin{bmatrix} x_s & 0 \\ 0 & \frac{1+2\alpha}{4} \end{bmatrix}.$$

The resulting optimal controls are

$$u_1^*(t) = -\frac{x_s}{\alpha}x_1(t) \text{ and } u_2^*(t) = -\frac{x_s}{3(1-\alpha)}x_1(t),\ \text{where } x_1(t) = [1\ 0]x(t).$$

This control yields the closed-loop system

$$A_{cl} = \begin{bmatrix} 1-\beta & 0 \\ 0 & -2 \end{bmatrix}.$$

The corresponding costs are obtained by solving the Lyapunov equations (see (2.18))

$$A_{cl}^T\tilde{M}_1 + \tilde{M}_1A_{cl} =$$

$$= -\begin{bmatrix} 1 & 0 & -\frac{x_s}{\alpha} & -\frac{x_s}{3(1-\alpha)} \\ 0 & 1 & 0 & 0 \end{bmatrix} \begin{bmatrix} 3 & 0 & 0 & 0 \\ 0 & 3 & 0 & 0 \\ 0 & 0 & 1 & 0 \\ 0 & 0 & 0 & 0 \end{bmatrix} \begin{bmatrix} 1 & 0 & -\frac{x_s}{\alpha} & -\frac{x_s}{3(1-\alpha)} \\ 0 & 1 & 0 & 0 \end{bmatrix}^T$$

and

$$A_{cl}^T\tilde{M}_2+\tilde{M}_2A_{cl}=$$

$$=-\begin{bmatrix}1&0&-\frac{x_s}{\alpha}&-\frac{x_s}{3(1-\alpha)}\\0&1&0&0\end{bmatrix}\begin{bmatrix}1&0&0&0\\0&1&0&0\\0&0&0&0\\0&0&0&3\end{bmatrix}\begin{bmatrix}1&0&-\frac{x_s}{\alpha}&-\frac{x_s}{3(1-\alpha)}\\0&1&0&0\end{bmatrix}^T.$$

Or, equivalently,

$$\begin{bmatrix}1-\beta&0\\0&-2\end{bmatrix}\tilde{M}_1+\tilde{M}_1\begin{bmatrix}1-\beta&0\\0&-2\end{bmatrix}=-\begin{bmatrix}3+\frac{x_s^2}{\alpha^2}&0\\0&3\end{bmatrix}$$

and

$$\begin{bmatrix}1-\beta&0\\0&-2\end{bmatrix}\tilde{M}_2+\tilde{M}_2\begin{bmatrix}1-\beta&0\\0&-2\end{bmatrix}=-\begin{bmatrix}1+\frac{3x_s^2}{9(1-\alpha)^2}&0\\0&1\end{bmatrix}.$$

The solutions to these Lyapunov equations are

$$\tilde{M}_1=\begin{bmatrix}\frac{3+\frac{x_s^2}{\alpha^2}}{2(\beta-1)}&0\\0&\frac{3}{4}\end{bmatrix}\text{ and }\tilde{M}_2=\begin{bmatrix}\frac{1+\frac{3x_s^2}{9(1-\alpha)^2}}{2(\beta-1)}&0\\0&\frac{1}{4}\end{bmatrix}.$$

So, the with $0<\alpha<1$, corresponding set of cooperative solutions is

$$J_1^* = \frac{3+\frac{x_s^2}{\alpha^2}}{2(\beta-1)}\bar{x}^2+\frac{3}{4}\bar{y}^2,$$

$$J_2^* = \frac{1+\frac{3x_s^2}{9(1-\alpha)^2}}{2(\beta-1)}\bar{x}^2+\frac{1}{4}\bar{y}^2,$$

if $x_0=[\bar{x},\ \bar{y}]^T$. For $x_0=[1,\ 2]^T$ we plotted this Pareto frontier in Figure 2.1.□

Example 2.12 *Consider the minimization of*

$$J_1:=\int_0^\infty\{3x^T(t)x(t)+u_1^2(t)\}dt\text{ and }J_2:=\int_0^\infty\{x^T(t)x(t)+3u_2^2(t)\}dt,$$

subject to the system

$$\dot{x}(t)=\begin{bmatrix}1&1\\0&-2\end{bmatrix}x(t)+\begin{bmatrix}1\\0\end{bmatrix}u_1(t)+\begin{bmatrix}1\\0\end{bmatrix}u_2(t),\ x(0)=[1,\ 2]^T.$$

The system $\left(\begin{bmatrix}1&1\\0&-2\end{bmatrix},\begin{bmatrix}1&1\\0&0\end{bmatrix}\right)$ *is stabilizable. So, for $\alpha\in A$ (see Theorem 2.16), the problem has a cooperative solution if the ARE*

$$Q+A^TX+XA-XSX=0,$$

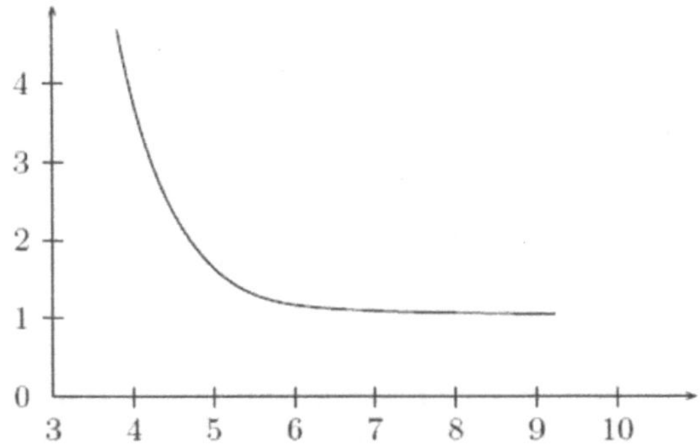

Figure 2.1: Part of Pareto frontier for Example 2.11 if $x_0^T = [1, 2]$.

with (see Example 2.11)

$$Q = \begin{bmatrix} 1+2\alpha & 0 \\ 0 & 1+2\alpha \end{bmatrix},\ A = \begin{bmatrix} 1 & 1 \\ 0 & -2 \end{bmatrix} \text{ and } S = \frac{3-2\alpha}{3\alpha(1-\alpha)} \begin{bmatrix} 1 & 0 \\ 0 & 0 \end{bmatrix}$$

has a stabilizing solution.
To determine the solution we proceed along the lines of Algorithm 2.1.
For a fixed $\alpha \in (0, 1)$ we calculate the eigenstructure of matrix

$$\begin{bmatrix} 1 & 1 & -\frac{3-2\alpha}{3\alpha(1-\alpha)} & 0 \\ 0 & -2 & 0 & 0 \\ -(1+2\alpha) & 0 & -1 & 0 \\ 0 & -(1+2\alpha) & -1 & -2 \end{bmatrix}.$$

By determining a basis for the eigenspace corresponding with the stable eigenvalues of this matrix, the stabilizing solution X_s of the Riccati equation is determined.
From this the closed-loop system matrix $A_{cl} := A - SX_s$ is then obtained.

The corresponding costs are next determined by solving the Lyapunov equations (see (2.18))

$$A_{cl}^T \tilde{M_1} + \tilde{M_1} A_{cl} =$$

$$= -\left[\begin{bmatrix} 1 & 0 \\ 0 & 1 \end{bmatrix}, \begin{bmatrix} \frac{-1}{\alpha} & \frac{-1}{3(1-\alpha)} \\ 0 & 0 \end{bmatrix} X_s\right] \begin{bmatrix} 3 & 0 & 0 & 0 \\ 0 & 3 & 0 & 0 \\ 0 & 0 & 1 & 0 \\ 0 & 0 & 0 & 0 \end{bmatrix} \begin{bmatrix} \begin{bmatrix} 1 & 0 \\ 0 & 1 \end{bmatrix} \\ \begin{bmatrix} \frac{-1}{\alpha} & 0 \\ \frac{-1}{3(1-\alpha)} & 0 \end{bmatrix} X_s \end{bmatrix}$$

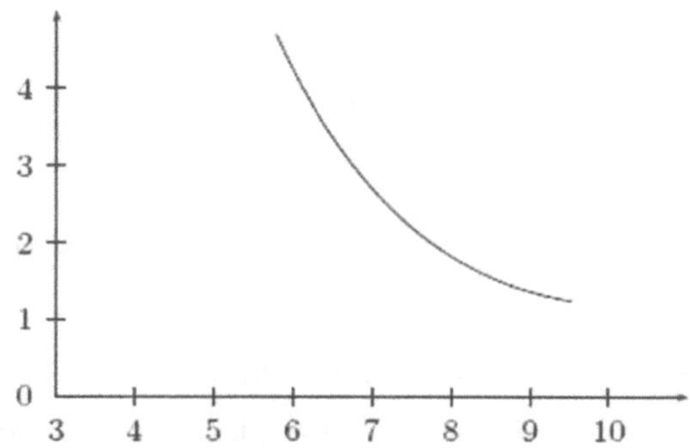

Figure 2.2: Part of Pareto frontier for Example 2.12 if $x_0^T = [1, 2]$

and

$$A_{cl}^T \tilde{M}_2 + \tilde{M}_2 A_{cl} =$$

$$= -\left[\begin{bmatrix} 1 & 0 \\ 0 & 1 \end{bmatrix}, \begin{bmatrix} \frac{-1}{\alpha} & \frac{-1}{3(1-\alpha)} \\ 0 & 0 \end{bmatrix}\right] X_s \begin{bmatrix} 1 & 0 & 0 & 0 \\ 0 & 1 & 0 & 0 \\ 0 & 0 & 0 & 0 \\ 0 & 0 & 0 & 3 \end{bmatrix} \left[\begin{matrix} \begin{bmatrix} 1 & 0 \\ 0 & 1 \end{bmatrix} \\ \begin{bmatrix} \frac{-1}{\alpha} & 0 \\ \frac{-1}{3(1-\alpha)} & 0 \end{bmatrix} \end{matrix} X_s\right].$$

The corresponding cooperative solution is then

$$J_i^* = [1\ 2]\tilde{M}_i \begin{bmatrix} 1 \\ 2 \end{bmatrix}.$$

By varying α *between* 0 *and* 1, *one obtains all Pareto solutions then. We plotted a part of the resulting Pareto frontier in Figure 2.2. As we already noticed in Example 2.10, the fact that in contrast to the previous example, the first state component is now continuously disrupted by the second state component. This implies a more active control policy of both players and increases their costs. This is visualized in the graphs. As one can clearly see, the Pareto frontier for Example 2.11 lies entirely below the Pareto frontier sketched in Figure 2.2.* □

2.5 The non-cooperative game

Non-cooperative differential games were first introduced in Isaacs (1954-1955) within the framework of two-person zero-sum games. Nonzero-sum differential games were introduced in Starr and Ho (1969a, 1969b); Engwerda (2005a) gives a good overview of the state-of-the-art of this theory and additional references. Our starting point in this section is again the cost and system dynamics introduced in Section 2.4. That is, we assume that there are two players who like to minimize their cost function given by

$$J_i(u_1,u_2) := \int_0^\infty [x^T(t),\ u_1^T(t),\ u_2^T(t)]M_i \begin{bmatrix} x(t) \\ u_1(t) \\ u_2(t) \end{bmatrix} dt, \qquad (2.19)$$

where $M_i = \begin{bmatrix} Q_i & P_i & L_i \\ P_i^T & R_{1i} & N_i \\ L_i^T & N_i^T & R_{2i} \end{bmatrix} \geq 0,\ R_{ii} > 0, i = 1,2$, subject to the system dynamics

$$\dot{x}(t) = Ax(t) + B_1u_1(t) + B_2u_2(t),\ x(0) = x_0. \qquad (2.20)$$

The non-cooperative aspect implies that the players are assumed not to cooperate in trying to attain this goal. Obviously, the value of the cost function depends for each player i also on the pursued actions of the other player. So, the question arises how a player will deal with this aspect in determining her control action. Now, assume that both players may propose in turn an action in a negotiation process that precedes the actual implementation of the control. So, the players can react on each other's proposal. Then, assuming that ultimately the proposition process ends, it seems reasonable that in that final situation each player likes to play an action which she cannot improve upon anymore. That is, any unilateral deviation from the action she has in mind will lead to a worse value of her cost function J_i. Nash argued in Nash (1950b, 1951) that this is a natural concept to be used in a non-cooperative context. He defined the (non-cooperative) Nash equilibrium in the following way.

Definition 2.5 *An admissible set of actions (u_1^*, u_2^*) is a Nash equilibrium for a 2-player game, where each player has a cost function $J_i(u_1,u_2)$, if for all admissible (u_1,u_2) the following inequalities hold:*

$$J_1(u_1^*,u_2^*) \leqq J_1(u_1,u_2^*) \text{ and } J_2(u_1^*,u_2^*) \leqq J_2(u_1^*,u_2). \qquad \square$$

Here, admissibility is meant in the sense that $u_i(.)$ belongs to some restricted set, where this set depends on the information players have on the game and the set of strategies the players like to use to control the system.

So, the Nash equilibrium is defined such that it has the property that there is no incentive for any unilateral deviation by any one of the players. Notice that in general one cannot expect to have a unique Nash equilibrium.

Obviously, since according to the *open-loop* information structure followed in this book, the participating parties cannot react to each other's policies, its economic relevance is limited. However, as a benchmark to see how much parties can gain by playing other strategies, it plays a fundamental role. A big advantage of this scenario is, as we will see in the remainder of this section, that it is both analytically and computationally tractable. This is, usually, not the case for most other information structures.

More precisely, the assumptions we make are as follows. First, since we consider an infinite planning horizon, we will assume that the matrix pairs (A, B_i), $i = 1,2$, are stabilizable. This formalizes the assumption that, in principle, each player is capable to stabilize the system on his own. The open-loop information structure of the game means that we assume that both players only know the initial state of the system and that the set of admissible control actions are functions of time, where time runs from zero to infinity. Like in the previous sections, we assume that the players choose control functions belonging to the set $\mathcal{U}_s$.

For notational convenience we introduce some shorthand notation. Let $S_i := B_i R_{ii}^{-1} B_i^T$; $Q := \begin{bmatrix} Q_1 \\ Q_2 \end{bmatrix}$; $G := \begin{bmatrix} [0\ I\ 0]\, M_1 \\ [0\ 0\ I]\, M_2 \end{bmatrix} \begin{bmatrix} 0 & 0 \\ I & 0 \\ 0 & I \end{bmatrix} = \begin{bmatrix} R_{11} & N_1 \\ N_2^T & R_{22} \end{bmatrix}$, where it will be assumed throughout that this matrix G is invertible; $A_2 := \text{diag}\{A, A\}$; $B := [B_1,\ B_2]$; $\tilde{B}^T := \text{diag}\{B_1^T, B_2^T\}$; $\tilde{B}_1^T := \begin{bmatrix} B_1^T \\ 0 \end{bmatrix}$; $\tilde{B}_2^T := \begin{bmatrix} 0 \\ B_2^T \end{bmatrix}$;
$Z := \begin{bmatrix} [0\ I\ 0]\, M_1 \\ [0\ 0\ I]\, M_2 \end{bmatrix} \begin{bmatrix} I \\ 0 \\ 0 \end{bmatrix} = \begin{bmatrix} P_1^T \\ L_2^T \end{bmatrix}$; $Z_i := [I\ 0\ 0] M_i \begin{bmatrix} 0 & 0 \\ I & 0 \\ 0 & I \end{bmatrix} = [P_i,\ L_i]$, for $i=1,2$;
$\tilde{A} := A - BG^{-1}Z$; $\tilde{S}_i := BG^{-1}\tilde{B}_i^T$; $\tilde{Q}_i := Q_i - Z_i G^{-1} Z$; $\tilde{A}_2^T := A_2^T - \begin{bmatrix} Z_1 \\ Z_2 \end{bmatrix} G^{-1}\tilde{B}^T$ and
$M := \begin{bmatrix} \tilde{A} & -\tilde{S} \\ -\tilde{Q} & -\tilde{A}_2^T \end{bmatrix}$, where $\tilde{S} := [\tilde{S}_1,\ \tilde{S}_2]$, $\tilde{Q} := \begin{bmatrix} \tilde{Q}_1 \\ \tilde{Q}_2 \end{bmatrix}$.

Notice that with this notation

$$M = \begin{bmatrix} A & 0 & 0 \\ -Q_1 & -A^T & 0 \\ -Q_2 & 0 & -A^T \end{bmatrix} + \begin{bmatrix} -B \\ Z_1 \\ Z_2 \end{bmatrix} G^{-1} \begin{bmatrix} Z, & \tilde{B}_1^T, & \tilde{B}_2^T \end{bmatrix}.$$

This representation more clearly shows the structure of M. From this, one may now derive in an obvious way matrix M in the case that the number of players is more than two. Something, which we will need in the next chapters.

Furthermore, consider the AREs

$$\begin{aligned} A^T K_1 + K_1 A - (K_1 B_1 + P_1) R_{11}^{-1} (B_1^T K_1 + P_1^T) + Q_1 &= 0, \\ A^T K_2 + K_2 A - (K_2 B_2 + L_2) R_{22}^{-1} (B_2^T K_2 + L_2^T) + Q_2 &= 0. \end{aligned} \tag{2.21}$$

and the non-symmetric (or set of coupled) ARE (s)

$$0 = \tilde{A}_2^T X + X\tilde{A} - XBG^{-1}\tilde{B}^T X + \tilde{Q}. \tag{2.22}$$

or, equivalently,

$$0 = A_2^T X + XA - (XB + \begin{bmatrix} Z_1 \\ Z_2 \end{bmatrix}) G^{-1} (\tilde{B}^T X + Z) + Q.$$

Then, by Definition 2.1, a solution X of (2.22) is called

a. *stabilizing*, if $\sigma(\tilde{A} - BG^{-1}\tilde{B}^T X) \subset \mathbb{C}^-$; and

b. *strongly stabilizing* if

i. it is a stabilizing solution, and

ii. $\sigma(\tilde{A}_2^T - XBG^{-1}\tilde{B}^T) \subset \mathbb{C}^-$;

From Engwerda (2005b) we recall the following result.

Theorem 2.17 *(Solution of open-loop non- cooperative game)*
Consider the linear-quadratic differential game (2.19)-(2.20), where (A, B_i) are stabilizable.
This game has a unique open-loop Nash equilibrium for every initial state if and only if

1. *The set of coupled AREs (2.22) has a strongly stabilizing solution X_s, and*

2. *the two AREs (2.21) have a stabilizing solution.*

Moreover, in the case that this game has a unique equilibrium, the unique equilibrium actions are given by

$$\begin{bmatrix} u_1^*(t) \\ u_2^*(t) \end{bmatrix} = -G^{-1}(Z + \tilde{B}^T X_s)\tilde{\Phi}(t,0)x_0, \tag{2.23}$$

where $\tilde{\Phi}(t,0)$ is the solution of the transition equation

$$\dot{\tilde{\Phi}}(t,0) = (A - BG^{-1}(Z + \tilde{B}^T X_s))\tilde{\Phi}(t,0);\ \tilde{\Phi}(0,0) = I.$$

□

Similar as in the previous section, we can exploit now the relationship between solutions of AREs and invariant subspaces of corresponding Hamiltonian matrices to derive a numerical algorithm to determine the solution of this game (if it exists).

Algorithm 2.2

Step 1: Calculate the eigenstructure of the matrices $H_i,\ i = 1, 2$, given by

$$\begin{bmatrix} A - B_1 R_{11}^{-1} P_1^T & -S_1 \\ -Q_1 + P_1 R_{11}^{-1} P_1^T & -(A - B_1 R_{11}^{-1} P_1^T)^T \end{bmatrix} \quad \text{and}$$

$$\begin{bmatrix} A - B_2 R_{22}^{-1} L_2^T & -S_2 \\ -Q_2 + L_2 R_{22}^{-1} L_2^T & -(A - B_2 R_{22}^{-1} L_2^T)^T \end{bmatrix},$$

respectively. If $H_i,\ i = 1, 2$, has an n-dimensional stable graph subspace, then proceed. Otherwise, go to Step 5.

Step 2: Calculate matrix $M := \begin{bmatrix} A & 0 & 0 \\ -Q_1 & -A^T & 0 \\ -Q_2 & 0 & -A^T \end{bmatrix} + \begin{bmatrix} -B \\ Z_1 \\ Z_2 \end{bmatrix} G^{-1} \left[Z,\ \tilde{B}_1^T,\ \tilde{B}_2^T \right].$

Next, calculate the spectrum of M. If exact n eigenvalues (counted with algebraic multiplicities) of M belong to $\mathbb{C}^-$, then proceed, otherwise, go to Step 5.

Step 3: Calculate the n-dimensional M-invariant subspace $\mathcal{V}$ corresponding with the n stable eigenvalues of M. Calculate $n \times n$ matrices X, Y and Z such that $\text{Im}\begin{bmatrix} X \\ Y \\ Z \end{bmatrix} = \mathcal{V}$.
If X is invertible then proceed. Otherwise, go to Step 5.

Step 4: Calculate $X_1 := YX^{-1}$ and $X_2 := ZX^{-1}$. Denote $X_s := \begin{bmatrix} X_1 \\ X_2 \end{bmatrix}$. Then

$$\begin{bmatrix} u_1^*(t) \\ u_2^*(t) \end{bmatrix} = -G^{-1}(Z + \tilde{B}^T X_s)\tilde{\Phi}(t,0)x_0,$$

where, with $A_{cl} := A - BG^{-1}(Z + \tilde{B}^T X_s)$, $\tilde{\Phi}(t,0)$ is the solution of the transition equation

$$\dot{\tilde{\Phi}}(t,0) = A_{cl}\tilde{\Phi}(t,0);\ \tilde{\Phi}(0,0) = I.$$

The spectrum of the involved closed-loop system matrix, A_{cl}, equals $\sigma(M|_{\mathcal{V}})$. The involved cost for player i is $x_0^T \bar{M}_i x_0$, where $\bar{M}_i$ is the unique solution of the Lyapunov equation:

$$A_{cl}^T \bar{M}_i + \bar{M}_i A_{cl} = -[I,\ -(X_s^T \tilde{B} + Z^T)G^{-1}]M_i \begin{bmatrix} I \\ -G^{-1}(\tilde{B}^T X_s + Z) \end{bmatrix}. \tag{2.24}$$

Step 5: End of the algorithm. □

Remark 2.4 *In the case that the algorithm terminates without providing an equilibrium, this does not mean that the game does not have an equilibrium. It can happen, e.g., that for some initial states an equilibrium exists whereas for other initial states there is no equilibrium. Another possibility is that the game has more than one equilibrium for every initial state. Details on the conditions under which these various cases occur can be found in Engwerda (2005a).* □

Examples 2.13 and 2.14, below, illustrate the algorithm.

Example 2.13 *Consider the problem where two players like to control the state of the system towards zero using as less as possible control efforts, but where each player has a different preference concerning the part of the system that should have highest priority in controlling it towards zero. That is, consider the* *minimization of*

$$\begin{aligned}
J_1 \; &: = \int_0^\infty \{x^T(t) \begin{bmatrix} 4 & 0 \\ 0 & 1 \end{bmatrix} x(t) + u_1^2(t)\}dt \\
&= \int_0^\infty \{[x^T(t),\; u_1(t),\; u_2(t)] \begin{bmatrix} 4 & 0 & 0 & 0 \\ 0 & 1 & 0 & 0 \\ 0 & 0 & 1 & 0 \\ 0 & 0 & 0 & 0 \end{bmatrix} \begin{bmatrix} x(t) \\ u_1(t) \\ u_2(t) \end{bmatrix}\}dt \\
&= : \int_0^\infty \{[x^T(t),\; u_1(t),\; u_2(t)] M_1 \begin{bmatrix} x(t) \\ u_1(t) \\ u_2(t) \end{bmatrix}\}dt \qquad \textit{and} \\
J_2 \; &: = \int_0^\infty \{x^T(t) \begin{bmatrix} 1 & 0 \\ 0 & 4 \end{bmatrix} x(t) + u_2^2(t)\}dt \\
&= \int_0^\infty \{[x^T(t),\; u_1(t),\; u_2(t)] \begin{bmatrix} 1 & 0 & 0 & 0 \\ 0 & 4 & 0 & 0 \\ 0 & 0 & 0 & 0 \\ 0 & 0 & 0 & 1 \end{bmatrix} \begin{bmatrix} x(t) \\ u_1(t) \\ u_2(t) \end{bmatrix}\}dt \\
&= : \int_0^\infty \{[x^T(t),\; u_1(t),\; u_2(t)] M_2 \begin{bmatrix} x(t) \\ u_1(t) \\ u_2(t) \end{bmatrix}\}dt
\end{aligned}$$

subject to the system

$$\dot{x}(t) = \begin{bmatrix} -\frac{3}{2} & 0 \\ 0 & -\frac{3}{2} \end{bmatrix} x(t) + \begin{bmatrix} 1 \\ 1 \end{bmatrix} u_1(t) + \begin{bmatrix} 1 \\ 1 \end{bmatrix} u_2(t),\; x(0) = [\bar{x},\; \bar{y}]^T.$$

Assume that both players do not cooperate to realize their goals. Following the notation of (2.19)-(2.20), we introduce

$$\begin{aligned}
A \; &: = \begin{bmatrix} -\frac{3}{2} & 0 \\ 0 & -\frac{3}{2} \end{bmatrix},\; B_i := \begin{bmatrix} 1 \\ 1 \end{bmatrix},\; Q_1 := \begin{bmatrix} 4 & 0 \\ 0 & 1 \end{bmatrix};\; Q_2 := \begin{bmatrix} 1 & 0 \\ 0 & 4 \end{bmatrix}, \\
P_i \; &: = L_i := [0,\; 0]^T,\; N_i := R_{12} := R_{21} := 0, \textit{ and } R_{ii} := 1 \textit{ for } i = 1, 2.
\end{aligned}$$

Notice that (A, B_i) *are stabilizable. So, according to Theorem 2.17, the problem has a unique open-loop Nash equilibrium if and only if the AREs*

$$Q_i + A^T K_i + K_i A - K_i S_i K_i = 0,$$

with $S_i = \begin{bmatrix} 1 & 1 \\ 1 & 1 \end{bmatrix}$, $i = 1, 2$, *have a stabilizing solution and the ARE*

$$\tilde{Q} + \tilde{A}_2^T X + X\tilde{A} - XBG^{-1}\tilde{B}^T X = 0$$

has a strongly stabilizing solution. Here

$$G \;:\; = \begin{bmatrix} 1 & 0 \\ 0 & 1 \end{bmatrix},\; B := \begin{bmatrix} 1 & 1 \\ 1 & 1 \end{bmatrix};\; \tilde{B}^T := \begin{bmatrix} 1 & 1 & 0 & 0 \\ 0 & 0 & 1 & 1 \end{bmatrix},$$

$$Z^T \;:\; = Z_i := [0,\ 0],\quad \tilde{A} := A,$$

$$\tilde{A}_2 \;:\; = \begin{bmatrix} -\frac{3}{2} & 0 & 0 & 0 \\ 0 & -\frac{3}{2} & 0 & 0 \\ 0 & 0 & -\frac{3}{2} & 0 \\ 0 & 0 & 0 & -\frac{3}{2} \end{bmatrix},\quad \textit{and}\ \tilde{Q} := \begin{bmatrix} 4 & 0 \\ 0 & 1 \\ 1 & 0 \\ 0 & 4 \end{bmatrix}.$$

Using this notation, it is easily verified that matrices H_i, $i = 1, 2$, in Step 1 of Algorithm 2.2 are given by

$$H_1 = \begin{bmatrix} -\frac{3}{2} & 0 & -1 & -1 \\ 0 & -\frac{3}{2} & -1 & -1 \\ -4 & 0 & \frac{3}{2} & 0 \\ 0 & -1 & 0 & \frac{3}{2} \end{bmatrix} \quad \textit{and}\ H_2 = \begin{bmatrix} -\frac{3}{2} & 0 & -1 & -1 \\ 0 & -\frac{3}{2} & -1 & -1 \\ -1 & 0 & \frac{3}{2} & 0 \\ 0 & -4 & 0 & \frac{3}{2} \end{bmatrix}.$$

It is straightforwardly verified that H_1 has eigenvalues $-\frac{3}{2}$ and $-\frac{1}{2}\sqrt{29}$. An eigenvector corresponding with $-\frac{3}{2}$ is $[3,\ -8,\ 4,\ -4]^T$, whereas $[\frac{3}{2} + \frac{1}{2}\sqrt{29},\ \frac{3}{2} + \frac{1}{2}\sqrt{29},\ 4,\ 1]^T$ is an eigenvector corresponding with the eigenvalue $-\frac{1}{2}\sqrt{29}$. Since matrix $\begin{bmatrix} 3 & \frac{3}{2} + \frac{1}{2}\sqrt{29} \\ -8 & \frac{3}{2} + \frac{1}{2}\sqrt{29} \end{bmatrix}$ is invertible it is clear that the with these eigenvalues corresponding eigenspace is a graph subspace.

Furthermore, H_2 has the same two stable eigenvalues as H_1. An eigenvector corresponding with the eigenvalue $-\frac{3}{2}$ is $[-8,\ 3,\ -4,\ 4]^T$, whereas $[\frac{3}{2} + \frac{1}{2}\sqrt{29},\ \frac{3}{2} + \frac{1}{2}\sqrt{29},\ 1,\ 4]^T$ is an eigenvector corresponding with the eigenvalue $-\frac{1}{2}\sqrt{29}$. From this it straightforwardly follows again that the with these stable eigenvalues corresponding eigenspace is a graph subspace.

So, both AREs (2.21) have a stabilizing solution and we may proceed with Step 2 of the algorithm.

Straightforward substitution shows that matrix M in Step 2 of the algorithm is given by

$$M = \begin{bmatrix} -\frac{3}{2} & 0 & -1 & -1 & -1 & -1 \\ 0 & -\frac{3}{2} & -1 & -1 & -1 & -1 \\ -4 & 0 & \frac{3}{2} & 0 & 0 & 0 \\ 0 & -1 & 0 & \frac{3}{2} & 0 & 0 \\ -1 & 0 & 0 & 0 & \frac{3}{2} & 0 \\ 0 & -4 & 0 & 0 & 0 & \frac{3}{2} \end{bmatrix}.$$

Next, we determine the eigenstructure of matrix M. It is easily verified that M has eigenvalues $\{-3\frac{1}{2},\ -1\frac{1}{2},\ 1\frac{1}{2},\ 1\frac{1}{2},\ 1\frac{1}{2},\ 3\frac{1}{2}\}$. So, it has two stable eigenvalues and four unstable eigenvalues. An eigenvector corresponding with the eigenvalue $-3\frac{1}{2}$ is $[5,\ 5,\ 4,\ 1,\ 1,\ 4]^T$ and an eigenvector corresponding with $-\frac{1}{2}$ is $[-3,\ 3,\ -4,\ 1,\ -1,\ 4]^T$. Since $X := \begin{bmatrix} 5 & -3 \\ 5 & 3 \end{bmatrix}$ is invertible, we conclude that the Riccati equation (2.22) has a strongly stabilizing solution.

Consequently, the game has a unique open-loop Nash equilibrium. To find the equilibrium actions we introduce the matrices

$$Y := \begin{bmatrix} 4 & -4 \\ 1 & 1 \end{bmatrix} \text{ and } Z := \begin{bmatrix} 1 & -1 \\ 4 & 4 \end{bmatrix}.$$

Then, according to Step 4 of the algorithm with

$$X_1 := YX^{-1} = \frac{1}{30}\begin{bmatrix} 32 & -8 \\ -2 & 8 \end{bmatrix} \text{ and } X_2 := ZX^{-1} = \frac{1}{30}\begin{bmatrix} 8 & -2 \\ -8 & 32 \end{bmatrix},$$

the equilibrium actions are

$$\begin{bmatrix} u_1^*(t) \\ u_2^*(t) \end{bmatrix} = -\tilde{B}^T \begin{bmatrix} X_1 \\ X_2 \end{bmatrix} x(t) = -\begin{bmatrix} 1 & 0 \\ 0 & 1 \end{bmatrix} x(t),$$

where $x(.)$ satisfies the differential equation

$$\begin{aligned} \dot{x}(t) &= \begin{bmatrix} -\frac{3}{2} & 0 \\ 0 & -\frac{3}{2} \end{bmatrix} x(t) - \begin{bmatrix} 1 \\ 1 \end{bmatrix} [1,\ 0]x(t) - \begin{bmatrix} 1 \\ 1 \end{bmatrix} [0,\ 1]x(t) \\ &= \begin{bmatrix} -\frac{5}{2} & -1 \\ -1 & -\frac{5}{2} \end{bmatrix} x(t) =: A_{cl}x(t), \text{ with } x(0) = [\bar{x},\ \bar{y}]^T. \end{aligned}$$

That is, the equilibrium action by player 1 is

$$\begin{aligned} u_1^*(t) &= -[1,\ 0]e^{A_{cl}t} \begin{bmatrix} \bar{x} \\ \bar{y} \end{bmatrix} \\ &= \frac{1}{2}[1,\ 0] \begin{bmatrix} 1 & 1 \\ 1 & -1 \end{bmatrix} \begin{bmatrix} e^{-3.5t} & 0 \\ 0 & e^{-1.5t} \end{bmatrix} \begin{bmatrix} -1 & -1 \\ -1 & 1 \end{bmatrix} \begin{bmatrix} \bar{x} \\ \bar{y} \end{bmatrix} \\ &= \frac{1}{2}(-(e^{-3.5t} + e^{-1.5t})\bar{x} + (e^{-1.5t} - e^{-3.5t})\bar{y}), \end{aligned}$$

whereas in a similar way it follows that

$$u_2^*(t) = -[0,\ 1]e^{A_{cl}t} \begin{bmatrix} \bar{x} \\ \bar{y} \end{bmatrix} = \frac{1}{2}(-(e^{-3.5t} - e^{-1.5t})\bar{x} - (e^{-1.5t} + e^{-3.5t})\bar{y}).$$

Finally, with $X_s := [X_1^T,\ X_2^T]^T$, the involved cost for player i are determined by calculating the solution $\bar{M}_i$ of the Lyapunov equation

$$A_{cl}^T \bar{M}_i + \bar{M}_i A_{cl} = -[I,\ -X_s^T \tilde{B}] M_i \begin{bmatrix} I \\ -\tilde{B}^T X_s \end{bmatrix}.$$

That is, $\bar{M}_1$ solves

$$\begin{bmatrix} -\frac{5}{2} & -1 \\ -1 & -\frac{5}{2} \end{bmatrix} \bar{M}_1 + \bar{M}_1 \begin{bmatrix} -\frac{5}{2} & -1 \\ -1 & -\frac{5}{2} \end{bmatrix} = -\begin{bmatrix} 5 & 0 \\ 0 & 1 \end{bmatrix}$$

and $\bar{M}_2$ solves

$$\begin{bmatrix} -\frac{5}{2} & -1 \\ -1 & -\frac{5}{2} \end{bmatrix} \bar{M}_1 + \bar{M}_1 \begin{bmatrix} -\frac{5}{2} & -1 \\ -1 & -\frac{5}{2} \end{bmatrix} = -\begin{bmatrix} 1 & 0 \\ 0 & 5 \end{bmatrix}.$$

The solutions of these equations are $\bar{M}_1 = \frac{1}{35}\begin{bmatrix} 39 & -10 \\ -10 & 11 \end{bmatrix}$ *and* $\bar{M}_2 = \frac{1}{35}\begin{bmatrix} 11 & -10 \\ -10 & 39 \end{bmatrix}$, *respectively. So, the cost for player 1 is* $\frac{1}{35}(39\bar{x}^2 - 20\bar{x}\bar{y} + 11\bar{y}^2)$ *and for player 2 is* $\frac{1}{35}(11\bar{x}^2 - 20\bar{x}\bar{y} + 39\bar{y}^2)$.
Notice that in case $\bar{x} = \bar{y}$ *the actions and costs for both players coincide. Furthermore,* $u_2^*(t) = u_1^*(t) + e^{-1.5t}(\bar{x} - \bar{y})$. *From this it follows that if, e.g.,* $0 \leqq \bar{x} \leqq \bar{y}$, *player 2 will use a more active control policy than player 1. This is what one intuitively also expects. If the second state variable is more out of its equilibrium value than the first state variable, one expects the player who is most concerned about this will also engage in the most active control policy.* □

Example 2.14 *Reconsider the optimization problems from Example 2.11. That is, consider the minimization of*

$$
\begin{aligned}
J_1 \ &: = \int_0^\infty \{3x^T(t)x(t) + u_1^2(t)\}dt = \\
&= \int_0^\infty \{[x^T(t),\ u_1(t),\ u_2(t)] \begin{bmatrix} 3 & 0 & 0 & 0 \\ 0 & 3 & 0 & 0 \\ 0 & 0 & 1 & 0 \\ 0 & 0 & 0 & 0 \end{bmatrix} \begin{bmatrix} x(t) \\ u_1(t) \\ u_2(t) \end{bmatrix}\}dt \\
&=: \int_0^\infty \{[x^T(t),\ u_1(t),\ u_2(t)] M_1 \begin{bmatrix} x(t) \\ u_1(t) \\ u_2(t) \end{bmatrix}\}dt \quad \text{and} \\
J_2 \ &: = \int_0^\infty \{x^T(t)x(t) + 3u_2^2(t)\}dt = \\
&= \int_0^\infty \{[x^T(t),\ u_1(t),\ u_2(t)] \begin{bmatrix} 1 & 0 & 0 & 0 \\ 0 & 1 & 0 & 0 \\ 0 & 0 & 0 & 0 \\ 0 & 0 & 0 & 3 \end{bmatrix} \begin{bmatrix} x(t) \\ u_1(t) \\ u_2(t) \end{bmatrix}\}dt \\
&=: \int_0^\infty \{[x^T(t),\ u_1(t),\ u_2(t)] M_2 \begin{bmatrix} x(t) \\ u_1(t) \\ u_2(t) \end{bmatrix}\}dt
\end{aligned}
$$

subject to the system

$$\dot{x}(t) = \begin{bmatrix} 1 & 0 \\ 0 & -2 \end{bmatrix} + \begin{bmatrix} 1 \\ 0 \end{bmatrix} u_1(t) + \begin{bmatrix} 1 \\ 0 \end{bmatrix} u_2(t),\ x(0) = [\bar{x},\ \bar{y}]^T.$$

But, different from Example 2.11, we now assume that both players do not cooperate to realize their goals.
Following the notation of (2.19)-(2.20), we introduce

$$
\begin{aligned}
A \ &: = \begin{bmatrix} 1 & 0 \\ 0 & -2 \end{bmatrix},\ B_i := \begin{bmatrix} 1 \\ 0 \end{bmatrix},\ Q_1 := \begin{bmatrix} 3 & 0 \\ 0 & 3 \end{bmatrix};\ Q_2 := \begin{bmatrix} 1 & 0 \\ 0 & 1 \end{bmatrix}, \\
R_{11} \ &: = 1,\ R_{22} := 3,\ P_i := L_i := [0,\ 0]^T,\ \text{and}\ N_i := R_{12} := R_{21} := 0,\ i = 1, 2.
\end{aligned}
$$

Notice that (A, B_i) is stabilizable. So, according to Theorem 2.17, the problem has a unique open-loop Nash equilibrium if and only if the AREs

$$Q_i + A^T K_i + K_i A - K_i S_i K_i = 0,$$

with $S_1 = \begin{bmatrix} 1 & 0 \\ 0 & 0 \end{bmatrix}$, $S_2 = \begin{bmatrix} \frac{1}{3} & 0 \\ 0 & 0 \end{bmatrix}$, *have a stabilizing solution and the ARE*

$$\tilde{Q} + \tilde{A}_2^T X + X\tilde{A} - XBG^{-1}\tilde{B}^T X = 0$$

has a strongly stabilizing solution. Here

$$G \; : \; = \begin{bmatrix} 1 & 0 \\ 0 & 3 \end{bmatrix}, \; B := \begin{bmatrix} 1 & 1 \\ 0 & 0 \end{bmatrix}; \; \tilde{B}^T := \begin{bmatrix} 1 & 0 & 0 & 0 \\ 0 & 0 & 1 & 0 \end{bmatrix}, \; Z^T := Z_i := [0, \; 0],$$

$$\tilde{A} \; : \; = A, \; \tilde{A}_2 := \begin{bmatrix} 1 & 0 & 0 & 0 \\ 0 & -2 & 0 & 0 \\ 0 & 0 & 1 & 0 \\ 0 & 0 & 0 & -2 \end{bmatrix}, \; \text{and} \; \tilde{Q} := \begin{bmatrix} 3 & 0 \\ 0 & 3 \\ 1 & 0 \\ 0 & 1 \end{bmatrix}.$$

Using this notation the matrices H_i, $i = 1, 2$, in Step 1 of Algorithm 2.2 are then given by

$$H_1 = \begin{bmatrix} 1 & 0 & -1 & 0 \\ 0 & -2 & 0 & 0 \\ -3 & 0 & -1 & 0 \\ 0 & -3 & 0 & 2 \end{bmatrix} \text{ and } H_2 = \begin{bmatrix} 1 & 0 & -\frac{1}{3} & 0 \\ 0 & -2 & 0 & 0 \\ -1 & 0 & -1 & 0 \\ 0 & -1 & 0 & 2 \end{bmatrix}, \text{ respectively.}$$

It is straightforwardly verified that H_1 has an eigenvalue -2 with algebraic multiplicity 2. A basis for the corresponding eigenspace is $\left\{ [1, \; 0, \; 3, \; 0]^T, [0, \; 4, \; 0, \; 3]^T \right\}$. *So, this eigenspace is a graph subspace.*

Furthermore, H_2 has two stable eigenvalues -2 and $-\sqrt{\frac{4}{3}}$. An eigenvector corresponding with the eigenvalue -2 is $[0, \; 4, \; 0, \; 1]^T$, whereas $\left[1, \; 0, \; 3\left(1 + \sqrt{\frac{4}{3}}\right), 0\right]^T$ *is an eigenvector corresponding with the eigenvalue $-\sqrt{\frac{4}{3}}$. So, the with these eigenvalues corresponding eigenspace is again a graph subspace.*

So, the AREs (2.21) have a stabilizing solution and we may proceed with Step 2 of the algorithm.

First, we calculate matrix M in Step 2 of the algorithm. Simple substitutions show that

$$M = \begin{bmatrix} 1 & 0 & -1 & 0 & -\frac{1}{3} & 0 \\ 0 & -2 & 0 & 0 & 0 & 0 \\ -3 & 0 & -1 & 0 & 0 & 0 \\ 0 & -3 & 0 & 2 & 0 & 0 \\ -1 & 0 & 0 & 0 & -1 & 0 \\ 0 & -1 & 0 & 0 & 0 & 2 \end{bmatrix}.$$

Next, we determine the eigenstructure of matrix M. It is easily verified that $M = TJT^{-1}$, where J is a diagonal matrix with entries $\{-\sqrt{\frac{13}{3}},\ -2,\ -1,\ 1,\ 2,\ \sqrt{\frac{13}{3}}\}$ and

$$T = \begin{bmatrix} -1+\sqrt{\frac{13}{3}} & 0 & 0 & 0 & 0 & -1-\sqrt{\frac{13}{3}} \\ 0 & 4 & 0 & 0 & 0 & 0 \\ 3 & 0 & 1 & 0 & 0 & 3 \\ 0 & 3 & 0 & 1 & 0 & 0 \\ 1 & 0 & -3 & 0 & 0 & 1 \\ 0 & 1 & 0 & 0 & 1 & 0 \end{bmatrix}.$$

Matrix M has three stable eigenvalues. Therefore, the ARE (2.22) has not a strongly stabilizing solution. Consequently, the game has not a unique open-loop Nash equilibrium. □

2.6 The game with coalitions

In this book we will also consider the possibility that some players in the game cooperate with other players. That is, we will study regimes where subgroups of players coordinate their policies but interact in a non-cooperative manner with the players that are not part of the coalition. In regimes of partial cooperation, important questions that arise are

(i) Why do certain coalitions arise and others not?

(ii) Are these coalitions stable over time?

(iii) How are the gains from cooperation distributed between the members of the coalitions?

(iv) How do differences in initial conditions, economic structures and policy preferences affect outcomes?

In this book we will try to shed some light on questions (i), (iii) and (iv) in a monetary union context.

Of course, before one can answer these questions, first the question must be addressed how to solve the involved optimization problems. It turns out that this can be relatively easily accomplished by merging the results from Sections 2.4 and 2.5. This is the subject of this section.

For simplicity, we consider a three-player game. That is, we consider the minimization of

$$J_i(u_1, u_2, u_3) := \int_0^{\infty} [x^T(t),\ u_1^T(t),\ u_2^T(t),\ u_3^T(t)]\hat{M}_i \begin{bmatrix} x(t) \\ u_1(t) \\ u_2(t) \\ u_3(t) \end{bmatrix} dt,$$

with

$$\hat{M}_i = \begin{bmatrix} Q_i & P_i & L_i & T_i \\ P_i^T & R_{1i} & N_i & V_i \\ L_i^T & N_i^T & R_{2i} & W_i \\ T_i^T & V_i^T & W_i^T & R_{3i} \end{bmatrix},$$

where $\hat{M}_i \geq 0$, $R_{ii} > 0$, $i = 1, 2, 3$, subject to the dynamic constraint

$$\dot{x}(t) = Ax(t) + \hat{B}_1 u_1(t) + \hat{B}_2 u_2(t) + \hat{B}_3 u_3(t),\ x(0) = x_0. \tag{2.25}$$

We will elaborate the case that players 1 and 3 coordinate their policies but act in a non-cooperative fashion with player 2. For this partial coalition we use the shorthand notation (1,3).

To determine the equilibrium actions for this (1,3) coalition, we rewrite the system equation (2.25) as:

$$\dot{x}(t) = Ax(t) + [\hat{B}_1,\ \hat{B}_3] \begin{bmatrix} u_1(t) \\ u_3(t) \end{bmatrix} + \hat{B}_2 u_2(t),\ x(0) = x_0,$$

and consider the cost function $J_{(1,3)} := \lambda_1 J_1 + \lambda_2 J_3$, with $\lambda_1 + \lambda_2 = 1$ (see Corollary 2.2) as the aggregate cost of players 1 and 3, and J_2 for player 2, respectively. Now, let

$$w(t) := \begin{bmatrix} x(t) \\ u_1(t) \\ u_2(t) \\ u_3(t) \end{bmatrix}.$$

Next, consider the with this (1,3) coalition corresponding permutation of $w(t)$

$$\tilde{w}(t) := \begin{bmatrix} x(t) \\ u_1(t) \\ u_3(t) \\ u_2(t) \end{bmatrix} = \begin{bmatrix} I & 0 & 0 & 0 \\ 0 & I & 0 & 0 \\ 0 & 0 & 0 & I \\ 0 & 0 & I & 0 \end{bmatrix} w(t) =: P_{(1,3)} w(t).$$

Notice that in the above *permutation matrix*[6] $P_{(1,3)}$ all entries have, in principle, a different dimension.

Now we can basically use Algorithm 2.2 to determine the equilibrium strategies.
To that end, first note that the inverse of a permutation matrix P is P^T. Using this, we can rewrite the cost functions and the system as follows:

$$J_i(u_1, u_3, u_2) := \int_0^\infty \tilde{w}^T(t) P_{(1,3)} \hat{M}_i P_{(1,3)}^T \tilde{w}(t) dt,$$

and

$$\dot{x}(t) = [A,\ \hat{B}_1,\ \hat{B}_2,\ \hat{B}_3] P_{(1,3)}^T \tilde{w}(t),\ x(0) = x_0.$$

Then, with

[6] A permutation matrix is an invertible matrix where all but one entry of every row are zero. The one entry that differs from zero contains a 1. So, premultiplication of a vector by such a matrix implies that the entries of the vector are reshuffled (permuted).

$$M_1{:=}\lambda_1 P_{(1,3)}\hat{M}_1 P_{(1,3)}^T{+}\lambda_2 P_{(1,3)}\hat{M}_2 P_{(1,3)}^T,\ M_2{:=}P_{(1,3)}M_2 P_{(1,3)}^T,\ B_1{:=}[\hat{B}_1,\ \hat{B}_3],$$

and $B_2{:=}\hat{B}_2$,we can use Algorithm 2.2 to calculate the open-loop Nash equilibrium of this two-person game $(u^*_{(1,3),1}, u^*_{(1,3),2})$. From this the equilibrium actions for the original game immediately result as $(u^*_{(1,3),1}, u^*_{(1,3),2}) = (u_1^*, u_3^*, u_2^*)$. The equilibrium cost $J_i(u_1^*, u_3^*, u_2^*)$ can be determined, e.g., as $x_0^T\bar{M}_i x_0$, where $\bar{M}_i$ is obtained in Step 4 of the algorithm as the solution of the Lyapunov equation (2.24) with M_i replaced by $P_{(1,3)}\hat{M}_i P_{(1,3)}^T$.

Example 2.15 *To study macroeconomic policy design in a Monetary Union (MU) the following model is considered. It is assumed that the MU consists of two (blocks of) countries that share a common Central Bank (CB). External interaction of the MU countries with the non-MU countries and also the dynamic implications of government debt and net foreign asset accumulation are ignored. Let s denote the competitiveness of country 2 vis-à-vis country 1, f_i the real fiscal deficit in country i and i_U the nominal interest rate set by the common central bank. The variables denote deviations from their long-term equilibrium (balanced growth path) that has been normalized to zero, for simplicity.*

The dynamics of the model are represented by the following first-order linear differential equation with competitiveness, $s(t)$, as the scalar state variable and the national fiscal deficits, $f_i(t)$ $i = 1, 2$, and the common interest rate, $i_U(t)$, as control variables:

$$\dot{s}(t) = -\phi_4 s(t) - \phi_1 f_1(t) + \phi_2 f_2(t) + \phi_3 i_U(t),\ s(0) = s_0. \tag{2.26}$$

The initial value of the state variable, s_0, measures any initial disequilibrium in intra-MU competitiveness. Such an initial disequilibrium in competitiveness could be the result of, e.g., differences in fiscal policies in the past or some initial disturbance in one country. It is assumed that all parameters ϕ_i are strictly positive.

The aim of the fiscal authorities is to use their fiscal policy instrument such that the following quadratic loss functions are minimized. The loss functions express the countries' concern towards differences in the competitiveness between the countries and domestic real fiscal deficits

$$\min_{f_i} J_i = \min_{f_i} \int_0^\infty e^{-\theta t}\{\alpha_i s^2(t) + \chi_i f_i^2(t)\}dt,\ i = 1, 2. \tag{2.27}$$

Here, θ denotes the rate of time preference and α_i, and χ_i ($i \in \{1, 2\}$) represent preference weights that are attached to the stabilization of competitiveness differentials and fiscal deficits, respectively. Preference for a low fiscal deficit reflects the goal to prevent excessive deficits. This aim may on the one hand be a reflection of the fact that excessive deficits are sanctioned in the MU. On the other hand, costs can also result from undesirable debt accumulation and intergenerational redistribution that high deficits imply and, in that interpretation, χ_i could also reflect the priority attached to fiscal retrenchment and consolidation.

Assume that the CB directs the common monetary policy at stabilizing inflation and, as long as not in contradiction to inflation stabilization, stabilizing the competitiveness gap in the aggregate MU economy. Moreover, assume that the active use of monetary policy implies costs for the monetary policymaker: other things equal it would like to keep its policy instrument constant, avoiding large swings. Then, it makes sense to assume that the CB considers the optimization problem:

$$\min_{i_U} J_U = \min_{i_U} \int_0^\infty e^{-\theta t}\{\alpha_3 s^2 + \chi_3 i_U^2(t)\}dt. \tag{2.28}$$

Defining $[x(t),\ u_1(t),\ u_2(t),\ u_3(t)] := e^{-\frac{1}{2}\theta t}[s(t),\ f_1(t),\ f_2(t),\ i_U(t)]$, *(2.27)-(2.28) can be rewritten as*

$$\min_{u_i} \int_0^\infty \{\alpha_i x^2(t) + \chi_i u_i^2(t)\}dt,\ i = 1,2,3,$$

subject to the dynamic system

$$\dot{x}(t) = -(\phi_4 + \frac{1}{2}\theta)x(t) - \phi_1 u_1(t) + \phi_2 u_2(t) + \phi_3 u_3(t),\ x(0) = s_0.$$

Below, we will calculate as well the cooperative solution as the non-cooperative Nash equilibrium as a partial coalitional equilibrium for this problem.

i) The cooperative solution

The set of cooperative solutions is obtained by solving for $0 \leqq \lambda_i \leqq 1$ *the problem*

$$\min_u \int_0^\infty \{\lambda_1(\alpha_1 x^2(t) + \chi_1 u_1^2(t)) + \lambda_2(\alpha_2 x^2(t) + \chi_2 u_2^2(t)) + \\ +(1-\lambda_1-\lambda_2)(\alpha_3 x^2(t) + \chi_3 u_3^2(t))\}dt,$$

subject to

$$\dot{x}(t) = ax(t) + Bu(t),\ x(0) = s_0,$$

where $a := -\phi_4 - \frac{1}{2}\theta$, $B := [-\phi_1,\ \phi_2,\ \phi_3]$, *and* $u := [u_1,\ u_2,\ u_3]^T$. *Introducing, moreover, for* $q := \lambda_1\alpha_1 + \lambda_2\alpha_2 + (1-\lambda_1-\lambda_2)\alpha_3$, $s_i := \frac{\phi_i^2}{\chi_i}$ *and* $R := \begin{bmatrix} \lambda_1\chi_1 & 0 & 0 \\ 0 & \lambda_2\chi_2 & 0 \\ 0 & 0 & (1-\lambda_1-\lambda_2)\chi_3 \end{bmatrix}$, *the cooperative cost function can be rewritten as*

$$\min_u \int_0^\infty \{qx^2(t) + u^T(t)Ru(t)\}dt.$$

For simplicity we restrict the analysis again to the set of points $\lambda_i > 0$. *To find the solution of this cooperative problem we consider the with this problem corresponding Hamiltonian matrix*

$$H = \begin{bmatrix} a & -BR^{-1}B^T \\ -q & -a \end{bmatrix}.$$

With $s := BR^{-1}B^T = \frac{s_1}{\lambda_1} + \frac{s_2}{\lambda_2} + \frac{s_3}{(1-\lambda_1-\lambda_2)}$ *the eigenvalues of* H *are* $\pm\sqrt{a^2+qs}$. *A with* $-\sqrt{a^2+qs}$ *corresponding eigenvector is* $[s, a+\sqrt{a^2+qs}]^T$. *So, the solution of the with this problem associated ARE is* $k = \frac{a+\sqrt{a^2+qs}}{s}$. *Consequently,*

$$u_1^* = \frac{\phi_1}{\lambda_1\chi_1}\frac{a+\sqrt{a^2+qs}}{s}x(t)$$

$$u_2^* = -\frac{\phi_2}{\lambda_2\chi_2}\frac{a+\sqrt{a^2+qs}}{s}x(t)$$

$$u_3^* = -\frac{\phi_3}{(1-\lambda_1-\lambda_2)\chi_3}\frac{a+\sqrt{a^2+qs}}{s}x(t),$$

with $x(t)$ *the solution of the differential equation*

$$\dot{x}(t) = -\sqrt{a^2+qs}x(t),\ x(0) = s_0.$$

The corresponding costs are

$$J_1^* = \frac{1}{2\sqrt{a^2+qs}}(\alpha_1 + \frac{s_1}{\lambda_1^2}\left(\frac{a+\sqrt{a^2+qs}}{s}\right)^2)s_0^2$$

$$J_2^* = \frac{1}{2\sqrt{a^2+qs}}(\alpha_2 + \frac{s_2}{\lambda_2^2}\left(\frac{a+\sqrt{a^2+qs}}{s}\right)^2)s_0^2$$

$$J_U^* = \frac{1}{2\sqrt{a^2+qs}}(\alpha_3 + \frac{s_3}{(1-\lambda_1-\lambda_2)^2}\left(\frac{a+\sqrt{a^2+qs}}{s}\right)^2)s_0^2.$$

ii) The non-cooperative case

Using the above introduced notation, the non-cooperative Nash equilibrium is obtained by solving the problem

$$\min_{u_i}\int_0^\infty \{\alpha_i x^2(t) + \chi_i u_i^2(t)\}dt,\ i = 1,2,3,$$

subject to

$$\dot{x}(t) = ax(t) - \phi_1 u_1(t) + \phi_2 u_2 + \phi_3 u_3,\ x(0) = s_0.$$

This problem has a unique Nash equilibrium for every initial state s_0 *if and only if the AREs*

$$2ak_i - s_i k_i^2 + \alpha_i = 0,\ i = 1,2,3, \tag{2.29}$$

have a stabilizing solution and the next (coupled) AREs have a strongly stabilizing solution:

$$0 = \begin{bmatrix} a & 0 & 0 \\ 0 & a & 0 \\ 0 & 0 & a \end{bmatrix} X + Xa - X[s_1,\ s_2,\ s_3]X + \begin{bmatrix} \alpha_1 \\ \alpha_2 \\ \alpha_3 \end{bmatrix}. \tag{2.30}$$

Obviously, $k_i = \frac{a-\sqrt{a^2+\alpha_i s_i}}{s_i}$ *is an appropriate solution of (2.29). To find the solution of (2.30), consider matrix (see Algorithm 2.2)*

$$M = \begin{bmatrix} a & -s_1 & -s_2 & -s_3 \\ -\alpha_1 & -a & 0 & 0 \\ -\alpha_2 & 0 & -a & 0 \\ -\alpha_3 & 0 & 0 & -a \end{bmatrix}.$$

To determine the eigenstructure of M introduce for notational convenience $\sigma := s_1\alpha_1 + s_2\alpha_2 + s_3\alpha_3$ *and* $\mu = \sqrt{a^2+\sigma}$. *Then straightforward calculations show (see also Engwerda (2005a)) that the eigenvalues of M are* $\{-\mu,\ -a,\ -a,\ \mu\}$. *So M has one stable eigenvalue and three unstable eigenvalues. Moreover, an eigenvector corresponding with* $-\mu$ *is* $[\sigma,\ (a+\mu)\alpha_1,\ (a+\mu)\alpha_2,\ (a+\mu)\alpha_3]^T$. *Therefore, (2.30) has a strongly stabilizing solution and the equilibrium actions are*

$$u_1^*(t) = \frac{\phi_1}{\chi_1}p_1x(t),\ u_2^*(t) = -\frac{\phi_2}{\chi_2}p_2x(t),\ u_3^*(t) = -\frac{\phi_3}{\chi_3}p_3x(t),$$

where $p_i = \frac{(a+\mu)\alpha_i}{\sigma}$ *and* $\dot{x}(t) = -\mu x(t)$, *with* $x(0) = s_0$.
The corresponding costs for player i in this equilibrium are: $J_i = \frac{\alpha_i + s_i p_i^2}{2\mu}s_0^2$, $i = 1, 2, U$.

iii) The partial (fiscal) coalition case

Here, we consider the case that both fiscal players cooperate but do not coordinate their actions with the Central Bank in order to realize their goal. Using the previously introduced notation again, together with $s_f := \frac{s_1}{\lambda} + \frac{s_2}{(1-\lambda)}$ *and* $q_f := \lambda\alpha_1 + (1-\lambda)\alpha_2$, *this problem can be formalized as follows.*

$$\min_{u_1,u_2} \int_0^\infty \{\lambda(\alpha_1 x^2(t) + \chi_1 u_1^2(t)) + (1-\lambda)(\alpha_2 x^2(t) + \chi_2 u_2^2(t))\}dt, \text{ with } 0 \leqq \lambda \leqq 1,$$

$$\text{and } \min_{u_3} \int_0^\infty \{\alpha_3 x^2(t) + \chi_3 u_3^2(t)\}dt$$

subject to

$$\dot{x}(t) = ax(t) + [-\phi_1,\ \phi_2]\begin{bmatrix} u_1(t) \\ u_2(t) \end{bmatrix} + \phi_3 u_3(t),\ x(0) = s_0.$$

This problem has a unique Nash equilibrium for every initial state s_0 *if and only if the AREs*

$$2ak - s_f k^2 + q_f = 0 \text{ and } 2ak_3 - s_3 k_3^2 + \alpha_3 = 0 \tag{2.31}$$

have a stabilizing solution and the next set of (coupled) ARES has a strongly stabilizing solution.

$$0 = \begin{bmatrix} a & 0 \\ 0 & a \end{bmatrix} X + Xa - X[s_f,\ s_3]X + \begin{bmatrix} q_f \\ \alpha_3 \end{bmatrix}. \tag{2.32}$$

Similar as in the non-cooperative case, one can easily verify that (2.31) has stabilizing solutions. To find the solution of (2.32), we consider matrix (see Algorithm 2.2)

$$M = \begin{bmatrix} a & -s_f & -s_3 \\ -q_f & -a & 0 \\ -\alpha_3 & 0 & -a \end{bmatrix}.$$

Introducing $\sigma_f := s_f q_f + s_3\alpha_3$ *and* $\mu_f = \sqrt{a^2 + \sigma_f}$ *it follows, similarly as in the non-cooperative case, that the eigenvalues of* M *are* $\{-\mu_f,\ -a,\ \mu_f\}$ *and an eigenvector corresponding with* $-\mu_f$ *is* $[\sigma_f,\ (a+\mu_f)q_f,\ (a+\mu_f)\alpha_3]^T$. *Therefore, (2.32) has a strongly stabilizing solution and the equilibrium actions are*

$$u_1^*(t) = \frac{\phi_1}{\lambda\chi_1} p_{f1} x(t),\ u_2^*(t) = -\frac{\phi_2}{(1-\lambda)\chi_2} p_{f1} x(t),\ u_3^*(t) = -\frac{\phi_3}{\chi_3} p_{f2} x(t),$$

where $p_{f1} = \frac{(a+\mu_f)q_f}{\sigma_f}$, $p_{f2} = \frac{(a+\mu_f)\alpha_3}{\sigma_f}$ *and* $\dot{x}(t) = -\mu_f x(t)$, *with* $x(0) = s_0$.
The corresponding costs for the players in this equilibrium are:

$$J_1 = \frac{\alpha_1 + \frac{s_1}{\lambda^2} p_{f1}^2}{2\mu_f} s_0^2,\ J_2 = \frac{\alpha_2 + \frac{s_2}{(1-\lambda)^2} p_{f1}^2}{2\mu_f} s_0^2,\ J_U = \frac{\alpha_3 + s_3 p_{f2}^2}{2\mu_f} s_0^2,$$

respectively.
The above expressions can be used for a detailed study of various aspects from this problem. Since at this moment the purpose of this example is just to demonstrate the algorithms we will not elaborate the example. A preliminary conclusion, however, that is easily seen is that any form of cooperation always leads to a closed-loop system which converges faster to the zero equilibrium than under the (full) non-cooperative situation. Another conclusion which readily follows, is that if players decide to cooperate, there is always a threshold for the coordination parameter λ_i *beyond which a player will abstain from further cooperation. This, because her cost becomes higher in the cooperative case than in the non-cooperative case. So, without side-payments it would be foolish for her to continue the cooperation under those conditions.* □

Chapter 3

The Basic Symmetric Two-Country Model

3.1 Introduction

This chapter presents a dynamic symmetric two-country model of a Monetary Union (MU). This model features short-term nominal rigidities, thus creating scope for active stabilization policies. To focus on the design and effects of fiscal policies in an MU, monetary policy is held fixed in this chapter. Three basic questions are focussed upon:

(i) How do fiscal policymakers interact in an MU and, more particular, what are the effects of uncoordinated and coordinated fiscal policies?

(ii) What are the effects of institutional constraints like the SGP?

(iii) What are the effects of asymmetric sizes of countries implying asymmetric bargaining power in case of fiscal cooperation?

Some attention is also directed to the introduction of a fiscal transfer system.

Our analysis builds on earlier works by Turnovsky *et al.* (1988) and Neck and Dockner (1995), who analyze the interaction of the monetary authorities in a similar dynamic two-country model by assuming that monetary policies of both countries affect short-term output in both the domestic and foreign economies. Thus, international interdependence creates a dynamic conflict between both monetary authorities. Output, inflation and exchange rate adjustments and their implications for social welfare are calculated for a number of different kinds of strategic interactions.

We extend the aforementioned two-country models into a setting of an MU, where the effects of fiscal policy in such a setting and the effects of fiscal stringency conditions and fiscal transfers on the outcomes are analyzed.

This chapter is organized as follows: Section 3.2 develops the analytical framework, Section 3.3 analyzes non-cooperative and cooperative fiscal policies under an MU, Section 3.4 presents numerical simulations of the model to illustrate its main characteristics, and the final section concludes.

3.2 A dynamic stabilization game in an MU

Consider a situation where a symmetric two-country MU has been fully implemented, implying that national currencies have been replaced by a common currency, national central banks by one common central bank (CB) as the ECB and that the internal exchange rate has disappeared as an adjustment instrument. Capital markets are assumed to be fully integrated and we abstain from any country risk premium, implying that any interest rate differential is arbitraged away instantaneously. On the other hand, we assume that there is no labour mobility between both MU parts (countries) and that goods and labour markets adjust sluggishly. Hence, the economies display (New-) Keynesian features in the short run.

We model a stylized symmetric two-country MU by the equations (3.1)-(3.5).

A stylized symmetric two-country MU model

$$y_1(t) \;:\; = \delta s(t) - \gamma r_1(t) + \rho y_2(t) + \eta f_1(t) \tag{3.1}$$
$$y_2(t) \;:\; = -\delta s(t) - \gamma r_2(t) + \rho y_1(t) + \eta f_2(t) \tag{3.2}$$
$$s(t) \;:\; = p_2(t) - p_1(t) \tag{3.3}$$
$$r_i(t) \;:\; = i_U(t) - \dot{p}_i(t),\; i \in \{1,2\} \tag{3.4}$$
$$\dot{p}_i(t) \;:\; = \xi y_i(t),\; i \in \{1,2\} \tag{3.5}$$

In the equations (3.1) to (3.5), y_i denotes the real output (gap), r_i the real interest rate, p_i the output price level, and f_i the real fiscal deficit of country (block) $i \in \{1,2\}$; moreover, s denotes the competitiveness of country 2 *vis-à-vis* country 1 and i_U the common nominal interest rate valid for the whole MU. All variables are in logarithms, except for the interest rate which is in perunages, and denote deviations from their long-term equilibrium (balanced growth path) that has been normalized to zero, for simplicity. A dot above a variable denotes its time derivative. We assume that both countries (country blocks) are symmetric and we ignore the interaction of this two-country MU with the rest of the world.

Equations (3.1) and (3.2) represent output (gap) in the MU countries as a function of competitiveness in *intra*-MU trade, the domestic real interest rate, the foreign output and the domestic real fiscal deficit. Competitiveness is defined in (3.3) as the output price differential. Real interest rates are defined in (3.4) as the difference between the MU-wide nominal interest rate, i_U, and domestic inflation. Note that equations (3.4) imply that real interest rates may diverge among countries if inflation rates are different. Domestic output and inflation are related through a Phillips curve type relation in (3.5), which is a short-run relation. Because of the nominal rigidities, implied by the Phillips curve, output and prices can diverge from their equilibrium values in the short run, but both economies adjust to a long-run equilibrium where output and prices are at their equilibrium values, which have been normalized to zero as indicated above. Notice that the structural model (3.1)-(3.5) is a model of an integrated economy with several kinds of cross-country effects. Besides the common nominal interest rate there are two other important direct cross-country spillovers that affect domestic output: (i) the *intra*-MU competitiveness channel (as measured by the elasticity δ) and (ii) the foreign output channel (as measured by the elasticity ρ).

Aggregate supply is assumed to be determined by a Phillips curve implied by the existence of some (nominal) rigidities in the goods (and/or labour) markets giving rise to a short-run trade-off between inflation and output. In this Phillips relationship the inflation rate of the other country could play a role if foreign inflation is passed through via domestic imports of foreign intermediate goods and also via the possibility that domestic wage claims rise, given the presence of a real wage wedge. We will introduce this extension in Chapter 6. In (3.5) some characteristics of the New-Keynesian Phillips curve, originating from the *New-Keynesian Economics* (NKE) with optimizing agents under some form of nominal inertia (e.g. sticky prices), are present. Goodfriend and King (1997) alternatively called this NKE the *New-Neoclassical Synthesis* (NNS; see also Woodford (2003)).[1] The NKE or the NNS provides a natural framework to study the interactions between fiscal and monetary policy, where the assumption of nominal inertia allows us to assess the implications of the microeconomic aspects of fiscal and monetary policies for macroeconomic stabilization.[2]

In agreement with our short-run stabilization focus, the effectiveness of fiscal policy is limited to its transitory impact on the output gap through the induced stimulus of the aggregate demand. We assume that its interest rate targeting policy enables the common CB to have perfect control over the nominal common interest rate, $i_U(t)$. Note, however, that also alternative interest rate rules like a Taylor rule could be introduced.

Both economies are connected by a number of channels through which price and output fluctuations in one part transmit themselves to the other part of the MU. Output fluctuations in both economies transmit themselves partly to the other MU country through the import channel. Therefore, the relative openness of both economies, as measured by ρ, implies an important interdependence

[1]The NKE implies a microeconomic underpinning with sluggish prices (and wages) for the traditional Keynesian economies During the seventies the Keynesians were under attack for being *ad hoc* and lacking serious microeconomic foundations. As van der Ploeg (2005) rightly asserts, the first attempts to provide a microeconomic foundation for Keynesian economics were made by Barro and Grossman (1971) and Malinvaud (1977). These publications had two main features. First, given that the price system does not work, quantity signals take over from price signals as a coordination device and second, general equilibrium interactions between labour, product and financial markets are important. Rationing in one market has spillover effects in other markets and effective rather than notional demands and supplies matter (see Meersman and Plasmans (1983) for a general introduction into (rationed) unemployment theories, Plasmans and Somers (1983) for econometric inference of a three-market disequilibrium model, and Plasmans (1984) for the varying impact of the simultaneous occurrence of various types of quantity and financial rationing). NKE models based on stickiness of prices and wages lead to coordination failures and imperfect competition and emerged only in the late nineties with Clarida *et al.* (1999), etc.. Coordination failures arise, because wage and price setters take into account what other wage and price setters do.

[2]These microeconomic aspects result from the consumers' and producers' optimizations in the NKE or NNS.

of both economies. Price fluctuations in the domestic or foreign economy affect *intra*-MU competitiveness, $s(t)$, and therefore output in both economies. Combining equations (3.1)-(3.5) enables to write output in both countries as a function of competitiveness, the policy instrument of the common CB, $i_U(t)$, and the fiscal deficit set by the two fiscal authorities, $f_i(t)$ $(i = 1, 2)$:

$$y_1(t) = bs(t) - ci_U(t) + af_1(t) + \frac{\rho}{k}af_2(t) \quad (3.6)$$

$$y_2(t) = -bs(t) - ci_U(t) + \frac{\rho}{k}af_1(t) + af_2(t) \quad (3.7)$$

with $a := \frac{\eta k}{k^2-\rho^2}$, $b := \frac{\delta}{k+\rho}$, $c := \frac{\gamma}{k-\rho}$ and $k := 1 - \gamma\xi$. Substituting equations (3.6) and (3.7) into equations (3.5) yields two first-order linear differential equations in the output price levels. Subtracting them from each other yields the dynamics of *intra*-MU competitiveness,

$$\dot{s}(t) = \phi_1 f_2(t) - \phi_1 f_1(t) + \phi_2 s(t) \quad (3.8)$$

with $\phi_1 := \frac{\xi\eta}{k+\rho}$ and $\phi_2 := -\frac{2\delta\xi}{k+\rho}$.

Having modelled the economies of both MU countries and derived the adjustment dynamics of output and prices over time, we still need to determine the fiscal policies and their dynamic adjustment over time as a consequence of the different modes of interaction of these macroeconomic policymakers. In order to do so, we need to specify the players' objective functions. These objectives are optimized subject to the dynamics of s in (3.8). Assuming that the players have quadratic objective functions, the policymakers' dynamic strategic interaction reduces to a linear-quadratic (LQ) differential game (see Chapter 2 for an extensive analysis of LQ differential games).

In particular, both fiscal authorities seek to minimize the following intertemporal loss functions that are assumed to be quadratic in the rate of inflation, output and fiscal deficits,

$$J_i = \frac{1}{2}\int_0^\infty \{\alpha\dot{p}_i^2(t) + \beta y_i^2(t) + \chi f_i^2(t)\}e^{-\theta t}dt, \; i \in \{1, 2\}. \quad (3.9)$$

Future losses are discounted at a rate θ. The costs of price and output fluctuations are standard in most analyses of macroeconomic policy design. The assumption that the fiscal authorities also value budget balance reflects the notion that high deficits, while beneficial to stimulate domestic output, are not costless: they to some extent crowd out private investment and lead to debt accumulation. Deficits in the loss function also feature the possibility that individual excessive deficits in e.g. the EMU countries will be subject to sanctions, as proposed in the SGP. Therefore, countries prefer low fiscal deficits, *ceteris paribus*, to high fiscal deficits. In case where $\chi \to \infty$, (cyclical) budget balance becomes the sole objective of the fiscal authority and fiscal activism is reduced accordingly. On the other hand, $\chi \to 0$ implies that fiscal stringency is minimal and that the fiscal authorities have maximal fiscal flexibility under EMU.

We consider the dynamic adjustment process caused by an initial disequilibrium in *intra*-MU competitiveness, implying that $s(0) \neq 0$. This initial disequilibrium or shock is practically identical with the relative preference shock of Subsection 1.4.2 Its anti-symmetric nature implies also anti-symmetric adjustment of output, prices and optimal policies in the adjustment towards equilibrium. We analyze how fiscal policies adjust over time as a result of the dynamic interaction between the macroeconomic policymakers in the MU. In this dynamic interaction, we focus on the different adjustment patterns that arise under non-cooperative and cooperative fiscal policy design in the MU and how these patterns are affected by different degrees of fiscal stringency and the introduction of a federal fiscal transfer system. Given our focus on fiscal policies in this chapter, we assume for the remainder of this chapter that the common CB pursues a fixed interest rate policy implying $i_U(t) = i_U^*$.

3.3 Non-cooperative and cooperative fiscal policies

3.3.1 The non-cooperative case

We first analyze the design of fiscal policy in the MU if the fiscal authorities implement non-cooperative fiscal policy strategies. In a Nash equilibrium setting the players implement their optimal strategies simultaneously. Following the notation of Chapter 2 the fiscal players' optimization problems can be written as:

$$\begin{aligned} \min_{u_i} \left\{ J_i \right. &= \left. \frac{1}{2} \int_0^\infty \{[x(t)^T \; u_1^T(t) \; u_2^T(t)]^T M_i \begin{bmatrix} x(t) \\ u_1(t) \\ u_2(t) \end{bmatrix} \} dt \right\} \\ \text{s.t. } \dot{x}(t) &= Ax(t) + B_1 u_1(t) + B_2 u_2(t), \;\; x(0) = x_0, \; i = 1, 2, \end{aligned}$$

in which

$$x(t) := e^{-\frac{1}{2}\theta t} \begin{bmatrix} s(t) \\ i_U^* \end{bmatrix}, \; x_0 = \begin{bmatrix} s_0 \\ i_U^* \end{bmatrix}, \; u_1(t) := e^{-\frac{1}{2}\theta t} f_1(t), \; u_2(t) := e^{-\frac{1}{2}\theta t} f_2(t).$$

The system parameters are

$$A := \begin{bmatrix} \phi_2 - \frac{1}{2}\theta & 0 \\ 0 & -\frac{1}{2}\theta \end{bmatrix}, \; B_1 := \begin{bmatrix} -\phi_1 \\ 0 \end{bmatrix}, \text{ and } B_2 := \begin{bmatrix} \phi_1 \\ 0 \end{bmatrix}$$

and M_i is a positive semi-definite matrix that can be factorized as,

$$M_i =: \begin{bmatrix} Q_i & P_i & L_i \\ P_i^T & R_{1i} & N_i \\ L_i^T & N_i^T & R_{2i} \end{bmatrix},$$

in which Q_i, P_i, L_i, N_i and R_{ii}, $(i = 1, 2)$, represent sub-matrices that are given in Appendix I.

Table 3.1: Parameter values and number of equilibria

No. of equilibria	Parameter values
1	$\varrho \leqq 1$
0	$\chi_1 < \chi < \chi_2,\ \varrho > 1$
1	$\chi \leqq \min(\chi_1, \chi_2),\ \varrho > 1$
1	$\chi \geqq \max(\chi_1, \chi_2),\ \varrho > 1$
more than 1	$\chi_2 < \chi < \chi_1,\ \varrho > 1$

Using the symbolic computational programme Mathematica, it is shown in Appendix I that (depending on the sign of the λ_is; see (3.14) in Appendix I) for an arbitrary initial state either the game has no solution, one solution in which case the closed-loop system dynamics satisfies the relationship

$$\dot{x}(t) = \begin{bmatrix} -\lambda & 0 \\ 0 & -\frac{1}{2}\theta \end{bmatrix} x(t), \tag{3.10}$$

or more than one solution. Here, $-\lambda = \min\{\lambda_1, \lambda_2\}$ is the adjustment speed of the output price differential, $s(t)$, towards its long-run equilibrium value zero. Assuming that the parameter k in (3.6), (3.7), and (3.8) is positive and denoting $\frac{\rho}{k}$ by ϱ, $\frac{\mu(\theta k+2\delta\xi)\eta^2\theta}{(\rho-k)(4\delta\xi+\theta(k+\rho))^2}$ by χ_1 and $\frac{\rho-k}{k}\mu\left(\frac{\eta k}{k^2-\rho^2}\right)^2$ by χ_2, Table 3.1 illustrates the possibilities.

Given our model we expect, normally, that $k > \rho$ will hold. In that case, the domestic fiscal instrument has a stronger impact on domestic output than the foreign fiscal instrument (see equation (3.6)). That is, $\varrho \leqq 1$ and therefore the closed-loop adjustment scheme will be uniquely determined by (3.10). In Figure 3.1 we illustrate the situations that can occur in case $k < \rho$. In this Figure, the number 2 should be interpreted as 'more than one' (see e.g. Engwerda (2005a), Chapter 7, for more details on this issue).

Figure 3.1 Number of equilibria as a function of fiscal stringency parameter χ

In particular, note that if ρ is much larger than k the situation occurs that the game permits more than one equilibrium. Which equilibrium actually will occur under these circumstances depends on additional requirements which are imposed on the outcome of the game. A natural choice seems to select that outcome of the game that increases the adjustment scheme for the closed-loop system towards its long-term equilibrium most. For, under such an adjustment scheme also unanticipated shocks to the system are dealt with best. Furthermore, this equilibrium seems to be a natural candidate that may be Pareto efficient (that is both players infer lower cost by playing this equilibrium). However, given the fact that we expect this to be a rare situation, we do not elaborate this subject here.

Finally, note that the state variable s in the closed-loop system (3.10) does not directly depend on the value of i_U^*. This variable i_U^* has only an indirect influence on the closed-loop dynamics of the model, that is via the parameters in the cost functionals.

3.3.2 The cooperative case

The various economic externalities between the two countries are not internalized if countries decide upon fiscal policies in a non-cooperative manner. In our case, national fiscal policies combined with initial disequilibria in *intra*-MU competitiveness imply important economic externalities. Domestic fiscal policies also have an impact on foreign output through the import channel. Any initial disequilibrium in *intra*-MU competitiveness, however, implies that both countries have opposite optimal policies. Therefore, national fiscal policy -while fostering domestic adjustment- at the same time increases the adjustment burden in the other economy. Coordination can help to reduce the working of such (economic) externalities caused by national fiscal policies in the presence of an initial disequilibrium in *intra*-MU competitiveness. Therefore, it is important to compare fiscal policies and macroeconomic outcomes under non-cooperative equilibria with outcomes under cooperation. The importance of surveillance and coordination of macroeconomic policies in e.g. the EU is stressed in the Maastricht Treaty which requires member states to regard their macroeconomic policies as a 'matter of common concern' and to coordinate these within the Council of Ministers. In these ECOFIN meetings, coordination and surveillance of macroeconomic policies has now been institutionalized.[3]

Under cooperation, fiscal policies are directed at minimizing a joined loss function, J^C,

$$J^C = \varpi J_1 + (1-\varpi)J_2 = \varpi\{J_1 + \frac{1-\varpi}{\varpi}J_2\} =: \varpi\{J_1 + \omega J_2\}, \tag{3.11}$$

rather than at minimizing the individual national loss functions (see Corollary 2.2 of Chapter 2), where $\omega := \frac{1-\varpi}{\varpi} \in (0,\infty)$ is the Pareto constant that measures the relative weight attached to both players' losses.[4] One could assume that it is the outcome of an earlier bargaining problem that the two players have solved to determine the relative weights of the individual objectives in the cooperative design of fiscal policies. In that case the Nash-bargaining solution (see e.g. Engwerda (2005a)) could be considered as the most natural outcome to such a bargaining problem associated with the cooperative decision making process.

[3] See Chapter 1, Section 1.5.4.

[4] Notice that in the actual minimization of (3.11), ϖ does not play a role and can therefore be dropped, which is done in the subsequent minimization.

Following Chapter 2 we can rewrite the cooperative decision making problem in the standard format as,

$$\min_{u_1,u_2}\left\{\begin{array}{rcl} J^C &=& \frac{1}{2}\int_0^{\infty}\{[x(t)^T\ u_1^T(t)\ u_2^T(t)]^T M(\omega)\left[\begin{array}{c} x(t) \\ u_1(t) \\ u_2(t)\end{array}\right]\}dt \end{array}\right\}$$

$$\begin{array}{rcl} \text{s.t. } \dot{x}(t) &=& Ax(t)+B_1u_1(t)+B_2u_2(t), \\ x(0) &=& x_0, \end{array} \tag{3.12}$$

where the positive definite matrix $M(\omega)$ is partitioned as,

$$M(\omega) := \left[\begin{array}{cc} \tilde{Q} & \tilde{P} \\ \tilde{P}^T & \tilde{R}\end{array}\right],$$

in which $\tilde{Q}, \tilde{R}$ and $\tilde{P}$ represent 2×2 sub-matrices that are given in Appendix II. Using Algorithm 2.1 of Chapter 2, the Pareto-efficient strategies are calculated in Appendix II. After some lengthy calculations, we find the following closed-loop system:

$$\dot{x}(t) = \left[\begin{array}{cc} -\lambda & v \\ 0 & -\frac{1}{2}\theta\end{array}\right]x(t), \tag{3.13}$$

where the adjustment speed λ is the positive square root that follows directly from (3.15) in Appendix II and v is a (in general nonzero) parameter that depends on the system parameters. Note that, different from the non-cooperative case, the variable i_U has now a direct impact via v on the closed-loop dynamics of the system.

Taking a closer look at λ as a function of the relative weight parameter ω, we see that it can be written as:

$$\lambda = \sqrt{\frac{\nu_1\omega+\nu_2(1+\omega)^2-\nu_3(1+\omega^2)}{\nu_4\omega+\nu_5(1+\omega)^2}},$$

where ν_i are positive constants (see Appendix V). Differentiation of this expression w.r.t. ω yields:

$$\lambda'(\omega) = \frac{1}{2\sqrt{\lambda}}\frac{(1-\omega^2)(\nu_1\nu_5-\nu_2\nu_4+\nu_3\nu_4+2\nu_5\nu_3)}{(\nu_4\omega+\nu_5(1+\omega)^2)^2}.$$

So, we conclude that, *ceteris paribus*, λ is maximized for $\omega = 1$ in case $\nu := \nu_1\nu_5 - \nu_2\nu_4 + \nu_3\nu_4 + 2\nu_5\nu_3$ is positive, and that λ is minimal for $\omega = 1$ in case $\nu < 0$. In Appendix III we show that $\nu < 0$ if and only if $(2a\varrho(\phi_2 - \frac{1}{2}\eta) - b\phi_1)(a^2\mu(\varrho^2-1)-\chi) - 2a^2b\phi_1\mu\varrho(\varrho+1) > 0$.

In Figure 3.2, below, we illustrated the behaviour of λ as a function of the coordination parameter ω.

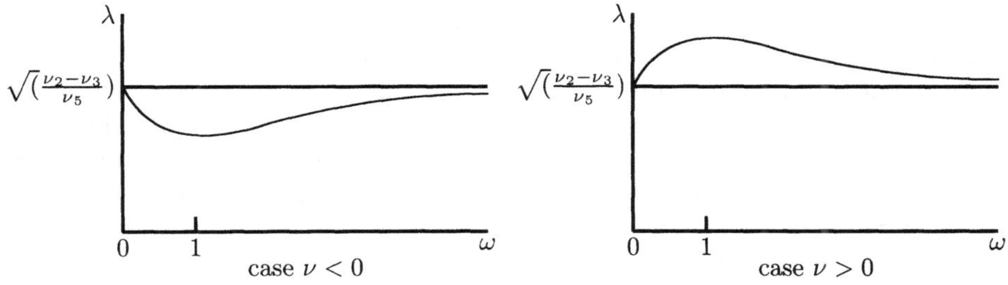

Figure 3.2 Adjustment speed λ as a function of coordination parameter ω

From this figure, we see that s converges as fast as possible to zero in the cooperative game if both cost functionals have an equal weight ($\varpi = \frac{1}{2}$) in case $\nu > 0$. So, under these parameter conditions, both players have an incentive to cooperate, since cooperation increases the adjustment speed of the closed-loop system (3.13) towards its long-term equilibrium. On the other hand, in case $\nu < 0$, s converges as fast as possible to zero in case either $\omega = 0$ or $\omega = \infty$. One might expect that cooperation under these parameter conditions will be much more difficult to achieve. For, whatever the value of the cooperation weight parameter ω is, both players observe that a different value of this parameter would increase the adjustment speed of their economy. Obviously, this is a desirable property as it implies that unanticipated shocks will have a less serious impact on the economy.

3.3.3 The effect of fiscal stringency conditions on adjustment speed λ

The impact of fiscal stringency is measured by the model parameter χ. In Section 3.3.1 we already analyzed the consequences of fiscal stringency on the number of non-cooperative equilibria. We saw that if the model parameter ϱ is smaller than or equal to one, fiscal stringency has no impact on the number of equilibria. There is always a unique equilibrium. However, in case $\varrho > 1$ fiscal stringency does have an impact. If fiscal stringency conditions are either rather weak or very strong, again a unique equilibrium will occur, whereas if fiscal stringency is in between a lower and upper bound, χ_1 and χ_2, either more than one or no equilibrium can occur.

In Section 3.3.2 we showed that in case the sign of the parameter ν is negative, one may expect that cooperation will be difficult to achieve. In fact this happens if and only if

$$(2a\varrho(\phi_2 - \tfrac{1}{2}\eta) - b\phi_1)(a^2\mu(\varrho^2 - 1) - \chi) - 2a^2b\phi_1\mu\varrho(\varrho + 1) > 0$$

or, stated differently in terms of the fiscal stringency measure χ,

$$\chi > \frac{a^2\mu(\varrho+1)(2a\varrho(\varrho-1)+b\phi_1(\varrho-\frac{1}{3}))}{b\phi_1-2a\varrho(\phi_2-\frac{1}{2}\theta)}.$$

In other words, there is always a threshold after which, if fiscal stringency is increased even more, the realization of a cooperative equilibrium will be more difficult to achieve. Tight fiscal stringency conditions imply that the domestic government is rather reluctant in using fiscal instruments to stabilize domestic output and prices. Since the foreign country has the same attitude, both countries are very reluctant to help out the other country in the achievement of an optimal performance. Note that in case $\varrho < \frac{1}{3}$, irrespective of the other parameter values, $\nu < 0$ always holds. In that case, foreign deficits have only a limited effect on domestic output (see equation (3.6)) and a cooperative equilibrium between both countries will be difficult to achieve if countries care about the internal stability of their economy (i.e. prefer a high adjustment speed λ).

Next, we analyze the impact of fiscal stringency conditions on the closed-loop dynamics of the system under both scenarios. In Table 3.2 we show the impact of χ on the closed-loop dynamics of the model under the assumption that $\varrho < 1$,where $a_{uc} := \phi_2 - \frac{1}{2}\theta$. Details of the calculations are given in Appendix IV.

Table 3.2 Impact of fiscal stringency on closed-loop dynamics

χ	Non-cooperative	Cooperative
0	$\lambda = \frac{1}{2}\theta$	$\lambda = \frac{1}{2}\theta$
:	Increasing	Increasing/(decreasing)
∞	$\lambda = -a_{uc}$	$\lambda = -a_{uc}$

Table 3.2 should be interpreted as follows. If χ increases, the corresponding λ for the non-cooperative case increases (monotonically) from $\frac{1}{2}\theta$ to $-a_{uc}$. For the cooperative case two different situations can occur depending on the sign of $\sigma := -b\phi_1(1+\omega)^2+2aa_{uc}(\varrho\omega^2-2\omega+\varrho)$. If $\sigma \geqq 0$, λ will increase (monotonically) in the cooperative case too. In case $\sigma < 0$, λ will first increase towards its maximum value (larger than $-a_{uc}$) and then decrease to $-a_{uc}$. We illustrate both cases in Figure 3.3.

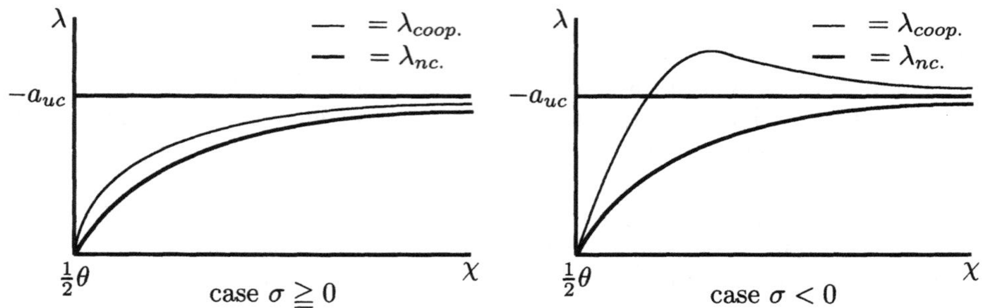

Figure 3.3 Adjustment speed as a function of fiscal stringency χ

From Table 3.2 and Figure 3.3 we see that the adjustment speed of s towards its long-term equilibrium always increases in case fiscal deficits are taken more seriously, at least in the non-cooperative case. In the latter case, the adjustment speed increases with higher values of χ: it reduces fiscal policy activism and, therefore, the negative externalities of national fiscal policies that occur when the dynamic system starts out of equilibrium. In the non-cooperative case, these externalities are less activated by the players in case the fiscal stringency requirements are imposed with more vigour, i.e. if χ is set higher, because with a higher valued χ the costs of high deficits and surpluses increase and policy activism is therefore reduced. For example, if $s_0 > 0$, country 1 has an initial competitive advantage compared to country 2 and would like to reduce output and inflation by means of a fiscal surplus. This, however, has also a contractional effect on country 2, whose economy is in recession already because of the initial disequilibrium and would suffer even more from a contractional fiscal policy in country 1.

In the cooperative case the convergence speed is larger than in the non-cooperative case: in case of an initial disequilibrium of the state variable s, the negative economic externalities from national fiscal policies are internalized when fiscal policies are set in a cooperative manner. In that case there exists, however, a threshold after which this convergence speed does not increase anymore (though it remains above that of the non-cooperative case). In case fiscal deficits are strongly taken into account, implying that χ is large, the impact on the convergence speed of s towards zero is almost the same in both scenarios. Note that this is also the case if in both scenarios fiscal deficits are (almost) neglected. Note also that if $\omega = 1$, σ is always positive and the monotonic relation between χ and λ applies. In case ω approaches either zero or infinity, implying that cooperative policy design is dominated by one country only, the case with $\sigma < 0$ applies and there exists some value for χ for which the adjustment speed is maximal.

Summarizing, we see that the adjustment speed of the output price differential is higher in the cooperative case than in the non-cooperative one. Furthermore, if fiscal stringency would be a design parameter, we observe that for a high adjustment speed it is best to increase fiscal stringency conditions as much as possible in case countries are non-cooperative (that is try to prevent the individual players to intervene in the economy) and if countries are cooperative, there exists some intermediate level of fiscal stringency where the adjustment speed is maximal (provided that the model parameter σ is negative). Moreover, in case fiscal deficits play either no role or a very important role it does not make any difference for the adjustment speed whether the countries cooperate or not.

3.3.4 Consequences of a European federal transfer system

It is well-known (see e.g. Weber (1991), Bayoumi and Eichengreen (1993), Bayoumi and Prassad (1995), and Christodoulakis *et al.* (1995)) that asymmetric macroeconomic shocks often occur and have considerable impact in most countries of the EU. Furthermore, Decressin and Fatás (1995) find that labour mobility is considerably smaller in the EU than in the US. Therefore, a European Fiscal Transfer System (EFTS) that aims at stabilizing asymmetric shocks in the EMU has been advocated by van der Ploeg (1991) and has been elaborated further by e.g. Italianer and van Heukelen (1993) and von Hagen and Hammond (1995). Such an EFTS could substitute for the stabilizing role of federal fiscal flows in mature fiscal federations like the US. Bayoumi and Masson (1995) find that for the US, 30 percent of short-term fluctuations is stabilized by federal fiscal flows. The stabilizing impact of the EU budget in contrast is not much more than 1 percent, reflecting its small size. On the other hand, the amount of stabilization provided by national government budgets in the EU countries is shown to be comparable to that which occurs in the US. Consequently, if national governments will be constrained to carry out stabilization policies given the need to comply with fiscal stringency requirements, a federal transfer system could be considered to alleviate the stabilization burden in the MU.

In this section we will include such an automatic stabilization rule into our model and analyze its consequences. In the context of the EMU a fiscal transfer system operating through the budget of the EU seems to be the most realistic institutional framework, e.g., in the form of an EU-wide scheme of unemployment benefits.

To that end we define net government expenditures as follows:

$$g_1 := f_1 - z \qquad \text{and} \qquad g_2 := f_2 + z,$$

where $z := \varepsilon(y_1 - y_2)$ is a net transfer from country 1 to country 2. The transfer system redirects demand from a country with a higher level of output to a country with a lower level of output. Thus, the transfer system contributes to automatic stabilization of *intra*-EU divergences in output fluctuations.

Note that transfer systems in practice may induce negative incentives in that countries postpone adjustment measures in the expectation of receiving transfers (consider e.g. the Mezzogiorno problem in the case of Italy where sustained transfers from north to south hampered structural adjustments in the South and created strong dependence from the South on the North). Our analysis - which deals with symmetric countries and cyclical fluctuations- disregards such incentive problems associated with fiscal transfer systems.[5]

The output equations (3.1) and (3.2) then become:

$$\begin{aligned} y_1(t) &= \delta s(t) - \gamma r_1(t) + \rho y_2(t) + \eta g_1(t) \\ y_2(t) &= -\delta s(t) - \gamma r_2(t) + \rho y_1(t) + \eta g_2(t). \end{aligned}$$

After some elementary calculations, we find that this model can be rewritten into the previous framework, with the following redefinition of parameters:

$$a := \frac{\eta X}{X^2 - Z^2};\ b := \frac{\delta}{X + Z};\ k := \frac{\rho X}{Z};\ \phi_1 := \frac{\xi\eta}{X + Z};\ \phi_2 := \frac{-2\delta\xi}{X + Z},$$

in which $X := 1 - \gamma\xi + \eta\varepsilon$ and $Z := \rho + \eta\varepsilon$.

Using these parameter redefinitions all results obtained in the previous sections can be applied now. Some elementary calculations show that the parameters a, b, ϕ_1 and ϕ_2 are in absolute terms smaller and k is larger than in the

[5] Welfare costs associated with a fiscal transfer system could be introduced by adding z to the welfare functions (3.9), implying that higher transfers are more costly.

original model, while c remains constant. According to equations (3.6)- (3.8), the consequences of the introduction of an EFTS for our model are that, due to the direct output transfer, divergences between both countries are automatically stabilized. In the EFTS case, therefore, less national fiscal policy activism is needed to stabilize output deviations. The role of the indirect stabilization mechanism via output price differentials (as measured by s) becomes less important. Consequently, initial output price differentials will be more persistent. In particular, if we recalculate the adjustment speed λ for the (non-)cooperative case we obtain the result given in Table 3.3.

Table 3.3 Effects of EFTS

χ	Benchmark model	Model with EFTS
0	$\lambda = \frac{1}{2}\theta$	$\lambda = \frac{1}{2}\theta$
∞	$\lambda = \frac{1}{2}\theta + 2\delta\xi / (1 - \gamma\xi + \rho)$	$\lambda = \frac{1}{2}\theta + 2\delta\xi / (1 - \gamma\xi + \rho + 2\eta\varepsilon)$

Since the parameter a_{uc} is in Table 3.3 in absolute value smaller in the EFTS model than in the benchmark model we see that the adjustment of the output price differential towards its long-run equilibrium is slower in the EFTS model if fiscal stringency conditions are getting tighter (for increasing χ).

3.4 Numerical simulations with the model

A numerical example is very useful to illustrate the main aspects of the functioning of the model and the analytical results established in the preceding section. For the model parameters we take values given in Table 3.4.

Table 3.4: Benchmark model parameters

$\delta = 0.2$	$\xi = 0.25$	$\theta = 0.15$
$\gamma = 0.4$	$\alpha = 2$	$\omega = 1$
$\rho = 0.4$	$\beta = 5$	$i_U(t) = i_U^* = 0$
$\eta = 1$	$\chi = 2, 5$	$s(0) = 0.05$

Figure 3.4 graphs the adjustment dynamics that result in the non-cooperative (solid line) and cooperative (dotted line) cases.

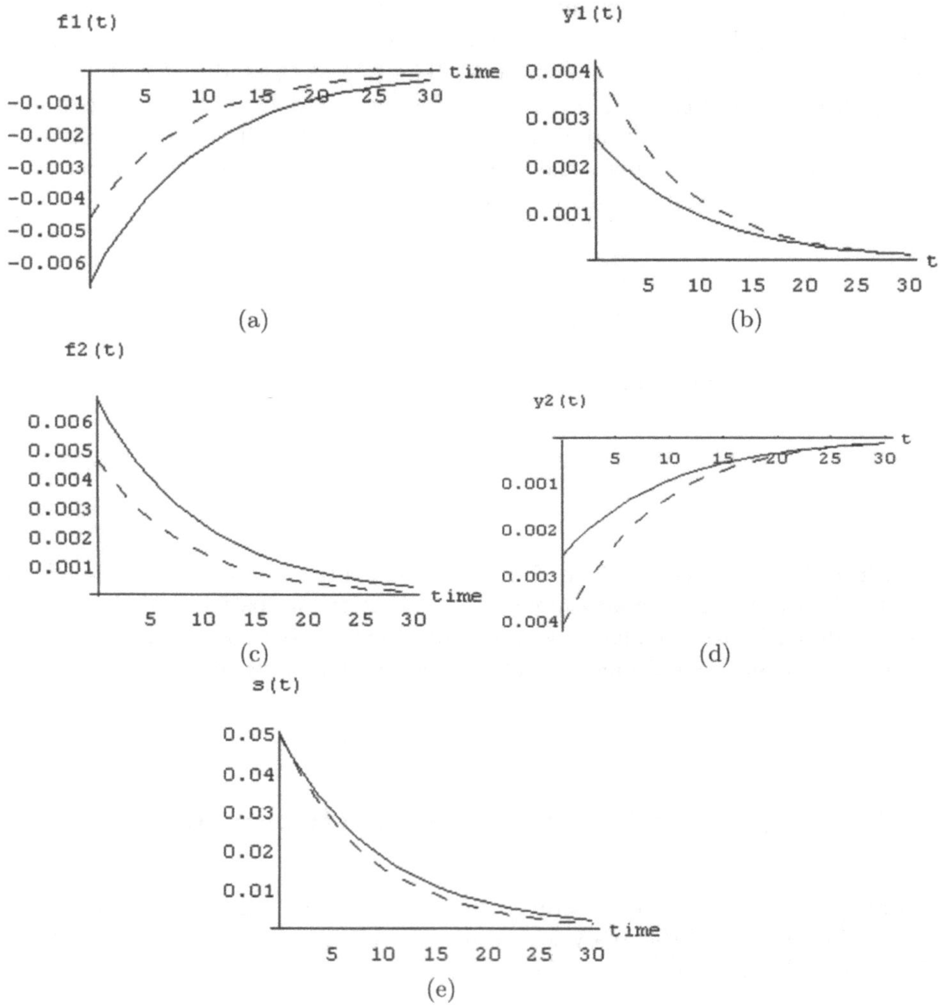

Figure 3.4

Non-cooperative (solid) and cooperative (dashed) fiscal policies.

Under fiscal policy coordination, adjustment of the state variable, $s(t)$ (panel (e)), is faster than under non-cooperative fiscal policies. Compared with uncoordinated fiscal policies, fiscal policy coordination leads to a less contractional fiscal policy in country 1 (panel (a)) and to a less expansionary fiscal policy in country 2 (panel (c)). A less contractional fiscal policy in country 1 leads to more output fluctuations in country 1 (compared with the non-cooperative case) but contributes to stabilizing the economy of country 2, which is facing a recession. Under cooperation these economic externalities of fiscal policies are internalized, producing more efficient policies than in the non-cooperative Nash case. This is also indicated by both players' (optimal) welfare losses, according to (3.9), which are calculated in the first row (I) of Table 3.5, both for the non-cooperative and the cooperative cases.

Table 3.5 Welfare losses

		J_1	J_2	
I	(a)	0.412	0.412	Non-coop
	(b)	0.368	0.368	Coop
II	(a)	0.013	0.013	Non-coop $\chi = 0$
	(b)	0.533	0.533	Non-coop $\chi = 5$
III	(a)	0.011	0.011	Coop $\chi = 0$
	(b)	0.474	0.474	Coop $\chi = 5$
IV	(a)	0.368	0.368	Coop $\omega = 1$
	(b)	0.302	0.470	Coop $\omega = 0.5$
V	(a)	0.308	0.308	Non-coop $\epsilon = 0.3$
	(b)	0.246	0.246	Coop $\epsilon = 0.3$

I: Base scenario for (a) the non-cooperative case and (b) the cooperative case.
II: Effect of either less (a) or stronger (b) interpretation of fiscal stringency in the non-cooperative case.
III: Similar as in II but now for the cooperative case.
IV: Effect of reducing bargaining weight for player 2 in the cooperative case.
V: Effect of a fiscal transfer system ($\varepsilon = 0.3$).

A stricter interpretation of the Maastricht restrictions on fiscal deficits reduces fiscal activism leading to more pronounced output fluctuations in the EMU. To analyze the effects of a higher degree of fiscal stringency on fiscal policies and macroeconomic adjustment in the EMU, we compare outcomes in two cases: (i) $\chi = 0$ (solid line) and (ii) $\chi = 5$ (dotted line). Figure 3.5 compares both cases under non-cooperative fiscal policy design. It turns out that the results for the cooperative case are similar. We, therefore, choose to plot these outcomes not separately. A higher degree of fiscal stringency reduces fiscal policy activism (panels (a) and (c)) in both countries both under non-cooperative and cooperative fiscal policy designs, implying larger short-run output fluctuations (panels (b) and (d)), and consequently high welfare losses. As noted in Section 3.3, the adjustment speed of the system dynamics increases when the degree of fiscal stringency is increased. In our example, the effects from a change in fiscal stringency on fiscal deficits and output turned out to be somewhat stronger in the case of policy coordination (not shown). Rows II and III of Table 3.5 display the (optimal) welfare losses that result in the non-cooperative and cooperative cases with no fiscal stringency ($\chi = 0$, line (a)) and with high fiscal stringency ($\chi = 5$, line (b)).

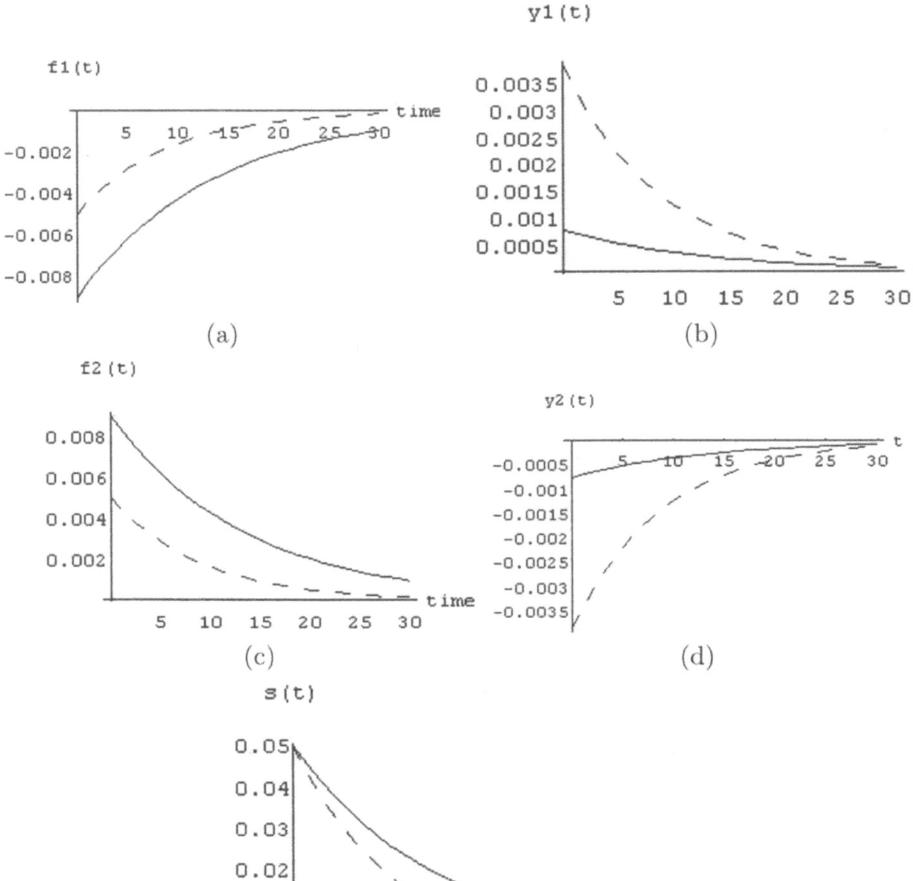

Figure 3.5 Non-cooperative fiscal policies: $\chi = 0$ (solid) vs. $\chi = 5$ (dashed).

In the case of fiscal policy coordination, the weighting parameter ω - that can also be interpreted as the relative bargaining strength of country 2 in the cooperative decision-making process - plays an important role as it determines how much weight is attributed to the preferences of both countries in policy design. In Figure 3.6, the effect of reducing ω from 1 (solid lines) to 0.5 (dashed lines) is displayed. Note that we have assumed that $\chi = 2.5$.

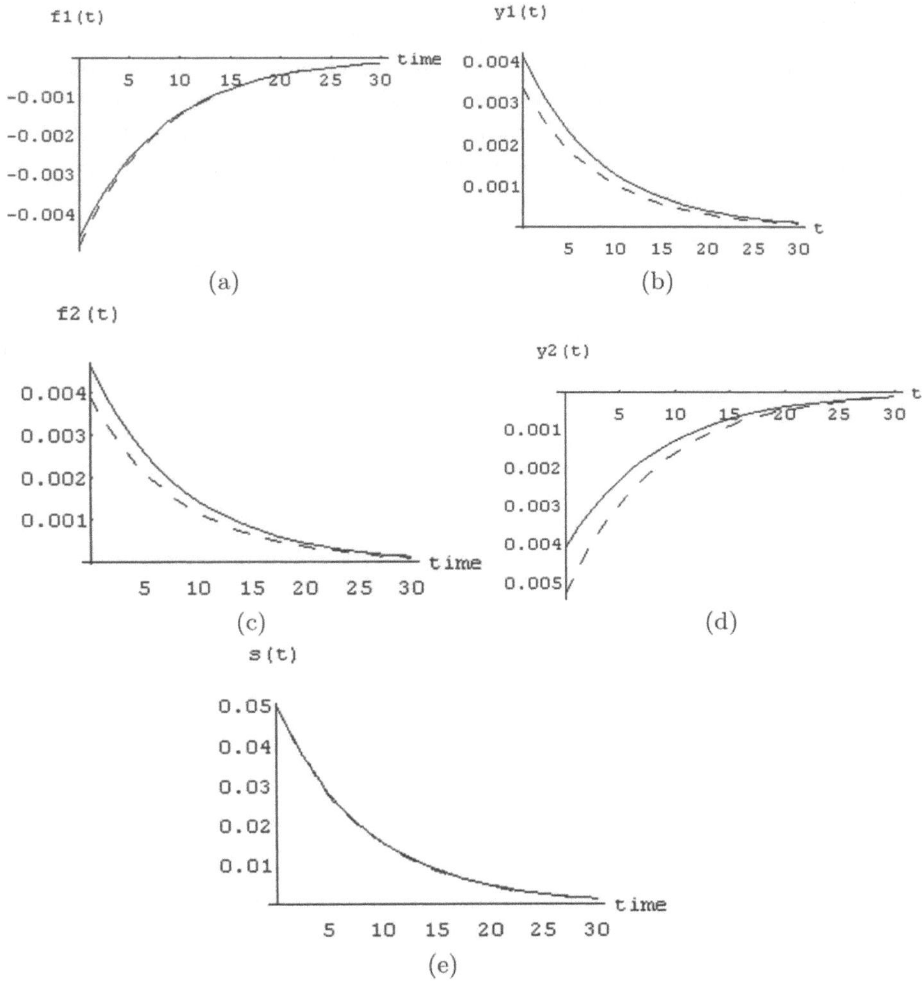

Figure 3.6
Cooperative fiscal policies: $\omega = 1$ (solid) vs. $\omega = 0.5$ (dashed).

With fiscal policies being more oriented to the needs of country 1, we in particular see a less expansionary fiscal policy in country 2 (panel (c)), which, therefore, faces larger output fluctuations (panel (d)), whereas country 1 features more stable output (panel (b)). The adjustment speed of the state variable $s(t)$ is slightly higher when ω is reduced to 0.5 (panel (e)). As noted in section 3.2, we are therefore in a case where $\nu < 0$. According to row IV of Table 3.5, (optimal) welfare losses are redistributed from country 1 to country 2 when its bargaining power increases. Therefore, such a situation is unlikely to support a cooperative arrangement, because country 2 is worse off under cooperation.

Issues of stability of coalitional cooperation will be introduced in Chapter 4 and studied extensively in the remainder of this book.

As discussed in section 3.4, a system of (federal) fiscal transfers may be a useful stabilization tool in an MU that features strong asynchronous business cycle fluctuations. To illustrate the functioning of the transfer system we consider in Figure 3.7 the adjustment dynamics in the case that $\varepsilon = 0.3$ (assuming again $\chi = 2.5$ and $\omega = 1$) in case of non-cooperative (solid lines) and cooperative (dashed lines) fiscal policies.

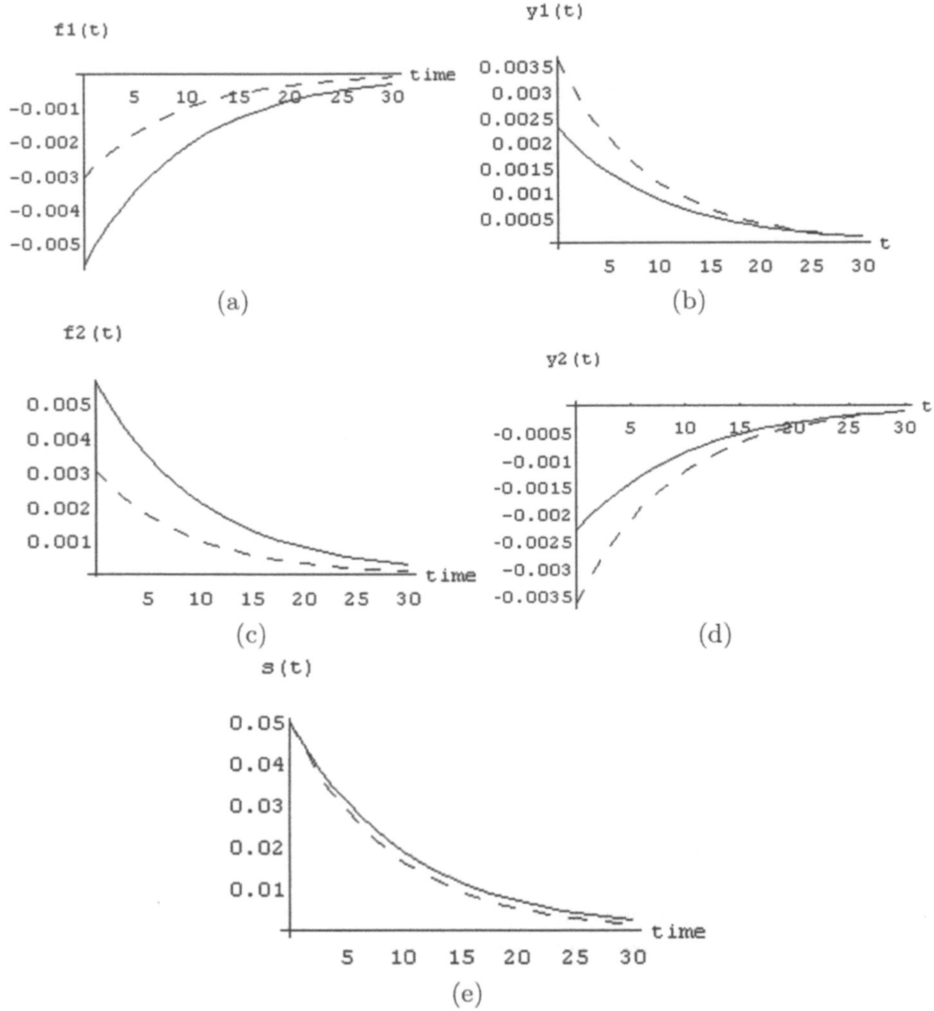

Figure 3.7
Non-cooperative (solid) and cooperative (dashed) fiscal policies with $\varepsilon = 0.3$.

Comparing with Figure 3.4, we find that the fiscal transfer system provides substantial automatic stabilization, resulting in lower output fluctuations (panels (b) and (d)) and less need for fiscal stabilization at the national level (panels (a) and (c)). Not visible, but reported in Subsection 3.3.4, is a reduced adjustment speed of the system dynamics when a federal transfer system is introduced. According to row V of Table 3.5, the transfer system enables to substantially reduce welfare losses compared to the base case of row I that features no fiscal transfer system. In that perspective, the introduction of the fiscal transfer system in a setting with asynchronous business cycle fluctuations and fiscal stringency conditions at the national level can be deemed as efficient.

3.5 Conclusions

This chapter has analyzed the design of fiscal policies under an MU as the EMU, with several explicit references to the latter. In an MU, countries lose monetary and exchange rate policies as macroeconomic stabilization tools. Therefore, the entire burden of stabilization is shifted to national fiscal policy adjustment. A symmetric two-country MU model with sluggish output and price adjustment in the short run was constructed. We modelled the design of fiscal stabilization policies in such an MU with special reference to the EMU as a linear quadratic differential game between national fiscal authorities. In this game we analyzed the Nash and the cooperative equilibria.

We imposed a number of simplifying restrictions in order to introduce the reader into the basics of our approach. The following specific limitations of the analysis in this chapter should be noted: (i) only a two-country MU was modelled; (ii) both countries were symmetric (iii) the interactions with non-MU countries are neglected; and (iv) a passive (non-strategic) common CB was assumed controlling the common nominal interest rate.

Within this framework, it was shown how fiscal stabilization policies were directed at stabilization of the business cycle fluctuations. The effects of a set of externally imposed constraints on fiscal flexibility, such as those involved in the SGP for the EMU countries, were studied in detail. In general, the fiscal stringency criteria reduce the degree of fiscal policy activism and by that the degree of effective stabilization of output and prices in the (E)MU. In that perspective, these constraints are causing suboptimal macroeconomic policies. We also showed that fiscal stringency may have an impact on the number of non-cooperative equilibria and on the internal stability of the economy. For the non-cooperative case, the adjustment speed of the economy increases if fiscal stringency increases, whereas for the cooperative case, there may exist a threshold for fiscal stringency after which this speed decreases again. For the cooperative case we looked in more detail at the effects of the bargaining power on the internal stability of the economy. It turned out that the adjustment speed is either maximized or minimized with symmetric bargaining shares. Though, obviously, the sum of welfare losses is minimized if bargaining shares are symmetric, the lower adjustment speed might be a reason for the occurrence of a difficult bargaining process. We showed that such a situation always occurs if e.g. fiscal stringency exceeds a certain threshold or if foreign deficits have only a limited direct effect on domestic output.

The effects of a fiscal transfer system in the (E)MU were considered. We showed that such a system increases the adjustment speed of the economy; hence, welfare costs may be considerably reduced. So, when national fiscal policies are restricted such a transfer system can be considered as a potentially powerful stabilization instrument in the presence of business cycle divergences.

Appendix

I. The non-cooperative case

From our model the next values for the matrices follow:

$$A = \begin{bmatrix} \phi_2 - \frac{1}{2}\theta & 0 \\ 0 & -\frac{1}{2}\theta \end{bmatrix}, \ B_1 = \begin{bmatrix} -\phi_1 \\ 0 \end{bmatrix}, \ B_2 = \begin{bmatrix} \phi_1 \\ 0 \end{bmatrix}, \ Q_1 = \mu \begin{bmatrix} b^2 & -bc \\ -bc & c^2 \end{bmatrix},$$

$$P_1 = \mu \begin{bmatrix} ab \\ -ac \end{bmatrix}, \ L_1 = \varrho P_1, \ R_{11} = \mu a^2 + \chi, \ N_1 = \varrho \mu a^2, \ R_{21} = \varrho^2 \mu a^2$$

and

$$Q_2 = \mu \begin{bmatrix} b^2 & bc \\ bc & c^2 \end{bmatrix}, \ P_2 = \varrho \mu \begin{bmatrix} -ab \\ -ac \end{bmatrix}, \ L_2 = \frac{1}{r} P_2, \ R_{12} = \varrho^2 \mu a^2, \ N_2 = \varrho \mu a^2, \ R_{22} = \mu a^2 + \chi.$$

From either Engwerda (2005a), Proposition 5.15, or a direct inspection of the eigenstructure of the matrices H_i in Algorithm 2.2 of Chapter 2, it immediately follows that the two algebraic Riccati equations (AREs) (2.21) have a stabilizing solution. Assuming that the matrix

$$G := \begin{bmatrix} R_{11} & N_1 \\ N_2^T & R_{22} \end{bmatrix} = \begin{bmatrix} \mu a^2 + \chi & \varrho \mu a^2 \\ \varrho \mu a^2 & \mu a^2 + \chi \end{bmatrix}$$

is invertible and denoting $\varrho := \frac{\varrho}{k}$, $(1-\varrho)\mu a^2 + \chi$ by α_1, $(1+\varrho)\mu a^2 + \chi$ by α_2, and $\phi_2 - \frac{1}{2}\theta$ by a_{uc}, matrix M in Step 2 of Algorithm 2.2 is given by:

$$M = - \begin{bmatrix} -a_{uc} - \frac{2\mu ab\phi_1}{\alpha_1} & 0 & \frac{\phi_1^2}{\alpha_1} & 0 & \frac{\phi_1^2}{\alpha_1} & 0 \\ 0 & \frac{1}{2}\theta & 0 & 0 & 0 & 0 \\ \frac{\mu b^2 \chi}{\alpha_1} & -\frac{\mu bc\chi}{\alpha_2} & a_{uc} + \frac{\mu ab\phi_1((1-\varrho^2)a^2\mu+\chi)}{\alpha_1\alpha_2} & 0 & -\frac{\varrho\mu ab\phi_1\chi}{\alpha_1\alpha_2} & 0 \\ -\frac{\mu bc\chi}{\alpha_1} & \frac{\mu c^2\chi}{\alpha_2} & -\frac{\mu ac\phi_1((1-\varrho^2)a^2\mu+\chi)}{\alpha_1\alpha_2} & -\frac{1}{2}\theta & \frac{\varrho\mu ac\phi_1\chi}{\alpha_1\alpha_2} & 0 \\ \frac{\mu b^2\chi}{\alpha_1} & \frac{\mu bc\chi}{\alpha_2} & -\frac{\varrho\mu ab\phi_1\chi}{\alpha_1\alpha_2} & 0 & a_{uc} + \frac{\mu ab\phi_1((1-\varrho^2)a^2\mu+\chi)}{\alpha_1\alpha_2} & 0 \\ \frac{\mu bc\chi}{\alpha_1} & \frac{\mu c^2\chi}{\alpha_2} & -\frac{\varrho\mu ac\phi_1\chi}{\alpha_1\alpha_2} & 0 & \frac{\mu ac\phi_1((1-\varrho^2)a^2\mu+\chi)}{\alpha_1\alpha_2} & -\frac{1}{2}\theta \end{bmatrix}.$$

The eigenvalues of M are:
$\{\frac{1}{2}\theta, \frac{1}{2}\theta, -\frac{1}{2}\theta, \zeta := \frac{1}{2}\theta - \phi_2 - \frac{\mu ab\phi_1}{\alpha_1\alpha_2}((1+\varrho)\chi + (1-\varrho^2)a^2\mu), \lambda_1, \lambda_2\}$, where

$$\lambda_{1,2} = \frac{1}{2}\left\{\frac{(1+\varrho)\mu ab\phi_1}{\alpha_1} \pm \sqrt{\left(\frac{-(1+\varrho)\mu ab\phi_1}{\alpha_1}\right)^2 - \frac{4\alpha_3}{\alpha_1^2}}\right\}, \tag{3.14}$$

in which $\alpha_3 := -\{(a_{uc}\alpha_1^2 + 2\mu ab\phi_1\alpha_1)(a_{uc} + \frac{1}{\alpha_1}\mu ab\phi_1(1-\varrho)) + 2\phi_1^2\mu b^2\chi\}$. Note that the square root term always exists as a real number, since this term can be rewritten as the sum of two positive numbers:

$$\frac{1}{\alpha_1^2}(\{(-3+\varrho)\mu ab\phi_1 - 2a_{uc}((1-\varrho)\mu a^2 + \chi)\}^2 + 8\mu\chi b^2\phi_1^2).$$

It is easily verified that the first entry of the eigenvector corresponding to the eigenvalue $-\frac{1}{2}\theta$ is always zero as is the second entry of the eigenvector corresponding to λ_i, $i = 1, 2$. From this immediately follows that, depending on the sign of λ_i, the model has either none ($\lambda_i \geqq 0$), one ($\lambda_1 < 0$ and $\lambda_2 \geqq 0$) or more than one equilibrium ($\lambda_i < 0$), respectively. Moreover, by calculating the exact structure of the eigenvalues corresponding to the eigenvalues $\frac{1}{2}\theta$ and λ_1, and using the above computational algorithm the closed-loop structure can be determined, as summarized in equation (3.10).
Some elementary rewriting shows that α_3 can be rewritten as

$$-\frac{1}{4}\frac{\alpha_1}{(k+\rho)^2}\{(4\delta\xi + \theta(k+\rho))^2\chi + \frac{\mu\eta^2\theta(\theta k + 2\delta\xi)}{k-\rho}\}.$$

It is now easily verified that if $k > \rho$ the parameters a and α_1 are positive and α_3 is, consequently, negative. So, M has exactly 2 negative eigenvalues. In case $k < \rho$, then $a < 0$. So there will be exactly one equilibrium if either $\alpha_1 < 0$ and $(4\delta\xi+\theta(k+\rho))^2\chi < \frac{\mu\eta^2\theta(\theta k+2\delta\xi)}{\rho-k}$ or $\alpha_1 > 0$ and $(4\delta\xi+\theta(k+\rho))^2\chi > \frac{\mu\eta^2\theta(\theta k+2\delta\xi)}{\rho-k}$. Denoting $(4\delta\xi + \theta(k+\rho))^2\chi$ by $\bar{y}_1$ and $\frac{\mu\eta^2\theta(\theta k+2\delta\xi)}{\rho-k}$ by $\bar{y}_2$, it is moreover easily verified that there exists no equilibrium in case $\alpha_1 < 0$ and $\bar{y}_1 > \bar{y}_2$, and that there are two equilibria in case $\alpha_1 > 0$ and $\bar{y}_1 < \bar{y}_2$. Using the definition of α_1 and denoting $\frac{\mu(\theta k+2\delta\xi)\eta^2\theta}{(\rho-k)(4\delta\xi+\theta(k+\rho))^2}$ by χ_1 and $\frac{\rho-k}{k}\mu\left(\frac{\eta k}{k^2-\rho^2}\right)^2$ by χ_2 we can rewrite these conditions in terms of inequalities that should be satisfied by the design parameter χ. That is, there is one equilibrium if either $\chi < \min(\chi_1, \chi_2)$ or $\chi > \max(\chi_1, \chi_2)$; there is no equilibrium if $\chi_1 < \chi < \chi_2$; and there is more than one equilibrium if $\chi_2 < \chi < \chi_1$. We summarized these results in Table 3.1.

II. The cooperative case

From our model the next values for the matrices follow:

$$A = \begin{bmatrix} \phi_2 - \frac{1}{2}\theta & 0 \\ 0 & -\frac{1}{2}\theta \end{bmatrix}, \; B := [B_1 \; B_2] = \begin{bmatrix} -\phi_1 & \phi_1 \\ 0 & 0 \end{bmatrix} \text{ and}$$

$$M(\omega) = \begin{bmatrix} (1+\omega)\mu b^2 & (\omega-1)\mu bc & (1-\omega\varrho)\mu ab & (\varrho-\omega)\mu ab \\ (-1+\omega)\mu bc & (1+\omega)\mu c^2 & (-1-\omega\varrho)\mu ac & (-\varrho-\omega)\mu ac \\ (1-\omega\varrho)\mu ab & (-1-\omega\varrho)\mu ac & (1+\omega\varrho^2)\mu a^2+\chi & \varrho(1+\omega)\mu a^2 \\ (\varrho-\omega)\mu ab & (-\varrho-\omega)\mu ac & \varrho(1+\omega)\mu a^2 & (\varrho^2+\omega)\mu a^2+\omega\chi \end{bmatrix}.$$

Following the notation of Theorem 2.16 and Algorithm 2.1 of Chapter 2 factorization of $M(\omega)$ yields the following parameter values for the matrices $\tilde{Q}$, $\tilde{P}$ and $\tilde{R}$:

$$\tilde{Q} = \begin{bmatrix} (1+\omega)\mu b^2 & (\omega-1)\mu bc \\ (-1+\omega)\mu bc & (1+\omega)\mu c^2 \end{bmatrix}, \; \tilde{P} = \begin{bmatrix} (1-\omega\varrho)\mu ab & (\varrho-\omega)\mu ab \\ (-1-\omega\varrho)\mu ac & (-\varrho-\omega)\mu ac \end{bmatrix}$$

$$\text{and } \tilde{R} = \begin{bmatrix} (1+\omega\varrho^2)\mu a^2 + \chi & \varrho(1+\omega)\mu a^2 \\ \varrho(1+\omega)\mu a^2 & (\varrho^2+\omega)\mu a^2 + \omega\chi \end{bmatrix}.$$

Note that matrix $\tilde{R}$ is invertible for all ω (and thus positive definite). Furthermore, (A, B) is stabilizable.
Following the lines of Algorithm 2.1 we next have to determine the eigenstructure of matrix

$$H := \begin{bmatrix} (A - B\tilde{R}^{-1}\tilde{P}^T) & -B\tilde{R}^{-1}B^T \\ -\tilde{Q} & -(A - B\tilde{R}^{-1}\tilde{P}^T)^T \end{bmatrix}.$$

Substitution of the above-mentioned parameter values into H yields, after some tedious manipulations, the eigenvalues for this Hamiltonian: $\{-\frac{1}{2}\theta, \frac{1}{2}\theta, \pm\lambda\}$, where:

$$\begin{aligned} \lambda^2 &= \frac{1}{4(\omega(\chi+\mu a^2(1-\varrho^2))^2 + \varrho^2\mu a^2\chi(1+\omega)^2)}\{(a\mu)^2\omega\{2(1-\varrho^2)aa_{uc} \\ &\quad +4(1+\varrho)b\phi_1\}^2 + \mu\chi\{-2(1+\omega^2)aa_{uc}(2(1-\varrho^2)aa_{uc} + 4(1+\varrho)b\phi_1) \\ &\quad +(1+\omega)^2(2aa_{uc} + 2b\phi_1)^2\} + 4\omega\chi^2 a_{uc}^2\}. \end{aligned} \tag{3.15}$$

By calculating the eigenvectors corresponding to the eigenvalues $-\frac{1}{2}\theta$ and $-\lambda$, and using Algorithm 2.1 the closed-loop structure (3.13) results.

III. A detailed look at parameter ν

By definition $\nu := \nu_1\nu_5 - \nu_2\nu_4 + \nu_3\nu_4 + 2\nu_5\nu_3$. This can be rewritten as

$$\begin{aligned} \nu &= (\nu_1 + 2\nu_3)\nu_5 + (\nu_3 - \nu_2)\nu_4 \\ &= 4[2a\mu(1-\varrho^2)aa_{uc} + 4a\mu(1+\varrho)b\phi_1 + 2\chi a_{uc}]^2\mu\chi\varrho^2a^2 - \\ &\quad 16\mu\chi(b\phi_1 - \varrho aa_{uc})^2(\chi + \mu a^2(1-\varrho^2))^2 \\ &= 16\mu\chi\{a^2\varrho^2[a_{uc}(\chi+\mu a^2(1-\varrho^2)) + 2a\mu b\phi_1(1+\varrho)]^2 - \\ &\quad (b\phi_1 - \varrho aa_{uc})^2(\chi+\mu a^2(1-\varrho^2))^2\} \\ &= -16\mu\chi b\phi_1(\chi+a^2\mu(1+\varrho)^2)[(2a\varrho a_{uc}-b\phi_1)(a^2\mu(\varrho^2-1)-\chi)-2a^2b\phi_1\mu\varrho(\varrho+1)]. \end{aligned}$$

The last equality can be verified, e.g., by straightforward expansion of both sides of the equation and then comparing terms.
Since $16\mu\chi b\phi_1(\chi + a^2\mu(1+\varrho)^2) > 0$, the conclusions concerning the sign of ν follow directly.

IV. Sensitivity analysis of the closed-loop eigenvalues w.r.t. χ

By substituting $\chi = 0$ and $\chi = \infty$ into the λs one obtains the numbers mentioned in Table 3.2.
To analyze the intermediate behaviour we consider the derivative of both λs w.r.t. χ. First, consider the non-cooperative case under the assumption that $\varrho < 1$. Then the appropriate λ is $\lambda = \frac{1}{2\alpha_1}\{-c_1 + \sqrt{c_1^2 - 4\alpha_3}\}$, where $c_1 := (1+\varrho)\mu ab\phi_1$ (see (3.14)). For analysis purposes we rewrite α_1 as $q_1 + \chi$ and α_3 as $-\frac{1}{4}\alpha_1(\zeta_1\chi + \zeta_2)$ (with $q_1 := (1-\varrho)\mu a^2$, $\zeta_1 := \frac{4\delta\xi + \theta(k+\rho))^2}{(k+\rho)^2}$ and $\zeta_2 := \frac{\mu\theta\eta^2(\theta k + 2\delta\xi)}{(k+\rho)^2(k-\rho)}$).
Next, we rewrite λ as

$$\begin{aligned} \lambda &= \frac{1}{2\alpha_1}\frac{-4\alpha_3}{c_1 + \sqrt{c_1^2 - 4\alpha_3}} \\ &= \frac{1}{2}\frac{\zeta_1\chi + \zeta_2}{c_1 + \sqrt{c_1^2 - 4\alpha_3}}. \end{aligned}$$

So,

$$\begin{aligned} 2\frac{d\lambda}{d\chi} &= \frac{\zeta_1(c_1 + \sqrt{c_1^2 - 4\alpha_3}) - \frac{1}{2\sqrt{c_1^2 - 4\alpha_3}}(\zeta_1\alpha_1 + \zeta_1\chi + \zeta_2)(\zeta_1\chi + \zeta_2)}{(c_1 + \sqrt{c_1^2 - 4\alpha_3})^2} \\ &= \frac{\zeta_1 c_1\sqrt{c_1^2 - 4\alpha_3} + \zeta_1(c_1^2 - 4\alpha_3) - \frac{1}{2}(\zeta_1\alpha_1 + \zeta_1\chi + \zeta_2)(\zeta_1\chi + \zeta_2)}{\sqrt{c_1^2 - 4\alpha_3}(c_1 + \sqrt{c_1^2 - 4\alpha_3})^2} \\ &= \frac{\zeta_1 c_1(\sqrt{c_1^2 - 4\alpha_3} + c_1) - \frac{1}{2}(\zeta_1\chi + \zeta_2)^2 + \frac{1}{2}\zeta_1\alpha_1(\zeta_1\chi + \zeta_2)}{\sqrt{c_1^2 - 4\alpha_3}(c_1 + \sqrt{c_1^2 - 4\alpha_3})^2} \\ &= \frac{\zeta_1 c_1(\sqrt{c_1^2 - 4\alpha_3} + c_1) + \frac{1}{2}(\zeta_1\chi + \zeta_2)(\zeta_1\alpha_1 - \zeta_1\chi - \zeta_2)}{\sqrt{c_1^2 - 4\alpha_3}(c_1 + \sqrt{c_1^2 - 4\alpha_3})^2} \\ &= \frac{\zeta_1 c_1(\sqrt{c_1^2 - 4\alpha_3} + c_1) + \frac{1}{2}(\zeta_1\chi + \zeta_2)(\zeta_1 q_1 - \zeta_2)}{\sqrt{c_1^2 - 4\alpha_3}(c_1 + \sqrt{c_1^2 - 4\alpha_3})^2}. \end{aligned}$$

From this it is clear that $\frac{d\lambda}{d\chi} > 0$ if we can show that $\zeta_1 q_1 - \zeta_2 > 0$. Substitution of the model parameters into this expression (see Table 3.A.1) yields (note that by assumption $\varrho < 1$, i.e. $k > \rho$)

$$\begin{aligned} sgn(\zeta_1 q_1 - \zeta_2) &= sgn\{\frac{(4\delta\xi + \theta(k+\rho))^2}{(k+\rho)^2}\frac{k-\rho}{k}\mu\frac{(k\eta)^2}{(k^2-\rho^2)^2} - \frac{\mu\theta\eta^2(\theta k + 2\delta\xi)}{(k+\rho)^2(k-\rho)}\} \\ &= sgn\{\frac{k}{(k+\rho)^2}(4\delta\xi + \theta(k+\rho))^2 - (\theta k + 2\delta\xi)\theta\} \\ &= sgn\{\frac{k}{(k+\rho)^2}(8\delta\xi\theta(k+\rho) + 16\delta^2\xi^2) - 2\delta\xi\theta\}. \end{aligned}$$

Next, we show that this last expression is always positive. To do so, we first note that since $k > \rho$, we have $2k > k + \rho$. Therefore,

$\frac{k}{(k+\rho)}8\delta\xi\theta - 2\delta\xi\theta > \frac{1}{2}8\delta\xi\theta - 2\delta\xi\theta > 0$. Using this inequality, the claim is obvious now. Which proves the positiveness of $\frac{d\lambda}{d\chi}$ for the non-cooperative case.
Next, we consider the cooperative case. Some elementary analysis shows that in that case the corresponding λ (see 3.15) can be rewritten as

$$\lambda = \sqrt{\frac{d_1\chi^2 + d_2\chi + d_3}{d_4\chi^2 + d_5\chi + d_6}},$$

where $d_i,\ i = 1,..,6$ are pointed out in Table 3.5.
Differentiation w.r.t. χ yields:

$$\frac{d\lambda}{d\chi} = \frac{1}{2\sqrt{\lambda}}\frac{e_1\chi^2 + 2e_2\chi + e_3}{(d_4\chi^2 + d_5\chi + d_6)^2},$$

where $e_i,\ i = 1, 2, 3$ are simple expressions in d_i (see either Table 3.5 or below). To analyze this derivative we first consider the sign of the parameters e_2 and e_3. By definition we have that

$$\begin{aligned} e_2 &= d_1d_6 - d_4d_3 \\ &= 64a^2\mu^2\omega^2 b\phi_1(1+\varrho)^2(-b\phi_1 + aa_{uc}(\varrho - 1)). \end{aligned}$$

Furthermore, by first substituting the appropriate model parameters into d_i and next comparing terms on both sides of the equality signs we obtain

$$\begin{aligned} e_3 &= d_2d_6 - d_3d_5 \\ &= 16\omega a^4 b\phi_1\mu^3(\varrho+1)^3[b\phi_1(1 + 2\varrho\omega + \omega^2) - 3b\phi_1(\varrho\omega^2 + 2\omega + \varrho) + \\ &\quad 2aa_{uc}(\varrho - 1)(\varrho\omega^2 + \varrho + 2\omega)] \\ &= 16\omega a^4 b\phi_1\mu^3(\varrho+1)^3[b\phi_1(1-\varrho)(1+\omega)^2 + 2(aa_{uc}(\varrho-1) - b\phi_1)(\varrho\omega^2 + \varrho + 2\omega)]. \end{aligned}$$

From the above expressions we see that both e_2 and e_3 are positive if we can show that $(aa_{uc}(\varrho - 1) - b\phi_1) > 0$. Using the definition of these parameters it is easily verified that $(aa_{uc}(\varrho - 1) - b\phi_1) = \frac{\frac{1}{2}\theta\eta}{k+\rho}$, from which the above inequality follows. So, both $e_2 > 0$ and $e_3 > 0$.
Finally, we consider e_1. Some elementary rewriting shows:

$$\begin{aligned} e_1 &= d_1d_5 - d_2d_4 \\ &= 16\omega\mu b\phi_1(-b\phi_1(1+\omega)^2 + 2aa_{uc}(\varrho\omega^2 - 2\omega + \varrho)). \end{aligned}$$

So, denoting $-b\phi_1(1+\omega)^2 + 2aa_{uc}(\varrho\omega^2 - 2\omega + \varrho)$ by σ, we have that $e_1 = 16\omega\mu b\phi_1\sigma$.
Note that the sign of the derivative is completely determined by the sign of $e_1\chi^2 + 2e_2\chi + e_3$. Using the above-derived information concerning the signs of $e_i,\ i = 1, 2, 3$ it is clear that if $\sigma > 0$, $\frac{d\lambda}{d\chi} > 0$ for all $\chi > 0$, and that if $\sigma < 0$, $\frac{d\lambda}{d\chi}$ will be positive for small χ and becomes negative if χ is large. From this the conclusions w.r.t. the behaviour of λ as a function of χ summarized in Table 3.2 and Figure 3.3, respectively, are obvious then.

V. List of parameters

Table 3.A.1

name	value
a	$\frac{k\eta}{k^2-\rho^2}$
a_{uc}	$\phi_2 - \frac{1}{2}\theta$
α_1	$(1-\varrho)\mu a^2 + \chi$
α_2	$(1+\varrho)\mu a^2 + \chi$
α_3	$-((a_{uc}\alpha_1^2 + 2\mu ab\phi_1\alpha_1)\ (a_{uc} + \frac{1}{\alpha_1}\mu ab\phi_1(1-\varrho))\ + 2\phi_1^2\mu b^2\chi)$
b	$\frac{\delta}{k+\rho}$
c	$\frac{\gamma}{k-\rho}$
d_1	$4\omega a_{uc}^2$
d_2	$\mu\{-2(1+\omega^2)aa_{uc}(2(1-\varrho^2)aa_{uc} + 4(1+\varrho)b\phi_1) +$ $+(1+\omega)^2(2aa_{uc} + 2b\phi_1)^2\}$
d_3	$(a\mu)^2\omega\{2(1-\varrho^2)aa_{uc} + 4(1+\varrho)b\phi_1\}^2$
d_4	4ω
d_5	$8\omega\mu a^2(1-\varrho^2) + 4\varrho^2\mu a^2(1+\omega)^2$
d_6	$4\omega\mu^2 a^4(1-\varrho^2)^2$
e_1	$d_1d_5 - d_2d_4$
e_2	$d_1d_6 - d_4d_3$
e_3	$d_2d_6 - d_3d_5$
k	$1-\gamma\xi$
μ	$\alpha\xi^2 + \beta$
ν_1	$(a\mu)^2\{2(1-\varrho^2)aa_{uc} + 4(1+\varrho)b\phi_1\}^2 + 4\chi^2 a_{uc}^2$
ν_2	$\mu\chi(2aa_{uc} + 2b\phi_1)^2$
ν_3	$2\mu\chi aa_{uc}(2(1-\varrho^2)aa_{uc} + 4(1+\varrho)b\phi_1)$
ν_4	$4(\chi + \mu a^2(1-\varrho^2))^2$
ν_5	$4\mu\chi\varrho^2 a^2$
ν	$\nu_1\nu_5 - \nu_2\nu_{4\,2} + \nu_3\nu_4 + 2\nu_5\nu_3$
ϕ_1	$\frac{\xi\eta}{k+\rho}$
ϕ_2	$\frac{-2\delta\xi}{k+\rho}$
q_1	$(1-\varrho)\mu a^2$
ϱ	$\frac{\rho}{k}$
σ	$-b\phi_1(1+\omega)^2 + 2aa_{uc}(\varrho\omega^2 - 2\omega + \varrho)$

Chapter 4

An MU Model with Active Monetary Policy

4.1 Introduction

This chapter analyzes the effects of active monetary stabilization policy in an MU. It extends the analysis of the previous chapter, where monetary policy was held passive and the focus was entirely concentrated on (the coordination of) fiscal policies. In this chapter we will study the effects of active monetary policy and alternative regimes of macroeconomic policy cooperation with their impact in a dynamic model of macroeconomic adjustment in an MU.

In fact with active monetary policy, three MU-policy regimes can be distinguished: (i) non-cooperative monetary and fiscal policies, (ii) full cooperation, and (iii) partial cooperation. Coalitions between countries and between the common central bank (CB) and one country are studied in case (iii). In case (ii), full co-ordination of all macroeconomic policies occurs, i.e. the national fiscal policies and the monetary policy of the common CB are implemented in a cooperative framework. We analyze the effects of these different policy regimes in an MU. We also consider the effects of asymmetries in players' preferences and structural parameters of the model.

As already noted in Chapter 3, our analysis is also motivated by the actual configuration of EMU where monetary policy has been delegated to a *supra*-national authority, the ECB, with a complex framework of objectives, policy instruments and decision-making procedures. According to the Maastricht Treaty (December 1991), the ECB should safeguard price stability in the EMU and - subject to the condition that it does not interfere with price stability- promote economic growth in the EMU. Its policies are therefore directed at controlling economic developments of the EMU economy as a whole rather than on individual countries. The design of fiscal policies in the EMU is complicated by the set of constraints on national fiscal policy imposed by the Stability and Growth Pact (SGP). According to the SGP, excessive deficits are to be avoided and are subject to sanctions.

Decision-making procedures, coalition formation, voting power and rent sharing inside the EU institutions have been studied in detail by e.g. Widgrén (1994), Laruelle and Widgrén (1996), Hosli (1996), Bindseil (1996), Bindseil and Hantke (1997), Sutter (1998) and Levinsky and Silarsky (1998). These studies - while enabling us insights into issues of power distribution and coalition formation in community policy formation -, however, do not consider a next step, namely the analysis of the effects of coalition formation and power distribution on economic policies.

Engwerda *et al.* (1999) have studied the effects of non-cooperative macroeconomic policies in the EMU. They analyze macroeconomic stabilization among three players (two countries and the ECB) in a dynamic model of the EMU. Cooperation has been analyzed in Hughes Hallett and Ma (1996) and Acocella and Di Bartolomeo (2001). This chapter extends these analyses and Chapter 3 by introducing coalition formation and studies how these coalitions affect policies and adjustment in the EMU.

The analysis is structured as follows: Section 4.2 proposes a simple dynamic model of an MU and formulates the dynamic stabilization game between the monetary and fiscal policymakers in this setup. Sections 4.3 and 4.4 study, theoretically, the various equilibria of this dynamic stabilization game and the resulting design of the common monetary policy and the national fiscal policies. Section 4.5 gives an analysis of the symmetric benchmark case. Section 4.6 studies in detail numerical examples to obtain a deeper insight into the economic properties of the model. The appendices provide details about algorithms and calculations in the analytical part of this chapter.

4.2 An MU model with active monetary policy

To study the interaction of monetary and fiscal policies in an MU, we extend the analysis of Chapter 3 by introducing active monetary policy of the common CB. The decision problem of this common CB is analyzed. In addition, Chapter 3 assumed that the MU consists of two symmetric, equally sized (blocks of) countries. In this chapter we also consider asymmetric settings and the symmetric model is interpreted as a benchmark scenario. As before, the model ignores the external interaction of the MU countries with the non-MU countries and also the dynamic implications of government debt and net foreign asset accumulation. It consists of the following equations:

$$
\begin{aligned}
y_1(t) &= \delta_1 s(t) - \gamma_1 r_1(t) + \rho_1 y_2(t) + \eta_1 f_1(t) && (4.1)\\
y_2(t) &= -\delta_2 s(t) - \gamma_2 r_2(t) + \rho_2 y_1(t) + \eta_2 f_2(t) && (4.2)\\
s(t) &= p_2(t) - p_1(t) && (4.3)\\
r_i(t) &= i_U(t) - \dot{p}_i(t),\ i \in \{1,2\} && (4.4)\\
m_i(t) - p_i(t) &= \kappa_i y_i(t) - \lambda_i i_U(t),\ i \in \{1,2\} && (4.5)\\
\dot{p}_i(t) &= \xi_i y_i(t),\ i \in \{1,2\}, && (4.6)
\end{aligned}
$$

which is a direct extension of the symmetric model (3.1)-(3.5) in Chapter 3 allowing for asymmetric (blocks of) countries and including the real money balances given by equation (4.5), where m_i are the nominal money balances of country (block) $i \in \{1,2\}$. All other variables are as defined in Chapter 3.

Equations (4.1) and (4.2) represent output in the MU countries as a function of competitiveness in *intra*-MU trade, the domestic real interest rate, the foreign (real) output and the domestic real fiscal deficit. Competitiveness is defined in (4.3) as the output price differential. Real interest rates are defined in (4.4) as the difference between the EMU-wide nominal interest rate, i_U, and domestic inflation. Equations (4.5) provide the demand for the common currency where it is assumed that the money market is in equilibrium. Domestic output and inflation are related through a Phillips curve type relation in (4.6).

We assume as in Chapter 3 that the fiscal authorities control their fiscal policy instrument so as to minimize the following quadratic loss functions that feature the countries' concern towards domestic nominal inflation, domestic real output and domestic real fiscal deficit:[1]

$$J_i = \int_0^\infty \{\alpha_i \dot{p}_i^2(t) + \beta_i y_i^2(t) + \chi_i f_i^2(t)\} e^{-\theta t} dt, \ i \in \{1,2\}, \tag{4.7}$$

in which θ denotes the rate of time preference and α_i, β_i and χ_i ($i \in \{1,2\}$) represent preference weights that are attached to the stabilization of inflation, output and fiscal deficits, respectively. Preference for a low fiscal deficit could reflect the costs of excessive deficits such as proposed in the SGP that sanctions such excessive deficits in the EMU. Moreover, costs could also result from undesirable debt accumulation and inter-generational redistribution that high deficits imply and, in that interpretation, χ_i could also reflect the priority attached to fiscal retrenchment and consolidation.

4.3 Monetary policy management in an MU

So far, the setup is principally similar as in the previous chapter. The crucial step is therefore to introduce the common monetary policy into the analysis. It is assumed that the common nominal interest rate is set by the common CB. The CB directs the common monetary policy at stabilizing inflation and stabilizing output in the aggregate MU economy. Moreover, we will assume that the active use of monetary policy invokes costs for the monetary policymaker: other things equal it would like to keep its policy instrument constant, avoiding large swings. Consequently, we assume that the CB is confronted with the following optimization problem:[2]

[1] Note that in an MU, the fiscal players are assumed not to have any direct control over the nominal interest rate, since this control is generally left for the common CB (see, among others, Gros and Hefeker (2000) and Acocella and Di Bartolomeo (2001)).

[2] α_U and β_U are the preference parameters w.r.t. inflation and output, respectively, of equation (14) in Engwerda *et al.* (1999), where $\alpha_U := 1$ because of normalization (see also equation (3.11) in the previous chapter).

$$\min_{i_U} J_U^A = \min_{i_U} \int_0^\infty \{(\alpha_{1U}\dot{p}_1(t)+\alpha_{2U}\dot{p}_2(t))^2 + (\beta_{1U}y_1(t)+\beta_{2U}y_2(t))^2 + \chi_U i_U^2(t)\}e^{-\theta t}dt \tag{4.8}$$

Alternatively, we could consider a case where the CB is governed by national interests rather than by MU-wide objectives.[3] In that scenario, the CB would be a coalition of the (former) national central banks that decide cooperatively on the common monetary policy that is based on individual, national interests rather than on MU-wide objectives. In this scenario the monetary policy of the CB will typically be more sensitive to individual country variables. In that case, the CB seeks to minimize a loss function, which is assumed to be quadratic in the individual countries' inflation rates and outputs - rather than in MU-wide inflation and output as in (4.8) - and the common interest rate:

$$\min_{i_U} J_U^N = \min_{i_U} \int_0^\infty \{\alpha'_{1U}\dot{p}_1^2(t)+\alpha'_{2U}\dot{p}_2^2(t)+\beta'_{1U}y_1^2(t)+\beta'_{2U}y_2^2(t)+\chi_U i_U^2(t)\}e^{-\theta t}dt \tag{4.9}$$

The objective (4.8) can be seen as a generalization of the loss function used in Engwerda *et al.* (1999), expression (14), p.262, and of objective (4.9), allowing any scheme of country and preference weights in the decision-making problem of the CB. The loss function in (4.9) can also be interpreted as a loss function in which the CB is a coalition of national central banks, which all have a share in the decision making proportional to the size of their economies.

Below, we will only elaborate the problem if the CB's objective is the most general one, i.e. (4.8).[4]

Using (4.6) we can rewrite (4.7) and (4.8) as follows:

$$J_i = d_i \int_0^\infty \{y_i^2(t)+\frac{\chi_i}{d_i} f_i^2(t)\}e^{-\theta t}dt, \ i \in \{1,2\}, \tag{4.10}$$

$$J_U^A = \int_0^\infty \{d_{1U}y_1^2(t)+d_{2U}y_2^2(t)+2d_{3U}y_1(t)y_2(t)+\chi_U i_U^2(t)\}e^{-\theta t}dt \tag{4.11}$$

where $d_i := \alpha_i\xi_i^2 + \beta_i$, $d_{iU} := \alpha_{iU}^2\xi_i^2 + \beta_{iU}^2$ with $i \in \{1,2\}$ and $d_{3U} := \alpha_{1U}\alpha_{2U}\xi_1\xi_2 + \beta_{1U}\beta_{2U}$.[5]

The model (4.1)-(4.6) can be reduced to two output equations:

[3] See also Gros and Hefeker (2000). These authors compare, in a static framework, a specification of the ECB's cost function based on national variables with the standard one (4.8) as in Cukierman (1992). They discuss the welfare implications of the two specifications. Also van Aarle *et al.* (1995) and De Grauwe (2000) compare outcomes under an ECB's objective function based on aggregate and national variables, respectively.

[4] Appropriate formulae as special cases can directly be obtained if (4.9) is used as the ECB's performance criterion.

[5] In the case that national variables feature in the CB's objective function, as in (4.9), we have $d_{iU} = \alpha_{iU}\xi_i^2 + \beta_{iU}$ with $i = \{1,2\}$ and $d_{3U} = 0$.

$$y_1(t) = b_1 s(t) - c_1 i_U(t) + a_1 f_1(t) + \frac{\rho_1}{k_1} a_2 f_2(t) \quad (4.12)$$

$$y_2(t) = -b_2 s(t) - c_2 i_U(t) + \frac{\rho_2}{k_2} a_1 f_1(t) + a_2 f_2(t) \quad (4.13)$$

in which $a_1 := \frac{\eta_1 k_2}{k_1 k_2 - \rho_1 \rho_2}$, $a_2 := \frac{\eta_2 k_1}{k_1 k_2 - \rho_1 \rho_2}$, $b_1 := \frac{\delta_1 k_2 - \rho_1 \delta_2}{k_1 k_2 - \rho_1 \rho_2}$, $b_2 := \frac{\delta_2 k_1 - \rho_2 \delta_1}{k_1 k_2 - \rho_1 \rho_2}$, $c_1 := \frac{\gamma_1 k_2 + \rho_1 \gamma_2}{k_1 k_2 - \rho_1 \rho_2}$, $c_2 := \frac{\gamma_2 k_1 + \rho_2 \gamma_1}{k_1 k_2 - \rho_1 \rho_2}$, $k_1 := 1 - \gamma_1 \xi_1$, $k_2 := 1 - \gamma_2 \xi_2$. The dynamics of the model are then represented by the following first-order linear differential equation with competitiveness, $s(t)$, as the scalar state variable and the national fiscal deficits, $f_i(t)$ $i \in \{1, 2\}$, and the common interest rate, $i_U(t)$, as control variables:

$$\dot{s}(t) = \phi_4 s(t) - \phi_1 f_1(t) + \phi_2 f_2(t) + \phi_3 i_U(t) \qquad s(0) := s_0 \quad (4.14)$$

in which $\phi_1 := (\xi_1 - \xi_2 \frac{\rho_2}{k_2}) a_1$, $\phi_2 := (\xi_2 - \xi_1 \frac{\rho_1}{k_1}) a_2$, $\phi_3 := \xi_1 c_1 - \xi_2 c_2$ and $\phi_4 := -(\xi_2 b_2 + \xi_1 b_1)$. The initial value of the state variable, s_0, measures any initial disequilibrium in *intra*-MU competitiveness. Such an initial disequilibrium in competitiveness could be the result of, e.g., differences in fiscal policies in the past or some initial disturbance in one country.

Defining $v^T(t) := (s(t),\ f_1(t),\ f_2(t),\ i_U(t))$, we can rewrite (4.12) and (4.13) as,

$$y_1(t) = (b_1, a_1, \frac{\rho_1}{k_1} a_2, -c_1) v(t) =: m_1 v(t)$$

$$y_2(t) = (-b_2, \frac{\rho_2}{k_2} a_1, a_2, -c_2) v(t) =: m_2 v(t)$$

Introducing e_j as the jth standard basis vector of $\mathbb{R}^4$ (i.e. $e_1 := (1\ 0\ 0\ 0)^T$, etc.), $M_i := m_i^T m_i + \frac{\chi_i}{d_i} e_{i+1}^T e_{i+1}$, $i \in \{1, 2\}$ and $M_U^A := d_{1U} m_1^T m_1 + d_{2U} m_2^T m_2 + 2 d_{3U} m_1^T m_2 + \chi_E e_4^T e_4$ the policymakers' loss functions (4.10)-(4.11) can be written as:

$$J_i =: d_i \int_0^\infty \{v^T(t) M_i v(t)\} e^{-\theta t} dt,\ i \in \{1, 2\}, \quad (4.15)$$

$$J_U^A =: \int_0^\infty \{v^T(t) M_U^A v(t)\} e^{-\theta t} dt \quad (4.16)$$

Henceforth, for reasons of convenience, we assume that $\theta = 0$. If θ differs from zero, the model can be easily solved using a simple transformation of variables (see Remark 2.1 of Chapter 2). All that changes in the ensuing results is that the parameter ϕ_4 has to be substituted by $\phi_4 - \frac{1}{2}\theta$. Since in this analysis the specific choice of the loss function from the CB does not play any role, for notational convenience this dependency is dropped and we will just use e.g. M_U instead of M_U^A and M_U^N.

A number of additional remarks on the monetary policy of the CB are relevant. First, note that the transmission of the common monetary policy in this setting is principally through the interest rate channel: by varying the nominal interest, the CB influences the real interest rates and thereby output in the short run. Countries in an MU may not only be subject to asymmetric shocks but also feature asymmetries in their monetary (and fiscal) policy transmissions, here measured by $c_1$and c_2. Second, the interesting targeting strategy of the CB outlined above can be changed. E.g. we could have assumed - as in Engwerda *et al.* (1999) and van Aarle *et al.* (2001) - that a monetary targeting strategy is implemented by the CB. In that scenario, the CB controls the common money supply and the common money market is cleared by the common interest rate. Clearly both approaches are related: by targeting the money supply, the CB, through the LM functions, controls the interest rate. Rather than the monetary targeting approach, the interest rate targeting approach is proposed here. This seems to be somewhat closer to the policy strategy adopted by the ECB in practice. In open-MU context as to be analyzed later in Chapters 6-8, also interest rate targeting and exchange rate targeting are directly related with each other in the presence of an uncovered interest rate parity condition.

Moreover, this representation of monetary policy is also related to inflation targeting: strict inflation targeting would imply that only inflation features as argument in the CB's preference functional. The representation above would therefore be consistent with the Svennson's (1999) notion of flexible inflation targeting where apart from inflation the CB is also concerned with output fluctuations and interest rate smoothing.

An alternative manner to introduce monetary policy is undertaken by Rossiter and Tang (2004) and implies the introduction of instrument rules. In their study, a Taylor rule is added to the model of Chapter 3 to analyze the effects of active monetary policy in an MU. Moreover, they introduce a real interest rate risk premium that may depend on the level of the fiscal debt of a country and/or the aggregate fiscal deficit in an MU, the latter capturing a common interest rate spillover. It is shown that if this spillover and resulting externality are larger, the cooperative and non-cooperative equilibria become more and more similar, so that in other words the gains from coordination become smaller.

4.4 Macroeconomic policy design in the MU

This section studies alternative modes of policy cooperation in an MU. We study macroeconomic policy design and macroeconomic adjustment in three alternative macroeconomic policy regimes: (*i*) non-cooperative macroeconomic policies, (*ii*) full cooperation and (*iii*) partial cooperation. The first two regimes are standard in macroeconomic policy analysis. The regimes, where subgroups of players form coalitions in which they coordinate their policies, but interact in a non-cooperative manner with the players that are not part of the coalition, is not usually dealt with, certainly not in a dynamic context. This is not because such cases would be less interesting or less relevant in practice, but rather because of a lack of analytical tools to analyze such cases. In regimes of partial cooperation, important questions need to be answered, like (*i*) Why certain coalitions arise and others not?, (*ii*) Do these coalitions display stability over time?, (*iii*) How are the gains from cooperation distributed between the members of the coalitions?, (*iv*) How do differences in initial conditions, economic structures and policy preferences affect outcomes in this scenario? In this chapter the issues (*iii*) and (*iv*) can be answered whereas some insight can be provided about the coalition formation issue. The stability issue will not be dealt with in this chapter but will be analyzed in detail in Chapters 6-8.

A study of all three regimes is necessary for a complete insight on macroeconomic policy design in an MU. The regimes with either fully non-cooperative or fully cooperative policies are clearly the two extreme forms of policy formulation. Forms of partial cooperation combine elements of these opposite policy regimes as the following analysis shows.

4.4.1 The non-cooperative case

In the non-cooperative case players minimize their cost functionals (4.15) and (4.16) with respect to the dynamic law of motion (4.14) of the system. From Appendix A.1 we find as equilibrium strategies in the non-cooperative open-loop case:

$$\begin{pmatrix} f_1(t) \\ f_2(t) \\ i_U(t) \end{pmatrix} = -G^{-1} \begin{pmatrix} a_1 b_1 - \phi_1 K_1 \\ -a_2 b_2 + \phi_1 K_2 \\ -b_1 c_1 d_{1U} + b_2 c_2 d_{2U} + (b_2 c_1 - b_1 c_2)\, d_{3U} + \phi_3 K_3 \end{pmatrix} s(t) =: H_{nc} s(t)$$

where the contents of matrices G and K_i $(i = 1, 2, 3)$ can be obtained from the Appendix. The cost of the players will be denoted by $J_{i,j}$, $i \in \{1, 2, U\}$ and $j \in \{nc, c, (1,2), (1,U), (2,U)\}$, where nc refers to the non-cooperative game, c to the full cooperative game, f to the fiscal coordination game, and $(1, U)$ and $(2, U)$ refer to partial coordination games between a fiscal player and the CB. Furthermore, the resulting system is described by the differential equation $\dot{s}(t) = -a_{nc} s(t)$ with $s(0) := s_0$, where the adjustment speed, a_{nc}, is obtained as the positive eigenvalue of some related matrix that is defined in Appendix A.1. Using these equilibrium controls we obtain then the corresponding fiscal players' optimal costs:

$$J_{i,j} = d_i (1 \;\; H_j^T) M_i \begin{pmatrix} 1 \\ H_j \end{pmatrix} s_0^2 \frac{1}{2a_j} \quad i \in \{1, 2\}, \tag{4.17}$$

and the CB's optimal costs:

$$J_{Uj} = (1 \;\; H_j^T) M_U \begin{pmatrix} 1 \\ H_j \end{pmatrix} s_0^2 \frac{1}{2a_j} \,. \tag{4.18}$$

4.4.2 The cooperative case

In the full cooperative case players minimize a common cost function: $J^C := \tau_1 J_1 + \tau_2 J_2 + \tau_3 J_U$ subject to (4.14); τ_i $(i \in \{1,2,3\})$ equals player i's bargaining power with $\tau_1 + \tau_2 + \tau_3 = 1$ and $\tau_i \geqq 0$. In Appendix A.2 we show that the equilibrium cooperative controls can be written as:

$$\begin{pmatrix} f_1(t) \\ f_2(t) \\ i_U(t) \end{pmatrix} := H_c s(t),$$

Using these controls the dynamic behaviour of this system is described as: $\dot{s}(t) = -a_c s(t)$ with $s(0) := s_0$, where a_c is again a positive eigenvalue of some matrix that is defined in Appendix A.2. The corresponding optimal costs for the players are (4.17) and (4.18) with $j = c$.

4.4.3 Cases with policymakers' coalitions

To determine the equilibrium solution for partial coalitions we will concentrate on the case that the fiscal authority of country 1 and the CB coordinate their policies but act in a non-cooperative fashion with the fiscal authority of country 2. For this case we will use the shorthand notation coalition $(1, U)$.

To determine the equilibrium solution for the $(1, U)$ coalition we rewrite the system equation as:

$$\dot{s} = \phi_4 s + (-\phi_1 \ \phi_3) \begin{pmatrix} f_1(t) \\ i_U(t) \end{pmatrix} + \phi_2 f_2(t) \qquad s(0) := s_0$$

and consider the performance criterion $J_{(1,U)} := \tau_1 J_1 + \tau_2 J_U$ with $\tau_1 + \tau_2 = 1$, $\tau_i \geqq 0$, as the aggregate performance of player 1 and the CB, and J_2 for player 2, respectively. Next, we consider a with this $(1, U)$ coalition form corresponding permutation of $v(t)$ (see also Section (2.6) in Chapter 2):

$$\tilde{v}(t) := \begin{pmatrix} s(t) \\ f_1(t) \\ i_U(t) \\ f_2(t) \end{pmatrix} = \begin{pmatrix} 1 & 0 & 0 & 0 \\ 0 & 1 & 0 & 0 \\ 0 & 0 & 0 & 1 \\ 0 & 0 & 1 & 0 \end{pmatrix} v(t) =: P_{(1,U)} v(t).$$

Now, we can, basically, use the non-cooperative algorithm to determine the equilibrium strategies (see Appendix A.3)

$$\begin{pmatrix} f_1(t) \\ i_U(t) \\ f_2(t) \end{pmatrix} := H_{(1,U)} s(t).$$

Using these equilibrium strategies, the system is described by $\dot{s}(t) = -a_{(1,U)} s(t)$ with $s(0) := s_0$, where $a_{(1,U)}$ is again obtained as the positive eigenvalue of some matrix. The optimal costs for the players are (4.17) and (4.18) with $j = (1, U)$. The partial coalitions $(2, U)$ and (1,2) are defined similarly and the equilibrium strategies are derived analogously.

4.4.4 Some coalition formation terminology

In order to obtain some insight into the question which coalition(s) might be realized and which is (are) less plausible, we introduce some terminology. Each of the five policy regimes outlined in the above subsections is called a *coalition form* and each group of two or more players that cooperate in a coalition form a *coalition*. We say that a certain coalition form is *supported by player i*, if player i has no incentive to deviate from this coalition form. If a coalition form has a coalition, then we say that this coalition form is *internally supported* if all players in the coalition support the coalition form. A coalition form is called *externally supported* if all players outside the coalition support the coalition form. If a coalition form is both externally and internally supported, then we will call this coalition form *sustainable*, that is, in such a coalition form no player has an incentive to deviate (leave this coalition form). Finally, we call a coalition form *non-sustainable* if as well players inside as outside the coalition can improve by joining another coalition form.

Note that a coalition form, which is internally supported, is in principle *viable*. One reason why such a coalition form might not be realized is that e.g. side-payments take place. Here we will ignore these issues. A similar remark holds w.r.t. the non-sustainable coalition form. Such a coalition form is in principle not viable, this contrary to a coalition form which is partially supported (i.e. supported by not all players in the coalition). Such a coalition form might be viable, but this typically depends on what other coalition forms have to offer for all the different player(s). So, this requires a more detailed description of the negotiation process, something we will not go into here. The notions introduced above will in particular be used in the simulation study.

4.5 The symmetric case

In this section we consider the model described in the previous sections under the assumption of symmetry of countries 1 and 2. In that case one can obtain theoretical results. The outcomes of this analysis are not only interesting on their own, but may also be helpful in analyzing the properties of the non-symmetric model. We make the following assumptions w.r.t. the various parameters: $\alpha_1 = \alpha_2$; $\alpha_{1U} = \alpha_{2U}$; $\beta_1 = \beta_2$; $\beta_{1U} = \beta_{2U}$; $\chi_1 = \chi_2$; $\xi_1 = \xi_2$; $\gamma_1 = \gamma_2$; $\rho_1 = \rho_2$; $\delta_1 = \delta_2$; $\eta_1 = \eta_2$ $\lambda_1 = \lambda_2$ and $\kappa_1 = \kappa_2$. Furthermore we introduce for notational convenience the following parameters: $a := a_1$, $e := \frac{\rho_1}{k_1}a_2$, $c := c_1$; $b := b_1$; $d := d_1$; $d_U^A := \alpha_{1U}^2\xi_1^2 + \beta_{1U}^2$; $d_U^N := \alpha_{1U}\xi_1^2 + \beta_{1U}$; $g := \frac{\chi_1}{d}$; $g_U^A := \frac{\chi_U}{2d_U^A}$ and $g_U^N := \frac{\chi_U}{d_U^N}$. Then, the dynamics are given by the state equation

$$\dot{s} = \phi_4 s - \phi_1 f_1 + \phi_1 f_2;\ s(0) = s_0,$$

whereas the performance criteria reduce to:

$$J_i = d_i \int_0^\infty \{v^T(t)M_i v(t)\}dt,\ i \in \{1,2\} \text{ and } J_U^j = d_U^j \int_0^\infty \{v^T(t)M_U^j v(t)\}dt,\ j \in \{A,N\}.$$

with

$$M_1 := \begin{pmatrix} b^2 & ab & be & -bc \\ ab & a^2+g & ae & -ac \\ be & ae & e^2 & -ce \\ -bc & -ac & -ce & c^2 \end{pmatrix}; M_2 := \begin{pmatrix} b^2 & -be & -ab & bc \\ -be & e^2 & ae & -ce \\ -ab & ae & a^2+g & -ac \\ bc & -ce & -ac & c^2 \end{pmatrix};$$

$$M_U^N := \begin{pmatrix} 2b^2 & b(a-e) & -b(a-e) & 0 \\ b(a-e) & a^2+e^2 & 2ae & -c(a+e) \\ -b(a-e) & 2ae & a^2+e^2 & -c(a+e) \\ 0 & -c(a+e) & -c(a+e) & 2c^2+g_U^N \end{pmatrix};$$

and

$$M_U^A := \begin{pmatrix} 0 & 0 & 0 & 0 \\ 0 & (a+e)^2 & (a+e)^2 & -2c(a+e) \\ 0 & (a+e)^2 & (a+e)^2 & -2c(a+e) \\ 0 & -2c(a+e) & -2c(a+e) & 4c^2+2g_U^A \end{pmatrix}.$$

4.5.1 The various equilibrium strategies

In Appendix B, we calculate various parameters that are essential for computing the equilibrium strategies for the non-cooperative coalition (nc), the cooperative coalition (c) with $\tau_1 = \tau_2 = \tau$ and $\tau_3 = 1 - 2\tau$, where $0 \leqq \tau \leqq \frac{1}{2}$ and the fiscal coalition (1,2), with $\tau_1 = \tau_2 = \frac{1}{2}$. These parameters are presented in Table 4.1. Substitution of these parameters into the equilibrium strategies determined in Appendix A straightforwardly yields the equilibrium strategies presented below. It turns out that as well for the non-cooperative as the fiscal coalition case, the strategies for the national and aggregate performance cases are the same. Only for the cooperative case the strategies depend on the CB's preference function. For that reason we discern below two cooperative cases, the national one (cN) and the aggregate one (cA). The equilibrium strategies are:

$$\begin{pmatrix} f_1(t) \\ f_2(t) \\ i_U(t) \end{pmatrix}_i = \begin{pmatrix} 1 \\ -1 \\ 0 \end{pmatrix} \zeta_i s(t),$$

and the corresponding costs for the players are:

$$J_{1,i} = J_{2,i} = \frac{1}{2}\frac{d}{a_i}\{(b + \zeta_i(a-e))^2 + \zeta_i^2 g\} s^2(0) \tag{4.19}$$

$$J_{U,i}^N = \frac{1}{2}\frac{d_U^N}{a_i}(b + \zeta_i(a-e))^2 s^2(0), \; J_{U,i}^A = 0, \tag{4.20}$$

for $i = nc, cA, cN, (1,2)$. Here:

Table 4.1 - Policy parameters for the symmetric case

$i =$	nc	cN	cA	(1,2)
u_i	$a(a-e)+g$	$\tau g + d_U^N(a-e)^2$	$\tau(g+(a-e)^2)$	$g+(a-e)^2$
a_i^2	$(\phi_4 - 2\phi_1 p_{nc})^2$	$\frac{\tau g \phi_4^2}{u_{cN}}$	$\frac{g\phi_4^2}{g+(a-e)^2}$	$\frac{g\phi_4^2}{u_{(1,2)}}$
K_i	$\frac{-2b^2 g}{u-\sqrt{u^2+8gb^2\phi_1^2}}$	$\frac{(\phi_4+a_c)u_{cN}+2d_U^N\phi_1 b(a-e)}{2\phi_1^2}$	$\frac{\phi_4\tau g + a_{cA}u_{cA}}{2\phi_1^2}$	$\frac{-gb^2}{\phi_4 g - u_{(1,2)}a_{(1,2)}}$
ζ_i	$\frac{\phi_1 K_{nc} - ab}{u_{nc}}$	$\frac{\phi_1 K_{cN} - d_U^N b(a-e)}{u_{cN}}$	$\frac{\phi_1 K_{cA} - \tau b(a-e)}{u_{cA}}$	$\frac{2\phi_1 K_{(1,2)} - b(a-e)}{u_{(1,2)}}$

with $u := 2\phi_4 u_{nc} + b\phi_1(3a-e)$.

If the coalition $(1,U)$ occurs (or its symmetric counterpart $(2,U)$), the MU is directly involved in the game (i.e. the common interest rate differs in general from zero). As a consequence, the theoretical formulae become much more involved. Therefore they are omitted.

4.5.2 First findings

First, we summarize some conclusions w.r.t. the number of equilibria that may appear in the game.

Theorem 4.1 *The game has always a unique equilibrium for the cooperative and (1,2) coalitions if* $e < a$, *the non-cooperative game has also a unique equilibrium. If* $e \geqq a$, *the game may have either none or more than one equilibrium (see Chapter 3).*

In the rest of this section, we will restrict to the case where $e < a$ and will assume, moreover, that as well $-\phi_4$ as a are positive. For a broad class of realistic model parameters, these assumptions hold (in particular the positivity condition on $-\phi_4$ is satisfied if one chooses the discount factor θ large enough). As a consequence, the non-cooperative game has a unique equilibrium. Furthermore, unless stated otherwise, we will restrict our analysis to the non-cooperative case, the cooperative case and the fiscal coalition (1,2).

We observe two striking things from the previous section, i.e. $f_1(t) = -f_2(t)$ and the CB does not influence the game, neither in a direct way (i.e. $i_U(t) = 0$) nor in an indirect way (i.e. via its parameters). These statements do not hold for the coalition form $(1,U)$. There, the fiscal instruments differ and the CB uses its instruments actively to reach its goals. The symmetry assumptions are crucial here, if they are dropped the CB gets also actively involved into all games.

Since we have explicit formulae for the various cost functionals, we can exploit these to derive some further general conclusions. Our first observation (see Appendix C) is that the convergence speed of the resulting systems satisfy some nice properties:

Lemma 4.1 *i)* $a_{cN} \leqq a_{(1,2)}$.
ii) $a_{nc} \leqq a_{cN}$ *if* $3\tau \geqq 2d_N$, *where* $d_N := \tau + (1-2\tau)\frac{d_U^N}{d}$.
iii) $a_i(g)$ *is an increasing function with* $a_i(0) = 0$ *and* $a_i(\infty) = -\phi_4$, $i \in$

$\{nc, c, (1,2)\}$.
iv) $a_{cN} \leqq a_{cA}$.

With respect to the performance criteria, we first note that the fiscal players' cost in the coalition case, with the CB considering an aggregate performance criterion, and the (1,2) coalition coincide. In other words, the fiscal players are indifferent between these modes of play. This is most easily seen by first noting that both a_{cA} and ζ_{cA} are independent of τ. As a consequence, the corresponding cost for the fiscal players is in this cooperative case independent of τ too. Next, substitute $\tau = \frac{1}{2}$ into the 'aggregate' coalition cost function. It is easily verified that this cost function coincides with the cost for the (1,2) coalition, which shows the correctness of the claim for an arbitrarily chosen τ.

Our next results concern the national performance criterion. We show, amongst others, that the CB will prefer a non-cooperative to a cooperative mode of play if the cooperation parameter τ becomes large and that the fiscal players will prefer a partial coalition to a cooperative mode of play. The proof is again deferred to Appendix C. We used the notation sgn(a) here to denote the sign of variable a.

Lemma 4.2 *i)* $\mathrm{sgn}(J^N_{E,nc} - J^N_{E,cN}) = \mathrm{sgn}(a_{nc} - a_{cN})$.
ii) $J_{i,cN} \geqq J_{i,(1,2)}$, $i \in \{1,2\}$.

From the Lemmas 4.1 ii) and 4.2 i) it follows that if, e.g., $3\tau \geqq 2d_N$, always $J^N_{U,cN} \geqq J^N_{U,nc}$. A more detailed analysis shows that if $\tau = 0$, $J^N_{U,cN} < J^N_{U,nc}$, and, therefore, it is easily seen from the proof of 4.1 ii) that there is always a threshold τ^* such that for all $\tau \geqq \tau^*$, $J^N_{U,cN} \geqq J^N_{U,nc}$ and for all $\tau < \tau^*$, $J^N_{U,cN} < J^N_{U,nc}$.

Now, consider the case that $\tau \geqq \tau^*$. Since aggregate performance is minimized in the cooperative situation and according to Lemma 4.1 ii) the CB's cost is higher in this situation than in the non-cooperative mode, the fiscal players' cost will be less in the cooperative mode of play than in the non-cooperative mode. A similar reasoning shows that since $J_{i,cN} \geqq J_{i,(1,2)}$, $i \in \{1,2\}$, the CB's cost in the coalition (1,2) mode of play will always be larger than in the cooperative mode. Stated differently, we see that under this assumption the CB will always prefer the non-cooperative mode of play, whereas the fiscal players prefer the coalition (1,2) mode of play. So, summarizing, we have:

Theorem 4.2 *Assume that the CB considers the national performance criterion. Then, there exists a number* τ^* *such that if* $\tau \geqq \tau^*$*, the cooperative mode of play is non-sustainable.*

4.6 A simulation study

In this section, we consider the differential game on macroeconomic stabilization in the MU that was set up in Section 4.2, using simulations of a stylized example. We analyze five scenarios:

(*i*) a symmetric baseline case in which countries are of equal size, all structural and preference parameters are the same in both countries,

(*ii*) an asymmetric case where the MU countries differ in stabilization preferences,

(*iii*) an asymmetric case where countries differ in monetary policy transmission,

(*iv*) an asymmetric case where countries differ in bargaining powers in case they enter coalitions, and

(*v*) an asymmetric case where countries differ in sensitivity to *intra*-MU competitiveness.

In this way our analysis contributes to the important discussion about the implications for policymaking in an MU in case countries differ in their structural characteristics. Outcomes are analyzed for all the five different equilibria outlined in Section 4.4

4.6.1 Baseline: A symmetric MU

In the symmetric baseline case both countries are of equal size and all structural and preference parameters are the same. The following values for the structural model parameters are used:[6] $\gamma = 0.4$, $\delta = 0.2$, $\rho = 0.4$, $\eta = 1$, $\kappa = 1$, $\lambda = 1$ and $\xi = 0.25$. The initial state of *intra*-MU competitiveness equals $s_0 = 0.05$ (implying an initial disequilibrium of 5 % in competitiveness between the two countries). Concerning the preference weights in the fiscal players' objective functions, the following values have been assumed: $\alpha = 2$, $\beta = 5$, $\chi = 2.5$ and $\theta = 0.15$. In the CB's loss function both countries are equally weighted. Furthermore, the CB -in contrast to the fiscal players- cares more about inflation than about output stabilization and has also an interest rate smoothing objective: $\alpha_{1U} = \alpha_{2U} = 0.8$, $\beta_{1U} = \beta_{2U} = 0.5$, and χ_U equals 2.5. Figure 4.1 displays the adjustment in the case the CB's aggregate objective function (4.8) is used (adjustment in the case where the CB's national objective function (4.9) is almost identical and therefore not displayed here),

[6] See Engwerda *et al.* (2001) for a similar simulation set up. The parameter choices are related to those used in Turnovsky *et al.* (1988) and Neck and Dockner (1995).

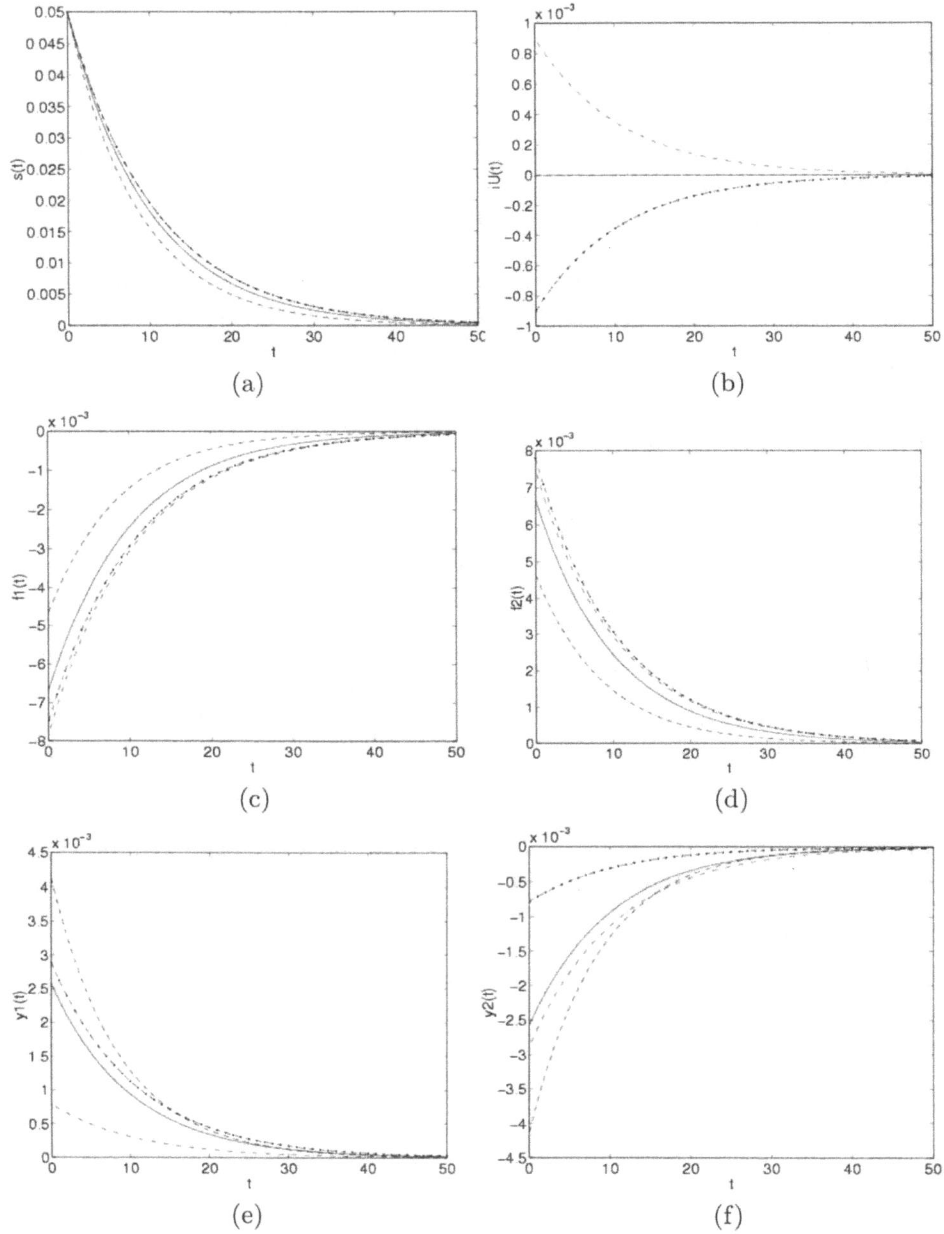

Figure 4.1

Symmetric Baseline. Aggregate Objective Function CB.

—— Nash, - - - - Pareto, ...(1,2), — – —$(1, U)$, — · — $(2, U)$

The adjustment of *intra*-MU competitiveness is given in panel (a). The adjustments of the policy variables are found in panels (b)-(d). The initial disequilibrium in *intra*-MU competitiveness implies that output in country 1 is initially above the long-run equilibrium in country 1 and below the long-run equilibrium in country 2. This induces restrictive fiscal policies in country 1 and expansionary fiscal policies in country 2. The magnitude of this fiscal stabilization, however, varies according to the type of equilibrium. In the MU there is a stabilization externality: the restrictive fiscal policy implemented by country 1 to stabilize its economy, is harmful for country 2 which would benefit from an expansionary fiscal policy in country 1. Coalitions potentially offer a solution to such policy coordination problems. In the Pareto case and the fiscal cooperation case (which coincide in this symmetric case), the fiscal players internalize the externalities from their fiscal instrument on the other country. A similar externality results from the fiscal policy in country 2. The common interest rate, panel (b), only reacts in the case of a coalition with one fiscal policymaker: in that case the common interest rate is partly targeted at the situation in the country with which the CB has formed a coalition. This leads to a higher interest rate in case a coalition is formed with country 1 and a lower interest rate when a coalition is formed with country 2. Panels (e) and (f) display output in country 1 and 2 in the different cases. Table 4.2 gives the resulting welfare losses that the players incur in this example. Aggregate cost refers to the case where the CB has (4.8) as its objective function, national cost to (4.9).

Table 4.2 - Cost functions baseline (multiplied by 1,000)

Aggregate Cost					
	Nash	*Pareto*	(1,2)	$(1,U)$	$(2,U)$
J_1	0.3596	0.3032	0.3032	0.4145	0.6228
J_2	0.3596	0.3032	0.3032	0.6228	0.4145
J_U	0	0	0	0.0088	0.0088
a_{cl}	0.1007	0.1162	0.1162	0.0933	0.0933
National Cost					
	Nash	*Pareto*	(1,2)	$(1,U)$	$(2,U)$
J_1	0.3596	0.3040	0.3032	0.4169	0.6227
J_2	0.3596	0.3040	0.3032	0.6227	0.4169
J_U	0.0189	0.0390	0.0423	0.0188	0.0188
a_{cl}	0.1007	0.1143	0.1162	0.0932	0.0932

In this symmetric case we recognize from Figure 4.1 and Table 4.2 the features that we have analytically derived in Section 4.4. In the case that the CB is using aggregate variables in its objective function, we know that the adjustment speed and losses in the Pareto and fiscal coalition form will coincide. Both equilibria are sustainable in this case, whereas the coalitions $(1,U)$ and $(2,U)$ are non-sustainable. One reason for this last finding is likely to be the fact that the countries and the CB have very different objectives. First, the CB is here oriented towards stabilization of aggregate fluctuations in the MU and, second, it cares more about inflation than output stabilization. The fiscal players on the other hand are only interested in stabilization of their own economy and attach a larger weight to output than to inflation stabilization. The coalitions between a fiscal player and the CB result in a slow adjustment speed, a feature that we will notice also in the other cases. This is also suggestive for the possible inefficient policies that may result when these coalitions are chosen. For the case of the loss function (4.9) of the CB, we know from Lemma 4.2 that the adjustment speed (measured by the size of the a_is) is fastest under fiscal cooperation, which is in addition an internally supported equilibrium in the symmetric case. Note that both the $(1, U)$ and $(2, U)$ coalitions are supported by the CB and that the Pareto coalition is non-sustainable (conform Theorem 4.2).

4.6.2 Asymmetric fiscal policy preferences

An important form of asymmetry that is likely to arise in an MU are different objectives for the fiscal authorities of the participating countries. In this second example, we analyze the consequences of such asymmetries in preferences. To do so, assume that the fiscal authority of the second country has now a higher preference for output stability than country 2: $\beta_1 = 5$ and $\beta_2 = 10$.[7] In that case the adjustments in Figure 4.2 patterns result. We see that optimal policies and adjustment are quite different from the baseline case and also between the two different objective functions of the CB. With a larger desire to reduce output fluctuations, country 2 wants to use its instrument with a larger intensity. However, a larger use increases the instrument costs and implies costs, also for country 1, which prefers a less active stabilization policy of country 2. Table 4.3 indeed indicates that the fiscal players have larger losses in the Nash case compared to the symmetric case. In the fiscal coalition case, country 1 is forced to share in the larger adjustment needs of country 2: it pursues a less active fiscal stabilization policy since its fiscal surpluses also negatively affect country 2. In case the CB participates in a coalition (i.e. in the Pareto, the $(1, U)$ and $(2, U)$) and has aggregate variables in its objective function, it also shares in the increased stabilization problem of country 2 (and the reduced problems of country 1): it sets a low interest rate which helps the stabilization of output in country 2. This, however, at the cost of country 1 for whom this policy is counterproductive. In case national variables are featuring in the objective function of the CB, on the other hand, the CB sets a restrictive interest policy, this reduces inflation in country 2 but also the amount of output stabilization in that country.

[7] In Engwerda *et al.* (1999) and Engwerda *et al.* (2001), we extensively experimented with variations of the fiscal players' χ-parameter, which measures the preference for deficit smoothing.

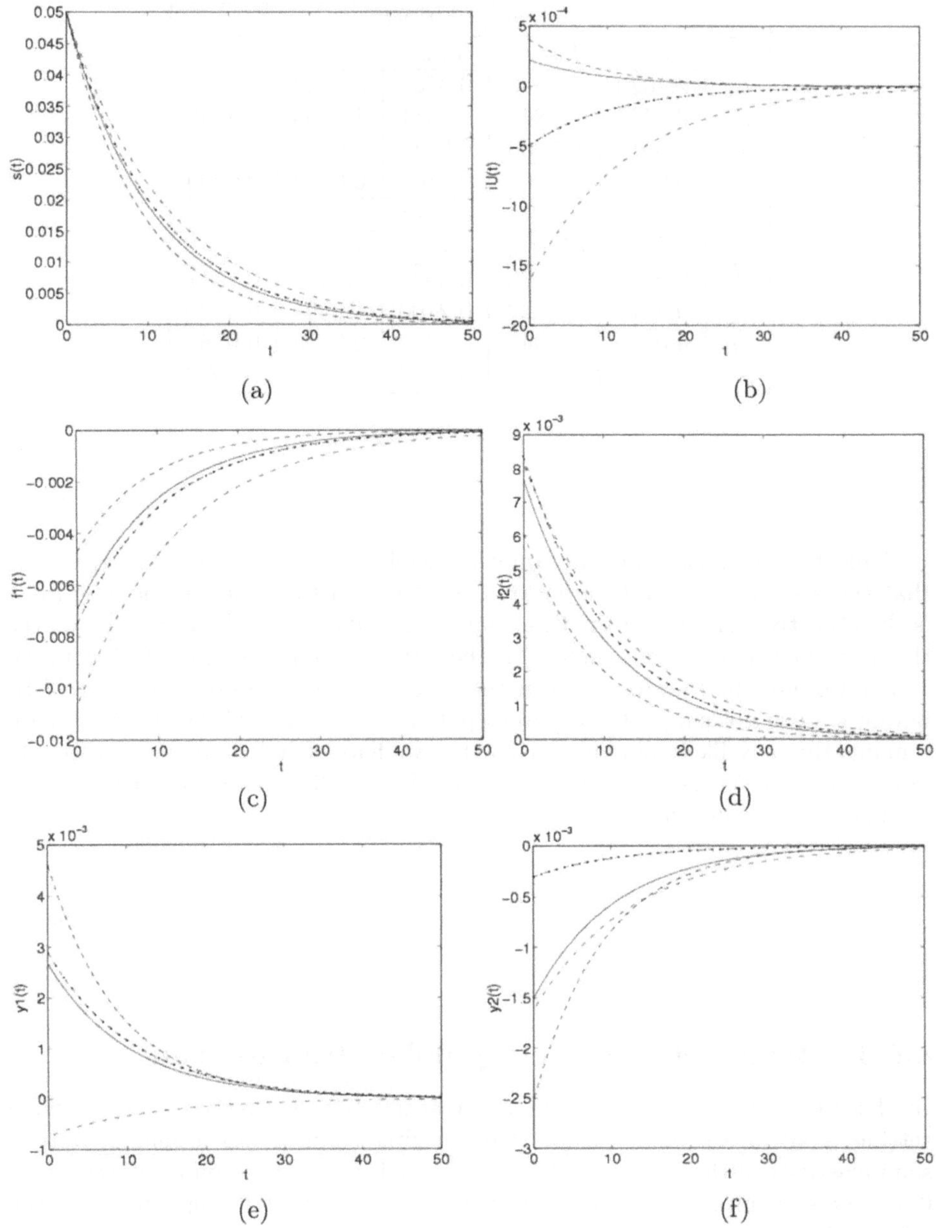

Figure 4.2

Asymmetric policy preferences, $\beta_1 = 5, \beta_2 = 10$. Aggregate Objective Function CB.

—— Nash, - - - - Pareto, ...(1,2), — – —$(1,U)$, — · — $(2,U)$

Table 4.3 - Cost functions asymmetric fiscal policy preferences

	Aggregate Cost				
	Nash	*Pareto*	(1,2)	$(1, U)$	$(2, U)$
J_1	0.4070	0.3842	0.3707	0.9028	1.2859
J_2	0.4432	0.3343	0.3511	1.5460	0.4848
J_U	0.0013	0.0033	0.0038	0.0257	0.0070
a_{cl}	0.0958	0.1107	0.1105	0.0794	0.0909
	National Cost				
	Nash	*Pareto*	(1,2)	$(1, U)$	$(2, U)$
J_1	0.4628	0.3973	0.3981	0.4645	0.7511
J_2	0.4175	0.2127	0.2100	1.2597	0.4169
J_U	0.0089	0.0346	0.0399	0.0115	0.0188
a_{cl}	0.0906	0.1084	0.1100	0.0884	0.0932

Unfortunately, coalitions are unlikely to offer a solution here. The reason is that there are no internally supported coalitions in this case: in the case (4.8) is the objective function of the CB, country 2 would prefer the Pareto case over the fiscal coalition and in case (4.9) is the objective function of the CB, country 1 would prefer the Pareto case over the fiscal coalition. In both cases, the CB, however, does not support the Pareto policy design. Therefore, the Nash case remains the only likely outcome given that we had excluded any side-payments in the coalition formation problem or any other binding arrangement to sustain policymakers' coalitions.

4.6.3 Asymmetric monetary policy transmission

In this example asymmetric monetary transmission is analyzed: the baseline setting is again assumed, except that the first country has a smaller output semi-elasticity of the real interest rate ($\gamma_1 = 0.4$) than the second country ($\gamma_2 = 0.8$). This example is useful to illustrate the important discussion about the effects of a common monetary policy in a situation where countries differ in the transmission of monetary policy. Figure 4.3 displays the resulting adjustments. Since adjustment with MU aggregate and national variables in the CB loss function is rather similar, we depict only the first case here,

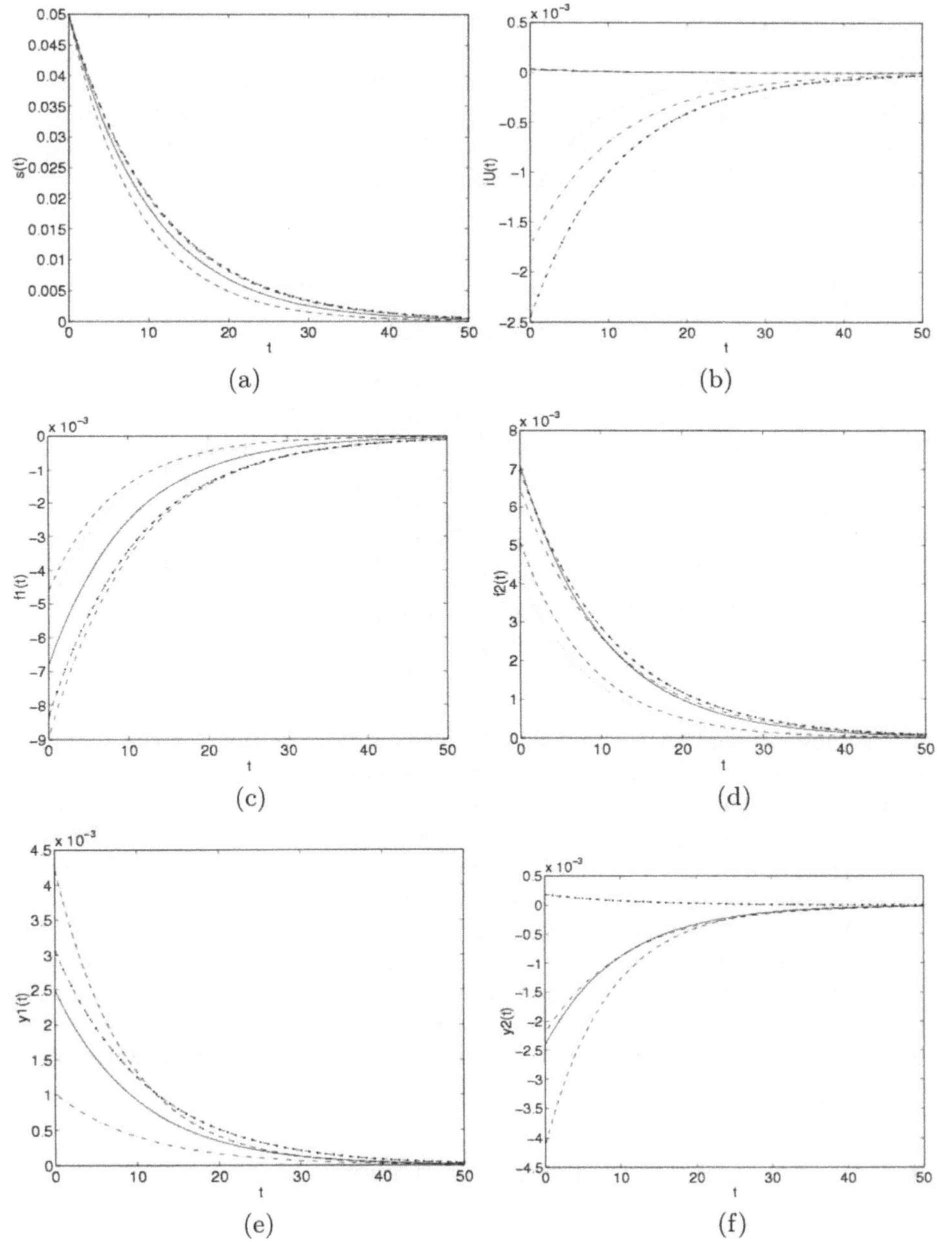

Figure 4.3

Asymmetric monetary transmission $\gamma_1 = 0.4, \gamma_2 = 0.8$. Aggregate Objective Function CB.

—— Nash, - - - - Pareto, ...(1,2), — – —(1, U), — · — (2, U)

In this asymmetric setting, the adjustment and policy strategies are not symmetric in both countries, although the deviations from the symmetric baseline case are not as large as in the previous example. The CB now reacts in all strategic settings as its objective functions imply that its optimal strategy is sensitive to any asymmetry. Because the economy of country 2 is more sensitive to the common monetary policy, the monetary policy of the CB is more directed to stabilization in country 2, in particular when the CB enters into a coalition with country 2. Table 4.4 shows the losses in this case.

Table 4.4 - Costs with asymmetric monetary policy transmission

	Aggregate Cost				
	Nash	*Pareto*	(1,2)	$(1, U)$	$(2, U)$
J_1	0.3697	0.3437	0.3065	0.5596	0.7890
J_2	0.3919	0.2596	0.3221	0.4537	0.3405
J_U	0	0.0091	0	0.0217	0.0502
a_{cl}	0.0994	0.1155	0.1165	0.0910	0.0894
	National Cost				
	Nash	*Pareto*	(1,2)	$(1, U)$	$(2, U)$
J_1	0.3759	0.3483	0.3140	0.5608	0.7890
J_2	0.3812	0.2557	0.3084	0.4527	0.3405
J_U	0.0174	0.0430	0.0430	0.0301	0.0569
a_{cl}	0.0994	0.1135	0.1165	0.0909	0.0894

We observe that there is no sustainable coalition, neither for the aggregate variables' case nor for the national variables' case. Without side-payments or other institutional arrangements that would make a coalition binding, we would find the Nash case to be the likely outcome. We further observe that for both welfare loss functions the Pareto coalition form is supported by player 2, whereas player 1 supports the governments' coalition form. Furthermore, we see that both other partial equilibrium forms are non-sustainable. Note that the fiscal coalition is now only second best for country 2. Because of its stronger exposure now to the monetary policy of the CB, country 2 would definitely prefer the CB to be included into policy cooperation. However, the CB is not benefiting from full cooperation; it incurs a relatively large cost by joining this coalition form (in the aggregate case).

4.6.4 Asymmetric bargaining powers

In cases with policy coordination, players' bargaining strengths become important, since these will determine too how collective decision making will be influenced by the players' objectives in the coalition. This will, therefore, have important consequences for macroeconomic policy formulation and adjustment in the MU. This example, therefore, analyzes the effects of different bargaining powers under cooperative policymaking in the MU.

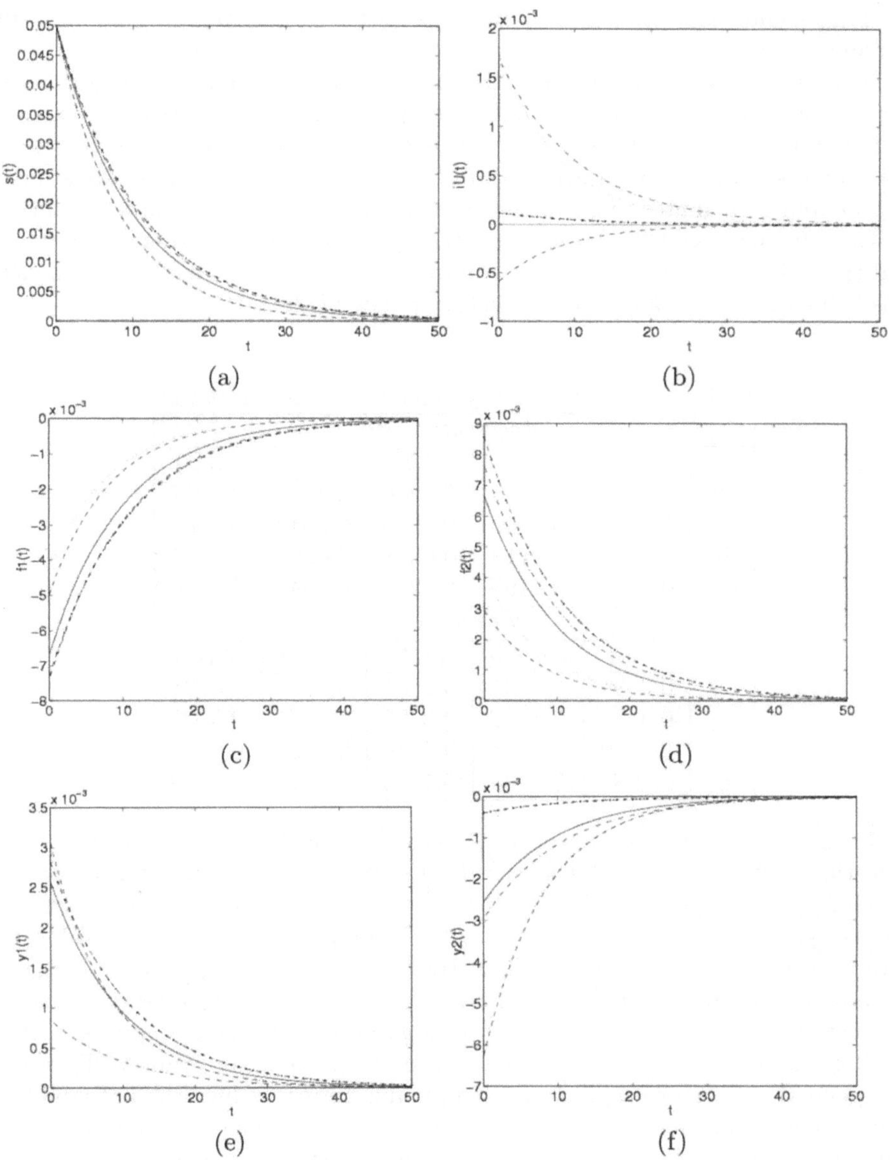

Figure 4.4
Asymmetric bargaining weights. Aggregate Objective Function CB.
—— Nash, - - - - Pareto, ...(1,2), — - —(1, U), — · — (2, U)

We assume the following scheme of bargaining powers: $\tau^c = \{3/6, 1/6, 2/6\}$, $\tau^{(1,2)} = \{3/4, 1/4\}$, $\tau^{(1,U)} = \{3/5, 2/5\}$, $\tau^{(2,U)} = \{1/3, 2/3\}$, implying that in a coalition country 1 has three times as many votes as country 2 and 1,5 as many votes as the CB, whereas the CB has two times as many votes as country

2. This asymmetric bargaining power case leads to the following adjustment dynamics as shown in Figure 4.4.

The Nash case is not affected by the different bargaining strengths as it implies entirely non-cooperative policy design. In the other cases, the balance of power is turning against country 2 in particular when it enters the fiscal coalition and a coalition with the CB. In those cases, it faces a larger adjustment burden and contributes more to the stabilization burden of the other coalition partner. In the case it acts non-cooperatively against the coalition of country 1 and the CB, the adverse effects for country 2 are much less. In the Pareto case it is helped by an expansionary monetary policy of the CB.

Table 4.5 - Cost with asymmetric bargaining powers

	Aggregate Cost				
	Nash	*Pareto*	(1,2)	$(1,U)$	$(2,U)$
J_1	0.3596	0.1866	0.2266	0.3724	0.6067
J_2	0.3596	0.4759	0.4546	0.6543	0.5062
J_U	0	0.0213	0.0078	0.0222	0.0047
a_{cl}	0.1007	0.1199	0.1215	0.0940	0.0910
	National Cost				
	Nash	*Pareto*	(1,2)	$(1,U)$	$(2,U)$
J_1	0.3596	0.2534	0.2555	0.4663	0.6228
J_2	0.3596	0.3672	0.3755	0.6076	0.5900
J_U	0.0189	0.0416	0.0486	0.0134	0.0151
a_{cl}	0.1007	0.1135	0.1183	0.0921	0.0888

In this case player 1 supports the Pareto coalition form, since it is very powerful there. Furthermore, all coalition forms are non-sustainable. Since none of the coalitions is supported by more than one player, the Nash outcome might be the ultimate outcome in this case. Therefore, comparing the results of Table 4.5 with that of Table 4.2, we observe that the introduction of asymmetric bargaining powers crucially changes the results of the game. The asymmetry increases the cost of the country with the smaller bargaining power as its importance in a coalition is reduced, while it decreases the costs of the other country. To put it in a general way: more asymmetric bargaining powers reduce the probabilities of coalitions -and therefore of policy cooperation- as policies will be biased towards the needs of the stronger player(s), and the smaller players are less likely to stay in such 'asymmetric' coalitions. This last result differs from that found in Hughes Hallett and Ma (1996) in analyzing the full coordination problem.

4.6.5 Asymmetric degree of competitiveness

Next, we assume that the first country's output elasticity of competitiveness is lower ($\delta_1 = 0.2$) than that of the second country ($\delta_2 = 0.4$). Such an asymmetry in the sensitiveness to competitive pressures has quite a dramatic impact as a comparison of Figures 4.1 and 4.5 shows.

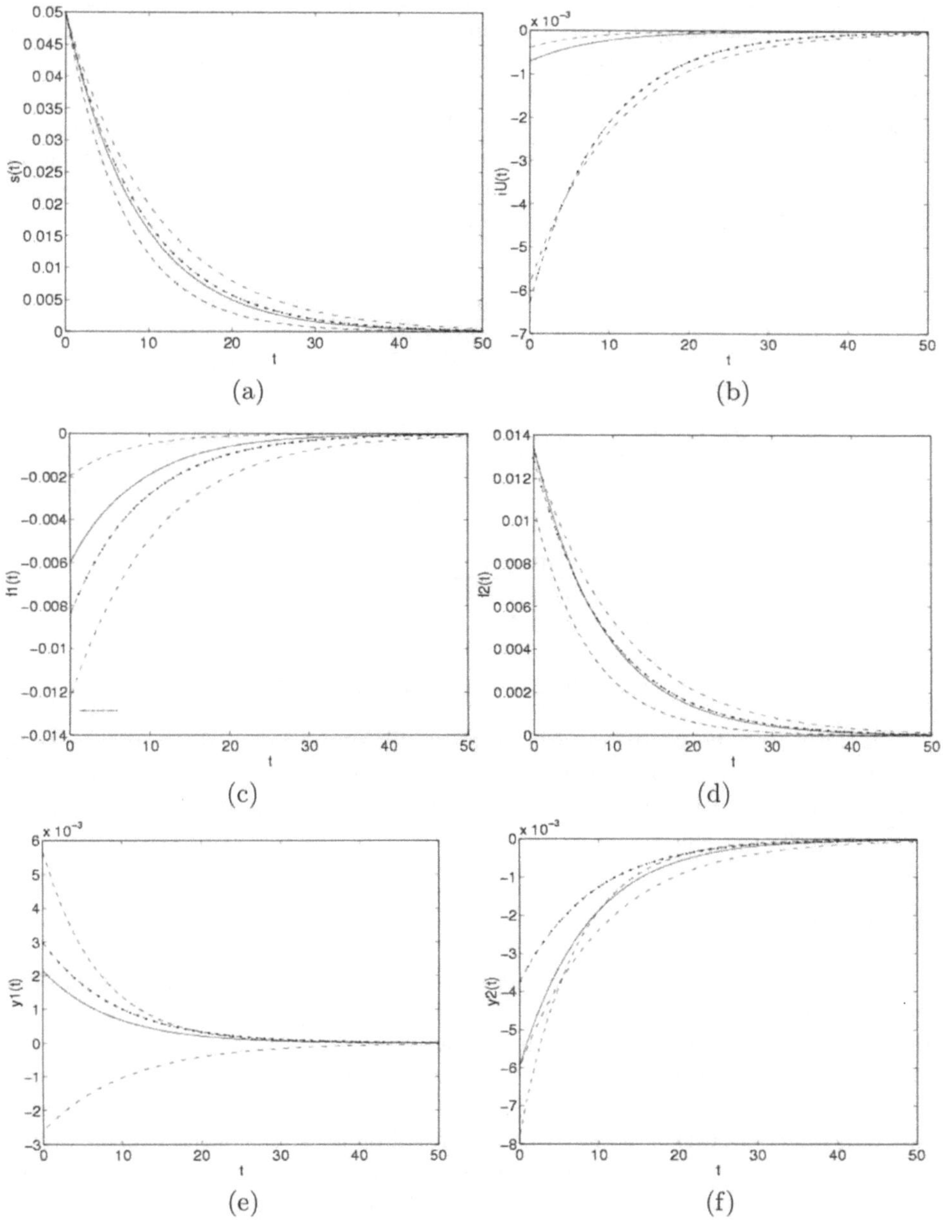

Figure 4.5
Asymmetric sensitivity to *intra*-MU competitiveness. Aggregate Objective Function CB.

—— Nash, - - - - Pareto, ...(1,2), — - —(1, U), — · — (2, U)

In this case there are no marked differences between the cases where the CB's objectives are governed by aggregate variables and where it is governed by national variables and, therefore, only the first case is displayed. Country 2 is now in a more disadvantaged position than in the baseline case: its higher sensitivity to the *intra*-MU competitiveness variable imply that it faces a deeper recession and a higher fiscal stabilization burden. The reduction of interest rates by the CB that occurs in all cases is helpful to stabilize prices and output in country 2 but inadequate from the perspective of country 1. Table 4.6 gives the losses that the players incur in this case.

Table 4.6 - Costs with asymmetric competitiveness

Aggregate Cost					
	Nash	*Pareto*	(1,2)	$(1,U)$	$(2,U)$
J_1	0.2449	0.3479	0.3050	1.1165	0.6461
J_2	1.3824	0.9283	1.0375	2.1857	1.1306
J_U	0.0117	0.0359	0.0029	0.2877	0.2253
a_{cl}	0.1153	0.1412	0.1420	0.0919	0.1085
National Cost					
	Nash	*Pareto*	(1,2)	$(1,U)$	$(2,U)$
J_1	0.2449	0.3347	0.3050	1.0995	1.2418
J_2	1.3824	0.9437	1.0375	2.1835	1.1381
J_U	0.0524	0.1202	0.0944	0.2898	0.2509
a_{cl}	0.1153	0.1382	0.1420	0.0921	0.1083

In both cases no coalition form is internally supported and its emergence is therefore hard to sustain without any form of other binding element. Coalitions $(1,U)$ and $(2,U)$ are non-sustainable, while in the aggregate case the coalition (1,2) is externally supported by the CB.

Conclusion

Macroeconomic policy cooperation is a crucial issue in a highly integrated economic and political union such as the EU. To study the effects of policy coordination in a two-country MU model, we compared the optimal policies and the effects of five alternative policy regimes under a stylized model: (i) non-cooperative monetary and fiscal policies, (ii) three partial cooperative schemes and (iii) full cooperation of monetary and fiscal policies. In contrast to the previous chapter, we explicitly incorporated into our analysis a strategically behaving CB and we studied asymmetric cases, in which countries differ in parameters and policy preferences.

Using numerical examples, we illustrated the sometimes complex effects that are produced by the various coalitions. We found that the sustainability of a certain type of coalition and its implications for the optimal strategies and the resulting macroeconomic adjustment, is highly sensitive to initial settings of preferences and the structural model parameters. Cooperation is often efficient for the fiscal players and, moreover, we saw that the fiscal players' cooperation (against the CB) often leads to a Pareto improvement for them, provided that they are not very asymmetric in preferences, structural characteristics and bargaining strength. The non-cooperative Nash equilibrium is most likely to be the outcome when countries are more asymmetric. In most simulations, full cooperation does not induce a Pareto improvement for the CB, while the governments' coalitions imply a considerable loss for the CB compared to the non-cooperative and full cooperative cases. That implies that the Pareto form is often non-sustainable. This was also shown theoretically for the symmetric case. Cases where the CB cooperates with one government against the other, generally produce suboptimal monetary and fiscal stabilization policies and are unlikely to be feasible in practice.

Considering current European discussions, it is found that the ECB has a rationale to pursue an institutional design that does not enforce cooperation, so that a high degree of independence is left to the monetary authority. Therefore, the ECB will try to promote fixed rules for European policy targets. On the other hand, governments may pursue a design based on fiscal cooperation, which leave them independent in interacting their policies with the monetary policy of the ECB.

The remaining limitations are: (i) the number of countries modelled is too small to analyze all interesting shocks' configurations; and (ii) we neglected interactions of members of an MU with outside countries.

Appendix A

1. The non-cooperative case

Let $x(t) := s(t)$, $u_1(t) := f_1(t)$, $u_2(t) := f_2(t)$ and $u_3(t) := i_E(t)$. Then, with $A := \phi_4$, $B_1 := -\phi_1$, $B_2 := \phi_2$ and $B_3 := \phi_3$ the system is described by

$$\dot{x}(t) = Ax(t) + B_1u_1(t) + B_2u_2(t) + B_3u_3(t); x(0) = s_0,$$

and the performance criterion of player i can be rewritten, with

$v^T(t) = [x(t), u_1(t), u_2(t), u_3(t)]^T$, as $\int_0^\infty v^T(t)M_iv(t)dt$, $i \in \{1, 2, U = 3\}$.

Next, factorize the above mentioned matrices M_i. That is,

$$M_i =: \begin{bmatrix} Q_i & P_i & L_i & W_i \\ P_i^T & R_{1i} & N_i & T_i \\ L_i^T & N_i^T & R_{2i} & V_i \\ W_i^T & T_i^T & V_i^T & R_{3i} \end{bmatrix},$$

where all entries are scalars. Following Algorithm 2.2, the non-cooperative Nash solution is then found as follows.

Step 1: Calculate the eigenstructure of the matrices

$$\begin{aligned} H_1 &:= \begin{bmatrix} A - B_1R_{11}^{-1}P_1^T & -B_1R_{11}^{-1}B_1^T \\ -Q_1 + P_1R_{11}^{-1}P_1^T & -(A - B_1R_{11}^{-1}P_1^T) \end{bmatrix}, \\ H_2 &:= \begin{bmatrix} A - B_2R_{22}^{-1}L_2^T & -B_2R_{22}^{-1}B_2^T \\ -Q_2 + L_2R_{22}^{-1}L_2^T & -(A - B_2R_{22}^{-1}L_2^T) \end{bmatrix}, \text{ and} \\ H_3 &:= \begin{bmatrix} A - B_3R_{33}^{-1}W_3^T & -B_3R_{33}^{-1}B_3^T \\ -Q_3 + W_3R_{33}^{-1}W_3^T & -(A - B_3R_{33}^{-1}W_3^T) \end{bmatrix}. \end{aligned}$$

Simple calculations show that all these matrices have a stable invariant graph subspace. So the AREs (2.21) in Chapter 2 have a stabilizing solution (one could also use e.g. Proposition 5.15 in Engwerda (2005a) to conclude this).

Step 2: Calculate $G := \begin{bmatrix} R_{11} & N_1 & T_1 \\ N_2^T & R_{22} & V_2 \\ T_3^T & V_3^T & R_{33} \end{bmatrix}$

and $M := \begin{bmatrix} A & 0 & 0 & 0 \\ -Q_1 & -A^T & 0 & 0 \\ -Q_2 & 0 & -A^T & 0 \\ -Q_3 & 0 & 0 & -A^T \end{bmatrix} + \begin{bmatrix} -B \\ Z_1 \\ Z_2 \\ Z_3 \end{bmatrix} G^{-1} \begin{bmatrix} P_1^T & B_1^T & 0 & 0 \\ L_2^T & 0 & B_2^T & 0 \\ W_3^T & 0 & 0 & B_3^T \end{bmatrix}.$

Here $B := [B_1\ B_2\ B_3]$ and $Z_i := [P_i\ L_i\ W_i]$, $i \in \{1, 2, 3\}$.

Step 3: Next, calculate the eigenstructure of M Assume M has one negative and three nonnegative eigenvalues. Then we proceed by calculating an eigenvector, w, associated with this negative eigenvalue, $-a_{nc}$ of M. With $w := [w_0\ w_1\ w_2\ w_3]^T$, provided $w_0 \neq 0$, the equilibrium strategies are $\begin{bmatrix} u_1(t) \\ u_2(t) \\ u_3(t) \end{bmatrix} := -G^{-1} \begin{bmatrix} P_1^T + B_1^T K_1 \\ L_2^T + B_2^T K_2 \\ W_3^T + B_3^T K_3 \end{bmatrix} x(t)$, where $K_i := \frac{w_i}{w_0}$. Using these equilibrium strategies the resulting system is described by $\dot{x}(t) = -a_{nc}x(t),\ x(0) = s_0$.

Step 4: Finally, from (2.24), it follows that the involved costs for the players are (4.17).

2. The cooperative case

To determine the cooperative strategies for this model we consider: $J^C := \tau_1 J_1 + \tau_2 J_2 + \tau_3 J_E$ with $\tau_1 + \tau_2 + \tau_3 = 1$. Introducing $\mu_1 := d_1\tau_1$, $\mu_2 := d_2\tau_2$ and $\mu_3^i := d_E^i\tau_3$, then $J_C^i = \int_0^\infty \{v^T(t)M_C^i v(t)\}dt$, where $M_C^i := \mu_1 M_1 + \mu_2 M_2 + \mu_3^i M_U^i$, $i \in \{A, N\}$.
With the notation of Appendix A.1 the unique equilibrium strategies are then obtained as follows (see Section (2.4)):

Step 1: Factorize matrix M_C^i as $\begin{bmatrix} Q & P \\ P^T & R \end{bmatrix}$, where Q is a scalar; S a 1×3 matrix and R a 3×3 matrix.

Step 2: Calculate the Hamiltonian matrix $H := \begin{bmatrix} (A - BR^{-1}P^T) & -BR^{-1}B^T \\ -Q + PR^{-1}P^T & -(A - BR^{-1}P^T)^T \end{bmatrix}$.

Step 3: Determine the negative eigenvalue $a_c$of H andi ts corresponding eigenvector $v =: [v_0\ v_1]^T$. Calculate $K := \frac{v_1}{v_0}$.

Then the unique equilibrium strategies are $\begin{bmatrix} f_1(t) \\ f_2(t) \\ i_U(t) \end{bmatrix} := -R^{-1}(P^T + B^T K)s(t) =: H_c s(t)$, and the resulting system satisfies $\dot{s}(t) = -a_c s(t),\ s(0) = s_0$.

3. Partial coalitions

We will elaborate the $(1, U)$ coalition. The results for the other cases are obtained similarly by considering the permutation matrix obtained from the appropriate redefined state $v(t)$.
First note that the inverse of the permutation matrix $P_{(1,U)}$is $P_{(1,U)}^T$ so that $v(t) = P_{(1,U)}^T \tilde{v}(t)$. Then, with $M_i^{(1,U)} := P_{(1,U)} M_i P_{(1,U)}^T$, $i \in \{1, 2, U\}$ we find $M_{(1,U),c} := \tau_1 d_1 M_1^{(1,U)} + \tau_2 M_U^{(1,U)}$, so that $J_{(1,U)} = \int_0^\infty \{\tilde{v}^T(t) M_{(1,U),c} \tilde{v}(t)\}dt$.

Next, introduce $B_1 := [-\phi_1\ \phi_3]$; $B_2 := \phi_2$ and $B := [B_1\ B_2]$.
Then, apply Step 1 and 2 described in the above Appendix A.1 for the two-player case to find a corresponding matrix M.
Determine the negative eigenvalue of M. If $a_{(1,U)}$is the negative eigenvalue of this matrix and $w =: [w_0\ w_1\ w_2]$ a corresponding eigenvector, then (generically) an equilibrium strategy is $\begin{bmatrix} f_1(t) \\ i_U(t) \\ f_2(t) \end{bmatrix} := -G^{-1} \begin{bmatrix} P_1^T + B_1^T K_1 \\ L_2^T + B_2^T K_2 \end{bmatrix} s(t) =: H_{(1,U)} s(t)$, where $K_i := \frac{w_i}{w_0}$. The resulting system is then $\dot{s}(t) = -a_{(1,U)} s(t), s(0) = s_0$.

Appendix B

The non-cooperative case

Note that for the determination of the optimal strategies the scaling parameters in the performance criteria are irrelevant in this case. Therefore, we assume $d_i = 1$. First, we consider the national performance criterion J_U^N.
To determine the equilibrium strategies, we have to calculate the eigenvalues and eigenvectors of the corresponding matrix M (see Appendix A.1). By substitution of the various parameters (with $g_U := g_U^N$) we obtain

$$G := \begin{bmatrix} a^2+g & ae & -ac \\ ae & a^2+g & -ac \\ -c(a+e) & -c(a+e) & 2c^2+g_U \end{bmatrix}.$$

Elementary calculations show that the determinant of G, det, equals $u_{1nc}u_{nc}$, where $u_{1nc} := a^2 g_U + aeg_U + gg_U + 2gc^2$. Moreover, $det * G^{-1}$ equals:

$$\begin{bmatrix} g(2c^2+g_U)+a(ag_U+c^2(a-e)) & a(c^2(a-e)-eg_U) & acu_{nc} \\ a(c^2(a-e)-eg_U) & g(2c^2+g_U)+a(ag_U+c^2(a-e)) & acu_{nc} \\ c(a+e)u_{nc} & c(a+e)u_{nc} & u_{nc}(a^2+ae+g) \end{bmatrix}.$$

Consequently, matrix M satisfies

$$det{*}M = -\begin{bmatrix} -\phi_4 det - 2ab\phi_1 u_{1nc} & \phi_1^2 u_{1nc} & \phi_1^2 u_{1nc} & 0 \\ b^2 g u_{1nc} & \phi_4 det + b\phi_1 u_{2nc} & b\phi_1 g u_{3nc} & 0 \\ b^2 g u_{1nc} & b\phi_1 g u_{3nc} & \phi_4 det + b\phi_1 u_{2nc} & 0 \\ 2b^2 g u_{1nc} & b\phi_1(a-e)u_{1nc} & b\phi_1(a-e)u_{1nc} & \phi_4 det \end{bmatrix},$$

where we used the shorthand notations $u_{2nc} := a^3 g_U + ac^2 g + agg_U - e^2 ag_U - c^2 ge$ and $u_{3nc} := -c^2 e - g_U e + ac^2$. Note that $u_{2nc} + gu_{3nc} = (a-e)u_{1nc}$, a relationship which is useful in elaborating details. The structure of matrix $det * M$ is:

$$M1 = -\begin{bmatrix} \tilde{a} & \tilde{c} & \tilde{c} & 0 \\ \tilde{b} & \tilde{d} & \tilde{e} & 0 \\ \tilde{b} & \tilde{e} & \tilde{d} & 0 \\ 2\tilde{b} & \tilde{f} & \tilde{f} & \tilde{g} \end{bmatrix}$$

The eigenvalues of $M1$ are $-\tilde{g}$, $-\tilde{d}+\tilde{e}$, $-\frac{1}{2}(\tilde{a}+\tilde{d}+\tilde{e})+\frac{1}{2}\sqrt{(\tilde{a}-\tilde{d}-\tilde{e})^2+8\tilde{b}\tilde{c}}$ and $-\frac{1}{2}(\tilde{a}+\tilde{d}+\tilde{e})+-\frac{1}{2}\sqrt{(\tilde{a}-\tilde{d}-\tilde{e})^2+8\tilde{b}\tilde{c}}$. Note that $-\tilde{g}>0$. Given the parametric restrictions, it is easily verified that if $r:=\frac{\rho_1}{k_1}<1$ (which implies that $0<e<a$) $-(\tilde{a}+\tilde{d}+\tilde{e})$ is positive and

$$\lambda := -\frac{1}{2}(\tilde{a}+\tilde{d}+\tilde{e})-\frac{1}{2}\sqrt{(\tilde{a}-\tilde{d}-\tilde{e})^2+8\tilde{b}\tilde{c}}<0.$$

Furthermore it follows after some tedious calculations that under this condition also $-\tilde{d}+\tilde{e}>0$. So, under this assumption there is a unique equilibrium. The with λ corresponding eigenvector is: $\begin{bmatrix} -(\tilde{e}+\tilde{d}-\lambda)/\tilde{b} \\ 1 \\ 1 \\ -2(\tilde{f}-\tilde{d}-\tilde{e}+\lambda)/(\tilde{g}-\lambda) \end{bmatrix}$.

Substitution of the corresponding parameters from M shows that

$$\begin{aligned} \lambda \quad &: \quad = \frac{1}{2}b\phi_1(a+e)u_{1nc}-\frac{1}{2}\sqrt{(-2\phi_4 det - b\phi_1(3a-e)u_{1nc})^2+8gb^2\phi_1^2u_{1nc}^2} \\ &= \quad -\frac{1}{2}u_{1nc}\{-b\phi_1(a+e)+\sqrt{(-2\phi_4u_{nc}-b\phi_1(3a-e))^2+8gb^2\phi_1^2}\}. \end{aligned}$$

Consequently, the eigenvalue of M we are looking for is $\frac{\lambda}{det}$ and $K:=K_1=K_2=$

$$\frac{2b^2g}{-2\phi_4u_{nc}-b\phi_1(3a-e)+\sqrt{(-2\phi_4u_{nc}-b\phi_1(3a-e))^2+8gb^2\phi_1^2}}.$$

Using this, the rest of the claims follow straightforwardly.
Next, consider the aggregate performance criterion J_U^A.
Substitution of the various parameters into Appendix A.1 shows that, except for the entries (4,1), (4,2) and (4,3) which are now zero, matrix M in step ii) of the algorithm coincides with the matrix M we determined above for the national performance case. Therefore, it is easily verified that the equilibrium strategies coincide. As a consequence, the resulting systems coincide too.

The cooperative case

First, we again consider the national performance case. Let $d_N:=\tau+(1-2\tau)\frac{d_U^N}{d}$. After substitution of the parameters we see that matrix $M_{C,N}$ (see Appendix A.2) is given by:

$$M_C^N = d\begin{bmatrix} 2d_Nb^2 & d_Nb(a-e) & -d_Nb(a-e) & 0 \\ d_Nb(a-e) & d_N(a^2+e^2)+\tau g & 2d_Nae & -d_Nc(a+e) \\ -d_Nb(a-e) & 2d_Nae & d_N(a^2+e^2)+\tau g & -d_Nc(a+e) \\ 0 & -d_Nc(a+e) & -d_Nc(a+e) & 2d_Nc^2+(d_N-\tau)g_E \end{bmatrix}$$

So, with $A := \phi_4$, $B := \phi_1[-1\ 1\ 0]$, $Q := 2d_N b^2$, $S := d_N b(a-e)[1\ -1\ 0]$ and

$$R := \begin{bmatrix} d_N(a^2+e^2)+\tau g & 2d_N ae & -d_N c(a+e) \\ 2d_N ae & d_N(a^2+e^2)+\tau g & -d_N c(a+e) \\ -d_N c(a+e) & -d_N c(a+e) & 2d_N c^2 + (d_N-\tau)g_U \end{bmatrix},$$

we can calculate the Hamiltonian of the system H. Since all entries of this matrix are scalar, it is easily verified that the negative eigenvalue equals $a_{cN} := -\sqrt{(A-BR^{-1}S^T)^2 + BR^{-1}B^T(Q-SR^{-1}S^T)}$ and its corresponding eigenvector $\begin{bmatrix} BR^{-1}B^T \\ (A-BR^{-1}S^T+a_{cN}) \end{bmatrix}$. From this, K_{cN} immediately results. Apart from the determination of the inverse of R things can be calculated straightforwardly now. Therefore, we conclude this part of the subsection with the exposition of matrix R^{-1} (from which the verification of correctness is left to the reader). Introducing $u_{1cN} := (d_N-\tau)(\tau g g_U + (a+e)^2 d_N g_U) + 2\tau g d_N c^2$, $u_{2cN} := d_N(d_N c^2(a-e)^2 - 2aeg_U(d_N-\tau))$ and the determinant of R, $det := u_{1cN}u_{cN}$, we have

$$det * R^{-1} = \begin{bmatrix} u_{1cN}+u_{2cN} & u_{2cN} & (a+e)cd_N u_{cN} \\ u_{2cN} & u_{1cN}+u_{2cN} & (a+e)cd_N u_{cN} \\ (a+e)cd_N u_{cN} & (a+e)cd_N u_{cN} & (d_N(a+e)^2+\tau g)u_{cN} \end{bmatrix},$$

Next, we consider the aggregate performance case. Let $d_A := (1-2\tau)\frac{d_E^A}{d}$. After substitution of the parameters we see that matrix M_C^A (see Appendix A.2) is given by:

$$\begin{bmatrix} 2\tau b^2 & \tau b(a-e) & -\tau b(a-e) & 0 \\ \tau b(a-e) & \tau(a^2+e^2+g)+d_A(a+e)^2 & 2\tau ae + d_A(a+e)^2 & -c(a+e)(\tau+2d_A) \\ -\tau b(a-e) & 2\tau ae+d_A(a+e)^2 & \tau(a^2+e^2+g)+d_A(a+e)^2 & -c(a+e)(\tau+2d_A) \\ 0 & -c(a+e)(\tau+2d_A) & -c(a+e)(\tau+2d_A) & 2\tau c^2 + d_A(4c^2+2g_E^A) \end{bmatrix}$$

From this, the matrices Q, S and R result in a similar way as in the national case. Introducing $u_{1cA} := \tau(\tau+2d_A)gc^2 + d_A g_U^A(\tau g + (\tau+2d_A)(a+e)^2)$; $u_{2cA} := \tau c^2(\tau+2d_A)(a-e)^2 - 2d_A g_U^A(2\tau ae + d_A(a+e)^2)$ and $u_{cA} := \tau(g+(a-e)^2)$ the determinant of R, det, is $2u_{1cA}u_{cA}$ and

$$det*R^{-1} = \begin{bmatrix} u_{2cA}+2u_{1cA} & u_{2cA} & (\tau+2d_A)(a+e)cu_{cA} \\ u_{2cA} & u_{2cA}+2u_{1cA} & (\tau+2d_A)(a+e)cu_{cA} \\ (\tau+2d_A)(a+e)cu_{cA} & (\tau+2d_A)(a+e)cu_{cA} & (\tau g+(a+e)^2(\tau+2d_A))u_{cA} \end{bmatrix}.$$

From this, it is easily verified (using the fact that $\phi_1 = -\frac{\phi_4(a-e)}{2b}$) that the Hamiltonian H equals $\frac{-1}{g+(a-e)^2}\begin{bmatrix} -\phi_4 g & \frac{\frac{1}{2}\phi_4^2(a-e)^2}{\tau b^2} \\ 2\tau b^2 g & \phi_4 g \end{bmatrix}$. Analogous to the national case it follows from this straightforwardly that the negative eigenvalue a_{cA} is $\frac{-\phi_4\sqrt{g}}{\sqrt{g+(a-e)^2}}$ and $K_{cA} = \tau\frac{\phi_4 g + a_{cA}((a-e)^2+g)}{2\phi_1^2}$.

The coalition form (1,2)

First, we consider again the national case. After substitution of the parameters we see that matrix $M_{(1,2)}$ (see Appendix A.3) is given by:

$$M_{(1,2),c} = \frac{1}{2}\begin{bmatrix} 2b^2 & b(a-e) & -b(a-e) & 0 \\ b(a-e) & a^2+e^2+g & 2ae & -c(a+e) \\ -b(a-e) & 2ae & a^2+e^2+g & -c(a+e) \\ 0 & -c(a+e) & -c(a+e) & 2c^2 \end{bmatrix}.$$

Consequently,

$$G := \frac{1}{2}\begin{bmatrix} a^2+e^2+g & 2ae & -c(a+e) \\ 2ae & a^2+e^2+g & -c(a+e) \\ -2c(a+e) & -2c(a+e) & 4c^2+2g_U^N \end{bmatrix}. \quad (4.21)$$

Using the notation $u_{1,(1,2)} := (a+e)^2 g_U + g(2c^2+g_U)$ and $u_{2,(1,2)} := c^2(a-e)^2 - 2aeg_U^N$, elementary calculations show that the determinant of G, det, equals $\frac{1}{4}u_{1,(1,2)}u_{(1,2)}$. Moreover, $det * G^{-1}$ equals:

$$\frac{1}{2}\begin{bmatrix} u_{1,(1,2)}+2u_{2,(1,2)} & 2u_{2,(1,2)} & \frac{1}{2}u_{(1,2)}c(a+e) \\ 2u_{2,(1,2)} & u_{1,(1,2)}+2u_{2,(1,2)} & \frac{1}{2}u_{(1,2)}c(a+e) \\ u_{(1,2)}c(a+e) & u_{(1,2)}c(a+e) & u_{(1,2)}(g+(a+e)^2) \end{bmatrix}.$$

Consequently,

$$det{*}M = -\begin{bmatrix} -\phi_4 det - \frac{1}{2}\phi_1 b(a-e)u_{1,(1,2)} & \phi_1^2 u_{1,(1,2)} & 0 \\ \frac{1}{4}b^2 g u_{1,(1,2)} & \phi_4 det + \frac{1}{2}\phi_1 b(a-e)u_{1,(1,2)} & 0 \\ \frac{1}{2}b^2 g u_{1,(1,2)} & \phi_1 b(a-e)u_{1,(1,2)} & \phi_4 det \end{bmatrix}.$$

The eigenvalues of M are $-\phi_4$, $-a_{(1,2)}$ and $a_{(1,2)}$, with $a_{(1,2)}^2 := \phi_4^2 + 4\phi_1 b\frac{\phi_4(a-e)+b\phi_1}{u_{(1,2)}} = \frac{g\phi_4^2}{u_{(1,2)}}$. So, there is always a unique equilibrium. The with $-a_{(1,2)}$ corresponding eigenvector is $[-\frac{u_{(1,2)}\phi_4+2\phi_1 b(a-e)-u_{(1,2)}a_{(1,2)}}{2gb^2}, \frac{1}{2}, 1]^T$. The rest of the conclusions follow then immediately.

Next, we consider the aggregate performance case. After substitution of the parameters in the algorithm described in Appendix A.3 we see that matrix G coincides with (4.21) except for the last row which is multiplied by a factor two. Consequently the determinant of G, det, equals $\frac{1}{2}u_{1,(1,2)}u_{(1,2)}$. After some elementary calculations we see that $det * G^{-1}$ equals:

$$\begin{bmatrix} u_{1,(1,2)}+u_{2,(1,2)} & u_{2,(1,2)} & \frac{1}{4}u_{(1,2)}c(a+e) \\ u_{2,(1,2)} & u_{1,(1,2)}+u_{2,(1,2)} & \frac{1}{4}u_{(1,2)}c(a+e) \\ u_{(1,2)}c(a+e) & u_{(1,2)}c(a+e) & \frac{1}{4}u_{(1,2)}(g+(a+e)^2) \end{bmatrix},$$

and matrix M satisfies:

$$det{*}M = -\begin{bmatrix} -\phi_4 det - \phi_1 b(a-e)u_{1,(1,2)} & 2\phi_1^2 u_{1,(1,2)} & 0 \\ \frac{1}{2}b^2 g u_{1,(1,2)} & \phi_4 det + \phi_1 b(a-e)u_{1,(1,2)} & 0 \\ 0 & 0 & \phi_4 det \end{bmatrix}$$

From this it is easily deduced that the only negative eigenvalue $-a_{(1,2)A}$ coincides with $-a_{(1,2)}$. Moreover, it is also easily verified that the corresponding K and strategies coincide with the national case.

Appendix C

Proof of Lemma 2:

i) To show that $a_{cN} \leqq a_{(1,2)}$, we note that

$$\begin{aligned} a_{(1,2)}^2 - a_{cN}^2 &= \phi_4^2 \frac{g}{g+(a-e)^2} - \phi_4^2 \frac{\tau g}{\tau g + d_N(a-e)^2} \\ &= \phi_4^2 \frac{g(a-e)^2(d_N-\tau)}{(g+(a-e)^2)(\tau g + d_N(a-e)^2)} \\ &\geqq 0. \end{aligned}$$

ii) First note that, using the equality $\phi_4(a-e) = -2b\phi_1$, a_{nc} can be rewritten as:

$$\frac{\frac{1}{2}\phi_4(a-e)(a+e) + \|\phi_4\|\sqrt{(\frac{1}{2}(a+e)(a-e)+2g)^2 + 2g(a-e)^2}}{2(a(a-e)+g)}.$$

Consequently,

$$\begin{aligned} a_{cN}^2 - a_{nc}^2 &= -\phi_4^2\{\frac{\frac{1}{2}(a^2-e^2)^2 + 4gu_{nc}}{4u_{nc}^2} - \frac{\tau g}{u_{cN}}\} + \\ &\quad \phi_4^2 \frac{(a^2-e^2)\sqrt{(\frac{1}{2}(a^2-e^2)+2g)^2 + 2g(a-e)^2}}{4u_{nc}^2} \\ &= : -t_1 + t_2. \end{aligned}$$

Since $t_2 \geqq 0$, it is obvious that if t_1 in the above expression is negative also $a_{cN}^2 - a_{nc}^2 \geqq 0$. Next, assume that t_1 is positive. Then, $a_{cN}^2 - a_{nc}^2 \geqq 0$ if and only if $t_2^2 - t_1^2 \geqq 0$. Elementary calculations show that

$$\begin{aligned} t_2^2 - t_1^2 &= \frac{\phi_4^4 g}{u_{nc}^2 u_{cN}^2}\{-g(u_{cN} - \tau u_{nc})^2 + \frac{1}{4}\tau(a^2-e^2)^2 u_{cN}\} \\ &= \frac{\phi_4^4 g(a-e)^3}{u_{nc}^2 u_{cN}^2}\{-\frac{\tau^2 g}{4}(3a+e) - g d_N(d_N(a-e) - 2a\tau) \\ &\quad + \frac{1}{4}\tau d_N(a-e)(a+e)^2\} \\ &= \frac{\phi_4^4 g(a-e)^3}{u_{nc}^2 u_{cN}^2}\{\frac{1}{4}g(2d_N-\tau)(a(3\tau-2d_N) + (2d_N+\tau)e) \\ &\quad + \frac{1}{4}\tau d_N(a-e)(a+e)^2\}. \end{aligned}$$

Obviously, this last expression is positive, if $3\tau - 2d_N \geqq 0$, which concludes the proof.

iii) For the non-cooperative case, one can show this result along the lines of the analysis we performed in Chapter 3. The proof of the other two cases is found by straightforward differentiation.

iv)

$$\begin{aligned} a_{cA}^2 - a_{cN}^2 &= \frac{g\phi_4^2}{g+(a-e)^2} - \tau\frac{g\phi_4^2}{\tau g + d_N(a-e)^2} \\ &= \frac{\phi_4^2}{g+(a-e)^2}\frac{g}{\tau g + d_N(a-e)^2}(a-e)^2(1-2\tau)\frac{d_U^N}{d} \\ &\gtreqless 0. \end{aligned}$$

□

<u>Proof of Lemma 3:</u>

i) From the cost functional (4.20) we have that

$$J_{U,cN}^N - J_{U,nc}^N = \frac{1}{4}\frac{d_U^N s^2(0)}{a_{cN}a_{nc}}\{a_{nc}(b+p_{cN}(a-e))^2 - a_{cN}(b+p_{nc}(a-e))^2\}.$$

Since, $p_i = \frac{\phi_4 + a_i}{2\phi_1}$, $i \in \{cN, nc\}$, and $\phi_4(a-e) = -2b\phi_1$ we have

$$\begin{aligned} \text{sgn}(J_{U,cN}^N - J_{U,nc}^N) &= \text{sgn}(a_{nc}(2b\phi_1 + (\phi_4 + a_{cN})(a-e))^2 - \\ &\quad -a_{cN}(2b\phi_1 + (\phi_4 + a_{nc})(a-e))^2) \\ &= \text{sgn}((a_{cN} - a_{nc})a_{nc}a_{cN}(a-e)^2) \\ &= \text{sgn}(a_{cN} - a_{nc}). \end{aligned}$$

ii) From (4.19) we have that

$$\begin{aligned} J_{i,cN} - J_{i,(1,2)} &= \frac{1}{4}\frac{ds^2(0)}{a_c a_{(1,2)}}\{a_{(1,2)}((b+p_{cN}(a-e))^2 + p_{cN}^2 g) - \\ &\quad -a_{cN}((b+p_{(1,2)}(a-e))^2 + p_{(1,2)}^2 g)\}. \end{aligned}$$

Using again the facts that $p_i = \frac{\phi_4 + a_i}{2\phi_1}$, $i \in \{cN, (1,2)\}$ and $\phi_4(a-e) = -2b\phi_1$ we have that $\text{sgn}(J_{i,cN} - J_{i,(1,2)})$ can be rewritten as:

$$\begin{aligned} &\text{sgn}(a_{(1,2)}(a_{cN}^2(a-e)^2 + (\phi_4 + a_{cN})^2 g) - a_{cN}(a_{(1,2)}^2(a-e)^2 + (\phi_4 + a_{(1,2)})^2 g)) = \\ &\qquad \text{sgn}(\phi_4^2 g(a_{(1,2)} - a_{cN}) + ((a-e)^2 + g)(a_{(1,2)}a_{cN}^2 - a_{cN}a_{(1,2)}^2)) = \end{aligned}$$

$$= \text{sgn}((a_{cN} - a_{(1,2)})(-\phi_4^2 g + ((a-e)^2 + g)a_{(1,2)}a_{cN})).$$

From Lemma 2.i) we therefore conclude that $\text{sgn}(J_{i,cN} - J_{i,(1,2)}) = \text{sgn}(\phi_4^2 g - ((a-e)^2 + g)a_{(1,2)}a_{cN})$. Since $a_{(1,2)}^2 = \phi_4^2 \frac{g}{u_{(1,2)}}$ and $a_{cN}^2 = \phi_4^2 \frac{\tau g}{u_{cN}}$, we finally have

$$\begin{aligned} \text{sgn}(J_{i,cN} - J_{i,(1,2)}) &= \text{sgn}(\phi_4^4 g^2(1 - \frac{\tau u_{(1,2)}}{u_{cN}})) \\ &= \text{sgn}((d_N - \tau)(a-e)^2) \gtreqless 0, \end{aligned}$$

which concludes the proof. □

Chapter 5

Endogenous Coalition Formation Concepts

5.1 Introduction

The recent large interest in endogenous coalition formation theory was boosted by several factors. International agreements among nations are more and more important in the globalizing economy. Examples of transnational issues range from economic cooperation, migration liberalization, technological cooperation and so on, to environmental protection. Especially studies on this last issue delivered very interesting developments in the endogenous coalition formation theory.[1] The common characteristic of all these problems is that welfare of each country depends not only on its own actions but also on actions of other nations. In other words, actions of each agent induce externalities, which can (but does not have to) deliver strong incentives to cooperate. Apart from international agreements, endogenous coalition formation theory has been utilized in various other important research fields, such as R&D, creation of oligopolies, etc. Again, the common feature of all these settings are externalities from coalition formation, which make a coalitional approach relevant for players' welfare.

In order to understand the logic of coalition formation in the presence of externalities, the economic literature has followed two main directions: cooperative games and non-cooperative games. In cooperative game theory, the focus of analysis lies on the so-called grand coalition of players and on the characteristic function (i.e. the function determining the total net benefits that the grand coalition can share), whereas non-cooperative game theory focuses on individual agents, who maximize their own welfare, subject to the individual welfare maximizing behaviour of other agents. From now

[1] See, for instance, Finus (2001, 2003), Eyckmans and Finus (2003), Carraro and Siniscalco (1998).

on we follow this latter approach, assuming that each player (a fiscal player or a monetary player) is purely self-oriented, i.e. aims to maximize her own welfare. Moreover, we assume that there is no central body that supervises coalition formation, which is consistent with the current EU/EMU institutional design implying that there is no institution which is directly responsible for coordination of macroeconomic policies. Consequently, all the possible cooperation agreements between different agents (countries and the CBs) must be self-enforcing, i.e. must be profitable for all the signatories.

The central problem of cooperation is free-riding. Two types of free-riding can be distinguished (see Finus (2003)). The first one relates to the situation when a player joins an agreement but does not comply with its rules, which brings her higher profits in relation to her inputs. The second type of free-riding comes from externalities from coalition formation, which can deliver incentives for a country to stay outside an agreement but still get profits from it. In this book, we focus on the latter type of free-riding. Models of coalition formation that regard this type of free-riding are called the 'new coalition theory' by Finus (2003) and they will be discussed in this chapter. For clarity, the first type of free-riding will be neglected, i.e. it is assumed that binding agreements to cooperate signed by players (coalitions) are fully enforceable.

Unfortunately, game theory is far from having achieved a well-defined non-cooperative theory of coalition formation under general assumptions and definitions. Therefore, there are several stability concepts and rules of coalition formation and each combination of them may lead to (a) different equilibrium coalition structure(s). These concepts and rules are based on different initial assumptions and, in our context, can be interpreted as different institutional settings of an MU. In other words, our game-theoretic analysis intends to examine different institutional settings, in which a coordination of monetary and fiscal policies takes place, and derive from that sound policy recommendations.

5.2 General setting and definitions

Assume that players from the set $N = \{1, 2, ..., n\}$ take part in a game in which (possibly multiple) coalitions may be created. A *coalition* is any non-empty subset of N. Therefore, C_k is a coalition if $C_k \subseteq N$ and $C_k \neq \emptyset$. The cardinality of a coalition C_k is the number of players in this coalition and will be denoted by $|C_k|$. If player $i \in C_k$ left this coalition we write $C_{k_{-i}}$.

Definition 5.1 *A coalition structure $\pi := \{C_1, C_2, ..., C_m\}$ is a partition of the player set N into coalitions; hence, it satisfies:*

$$C_k \neq \emptyset \text{ for } k = 1, 2, ..., m; \ \cup_{k=1}^{m} C_k = N \text{ and } C_k \cap C_l = \varnothing \text{ if } k \neq l.$$

We denote by Π the set of all possible coalition structures and we abbreviate a coalition structure by CS.

Remark 5.1 (Number of coalition structures) *The number of all possible coalition structures is a function of $n = |N|$ and can be obtained from the Bell numbers. The Bell number B_n is equal to the number of ways a set of n elements can be partitioned into non-empty subsets. The following Dobinski's formula is one way to compute Bell numbers (Comtet (1974)):* $B_n = \frac{1}{e}\sum_{i=0}^{\infty}\frac{i^n}{i!}$.

Note that, in particular, coalitions C_i of cardinality one are *singletons*. They will also be referred to as *trivial coalitions*, whereas all the other coalitions, i.e. those for which $|C_i| \geqq 2$, will be referred to as *non-trivial coalitions*. To simplify the presentation of CSs we will use the following shorthand notation: $[C_1|C_2|...|C_m]$ where C_i is represented by the sequence of players that belong to this coalition. For example: [123|4|56] stands for {(1,2,3),4,(5,6)}. Sometimes, to indicate different characteristics of players (countries and central banks) we will denote them by e.g. $C1$ and CB. However, to abbreviate notation we will still use notation in natural numbers while reporting CSs. For instance, for the set of players defined as $N := \{C1, C2, CB\}$ we will denote a CS made of one coalition consisting of all the players by [123]. Notations $[C1C2CB]$ and $\{(C1, C2, CB)\}$ will also be possible, depending on the context.

Example 5.1 *Let $N = \{1, 2, 3, 4\}$. Listing all the possible partitions of the set N into coalitions, we obtain:* [1234], [123|4], [124|3], [134|2], [1|234], [12|3|4], [13|2|4], [14|2|3], [23|1|4], [24|1|3], [1|2|34], [12|34], [13|24], [14|23], [1|2|3|4]. *Indeed, using simple recursive software to compute Dobinski's formula we obtain:* $B_4 = 15$. *It is very characteristic that the number of possible partitions increases extremely quickly with an increase of n. For $n = |N| = 1, 2, ..., 15$, we have the following numbers of coalitions according to Dobinski's formula:* $B_1 = 1$, $B_2 = 2$, $B_3 = 5$, $B_4 = 15$, $B_5 = 52$; $B_6 = 203$, $B_7 = 877$, $B_8 = 4140$; $B_9 = 21147$, $B_{10} = 115975$, $B_{11} = 678570$, $B_{12} = 4213597$, $B_{13} = 27644437$; $B_{14} = 190899322$, $B_{15} = 1382958545$.

It is clear that an examination of all possible CSs for $n > 10$ is a hopeless task, and the researcher should choose and restrict her attention to the most probable CSs. One may assume that all the parties, negotiating any international settlement, start talks with some pre-assumptions about preferable coalitions. It is rather unusual to assume that for a high number of players all the possible combinations of coalitions are taken into account. It would mean that in the EU negotiations each player considers $B_{25} \simeq 4638590332230000000$ CSs, which is not realistic. Consequently, throughout the book for $n>2$ we will study only those CSs which we consider relevant in our MU setting. We will (usually) exclude, for instance, the possibility to create a coalition between the CB of an MU and the central bank of a country which is outside the MU.

Definition 5.2 (Full and reduced set of feasible coalition structures) *Let Π be the set of feasible coalition structures for the coalition formation game of $N = \{1, 2, ..., n\}$ players. Then:*

a) If $|\Pi| = B_n$ we will call Π the full set of feasible coalition structures and denote it by Π^F.

b) If $|\Pi| < B_n$ we will call Π the reduced set of feasible coalition structures and denote it by Π^R.

We have $\Pi^R \subset \Pi^F$. If we just use the symbol Π, it means that we do not make a distinction between Π^F and Π^R.

Note, however, that not all reduced sets of feasible CSs meet the (implicit) assumption of independence of players. For example, if the coalition formation game is defined in such a way that the resulting $\Pi^R = \{[12|3|4], [12|34]\}$, then players 1 and 2 are, in fact, forced to play cooperatively. We assume that this cannot be the case. If such situation occurs players 1 and 2 will be modelled as one player in the coalition formation game. A direct consequence of this assumption is that if $[12|3|4] \in \Pi^R$ then also $[1|2|3|4]$ must belong to Π^R; that is players 1 and 2 have a possibility not to cooperate. We call this property of the (possibly reduced) set of feasible coalition structure the *independence property.* The formal definition is as follows:

Definition 5.3 (Independence property) *Let $\Pi = \{\pi_1, ..., \pi_s\}$ be the (possibly reduced) set of feasible coalition structures for the coalition formation game. Π has the independence property if for every $\pi_j = \{C_1, C_2, ..., C_{k-1}, C_k, C_{k+1}, ..., C_m\} \in \Pi$, $j = 1, ..., s$ and every non-trivial coalition $C_k = (i_1, i_2, ..., i_r) \in \pi_j$, (where $k = 1, ..., m$; $r \leqq n$ and $i_1, i_2, ..., i_r \in N$, indicate arbitrary players creating the coalition $C_k \subset N$) there exists a coalition structure $\pi_h = \{C_1, C_2, ..., C_{k-1}, (i_1), (i_2), ..., (i_r), C_{k+1}, ..., C_m\}$ that belongs to Π, $h \neq j$.*

Definition 5.4 (Independent coalition structure) *Coalition structure π_h from Definition 5.3, will be called the independent coalition structure of π_j w.r.t. C_k and will be denoted by $\pi_h^I(\pi_j, C_k)$.*

There are two special CSs:

1. A CS which consists of only singletons, i.e. $[1|2|...|n]$, will be called the non-cooperative CS, or the non-cooperative regime, and will be abbreviated by NC.

2. A CS which consists of only one coalition, which is made of all players. This will be called the full cooperative CS, the full cooperative regime, or full coalition and will be abbreviated by $C \equiv [12...n]$.

All the other CSs will be called partial cooperation CSs (or partial cooperation regimes).

Per-membership partition function In Section 2.6 of Chapter 2 we have already presented an LQ 3-player game with partial coalitions, where we derived cooperative and non-cooperative optimal strategies. Having computed these optimal strategies for every desired coalition we introduced in Chapter 4 some coalition formation concepts. We will now elaborate them in more detail. In fact, our game can be divided into two stages (is a *two-stage game*). In the first stage, all policymakers decide to sign or not the (possibly multiple) cooperation agreement(s). In the second stage, when coalitions are already formed, inside each coalition, policymakers act cooperatively by sharing their loss function in order to maximize the coalitional surplus whereas coalitions (and/or singletons) compete with each other in a non-cooperative way. The second stage of the game is assumed to have a unique Nash equilibrium for any division of players into coalitions. Under these assumptions, the second stage of the game can be reduced to the first stage of the game with known payoffs for every feasible CS. The study of coalition formation consists of the study of the first stage of the game where the agreement is negotiated (see Yi (1997)).

Following the approach described above, policymakers facing a stabilization problem (an initial shock) play a two-stage game, illustrated in Figure 5.1. In the first stage ($t = 1$) – the coalition game – they decide non-cooperatively whether or not to sign the agreement about policy coordination after a price shock was observed at $t = 0$. In the second stage ($t = 2$) – the stabilization game – they play the non-cooperative Nash game, where the policymakers who sign the agreement play as a single player sharing a common loss function.

Figure 5.1

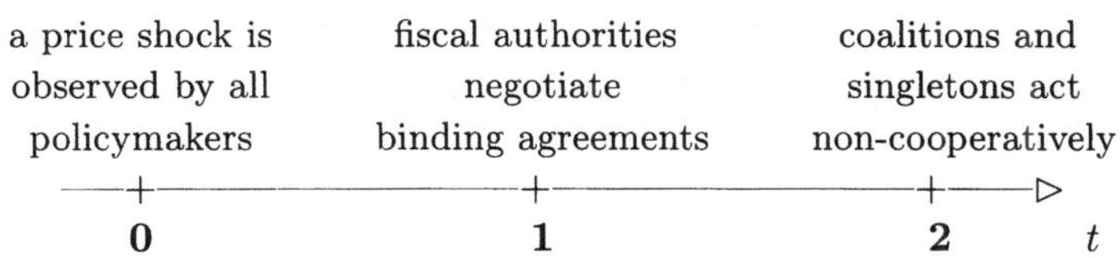

In order to reduce the game to a partition form, we need to assume that binding agreements can be written, i.e. once all the coalitions are formed, policymakers cannot deviate in the second stage of the game. In other words, in the second stage of the game agents belonging to a certain coalition have to play cooperatively for the whole time horizon until output and price stabilization is reached. We also assume that a transfer mechanism, which compensates those agents who may lose by joining (leaving) the coalition (e.g. side-payments), does not exist. Though this assumption can be removed along the lines of Chapter 4, it seems compatible with an MU context, where a transfer mechanism is difficult to be designed.[2]

The players' payoff, derived in the second stage of the game, depends on the particular CS created by the players. In other words, to each CS corresponds

[2] A transfer mechanism is analyzed in Chapter 3 (see also Casella (1999) and Engwerda *et al.* (2002)).

a payoff derived in the second stage of the game. The set of all possible *payoff vectors* will be denoted by Φ and player i's particular loss in coalition structure π_j by $\phi_i(\pi_j)$. Now, we can define the concept of the per-membership partition function:

Definition 5.5 (Per-membership partition function) *A per-membership partition function is a mapping $\phi : \Pi \rightarrow \Phi$, which associates to each coalition structure $\pi \in \Pi$ a vector of individual payoffs/losses $\phi(\pi) \in \Phi$.*[3]

A per-membership partition function can be defined in terms of payoffs or losses. Throughout the book we will represent the partition function in the form of a table. For instance, Example 5.2 shows the partition function for a four-player game with the full set of feasible CSs:

Example 5.2 (Partition function) *A partition function for the 4-player coalition formation game:*

Table 5.1 Partition function[4]

	π_1	π_2	π_3	π_4	π_5
	[1234]	[123|4]	[124|3]	[134|2]	[1|234]
$P1$	1	2	7	2	3
$P2$	5	2	1	3	4
$P3$	3	1	4	1	11
$P4$	2	4	7	5	4
	π_6	π_7	π_8	π_9	π_{10}
	[12|3|4]	[13|2|4]	[14|2|3]	[23|1|4]	[24|1|3]
$P1$	8	3	3	3	2
$P2$	6	2	1	5	4
$P3$	3	4	9	3	1
$P4$	11	10	3	2	4
	π_{11}	π_{12}	π_{13}	π_{14}	π_{15}
	[1|2|34]	[12|34]	[13|24]	[14|23]	[1|2|3|4]
$P1$	7	2	3	8	16
$P2$	1	3	4	5	21
$P3$	4	1	11	5	4
$P4$	7	5	4	21	1

Externalities from coalition formation Table 5.1 reports losses; hence, lower values are preferable to higher values. Looking at Table 5.1, we see that each player's loss depends on the particular CS. In other words, it matters for a player not only in which coalition she participates but also which coalitions other players create. Consider, for instance, the loss of Player 3 ($P3$) in two different CSs. We have $\phi_{P3}(\pi_6 := [12|3|4]) = 3$ and $\phi_{P3}(\pi_8 := [14|2|3]) = 9$.

[3] Note that values of $\phi_i(.)$ are obtained in the second stage of the game; hence, they equal $J_i(.)$, which are for the first time defined in Chapter 2.

[4] Per-membership partition function defined in terms of losses.

This means that for $P3$ it is relevant whether $P1$ cooperates with $P2$, or with $P4$. Dependence of payoffs on the cooperative/non-cooperative decision of the other player(s) is called an *externality from a coalition formation.* A partition function form of a game is a very convenient form to model and study such externalities from coalition formation. Yi ((1997), p. 202) summarizes that in the following way: "(...) a partition function (...) assigns a pay-off to each coalition in a coalition structure as a function of the entire coalition structure, not just the coalition in question. Thus, an important novelty of these models is that they can capture the possibilities of externalities across coalitions. In the traditional characteristic function approach, as in Aumann and Drèze (1974) and Shenoy (1979), these externalities across coalitions are assumed not to be present."

The main question, which endogenous coalition formation intends to answer, is to point out those CSs in the game, which are *stable* (i.e. are supported by an assumed equilibrium concept). In Table 5.1 $P1$ prefers to create [1234], $P2$ is indifferent between [124|3], [14|2|3], or [1|2|34], $P3$ is indifferent between [123|4], [134|2], [24|1|3], or [12|34] and $P4$ prefers the non-cooperative CS: [1|2|3|4]. If we assume that transfers are impossible, what will be the outcome of negotiations between players? It is obvious that without any further assumptions about the rules, the game in Table 5.1 cannot be solved, since every player prefers different CSs. After all, each player could stick to her first-best choice and there would be no cooperation at all. Does it mean that the outcome would be $\pi_{15} = [1|2|3|4]$? We cannot come to this conclusion as non-cooperation is also never satisfactory for $P1$, $P2$, and $P3$. Hence, when the current state of affairs is non-cooperation, these players would look for another solution, and possibly come back to non-cooperation, and so on.

There can be two special (extreme) cases of games with externalities - *positive* and *negative externality* games.

Definition 5.6 (Positive/negative externality games) *The following three conditions characterize a positive (negative) externality game:*

(a) Assume that coalition structure π' was created from coalition structure $\pi \neq \pi'$ by a merge of certain (possibly also trivial) coalitions that consist of k players, $k \in N$. By this merge larger coalitions were created. In the game of positive (negative) externalities it always holds that all the players who are not involved in the merge are better (worse) off. More formally, if the per-membership partition function $\phi(.)$ is defined in terms of losses: $\phi_i(\pi') \leqq \phi_i(\pi)$ $(\phi_i(\pi') \geqq \phi_i(\pi))$ for $i \in N \backslash k$.

(b) Members of smaller coalitions are better (worse) off than members of larger coalitions for any given coalition structure (Finus (2001), p. 287); and

(c) If a member i of a certain coalition k leaves its coalition to join a larger or equal-sized coalition l, then the other members of the coalition k are better (worse) off.

In short, we have a positive externality game when a creation (a merge) of some coalitions in a certain CS makes other players, who are not involved in a merge, better off. For a negative externality game the opposite holds. Examples of a positive externality game are output cartels in oligopoly and public goods coalitions (see Yi (1997)), like environmental coalitions. Examples of negative externalities are Research Joint Ventures between the inventor and important users of knowledge: the leakage of knowledge is prevented by internalizing the negative effects of knowledge spillovers from the viewpoint of the inventor. Another example of a negative externality game is a customs union.

However, it has to be noted that in many games of our interest, coalition formation creates both negative and positive externalities for non-members. Such games will be called henceforth *mixed externality* games.

Definition 5.7 (Mixed externality game) *A mixed externality game is a game which is neither a positive nor a negative externality game.*

Example 5.3 *The game in Example 5.2 is an example of a mixed externality game. The reader can verify this by applying both definitions of positive and negative externalities. For instance, when $P1$ and $P2$ form coalition $(P1, P2)$ player $P3$ becomes better off, since $\phi_{P3}([P1P2|P3|P4]) = 3$. However, if $P1$ and $P4$ create coalition $(P1, P4)$, then $P3$ becomes worse off, since $\phi_{P3}([P1P4|P2|P3])=$ 9. Clearly, neither the definition of a positive nor a negative externality game applies.*

Each player $i \in N$ has an own strategy space Σ_i. Its exact definition depends on the particular form of the coalition game and will be reported accordingly. The total strategy space is defined as the product of all players' strategy spaces, or $\Sigma := \Sigma_1 \times \Sigma_2 \times ... \times \Sigma_n$. An element of the total strategy space $\sigma \in \Sigma$ will be called a *strategy vector.*

Definition 5.8 (Coalition function) *A function that maps each strategy vector $\sigma \in \Sigma$ into a CS $\pi \in \Pi$ is called a coalition function and is denoted by $\psi(.)$. Hence, we have $\psi : \Sigma \rightarrow \Pi$, or $\pi = \psi(\sigma)$.*

Using these concepts we can formalize the notion of a coalition formation game:

Definition 5.9 (Coalition formation game) *A coalition formation game is characterized by:*

- *players $i \in N$,*
- *strategy vectors $\sigma \in \Sigma$,*
- *coalition function $\psi(.)$; and*
- *payoff vectors $\phi(\pi = \psi(\sigma)) \in \Phi$,*

and will be denoted by $\Gamma(N, \Sigma, \phi(\pi))$, where $\pi = \psi(\sigma)$.

Note that strategy spaces/vectors and coalition functions imply rules of coalition formation. Sometimes we will be interested in certain characteristics of the coalition formation game which are independent of payoffs but will not be interested in the particular values of the per-membership partition function. Hence, we define the following concept of a class of coalition formation games:

Definition 5.10 (Class of coalition formation games) *The class of coalition formation games consists of all the games, which:*

1. *are based on the same rules of coalition formation (i.e. the same strategy spaces/vectors and the coalition function), and*

2. *are played by the same set N of players but can be different w.r.t. the specific values $\phi(\pi) \in \Phi$ of the per-membership partition function.*

The class of coalition formation games will be denoted as $\Gamma(N, \Sigma, \psi(.))$ or Γ^C.

Simultaneous and sequential games A decision to create (a) certain coalition(s) can be made by players simultaneously or sequentially. Intuitively, in the simultaneous case, players do not know other players' decisions while choosing their own strategy at the moment the game is played.[5] On the contrary, in the sequential games utilized in this book, players at a certain stage of the game have full information about its history.

Single- and multiple-agreement games Depending on the problem considered, *single-agreement* or *multiple-agreement* assumptions can be made. In the latter approach it is assumed that in a particular CS there can be more than one non-trivial coalition. In contrast, the single-agreement approach imposes the restriction that only one (non-trivial) coalition may be created. Hence, the players' strategy space Σ consists of two decisions: cooperate and not cooperate, or $\Sigma = \{\text{cooperate, not cooperate}\}$, and all the players who decide not to cooperate play as singletons. Formally, a single-agreement CS can be represented as: $[\tilde{C}|\ \textit{singletons}]$, where $\tilde{C}$ is a coalition created by the (single) agreement.

Example 5.4 *If all 15 CSs from the previous 4-player Example 5.2 are taken into account we have a multiple-agreement game, as* [12|34], [13|24], [14|23] *are multiple-agreement CSs. However, when these 3 CSs are excluded, we have a single-agreement game which consist of 12 CSs:* [1234], [123|4], [124|3], [134|2], [1|234], [12|3|4], [13|2|4], [14|2|3], [23|1|4], [24|1|3], [1|2|34], [1|2|3|4].

Single-agreement games were extensively studied in the context of international environmental agreements. For instance, the Kyoto protocol was designed as a club, to which each country has a free access. Clearly, this may be modelled as a single-agreement game. The example above shows that CSs of single-agreement games are a subset of multiple-agreement CSs. Consequently, single-agreement games do not have to be discussed separately, but we will study this approach first due to its relative simplicity.

---

[5] While choosing her strategy a player in a simultaneous perfect-information game knows all the possible strategies of opponents but does not know which exact combination of strategies will be actually played by them.

Equilibrium Concepts Certain assumptions like single- vs. multiple-agreement CSs or simultaneous vs. sequential decision making are called *rules of coalition formation.* To define an endogenous coalition formation game we have to list all assumptions on rules of coalition formation in this game. These rules should be distinguished from equilibrium concepts, which concern the choice of an optimal strategy of players in the assumed framework (of rules). This distinction is very important for sound policy recommendations. [6] In the endogenous coalition formation literature the equilibrium (stable) CSs are often determined by the following equilibrium concepts: Nash Equilibrium (NE), Strong Nash Equilibrium, and Coalitional-Proof Nash Equilibrium. All of them may be utilized for games discussed in this chapter; however, we are going to concentrate on the concept of NE.[7]

Definition 5.11 (Stability of a coalition structure) *A coalition structure π^* is said to be stable if there exists a coalition strategy $\sigma^* \in \Sigma$ generating π^* such that for all $i \in N$ and for all $\sigma_i \in \Sigma_i$ with $(\sigma_i, \sigma^*_{-i}) \in \Sigma_i$ it holds that $\pi^* \succ \pi$, where $\pi^* = \psi(\sigma^*)$ and $\pi = \psi(\sigma_i, \sigma^*_{-i})$. In other words, π^* is stable if and only if it can be supported by an announcement strategy vector σ^* that constitutes a Nash Equilibrium in the coalition formation game.*[8]

We will denote stable coalition structures as Γ^{ST}, where Γ will be replaced by the particular name of the game.

5.3 Single-agreement games

5.3.1 External and internal stability

In this section we will discuss in more detail the concepts of *internal* and *external stability*, which have already been applied in Chapter 4. We will use the following simple single-agreement game as an illustration:

[6] As Finus (2003) writes "for analytical reasons but also to derive sound policy recommendations it is crucial to distinguish between the rules of coalition formation and the equilibrium concepts applied to determine the outcome in a coalition game".

[7] For this definition and for detailed discussion of the other two concepts, see Finus and Rundshagen (2002). Less formally, the NE occurs if all players have chosen such strategies that no one player can increase her payoff by unilaterally deviating from her chosen strategy.

[8] By writing that for player $i \in N$, $\pi^* \succ \pi$, we mean that the coalition structure π^* is preferred by a particular player i to coalition structure π w.r.t. payoffs/losses (i.e. $\phi_i(\pi^*) > \phi_i(\pi)$ if the per-membership coalition function is defined in terms of payoffs or $\phi_i(\pi^*) < \phi_i(\pi)$ if the per-membership coalition function is defined in terms of losses). For $\pi^* \prec \pi$ the opposite holds.

Table 5.2 Losses for a simple coalition formation game

	π_1	π_2	π_3	π_4	π_5
	[123]	[12|3]	[13|2]	[1|23]	[1|2|3]
$P1$	1	2	7	2	3
$P2$	5	2	1	3	6
$P3$	3	5	4	1	9

First, consider π_1, which is the full cooperative CS, or the full coalition. Each player considers to leave the full coalition assuming that all the other players do not change their strategies and do not leave the remaining coalition. It means, for instance, that a possible CS π_1 without $P1$ is perceived by this player as a change of the coalition structure from $\pi_1 = [123]$ to $\pi_4 = [1|23]$. Similarly, for $P2$ and $P3$ the abandonment of the full coalition means a switch from π_1 to $\pi_3 = [13|2]$ and $\pi_2 = [12|3]$, respectively. Would these changes take place? In fact, $\phi_{P1}(\pi_4) > \phi_{P1}(\pi_1), \phi_{P2}(\pi_3) < \phi_{P2}(\pi_1)$, and $\phi_{P3}(\pi_2) > \phi_{P3}(\pi_1)$, which means that the abandonment of the full coalition is preferred only by $P2$, whereas the other players do not consider it to be profitable. However, we may conclude that CS π_1 cannot be a stable agreement as there is at least one player (here $P2$) who would not like to sign it. More precisely, we may say that π_1 is not internally stable, as the instability is caused by players inside the coalition. Next consider $\pi_4 := [1|23]$. If any of the players $P2$ or $P3$ leaves the coalition $(2, 3)$ then π_5 emerges. However, both prefer π_4 to π_5 and, therefore, this coalition is internally stable. Nevertheless, we see that $P1$ would prefer to join coalition $(2, 3)$ in order to create the full coalition (π_1). Again, it makes π_4 unstable. This kind of instability is called external, since a player from outside causes instability by joining an existing coalition. Formal definitions of internal and external stability are the following:

Definition 5.12 (Internal and external stability) *Consider a single-agreement game $\Gamma(N, \Sigma, \phi(\pi))$, with $\pi = \psi(\sigma)$ and per-membership partition function $\phi(\pi)$ defined in terms of losses. A coalition structure $\pi := [\hat{C}|\ singletons]$ is:*

(a) internally stable if and only if $\phi_i([\hat{C}|singletons]) \leqq \phi_i([\hat{C}_{-i}|singletons|i])$ for all $i \in \hat{C}$; and

(b) externally stable if and only if $\phi_i([\hat{C}|singletons]) > \phi_i([\hat{C} \cup \{i\}|singletons_{-i}])$ for all $i \in singletons$.

The above definition of stability coincides with the definition of a stable cartel provided in the oligopoly literature (see d'Aspremont *et al.* (1983)). In other words, when leaving a coalition, each agent assumes that the other agents belonging to this coalition do not follow her. Therefore, this assumption is equivalent to the assumption of the Nash conjectures in a simultaneous oligopoly game where a player assumes no change in the other players' decision variable when she modifies her own decision variable.

Some points should be stressed here. First of all, as it has already been said, players, while considering to change decisions, assume that all the other players do stick to their strategies. Second, players are *myopic*, i.e. they do not look further than one step ahead. For instance, in Table 5.2 player $P2$ does not care whether π_4 is stable, when deciding to abandon π_1. If this assumption on myopic behaviour is waived and players anticipate next possible changes, we will have a game with *farsightedness*. Third, it is assumed that when considering external stability, players can freely join a coalition, which is called an *open-membership* assumption.

The main drawback of the concepts of internal and external stability presented above is that they are suitable only for single-agreement games. Consequently, we propose other concepts of CS stability, which can also be utilized for multiple-agreement games.

5.4 Multiple-agreement games

5.4.1 Simultaneous games - classic setting

Open-membership game

The Open-Membership Game (OMG) was introduced by Yi and Shin (1995). Players simultaneously make their decisions by announcing a message. Coalitions are created by those players who announce the same message. The basic assumption of the OMG is that insiders cannot exclude outsiders from joining a coalition (open-membership assumption). Thus, every player is entitled to join whatever coalition she wants including trivial ones.[9]

Definition 5.13 (***Open-Membership Game***) *Each player $i \in N = \{1, ..., n\}$ announces a message $\sigma_i \in \Sigma_i := \{\bar{A}, \bar{B}, ..., \bar{N}\}$.[10] Players who announce the same message form a coalition, i.e. the coalition function $\psi^{OMG}(.)$ maps the strategy vector $\sigma := [\sigma_1, ..., \sigma_i, ..., \sigma_j, ..., \sigma_n]^T$ into a coalition structure $\pi := \{C_1, C_2, ..., C_k, ..., C_m\}$ according to the rule: $C_k = \{i\} \cup \{j | \sigma_i = \sigma_j\}$.*

The open-membership game will be denoted by OMG($N, \Sigma, \psi^{OMG}(.), \phi(.)$) or by OMG and the class of open-membership games by OMG($N, \Sigma, \psi^{OMG}(.)$) or by OMG^C.

[9] In fact, due to the open-membership assumption the OMG is very close to the internal and external stability concepts.

[10] The cardinality of a strategy space Σ_i in the OMG is assumed to be equal to or higher than the number of players, or $|\Sigma_i| \geqq n$. This assumption is made because, when $|\Sigma_i| < n$ it would be impossible for players to announce a combination of messages to create a coalition structure of singletons. Moreover, we assume that $\Sigma_1 = \Sigma_2 = ... = \Sigma_n$.

Table 5.3 Example of a coalition function for the OMG

		P2			P2			P2		
		A	B	C	A	B	C	A	B	C
P1	A	π_1	π_3	π_3	π_2	π_4	π_5	π_2	π_5	π_4
	B	π_4	π_2	π_5	π_3	π_1	π_3	π_5	π_2	π_4
	C	π_4	π_5	π_2	π_5	π_4	π_2	π_3	π_3	π_1
		A			B			C		
		P3								

Example 5.5 *Consider a three-player game ($N = \{1, 2, 3\}$) with strategy spaces defined as $\Sigma_{i=1,2,3} := \{\bar{A}, \bar{B}, \bar{C}\}$. Then, 5 CSs can be created out of 3 players (see e.g. Table 5.2). Table 5.3 presents the coalition function in its strategic representation and is constructed in the following way. When players simultaneously announce $\sigma_1 = \bar{A}, \sigma_2 = \bar{A}, \sigma_3 = \bar{C}$ the $\pi_2 = \{12|3\}$ forms. If the third player changes her message to $\sigma_3 = \bar{A}$ the $\pi_1 = \{123\}$ forms, and so on. Note that there are usually many combinations of players' actions that support a certain CS. For instance, π_1 is supported by $\{\bar{A}, \bar{A}, \bar{A}\}, \{\bar{B}, \bar{B}, \bar{B}\}$ and $\{\bar{C}, \bar{C}, \bar{C}\}$.*

Next, assume that the game is characterized by the per-membership partition function as in Table 5.2. Substituting losses into Table 5.3 we obtain Table 5.4. Now we can look for an NE in this game:

Table 5.4 Example of the strategic representation of the OMG[11]

		P2			P2			P2		
		A	B	C	A	B	C	A	B	C
P1	A	1/5/3	7/1/4	7/1/4	2/2/5	2/3/1	3/6/9	2/2/5	3/6/9	2/3/1
	B	2/3/1	2/2/5	3/6/9	7/1/4	1/5/3	7/1/4	3/6/9	2/2/5	2/3/1
	C	2/3/1	3/6/9	2/2/5	3/6/9	2/3/1	2/2/5	7/1/4	7/1/4	1/5/3
		A			B			C		
		P3								

It is not difficult to show that there is no NE in the game of Table 5.4. In other words, for the OMG considered, there are no stable CSs, or $OMG^{ST} = \emptyset$.

Note that player's payoffs may be equal in many different coalitions. Consequently, to define a game completely we have to characterize player's preferences in a situation when she is indifferent w.r.t. losses. We call this *distinction assumptions.*

Definition 5.14 (Distinction assumptions) *If a player in her choice is indifferent between two different coalitions, then we make the following set of distinction assumptions:*

1. A player always prefers a larger coalition to a smaller one (the *size assumption*) and

[11] Per-membership partition function in terms of losses.

2. If a player is in a non-trivial coalition and has a possibility to alter her strategy to be in another coalition of equal size, then this player prefers to stay in the present coalition (the *status quo assumption*).

While looking for a NE we always compare only pairs of payoffs/coalitions. Hence, the distinction assumptions completely define preferences of a player in the case when she is indifferent between two coalitions w.r.t. payoffs.

Example 5.6 *If P1 is indifferent w.r.t. losses between coalitions (1,7,8) and (1,2), then she prefers (1,7,8) to (1,2) due to the size assumption. If P1 being in (1,7) is indifferent w.r.t. losses between coalitions (1,7) and (1,2), then she prefers to stay in (1,7) due to the status quo assumption.*

Restricted open-membership game

The main drawback of the OMG is that players cannot play as singletons even if they wish. For that reason the concept of the *Restricted Open-Membership Game* (ROMG), suggested by Bloch (1997) and formalized by Rundshagen (2002), was introduced which aims to remove this deficiency. Only a slight modification of the OMG definition is required, i.e. enlargement of player i's strategy space by the message that announces her preference of playing non-cooperatively. Technically, it can be done by enlarging each Σ_i by a message $\{\bar{0}\}$. Hence, when player i announces message $\sigma_i = \{\bar{0}\}$, it means that she wants to play as a singleton, and nobody else can create a coalition with her.

Definition 5.15 (Restricted Open-Membership Game (ROMG)) *Each player $i \in N = \{1, ..., n\}$ announces a message $\sigma_i \in \Sigma_i := \{\bar{A}, \bar{B}, ..., \bar{N}, \bar{0}\}$. Players who announce the same message form a coalition unless this message is $\{\bar{0}\}$. In this case, at least those players who announced $\{\bar{0}\}$ play as singletons. A coalition function $\psi^{ROMG}(.)$ maps the strategy vector $\sigma := [\sigma_1, ..., \sigma_i, ..., \sigma_j, ..., \sigma_n]^T$ into a coalition structure $\pi := \{C_1, C_2, ..., C_k, ..., C_m\}$ according to the rule: $C_k = \{i\} \cup \{j | \sigma_i = \sigma_j \neq \{\bar{0}\}\}$.*

The restricted open-membership game will be denoted by ROMG($N, \Sigma, \psi^{ROMG}(.), \phi(.)$) or by ROMG and the class of restricted open-membership games by ROMG(N, Σ, $\psi^{ROMG}(.)$) or by $ROMG^C$.

Example 5.7 *Consider again the game from Example 5.5, where to each player's strategy space we add a message $\bar{0}$. Table 5.5 depicts the strategic representation for this game. The only NE is $\{\bar{0}, \bar{0}, \bar{0}\}$, which supports CS π_5, in which all players play non-cooperatively. Note that it is enough to find one NE that supports a certain CS to conclude that this CS is stable.*

Table 5.5 Example of the ROMG (strategic representation)[12]

		P2				P2			
		A	B	C	$\bar{0}$	A	B	C	$\bar{0}$
P1	A	1/5/3	7/1/4	7/1/4	7/1/4	2/2/5	2/3/1	3/6/9	3/6/9
	B	2/3/1	3/6/9	3/6/9	3/6/9	7/1/4	1/5/3	7/1/4	7/1/4
	C	2/3/1	2/2/5	3/6/9	3/6/9	3/6/9	2/3/1	2/2/5	3/6/9
	$\bar{0}$	2/3/1	3/6/9	2/2/5	3/6/9	3/6/9	2/3/1	2/3/1	3/6/9
		A				B			
		P3							

		P2				P2			
		A	B	C	$\bar{0}$	A	B	C	$\bar{0}$
P1	A	2/2/5	3/6/9	2/3/1	3/6/9	2/2/5	3/6/9	3/6/9	3/6/9
	B	3/6/9	2/2/5	2/3/1	3/6/9	3/6/9	2/2/5	3/6/9	3/6/9
	C	7/1/4	7/1/4	1/5/3	7/1/4	3/6/9	3/6/9	2/2/5	3/6/9
	$\bar{0}$	3/6/9	3/6/9	2/3/1	3/6/9	3/6/9	3/6/9	3/6/9	**3/6/9**
		C				$\bar{0}$			
		P3							

The result of the above example is not surprising. In every ROMG a non-cooperative CS is always stable. It comes from the definition of this game, where it is assumed that players are not allowed to join singletons. Hence, when all the players announce message $\bar{0}$, no player can unilaterally change the non-cooperative CS that emerges, since there is no coalition to join. This property of the ROMG game is visible in Table 5.5 in the bottom-right box, where $NE = \{\bar{0}, \bar{0}, \bar{0}\}$ is found. The change of $P1's$ message to any other than $\bar{0}$ cannot change the CS π_5 (we move along the last column of the bottom-right box of Table 5.5). Similarly, the change of $P2's$ message cannot alter the situation (we move along the last row of the bottom-right box of Table 5.5). Finally, to check the ability of $P3$ to successfully change her initial strategy we compare a bottom-right cell of each of the four boxes. Also here no change of the non-cooperative CS is possible. Hence, in our example $ROMG^{ST} = \{\pi_5\}$.

The EMU, established by the Maastricht Treaty ((1991); see Chapter 1), may be considered as an example of a (n) (R)OMG.

Exclusive-membership game

The concept of Exclusive-Membership Games (EMGs) was introduced by Hart and Kurz (1983) and belongs to the class of games with *unanimous agreement.* The first definition presented below is of the form proposed by Eyckmans and Finus (2003) and corresponds to the Δ-game of Hart and Kurz (1983). All the players simultaneously announce the composition of a coalition they want to form, under the condition that the player belongs to the coalition which she announces. More formally $\Sigma_i = \{C_j | i \in C_j\}$. In particular, it can be a trivial coalition, i.e. $\sigma_i = \{i\}$. In the Δ-game a coalition is formed by those players who want to play together, even if not all the players from the proposed coalitions

[12] Per-membership partition function in terms of losses.

actually want it. For example, when $\sigma_1 = \sigma_2 = (1,2,3), \sigma_3 = (3), \sigma_4 = (4,5,6)$ and $\sigma_5 = \sigma_6 = (5,6)$ the outcome is [12|3|4|56]. Players 1 and 2 propose the coalition they both belong to and therefore form it. Player 3 decided to play non-cooperatively and therefore plays it, as she cannot be forced to cooperation with players 1 and 2. Player 4 remains a singleton as players 5 and 6 did not include her to a proposed coalition.

Definition 5.16 (Exclusive-Membership Game (Δ-version)) *The strategy space of a player $i \in N = \{1, ..., n\}$ is given by messages that correspond to all the possible combinations of players forming coalitions of which player i is part of (including trivial ones). More formally: $\Sigma_i = \{C_j | i \in C_j\}$. A coalition function $\psi^{EMG(\Delta)}(.)$ maps a strategy vector $\sigma := [\sigma_1, ..., \sigma_i, ..., \sigma_j, ..., \sigma_n]^T$ into a coalition structure $\pi := \{C_1, C_2, ..., C_k, ..., C_m\}$, according to the rule: $C_k = \{i\} \cup \{j | \sigma_i = \sigma_j\}$.*

The exclusive-membership game will be denoted by $EMG(N, \Sigma^{\Delta}, \psi^{EMG(\Delta)}(.), \phi(.))$ or by EMG(Δ) and the class of exclusive-membership games by $EMG(N, \Sigma^{\Delta}, \psi^{EMG(\Delta)}(.))$ or by $EMG^C(\Delta)$.

Table 5.6 Example of an EMG(Δ - version, strategic representation)[13]

		P3: C_3^1				P3: C_3^2			
		P2: C_2^1	C_2^2	C_2^3	C_2^4	P2: C_2^1	C_2^2	C_2^3	C_2^4
P1	C_1^1	**3/6/9**	3/6/9	3/6/9	3/6/9	**3/6/9**	3/6/9	3/6/9	3/6/9
	C_1^2	3/6/9	**2/2/5**	3/6/9	3/6/9	3/6/9	**2/2/5**	3/6/9	3/6/9
	C_1^3	3/6/9	3/6/9	3/6/9	3/6/9	7/1/4	7/1/4	7/1/4	7/1/4
	C_1^4	3/6/9	3/6/9	3/6/9	2/2/5	3/6/9	3/6/9	3/6/9	2/2/5

		P3: C_3^3				P3: C_3^4			
		P2: C_2^1	C_2^2	C_2^3	C_2^4	P2: C_2^1	C_2^2	C_2^3	C_2^4
P1	C_1^1	3/6/9	3/6/9	**2/3/1**	3/6/9	3/6/9	3/6/9	3/6/9	2/3/1
	C_1^2	3/6/9	**2/2/5**	2/3/1	3/6/9	3/6/9	**2/2/5**	3/6/9	2/3/1
	C_1^3	3/6/9	3/6/9	**2/3/1**	3/6/9	3/6/9	3/6/9	3/6/9	2/3/1
	C_1^4	3/6/9	3/6/9	2/3/1	2/2/5	7/1/4	7/1/4	7/1/4	1/5/3

Example 5.8 *Consider again the game from Example 5.5 but define the strategy spaces as:*

$$\Sigma_1 := \{C_1^1 := (1), C_1^2 := (1,2), C_1^3 := (1,3), C_1^4 := (1,2,3)\},$$
$$\Sigma_2 := \{C_2^1 := (2), C_2^2 := (1,2), C_2^3 := (2,3), C_2^4 := (1,2,3)\},$$
$$\Sigma_3 := \{C_3^1 := (3), C_3^2 := (1,3), C_3^3 := (2,3), C_3^4 := (1,2,3)\}.$$

In Table 5.6 we present the EMG(Δ) in its strategic form. It is not difficult to show that there are 8 NEs in this game:[14] $NE_1 = \{C_1^1, C_2^1, C_3^1\}$,

[13]Per-membership partition function in terms of losses.

[14]In all tables NEs are in bold.

$NE_2 = \{C_1^2, C_2^2, C_3^1\}$, $NE_3 = \{C_1^1, C_2^1, C_3^2\}$, $NE_4 = \{C_1^2, C_2^2, C_3^2\}$, $NE_5 = \{C_1^2, C_2^2, C_3^3\}$, $NE_6 = \{C_1^1, C_2^3, C_3^3\}$, $NE_7 = \{C_1^3, C_2^3, C_3^3\}$, $NE_8 = \{C_1^2, C_2^2, C_3^4\}$. NE_1 and NE_3 support CS π_5, NE_2, NE_4, NE_5, and NE_8 support CS π_2, NE_6 and NE_7 support CS π_4. Hence, $EMG^{ST}(\Delta) = \{\pi_2, \pi_4, \pi_5\}$.

For example, the recent accession of 10 new countries to the EU may be modelled as an EMG(Δ),[15] because when one of the accession countries did not accept the proposal to create an extended EU of 25 countries, this country would not be a member of the extended EU. In some real-life situations, parties which are going to sign an agreement may condition their involvement on the participation in the proposed 'coalition' of all other players that the 'coalition' is actually made of. The Treaty Establishing a Constitution for Europe (2004) is an example of such an agreement which is in force if and only if it is ratified by all prospective members. In other words, players do not want to form any smaller coalition if some of the players drop out from the initial proposal. For these cases the Γ-game of Hart and Kurz (1983) is useful.

Definition 5.17 (Exclusive-Membership Game (Γ-version, EMG(Γ))) *The strategy space of a player $i \in N = \{1, ..., n\}$ is given by messages that correspond to all the possible combinations of players forming coalitions of which player i takes part (including trivial ones). More formally: $\Sigma_i = \{C_j | i \in C_j\}$. A coalition function $\psi^{EMG(\Gamma)}(.)$ maps a strategy vector $\sigma := [\sigma_1, ..., \sigma_i, ..., \sigma_j, ..., \sigma_n]^T$ into a coalition structure $\pi := \{C_1, C_2, ..., C_k, ..., C_m\}$, according to the rule: $C_k = \{i\} \cup \{j \in (\sigma_i)_{-i} \mid \underset{k \in (\sigma_i)_{-i}}{\forall} \sigma_k = \sigma_i\}$.*

The exclusive-membership game will be denoted by $EMG(N, \Sigma^\Gamma, \psi^{EMG(\Gamma)}(.), \phi(.))$ or by $EMG(\Gamma)$ and the class of exclusive-membership games by $EMG(N, \Sigma^\Gamma, \psi^{EMG(\Gamma)}(.))$ or by $EMG^C(\Gamma)$.

The announced coalitions for the combination $\sigma_1 = \sigma_2 = (1,2,3)$, $\sigma_3 = (3)$, $\sigma_4 = (4,5,6)$ and $\sigma_5 = \sigma_6 = (5,6)$ would lead in an EMG(Γ) to the following coalitional structure: [1|2|3|4|56]. The coalition $(1,2)$ is not formed as it was not proposed. Instead, $(1,2,3)$ was proposed but the third player does not want this coalition.

[15] With some additional assumptions concerning the old 15 EU countries.

Table 5.7 Example of an EMG(Γ - version, strategic representation)[16]

		P2				P2			
		C_2^1	C_2^2	C_2^3	C_2^4	C_2^1	C_2^2	C_2^3	C_2^4
P1	C_1^1	**3/6/9**	3/6/9	3/6/9	3/6/9	**3/6/9**	3/6/9	3/6/9	**3/6/9**
	C_1^2	3/6/9	**2/2/5**	3/6/9	3/6/9	3/6/9	**2/2/5**	3/6/9	3/6/9
	C_1^3	3/6/9	3/6/9	3/6/9	3/6/9	7/1/4	7/1/4	7/1/4	7/1/4
	C_1^4	**3/6/9**	3/6/9	3/6/9	3/6/9	**3/6/9**	3/6/9	3/6/9	3/6/9
		C_3^1				C_3^2			
		P3							

		P2				P2			
		C_2^1	C_2^2	C_2^3	C_2^4	C_2^1	C_2^2	C_2^3	C_2^4
P1	C_1^1	3/6/9	3/6/9	**2/3/1**	3/6/9	**3/6/9**	3/6/9	3/6/9	**3/6/9**
	C_1^2	3/6/9	**2/2/5**	2/3/1	3/6/9	3/6/9	**2/2/5**	3/6/9	3/6/9
	C_1^3	3/6/9	3/6/9	**2/3/1**	3/6/9	3/6/9	3/6/9	3/6/9	3/6/9
	C_1^4	3/6/9	3/6/9	**2/3/1**	3/6/9	3/6/9	3/6/9	3/6/9	**1/5/3**
		C_3^3				C_3^4			
		P3							

Example 5.9 *Using the strategy spaces defined for the game from Example 5.8 but applying the coalition function from Definition 5.17 we obtain Table 5.7. It can be shown that there are 15 NEs in the game. They support four CSs:* $\pi_1, \pi_2, \pi_4,$ *and* π_5*. Hence,* $EMG^{ST}(\Gamma) = \{\pi_1, \pi_2, \pi_4, \pi_5\}$.

Relations between the OMG, the ROMG and the EMG It can be shown that the following theorem holds:[17]

Theorem 5.1

$$OMG^{ST} \subset ROMG^{ST} \subset EMG^{ST}(\Delta).$$

Intuitively, the stability of a CS depends on the number of possible deviations in each game. In the OMG players can join any other coalition including trivial ones; hence, the number of possible deviation is the highest. In the ROMG deviations are more limited since players can announce the message $\bar{0}$, that prevents from joining such players. Finally, in the EMG(Δ) the number of deviations is the lowest of all three games considered. It is because a player can join other players if and only if she is in the coalition proposed by these players.

The next property has already been mentioned above:

$$NC \subset ROMG^{ST},\ NC \subset EMG^{ST}(\Delta),\ \text{and}\ NC \subset EMG^{ST}(\Gamma).$$

Intuitively, in the ROMG, the EMG(Δ) and EMG(Γ) a CS made of singletons is stable since no deviation is possible (see, for instance, Example 5.7).

[16] Per-membership partition function in terms of losses.
[17] For the proof of this result see Finus and Rundshagen (2003).

5.4.2 Simultaneous games - MU setting

As it was mentioned at the beginning of this chapter, even for a relatively low number of players the full set of feasible CSs can be so big that the analysis of all of them would be extremely difficult. Moreover, some coalitions are rather implausible like a coalition between a (relatively) large member of an MU and a bank of a small outside country. This automatically reduces the number of CSs taken into account. Consequently, in this book our attention will (usually) be restricted only to a subset of CSs, which seems to be plausible and interesting from the policy-recommendation point of view. However, any restriction on the set of feasible CSs has important consequences on both:

- the definition of the coalition function $\psi(.)$, and/or
- the stability of CSs.

The latter effect can be caused by the fact that a lower number of feasible CSs in the game reduces the number of players' possibilities to alter their strategies changing a CS. This result is not in contrast to reality. In the real world, some coalitions are not feasible and nobody considers them as possible outcomes of negotiations. This may increase the number of stable CSs.

The influence of the reduced set of feasible CSs on the definition of the coalition function is more challenging. The aim is to find a coalition function which results in the desired Π^R. Definitions 5.13, 5.15, 5.16 and 5.17 from the previous section only boil down to the full set of feasible CSs. Hence, in order to obtain the OMG, the ROMG, and both Δ- and Γ-versions of EMG, which result in the (specific) reduced set of feasible coalition structures, we have to redefine the rules of coalition formation embodied in the coalition function $\psi(.)$ and strategy spaces Σ_i. For example, in the OMG, every combination of players' messages is plausible; hence, all partitions of players into coalitions have to be considered.

Assume that in a five-player application some coalitions are not plausible and a coalition function should result in the following reduced set of feasible CSs: $\Pi^R = \{[12|3|4|5], [1|23|4|5], [1234|5], [1|2|3|4|5]\}$. It is clear that Definition 5.13 of the OMG does not allow to obtain Π^R. Consider, for instance, the following combination of strategies $\left(\sigma_1 = \bar{A}, \sigma_2 = \bar{A}, \sigma_3 = \bar{A}, \sigma_4 = \bar{A}, \sigma_5 = \bar{A}\right)$. Which CS if any is created since there is no full coalition in Π^R? In such a situation, it could be assumed that players create [1234|5] as this is the largest possible coalition made by the players with the same message. However, which CS is reached when the combination of strategies becomes ($\sigma_1 = \bar{A}$, $\sigma_2 = \bar{A}$, $\sigma_3 = \bar{A}$, $\sigma_4 = \bar{B}$, $\sigma_5 = \bar{C}$)? In the CSs [12|3|4|5] and [1|23|4|5], we can find as the largest coalitions made by players with the same message the coalitions (1,2) in the former CS and (2,3) in the latter CS. Hence, the assumption to create the largest possible coalition made by the players with the same message does not discriminate enough to obtain a well-defined coalition function (the same strategy vector leads to two different CSs). A way out of this problem in our example would be the introduction of another assumption, where a player with a lower index has priority over a player with a higher index. So, for $(\sigma_1 = \bar{A},\ \sigma_2 = \bar{A},\ \sigma_3 = \bar{A},\ \sigma_4 = \bar{B},\ \sigma_5 = \bar{C})$ CS [12|3|4|5] emerges, since under this assumption $P1$ has priority over $P2$. However, such a discrimination collides with the spirit of simultaneous games, where all the players of the same type should be equal (in principle).

Consequently, we propose refinements in the definition of the OMG, the ROMG and both Δ- and Γ-versions of the EMG which are suitable for our MU setting. In this book, we exclude the possibility that a central bank cooperates with partial (possibly trivial) coalitions of fiscal players of whose monetary policy management this bank is responsible for. This is the central assumption, which reduces the number of feasible CSs. Moreover, we assume that central banks cannot cooperate with each other.[18] Hence, we have to define rules of coalition formation, i.e. players' strategy spaces and the coalition function, in such a way that all the desired characteristics of Π^R hold.

First, we introduce some additional terminology. We divide a set $N := \{1, 2, ..., n\}$ of players in two subsets: central banks $b \in B$ and fiscal players $i^b \in F$, where superscript b in i^b means that bank b is responsible for the monetary policy management for fiscal player (country) i and $B \cup F = N$, $B \cap F = \emptyset$, $n_f := |F| \leqq n - 1$, $n_b := |B| \geqq 1$, $n_f + n_b = n$. This leads to the following definition:

Definition 5.18 (Bank jurisdictional set) *The set of all the countries for which a bank b is liable is called a bank-b jurisdictional set (BJS) and is denoted by $BJS(b)$. More formally, $BJS(b) := \{i^b \in N\}$.*

Clearly, each MU consists of the following set of players $\{BJS(b), b\}$. In particular, if bank b is responsible for monetary policy management in only one country, i.e. $|BJS(b)| = 1$ or $BJS(b) = \{i^b\}$, we say that players from set $\{i^b, b\}$ constitute a trivial MU. A non-trivial MU consists of the set of players $\{BJS(b), b\}$ such that $|BJS(b)| \geqq 2$. Formally, to denote a specific MU we will write MU(b) where b is a bank responsible for the monetary policy management within the MU considered. However, in most of our applications there is only one non-trivial MU; hence the above more formal notation will be omitted. A coalition of all fiscal players in an MU(b) is called a *full MU fiscal coalition* (or more formally a *full MU b fiscal coalition*) and denoted by F^b,[19] whereas a coalition of all the fiscal players in a game is called the *grand fiscal coalition* (denoted by F). All other coalitions between fiscal players are called *partial fiscal coalitions*. When a central bank b joins the relevant full fiscal coalition F^b, then it becomes a *full MU coalition* (or more formally a *full MU(b) coalition*). For trivial MU(b) a coalition (i^b, b) will be called a *full national coalition.* If we talk about players which are members of the particular MU we will refer to all the other players in the game as to *outsiders* and to the MU members as to *insiders.*

[18] This assumption can easily be waived in our setting, as it will be shown in Chapter 8.
[19] Note that the full fiscal coalition is, in fact, the BJS of a central bank of an MU.

For our (possibly multiple) MU(s) settings we define the specific kind of reduced set of feasible CSs, which we call the MU-reduced set of feasible CSs.

Definition 5.19 (MU-reduced set of feasible coalition structures) *Let Π be the set of feasible coalition structures for the class of coalition formation games $\Gamma(N, \Sigma, \psi(.))$, in which players from the set N can be divided in two groups: central banks $b \in B$ and fiscal players $i^b \in F$ where $B \cup F = N$, $B \cap F = \emptyset$, $n_f = |F| \leqq n-1$, $n_b = |B| \geqq 1$, and $n_f + n_b = n$. Let Π' be the subset of Π consisting of only those coalition structures in which every central bank plays non-cooperatively or is in either the full MU coalition or in the full national coalition. Then Π' is called the MU-reduced set of feasible coalition structures and is denoted by Π^{MU}.*

Remark 5.2 *The MU-reduced set of feasible coalition structures meets the independence property.*

Example 5.10 *Assume that $N = 4$. The central bank (4) is responsible for monetary policy management in three countries (1,2, and 3). Then, from Example 5.1 we already know that* $\Pi = \{[1234], [123|4], [124|3], [134|2], [1|234], [12|3|4], [13|2|4], [14|2|3], [23|1|4], [24|1|3], [1|2|34], [1|2|3|4].[12|34], [13|24], [14|23]\}$. *To construct Π^{MU} we choose only those $\pi \in \Pi$ in which central bank 4 as P4 plays non-cooperatively or is in the full MU coalition. Consequently,* $\Pi^{MU} = \{[1|2|3|4], [1234]; [123|4]; [12|3|4]; [13|2|4]; [1|23|4]\}$.

Of course, the exact definition of the MU-reduced set of feasible CSs depends on the particular MU setting considered. In the MU setting of Chapter 6 we will utilize the Π^{MU} from Example 5.10. In Chapter 7, there will also be one MU but, additionally, outsiders (countries and corresponding central banks) will be present in the game. Hence, in this setting we will have one common CB for k countries in the MU and $n_b - 1$ other CB_js for the $n_f - k$ countries being outside the MU. In Chapter 8 we will study the case of two MUs and 2 outside countries with corresponding central banks, but we will not consider all the CSs from the set of feasible CSs for brevity.[20]

Now, we will redefine the OMG, the ROMG and the EMG(Δ/Γ) in such a way that the resulting set of feasible coalition structures will be Π^{MU}.

Open-membership game for an MU

The following definition is the MU refinement of Definition 5.13.

Definition 5.20 (Open-Membership Game for an MU) *Let the strategy spaces of both fiscal and monetary players $i \in N = \{1, ..., n\}$ (which are defined as in Definition 5.19) be $\Sigma_i := \{\bar{A}, \bar{B}, ..., \bar{N}\}$.*[21] *Each player announces*

---

[20] The set of feasible CSs in Chapter 8 will not be, in fact, the MU-reduced set of feasible CSs as defined in Definition 5.19 as we will allow for the existence of a coalition of CBs. Hence, in Chapter 8 we will not study any of the simultaneous coalition formation mechanisms.

[21] Note that the cardinality of the players' strategy space equals the number of fiscal players, i.e. $|\Sigma_{i^k_r}| = i$.

a message. The coalition function $\psi^{OMG(MU)}(.)$ maps the strategy vector $\sigma := [\sigma_1, ..., \sigma_i, ..., \sigma_j, ..., \sigma_n]^T$ to a coalition structure $\pi := \{C_1, C_2, ..., C_k, ..., C_m\}$ in the following way:

1. *If:*

   (i) all fiscal players who have the same central bank announce the same message, and

   (ii) those messages are the same as the message announced by their central bank,

   then a full MU/national coalition is created (i.e. a coalition consisting of all fiscal players with the same message and the relevant bank). More formally, if $\underset{i^b \in BJS(b)}{\forall} \sigma_{i^b} = \sigma_b$ *and* $\underset{i \notin R(b)}{\forall} \sigma_i \neq \sigma_b$, *then a coalition* $C_k = \{b\} \cup \{i^b : i^b \in R(b)\}$ *emerges.*

2. *All fiscal players, $i \in F$, who did not create full MU/national coalitions in point 1 and who announce the same message form a coalition, i.e. $C_k = \{i\} \cup \{j | \sigma_i = \sigma_j\}$.*

3. *All monetary players who did not create full MU/national coalitions in point 1 play as singletons.*[22]

The open-membership game for an MU will be denoted by $OMG(N, \Sigma, \psi^{OMG(MU)}(.), \phi(.))$ or by OMG(MU) and the class of open-membership games for an MU by $OMG(N, \Sigma, \psi^{OMG(MU)}(.))$ or by $OMG^C(MU)$.

It is not difficult to show that the above definition guarantees that the coalition function results in the reduced set of feasible coalition structures and that this set is the MU-reduced set of feasible coalition structures (Π^{MU}). Example 5.11 helps to grasp the difference between the standard OMG and the OMG(MU).

Example 5.11 *Assume that $N = 4$. There are two central banks (B1 and B2) and two fiscal players (countries C1 and C2). B1 is responsible for monetary policy management in country 1 and B2 in country 2, or $BJS(B1) := \{C1\}$ and $BJS(B2) := \{C2\}$. According to Definition 5.20 we have the following strategy spaces: Σ_{C1}, Σ_{C2}, Σ_{B1}, $\Sigma_{B2} := \{\bar{A}, \bar{B}\}$. We present the coalition function $\psi^{OMG(MU)}(.)$ using the strategic form of the game:*

Table 5.8 Example of the coalition function for the OMG(MU)

		$C2$		$C2$		$C2$		$C2$	
		A	B	A	B	A	B	A	B
$C1$	A	π_1	π_3	π_3	π_1	π_2	π_5	π_4	π_2
	B	π_2	π_4	π_5	π_2	π_1	π_3	π_3	π_1
		A,A		A,B		B, A		B,B	
		$B1, B2$							

[22] Note that, according to this definition, any coalition between banks is impossible.

where $\pi_1 = [C1B1|C2B2]$*;* $\pi_2 = [C1|B1|C2B2]$; $\pi_3 = [C1B1|C2|B2]$*;* $\pi_4 = [C1C2|B1|B2]$*;* $\pi_5 = [C1|B1|C2|B2]\}$*. It is easy to check that* $\Pi^{MU} = \{\pi_1, \pi_2, \pi_3, \pi_4\}$ *is the MU-reduced set of feasible coalition structures.*[23]

Note that there is a slight difference between the spirit of the standard OMG and the OMG(MU). In the former game $B1$ cannot enter coalition $(C1, C2)$ and exclude player $C2$, whereas in the latter game it is possible, i.e. $B2$ can exclude $C2$ from ($C1$,$C2$) and create ($C1$,$B1$). It can be interpreted as a stronger fiscal players' preference to cooperate with their central banks.

Restricted open-membership game for an MU

The following definition is the MU refinement of Definition 5.15.

Definition 5.21 (Restricted Open-Membership Game for an MU) *With the notation of Definition 5.19, define the strategy spaces of both fiscal and monetary players* $i \in N$ *as* $\Sigma_i := \{\bar{A}, \bar{B}, ..., \bar{N}, \bar{0}\}$*. Each player announces a message. The coalition function* $\psi^{ROMG(MU)}(.)$ *maps a strategy vector* $\sigma := [\sigma_1, ..., \sigma_i, ..., \sigma_j, ..., \sigma_n]^T$ *to a coalition structure* $\pi := \{C_1, C_2, ..., C_k, ..., C_m\}$ *in the following way:*

1. *If:*

(i) all fiscal players who have the same central bank announce the same message different from $\{\bar{0}\}$*, and*

(ii) those messages are equal to the message announced by their central bank, then a full MU/national coalition is created (i.e. a coalition consisting of all fiscal players with the same message and the relevant bank). More formally, if $\underset{i^b \in BJS(b)}{\forall} \sigma_{i^b} = \sigma_b$ *and* $\underset{i \notin BJS(b)}{\forall} \sigma_i \neq \sigma_b$*, then a coalition* $C_k = \{b\} \cup \{i^b : i^b \in R(b)\}$ *emerges.*

2. *All fiscal players,* $i \in F$*, who did not create full MU/national coalitions in point 1 and who announce the same message different from* $\{\bar{0}\}$ *form a coalition, i.e.* $C_k = \{i\} \cup \{j | \sigma_i = \sigma_j\}$*.*

3. *All monetary players who did not create full MU/national coalitions in point 1 play as singletons.*

The restricted open-membership game for an MU will be denoted by ROMG($N, \Sigma, \psi^{ROMG(MU)}(.), \phi(.)$*) or by ROMG(MU) and the class of restricted open-membership games for an MU by ROMG(*$N, \Sigma, \psi^{ROMG(MU)}(.)$*) or by ROMG*^{C}*(MU).*

Again, it is not difficult to show that the above definition guarantees that the coalition function results in the set of feasible coalition structures Π^{MU}.

[23] Refer to Example 5.1, where all the possible partitions of the set $N = \{1, 2, 3, 4\}$ are listed. Choose there only those CSs in which both CBs play non-cooperatively or are in full national coalitions.

Example 5.12 *Following the setting of the previous example, we consider now strategy sets:* $\Sigma_{C1}, \Sigma_{C2}, \Sigma_{B1}, \Sigma_{B2} := \{\bar{A}, \bar{B}, \bar{0}\}$ *. The coalition function* $\psi^{ROMG(MU)}(.)$ *becomes:*

Table 5.9 Example of the coalition function for ROMG(MU)

		C2			C2			C2		
		A	B	0	A	B	0	A	B	0
C1	A	π_1	π_3	π_3	π_3	π_1	π_3	π_2	π_5	π_5
	B	π_2	π_4	π_5	π_5	π_2	π_5	π_1	π_3	π_3
	0	π_2	π_5	π_5	π_5	π_2	π_5	π_2	π_5	π_5
		A,A			A,B			B, A		
		$B1, B2$								

		C2			C2			C2		
		A	B	0	A	B	0	A	B	0
C1	A	π_4	π_2	π_5	π_3	π_3	π_3	π_4	π_5	π_5
	B	π_3	π_1	π_3	π_5	π_4	π_5	π_3	π_3	π_3
	0	π_5	π_2	π_5	π_5	π_5	π_5	π_5	π_5	π_5
		B,B			A,0			B,0		
		$B1, B2$								

		C2			C2			C2		
		A	B	0	A	B	0	A	B	0
C1	A	π_2	π_5	π_5	π_4	π_2	π_5	π_4	π_5	π_5
	B	π_2	π_4	π_5	π_5	π_2	π_5	π_5	π_4	π_5
	0	π_2	π_5	π_5	π_5	π_2	π_5	π_5	π_5	π_5
		0,A			0,B			0, 0		
		$B1, B2$								

where $\pi_1 = [C1B1|C2B2]$; $\pi_2 = [C1|B1|C2B2]$; $\pi_3 = [C1B1|C2|B2]$; $\pi_4 = [C1C2|B1|B2]$, $\pi_5 = [C1|B1|C2|B2]\}$*. Hence, we obtain* Π^{MU}*, which is the same as in Example 5.11.*

Exclusive-membership game for an MU

The next definition is the MU refinement of Definition 5.16.

Definition 5.22 (Exclusive-Membership Game for MU (Δ-version)) *Let fiscal and monetary players* $i \in N$ *be defined as in Definition 5.19. The strategy space of a fiscal player* $i^b \in F$ *is given by messages that correspond to all the possible coalitions between the fiscal players she is part of (including trivial ones) and also by the full MU/national coalitions with the respective central banks. More formally:* $\Sigma_{i^b} := \{C_j | i^b \in C_j$*, where* C_j *consists of only fiscal players, is the full MU/national coalition of player* $j\}$*. The strategy space of monetary player* $b \in B$ *is given by either the trivial coalition message* (b) *or the full MU/national coalition message* $(b, BJS(b))$*, i.e.* $\Sigma_b := \{(b), (b, BJS(b))\}$*. Both for fiscal and monetary players, coalition function* $\psi^{EMG(\Delta,MU)}(.)$ *maps the strategy vector* σ *into a coalition structure* π *as follows:* $C_k = \{i\} \cup \{j | \sigma_i = \sigma_j\}$

with the following exception: a central bank can be a member of a non-trivial coalition (the full MU/national coalition) if and only if all other members participate in this coalition. The exclusive-membership game for MU ($\Delta-$version) will be denoted by EMG(N, Σ^{EMG}, $\psi^{EMG(\Delta)}(.)$, $\phi(.)$, MU) or by EMG(Δ, MU) and the class of open-membership games for an MU by EMG(N, Σ^{EMG}, $\psi^{EMG(\Delta)}(.)$, MU) or by EMG^C(Δ, MU).

Example 5.13 *Consider the EMG(Δ) with 3 players, where players $C1$ and $C2$ are fiscal players and $B1$ is a monetary player with $BJS(B1) := \{C1, C2\}$. Following the Definition 5.22 we define the players' strategy spaces as:*

$$\Sigma_1 := \left\{C_1^1 := (C1), C_1^2 := (C1, C2), C_1^3 := (C1, C2, B1)\right\},$$
$$\Sigma_2 := \left\{C_2^1 := (C2), C_2^2 := (C1, C2), C_2^3 := (C1, C2, B1)\right\},$$
$$\Sigma_3 := \left\{C_3^1 := (B1), C_3^2 := (C1, C2, B1)\right\}.$$

Table 5.10 presents the coalition function for this game:

Table 5.10 Example of the coalition function for EMG(Δ, MU)

		$C2$			$C2$		
		C_2^1	C_2^2	C_2^3	C_2^1	C_2^2	C_2^3
$C1$	C_1^1	π_1	π_1	π_1	π_1	π_1	π_1
	C_1^2	π_1	π_2	π_1	π_1	π_2	π_1
	C_1^3	π_1	π_1	π_2	π_1	π_1	π_3
		C_3^1			C_3^2		
		$B1$					

where $\pi_1 = [1|2|3]$, $\pi_2 = [12|3]$, $\pi_3 = [123]$. Hence, the resulting reduced set of feasible coalition structures is Π^{MU}.

Also in Definition 5.17 of the EMG(Γ) a similar change in the definition of players' strategy spaces is required.

Definition 5.23 (Exclusive-Membership Game for MU (Γ-version)) *Let fiscal and monetary players $i \in N$ and their respective strategy spaces be defined as in Definition 5.22. Both for fiscal and monetary players, coalition function $\psi^{EMG(\Gamma,MU)}(.)$ maps a strategy vector σ into a coalition structure π as follows: $C_k = \{i\} \cup \{j \in (\sigma_i)_{-i} | \underset{k \in (\sigma_i)_{-i}}{\forall} \sigma_k = \sigma_i\}$. The exclusive-membership game for MU (Γ-version) is denoted as EMG(Γ, MU) and the class of exclusive-membership games as EMG(N, Σ^{EMG}, $\psi^{EMG(\Gamma)}(.)$, $\phi(.)$, MU) (or, alternatively, by EMG(Γ) and EMG^C(Γ, MU), respectively).*

Example 5.14 *Consider the EMG(Γ, MU) with 3 players and relevant strategy spaces as in Example 5.13. Coalition function $\psi^{EMG(\Gamma,MU)}(.)$ yields:*

Table 5.11 Example of the coalition function for EMG(Γ, MU)

		$C2$			$C2$		
		C_2^1	C_2^2	C_2^3	C_2^1	C_2^2	C_2^3
$C1$	C_1^1	π_1	π_1	π_1	π_1	π_1	π_1
	C_1^2	π_1	π_2	π_1	π_1	π_2	π_1
	C_1^3	π_1	π_1	π_1	π_1	π_1	π_3
		C_3^1			C_3^2		
		$B1$					

where $\pi_1 = [1|2|3]$, $\pi_2 = [12|3]$, $\pi_3 = [123]$. *Again the resulting reduced set of feasible coalition structures is* Π^{MU}. *The only difference with Example 5.13 is for the strategy combination* (C_1^3, C_2^3, C_3^1), *which results in* π_1 *(non-cooperative regime) instead of* π_2 *(partial cooperation). This difference occurs because in the EMG(*Γ, MU*) the coalition is created if and only if all the players from the proposed coalition actually propose it. In this case* $B1$ *chooses to play non-cooperatively; hence,* π_2 *does not emerge.*

5.4.3 Alternative way to find stable coalition structures in simultaneous games

In practice, when the number of players increases it is difficult to find the set of stable CSs in the simultaneous games using their strategic representation. For instance, in the case of 6 players, $6^6 = 46.656$ for the OMG and $7^7 = 117.649$ for the ROMG combinations of different strategies should be examined while looking for the NE. However, we can develop more convenient methods to find stable CSs for our simultaneous games. This will be the subject of this subsection. We will try to provide the reader with some intuition why and how calculation speed can be considerably increased for the games in question. A more formal description of the algorithms to find stable CSs in our simultaneous games are presented in the Appendix. Now, we will show that it is not necessary to consider the strategic form of a game to look for stable CSs. To demonstrate this, the per-membership partition function representation can be utilized. To grasp the basic idea, consider again the game in Table 5.3, which is reproduced in Table 5.12 for convenience:

Table 5.12

	π_1	π_2	π_3	π_4	π_5
	[123]	[12|3]	[13|2]	[1|23]	[1|2|3]
$P1$	1	2	7	2	3
$P2$	5	2	1	3	6
$P3$	3	5	4	1	9

Informally, it can be said that the NE occurs when we can find at least one combination of strategies which is considered to be optimal by every player, assuming that all the other players stick to their strategies. The CS, which is supported by an NE combination of strategies, is stable (see Definition 5.11). Consequently, we will try to find stable CSs, first by elimination of those CSs, which are not stable, i.e. for which no such combination of strategies exists.

Assume that there is a combination of strategies $(\sigma_1, \sigma_2, \sigma_3)$ that leads to π_1. Does this combination constitute an NE? To answer this question consider a situation of P_i $i = 1, 2, 3$. First, note that in the OMG, the ROMG, and the EMG to achieve π_1 it must be that: $\sigma_1 = \sigma_2 = \sigma_3$. This is the only type of combination of strategies that leads to the first CS. Hence, for instance, any change of $P1$'s strategy means that $\sigma_1^* \neq (\sigma_2 = \sigma_3)$. Considering $P1$ in π_1 (Table 5.12), we find that any unilateral change of this player's strategy (i.e. $\sigma_1^* \neq (\sigma_2 = \sigma_3)$) leads to π_4. Finding that $\phi_1(\pi_1) < \phi_1(\pi_4)$, we conclude that $P1$ does not want to deviate her strategy; i.e. this player's current strategy is optimal (assuming that other players stick to their strategies). Consequently, $P1$ does not cause instability of π_1. However, the situation is different for $P2$ for whom $\phi_2(\pi_1) > \phi_2(\pi_3)$. Hence, $P2$ has an incentive to change her strategy and we can conclude that π_1 is not stable. More formally, there exists $\sigma_1^* \neq \sigma_1$ such that $\phi_2(\psi(\sigma_1^*, \sigma_2, \sigma_3)) < \phi_2(\psi(\sigma_1, \sigma_2, \sigma_3))$. Following this logic we could check all 5 CSs in Table 5.12. In the OMG the CS π_2 is not stable as $P3$ prefers to change her decision and join $P1$ and $P2$ in order to create $(P1, P2, P3)$. CS π_3 is not stable as $P1$ wants to leave $(P1, P3)$ and play non-cooperatively in π_5. CS π_4 is not stable as $P1$ would like to join $P2$ and $P3$ and create $(P1, P2, P3)$. The last CS π_5 is not stable because $P2$ wants to join $P3$ or $P1$ and *vice versa* for both cases. We see that the result, obtained in a formal way in Example 5.5, is confirmed, i.e. $OMG^{ST} = \emptyset$.

To formalize elements of the above analysis, we have to introduce some definitions and theorems. In the remainder of this section, Π means either Π^F or Π^{MU}.

Definition 5.24 (Coalition structure strategy set) *Let* $\Pi := \{\pi_1, ..., \pi_m\}$ *be the set of all possible coalition structures for the class of coalition formation games* $\Gamma(N, \Sigma, \psi(.))$. *Then, a coalition structure strategy set (CSSS)* $\Sigma^{\pi_i} \subset \Sigma$ *is defined as the set of all strategy vectors that support* π_i, *or* $\Sigma^{\pi_i} := \left\{\sigma := [\sigma_1, ..., \sigma_N]^T : \pi_i = \psi(\sigma)\right\}$. *Hence, each* Σ^{π_i} *satisfies:*

$$\Sigma^{\pi_i} \neq \varnothing \text{ for } i = 1, 2, ..., m \; ; \quad \cup_{i=1}^{m} \Sigma^{\pi_i} = \Sigma \text{ and } \Sigma^{\pi_i} \cap \Sigma^{\pi_j} = \varnothing \text{ if } i \neq j.$$

The above definition implies the following corollaries:

Corollary 5.1 *Assume that* $\pi = \psi(\sigma_1, ..., \sigma_N)$ *and that player* $i \in N$ *considers to change her strategy. Every change of the strategy* σ_i *to* $\sigma_i' \neq \sigma_i$, *such that* $\sigma' := [\sigma_1, ..., \sigma_i', ..., \sigma_N]^T \in \Sigma^{\pi} \ni [\sigma_1, ..., \sigma_i, ..., \sigma_N]^T := \sigma$ *leads to the same coalition structure* π.

Corollary 5.2 *Assume that* $\pi = \psi(\sigma_1, ..., \sigma_N)$ *and that player* $i \in N$ *considers to change her strategy. Every change of the strategy* σ_i *to* $\sigma_i' \neq \sigma_i$, *such that* $\sigma' := [\sigma_1, ..., \sigma_i', ..., \sigma_N]^T \notin \Sigma^{\pi} \ni [\sigma_1, ..., \sigma_i, ..., \sigma_N]^T =: \sigma$ *leads to a different coalition structure* π', *or* $\pi' \neq \pi$, *where* $\pi = \phi(\sigma)$ *and* $\pi' = \phi(\sigma')$.

Using Corollary 5.2 we can introduce the concept of a deviation:

Definition 5.25 (Full deviation) *Assume that* $\pi = \psi(\sigma_1, ..., \sigma_N)$ *and that player* $i \in N$ *considers to change her strategy. A change of the strategy* σ_i *to* $\sigma_i' \neq \sigma_i$ *such that* $\sigma' := [\sigma_1, ..., \sigma_i', ..., \sigma_N]^T \notin \Sigma^\pi \ni [\sigma_1, ..., \sigma_i, ..., \sigma_N]^T =: \sigma$ *is called player i's full deviation from coalition structure* π *(origin CS) to coalition structure* π' *(end CS). A deviation will be denoted by* $d(i, \sigma, \sigma', \pi, \pi')$.

Note that a player's full deviation is independent of the per-membership partition function $\phi(.)$ and indicates the possibility to deviate. It does not say whether the player actually exercises this full deviation. Player $i \in N$ will deviate if and only if $\pi' \succ \pi$.

Definition 5.26 (Full deviation set) *Let* $\Gamma(N, \Sigma, \psi(.))$ *be the class of coalition formation games. The set of all possible full deviations of all players* $i \in N$ *from all coalition structures* $\pi \in \Pi$ *will be called the full deviation set and will be denoted by* $D^F(\Pi)$ *or* D^F.

It is worth underlining that because a deviation set is irrelevant for the per-membership partition function $\phi(.)$, each class of the coalition formation games has its own deviation set.

Example 5.15 *For the 3-player OMG in Table 5.12 full deviation set* $D^{F,OMG}$ $(\Pi = \{\pi_1, ..., \pi_5\})$ *consists of:*

Table 5.13 Example of a full deviation set

$d_1 = \left(P1, \left(\bar{A}, \bar{A}, \bar{A}\right), \left(\bar{B}, \bar{A}, \bar{A}\right), \pi_1, \pi_4\right)$	$d_{z+1} = \left(P1, \left(\bar{B}, \bar{A}, \bar{A}\right), \left(\bar{A}, \bar{A}, \bar{A}\right), \pi_4, \pi_1\right)$
$d_2 = \left(P1, \left(\bar{A}, \bar{A}, \bar{A}\right), \left(\bar{C}, \bar{A}, \bar{A}\right), \pi_1, \pi_4\right)$	$d_{z+2} = \left(P1, \left(\bar{C}, \bar{A}, \bar{A}\right), \left(\bar{A}, \bar{A}, \bar{A}\right), \pi_1, \pi_4\right)$
$d_3 = \left(P2, \left(\bar{A}, \bar{A}, \bar{A}\right), \left(\bar{A}, \bar{B}, \bar{A}\right), \pi_1, \pi_3\right)$	$d_{z+3} = \left(P2, \left(\bar{A}, \bar{A}, \bar{A}\right), \left(\bar{A}, \bar{A}, \bar{A}\right), \pi_1, \pi_3\right)$
$d_4 = \left(P2, \left(\bar{A}, \bar{A}, \bar{A}\right), \left(\bar{A}, \bar{C}, \bar{A}\right), \pi_1, \pi_3\right)$	$d_{z+4} = \left(P2, \left(\bar{A}, \bar{A}, \bar{A}\right), \left(\bar{A}, \bar{A}, \bar{A}\right), \pi_1, \pi_3\right)$
$d_5 = \left(P3, \left(\bar{A}, \bar{A}, \bar{A}\right), \left(\bar{A}, \bar{A}, \bar{B}\right), \pi_1, \pi_2\right)$	$d_{z+5} = \left(P3, \left(\bar{A}, \bar{A}, \bar{A}\right), \left(\bar{A}, \bar{A}, \bar{A}\right), \pi_1, \pi_2\right)$
$d_6 = \left(P3, \left(\bar{A}, \bar{A}, \bar{A}\right), \left(\bar{A}, \bar{A}, \bar{C}\right), \pi_1, \pi_2\right)$	$d_{z+6} = \left(P3, \left(\bar{A}, \bar{A}, \bar{A}\right), \left(\bar{A}, \bar{A}, \bar{A}\right), \pi_1, \pi_2\right)$
$d_7 = \left(P2, \left(\bar{B}, \bar{A}, \bar{A}\right), \left(\bar{B}, \bar{B}, \bar{A}\right), \pi_4, \pi_2\right)$	$d_{z+7} = \left(P2, \left(\bar{B}, \bar{B}, \bar{A}\right), \left(\bar{B}, \bar{A}, \bar{A}\right), \pi_2, \pi_4\right)$
$d_8 = \left(P2, \left(\bar{B}, \bar{A}, \bar{A}\right), \left(\bar{B}, \bar{C}, \bar{A}\right), \pi_4, \pi_5\right)$	$d_{z+8} = \left(P2, \left(\bar{B}, \bar{C}, \bar{A}\right), \left(\bar{B}, \bar{A}, \bar{A}\right), \pi_5, \pi_4\right)$
$d_9 = \left(P3, \left(\bar{B}, \bar{A}, \bar{A}\right), \left(\bar{B}, \bar{A}, \bar{B}\right), \pi_4, \pi_3\right)$	$d_{z+9} = \left(P3, \left(\bar{B}, \bar{A}, \bar{B}\right), \left(\bar{B}, \bar{A}, \bar{A}\right), \pi_2, \pi_4\right)$
$d_{10} = \left(P3, \left(\bar{B}, \bar{A}, \bar{A}\right), \left(\bar{B}, \bar{A}, \bar{C}\right), \pi_4, \pi_5\right)$	$d_{z+10} = \left(P3, \left(\bar{B}, \bar{A}, \bar{C}\right), \left(\bar{B}, \bar{A}, \bar{A}\right), \pi_5, \pi_4\right)$
...	...
$d_z = \left(P1, \left(\bar{A}, \bar{B}, \bar{A}\right), \left(\bar{C}, \bar{B}, \bar{A}\right), \pi_3, \pi_5\right)$	$d_{2z} = \left(P1, \left(\bar{C}, \bar{B}, \bar{A}\right), \left(\bar{A}, \bar{B}, \bar{A}\right), \pi_5, \pi_3\right)$

As the total number of full deviations, $2z$, in $D^{F,OMG}(\Pi = \{\pi_1, ..., \pi_5\})$, i.e. $2z = D^{F,OMG}(\Pi)$ is very high, we do not report all of them. Note that $D^{F,OMG}(\Pi = \{\pi_1, ..., \pi_5\})$ has an interesting property: each full deviation has its counterpart full deviation, i.e. the full deviation in the opposite direction. More formally:

Lemma 5.1 *Let* Π *be the set of all possible coalition structures and* $D^F(\Pi)$ *the full deviation set for the coalition formation game* $\Gamma(N, \Sigma, \psi(.))$. *If there exists* $d(i \in N, \sigma \in \Sigma, \sigma' \in \Sigma, \pi \in \Pi, \pi' \in \Pi) \in D^F$, *then there also exists*
$d(i \in N,\ \sigma' \in \Sigma,\ \sigma \in \Sigma,\ \pi' \in \Pi,\ \pi \in \Pi) \in D^F$.

Intuitively, if player $i \in N$ can deviate from π to π' by changing her strategy, she can also deviate in the opposite direction, i.e. from π' to π. Next, notice that many full deviations from Table 5.13 coincide as far as players involved, the origin CS and the end CS are concerned. What differentiate them are different strategy vectors that lead to the origin CS and/or the end CS. In fact, each group of such similar full deviations describes the same deviation of a player, namely of a player i from π to π'. An actual player's decision to deviate will be based on her payoffs in both CSs considered (in other words on the per-membership partition function). Hence, once we identified the full deviation set, we are no more interested in strategy vectors that lead both to π and to π' but we focus on full deviations as such and evaluate feasibility of them in the context of the per-membership partition function.

Definition 5.27 (Deviation set and deviations) *Let $D^F(\Pi)$ be the full deviation set for the class of coalition formation games $\Gamma(N, \Sigma, \psi(.))$.*

Then, $D = \{(i \in N, \pi \in \Pi, \pi' \in \Pi) : (i, \sigma, \sigma', \pi, \pi') \in D^F$ for some $\sigma,\ \sigma' \in \Sigma\}$ will be called the deviation set and denoted by $D(\Pi)$ or D. The elements of this set, denoted by $\pi \xrightarrow{i} \pi'$, will be called deviations.

Example 5.16 *For the OMG in Table 5.12 the deviation set is $D^{OMG}(\Pi)$*

$$= \left\{ \begin{array}{l} \pi_1 \xrightarrow{P1} \pi_4, \pi_1 \xrightarrow{P2} \pi_3, \pi_1 \xrightarrow{P3} \pi_2, \pi_2 \xrightarrow{P1} \pi_5, \pi_2 \xrightarrow{P2} \pi_5, \pi_2 \xrightarrow{P3} \pi_1, \\ \pi_2 \xrightarrow{P1} \pi_3, \pi_2 \xrightarrow{P2} \pi_4, \pi_3 \xrightarrow{P1} \pi_5, \pi_3 \xrightarrow{P2} \pi_1, \pi_3 \xrightarrow{P3} \pi_5, \pi_3 \xrightarrow{P1} \pi_2, \\ \pi_3 \xrightarrow{P3} \pi_4, \pi_4 \xrightarrow{P1} \pi_1, \pi_4 \xrightarrow{P2} \pi_5, \pi_4 \xrightarrow{P3} \pi_1, \pi_4 \xrightarrow{P2} \pi_2, \pi_4 \xrightarrow{P3} \pi_3, \\ \pi_5 \xrightarrow{P1} \pi_2, \pi_5 \xrightarrow{P1} \pi_3, \pi_5 \xrightarrow{P2} \pi_2, \pi_5 \xrightarrow{P2} \pi_4, \pi_5 \xrightarrow{P3} \pi_3, \pi_5 \xrightarrow{P3} \pi_4. \end{array} \right\}$$

Of course, a deviation set is also symmetric, i.e. if $d := \left(\pi \xrightarrow{i} \pi'\right) \in D$, then $d' := \left(\pi' \xrightarrow{i} \pi\right) \in D$.

The following theorem holds for the OMG:

Theorem 5.2 *In coalition formation game $OMG(N, \Sigma, \psi(.), \phi(.))$ a coalition structure $\pi \in \Pi$ is stable, i.e. there exists at least one NE that supports π, if there is no player $i \in N$, who prefers to deviate from π given the deviation set $D(\Pi)$ and the per-membership partition function $\phi(.)$. In other words, for no player $i \in N$ there exists a $\bar{d}\left(\pi \xrightarrow{i} \pi'\right) \in D(\Pi)$ such that $\pi' \succ \pi$.*

Proof. See Michalak *et al.* (2005). ∎

Theorem 5.2 says that for the OMG it is possible to consider the deviation set to find stable CSs. However, as far as now, we did not manage to reduce the complexity of the solution, as this set has to be found using a strategic representation of the game. The question is whether it is possible and, if yes, how to construct the deviation set without referring to the strategic form. In the algorithms outlinedbelow, we will present a method of looking for stable CSs without considering the strategic form of the game in detail. Instead, mainly the partition form is considered.

Algorithms to look for stable coalition structures

By definition, each player in the OMG can join another player or a coalition or leave her current (non-trivial) coalition and play as a singleton. Hence, each player in each CS has at least one possibility to deviate. More formally:

Corollary 5.3 *In each OMG^C and $OMG^C(MU)$, for each combination of $\pi \in \Pi$ and $i \in N$ there exists $\pi' \in \Pi^F$ such that $d := \left(\pi \xrightarrow{i} \pi'\right) \in D$.*

Example 5.17 *In Table 5.12 we have 3 players and 5 CSs which gives 15 combinations of i and π. Referring to Example 5.16, we see that there are 24 feasible deviations and every player in any coalition structure has at least one deviation. Not surprisingly, in π_5 players have two deviations as each player can join one of the other players to create a partial coalition. Also in CSs with partial coalitions, each player can either decide to play non-cooperatively or join a singleton, who stays outside the partial coalition.*

Using the above analysis we propose a more formal algorithm in the Appendix. The intuition behind it is straightforward from the definition of the OMG: every player can leave the current (possibly trivial) coalition and join any other (possibly trivial) one.

Clearly, for the class of MU-coalition formation games as the OMG($|N| \geqq 2, \Sigma, MU$) we have to construct a different algorithm. It is caused by the fact that in the $\text{OMG}^C(MU)$ our special assumptions concerning strategies, coalition function, and (consequently) Π^{MU} must be taken into account. Comparing Algorithm 5.1 to Algorithm 5.2 (see Appendix) the most important difference is that in the latter players are no more homogeneous since we have to discriminate between fiscal and monetary players in order to apply to each group different rules of coalition formation (see Definition 5.21). The intuition behind Algorithm 5.2 is not so straightforward. For this reason, we present its main aspects below.

Consider CS $\pi = \{C_1, C_2, ..., C_m\} \in \Pi^{MU} := \{\pi_1, \pi_2, ..., \pi_w\}$ and player i which belongs to coalition $C_j \in \pi$. The following five possibilities result:[24]

1. Player i is a central bank playing in π as a singleton. Then bank i can join its full fiscal coalition if this coalition belongs to π, i.e. if $BJS(i) =: C_k \in \pi$. Moreover, if there is a coalition in π of which $BJS(i)$ is a subset, i.e. if there is $C_k \in \pi$ such that $BJS(i) \subset C_k$ then i breaks up this coalition into $BJS(i)$ and $C_{k_{-BJS(i)}}$ and joins $BJS(i)$. Otherwise, no deviation of a bank i from π is possible (Step 5.1 in Algorithm 5.2).

2. Player i is a central bank playing in π as a member of a full MU(i) coalition, i.e. $i \in C_k := (BJS(i), i)$. Then bank i can leave this coalition and play as a singleton. The remaining (fiscal) players from the full MU(i) coalition play in a full fiscal MU(i) coalition, i.e. in $C_{k_{-i}} = BJS(i)$ (Step 5.2 in Algorithm 5.2).

[24] The correctness of this intuition will be proven in the remaining of this section.

3. Player i is a fiscal player playing in π as a member of a non-trivial fiscal coalition C_k. Then player i can leave this coalition and join any other fiscal (possibly trivial) coalition, she can decide to play as a singleton, or she can join her CB b if and only if $JCB(b) := \{i^b\}$. The remaining players of coalition C_k play in coalition $C_{k_{-i}}$ (Step 5.3 in Algorithm 5.2).

4. Player i is a fiscal player playing in π as a singleton. Then player i can join any other fiscal (possibly trivial) coalition (Step 5.3 in Algorithm 5.2).

5. Player i is a fiscal player playing in π as a member of a full MU(b) coalition, i.e. $i = i^b \in C_k := (BJS(b), b)$. Then player i can leave this coalition and join any other (possibly trivial) fiscal coalition or she can decide to play as a singleton. Since central bank b cannot be in a coalition with only a partial coalition of fiscal players from $BJS(b)$ the remaining players of coalition C_k break up into two coalitions: (i) a trivial coalition (b), and (ii) partial coalition of fiscal players $C_{k_{-i^b -b}}$. In particular, if C_k is a trivial MU(b) then $C_{k_{-i^b -b}} = \{\emptyset\}$ (Step 5.4 in Algorithm 5.2).

Is Algorithm 5.2 complete? In other words, does it consider all possible cases? In fact, one could claim that in the 3-player OMG($N := \{C1^{CB}, C2^{CB}, CB\}$, $\Sigma, \psi^{OMG(MU)}, MU$) that results in $\Pi^{MU} := \{\pi_1 := [C1C2CB], \pi_2 := [C1C2|CB], \pi_3 := [C1|C2|CB]\}$, there is a feasible situation which is not taken into account in the above intuition and, hence, in the Algorithm 5.2. More in detail, assume that $\pi_3 = \psi^{OMG(MU)}([\sigma_{C1} = \bar{A}, \sigma_{C2} = \bar{B}, \sigma_{CB} = \bar{A}]^T)$. Obviously, player $C2$ can change her strategy σ_{C2} to $\bar{A}$ and by doing that deviate to $[C1C2CB] =: \pi_1 = \psi^{OMG(MU)}([\sigma_{C1} = \bar{A},\ \sigma_{C2} = \bar{A},\ \sigma_{CB} = \bar{A}]^T)$. Note that such a deviation is not included in the above intuition as neither in Point 3, nor in Point 4 and nor in Point 5 a fiscal player can (by a deviation) create a full MU coalition. Does it mean that Algorithm 5.2 is ill-defined?

Note that the above problem is caused by the assumption that a CB cannot cooperate with a partial coalition of relevant fiscal players. If we consider OMG($N := \{C1, C2, CB\}, \Sigma, \psi^{OMG}$) instead of OMG($N, \Sigma, \psi^{OMG(MU)}, MU$), this problem would not exist as a strategy vector $[\sigma_{C1} = \bar{A}, \sigma_{C2} = \bar{B}, \sigma_{CB} = \bar{A}]^T$ would support $\Pi^F \ni \pi := [C1CB|C2]$. However, it is not only the special MU definition of $\psi^{OMG(MU)}$ that can cause a problem of the kind as described above. Every restriction on ψ or on Σ may have similar effects, i.e. it will be no more obvious which deviations are plausible in a given CS unless we consider the full deviation set. But the analysis of the full deviation set involves the study of, by far, a lot more possibilities. and this is actually something that we want to avoid.

To make our argument more transparent, consider the simple game which illustrates the problem raised above. In the ROMG($N := \{1, 2\}$), the resulting set of feasible CSs is $\Pi^F = \{\pi_1 := [12], \pi_2 := [1|2]\}$. CS π_2 can be created by the following strategy vectors: $\sigma^{(1)} = [\bar{A},\ \bar{B}]^T$, $\sigma^{(2)} = [\bar{B},\ \bar{A}]^T$, $\sigma^{(3)} = [\bar{A}, \bar{0}]^T$, $\sigma^{(4)} = [\bar{B}, \bar{0}]^T$, $\sigma^{(5)} = [\bar{0}, \bar{A}]^T$, $\sigma^{(6)} = [\bar{0}, \bar{B}]^T$, $\sigma^{(6)} = [\bar{0}, \bar{0}]^T$. In the

OMG($N := \{1,2\}$) we do not have to know which strategy vectors actually created $\pi_2 = [1|2]$. We only know that the messages were different and that each player by changing her strategy could join the other player in order to create $\pi_1 = [12]$. Now, the situations seem to be much more complicated since, if $\pi_1 = [1|2]$ is created by $\sigma^{(3)} = [\bar{A}, \bar{0}]^T$, then a deviation of $P1$ from π_2 to π_1 is impossible because $P2$ announced message $\{\bar{0}\}$ and nobody can join her. Moreover, for strategy vector $\sigma^{(6)} = [\bar{0}, \bar{0}]^T$ no deviation at all is feasible.

Should we consider all those possibilities? Fortunately, the answer is negative. It should be stressed again that to prove that a CS is stable it is enough to show that there is only one strategy vector supporting this CS which constitutes an NE. It is obvious that in the ROMG($N := \{1,2\}$) example, CS π_2 is stable since strategy vector $\sigma^{(6)} = [\bar{0}, \bar{0}]^T$ is an NE by definition. In the remaining of this section we will show that in general only some special combinations of strategies have to be taken into account to evaluate whether a CS is stable or not. Those special combinations are, in fact, the most restrictive strategy vectors.[25] Intuitively, by the most restrictive strategy vectors we mean such strategy vectors which result in CSs characterized by the lowest number of feasible deviations of players. We will need the following two definitions:

Definition 5.28 (Coalition Structure Full Deviation Set (CSDS^F)) *The set of all full deviations in which a certain coalition structure π_j is an origin coalition structure is called a coalition structure π_j full deviation set (CSDS^F) and will be denoted by $D^F(\pi_j)$. Its elements are called full coalition structure π_j deviations or full π_j-deviations.*

Clearly, we have $D^F(\pi_j) \subseteq D^F$ and $\cup_{i=1}^{s} D^F(\pi_i) = D^F$ and $D^F(\pi_i) \cap D^F(\pi_j) = \varnothing$ if $i \neq j$ and s is the total number of CSs in the game.

Definition 5.29 (Coalition Structure Deviation Set (CSDS)) *The set of all deviations in which the origin coalition structure is π_j is called a coalition structure deviation set (CSDS) and will be denoted by $D(\pi_j)$. Its elements are called coalition structure deviations or π_j-deviations.*

Similarly, we have $D(\pi_j) \subseteq D$ and $\cup_{i=1}^{s} D(\pi_i) = D$ and $D(\pi_i) \cap D(\pi_j) = \emptyset$ if $i \neq j$ with s defined as before.

Now we will analyze CSDSs in the ROMG looking for a relationship between a strategy vector that created a certain CS and the number of possible deviations from this CS. Consider the ROMG($n \geqq 2$). Let $\pi = \{C_1, C_2, ..., C_m\} \in \Pi$ and let two strategy vectors $\sigma, \sigma' \in \Sigma^\pi$ be defined as follows:

(i) case A: $\sigma := [\overline{m}_1, ..., \overline{m}_n]$ where $\overline{m}_j$ is a message and some of them may be $\{\bar{0}\}$ but $\overline{m}_i \neq \{\bar{0}\}$.

(ii) case A': $\sigma' := [\overline{m}'_1, ..., \overline{m}'_n]$ where $\overline{m}'_j$ is a message and for $j = 1, ..., i-1, i+1, ..., n$ we have $\overline{m}'_j = \overline{m}_j$but $\overline{m}'_i = \{\bar{0}\}$.

Hence, strategy vectors σ and σ' differ only w.r.t. message m'_i. We may say that strategy vector σ' is more restrictive than strategy vector σ. Moreover, note that the above assumptions (i.e. $\sigma, \sigma' \in \Sigma^\pi$) imply that player i

[25]This property is also used, for instance, in Finus and Rundshagen (2003).

in both cases plays as a singleton; hence, a CS π created by these two strategy vectors ($\pi = \psi(\sigma) = \psi(\sigma')$) is of the form $\{C_1, C_2, ..., (i), ..., C_m\} \in \Pi$ and $\overline{m}_i \neq \overline{m}_1, ..., \overline{m}_{i-1}, \overline{m}_{i+1}, ..., \overline{m}_n$. How does this difference in strategy vectors influence the composition of the CSDS and the number of its elements in particular?

From Definition 5.15 of the ROMG and the previous analysis we know that:

1. For both σ and σ' all the players $1, ..., n$ have a possibility to unilaterally alter their strategy in such a way that they may join any different coalition:
   (a) a non-trivial coalition from the set $\{C_1, C_2, ..., C_{k-1}, C_{k+1}, ..., C_m\}$ if such a coalition exists;
   (b) any trivial coalition from the set $\{C_1, C_2, ..., C_{k-1}, C_{k+1}, ..., C_m\}$ if such a coalition exists and is not created by a strategy $\{\bar{0}\}$.
2. For both σ and σ' any player $1, ..., i-1, i+1, ..., n$, who belongs to a non-trivial coalition, may alter her strategy and become a singleton.

In other words, the fact, that player i's initial strategy in the case A' is $\{\bar{0}\}$, does not decrease this player's number of deviations (which are embodied in point 1 above). Now, denote all the π-deviations defined in points 1 and 2 by $\tilde{D}(\pi)$ and $\tilde{D}'(\pi)$ in cases A and A', respectively. We have:

$$\tilde{D}(\pi) = \tilde{D}'(\pi); \; \tilde{D}(\pi) \subseteq D(\pi); \text{ and } \tilde{D}'(\pi) \subseteq D(\pi). \tag{5.1}$$

In particular, if all $C_1, C_2, ..., C_{k-1}, C_{k+1}, ..., C_m$ are singletons created by messages $\{\bar{0}\}$, then: $\tilde{D}(\pi) = \tilde{D}'(\pi) = \emptyset$.

In points 1 and 2, we have not defined all possible deviations in case A. In particular, in point 1.b) we did not define a possibility for all the players $1, ..., n$ to unilaterally alter their strategy in such a way that they may join a trivial coalition $C_k := (i)$. Again, these new deviations exist only for the case A. Denote them by $\hat{D}(\pi)$. Notice, that this set is never empty, i.e. $\hat{D}(\pi) \neq \emptyset$, since in the case A every other player $-i$ can join player i who announced $m_i \neq \{\bar{0}\}$. Moreover, $\hat{D}(\pi) \subseteq D(\pi)$ and there are no other deviations possible in both cases considered. Denote all the deviations possible in the case A by $\breve{D}(\pi)$. We have:

$$\breve{D}(\pi) = \tilde{D}(\pi) \cup \hat{D}(\pi). \tag{5.2}$$

Hence, combining (5.1) and (5.2) we obtain the following relationship:

$$\tilde{D}'(\pi = \psi(\sigma')) \subset \breve{D}(\pi = \psi(\sigma)).$$

Summarizing, we proved that the number of deviations in case A' is a subset of those in case A. Hence, by mathematical induction we may prove that the strategy vector from the CSSS, which features the highest number of restrictions has the lowest number of possible deviations. Moreover, such a set of deviations is contained in any other set of deviations from this CS. Hence, if the CS is not stable because there is at least one player who wants to exercise her deviation in the most restrictive case, then for any other deviation set from a given CS this deviation will exist and will be exercised by this player. Consequently, in such a case we can say that there exists no strategy vector constituting an NE and the CS considered cannot be stable. On the other hand, to show that a CS is stable it is sufficient to show that this CS is stable for the most restrictive strategy vector (i.e. no feasible deviation is exercised by any of the players).

Although this analysis was conducted under the assumption of (a) restriction(s) on the open-membership in the ROMG, its conclusions also apply to other games, as well in the standard as in the MU setting.[26] The question which remains to be answered is which strategy vectors (and, hence, deviation sets) are the most restrictive ones in every game. In the Appendix, we propose some algorithms to look for the (most restrictive) deviation sets in the ROMG^C, the EMG$^C(\Delta)$, the EMG$^C(\Gamma)$, the ROMG$^C(MU)$, the EMG$^C(\Delta, MU)$, and the EMG$^C(\Gamma, MU)$. The intuition for those algorithms is as follows. For the ROMG^C we assume that every player who plays as a singleton announced message $\bar{0}$. Hence, we redefine Algorithm 5.1 in such a way that no player can join a singleton. While looking for deviations in the EMG$^C(\Delta)$ we assume that:

(i) every player i who plays as a singleton announced message $C^i = (i)$ so that no other player can join player i and

(ii) every player in a non-trivial coalition actually announced this coalition as her strategy, i.e., if in a CS π there is a coalition $(1, 2)$ it means $P1$'s and $P2$'s strategies were $C^1 = C^2 = (1, 2)$ and not, for instance, $C^1 = C^2 = (1, 2, 3)$ (and $C^3 \neq (1, 2, 3)$). This latter strategy combination would also result in $(1, 2)$ but $P3$ would have a possibility to join $(1, 2)$ by changing her strategy to $C^{3\prime} = (1, 2, 3)$. However, by assuming that a coalition $(1, 2)$ is created by $C^1 = C^2 = (1, 2)$ we restrict any such deviation, i.e. nobody can join a non-trivial coalition.

Consequently, in Algorithm 5.5 for EMG$^C(\Delta)$:

(a) a singleton player does not deviate since she cannot join any other singleton or a non-trivial coalition;

(b) player i who deviates from non-trivial coalition C_k becomes a singleton. Remaining players from C_k play in $C_{k_{-i}}$.

In Algorithm 5.7 for EMG$^C(\Gamma)$ we make the same assumptions as for the EMG$^C(\Delta)$; however, with one exception: after player i leaves a non-trivial coalition C_k then this coalition breaks up and its players play as singletons. Hence, for every player i who belongs to a non-trivial coalition C_k there is only one deviation, namely from the CS π to an independent coalition structure of π w.r.t. C_k, i.e. $\pi^I(\pi, C_k)$ (see Definition 5.4).

In the Algorithms looking for deviation sets in ROMG$^C(MU)$, the EMG$^C(\Delta, MU)$, and the EMG$^C(\Gamma, MU)$ additionally to the above assumptions for ROMG^C, the EMG$^C(\Delta)$, and the EMG$^C(\Gamma)$ we have to take into account special characteristics of our MU setting. Hence, in the case of ROMG$^C(MU)$, we follow Algorithm 5.3 but similar to Algorithm 5.2 we assume that:

[26] See Michalak *et al.* (2005).

1. If player i is a central bank playing in π as a singleton, then bank i can join its full fiscal coalition if such a coalition belongs to π, i.e. if $BJS(i) =: C_k \in \pi$. Moreover, if there is a coalition in π to which $BJS(i)$ belongs to, i.e. if there is $C_k \in \pi$ such that $BJS(i) \subset C_k$ then i breaks up this coalition into $BJS(i)$ and $C_{k_{-BJS(i)}}$ and joins $BJS(i)$. Otherwise no deviation of a bank i from π is possible.

2. If player i is a central bank playing in π as a member of a full MU(i) coalition, i.e. $i \in C_k := (BJS(i), i)$, then bank i can leave this coalition and play as a singleton. The remaining (fiscal) players from the full $MU(i)$ coalition play in a full fiscal MU(i) coalition, i.e. in $C_{k_{-i}} = BJS(i)$.

3. If player i is a fiscal player playing in π as a member of a non-trivial fiscal coalition C_k, then player i can either leave this coalition and join any other non-trivial fiscal coalition, or she can decide to play as a singleton. The remaining players from coalition C_k play in coalition $C_{k_{-i}}$.

4. If player i is a fiscal player playing in π as a singleton, then player i can join any non-trivial fiscal coalition.

5. If a player i is a fiscal player who in π belongs to a full MU(b) coalition, i.e. $i = i^b \in C_k := (BJS(b), b)$. Then player i can leave this coalition and join any other non-trivial fiscal coalition or she can decide to play as a singleton. Since central bank b cannot be in a coalition with only a partial coalition of fiscal players from $BJS(b)$, the remaining players from coalition C_k break up into two coalitions: (i) a trivial coalition (b), and (ii) a partial coalition of fiscal players $C_{k_{-i^b-b}}$. In particular, if C_k is a trivial MU(b) then $C_{k_{-i^b-b}} = \emptyset$.

In Algorithm 5.6 for EMG$^C(\Delta, MU)$ we find the most restrictive deviation sets in the following way:

1. A singleton player does not deviate since she cannot join any other singleton or a non-trivial coalition (as in Algorithm 5.5).

2. Monetary player $i := b$ who deviates from full MU(b) coalition C_k becomes a singleton; remaining players from C_k play in $C_{k_{-b}}$.

3. Fiscal player i who deviates from non-trivial fiscal coalition C_k becomes a singleton; remaining players from C_k play in $C_{k_{-i}}$.

4. Player i who deviates from a full MU(b) coalition, i.e. $i = i^b \in C_k := (BJS(b), b)$, becomes a singleton. Since central bank b cannot be in a coalition with only a partial coalition of fiscal players from $BJS(b)$, the remaining players from coalition C_k break up into two coalitions: (i) a trivial coalition (b), and (ii) partial coalition of fiscal players $C_{k_{-i^b-b}}$. In particular, if C_k is a trivial MU(b) then $C_{k_{-i^b-b}} = \emptyset$.

The algorithm for the $\text{EMG}^C(\Gamma, MU)$ is the same as Algorithm 5.7 for the $\text{EMG}^C(\Gamma)$: after player i leaves a non-trivial coalition C_k then this coalition breaks up and its players play as singletons. Hence, for every player i who belongs to a non-trivial coalition C_k there is only one deviation, namely from the CS π to an independent CS of π w.r.t. C_k, i.e. $\pi^I(\pi, C_k)$. Note that it does not matter whether player i is a fiscal authority or a central bank; hence, the same Algorithm 5.7 can be used for the $\text{EMG}^C(\Gamma)$ and the $\text{EMG}^C(\Gamma, MU)$.

5.4.4 Sequential negotiation game

Finally, consider the case that the macroeconomic coordination is built on the basis of a hierarchical sequential negotiation process (Sequential Negotiation Game, SNG, see Bloch (1996)). The multi-stage negotiation starts with one policymaker who proposes a coalition. The order in which the agents can propose or are being proposed a coalition is given by a rule (i.e. a rule of order). Each prospective member can accept or reject the proposal in the order determined by this rule. If one policymaker rejects the proposal, he must make a counter-offer. If all members accept, the coalition is formed and all members of that coalition withdraw from the negotiations. One player after the other decides to accept an ongoing proposal or rejects and proposes another (possibly trivial) coalition. These decisions are determined by non-cooperative best-reply rules, given the coalition structure and the allocation in the previous rounds. An equilibrium of the SNG is formed when all agents quit.

The following example introduces the basic rules of the SNG:

Table 5.14[27]

	NC	C
$P1$	5	6
$P2$	4	3
$P3$	3	2

Any player can either propose cooperation (C) or decide to play non-cooperatively (NC). In the game in Table 5.14 there is a degenerated set of feasible CSs $\Pi := \{NC, C\}$. We assume the standard rule of order ($P1$, $P2$, $P3$). $P1$ is the first player in the queue. To solve the SNG we have to construct a game tree. Hence, the game tree starts from a decision node of $P1$, which has two branches - left (NC) and right (C). If $P1$ decides to cooperate, coalition $(P1, P2, P3)$ becomes an ongoing proposal and the next player in the rule of order, $P2$, is supposed to make a decision - either to accept or reject the proposal. In the latter case $P2$ has to make a counter offer. If $P2$ accepts the cooperation, the next player in the queue, $P3$, also has to choose between cooperation and non-cooperation. If this player prefers cooperation a coalition proposed by $P1$, i.e. $(P1, P2, P3)$, is accepted by all other players involved (i.e. $P2$ and $P3$) and,

[27] Per-membership function defined in terms of losses.

therefore, this coalition is created. Then, $P1$, $P2$ and $P3$ leave the game. As there are no other players, the right-hand branch of the game tree is finished with a terminal node with payoffs related to cooperation.

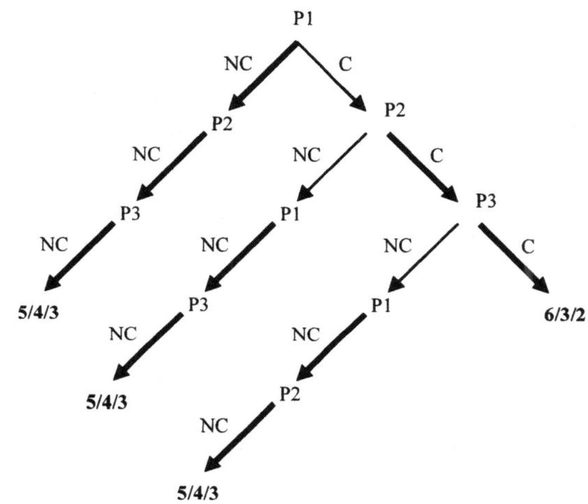

Figure 5.1 Example of the game tree for the SNG in Table 5.14

Note that in this very simple setting of two CSs, each player's decision to play non-cooperatively automatically leads to NC. If $P1$ chooses at the top decision node to play NC, she excludes coalition $(P1, P2, P3)$ from the plausible outcomes of the game. Consequently, the next in the queue $P2$ has to announce NC. $P3$ analogously. Concerning the rule of order in the book, we will usually follow the assumption that, if a just-created coalition leaves the game, the next to move is a player still in the game with the first position in the rule of order. Consider again Figure 5.1. When $P2$ decides to play non-cooperatively and leaves the game, the rule of order of players still in the game is reduced to ($P1$,$P3$). Following our assumption, the next to move is $P1$ instead of $P3$.

After a creation of the game tree, we can solve the game by backward induction. In all the left-hand branches of Figure 5.1, players have, in fact, no alternative and they follow non-cooperative actions. Consequently, the real choice is on the right-hand branches. Starting from $P3$'s right-bottom decision node, the choice to play non-cooperatively (NC) would bring her a loss 3, whereas cooperative action (C) yields a loss 2. Hence, $P3$ chooses cooperation. Now, we consider a $P2$'s move at a decision node in the middle of the right-hand branch.

This player already knows that $P3$ at a decision node below agrees to cooperate, so the action C would lead $P2$ to cooperation. Indeed, $P2$ chooses C as her loss is lower under cooperation than under non-cooperation. Finally, we consider the choice of $P1$, who knows that the left-hand branch leads to non-cooperation and the right-hand branch to cooperation. $P1$ chooses non-cooperation as her loss is lower under NC. The NE of the game in Table 5.14 is shown in Figure 5.1 with bold arrows

The following set of definitions, that formally characterize the SNG (which follows the original concept of Bloch (1996)), is based on Finus (2001, p. 304) with a modification concerning the rule of order.[28] We assume that a certain coalition can be proposed only once and we define a rule of order by a one-to-one function $\Theta : \{1, 2, ..., g, ..., n\} \rightarrow N$. For instance, $\Theta(g)$ denotes the player on the gth position in the rule of order.

Definition 5.30 (History of the SNG) *A history h^V at stage V is a list of all actions taken from stage 0 to $V - 1$. Possible actions are coalition offers, acceptances and rejections up to stage $V-1$. At any point in the game, a history h^V determines:*

1. a set $N^{(-)}$ of players who have already formed coalitions;
2. a coalition structure $\pi_{N^{(-)}}$ formed by the players in $N^{(-)}$;
3. an ongoing proposal (if any) $\hat{C}_j$;
4. a set of players N^A who has already accepted the proposal (including the initiator);
5. a list of rejected coalitions $\digamma$ and
6. a player i who moves at stage V.

Player i is called *active* at stage V if it is her turn to move after history h^V. The set of histories at which player i is active is denoted by H_i.

Definition 5.31 (A player's (continuation) SNG strategy) *A continuation strategy σ_i of player i is a mapping from H_i to her set of actions, namely:*

For $i \in N \backslash N^{(-)}$ (i.e. for all the players who have not created a coalition and left the game yet) we have:

1. $\sigma_i(h^V) \in \{C_j \subset N \backslash N^{(-)} \backslash \digamma\}$ if $\hat{C}_j = 0$ (A player can propose a coalition when there is no ongoing proposal. This proposal must be a coalition containing players who have not left the game yet and it has to be a feasible coalition). Moreover, if $\sigma_i(h^V) = \{i\}$, then $i^{V+1} := (\Theta(\Theta^{-1}(i)+1)) \backslash N^{(-)}$; else $i^{V+1} := ((\Theta(\Theta^{-1}(i) + 1)) \in \hat{C}_j)$ (i.e.: if player i proposes to play as a singleton, then the next player to move is the next player in the rule of order);

[28] Finus (2001) calls this game the Sequential Move Unanimity Game (SMUG).

2. $\sigma_i(h^V) \in \{yes, no\}$ if $\hat{C}_j \neq 0$, $i \notin N^A$ (player i's strategy set consists of *yes* and *no* if there is a non-empty ongoing proposal and if player i does not belong to a set of players who have already accepted the coalition). Then:

- if $\sigma_i(h^V) = no$, then $F = F \cup \hat{C}_j$ and $\hat{C}_j := 0, i^{V+1} := i$ (if player i rejects the ongoing proposal, then this coalition becomes an element of the list of rejected coalitions and the ongoing proposal is set to zero; player i is the next in line to submit a proposal);
- if $\sigma_i(h^V) = yes$, and $N^A \cup \{i\} = \hat{C}_j$, then $N^{(-)} = N^{(-)} \cup \hat{C}_j$ and $i^{t+1} := \Theta(\min(\Theta^{-1}(N \backslash N^{(-)})))$ (if player i accepts the ongoing proposal and all the other players in the proposed coalition have already accepted it, then these players join the set of players who have already formed coalitions and withdrew from the game; the next player to propose is the one who has not left the game and occupies the first position in the rule of order);
- if $\sigma_i(h^V) = yes$, and $N^A \cup \{i\} \subset \hat{C}_j$, $N^A \cup \{i\} \neq \hat{C}_j$ then $i^{V+1} := ((\Theta(\Theta^{-1}(i) + 1)) \in \hat{C}_j)$ (if player i accepts the ongoing proposal and not all the other players in the proposed coalition have accepted it yet, then player i joins the set of players who have already accepted the ongoing proposal; the next player in turn is the next player in the rule of order who belongs to the currently proposed coalition).

With these definitions a Sequential Negotiation Game Equilibrium (SNGE) in the sequential unanimity game SNG can be defined as follows:

Definition 5.32 (Sequential Negotiation Game Equilibrium (SNGE)) *An SNGE in a sequential move unanimity game is a subgame-perfect continuation strategy combination* $\sigma_i^*(h^V)$ *for which* $\phi_i(\sigma_i^*(h^V), \sigma_{-i}^*(h^V)) \succ \phi_i(\sigma_i'(h^V), \sigma_{-i}^*(h^V))$ *for all* $i \in N$, $h^V \in H_i$ *and* $V = \{1, 2, ..., t\}$, *where* t *is the final stage of the game.*

The assumption that a certain coalition can be proposed only once makes the original Bloch (1996) game finite and solvable by backward induction. It means that SNG - in contrast to the myopic OMG, ROMG and EMG - takes players' farsightedness into account.[29]

Example 5.18 *Unfortunately, game trees for the game settings utilized in this book (i.e. a game with five players and nine possible coalition structures) may have more than 2,000,000 decision nodes. Therefore, as a second example we present losses for a very simple 3-player game (Country 1, Country 2, CB) and three feasible coalition structures (NC - non-cooperation, C - full cooperation, F - fiscal cooperation):*

[29] Farsightedness is a characteristic of the backward-induction solution concept of the game tree.

Table 5.15 Example of SNG

	NC	*C*	*F*
Country 1	*5*	*6*	*2*
Country 2	*4*	*3*	*4*
CB	*3*	*2*	*3*

The game tree for the natural order of players [C1,C2,CB] is presented in Figure 5.2. Solving the game with backward induction leads to the outcome F.

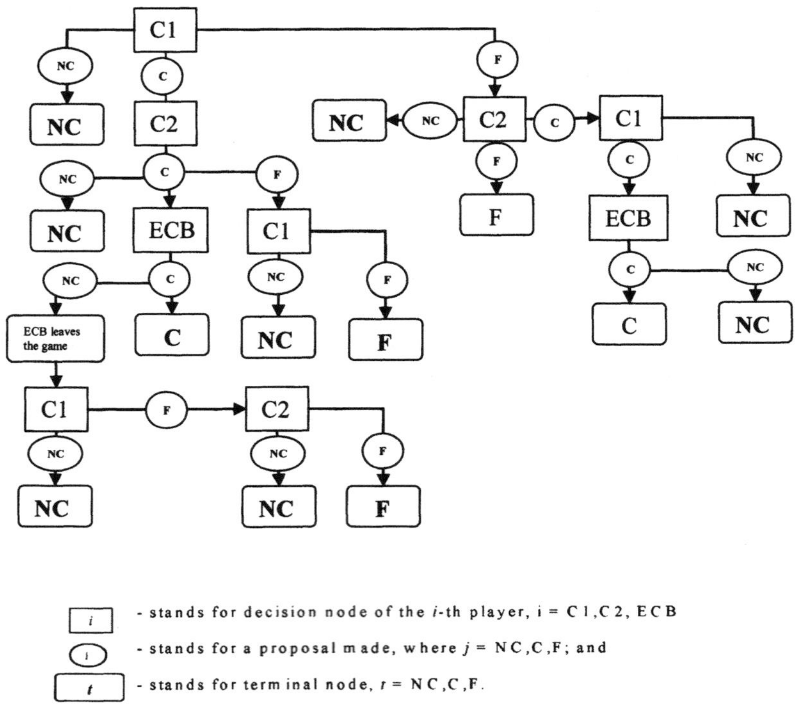

where :

Figure 5.2 SNG game tree for the example in Table 5.15

The distinction assumptions from simultaneous games have to be redefined for the SNG. First of all, the status quo assumption concerns deviations which are not present in the SNG. Secondly, the size assumption is insufficient to distinguish between coalitions in some special cases. Consider, for instance, a situation, where $P1$ is the next to make a move and that she is indifferent w.r.t. losses of four coalitions (1,2), (1,3), (1,8) and (1,7). Clearly, the size assumption cannot be the only rule, because this does not distinguish between coalitions of the same size.

Definition 5.33 (SNG distinction assumptions) *If in the SNG a player is in her choice indifferent between (possibly many) various coalitions, then her decision is based on the following set of the SNG distinction assumptions:*

1. A player always prefers a coalition containing the most important players according to the rule of order (SNG rank assumption) and

2. If there is more than one coalition satisfying 1., then a player prefers that coalition which contains the highest number of players (SNG size assumption).

Example 5.19 *Assume a natural rule of order, i.e. P*1*, P*2*, P*3*,... If P*1 *is indifferent w.r.t. losses between coalitions (1,2) and (1,4), then she prefers (1,2) to (1,4) due to the SNG rank assumption. If P*1*, being indifferent w.r.t. losses, has to choose between (1,2,3), (1,2,3,5), and (1,2,3,6), she prefers (1,2,3,5) to (1,2,3) due to the SNG size assumption and (1,2,3,5) to (1,2,3,6) due to the SNG rank assumption.*

5.5 Institutional design and equilibrium concepts

In general, two kinds of coordination can be distinguished (Beetsma *et al.* (2001)).

1. institutional or *ex-ante* coordination and

2. policy or *ex-post* coordination.

This division is related to Figure 5.1. The *ex-ante* coordination is related to the institutional framework, the coordination procedures, and the design of policy rules, whereas *ex-post* coordination takes place from the current state of affairs and concerns the actual policy decisions. More in particular, *ex-ante* coordination operates through formal binding agreements recognized by the policymakers as international obligations (e.g. the Maastricht Treaty and the SGP). By contrast, *ex-post* coordination has an informal character and refers to discretionary and *ad hoc* informal agreements stipulated among the countries.[30] The two kinds of coordination are strictly interconnected. In fact, e.g. the SGP might strongly reduce the room for discretionary coordination of the national fiscal policies. Similarly, discretionary agreements among the countries might depend on the design of the European institutions concerning fiscal cooperation as, e.g. the ECOFIN Council.

Our two-stage approach captures both *ex-ante* and *ex-post* coordination. *Ex-ante* coordination is described by the institutional setting embodied in the rules of the game during the negotiation, while *ex-post* coordination is related to the emerging equilibrium once the rules are fixed. More specifically, in the first

[30] As it is pointed out by Beetsma *et al.* (2001), we can think of the *Eurogroup*, in which the Finance Ministers of the EMU area discuss fiscal policies in an informal way, as a forum of *ex-post* co-ordination. Furthermore, also the *ECOFIN Council*, notwithstanding its more formal nature, is characterized by largely-discretionary decisions and can, therefore, be interpreted as a formal institution where not only formal but also informal agreements take place (see Chapter 1).

stage of the endogenous coalition games, different negotiation rules can lead to different equilibria. CSs with different rules correspond to different initial assumptions that can be interpreted as different institutional settings of the monetary union and can be justified on the basis of economic theory.[31] The rest of this section will discuss the economic interpretation of the negotiation rules in an MU context.

Different assumptions can be made on stability as open- or exclusive-membership rules. A particular disadvantage of OMGs is the assumption that each country can freely join any coalition. In the current EU/EMU-institutional setting there is no obvious reason why a coalition (or singleton) cannot restrict membership if the accession of outsiders implies a welfare loss. Consequently, comparing with OMG and ROMG we may assume that the EMG describes the current state of art of European institutions better. In fact, the *EU* itself is an EMG club, as every single Member State has to agree on the enlargement of the union. However, already the EMU is an open-membership club, which could be described by the OMG with only two possible messages in each player's strategy – to cooperate (monetary) or not to cooperate. Unanimity in some circumstances can also cause some EU problems since it implies a veto power that characterizes many European decisions, e.g. those about accession of new members. Assuming coalition unanimity means in fact that the whole coalition is assumed to collapse when one of its members defects. In the EMU context most economic policy measures should still be decided by all the members through a unanimous majority.

In modelling other institutions, the assumption of open membership can be more appropriate. For example, in international trade the accession to GATT/WTO is in general open to all countries if they obey the rules. The central characteristic of GATT/WTO negotiations is that they are highly institutionalized, which make them open due to political reasons. There is a possibility that a similar institutional reform may be introduced in the EMU/EU, concerning coordination of fiscal policies. Once the need for macroeconomic coordination is even more urgent and widely recognized, the member states can pursue a project of an institutionalized macroeconomic cooperation scheme based on the rules similar to GATT/WTO negotiations, in which (for political reason) membership is not exclusive. Such a cooperation could for instance be initiated by the European Commission and all EU members could be invited to participate.

Apart from coalition formation rules, an important role in our analysis is played by the concept of a Nash Equilibrium (NE); hence we list four common interpretations of an NE:

1. The self-enforcing agreement is probably the most common interpretation in which it is assumed that players reach a pre-play agreement about how they will actually play the game. There is no force which binds players so, no player should have an incentive to deviate from an agreed strategy combination. This condition is met only when each player chooses an optimal

[31] See Ecchia and Mariotti (1998) for a more general discussion on this methodology.

strategy (assuming that other players stick to their strategies). Hence, this agreement must constitute the NE. However, the main problem with this interpretation is that, if there are any pre-play negotiations, why they are not included in the game.[32]

2. The rationality argument implies that rational players would choose only a combination of strategies that constitutes an NE. If an NE is not chosen, it means that at least one player is not rational.

3. The social convention interpretation relies to common culture. It is a combination of strategies that enters people's minds. In order that this combination is stable it has to be an NE.

4. Rational beliefs/expectations say that players build up predictions how other players would play and use them to optimize own strategies. In this interpretation an NE is not a prediction of how the game is played, but it is a consistent theory of how the game might be played.

The Nash conjectures have also an economic interpretation regarding the institutional design. Nash conjectures imply a sort of the agents' myopic behaviour since agents look only at the immediate consequence of their actions without forecasting the final implication of their strategies. Several game-theoretical economists have defined some solution concepts based on the idea of indirect domination, where players foresee the other ones' reactions to their actions by making rational conjectures about the other players' behaviour in replying to their actions, i.e. each policymaker considers how many policymakers will leave the coalition if she will leave it. In such a case farsighted behaviour is introduced and different conditions for stability are requested. In other words, considering farsighted behaviour a CS can be an equilibrium of the game even if it violates the (Nash conjecture) stability condition if this violation leads to a (Nash conjecture) unstable coalition.

The main difference between the Nash conjectures and the farsighted behaviour lies in the information that players have. In the Nash conjecture it is assumed that agents cannot communicate whereas in the farsighted behaviour the opposite occurs. Thus, the Nash conjectures stress a situation in which either an 'institutional place', where negotiations can be performed, does not exist or shocks need quick policy reactions and, therefore, time for consultation is limited. The farsighted behaviour emphasizes the opposite situation and, therefore, it is linked to the assumption that a real mechanism of institutional coordination already exists (e.g. the ECOFIN Council in the EMU). However, both the above concepts do not capture the possible sequential features of the negotiation process. These features can be important in emphasizing the hegemony of a country or of a block of countries in the negotiation process. This feature is captured by SNG.

The SNG can be interpreted in two alternative ways:

[32] Note that not all NEs must be self-enforcing. Aumann (1990) offered an example in which an NE need not be self-enforcing.

1. It can be seen as a structured negotiation process taking place in the institutionalized body of negotiations.
2. It can describe a spontaneous creation of coalitions emerging from bilateral or multilateral negotiation.

The first interpretation emphasizes the possible role played by an international institution or single leader countries in the negotiation for achieving a coordination agreement. For instance, in an SNG, one can imagine that the temporary EU President Country determines the list of proponents among the Member Country Ministers, and then each minister, according to this list of order, proposes a coalition to a group of countries. Alternatively, one can assume that the list of order follows the relative power of countries and thus a list of order based on a relative country hegemony, which often characterizes the EMU history. It is worth noticing that this interpretation implies an additional element of heterogeneity among countries.[33]

The second interpretation assumes that there are no institutionalized negotiations between all the players, but that the SNG describes the spontaneous creation of coalitions from multilateral negotiations. After a shock is observed, negotiations start when a country which, for example: (a) has the strongest political power; or/and (b) is the most affected by the shock proposes a coalition. This assumption that some countries are more interested (entitled) to start negotiations is obviously plausible, even when there is no institutionalized body for macroeconomic coordination. However, when there is no exogenously given rule of order, the problem arises with the definition of the sequence of players who are supposed to move next. Either the game with a probabilistic choice of the next player in the queue may be utilized or other assumptions should be made. It is possible to construct the chance-move version of the SNG; however, it is difficult to apply it in a game with more than three players.[34]

In this book we utilize the natural rule of order $\Theta : \{1, 2, ..., n\} \to \{1, 2, ..., n\}$. The examples of the rule of order based on the standard deviation of optimal losses can be found in van Aarle *et al.* (2005).

[33] Indeed, this relative hegemony in the EMU can be exercised by one country, a block of countries or even by the central bank. All cases can be realistic under different points of view. The European Monetary System, e.g., was driven by the German economic policy and the same European Unionization process was based on the axis formed by Germany and France. An interesting application of the SNG is to consider the block of the largest countries as the leader and the block of the smallest countries as the follower and regarding the common CB as in a different institutional setting (i.e. according to its position in the rule of order, an hegemonous, a neutral or an accommodating CB). This classification can be seen as a new dimension in the study of CB independence.

[34] Finus and Rundshagen (2001) apply such a modification of the Bloch concept to 3-player games. They introduce the following rules that govern the sequence of players who move: in the ongoing proposal, the player who has the move decides who will be the next player whether to accept or rejct the proposal. Secondly, at the beginning of the game or when a coalition has been created the nature (chance-mechanism) chooses the next player to move. This concept is very appealing for our interpretation for spontanous SNGE negotiations, however, as it has been mentioned in the text, very difficult to apply in the game of more than 3 players.

The crucial element of the Bloch idea is that countries while creating a coalition make binding agreements and withdraw from the game. Apart from perfect information and the assumption that a particular coalition can be proposed only once, this is the only important requirement that must be met to ensure that sequential negotiation of coalitions actually works. It means that the indispensable institutional framework consists only of creating a mechanism of making binding agreements of cooperation, when a proposed coalition has been accepted by all the involved players. If such a mechanism exists, after the shock is observed, coalitions will be sequentially created, even when there is no other common body of negotiations.

Finally, two major assumptions of the game concepts should be stressed. As it was already said, all the presented simultaneous move games are solved with the NE-solution concept, which means that players are assumed to behave in a myopic way. This myopic behaviour assumption is waved when the SNG concept is considered. Moreover, in all the games we assume perfect information.

5.6 Social optimum and indices

From the policy-recommendation point of view, the most important question we would like to answer is which mechanism of coalition formation is the most effective, i.e. results in the most-desirable CSs from the social perspective. By social perspective we mean the point of view of a society as a whole, which aims to maximize the joint welfare of all the players. Since different games are based on different initial assumptions and correspond to different institutional settings, we can study how to structure the international policy coordination to enhance its *effectiveness* by comparing them. To setup a comparison-benchmark we define the concept of a *social optimum* CS.

Definition 5.34 (Social optimum CS) *Let $\Pi = \{\pi_1, ..., \pi_m\}$ be the set of all possible coalition structures for the coalition formation game $\Gamma(N, \Sigma, \psi(.), \phi(.))$ with per-membership partition function $\phi(.)$ defined in terms of losses. Then, a social optimum coalition structure is defined as: $\pi^{SOP} := \min_{j=1,...,m} \sum_{i=1}^{N} \phi_i(\pi_j)$, i.e. the coalition structure which features the lowest sum of all the players' losses. If there is more than one social optimum coalition structure then we talk about the social optimum coalition structure set (abbreviated by social optimum CS set and denoted by Π^{SOP}).*

For the games considered in this book the following theorem holds:

Theorem 5.3 *If the second stage of the game is solved by linear-quadratic differential games with symmetric bargaining powers and if the full-cooperation coalition structure belongs to the set of feasible coalition structures, or $C \in \Pi$, then this coalition structure belongs to the social optimum coalition structure set, or $C \in \Pi^{SOP}$.*

Proof. Trivial from Chapter 2. ■

A concept, closely related to the above definition is a *welfare index* (WIX), which shows the percentage difference between the sum of losses in the particular coalition and the social optimum CS:[35]

Definition 5.35 *The welfare index is defined as:*

$$WIX(\pi_j) := \frac{\sum_{i=1}^{N}\phi_i(\pi_j) - \sum_{i=1}^{N}\phi_i(\pi^{sop})}{\sum_{i=1}^{N}\phi_i(\pi^{sop})} 100\%.^{36}$$

Of course, we have $WIX(\pi^{SOP}) = 0$. *Note also that* WIX *is always non-negative.*

In simultaneous games more than one stable CS can be found. This raises the question how to evaluate CSs w.r.t. welfare using WIX? Hence, we introduce the concept of an *average welfare index,* denoted by $\overline{WIX}$ and defined as:

$$\overline{WIX} := \frac{1}{z}\sum_{i=1}^{z} WIX_i$$

where WIX_i are the welfare indices of all the stable CSs in the game considered; hence $z := |\Gamma^{ST}|$. Since we consider all the possible stable CSs to be equally probable, $\overline{WIX}$ may be interpreted as the expected WIX in the particular coalition formation game. In other words, $\overline{WIX}$ shows the (degree of) effectiveness of the given coalition formation game (mechanism).

Moreover, we introduce a *coalition formation index* (CFI):

Definition 5.36 *A coalition formation index is defined as:*

$$CFI(\pi_j) := \frac{\sum_{i=1}^{N}|\phi_i(\pi_j) - \phi_i(NC)|}{\sum_{i=1}^{N}\phi_i(NC)} 100\%.$$

Intuitively, CFI shows the magnitude of losses' volatility in a particular CS w.r.t. the non-cooperative regime (NC), when no non-trivial coalition exists. As our setting features mixed externalities from coalition formation, the numerator in Definition 5.36 is a sum of relevant absolute differences. Clearly, also the value of this index is always nonnegative.[37]

---

[35] We define all the indices in terms of percentages to avoid (possible) confusion with losses.

[36] WIX is comparable to the 'degree of externality index' (DEX) of Eyckmans and Finus (2003).

[37] One could also think about another index, which would be used to measure effects of coalition formation but in more relative terms than CFI. Note that the index from Definition 5.36 measures the total magnitude of changes in players' losses w.r.t. the non-cooperative regime. However, for each player the same change in losses may have a completely different meaning. For instance, if $N = \{1, 2\}$, $\phi_1(NC) = 1$; $\phi_2(NC) = 100$; $\phi_1(C) = \frac{1}{2}$; and

5.7 Appendix

Algorithm 5.1 (OMG($|N| \geqq 2, \Sigma$)) *Step 1: Let* $\Pi^F = \{\pi_1, ..., \pi_s\}$ *and* $r = 1$;
Step 2: Consider CS $\pi_r = \{C_1, C_2, ..., C_m\} \in \Pi^F$;
Step 3: Let $i = 1$;
Step 4: Find coalition C_j *such that* $i \in C_j$;
Step 5: If C_j *is a full coalition, i.e.* $C_j = C$, *then a new player i's deviation to end CS* $\pi_p = \{C_{j_{-i}}, (i)\} \in \Pi^F$, $(p \neq r)$, *is found.*[38] *Then:*
Step 5.1: If $i < n$ *then* $i = i + 1$. *Go back to Step 4;*
Step 5.2: If $i = n$ *and if* $r < s$ *then* $r = r + 1$. *Go back to Step 2;*
Step 5.3: Go to Step 12.
Step 6: If C_j *is a non-trivial coalition then a new player i's deviation is found. End CS* $\pi_p \in \Pi^F$, $(p \neq r)$ *is of the form* $\{C_1, C_2, ..., (i), C_{j_{-i}}, ..., C_m\}$;
Step 7: Let $k = 1$;
Step 8: If $k \neq j$ *then consider* $C_k \subset \pi_r$. *Merge player i with* C_k *and leave all the other coalitions in* π_r *unchanged. A new player i's deviation is found. End CS* $\pi_p \in \Pi^F$, $(p \neq r)$ *can have one of the following two forms:*
(a) $\pi_p := \{C_1, C_2, ..., C_{j_{-i}}, ..., (C_k, i), ..., C_m\} \in \Pi^F$ *if* C_j *is a non-trivial coalition.*
(b) $\pi_p := \{C_1, C_2, ..., (C_k, i), ..., C_m\} \in \Pi^F$ *if* C_j *is a trivial coalition.*
Step 9: If $k < m$ *then* $k = k + 1$. *Go back to Step 8;*
Step 10: If $i < n$ *then* $i = i + 1$. *Go back to Step 4;*
Step 11: If $r < s$ *then* $r = r + 1$. *Go back to Step 2;*
Step 12: All deviations have been found. End.

Example 5.20 *We will illustrate the functioning of the Algorithm 5.1 on the first two CSs in the OMG from Table 5.12.*[39]

(π_1) Let $r = 1$; *hence we consider* $\pi_1 = [123]$; $i = 1$. *We find that* $i \in C_{j=1} = (1, 2, 3)$, *which is the full coalition. From Step 5 we find the first end CS* $\pi_{p=4\neq r} \in \Pi^F$ *which has the form* $\{C_{1_{-1}}, (1)\}$, *i.e.* $\pi_4 = \{(1), (2, 3)\}$ *after rearranging. As* $i < n = 3$ *i becomes* 2 *and, again, we find that* $i \in C_j = (1, 2, 3)$ *and Step 5 follows. The same procedure is applied to the next and the last player* $i = 3$. *Till now three deviations have been found* $\left(\pi_1 \xrightarrow{P1} \pi_4\right)$, $\left(\pi_1 \xrightarrow{P2} \pi_3\right)$, $\left(\pi_1 \xrightarrow{P3} \pi_2\right)$. *As* $i = n = 3$ *and* $r = 1 < s = 5$ *then r becomes* 2 *and we return to Step 2.*

$\phi_2(C) = 99$ then $CFI(C) = 1.4851\%$. Hence, the value of the index is marginal but the difference in $P1$'s losses is substantial: 50%. An index which takes this issue into account can be defined as follows:
$RCFI(\pi_j) := \frac{1}{n}\sum_{i=1}^{n}\frac{|\phi_i(\pi_j) - \phi_i(NC)|}{\phi_i(NC)}100\%$ and is called the *relative coalition formation index*. However, in our simulations we will use CFI instead of $RCFI$.

[38] Intuitively, if a certain CS π_r is a full-coalition CS, then the only possible deviation of a player i is to play as a singleton, as there is no other (partial) coalition or singleton to join.

[39] Note that, in fact, obtained reduced deviations are valid for every game from this particular class of coalition formation OMGs.

(π_2) Consider $\pi_2 = [12|3]$ which can be also presented in the form $\{C_1, C_2\}$ where $C_1 = (1,2)$ and $C_3 = (3)$.[40] *Again $i = 1$ and we find that $i \in C_1$, so $j = 1$. Since C_1 is not the full-coalition we skip Step 5 and follow from Step 6. As C_1 is a non-trivial coalition then find the end CS $\pi_{p=5\neq r} \in \Pi^F$ which has the form $\{(1), C_{1_{-1}}, C_2\}$, i.e. $\pi_5 = \{(1),(2),(3)\}$. Hence, in Step 6 we find $\left(\pi_2 \xrightarrow{P1} \pi_5\right)$ and continue with Step 7. Let $k = 1$. Since $k = j$ we skip Step 8 and proceed from Step 9. As $k = 1 < m = 2$ then k becomes 2 and we proceed from Step 8 considering $C_2 = (3)$. Since $k \neq m$ we construct the end CS $\pi_{p=3\neq r}$ of the form $\{C_{1_{-1}}, (C_2, 1)\}$, i.e. $\pi_3 = \{(1,3),(2)\}$. Consequently, we find $\left(\pi_2 \xrightarrow{P1} \pi_3, \right)$,... etc.*

The reader can compare a set of deviations obtained in this example with the one reported in Example 5.16

Algorithm 5.2 (OMG($|N| \geqq 2, \Sigma, MU$)) *Step 1: Let $\Pi^{MU} := \{\pi_1, \pi_2, ..., \pi_w\}$ and $r = 1$;*

Step 2: Consider CS $\pi_r = \{C_1, C_2, ..., C_m\} \in \Pi^{MU}$;

Step 3: Let player $i = 1$;

Step 4: Find coalition C_j such that player $i \in C_j$;

Step 5: Consider player i:

Step 5.1: If player i is a singleton monetary player then:

Step 5.1.1: Let $k = 1$;

Step 5.1.2: If $k \neq j$ then consider $C_k \subset \pi_r$. If C_k is a fiscal coalition, such that $BJS(i) \subseteq C_k$, then a new player i's deviation is found. End CS $\pi_p \in \Pi^{MU}$, $(p \neq r)$, can have one of the following two forms:

(a)$\{C_1, C_2, ..., (BJS(i), i), C_{k_{-BJS(i)}} ..., C_m\}$ if $C_k \neq BJS(i)$; or

(b) $\{C_1, C_2, ..., (BJS(i), i), ..., C_m\}$ if $C_k = BJS(i)$.

Step 5.1.3: If $k < m$ then $k = k + 1$. Go back to Step 5.1.2;

Step 5.2: If player i is a monetary player and C_j is a full MU(i) coalition, i.e. $C_k = (i, BJS(i))$, then a new player i's deviation has been found. End CS $\pi_p \in \Pi^{MU}$, $(p \neq r)$, is of the form $\{C_1, C_2, ..., (i), C_{j_{-i}}, ..., C_m\}$.

Step 5.3: If player i is a fiscal player and C_j is a (possibly trivial) fiscal coalition then:

Step 5.3.1: C_j is a non-trivial coalition and a new player i's deviation is found. End CS $\pi_p \in \Pi^{MU}$, $(p \neq r)$, is of the form $\{C_1, C_2, ..., (i), C_{j_{-i}} ..., C_m\}$.

Step 5.3.2: Let $k = 1$;

Step 5.3.3: If $k \neq j$ then consider $C_k \subset \pi_r$:

(i) If C_k is a (possibly trivial) fiscal coalition then a new player i's deviation has been found. An end coalition structure $\pi_p \in \Pi^{MU}$, $(p \neq r)$, is of the form $\{C_1, C_2, ..., (i, C_k), ..., C_{j_{-i}}, ..., C_m\}$;

(ii) If $C_k = \{b\}$ and central bank b is responsible for monetary policy management in i, i.e. $i := i^b$, and if $BJS(b) := \{i^b\}$ then a new player i's deviation has been found. End CS $\pi_p \in \Pi^{MU}$, $(p \neq r)$is of the form$\{C_1, C_2, ..., (i, C_k), ..., C_{j_{-1}}, ..., C_m\}$;

Step 5.3.4: If $k < m$ then $k = k + 1$. Go back to Step 5.3.3;

[40] Note also that $m = 2$.

Step 5.4: If a player i is a fiscal player and C_j is a full MU(b) coalition, i.e.: $i := i^b \in C_j = (b, BJS(b))$, then:

Step 5.4.1: a new player i^b's deviation is found. End CS $\pi_p \in \Pi^{MU}$, $(p \neq r)$, can have one of the following two forms:

(a) $\left\{C_1, C_2, ..., (i^b), (b), C_{j_{-b-i^b}}, ..., C_m\right\}$ *if* $|BJS(b)| \geqq 2$.

(b) $\{C_1, C_2, ..., (i^b), (b), ..., C_m\}$ *if* $|BJS(b)| = \{i^b\}$.

Step 5.4.2: Let $k = 1$;

Step 5.4.3: If $k \neq j$ then consider $C_k \subset \pi_s$. If C_k is a (possibly trivial) fiscal coalition then a new player i^b's deviation is found. End CS $\pi_p \in \Pi^{MU}$, $(p \neq r)$, can have one of the following two forms:

(a) $\left\{C_1, C_2, ..., (C_k, i^b), (b), C_{j_{-b-i^b}}, ..., C_m\right\}$ *if* $|BJS(b)| \geqq 2$.

(b) $\{C_1, C_2, ..., (C_k, i^b), (b), ..., C_m\}$ *if* $|BJS(b)| = \{i^b\}$.

Step 5.4.4: If $k < m$ then $k = k + 1$. Go back to Step 5.4.3;

Step 6: If $i < n$ then $i = i + 1$. Go back to Step 4;

Step 7: If $r < w$ then all the possible deviations for CS r have been found; $r = r + 1$. Go back to Step 2;

Step 8: All deviations have been found. End.

Example 5.21 *To show the basic differences with Algorithm 5.1 we will illustrate the functioning of Algorithm 5.2 also on the 3-player game. Assume the class OMG($N := \{C1, C2, CB\}$, Σ, $\psi^{OMG(MU)}(.)$, MU) and $BJS(CB) := \{C1, C2\}$. The resulting set of the MU feasible CSs is $\Pi^{MU} = \{\pi_1 = [C1C2CB]$, $\pi_2 = [C1C2|CB]$, $\pi_3 = [C1|C2|CB]\}$.*

(π_1) Let $r = 1$; hence we consider $\pi_1 = [C1C2CB]$; $i = C1$; i.e. i is a fiscal player. We find that $i \in C_{j=1} = (C1, C2, CB)$ which is the full MU(CB) coalition; hence from Step 5.4 we find the first end CS $\pi_{p=3\neq r} \in \Pi^{MU}$ which has the form $\{(C1), (CB), C_{j_{-CB-C1}}\}$, i.e. $\pi_3 = \{(C1), (C2), (CB)\}$ after rearranging. As $k = m = 1$ and $i < n = 3$ in Step 6 i becomes 2 and we go back to Step 4. Again we find that $i = 2 \in C_{j=1} = (C1, C2, C3)$ and Step 5.4 follows. For the second time the end CS is π_3. As $k = m = 1$ and $i < n = 3$ in Step 6 i becomes 3 and we go back to Step 4. Player $i = 3 = CB$ is a monetary player. We find that $i \in C_{j=1} = (C1, C2, CB)$ which is the full MU(CB) coalition. In Step 5.2 we find the next end CS $\pi_{p=2\neq r} \in \Pi^{MU}$ which has the form $\{(CB), C_{j_{-CB}}\}$, i.e. $\pi_3 = \{(C1, C2), (CB)\}$ after rearranging. We have found 3 deviations from the CS π_1, i.e.: $\left(\pi_1 \xrightarrow{C1} \pi_3\right)$, $\left(\pi_1 \xrightarrow{C2} \pi_3\right)$, $\left(\pi_1 \xrightarrow{CB} \pi_2\right)$. As $r = 1 < w = 3$ in Step 7 r becomes 2.

(π_2) $\pi_2 = [C1C2|CB]$; $i = C1$; i.e. i is a fiscal player. We find that $i \in C_{j=1} = (C1, C2)$ which is the full fiscal MU(CB) coalition; hence from Step 5.3 we find the first end CS $\pi_{p=3\neq r} \in \Pi^{MU}$ which has the form $\{(C1), C_{j_{-C1}}, (CB)\}$, i.e. $\pi_3 = [C1|C2|CB]$. In Step 5.3.2 $k = 1$. As $k = j$ we skip Step 5.3.4. As $k < m = 2$ in Step 5.3.4 k becomes 2. We go back to Step 5.3.3 and find that $k \neq j$ but $C_k = (CB)$; hence C_k is not a fiscal coalition and player i cannot join it. In Step 6 i becomes 2 and we return to Step 4. Next a similar

procedure as for $i = 1$ *is applied to player* $i = 2$. *We find one deviation of* $C2$ *to end CS* $\pi_3 = [C1|C2|CB]$. *In Step 6* i *becomes* 3 *and we return to Step 4. We find that* $CB = i \in C_{j=2} = (CB)$, *i.e.* i *is a singleton monetary player. In Step 5.1.1* $k = 1$. *As* $k \neq j$ *we consider* $(C1, C2) =: C_1 \subset \pi_2$. *In fact,* $\{C1, C2\} =: BJS\,(i = CB) \subseteq C_1$; *hence a new player* i*'s deviation is found to an end CS of the form:* $\{(BJS\,(CB)\,, CB)\}$. *We can write the end CS* π_1 *in the more familiar form* $[C1C2CB]$.

Algorithm 5.3 (ROMG($|N| \geqq 2, \Sigma, \psi^{ROMG}$**))** *Step 1: Let* $\Pi^F = \{\pi_1, ..., \pi_s\}$ *and* $r = 1$;

Step 2: Consider CS $\pi_r = \{C_1, C_2, ..., C_m\} \in \Pi^F$;

Step 3: Let $i = 1$;

Step 4: Find coalition C_j *such that* $i \in C_j$;

Step 5: If C_j *is a full-coalition, i.e.* $C_j = C$, *then a new player* i*'s deviation to end CS* $\pi_p = \{C_{j_{-i}}, (i)\} \in \Pi^F$, $(p \neq r)$, *is found.*[41] *Then:*

(i) if $i < n$ *then* $i = i + 1$. *Go back to Step 4;*

(ii) if $i = n$ *and if* $r < s$ *then* $r = r + 1$. *Go back to Step 2;*

(iii) Go to Step 12.

Step 6: If C_j *is a non-trivial coalition then you find a new player* i*'s deviation is found. End CS* $\pi_p \in \Pi^F$, $(p \neq r)$ *is of the form* $\{C_1, C_2, ..., (i), C_{j_{-i}}, ..., C_m\}$;

Step 7: Let $k = 1$;

Step 8: If $k \neq j$ *then consider* $C_k \subset \pi_r$. *If* C_k *is a non-trivial coalition merge player* i *with* C_k *and leave all the other coalitions in* π_r *unchanged. a new player* i*'s deviation is found. End CS* $\pi_p \in \Pi^F$, $(p \neq r)$ *can have one of the following two forms:*

(i) $\pi_p := \{C_1, C_2, ..., C_{j_{-i}}, ..., (C_k, i), \ ..., C_m\} \in \Pi^F$ *if* C_j *is a non-trivial coalition.*

(ii) $\pi_p := \{C_1, C_2, ..., (C_k, i), ..., C_m\} \in \Pi^F$ *if* C_j *is a trivial coalition.*

Step 9: If $k < m$ *then* $k = k + 1$. *Go back to Step 8;*

Step 10: If $i < n$ *then* $i = i + 1$. *Go back to Step 4;*

Step 11: If $r < s$ *then* $r = r + 1$. *Go back to Step 2;*

Step 12: All deviations have been found. End.

Algorithm 5.4 (ROMG($|N| \geqq 2, \Sigma, \psi^{ROMG(MU)}$**))** *Step 1: Let* $\Pi^{MU} := \{\pi_1, \pi_2, ..., \pi_w\}$ *and* $r = 1$;

Step 2: Consider CS $\pi_r = \{C_1, C_2, ..., C_m\} \in \Pi^{MU}$;

Step 3: Let player $i = 1$;

Step 4: Find coalition C_j *such that player* $i \in C_j$;

Step 5: Consider player i:

Step 5.1: If player i *is a singleton monetary player then:*

Step 5.1.1: Let $k = 1$;

Step 5.1.2: If $k \neq j$ *then consider* $C_k \subset \pi_r$.

---

[41] Intuitively, if a considered CS π_r is a full-coalition CS, then the only possible deviation of a player i is to play as a singleton, as there is no other (partial) coalition or singleton to join.

(a) If C_k is a non-trivial fiscal coalition, such that $BJS(i) \subseteq C_k$, and $C_k \neq BJS(i)$ then a new player i's deviation is found. End CS $\pi_p \in \Pi^{MU}$, $(p \neq r)$, is of the form $\{C_1, C_2, ..., (BJS(i), i), C_{k_{-BJS(i)}}, ..., C_m\}$.

(b) If C_k is a non-trivial fiscal coalition, such that $BJS(i) = C_k$, then a new player i's deviation is found. End CS $\pi_p \in \Pi^{MU}$, $(p \neq r)$, is of the form $\{C_1, C_2, ..., (BJS(i), i), ..., C_m\}$.

Step 5.1.3: If $k < m$ then $k = k + 1$. Go back to Step 5.1.2;

Step 5.2: If player i is a monetary player and C_j is a full MU(i) coalition, i.e. $C_k = (i, BJS(i))$, then a new player i's deviation has been found. End CS $\pi_p \in \Pi^{MU}$, $(p \neq r)$, is of the form $\{C_1, C_2, ..., (i), C_{j_{-i}}, ..., C_m\}$.

Step 5.3: If a player i is a fiscal player and C_j is a fiscal coalition then:

Step 5.3.1: If C_j is a non-trivial coalition then a new player i's deviation is found. End CS $\pi_p \in \Pi^{MU}$, $(p \neq r)$, is of the form $\{C_1, C_2, ..., (i), C_{j_{-i}} ..., C_m\}$.

Step 5.3.2: Let $k = 1$;

Step 5.3.3: If $k \neq j$ then consider $C_k \subset \pi_r$:

(i) If C_k is a non-trivial fiscal coalition then a new player i's deviation has been found. End coalition structure $\pi_p \in \Pi^{MU}$, $(p \neq r)$, is of the form $\{C_1, C_2, ..., (i, C_k), ..., C_{j_{-1}}, ..., C_m\}$.

Step 5.3.4: If $k < m$ then $k = k + 1$. Go back to Step 5.3.3;

Step 5.4: If player i is a fiscal player and C_j is a full MU(b) coalition, i.e.: $i := i^b \in C_j = (b, BJS(b))$ then:

Step 5.4.1: a new player i^b's deviation is found. End coalition structure $\pi_p \in \Pi^{MU}$, $(p \neq r)$, can have one of the following two forms:

(a) $\left\{C_1, C_2, ..., (i^b), (b), C_{j_{-b-i^b}}, ..., C_m\right\}$ if $|BJS(b)| \geqq 2$.

(b) $\{C_1, C_2, ..., (i^b), (b), ..., C_m\}$ if $|BJS(b)| = \{i^b\}$.

Step 5.4.2: Let $k = 1$;

Step 5.4.3: If $k \neq j$ then consider $C_k \subset \pi_s$.

(i) If C_k is a non-trivial fiscal coalition then a new player i^b's deviation is found. a new player i^b's deviation is found. End coalition structure $\pi_p \in \Pi^{MU}$, $(p \neq r)$, can have one of the following two forms:

(a) $\left\{C_1, C_2, ..., (C_k, i^b), (b), C_{j_{-b-i^b}}, ..., C_m\right\}$ if $|BJS(b)| \geqq 2$.

(b) $\{C_1, C_2, ..., (C_k, i^b), (b), ..., C_m\}$ if $|BJS(b)| = \{i^b\}$.

Step 5.4.4: If $k < m$ then $k = k + 1$. Go back to Step 5.4.3;

Step 6: If $i < n$ then $i = i + 1$. Go back to Step 4;

Step 7: If $r < w$ then all the possible deviations for coalition structure r have been found; $r = r + 1$. Go back to Step 2;

Step 8: All deviations have been found. End.

Algorithm 5.5 (EMG($N, \Sigma^{\Delta}, \psi^{EMG(\Delta)}(.)$)) *Step 1: Let $\Pi^F := \{\pi_1, \pi_2, ..., \pi_s\}$ and $r = 1$;*

Step 2: Consider the coalition structure $\pi_r = \{C_1, C_2, ..., C_m\} \in \Pi^F$;

Step 3: Let player $i = 1$;

Step 4: Find a coalition C_j such that player $i \in C_j$;

Step 5: If C_j is a trivial coalition then go to Step 7

Step 6: If C_j is a non-trivial coalition then a new player i's deviation is found. End CS $\pi_p \in \Pi^F$, $(p \neq r)$, is of the form $\{C_1, C_2, ..., (i), C_{j_{-i}} ..., C_m\}$;

Step 7 If $i < N$ then $i = i + 1$. Go back to Step 4;

Step 8 If $r < s$ then all the possible deviations for coalition structure r have been found; $r = r + 1$. Go back to Step 2;

Step 9: All deviations have been found. End.

Algorithm 5.6 (EMG($N, \Sigma^\Delta, \psi^{EMG(\Delta,MU)}(.), MU$)) *Step 1: Let $\Pi^{MU} := \{\pi_1, \pi_2, ..., \pi_w\}$ and $r = 1$;*

Step 2: Consider the coalition structure $\pi_r = \{C_1, C_2, ..., C_m\} \in \Pi^{MU}$;

Step 3: Let player $i = 1$;

Step 4: Find a coalition C_j such that player $i \in C_j$;

Step 5: If C_j is a trivial coalition then go to Step 8;

Step 6: If C_j is a non-trivial coalition then:

Step 6.1: If C_j is a fiscal coalition then a new player i's deviation is found. End CS $\pi_p \in \Pi^{MU}$, $(p \neq r)$, is of the form $\{C_1, C_2, ..., (i), C_{j_{-i}} ..., C_m\}$;

Step 6.2: If C_j is a full MU coalition with the central bank b then a new player i's deviation:= i^b is found. End coalition structure $\pi_p \in \Pi^{MU}$, $(p \neq r)$ can have one of the following two forms:

(a) $\left\{C_1, C_2, ..., (i^b), (b), C_{j_{-b-i^b}}, ..., C_m\right\}$ if $|BJS(b)| \geqq 2$.

(b) $\{C_1, C_2, ..., (i^b), (b), ..., C_m\}$ if $|BJS(b)| = \{i^b\}$.

Step 7 If $i < N$ then $i = i + 1$. Go back to Step 4;

Step 8 If $r < s$ then all the possible deviations for coalition structure r have been found; $r = r + 1$. Go back to Step 2;

Step 9: All deviations have been found. End.

Algorithm 5.7(EMG($N, \Sigma^\Gamma, \psi^{EMG(\Gamma)}(.)$) and EMG ($N, \Sigma^\Gamma, \psi^{EMG(\Gamma,MU)}(.), MU$)) *Step 1: Let $\Pi^F := \{\pi_1, \pi_2, ..., \pi_s\}$[42] and $r = 1$;*

Step 2: Consider the coalition structure $\pi_r = \{C_1, C_2, ..., C_m\} \in \Pi^F$;

Step 3: Let player $i = 1$;

Step 4: Find a coalition C_j such that player $i \in C_j$;

Step 5: If C_j is a trivial coalition then go to Step 7;

Step 6: If C_j is a non-trivial coalition then a new player i's deviation is found. End CS $\pi_p \in \Pi^F$, $(p \neq r)$, is an independent coalition structure of π_r w.r.t. C_k, i.e. $\pi_p^I(\pi_r, C_k)$;

Step 7 If $i < N$ then $i = i + 1$. Go back to Step 4;

Step 8 If $r < s$ then all the possible deviations for coalition structure r have been found; $r = r + 1$. Go back to Step 2;

Step 9: All deviations have been found. End.

[42]Note that this algorithm can be used to solve any EMG(Γ) which results in the reduced set of feasible coalition structures characterized by the independence property.

Chapter 6

A Multi-Country Closed-Economy MU Model

6.1 Introduction

In Chapter 4 we analyzed monetary and fiscal policy interactions in a two-country monetary union (MU). While this setting yields many important insights, it also seems interesting to consider an MU with a larger number of participants. This chapter, therefore, seeks to generalize the previous analysis by introducing a multi-country MU model. Moreover, we consider a more general shock structure which is based on price levels instead of (relative price) competitiveness. Furthermore more general inflation dynamics are introduced, i.e. the effects of foreign inflation rates, as suggested by the recent open economies' literature.[1]

The emphasis of the analysis is put on the various spillovers in an MU and their effects on monetary and fiscal policies. As indicated in Section 1.3 of Chapter 1, the following spillovers might play a crucial role in the analysis via the 'trade channel', 'pass-through' hypothesis, 'competitiveness channel', 'interest rate channel', 'exchange rate channel', and 'fiscal deficit' channel, respectively: (i) output spillovers, (ii) price spillovers, (iii) competitiveness spillovers, (iv) interest rate spillovers, (v) exchange rate spillovers, and (vi) fiscal deficit spillovers via the real interest rate. In this chapter on a multi-country closed-economy MU, the effects of all these types of spillovers except type (v) will be analyzed.

The chapter is organized as follows. Section 6.2 provides a small dynamic macroeconomic model of a multi-country MU and the dynamic stabilization problem faced by the fiscal policymakers and the common monetary authority. Section 6.3 analyzes the consequences of an *ex-post* and an *ex-ante* policy coordination in a dynamic framework by studying numerical simulations of various examples. Three types of shocks are considered: symmetric shocks,

[1] Evidence of foreign inflation effects on the Phillips curve is provided by DiNardo and Moore (1999). See also Razin and Yuen (2001) and Plasmans *et al.* (2004).

anti-symmetric shocks and asymmetric shocks. Moreover, a detailed analysis of (the effects of) various above-mentioned spillovers is undertaken. The numerical analysis is concluded by studying two cases where countries are asymmetric in their economic structure and bargaining weights in cooperative decision making.

6.2 Model

In this section we further extend our model of Chapter 4 by allowing for $n_f = n-1$ countries (with a corresponding set of fiscal players $F := \{1, 2, ..., n_f\}$) to participate in an MU with a common central bank (CB). The IS curves (6.1) are not different from those of previous chapters, but rewritten in a more general form since in an n_f-country setting each country i has $n_f - 1$ bilateral trade relations, or for $i = 1, 2, ..., n_f$:

$$y_i(t) = -\gamma_i [i_U(t) - \dot{p}_i(t)] + \eta_i f_i(t) + \sum_{j \in F/i} \rho_{ij} y_j(t) + \sum_{j \in F/i} \delta_{ij} [p_j(t) - p_i(t)]; \tag{6.1}$$

moreover, foreign price spillovers are now added to the original Phillips curves:

$$\dot{p}_i(t) = \zeta_i y_i(t) + \sum_{j \in F/i} \varsigma_{ij} \dot{p}_j(t), \quad p_i(0) = p_{i0}. \tag{6.2}$$

The direct output and inflation spillovers are measured by ρ_{ij} and ς_{ij}, respectively. The competitiveness spillovers are given by δ_{ij}. The spillovers through the common interest rate in an MU are determined by γ_i and the fiscal deficit spillovers by the direct effects of fiscal deficits, η_i. The spillovers from foreign inflation on domestic inflation, ς_{ij}, reflect the pass-through in the pricing of foreign goods when sold on domestic markets. Clearly, if the size of these parameters increases, the effects from the spillovers increase and the potential benefits from policy coordination may rise. In the numerical analysis in the next section(s) we will look in more detail into the effects of these different spillovers and how the relative importance of these spillovers can be determined. Typically, in most cases not all spillovers are equally important at the same time.

In Chapters 3 and 4 our analysis concentrated on competitiveness shocks. Since any non-zero competitiveness gap implies asymmetry in price levels, by its very nature every competitiveness shock hits countries in an asymmetric way. However, as it was already mentioned in Chapter 1, symmetric shocks may play a very important role in an MU. Hence, from now on this type of shocks will be studied in detail.

Note that it is not possible to analyze effects of the symmetric shock with the loss functions introduced in Chapters 3 and 4 within the context of the model (6.1)-(6.2). Since, objectives from previous chapters are functions of inflation, output gap and control instruments only, players are indifferent to any initial symmetric shock in price levels. Consequently, to facilitate the analysis of symmetric shocks in the framework of our model we have to introduce price levels into players' loss functions explicitly. We propose the following objectives for the $n_f - 1$ fiscal players and the common CB, respectively (compare to Chadha and Nolan (2002)):□

$$\min_{f_i} J_i(t_0) = \min_{f_i} \frac{1}{2} \int_{t_0}^{\infty} \{\alpha_i (\dot{p}_i(t) - \varpi p_i(t))^2 + \beta_i y_i^2(t) + \chi_i f_i^2(t)\} e^{-\theta(t-t_0)} dt \tag{6.3}$$

for $i = 1, 2, \ldots, n_f$, and

$$\min_{i_U} J_U(t_0) = \min_{i_u} \frac{1}{2} \int_{t_0}^{\infty} \{\alpha_U \dot{p}_U^2(t) + \beta_U y_U^2(t) + \chi_U i_U^2(t)\} e^{-\theta(t-t_0)} dt, \tag{6.4}$$

where $\varpi p_i(t)$ is a state-dependent target inflation (being proportional to price levels), $\dot{p}_U := \sum_{i=1}^{n_f} \omega_i (\dot{p}_i(t) - \varpi p_i(t))$ is aggregate inflation in deviation from state-dependent target inflation, $y_U := \sum_{i=1}^{n_f} \omega_i y_i$ is loglinearized aggregate output,[2] and α_U and β_U indicate the relative preferences of the CB concerning inflation and output of the MU as a whole. Parameter ω_i indicates the relative weight of country i in the MU ($\sum_{i=1}^{n_f} \omega_i = 1$). The minimization of the CB's loss function w.r.t. $i_U(t)$ is consistent with the derivation of a standard monetary policy rule (see e.g. Clarida *et al.* (1999)), since it results in a linear function in its arguments.

We transform the structural form model (6.1)-(6.2) to the reduced form model:[3]

$$\begin{bmatrix} y(t) \\ \dot{p}(t) \end{bmatrix} = \begin{bmatrix} D & E & M \\ A & B & N \end{bmatrix} \begin{bmatrix} p(t) \\ f(t) \\ i_u(t) \end{bmatrix} \tag{6.5}$$

where $y(t)$ is an (n_f)-dimensional country-ordered vector of output gaps, $\dot{p}(t)$ is a country-ordered vector of inflation rates, $p(t)$ and $f(t)$ are the price level and (real) fiscal deficit vectors, respectively. The partitioned matrix $L := \begin{bmatrix} D & E & M \\ A & B & N \end{bmatrix}$ indicates the elasticities of the real output gap and the inflation rate with respect to price levels and control instruments. The upper part of matrix $L \in \mathbb{R}^{2n_f \times (2n_f+1)}$ indicates the (reduced-form) elasticities of the real

[2] The following two-country example illustrates the procedure of loglinearization. Assuming that the real output $X_i(t)$ is in the neighbourhood of the steady-state output $\overline{X}_i$, the following approximation holds: $\frac{X_i(t)}{\overline{X}_i} \simeq 1 + x_i(t)$. The aggregate-output equation for two countries is $X_U(t) := X_1(t) + X_2(t)$, which is directly rewritten as $1 = \frac{X_1(t)}{X_U(t)} + \frac{X_2(t)}{X_U(t)}$ and by rules of loglinearization transformed into $1 \simeq \frac{\overline{X}_1}{\overline{X}_U}(1 + x_1(t) - x_U(t)) + \frac{\overline{X}_2}{\overline{X}_U}(1 + x_2(t) - x_U(t))$. Simplifying, we obtain: $x_U(t) \equiv \log \frac{X_U(t)}{\overline{X}_U} = \sigma_1 x_1(t) + \sigma_2 x_2(t)$ where $\sigma_1 := \frac{\overline{X}_1}{\overline{X}_U}$ and $\sigma_2 := \frac{\overline{X}_2}{\overline{X}_U}$ are the relative weights of the countries' steady-state outputs. Hence, it follows that $x_U(t)$ is the *aggregate output gap*.

[3] Although the derivation of the reduced form of the model is similar to that in previous chapters, we report it in order to demonstrate the (impact of the general) notation for $n-1$ countries.

output gaps. The lower part of this matrix indicates the (reduced-form) elasticities of the inflation dynamics of the model. More in detail, the matrix $E \in \mathbb{R}^{n_f \times n_f}$ describes the effects of the domestic fiscal policy on the domestic real output gaps (main diagonal elements) and those of the foreign fiscal policies on the domestic real output gaps (off-diagonal elements); the latter elasticities are called (reduced-form) *fiscal spillovers*. Similarly, the matrix $B \in \mathbb{R}^{n_f \times n_f}$ describes the effects of the fiscal policy variables on the inflation rates. The matrices $D \in \mathbb{R}^{n_f \times n_f}$ and $A \in \mathbb{R}^{n_f \times n_f}$ indicate the effects of domestic and foreign price levels on the domestic real output gaps and inflation rates, respectively. Vectors $M \in \mathbb{R}^{n_f}$ and $N \in \mathbb{R}^{n_f}$ are the semi-elasticities of the real output gaps and inflation rates w.r.t. the common nominal interest rate.

6.3 Numerical solutions of the model

By analyzing the different cases of asymmetries, we may compare some conclusions of Buti and Sapir (1998) and Beetsma *et al.* (2001), but now in a dynamic and possibly asymmetric model setting. Buti and Sapir (1998) argue that fiscal coordination is desirable when large symmetric shocks are present, while Beetsma *et al.* (2001) argue that fiscal coordination is most desirable when there are asymmetric shocks, since fiscal authorities can internalize the economic externalities connected with opposite fiscal policies then.

We consider two different settings:

1. *Symmetric countries scenario* (sc_1): all countries are symmetric in the structural and preference parameters and sizes. However, preferences of fiscal players are asymmetric w.r.t. preferences of the CB.
2. *Asymmetric countries scenarios* (sc_2 and sc_3): in an asymmetric setting countries are marked by asymmetries in economic structures, policy preferences or bargaining weights. In particular, we assume that the relatively-closed country 1 ($C1$) faces two relatively open countries 2,3 ($C2$, $C3$) that are relatively more sensitive to foreign output and price changes. In addition, we analyze a case where countries are not only asymmetric in openness but also feature different bargaining powers in cooperative decision making (sc_3). More specifically, $C1$ and $C2$ are assumed to have a greater bargaining power than $C3$.

Three different types of shocks are analyzed (note that shocks always occur at $t = 0$ in the form of initial innovations to the state variables): (i) a symmetric negative supply shock: $p_{0S} = [0.01; 0.01; 0.01]^T$, (ii) an asymmetric supply shock that hits only country 1: $p_{0A} = [0.01; 0; 0]^T$; and (iii) an anti-symmetric supply shock that hits $C1$ and $C3$: $p_{0AS} = [0.01; 0; -0.01]^T$.

For each case considered we compute and analyze stable equilibria. Our aim is to analyze welfare effectiveness of different coalition formation mechanisms.

6.3.1 Symmetric baseline model

In the baseline, countries are assumed to be symmetric with respect to all structural parameters. It is assumed that policymakers' preferences are not symmetric. The CB's preferences differ from those of the (identical) national governments (preference asymmetry). The CB puts a larger weight on inflation stabilization than on output-gap stabilization. On the other hand, fiscal players are more concerned with output-gap stabilization than with inflation (-rate) stabilization. Moreover, the CB's objectives concern aggregate output and inflation in the MU while the fiscal players are only concerned about own output and inflation. The baseline parameters used in the simulations are listed in Table 6.1.

Table 6.1 – Baseline parameters $(i, j \in \{1,2,3\}, i \neq j)$

$\eta_i = 0.75$	$\delta_{ij} = 0.2$	$\gamma_i = 0.2$	$\zeta_i = 0.25$	$\rho_{ij} = 0.2$	$\varsigma_{ij} = 0.2$
$\alpha_i = 0.2$	$\beta_i = 0.4$	$\chi_i = 0.4$	$\alpha_U = 0.4$	$\beta_U = 0.2$	$\chi_U = 0.4$

This parameterization is based on various empirical studies for the euro area and will also be used in the next two chapters. Empirical studies suggest that the interest rate semi-elasticity of output (γ_i) lies in the range 0.1 to 0.3 (e.g. Angeloni *et al.* (2002) find a value of 0.19) and the other spillovers originate from the instantaneous multiplier of fiscal policy (η_i) lying between 0.5 and 1 (European Commission (2001) uses a value of 0.5 in its model), the competitiveness effect (δ_{ij}) and the elasticity w.r.t. the foreign output gap (ρ_{ij}), which are somewhere around 0.1 and 0.3, respectively (Hooper *et al.* (1998)). Considerable evidence also exists for the property that the output-gap elasticity in the Phillips curve (ζ_i) is relatively small (Smets (2000) estimates a value of 0.18) and that there is some effect from foreign inflation rates (ς_{ij}) (Laxton *et al.* (1998)).

Given the parameters of Table 6.1, the matrix of reduced form coefficients in this first scenario ($L_{(1)} := \left[\begin{array}{c|c|c} D_{(1)} & E_{(1)} & M_{(1)} \\ \hline A_{(1)} & B_{(1)} & N_{(1)} \end{array}\right]$) equals (the theoretical reduced form coefficients are derived in the Appendix):

$$L_{(1)} = \left[\begin{array}{ccc|ccc|c} -0.3453 & 0.1727 & 0.1727 & 0.9155 & 0.2680 & 0.2680 & -0.3871 \\ 0.1727 & -0.3453 & 0.1727 & 0.2680 & 0.9155 & 0.2680 & -0.3871 \\ 0.1727 & 0.1727 & -0.3453 & 0.2680 & 0.2680 & 0.9155 & -0.3871 \\ \hline -0.1219 & 0.0360 & 0.0360 & 0.2915 & 0.1566 & 0.1566 & -0.1613 \\ 0.0360 & -0.1219 & 0.0360 & 0.1566 & 0.2915 & 0.1566 & -0.1613 \\ 0.0360 & 0.0360 & -0.1219 & 0.1566 & 0.1566 & 0.2915 & -0.1613 \end{array}\right]$$

Since $E_{(1)}$ and $B_{(1)}$ contain only positive off-diagonal elements, the setting is characterized by positive reduced-form fiscal spillovers on the real output gaps(i.e. increases in the domestic fiscal deficit raise foreign output gaps) and negative reduced-form fiscal spillovers on the inflation rates (i.e. increases in the domestic fiscal deficit raise foreign inflation). Moreover, increases of domestic fiscal expenditures raise both the domestic real output gaps and inflation rates.

Common price shock

We first consider the common price shock $p_0 = [0.01, 0.01, 0.01]^T$, that hits the whole MU area (with an equal size). Following the notation from the previous chapter, NC indicates the non-cooperative regime, C the full cooperation regime, and F the set of all the fiscal players. For 3 fiscal players and one central bank the proposed reduced set of feasible coalition structures is $\Pi^{MU} = \{NC = [C1|C2|C3|CB];\ C = [C1C2C3CB];\ F = [C1C2C3|CB]; [C1C2|C3|CB]; [C1C3|C2|CB]; [C1|C2C3|CB]\}$. This set meets the conditions in Definition 5.19; hence, it is the MU-reduced set of feasible coalition structures. Table 6.2 contains (optimal) welfare losses in the form of the per-membership partition function for the symmetric benchmark scenario and the common price shock.

Table 6.2 Optimal losses for (sc_1, p_{0S})[4]

	NC	C	F	[12|3|4]	[13|2|4]	[1|23|4]
$C1$	2.4600	2.4665	2.4572	2.4598	2.4598	2.4555
$C2$	2.4600	2.4665	2.4572	2.4598	2.4555	2.4598
$C3$	2.4600	2.4665	2.4572	2.4555	2.4598	2.4598
CB	4.9148	4.8229	4.8781	4.8989	4.8989	4.8989
WIX	0.59%	0%	0.22%	0.42%	0.42%	0.42%
CFI	0%	0.91%	0.36%	0.17%	0.17%	0.17%

All the fiscal players have symmetric losses in each of the first three regimes NC, C and F, which is caused by the symmetry of the model parameters. Since these players are equal, it does not play a role whether the fiscal players cooperate or not - losses will be symmetric. Of course, different regimes feature different losses but in every single regime each fiscal player influences the others in exactly the same way and follows exactly the same optimization path. Also in the partial coalition regimes cooperating players have symmetric losses but the symmetry is broken for the player who plays as a singleton. The CB has different losses in the first three regimes as each form of fiscal players' cooperation is characterized by different optimizations. However, the CB's losses in the partial cooperation regimes [12|3|4],[13|2|4] and [1|23|4] are equal, which is again caused by the symmetry of the model. This is a good example of externalities from coalition formation. However, in our symmetric model this kind of externalities are (relatively) small - the coalition formation index CFI is according to Definition 5.36 lower than one percent in all the regimes. The welfare index WIX in Definition 5.35 is even smaller, so that the overall gains of full cooperation over other regimes are sizeably lower than one percent.

Figures 6.1 - 6.4 illustrate the macroeconomic adjustments of relevant variables. The first two figures represent the non-cooperative case and the other two the full cooperative case.

[4] All (optimal) losses are multiplied by the factor 10^7.

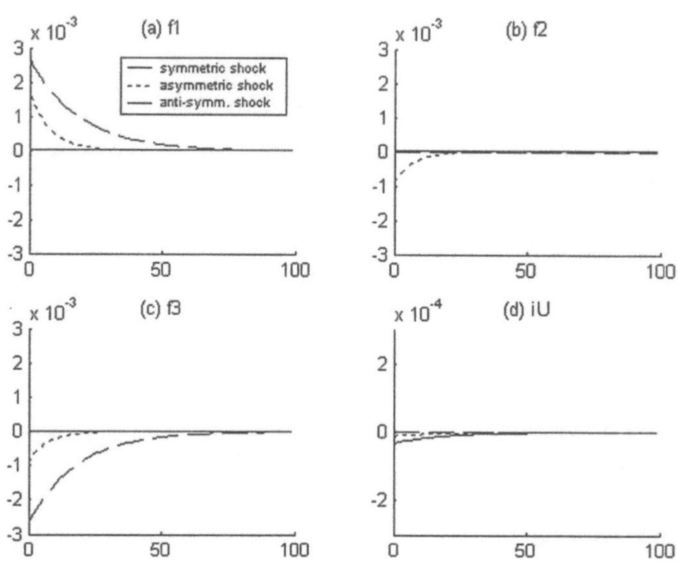

Figure 6.1 Control paths for sc_1, non-cooperative regime (NC)

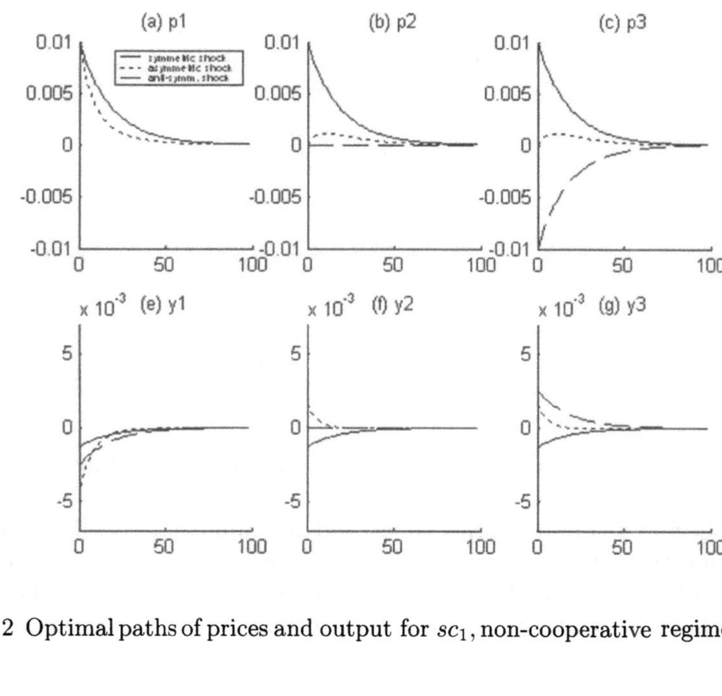

Figure 6.2 Optimal paths of prices and output for sc_1, non-cooperative regime (NC)

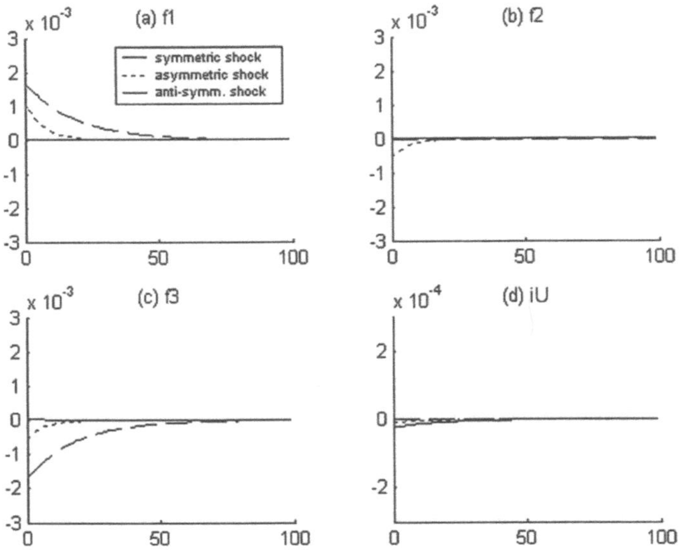

Figure 6.3 Controls' optimal paths for sc_1, full cooperation (C)

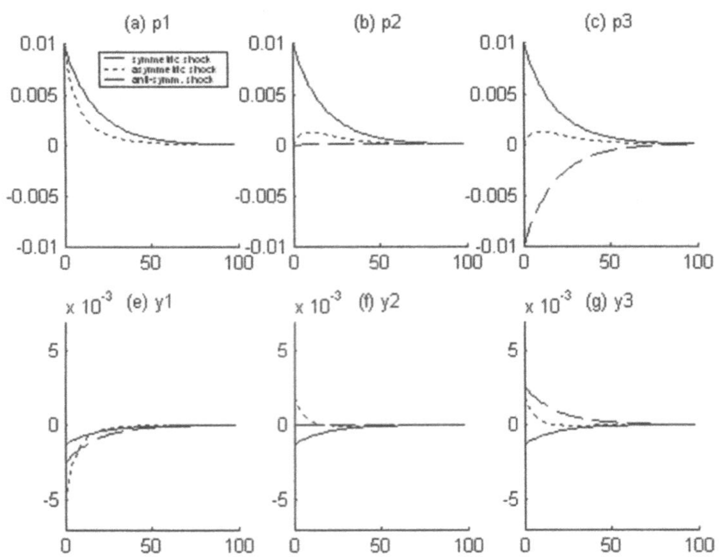

Figure 6.4 Optimal paths of prices and output for sc_1, full cooperation (C)

Observing a common price shock and the immediate decline in output, fiscal authorities pursue a very mildly expansionary fiscal policy, which is hardly visible in Figures 6.1 and 6.3. Since the countries are assumed to be symmetric, they behave in exactly the same way according to this expansionary fiscal policy. Next to the fiscal authorities, also the CB wants to stimulate the economy, this time by cutting the common nominal interest rate. Note that in the case of symmetric shocks and symmetric countries, all countries are always affected in the same manner by the monetary policy.

We observe that the differences between the cooperative and non-cooperative cases are pretty small for a common price shock, so that in this symmetric benchmark scenario the benefits from coordination between fiscal players are also small. It appears that output gaps and prices adjust practically in the same manner. Policy strategies, however, are somewhat different. In the non-cooperative regime, in fact, fiscal authorities tend to neutralize the effects of fiscal policies on competitiveness, whereas the CB tends to neutralize the deflationary and recessive effects of fiscal policies.[5]

In the above analysis we have mainly discussed *ex-post* policy coordination. However, the complex situation which emerged in Table 6.2 suggests that also different forms of *ex-ante* coordination should be studied. Table 6.3 presents stable coalition structures (CSs) of all the coalition formation games considered for the per-membership partition function in Table 6.2.

Table 6.3 Stable CSs for (sc_1, p_{0S})

(sc_1, p_{0S})	*Stable CSs*	WIX
OMG^{ST}	[12|3|4];[13|2|4];[1|23|4]	0.42%
$ROMG^{ST}$	NC;[12|3|4];[13|2|4];[1|23|4]	0.46%
$EMG^{ST}(\Delta)$	NC;[12|3|4];[13|2|4];[1|23|4]	0.46%
$EMG^{ST}(\Gamma)$	NC;F;[12|3|4];[13|2|4];[1|23|4]	0.41%
SNG^{ST}	[1|23|4]	0.42%

The definition of different games and relevant algorithms to derive stable CSs (or regimes) can be found in Chapter 5, Subsections 5.4.2, 5.4.3, and 5.4.4. The regimes C, F, and NC are not equilibria in the OMG, which confirms our first observations. Although the welfare index WIX in Table 6.2 shows that C is the social optimum, the optimization of all the MU losses in this full MU coalition have been made at the expense of fiscal players for whom full cooperation became the least preferred regime. In fact, the CB is the only player who benefits from C but its gains are sizeable enough to completely set off increases in the losses of fiscal players and still this regime is the social optimum. It is the least-preferred CS by all the fiscal players; hence, it cannot be an equilibrium in any of the games considered. The fiscal coalition F is not stable since the CB has an incentive to join this coalition and, moreover, each fiscal player has an incentive to deviate (in order to play as a singleton when the other two fiscal players cooperate in a partial coalition). Similarly, NC is not an equilibrium as all the fiscal players prefer to create partial coalitions, which are, consequently, the OMG equilibria. Note that the stability of the regimes [12|3|4], [13|2|4]

[5] With a (symmetric) negative price shock ($p_0 = [0.01, 0.01, 0.01]^T$), fiscal policy is expansionary (a deficit) and monetary policy is also expansionary (a cut in the interest rate), while with a (symmetric) positive price shock ($p_0 = [-0.01, -0.01, -0.01]^T$), we have the same (optimal) losses but with opposite policies: restrictive fiscal and monetary policies.

and [1|23|4] is due to distinction assumptions (see Definition 5.14). Whenever a fiscal player chooses between two partial coalitions and losses of this player in both CSs considered are equal, then this player prefers to stay in the current coalition. For instance, $C1$ could deviate from regime [12|3|4] to regime [13|2|4], but losses are equal and it prefers to stay in the present coalition. In the ROMG, the stability of partial coalitions has also another explanation. A deviation of $C1$ is not feasible since $C3$ plays as a singleton and does not want to join (to build F or C). Moreover, in the ROMG, the non-cooperative regime is stable by definition.

The EMG(Δ) features the same set of stable CSs as the ROMG. In fact, fiscal players prefer to deviate from both C and F in order to play non-cooperatively in a partial-coalition setting. All the other CSs are stable. In the EMG(Γ), where, in contrast to the EMG(Δ), the creation of a coalition requires a common consent of all players involved, also fiscal cooperation becomes stable because if any country deviates, then F breaks up and players end up in a non-cooperative regime, which is worse than F. However, for the fiscal players, regime C is still worse than NC; consequently, C cannot be stable in the EMG(Γ). Finally, it should be noted that the high number of stable CSs in the EMG(Γ) provides us with little information which CS would be actually played.

It is impossible to visualize a game tree for the SNG. Why does CS $[1|23|4] \in SNG^{ST}$ but not any other partial coalition? To answer this question we have to look at the assumed order of players, i.e. $C1, C2, C3, CB$, and the relevant part of the game tree which is presented in Figure 6.5.

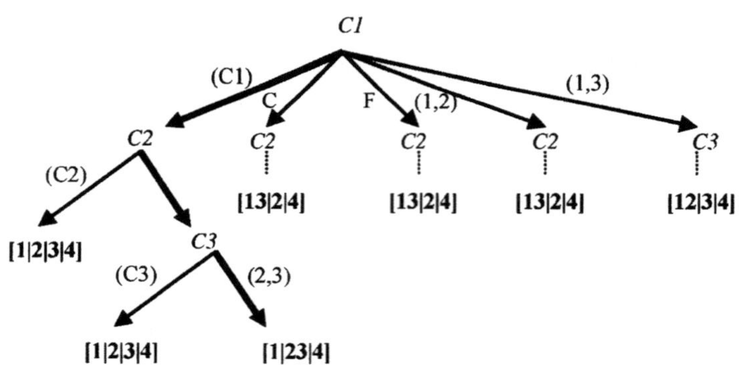

Figure 6.5. The fragment of the SNG game tree for (sc_1, p_{0S}) for a natural rule of order

$C1$ is entitled to propose a coalition or leave the game to play non-cooperatively. In fact, each fiscal player mostly prefers to play non-cooperatively, but only when both other fiscal players create a partial coalition. Indeed, $C1$ knows that if it proposes to play as a singleton, then $C2$ and $C3$ will decide to create a partial coalition. It is caused by the fact that $C1$'s decision to play as a singleton (proposal $(C1)$) and to leave the game reduces the set of feasible coalitions, which player $C2$ can propose (as being the next player in the rule of order). It happens because no coalition including $C1$ is now feasible. Hence, $C2$ can propose only (2,3) or can decide to play non-cooperatively by announcing ($C2$). This player prefers, of course, to create the former regime. What would happen if $C1$ decided to propose C, F, $(1,2)$? The next player in turn, i.e. $C2$, would reject this proposal and leave the game since $C2$ also knows that it would lead to partial cooperation between $C1$ and $C3$. Following the same logic, an initial proposal of $C1$ to $C3$ to create a coalition would end up in the regime [12|3|4], which is less preferred by $C1$. The conclusion is that the rule of order enables the first player to leave the game and, by that, to force both other players to play cooperatively, which leads to the most preferred regime of $C1$.

The last column of Table 6.3 presents the average WIX, i.e. $\overline{WIX}$. If we assume that effectiveness is measured by a relative deviation of welfare from the social optimum, this index shows the average effectiveness of each coalition formation mechanism from the point of view of the MU as a whole. We find that in Table 6.3 the most-efficient game equilibria are the OMG and the SNG. The EMG(Γ) is characterized by a lower $\overline{WIX}$ but, as it was mentioned before, there are too many stable CSs to derive a fruitful insight.

Note that the above analysis matches the case studied by Buti and Sapir (1998), where a common (price) shock is applied. The results confirm their conclusion that, in the case of a common symmetric shock, fiscal coordination emerges as an equilibrium but that the gains of coordination are likely to be relatively small then.

Asymmetric shock

Asymmetric shocks play an important role in the analysis of an MU: how e.g. should countries react in an MU if hit by asymmetric shocks and being restricted by fiscal stringency requirements? Policy coordination seems a potential strong instrument to alleviate the adjustment burden individual countries face when dealing with asymmetric shocks. On the other hand, policy coordination - despite these potential sizeable benefits- may be more difficult to implement as countries are more divergent and countries that are not affected by the asymmetric shocks may lose from policy coordination, creating strong dilemmas for policymakers in an MU.

Consider an asymmetric shock hitting $C1$: $p_{0A} = [0.01; 0; 0]^T$. In our symmetric baseline scenario this leads to a number of interesting outcomes. Table 6.4 provides the welfare losses produced by the asymmetric shock to $C1$.

Table 6.4. Optimal losses for (sc_1, p_{0A})

	NC	C	F	[12|3|4]	[13|2|4]	[1|23|4]
$C1$	73.7731	68.3581	68.5625	67.1665	67.1665	79.0785
$C2$	17.7538	16.7086	16.6049	18.6978	19.1054	17.6972
$C3$	17.7538	16.7086	16.6049	19.1054	18.6978	17.6972
CB	0.5461	0.5359	0.5420	0.5216	0.5216	0.7909
WIX	7.35%	0%	0.003%	3.11%	3.11%	12.67%
CFI	0%	6.843%	8.840%	8.13%	8.13%	5.16%

First, observe that fiscal players' losses are much higher than in the previous example with a symmetric shock, but that the CB features much lower losses. Full cooperation results in significant welfare gains for all the players, even though it is for none of the players the most preferred outcome. Figure 6.1 gives the controls' effects, produced by the asymmetric shocks with dotted lines. $C1$ implements an expansionary fiscal policy to stabilize output, which declined immediately after the negative price shock. The improved competitiveness of $C2$ and $C3$ *vis-à-vis* $C1$ increases their output at the cost of $C1$. Accordingly, they implement restrictive fiscal policies, which, however, are delaying the recovery in $C1$. Under coordination, therefore, $C2$ and $C3$ have a less restrictive fiscal policy. Some of the inflation in $C1$ is transmitted to $C2$ and $C3$. As to be expected, the monetary policy of the CB is not much affected by an asymmetric shock in one country. Also the CB has small gains if at least some form of policy coordination can be implemented, with the exception of the case where the two non-affected countries are cooperating.

Table 6.5 presents stable CSs of the coalition formation games for the symmetric scenario under an asymmetric shock:

Table 6.5 Stable CSs for (sc_1, p_{0A})

(sc_1, p_{0A})	*Stable CSs*	WIX
OMG^{ST}	C	0%
$ROMG^{ST}$	NC,C	3.67%
$EMG^{ST}(\Delta)$	NC,C,F, [1|23|4]	5.00%
$EMG^{ST}(\Gamma)$	NC,C,F, [1|23|4]	5.00%
SNG^{ST}	F	0.003%

The full cooperative regime is stable in the OMG and, hence, in the ROMG and the EMG(Δ). This is easily seen as no player wants to deviate unilaterally from C. In the EMG(Δ) also F and [1|23|4] become stable since the CB cannot join this fiscal coalition and $C1$ cannot join the partial coalition (2,3) due to exclusive-membership assumption. In this example the $EMG^{ST}(\Gamma) = EMG^{ST}(\Delta)$ coincide but it should be stressed that this does not have to be necessarily the case in other examples.

We will again have a closer look to the result of the SNG. $C1$ mostly prefers the partial coalitions (1,2) and (1,3). $C2$ and $C3$ can reject these proposals, respectively, and can propose F or C, which they prefer to partial coalitions with $C1$. As they obtain lower (optimal) losses in fiscal cooperation they would like to end up in F, whereas $C1$ would like to end up in C if partial cooperation is rejected. What does $C1$ propose? It has the following four possibilities:

(a) Assume $C1$ proposes (1,2). $C2$ rejects this coalition and proposes F, which is accepted by $C3$ but rejected by $C1$, which prefers C to F and the game finishes in C as F is no more feasible (because it is already proposed and rejected). Hence, $C2$, receiving the proposal (1,2), has to think about the way to end up in F, and not in C. To achieve this, $C2$, after rejecting (1,2), does not propose F, but proposes C. The first to react is $C1$. It can either accept C, propose F or (1,3). If it accepts C, it is rejected by $C3$ and F is proposed and accepted. If it proposes F, it is just accepted. If it rejects C and proposes (1,3), then $C3$ rejects (1,3) and proposes F. Hence, after an initial proposal of (1,2) by $C1$, the fiscal coalition F always emerges.

(b) Assume $C1$ proposes (1,3). The story follows the same logic as in (a). $C3$, after rejecting (1,3), proposes C in spite of the fact that it wants to have this coalition rejected. But $C3$ knows that C will be rejected by $C2$ because they have a common interest to create F. Hence, after this proposal, $C1$ is the first player to react. If it accepts C, it is rejected by $C2$ and F is proposed and accepted. If $C1$ proposes F, it is just accepted. If it proposes (1,2), then $C2$ rejects this coalition and proposes F, which is accepted.

(c) Assume $C1$ proposes F. Then it is just accepted by $C2$ and $C3$.

(d) Assume $C1$ proposes C. Then $C2$ rejects it and proposes F, which is accepted. $C1$ could reject F and propose a partial cooperation to any of the fiscal players, but it would be rejected as $C2$ and $C3$ prefer not to cooperate in a partial coalition.

Hence, all the possible proposals of $C1$ lead to F, in spite of the fact that $C1$ is the first in the rule of order and prefers mostly a partial coalition. This analysis illustrates a very interesting (strategic) characteristic of the SNG. Whenever there are two coalitions (say $(P1, P2)$ and $(P1, P2, P3)$) in which two subsequent players in the rule of order (say $P1$ and $P2$) take part, and if:

(i) $P1$ prefers $(P1, P2)$ to $(P1, P2, P3)$ and she prefers both these coalitions to all other coalitions/CSs in the game, and

(ii) $P2$ prefers $(P1, P2, P3)$ to $(P1, P2)$ and she prefers both these coalitions to all other coalitions/CSs in the game

then (*ceteris paribus*) the more power has $P2$, in spite of the fact that she is the second in the rule of order. This power comes from our assumption that a coalition, once rejected, cannot be proposed for the second time. Hence, $P2$ can reject the proposal of $P1$ and, by that, narrow the set of coalitions she can take part in. This power can be called the *power to reject*. This power has been extensively used in the previous example. We leave the analysis what would happen if the rule of order was changed to ($C2$,$C1$,$C3$,CB) to the reader.

Concerning the effectiveness it comes out that OMG mechanisms are the most efficient ones from the point of view of the MU as a whole. With the SNG we achieve just a slightly less efficient outcome.

Anti-symmetric shock

The analysis of symmetric and asymmetric shocks provided already a number of insights about the effects of policy coordination. Now we turn our interest on the final type of shock, an anti-symmetric shock. We consider a price shock that affects the prices in $C1$ and $C3$ in an opposite manner (an anti-symmetric country-specific shock, $p_{0AS} = [0.01, 0, -0.01]^T$). The resulting losses for the various regimes are reported in Table 6.6.

Table 6.6. Optimal losses for (sc_1, p_{0AS})

	NC	C	F	[12|3|4]	[13|2|4]	[1|23|4]
$C1$	162.6911	151.4297	151.4297	148.6954	151.4297	174.7063
$C2$	0.0000	0.0000	0.0000	8.0995	0.0000	8.0995
$C3$	162.6911	151.4297	151.4297	174.7063	151.4297	148.6954
CB	0.0000	0.0000	0.0000	0.3018	0.0000	0.3018
WIX	7.44%	0%	0%	9.56%	0%	9.56%
CFI	0%	6.92%	6.92%	10.58%	6.92%	10.58%

The most evident feature of Table 6.6 is that there are no differences between the grand coalition C, the fiscal coalition F, and the partial fiscal cooperation CS [13|2|4]. This occurs because the fiscal policy of the first country is exactly offset by the fiscal policy of the third country, due to the model symmetry and the preference symmetry among fiscal authorities.[6] More in detail, in regimes where $C1$ and $C3$ are either both in the same coalition or both outside, due to the equal sizes of the perfectly opposite shocks, the CB and $C2$ do not affect the adjustment dynamics in the MU since they are not affected by the anti-symmetric shock. Hence, because of the perfect structural symmetry of the model, $C2$ and the CB are not affected at all by the anti-symmetric shocks in $C1$ and $C3$.

In case the CB would react, this would affect all three countries in a different manner and would clearly affect the adjustment dynamics of the MU. Something similar could be said of $C2$: if it would react, it would affect $C1$ and $C3$ in a different way as they are facing different initial conditions, even though they are symmetric in all other respects. This 'neutrality' of the CB and $C2$ changes when partial fiscal coalitions with $C2$ are formed, even in this symmetric setting. With the partial fiscal coalitions $(1, 2)$ and $(2, 3)$ all the players, including the CB, are directly affected in their optimal policies and losses. Clearly, from the perspective of $C2$ it is not beneficial to enter a coalition with $C1$ or $C3$, which are hit by the shock, since in a cooperative arrangement $C2$'s policies will be partly directed at the problems in the other country.

Figure 6.1 shows the paths of the control variables after this anti-symmetric shock with dashed lines. Anti-symmetric shocks have a neutralizing effect in the countries involved and tend to compensate the effects of the policymakers' actions. Therefore, cooperation helps in reducing the losses from too expansionary (restrictive) fiscal policies: in the cooperative case $C1$ has a smaller deficit and $C3$ a smaller surplus than in the non-cooperative case. In this way negative fiscal externalities are internalized and, therefore, partially reduced.

The anti-symmetric shock analyzed in Table 6.6 is also studied by Beetsma *et al.* (2001) who find that fiscal coordination is desirable.

[6] See Chapter 4 for a more detailed description of this mechanism in a two-country model.

We confirm their result that fiscal authorities internalize the negative effects of opposite policies with coordination. But, we also find that, in this symmetric setting, no further gains are associated with full cooperation C, which is confirmed by Figure 6.1 (there are no more effects that can be internalized by the fiscal policy of $C2$ and/or the monetary policy of the CB).

Table 6.7 presents stable CSs of the various coalition formation games:

Table 6.7 Stable CSs for (sc_1, p_{0AS})

(sc_1, p_{0AS})	*Stable CSs*	WIX
OMG^{ST}	C	0%
$ROMG^{ST}$	NC,C	3.72%
$EMG^{ST}(\Delta)$	NC,C,F, [13|2|4]	1.86%
$EMG^{ST}(\Gamma)$	NC,C,F,[13|2|4]	1.86%
SNG^{ST}	C	0%

Coalitions including both $C1$ and $C3$ are clearly candidates for stable equilibria of the games since the first-best strategy for $C1$ occurs for CS [12|3|4], which is not stable since $C3$ wants to join, and the first-best strategies for $C3$ occur within these coalitions with $C1$ and $C3$. In fact, in the OMG the full cooperative regime C is stable. However, the regimes [13|2|4] and F are not stable since the players $C2$ and the CB, being indifferent w.r.t. losses, want to join larger coalitions (see Definition 5.14). As already suggested the partial coalitions [12|3|4] and [1|23|4] are not stable as singleton fiscal players want to join them to create the more preferred regime F. Consequently, F must be stable in the EMG(Δ) as no player wants to unilaterally leave this coalition as it would lead to partial coalitions. Also [13|2|4] is stable in the EMG(Δ) as $C1$ and $C3$ do not want to break this coalition and play as in the non-cooperative regime. A similar reasoning applies to the EMG(Γ) when assuming that a coalition considered breaks up when a player deviates. Clearly, full MU cooperation is stable in the SNG due to SNG distinction assumptions in Definition 5.14.

From the welfare point of view the most effective games are the OMG and the SNG, which result only in C. Other coordination mechanisms, apart from C, F, and [13|2|4], which are social optima, support also NC; hence, cannot be optimal compared to the OMG and the SNG.

Concluding, the above examples seem to advocate a need for coordination even though the welfare gains are in most cases limited in size. First, when a common price shock is considered in our symmetric setting, fiscal coordination of policies is required to internalize the externalities arising from excessive deficits. However, when the CB joins this fiscal coalition the joint optimization is not profitable for the fiscal players. Second, in the case of asymmetric shocks, externalities from coalition formation increase considerably; hence, players' interests become more diverse. On the other hand, they have often much more to gain from cooperation than under a symmetric shock. Third, when anti-symmetric country-specific shocks occur, coordination needs become weaker since there is no difference between the full MU coalition, the full fiscal coalition and the partial coalition of those countries which are hit by the (perfectly) anti-symmetric shock.

6.3.2 The role of spillovers

Having analyzed the three types of shocks and their implications for policy coordination in the baseline configuration, it is now of interest to analyze in more detail the implications of various types of spillovers. To do so, we confront in this section the outcomes of the symmetric baseline scenario outlined above with a number of alternative scenarios listed in Table 6.8.

Table 6.8 Alternative scenarios

No.	Sc.	Parameters	Description
1.	sc_1	Parameters as in Table 6.1	baseline
2.	sc_{1A}	$\chi_i, \chi_U \rightarrow \infty$	no-policy regime
3.	sc_{1B}	$\varsigma_{ij} = 0$	no inflation spillovers
4.	sc_{1C}	$\rho_{ij} = 0$	no output spillovers
5.	sc_{1D}	$\delta_{ij} = 0$	no competitiveness spillovers
6.	sc_{1E}	$\gamma_i = 0$	no interest rate spillovers
7.	sc_{1F}	$\varsigma_{ij} = \rho_{ij} = \delta_{ij} = \gamma_i = 0$	autarky
8.	sc_{1G}	$sc_{1A} + sc_{1F}$	autarky plus no-policy regime
9.	sc_{1H}	$\alpha_i = 0$	no inflation stabilization objective
10.	sc_{1I}	$\beta_i = 0$	no output stabilization objective

Scenario sc_{1A} is a 'no-policy' scenario: by letting welfare losses from active stabilization go to infinity for all players, this regime has no policy interventions at all (all equilibrium paths have been put at zero) and, therefore, all policy regimes will coincide. All other parameters are as in the baseline. Scenario sc_{1B} features no direct inflation spillovers. Scenario sc_{1C} has no direct output spillovers. In scenario sc_{1D} there is no competitiveness effect. Scenario sc_{1E} turns off the interest rate channel in the MU to isolate the effects from monetary policy, so that the analysis becomes relatively similar to the one of Chapter 3. Scenario sc_{1AF} combines scenarios $sc_{1B} - sc_{1E}$, implying that the MU basically consists of three autarkic economies. Scenario sc_{1G} in addition shuts off all policy interventions. In scenario sc_{1H}, the contribution from output stabilization is isolated by assuming that policymakers no longer have an inflation stabilization objective. In scenario sc_{1I} on the other hand, policymakers no longer have an output stabilization objective. Tables 6.9, 6.10 and 6.11 contain outcomes of numerical simulations in all alternative scenarios for the non-cooperative regime.[7]

[7]Please note that externality indices in the symmetric benchmark model show that for losses a shock symmetry is much more important than externalities from a coalition formation. Hence, we may expect that also changes in the model parameters will be relatively more influential than externalities from a coalition formation. Hence, to grasp main effects of those changes we can restrict our attention to the non-cooperative regime (NC).

Table 6.9 Symmetric price shock $p_{0S} = [0.01, 0.01, 0.01]^T$

NC	sc_1	sc_{1A}	sc_{1B}	sc_{1C}	sc_{1D}
$C1$	2.4600	2.5000	2.4853	2.4769	2.4602
$C2$	2.4600	2.5000	2.4853	2.4769	2.4602
$C3$	2.4600	2.5000	2.4853	2.4769	2.4602
CB	4.9148	5.0000	4.9654	4.9498	4.9162
$\max(WIX)$	*0.59%*	*0%*	*0.17%*	*0.52%*	*0.61%*
$\max(CFI)$	*0.91%*	*0%*	*0.31%*	*0.55%*	*0.91%*
NC	sc_{1E}	sc_{1F}	sc_{1G}	sc_{1H}	sc_{1I}
$C1$	2.4728	2.4930	2.5000	0.0000	2.5000
$C2$	2.4728	2.4930	2.5000	0.0000	2.5000
$C3$	2.4728	2.4930	2.5000	0.0000	2.5000
CB	4.9261	4.9734	5.0000	0.0000	5.0000
$\max(WIX)$	*0.69%*	*0.58%*	*0%*	*0%*	*0%*
$\max(CFI)$	*0.83%*	*0.17%*	*0%*	*0%*	*0%*

First, compare the no-policy scenario sc_{1A} with the baseline scenario sc_1. If players do not use their instruments losses increase (for all three shocks). Clearly, players use their instruments to internalize economic externalities and reduce losses. If policy instruments are abandoned, then there are no policy-induced economic externalities and we can determine the spillovers' effects of this unconstrained, no policy regime. In a way these are 'natural' effects of spillovers in the open MU setting: they represent the spillovers' effects that result in case there is no stabilization policy at all. Consequently, we can consider losses in Tables 6.9 - 6.11, column sc_{1A} as the unconstrained effects of spillovers.[8] Looking at it in a different way, we can argue that there are positive effects from allowing policymakers being flexible: in the case of policies being entirely fixed at level 0, losses are higher for all players in all cases than in the baseline with a certain degree of policy flexibility.

The next column in Tables 6.9 - 6.11, i.e. sc_{1B}, contains losses in the absence of price spillovers. Comparing to sc_1 we see that for the symmetric shock case losses are a bit higher for all players, suggesting that there are small but positive externalities under symmetric shocks. In the asymmetric shock losses are lower for the fiscal players and higher for the CB. In case of the anti-symmetric shock, $C2$ and the CB are not involved in the game as before. The countries hit by the anti-symmetric shock have lower losses suggesting that in this case the price spillovers impose significant negative externalities from the point of view of the fiscal players.

[8] In this section when we describe spillovers in a scenario, we consider respective columns in Tables 6.9, 6.10 and 6.11 jointly.

Table 6.10 Asymmetric price shock $p_{0A} = [0.01, 0, 0]^T$

NC	sc_1	sc_{1A}	sc_{1B}	sc_{1C}	sc_{1D}
$C1$	73.7731	80.9898	66.4293	83.9276	2.4848
$C2$	17.7538	19.1899	15.7502	20.0830	0.0008
$C3$	17.7538	19.1899	15.7502	20.0830	0.0008
CB	0.5461	0.5556	0.5517	0.5500	0.5462
$\max(WIX)$	*12.66%*	*0%*	*10.76%*	*1.77%*	*0.39%*
$\max(CFI)$	*8.13%*	*0%*	*7.12%*	*1.47%*	*0.98%*
NC	sc_{1E}	sc_{1F}	sc_{1G}	sc_{1H}	sc_{1I}
$C1$	69.9326	2.4930	2.5000	75.5150	5.4748
$C2$	16.6285	0.0000	0.0000	18.8787	0.3112
$C3$	16.6285	0.0000	0.0000	18.8787	0.3112
CB	0.5473	0.5526	0.5556	0.0000	0.5556
$\max(WIX)$	*9.24%*	*0.03%*	*0%*	*0%*	*0%*
$\max(CFI)$	*6.67%*	*0.07%*	*0%*	*0%*	*0%*

Compared to the baseline, the no-output spillover case, sc_{1C}, features higher losses for all players for all types of shocks, implying that there are in all cases positive externalities from output spillovers.

In case of symmetric shocks and symmetric countries the spillovers from competitiveness essentially do not matter as sc_{1D} shows. Spillovers from competitiveness are, on the other hand, very important in the case of asymmetric and anti-symmetric shocks. If there are no spillovers through this channel, welfare losses are much lower for the countries that are hit by asymmetric and anti-symmetric shocks; an indication that there are strong negative externalities for these countries coming through this channel.

Table 6.11 Anti-asymmetric price shock $p_{0A\text{-}S} = [0.01, 0, -0.01]^T$

NC	sc_1	sc_{1A}	sc_{1B}	sc_{1C}	sc_{1D}
$C1$	162.6911	177.8044	145.6518	184.9018	2.4994
$C2$	0.0000	0.0000	0.0000	0.0000	0.0000
$C3$	162.6911	177.8044	145.6518	184.9018	2.4994
CB	0.0000	0.0000	0.0000	0.0000	0.0000
$\max(WIX)$	*9.56%*	*0%*	*8.15%*	*1.32%*	*0.18%*
$\max(CFI)$	*10.56%*	*0%*	*9.47%*	*1.90%*	*0.22%*
NC	sc_{1E}	sc_{1F}	sc_{1G}	sc_{1H}	sc_{1I}
$C1$	69.9326	2.4930	2.5000	75.5150	5.4748
$C2$	16.6285	0.0000	0.0000	18.8787	0.3112
$C3$	16.6285	0.0000	0.0000	18.8787	0.3112
CB	0.5473	0.5526	0.5556	0.0000	0.5556
$\max(WIX)$	*6.97%*	*0%*	*0%*	*0%*	*0%*
$\max(CFI)$	*8.72%*	*0%*	*0%*	*0%*	*0%*

The effects of the interest rate spillovers, sc_{1E}, on the other hand, are similar to the case of the foreign price spillovers. In the case of symmetric shocks there are small positive externalities and there are larger negative externalities to the fiscal players in case of asymmetric and anti-symmetric shocks. In case of the anti-symmetric shock, $C2$ and the CB are not affected.

The total set of spillovers resulting from openness in an MU are analyzed in sc_{1F}. Since it is a mixture of the effects of sc_{1B} till sc_{1F}, we do not know *a priori* the directions of the externalities, except for the symmetric case where we find that openness implies (small) positive externalities: more open economies have lower welfare losses in case of symmetric shocks. Adjustment is enhanced by the openness making the open economy in our framework always perform better than the equivalent closed economy in case of symmetric shocks. However, note that the effects remain small. In case of asymmetric and anti-symmetric shocks, the negative spillovers dominate for the countries experiencing the shocks: they would have been better off if their economies were not open to the other countries of the MU and they were not subject to the common interest rate regime. In a way, these are results that are strongly related to the OCA theory: if countries are more (less) open and experience a high (low) degree of symmetric shocks, they are more (less) likely to represent an OCA. Clearly dominating -in a quantitative sense- are in this case the spillovers resulting from competitiveness in an MU. This underlines why the study of this channel is so important and will therefore be the subject of study throughout this book. Taking out policy in the closed-economy regime in sc_{1G} has much less effects as in the open economy.

A CB that has no inflation stabilization objective, sc_{1B}, imposes positive externalities in case of asymmetric and anti-symmetric shocks as it will react more strongly to the output effects produced by the shocks, which will be beneficial to stabilize the output of all countries: monetary and fiscal policies will then reinforce each other rather than counteract each other as in the baseline regime where monetary and fiscal authorities have asymmetric preferences in terms of output and inflation objectives.

A CB that is a strict inflation targeter sc_{1I}, is posing significant positive externalities on the fiscal players in the case of asymmetric and anti-symmetric shocks: they are in that case better of with this CB that is a strict inflation targeter than with the flexible inflation targeter in the baseline. On the other hand, in case of symmetric shocks there are small negative externalities from the strict inflation targeting by the CB.

6.3.3 Structural asymmetric setting

So far, Subsection 6.3.1 has analyzed the case of symmetric countries. Like in Chapter 4, it may be interesting to also look at the case where countries are asymmetric in their structural parameters. There, it was seen that asymmetries are likely to reduce the possibilities that sustainable coalitions arise: in case of asymmetries countries react differently to changing macroeconomic conditions and differ in the optimal policy adjustments. It is interesting to verify whether increasing the number of countries may cause additional insights on the setting of asymmetric countries. We consider the example presented in Table 6.12 that can be interpreted as a setup, where a relatively-closed $C1$ faces two open countries $C2$ and $C3$, which are more sensitive to foreign output and price changes.

Table 6.12 An example of a structural asymmetric setting

$\eta_1 = 0.75$	$\delta_{12} = 0.1$	$\gamma_1 = 0.2$	$\zeta_1 = 0.25$	$\rho_{12} = 0.1$	$\varsigma_{12} = 0$
$\eta_2 = 0.75$	$\delta_{13} = 0.1$	$\gamma_2 = 0.2$	$\zeta_2 = 0.25$	$\rho_{13} = 0.1$	$\varsigma_{13} = 0$
$\eta_3 = 0.75$	$\delta_{21} = 0.3$	$\gamma_3 = 0.2$	$\zeta_3 = 0.25$	$\rho_{21} = 0.3$	$\varsigma_{21} = 0.3$
	$\delta_{23} = 0.3$			$\rho_{23} = 0.3$	$\varsigma_{23} = 0.3$
	$\delta_{31} = 0.3$			$\rho_{31} = 0.3$	$\varsigma_{31} = 0.3$
	$\delta_{32} = 0.3$			$\rho_{32} = 0.3$	$\varsigma_{32} = 0.3$

The asymmetries imply that spillovers are no longer symmetric across the MU. This is also seen in matrix $L_{(2)}$, which corresponds to the (semi-)elasticities in Table 6.12. It features asymmetric positive fiscal spillovers for output gaps and negative fiscal spillovers for inflation rates and, similarly, asymmetric negative (foreign) price spillovers for (domestic) output gaps and negative.(foreign) price spillovers for (domestic) inflation rates. Also the semi-elasticities of the output gaps and inflation rates w.r.t. the common nominal interest rate are asymmetric between, on the one hand, $C1$ and, on the other hand, $C2$ and $C3$.

$$L_{(2)} = \left[\begin{array}{ccc|ccc|c} -0.1233 & 0.0617 & 0.0617 & 0.8847 & 0.1408 & 0.1408 & -0.311 \\ 0.4142 & -0.5638 & 0.1496 & 0.4524 & 0.9658 & 0.3713 & -0.4772 \\ 0.4142 & 0.1496 & -0.5638 & 0.4524 & 0.3713 & 0.9658 & -0.4772 \\ \hline -0.0808 & 0.0154 & 0.0154 & 0.2212 & 0.0352 & 0.0352 & -0.0777 \\ 0.1347 & -0.186 & 0.0012 & 0.2564 & 0.311 & 0.1967 & -0.2038 \\ 0.1347 & 0.0012 & -0.186 & 0.2564 & 0.1967 & 0.311 & -0.2038 \end{array}\right]$$

In such a context we consider the following country-specific (initial) price shock: $p_{0A2} = [0.01;\ 0.0075; 0.005]^T$.[9] The resulting optimal losses for this asymmetric scenario sc_2 are described in Table 6.13.

Table 6.13 Optimal losses for (sc_2, p_{0A2})

	NC	C	F	[12|3|4]	[13|2|4]	[1|23|4]
$C1$	4.2544	6.0294	5.6854	4.2058	5.5168	4.5258
$C2$	1.8150	1.7105	1.8143	1.7756	1.5502	2.5561
$C3$	23.2730	18.8049	19.8800	23.0975	20.5289	22.1761
CB	3.1998	3.2611	2.8511	3.1743	2.9223	3.0087
WIX	9.18%	0%	1.43%	8.21%	2.39%	8.26%
CFI	0%	19.69%	15.90%	0.88%	13.98%	7.07%

In Table 6.13 $C3$ has by far the highest losses in all regimes, whereas $C2$ has the lowest. As $C2$ and $C3$ are identical, an explanation of these outcomes

[9] Note that not only this price shock is completely different from the p_{0A} but that also various structural asymmetries were introduced. Hence, the result of these simulations cannot be directly compared with those for the previous asymmetric shock. However, in Table 6.11 we did a comparison of the model with structural asymmetries with the original asymmetric price shock p_{0A}.

is to be found in the asymmetry of the initial price shocks and the different adjustment dynamics produced by them. Due to the assumed country-specific (initial) price shocks $C1$ has a comparative price disadvantage w.r.t. $C2$ and $C3$. This causes a relatively high instability in output gap, especially for $C3$, which is an inflation importer. Moreover, the common monetary policy is based on an aggregate macroeconomic variable, hence, it tends to stabilize the average. Therefore, its policy is more in line with the situation in $C2$, because in this country an initial increase in prices equals the average of the (asymmetric) shock p_{0A2}. Moreover, for $C2$ spillovers and economic externalities from $C1$ and $C3$ tend to compensate each other to a large extent (for instance, $C2$ has a less comparative price disadvantage w.r.t. $C1$ and a more comparative price disadvantage w.r.t. $C3$). Consequently, this player features the lowest losses in spite of the fact that its shock is larger than the shock incurred by $C3$. $C2$ features the highest losses in a partial fiscal coalition with $C3$, because its policies are partly determined by the conditions in $C3$ and is less in line with the CB's objectives.

Figures 6.6 and 6.7 display the (optimal) adjustments of controls, prices and outputs in the non-cooperative and [12|3|4] regimes. Under non-cooperation, $C1$ has an expansionary policy since its output declines due to the unfavourable terms of trade and highest price shock, whereas $C3$ pursues a comparatively very restrictive fiscal policy, as an inflation importer. $C2$'s fiscal policy is somewhere in between that of $C1$ and $C3$; hence, it is close to the 0 axis. This confirms our presumptions that (indirect) fiscal spillovers and resulting economic externalities from $C1$ and $C3$ set off each other in the case of $C2$. This situation is somehow comparable to the anti-symmetric shock p_{0AS} and the symmetric model in sc_1, in which effects of foreign spillovers and economic externalities in case of symmetric CSs did not exist as they perfectly set off each other.

The monetary policy of the CB is restrictive to counteract the inflation in the aggregate MU economy. The inflation and output drops are largest in $C1$, also substantial in $C2$, whereas $C3$ experiences an increase in output as the positive competitiveness effects dominate the negative effects from the price shock and the negative output spillovers from $C1$ and $C2$.

On the same graph the optimal paths for the [12|3|4] regime were plotted (in dashed lines). Partial fiscal cooperation between $C1$ and $C2$ leads in the non-cooperative regime to more moderate stabilization policies in both countries. The influence of the formation of coalition (1,2) on the optimal control paths of the external players $C3$ and the CB is not visible. Moreover, there is no (noticeable) difference between the non-cooperative regime and [12|3|4] in Figure 6.7, i.e. the cooperation between $C1$ and $C2$ does not substantially affect the output gaps and price adjustments. Hence, lower losses of both players are caused by internalization of mutual fiscal externalities.

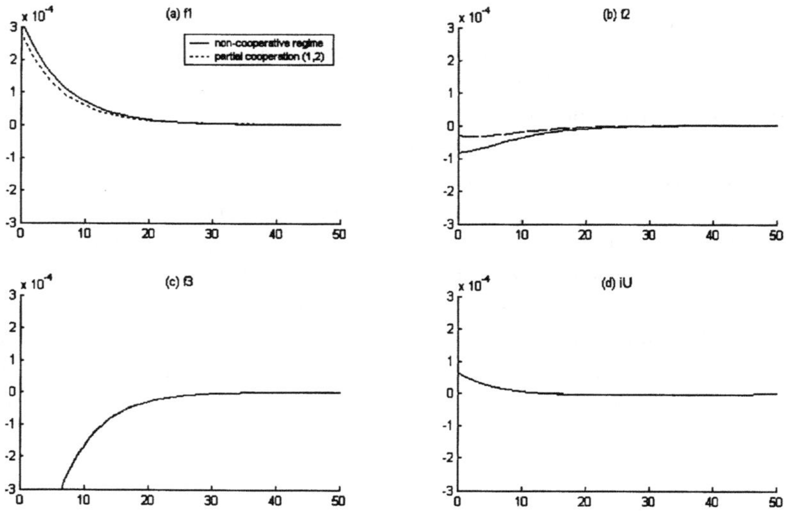

Figure 6.6 Optimal paths of controls for (sc_2, p_{0A2}), regimes NC and [12|3|4].

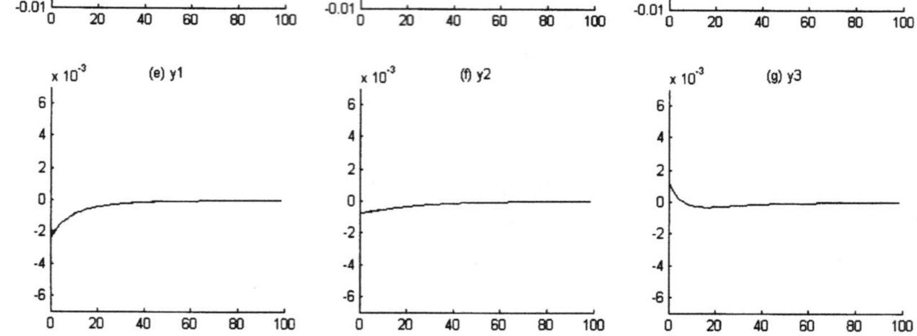

Figure 6.7 Optimal paths of prices and output for (sc_2, p_{0A2}), regimes NC and [12|3|4].

Table 6.14. Stable CS for (sc_2, p_{0A2})

(sc_2, p_{0A2})	*Stable CSs*	WIX
OMG^{ST}	–	–
$ROMG^{ST}$	NC	9.18%
$EMG^{ST}(\Delta)$	NC;[12|3|4]	8.69%
$EMG^{ST}(\Gamma)$	NC;[12|3|4]	8.69%
SNG^{ST}	[12|3|4]	8.21%

There are no stable non-trivial CSs in the open-membership games, whereas stable exclusive-membership games lead to [12|3|4] and to the trivial NC; the partial coalition is stable since both $C1$ and $C2$ prefer this regime to the non-cooperative regime. So, the small number of stable CSs indicate that in this asymmetric setting, the interests of players are very diverse.

CS [12|3|4] emerges also in the SNG, which is the most-efficient coalition formation mechanism from the MU-welfare point of view. In this example, another interesting characteristic of sequential negotiations can be observed. In Table 6.13 $C1$ prefers mostly [12|3|4]; then, it is obvious that it likes to propose it. Why does $C2$ accept this proposal, if it would prefer to play in C or be as a singleton in [13|2|4]? The answer is that both these latter CSs will not be accepted. C is the worst possible outcome for the CB and [13|2|4] is one of the worst outcomes for $C1$. In contrast to the previous example, $C2$ cannot direct the sequential game in the desired direction because in no situation the CB and $C1$ can be forced to accept. Clearly, the CB never wants to cooperate since its loss in C is the highest. To put it differently, if the CB plays non-cooperatively, no matter which strategy the other players will pursue, it is better off than in C. Also $C1$ never accepts (1,3) as it would prefer to play non-cooperatively (no matter what the other players do) than to be in this partial coalition. Clearly, the highest loss of a player as a singleton throughout all the CSs is an *SNG threat point* for $C1$. This player is not going to accept any proposal that yields a higher loss than the SNG threat point. $C1$'s threat point is $\phi_1([1|23|4]) = 4.5258$.[10] Any proposal to create a coalition in which $\phi_1(.) > 4.5258$ will not be accepted by this player as she can get at least the value of this threat point by non-cooperating no matter what other players do. Threat points for the other players $C2$, $C3$, and CB are 1.8150, 23.2730, and 3.1998, respectively.

6.3.4 Structural asymmetric setting with asymmetric bargaining power

In the next example we consider again the same structural asymmetric setting, but this time also with players' bargaining power asymmetry in the various coalitions. We denote this scenario by sc_3. It is assumed that $C3$ has always a

[10]Note that $\phi(.)$ is a per-membership partition function defined in Chapter 5 (Definition 5.5).

lower bargaining power when it cooperates with the (an)other policymaker(s).[11] More in detail, $C3$ is assumed to have a bargaining power equal to $\omega_3 = \frac{1}{5}$ in the grand coalition regime (while the other players share the rest, i.e. each of them has a bargaining power equal to $\omega_{1,2,U} = \frac{(1-\frac{1}{5})}{3}$), $C3$'s bargaining power is assumed to be equal to $\frac{1}{4}$ in the fiscal cooperation regime (others $\frac{3}{8}$), and it is assumed to be equal to $\frac{1}{3}$ when this country cooperates with only one of the other countries ($\frac{2}{3}$). Moreover, the power asymmetry is also reflected in the CB's loss function where $C3$'s weight is assumed to be $\omega_3 = \frac{1}{4}$ and weights of the other countries are equal: $\omega_1 = \omega_2 = \frac{3}{8}$, which means that the CB is relatively more concerned about the inflation and output in $C1$ and $C2$. In such a context we consider again asymmetric price shock $p_{0A} = [0.01; 0; 0]^T$.

The resulting (optimal) losses are described in Table 6.15 (lower part). For convenience, in the upper part we report again losses for the symmetric benchmark model (sc_1) under the initial asymmetric price shocks p_{0A} from Table 6.4 and we additionally present losses for the structural asymmetric model sc_2 under the same asymmetric shock (p_{0A}, in the middle part).

Table 6.15 Optimal losses for $(sc_1\text{-}sc_3, p_{0A})$

(sc_1, p_{0A})	NC	C	F	[12|3|4]	[13|2|4]	[1|23|4]
$C1$	73.7731	68.3581	68.5625	67.1665	67.1665	79.0785
$C2$	17.7538	16.7086	16.6049	18.6978	19.1054	17.6972
$C3$	17.7538	16.7086	16.6049	19.1054	18.6978	17.6972
CB	0.5461	0.5359	0.5420	0.5216	0.5216	0.7909
WIX	7.35%	0%	0.003%	3.11%	3.11%	12.67%
CFI	0%	6.843%	8.840%	8.13%	8.13%	5.16%
(sc_2, p_{0A})	NC	C	F	[12|3|4]	[13|2|4]	[1|23|4]
$C1$	14.5124	29.3021	25.7977	17.2511	17.2511	16.4875
$C2$	55.6306	38.8044	43.5807	48.5603	50.0623	55.5258
$C3$	55.6306	38.8044	43.5807	50.0623	48.5603	55.5258
CB	6.8193	5.6538	2.6664	4.8511	4.8511	4.9084
WIX	17.79%	0%	2.72%	7.25%	7.25%	17.66%
CFI	0%	37.41%	29.82%	13.08%	13.08%	3.09%
(sc_3, p_{0A})	NC	C	F	[12|3|4]	[13|2|4]	[1|23|4]
$C1$	14.5124	26.8828	22.6794	17.2511	14.3862	17.0198
$C2$	55.6306	39.7098	44.2456	48.5603	54.2682	51.1274
$C3$	55.6306	41.3574	46.3850	50.0623	52.1545	62.7278
CB	6.8193	4.9473	3.0921	4.8511	6.3503	4.4804
WIX	17.45%	0%	3.10%	6.93%	12.63%	19.89%
CFI	0%	33.51%	24.53%	13.08%	4.10%	12.40%

The reader may easily analyze the influence of model asymmetry on the players' losses by comparing the upper and middle parts of Table 6.15. In

[11] The bargaining power of a country can be assumed to be an increasing function of its relative size (e.g. the share of its GDP with respect to the aggregate GDP of the EMU; see before in Chapters 2-4).

fact, the middle part of Table 6.15 shows that the structural asymmetries in the model have a tremendous impact on the magnitude and distribution of losses. In (sc_1, p_{0A}) $C1$, which is hit by an asymmetric shock, experienced by far the highest losses, while other countries in the MU are in a comparatively better situation as they do not suffer from the (asymmetric) shock. However, in the asymmetric setting in which $C2$ and $C3$ become inflation importers, the situation changes dramatically. Now, losses of $C2$ and $C3$ are (much) higher than those of $C1$. This happens in spite of the fact that the shock p_{0A} hits only $C1$ but not other countries, which is another indication how important are output, price and competitiveness spillovers in our model. They vastly enhance the volatility of $C2$ and $C3$'s outputs and prices, increasing their losses and at the same time increasing the CB's loss, which is by far much higher in (sc_2, p_{0A}) than in (sc_1, p_{0A}).

By comparing the middle and the lower parts of Table 6.15, we investigate the influence of asymmetric bargaining power on losses. First, note that there is no difference between the non-cooperative regime in (sc_3, p_{0A}) and (sc_2, p_{0A}) since the asymmetric bargaining power does not play a role in this CS made of singletons. Moreover, since both $C1$ and $C2$ are equally powerful, there is no difference between losses in regime [12|3|4] for (sc_2, p_{0A}) and (sc_3, p_{0A}). Second, $C1$, which is more powerful than $C3$, is better off in every CS except for [1|23|4]. Also $C2$ has a higher bargaining power in (sc_3, p_{0A}) but its losses increase compared to (sc_2, p_{0A}). It means that in this case structural asymmetry is amplified by power asymmetry. In other words, $C1$ being less fragile to international spillovers, is able to take advantage of its bargaining power in a much more efficient way than open $C2$.

It should also be noted that the asymmetry of the model considerably increased the maximum value of WIX - from 12.67% in (sc_1, p_{0A}) to 17.79% in (sc_2, p_{0A}) and to 19.89% in (sc_3, p_{0A}). It indicates that coordination may bring a lot of advantages, but can be hard to emerge due to opposite interests of players. Table 6.16 presents results of the coalition formation games for (sc_3, p_A).

Table 6.16. Stable CSs (sc_3, p_{0A})

(sc_2, p_{0AS2})	*Stable CSs*	$\overline{WIX}$
OMG^{ST}	–	–
$ROMG^{ST}$	NC	17.45%
$EMG^{ST}(\Delta)$	NC;[13|2|4]	15.04%
$EMG^{ST}(\Gamma)$	NC;[13|2|4]	15.04%
SNG^{ST}	[13|2|4]	12.63%

Interests of players are so diverse that in the first two simultaneous games there are no stable CSs (except for NC in the ROMG). All the other mechanisms result in [13|2|4] It is not difficult to guess how this CS emerges in the SNG. [13|2|4] is the first-best choice for $C1$ but it is certainly not the first-best choice for $C3$. How is the sequential game played in this case? $C1$ can propose C or F but, then, these CSs would be immediately accepted as $C2$, $C3$ and CB obtain lower losses in these CSs than in the expected [13|2|4]. It means that, as the first move, $C1$ just proposes coalition (1,3). Why then $C3$ does not reject it and exclude this CS from the game? The SNG threat point of $C1$ that equals 17.0198 is the answer. If (1,3) is rejected then $C1$ plays non-cooperatively and that costs $C3$ either $\phi_3(NC) = 55.6306$ or $\phi_3([1|23|4]) = 62.7278$. Hence, $C3$ immediately agrees to the proposal of $C1$ and [13|2|4] is created. Again, the most efficient coalition formation mechanism is the SNG.

6.4 Concluding remarks

In this chapter we have studied the institutional design of the coordination of macroeconomic stabilization policies within a three-country MU and its consequences on macroeconomic outcomes and policies. We have taken into account both *ex-ante* and *ex-post* coordination. *Ex-ante* coordination is related to the institutional framework, the coordination procedure, and the design of policy rules within an MU, whereas *ex-post* coordination takes place from the current state of affairs and concerns the actual policy decisions of the national governments and the CB. In our simulations different kinds of spillovers and asymmetries have been considered since fiscal policy coordination is strongly connected with the resulting economic externalities and asymmetries that are present in the economy. The following extensions of the setting in Chapter 4 should be stressed: (i) we modelled a three-country MU, which enabled us to study much richer shock configurations than in a two-country setting; (ii) loss functions were extended to facilitate the study of a symmetric shock; (iii) foreign price spillovers have been added to the price equation of the model, which made the analysis more realistic.

From the simulations some more general conclusions can be drawn when several symmetries (but not all) are assumed. In the case of a common shock and symmetric countries the main result, which can be derived from our model, is that fiscal coordination is better for fiscal players than full coordination (with the CB), but because of the existence of free-riding incentives for each fiscal player from the coalition F, it is hardly sustainable. Hence, it is most probable that partial coalitions between fiscal players emerge; however, this outcome is suboptimal from the total welfare point of view w.r.t. both C and F. For a country-specific (asymmetric) shock, it appears that full policy coordination may be sometimes sustainable. This result is somehow in contrast to findings of Chapter 4 and the intuition that asymmetry of the shock makes a cooperation less probable since players have diverse interests. In case of an anti-symmetric shock, only the cooperation of affected countries is needed and full or fiscal cooperation is not associated with any extra gains in the policymakers' welfare. These results add new features to the debate between Buti and Sapir (1998) and Beetsma *et al.* (2001) on the effects of coordination in the presence of different types of shocks. Fiscal coordination can be deficient in the case of a common shock (as suggested by Beetsma *et al.* (2001)). In this situation the coordination among all policymakers improves the performance. However both regimes are hardly sustainable, as already mentioned. The same conclusion can be drawn when model asymmetries come into play, since players have very specific preferences concerning cooperation and often partial coalitions emerge. An interesting result comes from the analysis of the asymmetric model and the bargaining power scenario. First of all, asymmetry of the model (hence, real economic conditions) is more important than asymmetry of (political) power. Since players have only limited influence on the economies, mainly model asymmetries drive the stabilization process, whereas bargaining power is less important. Consequently, it is not surprising that an advantageous bargaining power enhances the effects of structural asymmetries in our model as it was shown in the last example.

Regarding the analysis of different coordination mechanisms in the present four-player setting, we can derive some more general conclusions and observations. As expected, the more restrictive is a membership rule, the more stable CSs can be found. More in detail, both the OMG and the ROMG did not produce any stable CSs, when structural (and also bargaining power) asymmetries were considered. However, it should be noted that not all the asymmetries make the above mechanisms unproductive. In the case of the asymmetric shock/symmetric model they led to the socially-optimal outcome C. The interesting observation is that from the welfare point of view sequential unanimous agreement coordination mechanisms (the SNG) is very often more effective than the exclusive-membership rule in the EMGs.[12] Especially, the EMG(Γ) can be compared to the SNG w.r.t. some coalition formation rules, as in both games unanimous consent of players is required to create a coalition structure. Hence, it could be argued that sequential negotiations with the unanimous/exclusive-membership rule is more effective than simultaneous coalition formation. However, this observation cannot be generalized because of two reasons:

1. In the simultaneous games we assumed myopic behaviour of players whereas in the SNG players are farsighted.
2. The comparatively low number of fiscal players and CSs causes that there are many NEs in the EMG; hence, welfare analysis, which has to be based on the average of welfare indices, has to be interpreted with caution.

To a large extent, the second impediment will be removed in the next chapter, in which we introduce exchange rates allowing for the existence of outside players and (possibly multiple) MUs.

[12] Compare relevant $\overline{WIX}$ in Tables 6.3, 6.5, 6.7, 6.10 and 6.12.

6.5 Appendix

Defining matrices $\eta := \begin{bmatrix} \eta_1 & 0 & \dots & 0 \\ 0 & \eta_2 & \dots & 0 \\ \dots & \dots & \dots & \dots \\ 0 & 0 & \dots & \eta_{n_f} \end{bmatrix}$, $\gamma := \begin{bmatrix} \gamma_1 & 0 & \dots & 0 \\ 0 & \gamma_2 & \dots & 0 \\ \dots & \dots & \dots & \dots \\ 0 & 0 & \dots & \gamma_{n_f} \end{bmatrix}$, $\rho :=$ $\begin{bmatrix} 0 & \rho_{12} & \dots & \rho_{1n_f} \\ \rho_{21} & 0 & \dots & \rho_{2n_f} \\ \dots & \dots & \dots & \dots \\ \rho_{n_f1} & \rho_{n_f2} & \dots & 0 \end{bmatrix}$, $\zeta := \begin{bmatrix} \zeta_1 & 0 & \dots & 0 \\ 0 & \zeta_2 & \dots & 0 \\ \dots & \dots & \dots & \dots \\ 0 & 0 & \dots & \zeta_{n_f} \end{bmatrix}$, $\varsigma := \begin{bmatrix} 0 & \varsigma_{12} & \dots & \varsigma_{1n_f} \\ \varsigma_{21} & 0 & \dots & \varsigma_{2n_f} \\ \dots & \dots & \dots & \dots \\ \varsigma_{n_f1} & \varsigma_{n_f2} & \dots & 0 \end{bmatrix}$,

$\delta := \begin{bmatrix} -\sum_{i\in n_f/1} \delta_{1i} & \delta_{12} & \dots & \delta_{1n_f} \\ \delta_{21} & -\sum_{i\in n_f/2} \delta_{2i} & \dots & \delta_{2n_f} \\ \dots & \dots & \dots & \dots \\ \delta_{n_f1} & \delta_{n_f2} & \dots & -\sum_{i\in n_f/n_f} \delta_{n_fi} \end{bmatrix}$, and $\iota_{n_f} := \begin{bmatrix} 1 \\ 1 \\ 1 \\ \dots \\ 1 \end{bmatrix}$, the structural form of the model can be rewritten as:

$$\begin{cases} y(t) = -\gamma\iota_{n_f} i_u(t) + \eta f(t) + \gamma\dot{p}(t) + \delta p(t) + \rho y(t) \\ \dot{p}(t) = \zeta y(t) + \varsigma\dot{p}(t), p(0) = p_0. \end{cases}$$

Therefore, by solving the inflation equation, $\dot{p}(t) = (I-\varsigma)^{-1}\zeta y(t)$, and plugging this result in the output-gap equation, we get:

$$y(t) = -\gamma\iota_{n_f} i_u(t) + \eta f(t) + \gamma (I-\varsigma)^{-1} \zeta y(t) + \delta p(t) + \rho y(t),$$

from which we obtain the reduced form for the real output gaps:

$$y(t) = \left(I - \gamma (I-\varsigma)^{-1} \zeta - \rho\right)^{-1} \left(-\gamma\iota_{n_f} i_u(t) + \eta f(t) + \delta p(t)\right)$$

and for the inflation rates:

$$\dot{p}(t) = (I-\varsigma)^{-1} \zeta \left(I - \gamma (I-\varsigma)^{-1} \zeta - \rho\right)^{-1} \left(-\gamma\iota_{n_f} i_u(t) + \eta f(t) + \delta p(t)\right).$$

Rearranging yields:

$$\begin{bmatrix} y(t) \\ \dot{p}(t) \end{bmatrix} = L \begin{bmatrix} p(t) \\ f(t) \\ i_u(t) \end{bmatrix} = \begin{bmatrix} D & E & M \\ A & B & N \end{bmatrix} \begin{bmatrix} p(t) \\ f(t) \\ i_u(t) \end{bmatrix},$$

where:

$$\begin{aligned}
D &:= \left(I - \gamma (I - \varsigma)^{-1} \zeta - \rho\right)^{-1} \delta \\
E &:= \left(I - \gamma (I - \varsigma)^{-1} \zeta - \rho\right)^{-1} \eta \\
M &:= -\left(I - \gamma (I - \varsigma)^{-1} \zeta - \rho\right)^{-1} \gamma \iota_{n_f} \\
A &:= (I - \varsigma)^{-1} \zeta \left(I - \gamma (I - \varsigma)^{-1} \zeta - \rho\right)^{-1} \delta \\
B &:= (I - \varsigma)^{-1} \zeta \left(I - \gamma (I - \varsigma)^{-1} \zeta - \rho\right)^{-1} \eta \\
N &:= -(I - \varsigma)^{-1} \zeta \left(I - \gamma (I - \varsigma)^{-1} \zeta - \rho\right)^{-1} \gamma \iota_{n_f},
\end{aligned}$$

we can rewrite the reduced-form equations for real outputs as:

$$\begin{cases}
y_1(t) =: L_1 z(t) \\
\dots \\
y_{n_f}(t) =: L_{n_f} z(t) \\
\dot{p}_1(t) =: L_{n_f+1} z(t) \\
\dots \\
\dot{p}_{n_f}(t) =: L_{2n_f} z(t),
\end{cases}$$

where L_i is the ith row of matrix L and $z^T(t) := \left[p_1(t), p_2(t), ...p_{n_f}(t),\ f_1(t),\ f_2(t), ...f_{n_f}(t),\ i_U(t)\right]$. Thus, government i's loss function becomes:

$$\begin{aligned}
J_i(t_0) &= \frac{1}{2}\int_{t_0}^{\infty} \left\{\alpha_i \left(\dot{p}_i(t) - \varpi p_i(t)\right)^2 + \beta_i y_i^2(t) + \chi_i f_i^2(t)\right\} e^{-\theta(t-t_0)} dt = \\
&= \frac{1}{2}\int_{t_0}^{\infty} \{z^T(t)(\alpha_i \left(L_{n_f+i}^T - \varpi e_i^T\right)\left(L_{n_f+i} - \varpi e_i\right) \\
&\quad +\beta_i L_i^T L_i + \chi_i e_{n_f+i}^T e_{n_f+i}) z(t)\} e^{-\theta(t-t_0)} dt = \\
&= \frac{1}{2}\int_{t_0}^{\infty} \{z^T(t) M_i z(t)\} e^{-\theta(t-t_0)} dt, \qquad M_i \in \mathbb{R}^{(2n_f+1)\times(2n_f+1)},
\end{aligned}$$

where $e_i \in \mathbb{R}^{2n_f+1}$ is a vector with all entries equal to zero, except for entry i that is equal to one.

Similarly, we can rewrite the CB's loss function as:

$$\begin{aligned}
J_U &= \frac{1}{2}\int_0^{\infty} \left\{\alpha_U \left(\sum_{i=1}^{n_f} \omega_{ii} \left(\dot{p}_i(t) - \varpi p_i(t)\right)\right)^2 + \beta_U \left(\sum_{i=1}^{n_f} \omega_i y_i(t)\right)^2 + \chi_U i_u^2(t)\right\} e^{-\theta(t-t_0)} dt = \\
&= \frac{1}{2}\int_{t_0}^{\infty} z^T(t) \left\{ \begin{array}{c} \alpha_U \left(\sum_{i\in n_f} \omega_i \left(L_{n_f+i} - \varpi e_i\right)\right)^T \left(\sum_{i\in n_f} \omega_i \left(L_{n_f+i} - \varpi e_i\right)\right) + \\ +\beta_U \left(\sum_{i\in n_f} \omega_i L_i\right)^T \left(\sum_{i\in n_f} \omega_i L_i\right) + \chi_U e_{2n_f+1}^T e_{2n_f+1} \end{array} \right\} z(t) e^{-\theta(t-t_0)} dt = \\
&= \frac{1}{2}\int_{t_0}^{\infty} \{z^T(t) M_U z(t)\} e^{-\theta(t-t_0)} dt, \text{ where } M_U \in \mathbb{R}^{(2n_f+1)\times(2n_f+1)}.
\end{aligned}$$

The basic algorithm to derive the game solutions

Similar to the computations in Chapter 2, the algorithm is described by the following 5 steps.

1. Factorize matrices M_i for any country or the central bank ($i = 1, 2, ..., n_f, U$) as

$$M_i =$$

$$\left(\begin{array}{cccccccc}
Q_i & S_{1i} & S_{2i} & S_{3i} & \dots & S_{(n_f-1)i} & S_{n_f i} & S_{Ui} \\
S_{1i}^T & R_{1i} & P_{11[i]} & P_{12[i]} & \dots & P_{1(n_f-2)[i]} & P_{1(n_f-1)[i]} & P_{1n_f[i]} \\
S_{2i}^T & P_{11[i]}^T & R_{2i} & P_{22[i]} & \dots & P_{2(n_f-2)[i]} & P_{2(n_f-1)[i]} & P_{2n_f[i]} \\
S_{3i}^T & P_{12[i]}^T & P_{22[i]}^T & R_{3i} & \dots & P_{3(n_f-2)[i]} & P_{3(n_f-1)[i]} & P_{3n_f[i]} \\
\dots & \dots & \dots & \dots & \dots & \dots & \dots & \dots \\
S_{(n_f-1)i}^T & P_{1(n_f-2)[i]}^T & P_{2(n_f-2)[i]}^T & & \dots & R_{(n_f-1)i} & P_{(n_f-1)(n_f-1)[i]} & P_{(n_f-1)n_f[} \\
S_{n_f i}^T & P_{1(n_f-1)[i]}^T & P_{2(n_f-1)[i]}^T & P_{3(n_f-1)[i]}^T & \dots & P_{(n_f-1)(n_f-1)[i]}^T & R_{n_f i} & P_{n_f n_f[i]} \\
S_{Ui}^T & P_{1n_f[i]}^T & P_{2n_f[i]}^T & P_{3n_f[i]}^T & \dots & P_{(n_f-1)n_f[i]}^T & P_{n_f n_f[i]}^T & R_{Ui}
\end{array}\right.$$

for $i \in \{n_f \cup U\}$, where $Q_i \in \mathbb{R}^{n_f \times n_f}$, $S_{ij} \in \mathbb{R}^{n_f \times 1}$, while R_{ij} for $j \in \{n_f \cup U\}$ and the other coefficients are scalars.

2. Compute the following matrices:

$$G := \begin{pmatrix}
R_{11} & P_{11[1]} & \dots & P_{1(n_f-1)[1]} & P_{1n_f[1]} \\
P_{n_f n_f[2]}^T & R_{22} & \dots & P_{2(n_f-1)[i]} & P_{2n_f[i]} \\
\dots & \dots & \dots & \dots & \dots \\
P_{2n_f[n_f]}^T & P_{2(n_f-1)[n_f]}^T & \dots & R_{n_f n_f} & P_{n_f n_f[n_f]} \\
P_{1n_f[U]}^T & P_{1(n_f-1)[U]}^T & \dots & P_{n_f n_f[U]}^T & R_{UU}
\end{pmatrix},$$

$$H_1 := \begin{pmatrix}
-A & 0 & 0 & 0 & \dots & 0 \\
Q_1 & A^T & 0 & 0 & \dots & 0 \\
Q_2 & 0 & A^T & 0 & \dots & 0 \\
\dots & \dots & \dots & \dots & \dots & \dots \\
Q_{n_f} & 0 & 0 & A^T & \dots & 0 \\
Q_U & 0 & 0 & 0 & \dots & A^T
\end{pmatrix},$$

$$H_2 := \begin{pmatrix}
B_1 & B_2 & \dots & B_{n_f} & M \\
-S_{11} & -S_{21} & \dots & -S_{n_f 1} & -S_{U1} \\
-S_{12} & -S_{22} & \dots & -S_{n_f 2} & -S_{U2} \\
\dots & \dots & \dots & \dots & \dots \\
-S_{1n_f} & -S_{2n_f} & \dots & -S_{n_f n_f} & -S_{Un_f} \\
-S_{1U} & -S_{2U} & \dots & -S_{n_f U} & -S_{UU}
\end{pmatrix}$$

$$H_3 := \begin{pmatrix} S_{11}^T & B_1^T & 0 & \ldots & 0 & 0 \\ S_{22}^T & 0 & B_2^T & \ldots & 0 & 0 \\ \ldots & \ldots & \ldots & \ldots & \ldots & \ldots \\ S_{n_f n_f}^T & 0 & 0 & \ldots & B_{n_f}^T & 0 \\ S_{UU}^T & 0 & 0 & \ldots & O & M^T \end{pmatrix},$$

where B_i is the ith column of matrix B. Then, we can define the following matrix:

$$H \ : \ = H_1 + H_2 G^{-1} H_3$$

4. After computing the eigenstructure of H, take n_f positive eigenvalues and the corresponding eigenvectors v_i to write the following expression:[13]

$$\begin{pmatrix} X \\ Y_1 \\ Y_2 \\ \ldots \\ Y_{n_f} \\ Y_U \end{pmatrix} := \begin{pmatrix} v_1 & v_2 & \ldots & v_{n_f} \end{pmatrix} := V \in \mathbb{R}^{n_f(n_f+2)\times n_f},$$

from which we can derive the optimal controls:

$$\begin{pmatrix} f_1(t) \\ f_2(t) \\ \ldots \\ f_{n_f}(t) \\ i_U(t) \end{pmatrix} = -G^{-1} \begin{pmatrix} S_{11}^T + B_1^T K_1 \\ S_{22}^T + B_2^T K_2 \\ \ldots \\ S_{n_f n_f}^T + B_{n_f}^T K_{n_f} \\ S_{UU}^T + M_U^T K_{n_f+1} \end{pmatrix} p =: Fp,$$

where $K_i := Y_i X^{-1}$ for $i \in \{n_f \cup U\}$.

5. Rewrite the policymakers' cost functions[14] and the dynamics of the model as $J_i(t) = \frac{1}{2}\int_0^\infty p^T \left[\left(I, F^T\right) M_i \begin{pmatrix} I \\ F \end{pmatrix} \right] p(t)\, dt$ and $\dot{p}(t) = (A + (Bn\ \ )_f F)\, p(t) =: A_{CL} p(t)$, respectively. The problem is then solved by considering:

$$J_i = p_0^T \tilde{L}_i p_0$$

[13]Notice that matrix H coincides up to a minus sign with the corresponding matrix in Chapter 2. If matrix H has more than n positive eigenvalues multiple equilibria arise, whereas if this matrix has less than n positive eigenvalues no equilibrium exists (for more details see Engwerda (2005a)).

[14]For reasons of convenience, we assume that $t_0 = 0$ and θ is equal to zero. Assuming θ different from zero, the model could easily be solved following the procedure used here after a simple transformation of variables, i.e. transforming $x(t)$ into $e^{-\frac{1}{2}\theta t}x(t)$ and substituting A by $A - \frac{1}{2}\theta I$ where $I \in \mathbb{R}^{n\times n}$ is a diagonal matrix with ones on the main diagonal (see Chapter 2).

where $\tilde{L}_i$ solves the following Lyapunov equation (for $i \in \{n_f \cup U\}$):

$$A_{CL}^T \tilde{L}_i + \tilde{L}_i A_{CL} + \frac{1}{2}\left(I, F^T\right) M_i \begin{pmatrix} I \\ F \end{pmatrix} = 0.$$

Cooperative solutions are achieved by using the same algorithm, but considering the minimization of joint optimal losses.[15]

[15] For more details, see Chapters 3 and 4.

Chapter 7

Accession to a Monetary Union

7.1 Introduction

In Chapter 6 the multi-country MU setting was analyzed. It was shown that many basic insights of the 2-country MU model of Chapters 3 and 4 carry over to a multi-country setting and that at the same time a multi-country MU features many new issues. These new issues were, in particular, related to the strongly increased number of interactions and economic externalities and the more complicated patterns in policy coordination due to the numerous opportunities of coalition formation. However, Chapter 6 did not address the questions why and when countries decide to participate (or not to participate) in an MU. Yet, this question seems of crucial importance in understanding the actual design and functioning of MUs.

This chapter wants to look more closely at such a decision by countries to participate (or not) in MUs. The accession to an MU raises several additional interesting and important questions. For example, what are the consequences for the accession countries and is the accession beneficial for the acceding countries and the current MU members? How does the accession of new members affect the monetary policy of the CB? How does the accession affect the coordination of fiscal policies? Is there any effect of accession on the interaction between the MU and the rest of the world?

Such questions are in many ways related to more fundamental questions on (i) the degree to which the MU constitutes an optimal currency area (OCA) before and after accession, and (ii) the effects of accession on the institutional framework in which decision making about macroeconomic policies in the MU takes place. In order to properly assess the effects of an enlargement of an MU, our analysis suggests that both aspects should be studied within one framework.

This chapter attempts to shed some more light on the questions raised above. It studies the economic and coalition formation externalities and the institutional design of the coordination of macroeconomic stabilization policies in the MU and the effects of accession of new members to the MU. In fact, we consider accession to the MU from the perspective of the more general issue of international policy cooperation. More in detail, not only the policy-coordination issues inside the MU and between the MU and non-MU countries are analyzed, but also the effects of the accession of additional countries to the MU and under which conditions such an accession is beneficial for the acceding countries and for existing members. These important questions can be addressed in a relatively straightforward manner in our approach. The OCA issues are approached in our analysis by a detailed study of the effects that comparable shocks produce in the pre-accession phase and the post-accession phase, respectively. The differences between both scenarios need to be completely attributed to the accession to the MU by new members. In this way we can also directly calculate the net benefits of accession for all players in the model.

As a specific example, consider the fourth enlargement of the EU on May 1, 2004, which is by any standard the most pervasive and diverse of all EU enlargements in history.[1] To enter the EU, the ten acceding countries had to fulfil a set of entrance conditions, the so-called Copenhagen criteria. In order to cope with such an enlargement of an unprecedented scale, the Treaty of Nice (2002) initiated a process of complete institutional redesign in the EU. Among many other obligations, the acceding countries also committed themselves to join the EMU as soon as they have fulfilled the entry conditions laid down in the Treaty of Maastricht. These so-called Maastricht Criteria (EU, 1992, article 109 j (1)) provide convergence criteria in terms of inflation, interest rates, debt and deficits for the countries to qualify for entrance into the EMU.[2] Depending on the amount of effort that countries invest in complying with these entrance criteria, there is a certain degree of freedom in choosing the exact point in time at which to enter. In the fastest track countries would immediately comply and enter the euro-area in the second half of 2006.[3] But Bohn (2004) rightly asserts regarding the prospective acceding countries: "However, care must be taken to avoid recession or overheating effects, in case interest and exchange rate impulses reinforce one another (instead of exhibiting trade-off effects). The

[1]The earlier enlargements in 1981-86 and in 1995 involved only three countries each. The 2004 enlargement has raised the EU population to about 480 million people from the 375 million in the EU-15 countries.

[2]For example, Hughes Hallett and McAdam (1997) and von Hagen and Lutz (1996) investigated the macroeconomic repercussions of implementing the fiscal convergence criteria of the Maastricht Treaty in the EMU-12.

[3]According to the Maastricht Treaty a candidate country should participate in the Exchange Rate Mechanism II (ERM II) without major tensions in the foreign exchange market. ERM II replaced the ERM of the European Monetary System created in 1979. ERM II was established in 1997 with the resolution of the European Council in order to link the currencies of the EU-member states outside the euro area and the euro. Like ERM I, ERM II is also a multilateral exchange rate arrangement with a fixed, but adjustable, central parity and a fluctuation band around it. Countries participating in ERM II peg their exchange rates to the euro, allowing for fluctuations within a symmetric band of 15 percent on each side of the central parity. Interventions at the margins are automatic, unless they conflict with the primary objective of price stability in the euro area.

right timing for joining a monetary union is crucial, if policymakers want to make sure that conditions are advantageous for all countries involved."

Moreover, it is very unlikely that a single strategy could be recommended to all acceding countries regarding macroeconomic stabilization on the road to the euro. Arguments in favour of adopting the euro as early as possible include a smaller financial risk due to the elimination of a currency mismatch in the balance sheets of banks and firms, interest rate convergence and overall gains in monetary credibility. Arguments for a slower pace to the euro include the need to remove financial distortions, creating moral hazard and, therefore, raising the country's default risk, easier relative-price adjustment without the need of costly nominal wage and price adjustments and the need to make fiscal and financial policy sustainable and compatible with a fixed exchange rate before participation in the EMU. The European Economic Advisory Group at CESifo recommends in its 2004 Report on the European Economy (p. 135) that: "Delaying participation in ERM II is a realistic option for countries that are currently unable to sustain hard pegs and have large domestic imbalances. The magnitude of domestic imbalances varies considerably across countries, so that ERM entry may be desirable at different times. Yet in all cases, the policy priority is achieving a sustainable fiscal situation and stabilizing inflation at the correct relative prices, a task that requires both institutional and policy reforms."[4]

As concerning the OCA questions,[5] several studies have analyzed whether the accession countries may form an OCA with the current euro-area. In terms of trade interdependence and business-cycle convergence with the E(M)U, the accession countries reach comparable scores like current member countries (see e.g. Boone and Maurel (1999)). On the other hand, the degree of symmetry of shocks is generally found to be lower (see e.g. Fidrmuc and Korhonen (2003)). The latter finding may be problematic in the sense that the accession countries by acceding to the euro-area give up national monetary policy independence and, in particular, the possibility of the exchange-rate adjustment *vis-à-vis* the euro-area in case they experience asymmetric shocks. Upon accession, their monetary policy will be set by the ECB. In addition, the accession countries will adopt the fiscal policy cooperation and surveillance procedures of the Stability and Growth Pact (SGP). During the recent years, monetary policy in the accession countries have displayed a large variation ranging from very strict euro pegging in the form of a currency board in small accession countries such as Estonia to informal euro-target zones in larger accession countries like Poland (see European Parliament (1999) for a detailed account). As a consequence of fixed bilateral exchange rates, asymmetric shocks have long been seen as the major problem for the EMU (see Favero *et al.* (2000)). It is generally argued that such shocks can be coped by structural reforms that have been advocated to improve flexibility on product and labour markets. However, an alternative way resides in the adoption of coordinated policies among EU countries.

[4] To provide an adequate analysis of this timing issue we want to consider a real strategic options approach in the very near future.

[5] See also Subsection 1.4.2 in Chapter 1.

As regarding the effects of accession on institutions and macroeconomic policies in the euro-area context, there is even less clarity. In particular, an accession will change the institutional framework in which macroeconomic policy design and cooperation is situated, this in the first place for the acceding countries but even for the existing euro-area countries and for the non-acceding non-euro-area countries. It is more than likely that various forms of policy cooperation that were active before accession will no longer be pursued after accession, given that they are no longer efficient from the policymaker's point of view. Similarly, forms of policy cooperation that were non-existing before accession may become very relevant once accession occurs.

This chapter is structured as follows: Section 7.2 provides a multiple-country dynamic macroeconomic model that underlies the analysis. It also treats the case where an MU between a subset of countries is introduced. Section 7.3 analyzes the policy-coordination issues that arise in an MU. In particular, we focus on the institutional setup and cooperative mechanisms in the MU. Section 7.4 studies the accession to the MU by non-members. Numerical simulations in Section 7.5 illustrate the main aspects of our approach. Last section concludes.

7.2 The basic economic framework

Our analytical framework is presented in its most general form, from which various specific settings can directly be chosen, e.g. by varying the number of countries and MUs and types of policy cooperation. Again, we consider the setting developed in Chapter 5, where players from the set N interact. They can be divided in two groups: n_f countries i ($i \in F$) and n_b central banks b ($b \in B$, with $N = F \cup B$). Considering Definition 5.18 about a bank-b jurisdictional set, we describe each economy j^b, i.e. each economy j for which central bank b is liable, by an aggregate demand/IS curve and an aggregate supply curve which are direct extensions of the closed-economy MU model (6.1)-(6.2) of the previous chapter.

The nominal exchange rates e_{j^b} are added to the IS curves (6.1), i.e.:[6]

$$\begin{aligned} y_{j^b}(t) &= -\gamma_{j^b}\left[i_{j^b}(t)-\dot{p}_{j^b}(t)\right]+\eta_{j^b}f_{j^b}(t)+ \\ &\sum_{\ell\in F/j^b}\rho_{j^b\ell}y_\ell(t)+\sum_{\ell\in F/j^b}\delta_{j^b\ell}\left[e_{j^b}(t)+p_\ell(t)-p_{j^b}(t)\right]. \end{aligned} \tag{7.1}$$

Nominal exchange rates, adjusted for relative prices, measure the international competitiveness of the economy and are determined according to the uncovered interest-rate parity (UIP) hypothesis, so that nominal exchange rates adjust to corresponding interest-rate differentials:

[6] As is conventional, nominal exchange rates are measured as the (logarithmic) price of one unit of foreign currency, expressed in domestic currency.

Notice also that we switched to a notation for country j^b and not country i^b, in order to prevent any confusion with the nominal interest rates i in this most general setting.

$$\dot{e}_{j^b}(t) = i_{j^b}(t) - i_{\ell^{b'}}(t), \quad e_{j^b}(0) = e_{j^b0}, \tag{7.2}$$

where the foreign currency of the nominal exchange rate is under the jurisdiction of central bank $b' \neq b$ and where $i_{j^b}(t)$ is the nominal interest rate valid for country j^b at time t.[7] The initial values of the exchange rates represent (initial) level shocks that hit the exchange rate at time zero, reflecting e.g. (initial) shocks in international financial markets, etc. In an open-MU setting, the external exchange rate of the MU with non-MU countries becomes a new shock absorber *viz.* the transmission mechanism of monetary policy.

Equations (7.3) are open-economy Phillips curves, where nominal exchange-rate changes are added to (6.2):

$$\dot{p}_{j^b}(t) = \zeta_{j^b} y_{j^b}(t) + \sum_{\ell \in F/j^b} \varsigma_{j^b\ell}(\dot{e}_\ell(t) + \dot{p}_\ell(t)), \quad p_{j^b}(0) = p_{j^b0}. \tag{7.3}$$

In this Phillips relationship, the inflation rates of the other countries play a role reflecting the effects of 'pass-through' of foreign inflation on domestic currency. As before, in accordance with our short-run stabilization focus, the effectiveness of fiscal policy is limited to its transitory impact on output through the induced stimulus of aggregate demand. In this more general open-economy setting, monetary policy affects output not only via the interest-rate channel but also through the exchange-rate channel (i.e. via influencing international competitiveness).

Loss functions of fiscal and monetary players are defined in a way similar to previous chapters, i.e. for country $j \in F$ and (central) bank $b \in B$ and for MU $u \in U$:

$$J_{j^b}(t_0) = \frac{1}{2}\int_{t_0}^{\infty} \{\alpha_{j^b}\left(\dot{p}_{j^b}(t) - \varpi p_{j^b}(t)\right)^2 + \beta_{j^b} y_{j^b}^2(t) + \chi_{j^b} f_{j^b}^2(t)\} e^{-\theta(t-t_0)} dt \tag{7.4}$$

$$\begin{aligned} J_u(t_0) &= \frac{1}{2}\int_{t_0}^{\infty} \left\{\alpha_u^M \left(\dot{p}_u(t) - \varpi p_u(t)\right)^2 + \beta_u^M y_u^2(t) + \chi_u^M i_u^2(t)\right\} e^{-\theta(t-t_0)} dt \\ &= \frac{1}{2}\int_{t_0}^{\infty} \left\{\alpha_u^M \bar{P}_u^2(t) + \beta_u^M \bar{Y}_u^2(t) + \chi_u^M i_u^2(t)\right\} e^{-\theta(t-t_0)} dt, \end{aligned} \tag{7.5}$$

[7] If there is only one non-trivial MU (with k countries) involved in the model and if the currency of this MU is the currency in which the exchange rates of the non-MU countries are expressed, we can simply rewrite the UIP hypothesis (7.2) as: $\dot{e}_j(t) = i_j(t) - i_U(t)$, $e_j(0) = e_{j0}$ $(j = 1, 2, \ldots, n-k+1)$, where $i_U(t)$ is the common nominal interest rate in the MU.

where $\bar{P}_u(t)$ and $\bar{Y}_u(t)$ are average prices and output in MU u defined as $\bar{P}_u(t) := \sum_{j^u=1}^{k_u} \omega_{j^u}(\dot{p}_{j^u}(t) - \varpi p_{j^u}(t))^2$ and $\bar{Y}_u(t) := \sum_{j^u=1}^{k_u} \omega_{j^u} y_{j^u}(t)$ with k_u being the number of countries and ω_{j^u} the weight of country j in the MU aggregate.

Policymakers, who are responsible for monetary management in only one country (i.e. are central banks of a trivial MU), feature the following form of loss functions:

$$J_{j^b}^M(t_0) = \frac{1}{2} \int_{t_0}^{\infty} \{\alpha_{j^b}^M \left(\dot{p}_{j^b}(t) - \varpi p_{j^b}(t)\right)^2 + \beta_{j^b}^M y_{j^b}^2(t) + \chi_{j^b}^M i_{j^b}^2(t)\} e^{-\theta(t-t_0)} dt, \quad (7.6)$$

which is, in fact, equation (7.5) for a single country, which can be seen as a single-country monetary area (i.e. a trivial MU).

Theoretically speaking, any subset of the n_f countries in the model could decide to form an MU, there could be several MUs at the same time, there could exist none at all or there could exist just one containing either a subset of countries or all the countries, in which case we would have one world currency. Since this chapter analyzes the problem of accession of one or more countries to a single MU, we concentrate on the situation that the set U contains only one element (see last footnote). As we aim to analyze international monetary and fiscal policy cooperation among countries divided over possibly more than one MU in the next chapter, we will extend the application of the model to multiple MUs there.

The OCA theory studies the costs and benefits of MUs for its participants. In particular, the OCA problem of MUs is related to the incidence of asymmetric shocks and asymmetric transmissions of shocks. In particular, the question is asked under which conditions a country that experiences an asymmetric shock may improve itself from being inside or outside an MU. Participating in an MU implies the loss of the exchange-rate adjustment towards other participating countries and the loss of an independent monetary policy as policy instruments. In addition, participation may imply the need to comply with fiscal and other policy restrictions; think in particular of the SGP requirements in the EMU context. In fact, the effects of fiscal-stringency requirements were studied in Chapter 3. On the other hand, alternative stabilizing mechanisms may replace the role of the exchange-rate adjustment and there may be sizeable benefits from participation to the MU that will compensate the costs. The OCA theory suggests that countries will establish an MU as soon as benefits start to outweigh costs. In the EMU context, the OCA aspect has received a lot of attention. A detailed survey of this literature is found in Buti and Sapir (1998) and the problem is also discussed in Subsection 1.4.2 of Chapter 1.

A way to assess these OCA issues in a theoretical framework like ours, is to compare the effects of an asymmetric shock in a country, when it continues its independent monetary policy, with the effects of the same shock when it has entered an MU. In fact, we will apply this concept in Section 7.4, while analyzing the effects of accession to the MU by new members.

As shown in Appendix A to this chapter, the structural-form model (7.1)-(7.3) can be transformed for one MU into the following reduced-form model (which is a direct extension of the reduced form (6.5) of the previous chapter; see Appendix A):

$$\begin{bmatrix} y(t) \\ \dot{p}(t) \\ \dot{e}(t) \end{bmatrix} = \begin{bmatrix} D & E & M \\ A & B & N \end{bmatrix} \begin{bmatrix} p(t) \\ e(t) \\ f(t) \\ i(t) \end{bmatrix}, \tag{7.7}$$

where $y(t)$, $p(t)$, and $f(t)$ are the country-ordered vectors of outputs, prices, and net-government expenditures, respectively, and $e(t)$ and $i(t)$ are the mixed MU/country-ordered vectors of exchange rates and interest rates.[8] The partitioned matrix $L = \begin{bmatrix} D & E & M \\ A & B & N \end{bmatrix}$ indicates the (reduced-form) elasticities of the price levels and control instruments with respect to the real output gap and inflation. The upper part of matrix $L \in \mathbb{R}^{(2n_f+n_b)\times(2n_f+2n_b)}$ indicates the instantaneous elasticities with respect to the real output gaps. The lower part of the matrix indicates the elasticities with respect to the price and exchange-rate dynamics of the model. Matrix L is crucial in the analysis of the spillovers. More in detail, matrix $E \in \mathbb{R}^{n_f \times n_f}$ describes the effects of the domestic fiscal policy on the domestic real output gaps (diagonal elements) and those of the foreign fiscal policies on the domestic real output gaps (off-diagonal elements), i.e. fiscal spillovers. Similarly, matrix $B \in \mathbb{R}^{(n_f+n_b)\times n_f}$ describes the effects of fiscal policy on the price and exchange-rate dynamics. Matrices $D \in \mathbb{R}^{n_f\times(n_f+n_b)}$ and $A \in \mathbb{R}^{(n_f+n_b)\times(n_f+n_b)}$ indicate the effects of price levels and exchange rates on the domestic real output gaps and price and exchange-rate dynamics, respectively. Matrices $M \in \mathbb{R}^{n_f\times n_b}$ and $N \in \mathbb{R}^{(n_f+n_b)\times n_b}$ are the semi-elasticities of the nominal interest rates on real output gaps and price and exchange-rate dynamics, respectively.

7.3 International economic interdependencies

In the case of the EMU, there are not only aspects of coordination of monetary and fiscal policy between the euro-area and the non-euro area countries (external coordination), but also important internal policy-coordination issues. Internal policy coordination in the EMU concerns: (i) fiscal policy coordination, in particular the coordination of the fiscal policies of individual countries in the context of the Broad Economic Policy Guidelines and the SGP (see e.g. Levine and Brociner (1994) and Beetsma *et al.* (2001) on fiscal policy coordination in the EMU). (ii) monetary and fiscal policy coordination, in particular the mix of the fiscal policies in the EMU and the monetary policy implemented by the ECB (see e.g. Hughes Hallett and Ma (1996), Issing (1999), and Bini Smaghi and Casini (2000)).

[8] The dimension of all vectors but $i(t)$ and $e(t)$ is n_f. The dimension of the vectors $i(t)$ and $e(t)$ is equal to the number of existing central banks n_b (by definition the logarithmic exchange rate of the anchor country is 0).

An important aspect concerns the actions of the ECB, which can neutralize the effects of fiscal cooperation if its targets are opposed to those of the national governments (see e.g. Beetsma and Bovenberg (1998) and Acocella and Di Bartolomeo (2001)). The sign and size of fiscal spillovers are particularly important as they partially determine how large economic externalities are (in absolute terms) and whether coordination should lead to a more expansionary or more restrictive fiscal stance in the Member States (Beetsma *et al.* (2001), pp. 4-5).

In the model spillovers are described by the matrix L involved in (7.7). Therefore, this matrix is crucial to understand the interplay of the national governments as well as the interplay between these and the ECB. In fact, the matrix L describes the effects of the policies, not only on the domestic outcomes, but also on the real output gaps, inflation rates and exchange-rate devaluations in the other countries. Both types of spillovers are relevant in order to evaluate the impact of coordination. Furthermore, also the initial shock structure has to be taken into account. Actually, each policymaker reacts to an initial shock. However, the policy actions also affect the other countries and imply a feedback from them. This feedback will be determined by the effects of the monetary and fiscal policies from the other countries and these effects are captured by matrix L as well.

7.4 General aspects of accession

The question arises what are the effects of the accession of additional countries to the MU and under which conditions such an accession is beneficial for the acceding countries and for existing members. The correct way to measure and evaluate accession effects (on macroeconomic adjustment, policy formation and cooperation, and the resulting welfare losses) is by comparing identical situations (in terms of shocks, structures, and preferences) under two scenarios: (i) before accession (called 'pre-accession') and (ii) after accession (called 'post-accession'). The net effects can then be attributed solely to the accession. Calculating welfare gains/losses and graphs of the situation without and with enlargement immediately provides the accession effects and this can be done, not only for the acceding countries, but also for the countries that were already participating in the MU and for the countries that do not accede at all.

We would expect that outsiders would like to accede if they are better off in the MU than staying outside. Similarly, we could expect that current member states agree to an MU enlargement if it makes them better off. Enlarging the MU when countries are asymmetric is likely to make it more heterogeneous. To study this feature and assess its consequences, we also need -apart from a symmetric baseline for reference purposes- cases where the acceding countries are different from the existing members, e.g. in shocks, structure, preferences, etc.

These important issues can be addressed in a relatively straightforward manner in our approach. In our model, acceding the MU implies that for an accession country: (i) exchange rate adjustments *vis-à-vis* countries that already participate in the MU are no longer possible; (ii) its monetary policy is now set by the common CB, the monetary policy of which may not be optimal for the acceding country because (a) it targets aggregate MU output and inflation and (b) it may have different preferences as reflected in the values of α_U^M, β_U^M, and χ_U^M; (iii) participating in the MU could require that fiscal flexibility is more constrained because of the necessary adoption of fiscal-stringency measures like the SGP; this would imply a higher value of χ_j when a country enters the MU; (iv) participation changes the strategic settings in the game and the possibilities for cooperation of policies for both acceding countries and existing member states.

For the common CB, the accession of additional countries implies that: (i) there is a redefinition of the aggregate target variables; this by itself may already induce changes in optimal policymaking; (ii) its preferences may change if the acceding countries have different preferences as reflected in the values of α_j, β_j, and χ_j; this will affect policymaking; (iii) the strategic configurations (coalition formation process) in which the common CB operates have changed: the number of fiscal players in the MU increases and the number of outside monetary and fiscal players decreases. The adjustment dynamics from exchange-rate adjustment are changed.

For the (fiscal players of) existing member countries, the accession implies: (i) changes in the policy reactions of the acceding countries and the common CB because of the reasons given above; (ii) the strategic configurations (coalition formation process) in which they operate have changed: the number of other fiscal players in the MU increases, while the number of outside monetary and fiscal players decreases.

Assuming that the economic structure is not affected by acceding the MU, we can determine the welfare effects of accession for (i) the acceding countries, (ii) the existing members by comparing losses under the no-accession scenario and the accession scenario, assuming a similar shock scenario. Incentive compatibility of accession would imply that both the acceding country and the existing member countries would not lose from the accession.

Given all the effects listed above it is, therefore, even in our highly-stylized model, by no means clear under which conditions the accession is likely to occur. The loss of exchange-rate and interest-rate flexibility is likely to entail negative costs for the acceding country, as does the possible increase in fiscal conservatism stemming from SGP-alike requirements. On the other hand, the change in the institutional settings, as reflected in the enhanced strategic position and coalition formation possibilities, may benefit the accession countries. The numerical analysis in the next section will elaborate on these insights about the net effects of accession.

7.5 Numerical solutions of the model

7.5.1 General setup

In our model different forms of asymmetry can be considered: countries may have asymmetric structural model parameters (model asymmetry), policymakers may have different preferences and different bargaining powers (preference asymmetry and bargaining-power asymmetry) and, finally, shocks may asymmetrically hit countries (shock asymmetry).

Our analysis considers a setting of 5 countries: countries 1 and 2 are already forming an MU at the beginning of the planning period (*pre-accession stage*). Countries 3 and 4 are initially outside the MU but country 3 considers the possibility to also enter the MU, already encompassing countries 1 and 2. Country 5 is never considering to enter the MU, whether enlarged or not. Therefore, there are 5 fiscal authorities (denoted as $C1, ..., C5$) and 4 monetary authorities (denoted as $CB, CB3, CB4, CB5$), initially. We assume that $C5$ is not entering in partial coalitions with other countries and is mostly focussed on its internal coordination problem in cooperation with its $CB5$. In that sense, it is assumed to be a reference/outside country. We will then consider the consequences of the accession of $C3$ on all players. This will be called the *post-accession stage.*

Out of all possible coalition structures (CSs) π_i, we choose 37 CSs at the pre-accession stage and 27 CSs at the post-accession stage. The first three CSs and the last two of both pre- and post-accession stages are reported as they are interesting reference points for comparison. In π_1-π_3, players $C5$ and $CB5$ play as singletons. However, in all the other CSs, but π_{36} and π_{37}, they play as a full national coalition $\{C5, CB5\}$, which is an assumption in our simulation made in order to decrease the number of possible CSs. All coalition formation computations will be made only for $\pi_4 - \pi_{35}$ at the pre-accession stage and for π_{41}-π_{62} at the post-accession stage. Both sets, i.e. $\{\pi_4, ..., \pi_{35}\}$ and $\{\pi_{41}, ..., \pi_{62}\}$ constitute the MU-reduced set of feasible CSs (see Definition 5.19 in Chapter 5). We assumed that the fiscal players $C1$,$C2$,$C3$ and $C4$ can freely cooperate with each other, forming whatever coalition. We will refer to players $C1, C2, CB$ and $C3$,$C4$,$CB3$,$CB4$ as to insiders and outsiders, respectively, at the pre-accession stage, and to $C1$,$C2$,$C3$,CB as to insiders in the post-accession stage. Coalitions $\{C1,C2\}$ and $\{C3,C4\}$ at the pre-accession stage are called a full fiscal coalition of insiders and outsiders, respectively. The coalition $\{C1,C2,C3,C4\}$ is called the grand fiscal coalition. At the post-accession stage $\{C1,C2,C3\}$ is the full fiscal coalition of insiders, whereas there is no full fiscal coalition of outsiders. All coalitions, like $\{C1,C3\}$ or $\{C2,C4\}$, are called partial fiscal coalitions. The CB can form a coalition only with all countries that belong to the MU and this coalition is called the full coalition. For outsiders, we refer to their coalitions with the own central banks as to full national coalitions (e.g. $\{C4,CB4\}$). All CSs considered are listed in Table 7.1. The relevant 37 CSs of the pre-accession stage are listed in the upper part of Table 7.1 and in the lower part the 27 post-accession CSs appear. Often one can find a natural correspondence between certain CSs before and after accession. The basic difference consists in taking over the activities of $CB3$ by the CB of the

MU upon accession (at the post-accession stage $CB3$ ceases to exist). From now on, we will refer to the ith CS by π_i, where $i = 1, ..., 64$.

Table 7.1 Pre- and post- accession coalition structures

PRE-ACCESSION COALITION STRUCTURES			
π_{1}	C1 C2 CB C3 CB3 C4 CB4 C5 CB5	π_{20}	(C1,C2,C3) CB CB3 (C4,CB4) (C5,CB5)
π_{2}	(C1,C2) CB C3 CB3 C4 CB4 C5 CB5	π_{21}	(C1,C3) C2 CB CB3 C4 CB4 (C5,CB5)
π_{3}	(C1,C2,CB) C3 CB3 C4 CB4 C5 CB5	π_{22}	(C1,C3) C2 CB CB3 (C4,CB4) (C5,CB5)
π_{4}	C1 C2 CB C3 CB3 C4 CB4 (C5,CB5)	π_{23}	(C2,C3) C1 CB CB3 C4 CB4 (C5,CB5)
π_{5}	C1 C2 CB (C3,CB3) C4 CB4 (C5,CB5)	π_{24}	(C2,C3) C1 CB CB3 (C4,CB4) (C5,CB5)
π_{6}	C1 C2 CB C3 CB3 (C4,CB4) (C5,CB5)	π_{25}	(C1,C2,C4) CB C3 CB3 CB4 (C5,CB5)
π_{7}	C1 C2 CB (C3,CB3) (C4,CB4) (C5,CB5)	π_{26}	(C1,C2,C4) CB (C3,CB3) CB4 (C5,CB5)
π_{8}	C1 C2 CB (C3,C4) CB3 CB4 (C5,CB5)	π_{27}	(C1,C4) C2 CB C3 CB3 CB4 (C5,CB5)
π_{9}	(C1,C2,CB) C3 CB3 C4 CB4 (C5,CB5)	π_{28}	(C1,C4) C2 CB (C3,CB3) CB4 (C5,CB5)
π_{10}	(C1,C2,CB) (C3,CB3) C4 CB4 (C5,CB5)	π_{29}	(C2,C4) C1 CB C3 CB3 CB4 (C5,CB5)
π_{11}	(C1,C2,CB) C3 CB3 (C4,CB4) (C5,CB5)	π_{30}	(C2,C4) C1 CB (C3,CB3) CB4 (C5,CB5)
π_{12}	(C1,C2,CB) (C3,CB3) (C4,CB4) (C5,CB5)	π_{31}	(C1,C2,C3,C4) CB CB3 CB4 (C5,CB5)
π_{13}	(C1,C2,CB) (C3,C4) CB3 CB4 (C5,CB5)	π_{32}	(C1,C4) (C2,C3) CB CB3 CB4 (C5,CB5)
π_{14}	(C1,C2) CB C3 CB3 C4 CB4 (C5,CB5)	π_{33}	(C1,C3,C4) C2 CB CB3 CB4 (C5,CB5)
π_{15}	(C1,C2) CB (C3,CB3) C4 CB4 (C5,CB5)	π_{34}	(C2,C3,C4) C1 CB CB3 CB4 (C5,CB5)
π_{16}	(C1,C2) CB C3 CB3 (C4,CB4) (C5,CB5)	π_{35}	(C1,C3) (C2,C4) CB CB3 CB4 (C5,CB5)
π_{17}	(C1,C2) CB (C3,CB3) (C4,CB4) (C5,CB5)	π_{36}	(C1,C2,C3,C4,C5) CB CB3 CB4 CB5
π_{18}	(C1,C2) CB (C3,C4) CB3 CB4 (C5,CB5)	π_{37}	(C1,C2,CB,C3,CB3,C4,CB4,C5,CB5)
π_{19}	(C1,C2,C3) CB CB3 C4 CB4 (C5,CB5)		
POST-ACCESSION COALITION STRUCTURES			
π_{38}	C1 C2 C3 CB C4 CB4 C5 CB5	π_{52}	(C1,C3) C2 CB (C4,CB4) (C5,CB5)
π_{39}	(C1,C2) C3 CB C4 CB4 C5 CB5	π_{53}	(C1,C4) C2 C3 CB CB4 (C5,CB5)
π_{40}	(C1,C2,C3,CB) C4 CB4 C5 CB5	π_{54}	C1 (C2,C4) C3 CB CB4 (C5,CB5)
π_{41}	C1 C2 C3 CB C4 CB4 (C5,CB5)	π_{55}	C1 C2 (C3,C4) CB CB4 (C5,CB5)
π_{42}	C1 C2 C3 CB (C4,CB4) (C5,CB5)	π_{56}	(C1,C2) (C3,C4) CB CB4 (C5,CB5)
π_{43}	(C1,C2,C3,CB) C4 CB4 (C5,CB5)	π_{57}	(C1,C3) (C2,C4) CB CB4 (C5,CB5)
π_{44}	(C1,C2,C3,CB) (C4,CB4) (C5,CB5)	π_{58}	(C1,C4) (C2,C3) CB CB4 (C5,CB5)
π_{45}	(C1,C2,C3) CB C4 CB4 (C5,CB5)	π_{59}	(C1,C2,C4) CB C3 CB4 (C5,CB5)
π_{46}	(C1,C2,C3) CB (C4,CB4) (C5,CB5)	π_{60}	(C1,C3,C4) CB C2 CB4 (C5,CB5)
π_{47}	(C1,C2) C3 CB C4 CB4 (C5,CB5)	π_{61}	(C2,C3,C4) CB C1 CB4 (C5,CB5)
π_{48}	(C1,C2) C3 CB (C4,CB4) (C5,CB5)	π_{62}	(C1,C2,C3,C4) CB CB4 (C5,CB5)
π_{49}	C1 (C2,C3) CB C4 CB4 (C5,CB5)	π_{63}	(C1,C2,C3,C4,C5) CB CB4 CB5
π_{50}	C1 (C2,C3) CB (C4,CB4) (C5,CB5)	π_{64}	(C1,C2,C3,CB,C4,CB4,C5,CB5)
π_{51}	(C1,C3) C2 CB C4 CB4 (C5,CB5)		

We consider three different scenarios:

1. The benchmark scenario with a symmetric economic structure (sc_1) - the MU consists of two countries, $C1$ and $C2$, while there is one accession country, $C3$, one non-accession country, $C4$, and an additional country, $C5$. All countries are assumed to be symmetric in the structural and preference parameters and sizes. However, preferences of fiscal players are asymmetric w.r.t. preferences of central banks. The following set of parameters underlies this baseline case: $\gamma_{j^b} = 0.2$, $\eta_{j^b} = 0.75$, $\rho_{j^b\ell} = 0.1$, $\delta_{j^b\ell} = 0.1$, $\zeta_{j^b} = 0.25$, $\varsigma_{j^b\ell} = 0.1$, $\alpha_{j^b} = 0.2$, $\beta_{j^b} = 0.4$, $\chi_{j^b} = \chi_U^M = \chi_{j^b}^M = 0.4$, $\alpha_U^M = \alpha_{j^b}^M = 0.4$, $\beta_U^M = \beta_{j^b}^M = 0.2$, $\omega_{j^b} = 0.5$, $\theta = 0.10$.

2. An asymmetric structural scenario (sc_2) - in this example, we consider a situation where the countries are marked by asymmetries in the economic structure and in policy preferences. Simplifying, these asymmetries may be interpreted in terms of the size of the country.[10] In particular, we assume that, compared with the symmetric baseline scenario:

   (i) $C1$ is two times bigger than $C2$ and the accession country $C3$ and of an equal size as $C4$ and $C5$. Hence, we assume the following parameter values for the matrices ρ, ς, δ defined in Appendix A, which are direct extensions of those from Chapter 6:[11]

$$\rho := \varsigma := \begin{bmatrix} 0 & 1/15 & 1/15 & 2/15 & 2/15 \\ 4/35 & 0 & 2/35 & 4/35 & 4/35 \\ 4/35 & 2/35 & 0 & 4/35 & 4/35 \\ 2/15 & 1/15 & 1/15 & 0 & 2/15 \\ 2/15 & 1/15 & 1/15 & 2/15 & 0 \end{bmatrix} \text{ and}$$

$$\delta := \begin{bmatrix} -4/10 & 1/15 & 1/15 & 2/15 & 2/15 \\ 4/35 & -4/10 & 2/35 & 4/35 & 4/35 \\ 4/35 & 2/35 & -4/10 & 4/35 & 4/35 \\ 2/15 & 1/15 & 1/15 & -4/10 & 2/15 \\ 2/15 & 1/15 & 1/15 & 2/15 & -4/10 \end{bmatrix}$$

   Because $C1$ and $C2$ have a different size, $CB1$ is more concerned with the economic performance in $C1$ than in $C2$, implying that countries' weights in $CB1$'s loss function are asymmetric: $\omega_1 = 2/3$, $\omega_2 = 1/3$ before accession and $\omega_1 = 1/2$, $\omega_2 = 1/4$, $\omega_3 = 1/4$ after accession.

   (ii) $C4$ has a less conservative central bank, $\alpha_4^M = 0.2$ and $\beta_4^M = 0.4$; hence, they coincide with the preferences of the fiscal authorities in $C4$.

[10] Both small and big countries can be either relatively open or relatively closed. A relatively closed but big country may still affect other countries via direct (or structural form) spillover channels more than a relatively open but small country. Hence, the interpretation of our direct spillover parameters $\rho_{j^b\ell}$, $\delta_{j^b\ell}$, $\varsigma_{j^b\ell}$ is not straightforward. They represent the mixed effects of size and openness. To have a clear interpretation we may assume either that countries are of equal size and the value of a spillover parameter indicates openness or that countries differ in size but are equally open. In the latter case the value of a spillover parameter shows relative size of a country. In this chapter and in the remaining of the book we will follow this interpretation.

[11] The off-diagonal elements of these matrices are the direct spillovers. Similarly to Chapter 6, all rows of the off-diagonal elements add to 0.4.

3. An asymmetric structural scenario with asymmetric bargaining power (sc_3), where we add asymmetric bargaining power τ to the previous case. More specifically, $C1$ is assumed to have a two times higher bargaining power than $C2$ and $C3$ in both pre- and post-accession stages and the same bargaining power as $C4$, while $C4$ has a three times higher bargaining power than $CB4$. The exact definition of τ is provided in Appendix B.

Note that scenario sc_3 is the most realistic one, since structural asymmetries are accompanied by corresponding bargaining power asymmetries (so that a larger country has a larger bargaining power).

Three different types of shocks are analyzed (shocks always occur at $t = 0$ in the form of initial innovations to the state variables): (i) a symmetric *(negative) supply shock:* $s_{0S}^P = [0.01;\ 0.01; 0.01; 0.01; 0.01, 0, 0, 0, 0]^T$, (ii) an asymmetric (negative) supply shock that hits only $C3$: $s_{0A}^P = [0; 0; 0.01; 0; 0; 0; 0; 0; 0]^T$, and (iii) an asymmetric exchange-rate shock that hits $C5$: $s_{0E}^P = [0; 0; 0; 0; 0; 0; 0; 0; 0.01]^T$ in the pre-accession stage. In the post-accession stage, these shocks are defined as $s_{0S}^A = [0.01;\ 0.01; 0.01; 0.01; 0.01, 0, 0, 0]^T$, (ii) $s_{0A}^A = [0; 0; 0.01; 0; 0; 0; 0; 0]^T$, and (iii) $s_{0E}^A = [0; 0; 0; 0; 0; 0; 0; 0.1]^T$.

Note that sc_1 in both post- and pre-accession stages is designed in such a way that the model's results can be directly compared to the relevant results obtained in Chapter 6. More in detail, in the previous 3-country setting, each country has 2 bilateral trade relations and the values of direct price, output and competitiveness spillovers were set to 0.2 in the symmetric benchmark scenario. Clearly, the total value of one kind of (direct) spillovers received by each country equalled 0.4 (as the model equations are linear). In the present setting each of 5 countries has 4 bilateral trade relations and all direct price, output and competitiveness spillover parameters are set to 0.1. Hence, the total value of spillovers is the same as in Chapter 6.

For clarity and in order to save space, we will characterize the pre- and post-accession scenarios by providing a superscript P and A, respectively (i.e., sc_1^P, sc_2^P, sc_3^P, sc_1^A, sc_2^A, sc_3^A).

7.5.2 Pre-accession stage, symmetric model

Tables 7.2, 7.3, and 7.4 report (optimal) losses for a symmetric model in the pre-accession stage under s_{0S}^P, s_{0A}^P, and s_{0E}^P, respectively.[12] As all the coalition formation games in this chapter will be played between π_4 and π_{35} in the pre-accession stage and between π_{41} and π_{62} in the post-accession stage, we assumed that both CSs π_4 and π_{41} of the form $[singletons|C5CB5]$ are the baseline in the computations of the coalition formation index CFI. Also, while looking for the social optimum CS(s), only CSs from π_4 to π_{35} and from π_{41} to π_{62} are taken into account.

[12] For tables with losses for asymmetric scenarios sc_2^P, sc_3^P and sc_2^A, sc_3^A see www.ua.ac.be/joseph.plasmans.

Table 7.2 - Optimal losses for (sc_1^P, s_{0S}^P)

	π_1	π_2	π_3	π_4	π_5	π_6	π_7	π_8	π_9	π_{10}
C1	0.2462	0.2462	0.2487	0.2461	0.2465	0.2465	0.2475	0.2461	0.2482	0.2480
C2	0.2462	0.2462	0.2487	0.2461	0.2465	0.2465	0.2475	0.2461	0.2482	0.2480
CB	0.4926	0.4915	0.4871	0.4905	0.4889	0.4889	0.4881	0.4900	0.4868	0.4881
C3	0.2462	0.2460	0.2465	0.2460	0.2484	0.2462	0.2479	0.2460	0.2474	0.2479
CB3	0.4926	0.4919	0.4889	0.4905	0.4870	0.4889	0.4863	0.4897	0.4883	0.4879
C4	0.2462	0.2460	0.2465	0.2460	0.2462	0.2484	0.2479	0.2460	0.2474	0.2492
CB4	0.4926	0.4919	0.4889	0.4905	0.4889	0.4870	0.4863	0.4897	0.4883	0.4891
C5	0.2462	0.2460	0.2465	0.2490	0.2484	0.2484	0.2479	0.2488	0.2480	0.2479
CB5	0.4926	0.4919	0.4889	0.4885	0.4870	0.4870	0.4863	0.4880	0.4867	0.4879
WIX	-	-	-	0.36%	0.22%	0.22%	0.18%	0.27%	0.31%	0.46%
CFI	0.28%	0.16%	0.52%	0.00%	0.41%	0.41%	0.71%	0.09%	0.62%	0.62%
	π_{11}	π_{12}	π_{13}	π_{14}	π_{15}	π_{16}	π_{17}	π_{18}	π_{19}	π_{20}
C1	0.2480	0.2480	0.2481	0.2461	0.2465	0.2465	0.2475	0.2461	0.2462	0.2465
C2	0.2480	0.2480	0.2481	0.2461	0.2465	0.2465	0.2475	0.2461	0.2462	0.2465
CB	0.4881	0.4921	0.4867	0.4898	0.4885	0.4885	0.4879	0.4893	0.4887	0.4878
C3	0.2492	0.2481	0.2474	0.2459	0.2483	0.2462	0.2478	0.2459	0.2460	0.2462
CB3	0.4891	0.4918	0.4881	0.4900	0.4867	0.4886	0.4862	0.4892	0.4887	0.4877
C4	0.2479	0.2481	0.2474	0.2459	0.2462	0.2483	0.2478	0.2459	0.2458	0.2480
CB4	0.4879	0.4918	0.4881	0.4900	0.4886	0.4867	0.4862	0.4892	0.4891	0.4863
C5	0.2479	0.2481	0.2479	0.2488	0.2483	0.2483	0.2478	0.2486	0.2484	0.2480
CB5	0.4879	0.4918	0.4866	0.4880	0.4867	0.4867	0.4862	0.4876	0.4872	0.4863
WIX	0.46%	0.85%	0.29%	0.28%	0.17%	0.17%	0.16%	0.20%	0.15%	0.09%
CFI	0.62%	0.49%	0.63%	0.08%	0.44%	0.44%	0.72%	0.17%	0.22%	0.52%
	π_{21}	π_{22}	π_{23}	π_{24}	π_{25}	π_{26}	π_{27}	π_{28}	π_{29}	π_{20}
C1	0.2462	0.2465	0.2460	0.2464	0.2462	0.2465	0.2462	0.2465	0.2460	0.2464
C2	0.2460	0.2464	0.2462	0.2465	0.2462	0.2465	0.2460	0.2464	0.2462	0.2465
CB	0.4899	0.4885	0.4899	0.4885	0.4887	0.4878	0.4899	0.4885	0.4899	0.4885
C3	0.2460	0.2462	0.2460	0.2462	0.2458	0.2480	0.2459	0.2482	0.2459	0.2482
CB3	0.4897	0.4884	0.4897	0.4884	0.4891	0.4863	0.4900	0.4867	0.4900	0.4867
C4	0.2459	0.2482	0.2459	0.2482	0.2460	0.2462	0.2460	0.2462	0.2460	0.2462
CB4	0.4900	0.4867	0.4900	0.4867	0.4887	0.4877	0.4897	0.4884	0.4897	0.4884
C5	0.2488	0.2482	0.2488	0.2482	0.2484	0.2480	0.2488	0.2482	0.2488	0.2482
CB5	0.4880	0.4867	0.4880	0.4867	0.4872	0.4863	0.4880	0.4867	0.4880	0.4867
WIX	0.28%	0.17%	0.28%	0.17%	0.15%	0.09%	0.28%	0.17%	0.28%	0.17%
CFI	0.09%	0.45%	0.09%	0.45%	0.22%	0.52%	0.09%	0.45%	0.09%	0.45%
	π_{31}	π_{32}	π_{33}	π_{34}	π_{35}	π_{36}	π_{37}			
C1	0.2462	0.2461	0.2462	0.2459	0.2461	0.2461	0.2498			
C2	0.2462	0.2461	0.2459	0.2462	0.2461	0.2461	0.2498			
CB	0.4876	0.4893	0.4889	0.4889	0.4893	0.4871	0.4775			
C3	0.2459	0.2459	0.2460	0.2460	0.2459	0.2459	0.2493			
CB3	0.4876	0.4893	0.4886	0.4886	0.4893	0.4870	0.4768			
C4	0.2459	0.2459	0.2460	0.2460	0.2459	0.2459	0.2493			
CB4	0.4876	0.4893	0.4886	0.4886	0.4893	0.4870	0.4768			
C5	0.2480	0.2486	0.2484	0.2484	0.2486	0.2459	0.2493			
CB5	0.4863	0.4876	0.4872	0.4872	0.4876	0.4870	0.4768			
WIX	0.00%	0.20%	0.14%	0.14%	0.20%	-	-			
CFI	0.37%	0.16%	0.24%	0.24%	0.16%	0.44%	2.22%			

Table 7.3 - Optimal losses for (sc_1^P, s_{0A}^P)

	π_1	π_2	π_3	π_4	π_5	π_6	π_7	π_8	π_9	π_{10}
C1	0.1737	0.1771	0.1027	0.1774	0.1677	0.1829	0.1689	0.1902	0.1005	0.1126
C2	0.1737	0.1771	0.1027	0.1774	0.1677	0.1829	0.1689	0.1902	0.1005	0.1126
CB	0.0950	0.0817	0.1492	0.0981	0.0913	0.1029	0.0920	0.1066	0.1626	0.1325
C3	3.0099	3.0397	2.9541	3.0050	2.3910	2.9976	2.4046	2.9187	2.9419	2.4060
CB3	2.3515	2.3749	2.2884	2.3407	2.4713	2.3276	2.4544	2.3537	2.2694	2.3805
C4	0.1643	0.1572	0.1831	0.1660	0.1631	0.1207	0.1339	0.1805	0.1906	0.1760
CB4	0.0956	0.0905	0.1169	0.0987	0.0918	0.1128	0.0957	0.1516	0.1275	0.1051
C5	0.1643	0.1572	0.1831	0.1233	0.1381	0.1207	0.1339	0.1305	0.1225	0.1329
CB5	0.0956	0.0905	0.1169	0.1063	0.0935	0.1128	0.0957	0.1157	0.1418	0.1123
WIX	-	-	-	12.64%	2.99%	11.97%	2.52%	13.16%	9.47%	0.78%
CFI	0.51%	1.70%	5.59%	0.00%	12.88%	1.58%	12.74%	3.31%	6.70%	13.51%

	π_{11}	π_{12}	π_{13}	π_{14}	π_{15}	π_{16}	π_{17}	π_{18}	π_{19}	π_{20}
C1	0.0988	0.1092	0.1062	0.1809	0.1701	0.1865	0.1714	0.1943	0.1844	0.1893
C2	0.0988	0.1092	0.1062	0.1809	0.1701	0.1865	0.1714	0.1943	0.1844	0.1893
CB	0.1812	0.1427	0.1754	0.0842	0.0789	0.0881	0.0792	0.0916	0.1384	0.1424
C3	2.9268	2.4195	2.8538	3.0354	2.4105	3.0289	2.4239	2.9500	2.8761	2.8684
CB3	2.2471	2.3501	2.2892	2.3654	2.4956	2.3538	2.4804	2.3778	2.3971	2.3886
C4	0.1219	0.1301	0.2017	0.1586	0.1566	0.1162	0.1294	0.1740	0.1793	0.1291
CB4	0.1599	0.1223	0.1808	0.0931	0.0875	0.1057	0.0905	0.1452	0.1086	0.1236
C5	0.1219	0.1301	0.1297	0.1187	0.1335	0.1162	0.1294	0.1257	0.1318	0.1291
CB5	0.1599	0.1223	0.1534	0.1001	0.0889	0.1057	0.0905	0.1090	0.1171	0.1236
WIX	8.39%	0.00%	9.85%	13.29%	3.46%	12.68%	3.03%	13.82%	12.73%	12.03%
CFI	8.53%	13.77%	8.91%	1.47%	13.26%	2.01%	13.14%	3.08%	4.33%	5.18%

	π_{21}	π_{22}	π_{23}	π_{24}	π_{25}	π_{26}	π_{27}	π_{28}	π_{29}	π_{20}
C1	0.1994	0.2042	0.1807	0.1864	0.1789	0.1683	0.1783	0.1684	0.1713	0.1622
C2	0.1807	0.1864	0.1994	0.2042	0.1789	0.1683	0.1713	0.1622	0.1783	0.1684
CB	0.1271	0.1320	0.1271	0.1320	0.0697	0.0663	0.0886	0.0831	0.0886	0.0831
C3	2.9171	2.9089	2.9171	2.9089	3.0873	2.4441	3.0348	2.4103	3.0348	2.4103
CB3	2.3575	2.3462	2.3575	2.3462	2.4072	2.5369	2.3647	2.4951	2.3647	2.4951
C4	0.1770	0.1276	0.1770	0.1276	0.1702	0.1650	0.1701	0.1658	0.1701	0.1658
CB4	0.1070	0.1224	0.1070	0.1224	0.0698	0.0665	0.0849	0.0794	0.0849	0.0794
C5	0.1303	0.1276	0.1303	0.1276	0.1112	0.1258	0.1188	0.1335	0.1188	0.1335
CB5	0.1154	0.1224	0.1154	0.1224	0.0902	0.0813	0.1003	0.0889	0.1003	0.0889
WIX	12.68%	11.98%	12.68%	11.98%	14.47%	4.32%	13.18%	3.37%	13.18%	3.37%
CFI	2.94%	3.85%	2.94%	3.85%	3.52%	13.86%	1.46%	13.32%	1.46%	13.32%

	π_{31}	π_{32}	π_{33}	π_{34}	π_{35}	π_{36}	π_{37}
C1	0.1775	0.1819	0.1908	0.1859	0.1940	0.1669	0.0908
C2	0.1775	0.1940	0.1859	0.1908	0.1819	0.1669	0.0908
CB	0.1239	0.1162	0.1230	0.1230	0.1162	0.1070	0.1892
C3	2.8707	2.9472	2.8764	2.8764	2.9472	2.8941	2.0675
CB3	2.4514	2.3807	2.3951	2.3951	2.3807	2.5172	2.5484
C4	0.1662	0.1815	0.1728	0.1728	0.1815	0.1579	0.1167
CB4	0.1241	0.0925	0.1392	0.1392	0.0925	0.1072	0.1520
C5	0.1292	0.1256	0.1319	0.1319	0.1256	0.1579	0.1167
CB5	0.1133	0.1090	0.1174	0.1174	0.1090	0.1072	0.1520
WIX	13.16%	13.21%	13.01%	13.01%	13.21%	-	-
CFI	4.89%	2.62%	4.57%	4.57%	2.62%	5.51%	24.94%

Table 7.4 - Optimal losses for (sc_1^P, s_{0E}^P)

	π_1	π_2	π_3	π_4	π_5	π_6	π_7	π_8	π_9	π_{10}
C1	0.1740	0.1774	0.1020	0.1651	0.1649	0.1649	0.1659	0.1587	0.1152	0.1114
C2	0.1740	0.1774	0.1020	0.1651	0.1649	0.1649	0.1659	0.1587	0.1152	0.1114
CB	0.0957	0.0822	0.1511	0.0895	0.0889	0.0889	0.0894	0.0857	0.1222	0.1281
C3	0.1642	0.1571	0.1835	0.1620	0.1367	0.1606	0.1325	0.1643	0.1702	0.1315
CB3	0.0963	0.0911	0.1186	0.0899	0.0909	0.0893	0.0927	0.0781	0.0972	0.1082
C4	0.1642	0.1571	0.1835	0.1620	0.1606	0.1367	0.1325	0.1643	0.1702	0.1728
CB4	0.0963	0.0911	0.1186	0.0899	0.0893	0.0909	0.0927	0.0781	0.0972	0.1013
C5	2.6688	2.6980	2.6074	1.9679	1.9810	1.9810	1.9934	1.9862	1.9812	1.9934
CB5	1.5827	1.6043	1.5147	1.7802	1.7645	1.7645	1.7458	1.8003	1.6971	1.6697
WIX	-	-	-	14.77%	11.39%	11.39%	8.34%	10.34%	10.31%	7.49%
CFI	4.46%	4.75%	31.20%	0.00%	3.16%	3.16%	7.18%	4.87%	17.73%	23.51%

	π_{11}	π_{12}	π_{13}	π_{14}	π_{15}	π_{16}	π_{17}	π_{18}	π_{19}	π_{20}
C1	0.1114	0.1081	0.1115	0.1673	0.1672	0.1672	0.1683	0.1609	0.1658	0.1655
C2	0.1114	0.1081	0.1115	0.1673	0.1672	0.1672	0.1683	0.1609	0.1658	0.1655
CB	0.1281	0.1375	0.1155	0.0776	0.0768	0.0768	0.0769	0.0744	0.0656	0.0646
C3	0.1728	0.1287	0.1730	0.1558	0.1321	0.1543	0.1281	0.1581	0.1635	0.1624
CB3	0.1013	0.1173	0.0836	0.0860	0.0864	0.0853	0.0878	0.0748	0.0657	0.0648
C4	0.1315	0.1287	0.1730	0.1558	0.1543	0.1321	0.1281	0.1581	0.1455	0.1245
CB4	0.1082	0.1173	0.0836	0.0860	0.0853	0.0864	0.0878	0.0748	0.0797	0.0793
C5	1.9934	2.0053	1.9995	1.9864	1.9993	1.9993	2.0115	2.0041	2.0184	2.0309
CB5	1.6697	1.6367	1.7231	1.8009	1.7866	1.7866	1.7697	1.8199	1.8365	1.8244
WIX	7.49%	5.11%	5.86%	11.34%	8.05%	8.05%	5.06%	7.13%	5.84%	2.74%
CFI	23.51%	30.69%	18.18%	3.94%	6.75%	6.75%	9.82%	6.66%	8.41%	10.74%

	π_{21}	π_{22}	π_{23}	π_{24}	π_{25}	π_{26}	π_{27}	π_{28}	π_{29}	π_{20}
C1	0.1659	0.1656	0.1599	0.1595	0.1658	0.1655	0.1659	0.1656	0.1599	0.1595
C2	0.1599	0.1595	0.1659	0.1656	0.1658	0.1655	0.1599	0.1595	0.1659	0.1656
CB	0.0817	0.0809	0.0817	0.0809	0.0656	0.0646	0.0817	0.0809	0.0817	0.0809
C3	0.1644	0.1632	0.1644	0.1632	0.1455	0.1245	0.1558	0.1322	0.1558	0.1322
CB3	0.0780	0.0773	0.0780	0.0773	0.0797	0.0793	0.0861	0.0865	0.0861	0.0865
C4	0.1558	0.1322	0.1558	0.1322	0.1635	0.1624	0.1644	0.1632	0.1644	0.1632
CB4	0.0861	0.0865	0.0861	0.0865	0.0657	0.0648	0.0780	0.0773	0.0780	0.0773
C5	1.9863	1.9992	1.9863	1.9992	2.0184	2.0309	1.9863	1.9992	1.9863	1.9992
CB5	1.8006	1.7862	1.8006	1.7862	1.8365	1.8244	1.8006	1.7862	1.8006	1.7862
WIX	10.83%	7.54%	10.83%	7.54%	5.84%	2.74%	10.83%	7.54%	10.83%	7.54%
CFI	4.13%	6.68%	4.13%	6.68%	8.41%	10.74%	4.13%	6.68%	4.13%	6.68%

	π_{31}	π_{32}	π_{33}	π_{34}	π_{35}	π_{36}	π_{37}
C1	0.1610	0.1607	0.1634	0.1500	0.1607	0.1664	0.0875
C2	0.1610	0.1607	0.1500	0.1634	0.1607	0.1664	0.0875
CB	0.0545	0.0745	0.0724	0.0724	0.0745	0.1057	0.1872
C3	0.1594	0.1582	0.1633	0.1633	0.1582	0.1574	0.1137
CB3	0.0546	0.0747	0.0659	0.0659	0.0747	0.1059	0.1493
C4	0.1594	0.1582	0.1633	0.1633	0.1582	0.1574	0.1137
CB4	0.0546	0.0747	0.0659	0.0659	0.0747	0.1059	0.1493
C5	2.0596	2.0041	2.0182	2.0182	2.0041	2.5594	1.6952
CB5	1.8812	1.8199	1.8359	1.8359	1.8199	1.7473	1.8083
WIX	0.00%	7.12%	4.95%	4.95%	7.12%	-	-
CFI	12.87%	6.67%	9.16%	9.16%	6.67%	6.50%	50.72%

The consequences of a symmetric shock in the symmetric model in the pre-accession stage are found in Table 7.2. The differences in (optimal) losses between the different CSs are relatively small as indicated by the small values of CFI, suggesting that policy coordination is of limited importance in the case of symmetric shocks and in the presence of symmetric countries.[13] The differences between being inside or outside the MU are essentially negligible in all regimes, so that it is practically irrelevant for countries if they are inside or outside the MU in this symmetric setting. It is worth analyzing the fully non-cooperative regime π_1 in Table 7.2. Losses of all fiscal players seems to be the same in Table 7.2, however, we expect that they may differ, due to the asymmetry of our setting. The model is symmetric w.r.t. all the structural and preference parameters, but there is an asymmetry in the interest rates, because the insiders are subject to the common interest rate set by the CB, while outsider have their own national CB. This expected difference between the fiscal insiders and outsiders and between CB and $CB3$, $CB4$, and $CB5$ is visible in Table 7.C.1 in Appendix C, where losses are reported with better precision. Clearly, the interest rate of CB differs from those set by other central banks. Moreover, notice that losses of countries are in general much lower than losses of central banks. It can indicate that the interest rate instrument is more used than the fiscal deficit.[14]

Losses in Table 7.2 for (sc_1^P, s_{0S}^P) are comparable to losses in Table 6.2 for (sc_1, p_{0S}). In fact, the differences in losses are reasonably small. These differences are caused by the fact that, now, there are a few central banks in the game. Depending on whether a central bank is responsible for one or more players, its interest rate (and indirectly also the exchange rate) policy differs. The welfare index WIX shows that, in almost all CSs, the welfare losses compared to the social optimum CS C are below one percent.[15] Hence, the practical value of policy coordination is rather limited. The most-efficient outcome from the social point of view is reached for π_{31} and the second-best one in π_{20}.

Table 7.3 presents the (optimal) losses in the various CSs in the case of an asymmetric shock hitting $C3$. Clearly, outcomes are different from the symmetric shock case. There is much more dispersion and many regimes entail substantial gains from the worst performing (π_{25}). In contrast to the symmetric model, full cooperation of all the players (including $C5$ and $CB5$) is not an efficient outcome from the social perspective point of view. Now, CS π_{12} is a social optimum, i.e. $\pi_{12} \in \Pi^{SOP}$.

The exchange rate shock to the currency of $C5$ in Table 7.4 works similarly to the anti-symmetric shock analyzed in Chapters 3, 4, and 6: the depreciation of the currency of $C5$ raises its competitiveness *vis-à-vis* the other countries. At the same time it increases inflation in $C5$ and reduces inflation in the other countries, therefore, this pass-through effect will start to mitigate the initial competitiveness effects. The effects are felt much stronger in $C5$ as the exchange rate shock implies that it initially depreciates against all other countries, whereas from the perspective of the other countries, they only initially appreciate *vis-à-*

[13] See also a similar observation for the symmetric base scenario in Chapter 6.

[14] Note the perfect anti-symmetry between preferences of countries and central banks w.r.t. inflation and output gap.

[15] Note that in computations of WIX in this chapter, losses of $C5$ and $CB5$ were omitted.

vis $C5$. Also in this 'quasi'-anti-symmetric shock, there are very large welfare gains in many cases from coordination so that externalities are large.

Externalities from coalition formation

In Chapter 6 we studied in detail different kinds of spillovers. In contrast, in this chapter we will focus more on externalities from coalition formation. Table 7.5 shows how the formation of some different types of pre-accession coalitions, both by insiders and outsiders, affects different players. A plus sign implies a positive impact (lower losses) and a negative sign a negative impact (higher losses). Hence, we can say that for players, who do not take part in a coalition, Table 7.5 presents externalities from coalition formation.[16]

Table 7.5 Example of externalities and impact of coalition formation (sc_1^P, s_{0S}^P)

	ACTION		C1 C2	CB	C3 C4	CB3 CB4
(1)	**Remaining players play as singletons**					
INSIDERS	form fiscal coalition	π_{14} vs. π_4	-	+	+	+
	form full coalition	π_9 vs. π_4	-	+	-	+
OUTSIDERS	form fiscal coalition	π_8 vs. π_4	+	+	+	+
	1 outsider forms full coalition	π_5 vs. π_4	-	+	-	+
	2 outsiders form full coalitions	π_7 vs. π_4	-	+	-	+
(2)	**Remaining players are in coalition(s)**					
INSIDERS	form fiscal coalition	π_{17} vs. π_7	-	+	+	+
	form full coalition	π_{12} vs. π_7	-	-	-	-
OUTSIDERS	form fiscal coalition	π_{13} vs. π_9	+	+	-	+
	1 outsider forms full coalition	π_{10} vs. π_9	+	-	-	+/-
	2 outsiders form full coalitions	π_{12} vs. π_9	+	-	-	-

The first observation is that the game considered is a mixed externality game (see Definition 5.7). Players who do not take part in a merge in some CSs are worse off and in others better off. For instance, when fiscal insiders (i.e. $C1$ and $C2$) form a fiscal coalition, then all the other players in the game (i.e. $CB, C3, C4, CB3$, and $CB4$) are better off as depicted in the first line of Table 7.5. However, when all the players of the MU create a full MU coalition ($C1$, $C2$, CB), fiscal outsiders, $C3$ and $C4$, are worse off, but monetary outsiders, $CB3$ and $CB4$, are better off. This situation is depicted in the second line of Table 7.5. Concluding, it is neither a positive nor a negative externality game, i.e. it is a mixed externality game.

In general, by analyzing the impact of the creation of different coalitions on the players' losses in the game, we may provide first hints on the stability of CSs in some of the coalition formation games. For instance, it is clear from Table 7.5 that neither π_9 nor π_{14} can be stable in any of the games, since

[16] Due to space limitations we had to restrict the presentation of losses in the tables to four decimals. Since, many of the results in Table 7.5 require a greater precision, we present losses for (sc_1, s_{0S}) again in the Appendix C but with six decimals precision (Table.7.C.1).

fiscal insiders would prefer non-cooperation in π_4 over a fiscal coalition and a full MU coalition. Also the creation of a full national coalition by an outsider (i.e. π_5) is not possible for the same reason - fiscal players $C3$ and $C4$ get worse off. Similarly, when both outsiders form two full national coalitions (i.e. π_7). However, when outsiders decide to pursue a fiscal cooperation between each other, all the players in the game gain. This result indicates that CS π_8 is stable in the EMG(Δ) and the EMG(Γ) (see Definitions 5.22 and 5.23 in Chapter 5), as $C3$ and $C4$ do not want to deviate from this CS by playing as singletons. However, this condition is not sufficient to conclude that π_8 is stable in the OMG and the ROMG since it must be checked whether other players do not want to deviate from this CS by creating a two-player coalition (in the OMG) or by joining coalition ($C3$, $C4$) (in the OMG and the ROMG). In both versions of the EMG such a move does not have to be considered; hence π_8 is stable in these games.[17]

When the outsiders are in a coalition and the insiders form a fiscal coalition (π_{17} in the lower part of Table 7.5), then the outsiders are better off. This indicates that CS π_7 might be (but does not have to be) stable. We can only conclude that $C1$ and $C2$ do not want to deviate from this CS. However, when we examine the difference between π_7 and π_6, it becomes obvious that the former CS cannot be stable since $C3$ has an incentive to deviate to the latter CS. When the outsiders form different coalitions and the insiders already cooperate (last three rows of Table 7.5) then fiscal outsiders are never better off. Hence, such a deviation is not feasible. Again, it can (but does not have to) indicate that the CS in which the insiders cooperate and the outsiders do not, are stable in the OMG game. In fact, π_9 is such a CS, but we already showed above that this CS cannot be stable as the fiscal insiders lose compared to the non-cooperative regime, rather they would prefer to deviate.

The more general conclusion from Table 7.5 is that in our setting, singletons may absorb externalities from coalition formation in a different way as coalitions.

7.5.3 Post-accession stage, symmetric model

Table 7.6 provides losses for a symmetric shock in the post-accession stage. Results can be directly compared to Table 7.2 for the pre-accession stage. Accession of $C3$ leads to only marginal changes in the case of symmetric shocks. As before, differences between CSs are small under symmetric shocks after accession, suggesting that in the case of symmetric shocks accession has no substantive effects, neither for the accession countries nor for the existing members.

Results are different for the asymmetric-shock case in the post-accession stage found in Table 7.7. With $C3$ now inside the MU, there are more externalities to the old members via the common monetary policy. $C3$ loses w.r.t.

[17] This result can be found in Table 7.11.

the pre-accession regimes, where it still could coordinate with its old CB. Under MU, it has a new CB but one that is far less receptive to asymmetric shocks to $C3$. From the perspective of $C3$, it raises doubts whether accession to the MU is an optimal choice in the presence of a high degree of asymmetry of its shocks. This example is therefore an indirect indication for the OCA problem, which is (could be) inherent to a decision to enter an MU.

Table 7.6 - Optimal losses for (sc_1^A, s_{0S}^A)

	π_{38}	π_{39}	π_{40}	π_{41}	π_{42}	π_{43}	π_{44}	π_{45}	π_{46}
C1	0.2462	0.2462	0.2486	0.2461	0.2465	0.2483	0.2483	0.2461	0.2465
C2	0.2462	0.2462	0.2486	0.2461	0.2465	0.2483	0.2483	0.2461	0.2465
C3	0.2462	0.2460	0.2486	0.2461	0.2465	0.2483	0.2483	0.2461	0.2465
CB	0.4926	0.4917	0.4864	0.4906	0.4890	0.4880	0.4923	0.4889	0.4879
C4	0.2462	0.2460	0.2475	0.2459	0.2483	0.2495	0.2480	0.2456	0.2479
CB4	0.4926	0.4919	0.4880	0.4905	0.4869	0.4891	0.4922	0.4892	0.4862
C5	0.2462	0.2460	0.2475	0.2490	0.2483	0.2477	0.2480	0.2484	0.2479
CB5	0.4926	0.4919	0.4880	0.4885	0.4869	0.4880	0.4922	0.4872	0.4862
WIX	-	-	-	0.30%	0.20%	0.61%	0.91%	0.13%	0.10%
CFI	0.24%	0.15%	0.80%	0.00%	0.45%	0.71%	0.61%	0.17%	0.52%
	π_{47}	π_{48}	π_{49}	π_{50}	π_{51}	π_{52}	π_{53}	π_{54}	π_{55}
C1	0.2461	0.2465	0.2460	0.2464	0.2461	0.2465	0.2462	0.2460	0.2460
C2	0.2461	0.2465	0.2461	0.2465	0.2460	0.2464	0.2460	0.2462	0.2460
C3	0.2460	0.2464	0.2461	0.2465	0.2461	0.2465	0.2460	0.2460	0.2462
CB	0.4900	0.4886	0.4900	0.4886	0.4900	0.4886	0.4900	0.4900	0.4900
C4	0.2458	0.2482	0.2458	0.2482	0.2458	0.2482	0.2459	0.2459	0.2459
CB4	0.4900	0.4866	0.4900	0.4866	0.4900	0.4866	0.4897	0.4897	0.4897
C5	0.2488	0.2482	0.2488	0.2482	0.2488	0.2482	0.2488	0.2488	0.2488
CB5	0.4880	0.4866	0.4880	0.4866	0.4880	0.4866	0.4880	0.4880	0.4880
WIX	0.23%	0.16%	0.23%	0.16%	0.23%	0.16%	0.22%	0.22%	0.22%
CFI	0.07%	0.47%	0.07%	0.47%	0.07%	0.47%	0.09%	0.09%	0.09%
	π_{56}	π_{57}	π_{58}	π_{59}	π_{60}	π_{61}	π_{62}	π_{63}	π_{64}
C1	0.2460	0.2460	0.2461	0.2462	0.2462	0.2459	0.2461	0.2461	0.2483
C2	0.2460	0.2461	0.2460	0.2462	0.2459	0.2462	0.2461	0.2461	0.2483
C3	0.2461	0.2460	0.2460	0.2459	0.2462	0.2462	0.2461	0.2461	0.2483
CB	0.4894	0.4894	0.4894	0.4890	0.4890	0.4890	0.4878	0.4872	0.4792
C4	0.2458	0.2458	0.2458	0.2458	0.2458	0.2458	0.2457	0.2457	0.2481
CB4	0.4893	0.4893	0.4893	0.4887	0.4887	0.4887	0.4876	0.4871	0.4785
C5	0.2486	0.2486	0.2486	0.2484	0.2484	0.2484	0.2480	0.2457	0.2481
CB5	0.4876	0.4876	0.4876	0.4872	0.4872	0.4872	0.4863	0.4871	0.4785
WIX	0.16%	0.16%	0.16%	0.11%	0.11%	0.11%	0.00%	-	-
CFI	0.14%	0.14%	0.14%	0.20%	0.20%	0.20%	0.31%	0.36%	1.64%

Table 7.7 - Optimal losses for (sc_1^A, s_{0A}^A)

	π_{38}	π_{39}	π_{40}	π_{41}	π_{42}	π_{43}	π_{44}	π_{45}	π_{46}
C1	0.8846	0.9020	1.0552	0.9121	0.9446	1.0630	1.0731	0.9236	0.9545
C2	0.8846	0.9020	1.0552	0.9121	0.9446	1.0630	1.0731	0.9236	0.9545
C3	7.0742	7.1785	6.4189	7.0122	6.9413	6.4087	6.3947	6.7798	6.7115
CB	0.1110	0.1358	0.1444	0.1104	0.1103	0.1400	0.1355	0.0965	0.0973
C4	0.1706	0.1569	0.1564	0.1725	0.1218	0.1559	0.1255	0.1865	0.1306
CB4	0.1020	0.0879	0.0879	0.1054	0.1210	0.0888	0.0954	0.1159	0.1322
C5	0.1706	0.1569	0.1564	0.1243	0.1218	0.1295	0.1255	0.1332	0.1306
CB5	0.1020	0.0879	0.0879	0.1144	0.1210	0.0912	0.0954	0.1259	0.1322
WIX	-	-	-	3.68%	3.22%	0.25%	0.00%	1.45%	0.94%
CFI	1.33%	2.65%	10.27%	0.00%	2.19%	10.49%	11.08%	3.19%	5.07%
	π_{47}	π_{48}	π_{49}	π_{50}	π_{51}	π_{52}	π_{53}	π_{54}	π_{55}
C1	0.9262	0.9547	0.9502	0.9857	0.9795	1.0119	0.8761	0.8635	1.0126
C2	0.9262	0.9547	0.9795	1.0119	0.9502	0.9857	0.8635	0.8761	1.0126
C3	7.1253	7.0645	6.8055	6.7303	6.8055	6.7303	7.1381	7.1381	6.7187
CB	0.1347	0.1339	0.0934	0.0943	0.0934	0.0943	0.1211	0.1211	0.1015
C4	0.1579	0.1149	0.1883	0.1304	0.1883	0.1304	0.2112	0.2112	0.2598
CB4	0.0900	0.1018	0.1204	0.1385	0.1204	0.1385	0.0749	0.0749	0.2083
C5	0.1174	0.1149	0.1329	0.1304	0.1329	0.1304	0.1184	0.1184	0.1347
CB5	0.0973	0.1018	0.1309	0.1385	0.1309	0.1385	0.1021	0.1021	0.1396
WIX	5.20%	4.80%	2.70%	2.18%	2.70%	2.18%	4.35%	4.35%	4.68%
CFI	2.12%	2.41%	3.90%	5.93%	3.90%	5.93%	3.15%	3.15%	7.52%
	π_{56}	π_{57}	π_{58}	π_{59}	π_{60}	π_{61}	π_{62}	π_{63}	π_{64}
C1	1.0306	0.9347	0.9144	0.8552	0.9935	0.9914	0.9135	0.8723	1.0957
C2	1.0306	0.9144	0.9347	0.8552	0.9914	0.9935	0.9135	0.8723	1.0957
C3	6.8330	6.9312	6.9312	7.3420	6.6818	6.6818	6.7807	6.8749	6.3081
CB	0.1220	0.1017	0.1017	0.1568	0.0952	0.0952	0.1046	0.1141	0.1983
C4	0.2534	0.2304	0.2304	0.2544	0.1951	0.1951	0.1726	0.1642	0.1020
CB4	0.1860	0.0869	0.0869	0.0461	0.1741	0.1741	0.1325	0.1151	0.0822
C5	0.1270	0.1267	0.1267	0.1085	0.1359	0.1359	0.1307	0.1642	0.1020
CB5	0.1181	0.1171	0.1171	0.0814	0.1394	0.1394	0.1221	0.1151	0.0822
WIX	6.28%	3.39%	3.39%	6.88%	2.63%	2.63%	1.35%	-	-
CFI	6.39%	2.07%	2.07%	6.84%	6.48%	6.48%	2.90%	2.59%	13.58%

Table 7.8 concerns an exchange-rate shock to the currency of $C5$ in the post-accession stage. All fiscal policymakers prefer full monetary and fiscal coordination π_{64} as in this way they get more influence on the monetary players, who can exert direct control on the exchange-rate dynamics in the presence of UIP hypothesis. The fiscal players lack this ability. For the CBs, however, coordination with the fiscal authorities involves large losses when compared to their preferred arrangements. This was also the case in the pre-accession phase in Table 7.4. Also in the post-accession stage, we observe substantial differences in the welfare and coalition formation indices across the different CSs, indicating that there are significant welfare effects and externalities from

different cooperative arrangements.

Table 7.8 - Optimal losses for (sc_1^A, s_{0E}^A)

	π_{38}	π_{39}	π_{40}	π_{41}	π_{42}	π_{43}	π_{44}	π_{45}	π_{46}
C1	0.1802	0.1820	0.0957	0.1672	0.1675	0.1055	0.1027	0.1675	0.1677
C2	0.1802	0.1820	0.0957	0.1672	0.1675	0.1055	0.1027	0.1675	0.1677
C3	0.1802	0.1745	0.0957	0.1672	0.1675	0.1055	0.1027	0.1675	0.1677
CB	0.0914	0.0810	0.1889	0.0884	0.0872	0.1531	0.1642	0.0646	0.0632
C4	0.1600	0.1533	0.2023	0.1607	0.1366	0.1838	0.1304	0.1445	0.1244
CB4	0.0921	0.0872	0.1418	0.0890	0.0889	0.1112	0.1323	0.0790	0.0778
C5	2.6869	2.7157	2.5678	1.9695	1.9829	1.9896	2.0028	2.0200	2.0329
CB5	1.6015	1.6227	1.4707	1.7902	1.7783	1.6245	1.5913	1.8454	1.8365
WIX	-	-	-	14.24%	10.91%	4.02%	0.00%	7.57%	4.56%
CFI	5.47%	6.39%	48.75%	0.00%	3.13%	35.16%	40.83%	6.07%	8.84%

	π_{47}	π_{48}	π_{49}	π_{50}	π_{51}	π_{52}	π_{53}	π_{54}	π_{55}
C1	0.1683	0.1686	0.1622	0.1623	0.1683	0.1686	0.1673	0.1613	0.1613
C2	0.1683	0.1686	0.1683	0.1686	0.1622	0.1623	0.1613	0.1673	0.1613
C3	0.1622	0.1623	0.1683	0.1686	0.1683	0.1686	0.1613	0.1613	0.1673
CB	0.0792	0.0779	0.0792	0.0779	0.0792	0.0779	0.0820	0.0820	0.0820
C4	0.1546	0.1321	0.1546	0.1321	0.1546	0.1321	0.1633	0.1633	0.1633
CB4	0.0853	0.0847	0.0853	0.0847	0.0853	0.0847	0.0772	0.0772	0.0772
C5	1.9879	2.0012	1.9879	2.0012	1.9879	2.0012	1.9878	1.9878	1.9878
CB5	1.8103	1.7996	1.8103	1.7996	1.8103	1.7996	1.8097	1.8097	1.8097
WIX	11.29%	8.07%	11.29%	8.07%	11.29%	8.07%	10.54%	10.54%	10.54%
CFI	3.13%	6.09%	3.13%	6.09%	3.13%	6.09%	3.88%	3.88%	3.88%

	π_{56}	π_{57}	π_{58}	π_{59}	π_{60}	π_{61}	π_{62}	π_{63}	π_{64}
C1	0.1625	0.1625	0.1623	0.1657	0.1657	0.1522	0.1623	0.1719	0.0784
C2	0.1625	0.1623	0.1625	0.1657	0.1522	0.1657	0.1623	0.1719	0.0784
C3	0.1623	0.1625	0.1625	0.1522	0.1657	0.1657	0.1623	0.1719	0.0784
CB	0.0735	0.0735	0.0735	0.0693	0.0693	0.0693	0.0538	0.1007	0.2892
C4	0.1572	0.1572	0.1572	0.1626	0.1626	0.1626	0.1589	0.1532	0.1242
CB4	0.0740	0.0740	0.0740	0.0652	0.0652	0.0652	0.0541	0.1007	0.2068
C5	2.0057	2.0057	2.0057	2.0197	2.0197	2.0197	2.0609	2.5773	1.6713
CB5	1.8288	1.8288	1.8288	1.8442	1.8442	1.8442	1.8882	1.7704	1.6529
WIX	7.78%	7.78%	7.78%	6.23%	6.23%	6.23%	2.54%	-	-
CFI	5.66%	5.66%	5.66%	7.47%	7.47%	7.47%	10.24%	5.43%	74.03%

Externalities from coalition formation

Table 7.9 presents (some) externalities for (sc_1^A, s_{0S}^A).[18] The obtained pattern is similar to that in pre-accession Table 7.5. When the fiscal insiders create a (full) fiscal coalition, then they are worse off and the outsiders are better off, exactly

[18] The losses for (sc_1^A, s_{0S}^A) are presented with a greater precision in Table 7.C.2. See also footnote 16).

as in the pre-accession stage. When two fiscal insiders merge to form a partial fiscal coalition, then they again lose but the other fiscal player in the MU gains. Similarly to Table 7.5, in Table 7.9 we see that when the outsider forms the full national coalition with respective CB all the fiscal players considered ($C1$, $C2$, $C3$, $C4$) are worse off and CBs are better off. When $C4$ and $CB4$ play in a coalition and countries of an MU form a (full) fiscal coalition, then the latter players lose and all the other players in the game gain.

Table 7.9 Example of externalities and impact of coalition formation (sc_1^A, s_{0S}^A)

	ACTION		C1 C2 C3	CB	C4	CB4
(1)	**Remaining players play as singletons**					
INSIDERS	form fiscal coalition	π_{45} vs. π_{41}	- - -	+	+	+
INSIDERS	form partial fiscal coalition	π_{47} vs. π_{41}	- - +	+	+	+
INSIDERS	form full coalition	π_{43} vs. π_{41}	- - -	+	-	+
OUTSIDERS	form fiscal coalition	not relevant	X	X	X	X
OUTSIDERS	1 outsider forms full coalition	π_{42} vs. π_{41}	- - -	+	-	+
OUTSIDERS	2 outsiders form full coalitions	not relevant	X	X	X	X
(2)	**Remaining players are in coalition(s)**					
INSIDERS	form fiscal coalition	π_{46} vs. π_{42}	- - -	+	+	+
INSIDERS	form full coalition	π_{44} vs. π_{42}	- - -	-	+	-
	Outsiders form full coalition	π_{44} vs. π_{43}	- - -	-	+	-

In the last two lines of Table 7.9 we observe a (slightly) different pattern of externalities than in Table 7.5. When $C4$ and $CB4$ play in a coalition and a full MU coalition is created, the outside country $C4$ gains in the post-accession stage, whereas in the pre-accession stage it loses. Hence, we see that spillovers from other countries to $C4$ depend on whether $C3$ is in the MU or not. Finally, when the full MU coalition already exists and full national coalition between $C4$ and $CB4$ is created, in contrast to Table 7.5 fiscal players of an MU are worse off and $C4$ is better off.

7.5.4 Asymmetry in the model

For reasons of brevity we do not report all the losses for asymmetric scenarios ($sc_2^P, sc_3^P, sc_2^A, sc_3^A$). To give a flavour of consequences of model and bargaining-power asymmetries we list in Table 7.15 optimal losses for all the combinations of scenarios and shocks in two regimes: $\pi_{12} = [C1C2CB|C3CB3|C4CB4|C5CB5]$ and $\pi_{44} = [C1C2C3CB|C4CB4|C5CB5]$. These CSs were chosen because of two reasons. First, they can be directly compared with each other and second, they are characterized by a high degree of players' cooperation, which will show the effects of the bargaining power asymmetries in sc_3^P and sc_3^A.

Table 7.10 Losses for CSs π_{12} and π_{44} in all combinations of scenarios and shocks

Sc:	Structural Symmetry ($sc_1^{P/A}$)			Structural Asymmetry ($sc_2^{P/A}$)			Structural and bargaining power asymmetry ($sc_3^{P/A}$)		
PRE-ACCESSION STAGE									
Pl.\S.	s_{0S}^P	s_{0A}^P	s_{0E}^P	s_{0S}^P	s_{0A}^P	s_{0E}^P	s_{0S}^P	s_{0A}^P	s_{0E}^P
C1	0.2480	0.1092	0.1081	0.2499	0.0511	0.1852	0.2483	0.0503	0.1823
C2	0.2480	0.1092	0.1081	0.2472	0.0374	0.1354	0.2492	0.0431	0.1559
CB	0.4921	0.1427	0.1375	0.4931	0.0631	0.2112	0.4934	0.0776	0.2589
C3	0.2481	2.4195	0.1287	0.2479	2.5014	0.1700	0.2481	2.4784	0.1848
CB3	0.4918	2.3501	0.1173	0.4929	2.6107	0.1734	0.4931	2.5531	0.2116
C4	0.2481	0.1301	0.1287	0.2463	0.0574	0.2078	0.2461	0.0353	0.1298
CB4	0.4918	0.1223	0.1173	0.2506	0.0602	0.2012	0.2506	0.1024	0.3478
C5	0.2481	0.1301	2.0053	0.2492	0.0592	1.9548	0.2495	0.0646	1.9077
CB5	0.4918	0.1223	1.6367	0.4927	0.0554	1.4787	0.4929	0.0675	1.3885
WIX	0.85%	0.00%	5.11%	0.94%	0.12%	4.75%	1.00%	0.00%	17.76%
CFI	0.49%	13.77%	30.69%	0.71%	13.85%	26.61%	0.76%	14.24%	46.12%
POST-ACCESSION STAGE									
Pl.\S.	s_{0S}^A	s_{0A}^A	s_{0E}^A	s_{0S}^A	s_{0A}^A	s_{0E}^A	s_{0S}^A	s_{0A}^A	s_{0E}^A
C1	0.2483	1.0731	0.1027	0.2509	0.8656	0.1759	0.2484	0.5756	0.1654
C2	0.2483	1.0731	0.1027	0.2475	0.7113	0.1239	0.2492	0.4753	0.1405
C3	0.2483	6.3947	0.1027	0.2475	6.5123	0.1239	0.2492	7.2718	0.1405
CB	0.4923	0.1355	0.1642	0.4944	0.1726	0.2559	0.4947	0.0688	0.3172
C4	0.2480	0.1255	0.1304	0.2463	0.0618	0.2109	0.2462	0.0348	0.1269
CB4	0.4922	0.0954	0.1323	0.2518	0.0350	0.2271	0.2519	0.1029	0.3923
C5	0.2480	0.1255	2.0028	0.2493	0.0627	1.9491	0.2496	0.0609	1.9021
CB5	0.4922	0.0954	1.5913	0.4940	0.0362	1.4295	0.4942	0.0722	1.3332
WIX	0.91%	0.00%	0.00%	1.11%	0.06%	0.00%	1.18%	0.03%	9.26%
CFI	0.61%	11.08%	40.83%	0.95%	20.88%	38.17%	1.01%	5.08%	60.30%

Comparing $(sc_2^{P/A}, s_{0S}^{P/A})$ to $(sc_1^{P/A}, s_{0S}^{P/A})$ we see the effects of the model asymmetries in case of a symmetric shock. Differences are limited both in the pre- and post accession cases. The large country $C1$ has higher losses than the smaller country $C2$ whereas in the symmetric scenario losses were identical. $C3$ and $C4$ also incur lower losses than in the benchmark.

The importance of model asymmetries is more profound in case of asymmetric shocks as a comparison of $(sc_2^{P/A}, s_{0A}^{P/A})$ to $(sc_1^{P/A}, s_{0A}^{P/A})$ suggests. Similarly, the asymmetries have substantial consequences in case of the exchange rate shock as $(sc_2^{P/A}, s_{0E}^{P/A})$ to $(sc_1^{P/A}, s_{0E}^{P/A})$. Note also, that in $sc_1^{P/A}$ -with the exception of $C3$, $CB3$, $C5$ and $CB5$-, the exchange rate shock leads to rather similar effects as the asymmetric shock.

These results on the role of asymmetries apply to both the pre- and post-accession cases. The effects from accession (of $C3$) itself are found from a comparison of the upper (pre-accession, sc^P) and lower (post-accession, sc^A) parts of Table 7.10. In case of the symmetric shock, the effects are rather small. The most striking are the effects of an asymmetric price shock that hits $C3$.

Before and after the accession losses of this country are very high compared to losses of other players. Moreover, as pointed out in previous tables, the costs incurred by $C3$ at the pre-accession stage is much lower than those at the post-accession stage. It suggests that the study of symmetric shocks is a good starting point but the real issue at stake are asymmetric shocks since their influence is the highest. Hence, in our model lack of the exchange rate adjustment (which also means sharing a common interest rate in an MU) is a big burden to the economy hit by an asymmetric shock.

If the structure of $C3$'s economy differs more from the economic structure of the existing MU countries and there is a higher risk of an asymmetric shock, it becomes less likely that the MU will be enlarged and it is in the interest of both current and prospective members of the MU that the enlargement is postponed until a larger degree of economic convergence is achieved. These findings are in line with conclusions of the OCA theory.

7.5.5 Stable coalition structures

Table 7.11 gives the stable CSs for all three scenarios and three types of shocks in the 4 simultaneous coalition formation mechanisms. As $C5$ and $CB5$ are always in coalition they do not take part in the coalition formation game and are omitted. Note that in the ROMG coalition structures π_4 and π_{41} are stable by definition because, after excluding $C5$ and $CB5$, they are the non-cooperative regimes. Stable CSs in Table 7.11 were found using the algorithms from Chapter 5.

Table 7.11 Stable coalition structures in the pre-accession stage

Scenario:	Game:	s_{0S}^P	s_{0A}^P	s_{0E}^P
sc_1^P	OMG	-	-	-
	ROMG	4	4	4
	EMG(Δ)	4, 8	4, 31	4
	EMG(Γ)	4, 8	4	4, 31
sc_2^P	OMG	-	-	-
	ROMG	4, 5	4, 6	4
	EMG(Δ)	4, 5	4, 6	4
	EMG(Γ)	4, 5	4, 6	4
sc_3^P	OMG	-	-	-
	ROMG	4	4, 31	4
	EMG(Δ)	4	4, 31, 33	4
	EMG(Γ)	4	4	4

The first and the most important observation is that there are relatively few stable CSs compared to the previous chapter. In other words, introducing exchange rates and extra players dramatically changed the situation. Now, in the game of seven players stable CSs are very seldom. For instance, in the case of the asymmetric exchange rate shock, s_{0E}^P, there is only one non-trivial stable CSs (in the EMG(Γ), sc_1^P). Second, note that there are no stable CSs in the OMG at all, even for the symmetric scenario and the symmetric shock. This contrasts to the outcomes in Chapter 6 where in some cases the OMG resulted in the full coalition as a stable CS. In the present, richer and more realistic setting this is not the case. Third, as expected, all the CSs that are stable in the ROMG are also stable in the EMG(Δ) (see Theorem 5.1). In contrast, CSs which are stable in the EMG(Γ) are not necessarily stable in the EMG(Δ) as, due to different rules of coalition formation, a set of deviations in the former type of game does not have to be the subset of a set of deviations in the latter game and *vice versa*. Such a situation occurs, for instance, in (sc_1^P, s_{0A}^P) and (sc_1^P, s_{0E}^P).

It is interesting to investigate the coalitional effects of the special assumptions made in our MU setting concerning the priority of central banks in the OMG and the ROMG to create a coalition with their respective bank jurisdictional sets. In (sc_1^P, s_{0A}^P) no fiscal player wants to unilaterally leave the full fiscal coalition $(C1, C2, C3, C4)$ in the ROMG. However the $CB4$ breaks up this regime since its loss in π_{20} is lower than in π_{31}. In contrast, π_{31} is stable in the EMG(Δ) as such a deviation of the $CB4$ is not possible in this game. However, this CS is not stable in the EMG(Γ). It is caused by the fact that any deviation of a fiscal player from π_{31} leads to π_4 and this latter CS is preferred by both $C1$ and $C2$.

Looking from a broader perspective at Table 7.11 we see that, except for π_4, there are 4 different CSs which appear to be stable under various coalition formation mechanisms in the pre-accession stage:

$$\begin{aligned}
\pi_6 &= [C1|C2|CB|C3|CB3|C4CB4|C5CB5] \\
\pi_8 &= [C1|C2|CB|C3C4|CB3|CB4|C5CB5] \\
\pi_{31} &= [C1C2C3C4|CB|CB3|CB4|C5CB5] \\
\pi_{33} &= [C1C3C4|C2|CB|CB3|CB4|C5CB5]
\end{aligned}$$

Note that three out of these four CSs consist of only the partial or full fiscal coalitions: ($C3$, $C4$), ($C1$, $C2$, $C3$, $C4$) and ($C1$, $C3$, $C4$) .[19] There is only one national MU coalition in the set of stable CSs. In other words, fiscal players prefer rather to cooperate with other fiscal players than with own central banks and/or *vice versa*. In 7 cases out of 10 when a cooperation emerges in Table 7.11 players choose fiscal coalitions. Hence, we may pose a more general hypothesis that partial or full fiscal cooperation has higher chances to emerge than full MU/national arrangements. It is interesting to see whether the situation after the enlargement of the union will confirm the above outcome. Stable coalition structures in the post-accession stage are listed in Table 7.12.

[19] Apart from coalition $(C5, CB5)$ which is not considered in our games.

Table 7.12 Stable coalition structures in the post-accession stage

Scenario:	Game:	s_{0S}^{A}	s_{0A}^{A}	s_{0E}^{A}
sc_1^A	OMG	-	-	42
	ROMG	41	41	41, 42
	EMG(Δ)	41	41, 45, 62	41, 42
	EMG(Γ)	41	41	41, 42, 62
sc_2^A	OMG	-	-	-
	ROMG	41	41, 42	41
	EMG(Δ)	41	41, 42	41
	EMG(Γ)	41	41, 42	41
sc_3^A	OMG	-	-	-
	ROMG	41	41, 62	41
	EMG(Δ)	41	41, 45, 60, 62	41
	EMG(Γ)	41	41	41

Except for non-cooperative regime π_{41}, also in the post-accession stage there are 4 different CSs which are stable under various coalition formation mechanisms:

$$\begin{aligned}
\pi_{42} &= [C1|C2|C3|CB|C4CB4|C5CB5] \\
\pi_{45} &= [C1C2C3|CB|C4|CB4|C5CB5] \\
\pi_{60} &= [C1C3C4|C2|CB|CB4|C5CB5] \\
\pi_{62} &= [C1C2C3C4|CB|CB4|C5CB5]
\end{aligned}$$

Similarly to the pre-accession stage only in π_{42}, we find that $C4$ cooperates with $CB4$. Three other CSs listed above, consist of only partial or full fiscal coalitions: $(C1, C2, C3)$, $(C1, C2, C3, C4)$ and $(C1, C3, C4)$. Note that two of these coalitions also occurred in the pre-accession stage. Moreover, one can find a natural correspondence between the stable CSs, i.e., π_{42} corresponds to π_6; π_{60} to π_{33}; and π_{62} to π_{31}. There is no natural correspondence only between π_{45} and π_8. Furthermore, note that the pattern of stable CSs in Table 7.12 is very similar to the pattern in Table 7.11:

1. For the symmetric shock, s_{0S}^A, in the post-accession stage (third column of Table 7.12) there is no stable CS in any game (except for trivial π_{41}). In the pre-accession stage only CS π_8 is stable in the symmetric scenario (sc_1^P, s_{0S}^P) in both EMGs;

2. For the asymmetric price shock, $s_{0A}^{P/A}$, the results in Tables 7.12 and 7.11 (fourth columns) coincide (except for π_{45} in the EMG(Δ) in (sc_1^A, s_{0A}^A) and (sc_3^A, s_{0A}^A));

3. For the asymmetric exchange rate shock, $s_{0E}^{P/A}$, the results in Table 7.12 (last column) are also very similar to the results in Table 7.11. The only difference is CS π_{42}, which appears to be stable in the symmetric scenario sc_1^A in all the games.

Consequently, we conclude that within the framework of our setting: (i) in a structurally asymmetric model with an asymmetric price shock hitting an accession country, the CS, in which fiscal outsiders cooperate with their monetary authorities, is likely to emerge; (ii) when asymmetries in bargaining power (sc_3^P and sc_3^A) are introduced full fiscal coalitions or partial fiscal coalitions are likely to emerge in the ROMG and the EMG(Δ) for $s_{0A}^{P/A}$; (iii) the full fiscal coalition emerges in the EMG(Γ) for $(sc_1^{P/A}, s_{0E}^{P/A})$.

The above results suggest that our results of coalition formation analysis are quite robust. From the fact that CSs with only fiscal coalitions emerge more often than CSs with a national coalition (π_6 or π_{42}), we conclude that, irrespective of monetary arrangements (a smaller or larger MU), fiscal players prefer fiscal coalitions over cooperation with the monetary authorities. This can (very probably) be explained by the opposite fiscal and monetary players' preferences about inflation and output (gap) stabilization. We can compare this result with our findings from Chapter 6. There, either a partial or full fiscal cooperation but not full MU cooperation emerged in the simultaneous coalition formation mechanisms under (sc_1, p_{0S}), (sc_2, p_{0A2}) and (sc_2, p_{0A2}) (see Tables 6.3, 6.10 and 6.14). However, in two other cases (sc_1, p_{0A}) and (sc_1, p_{0A-S}) the full MU cooperation is supported (see Tables 6.5 and 6.7). Note however, that the open-economy setting in the present chapter is much richer and closer to reality; hence its conclusions are superior to Chapter 6.

To compare the effectiveness (in the sense of social welfare) of simultaneous coalition formation mechanisms the average value of the welfare index (WIX) throughout all the combinations of scenarios and shocks was computed. The average values (denoted by $\overline{WIX}^P$ and $\overline{WIX}^A$) were computed for all the CSs that take part in the game in the pre- and post-accession stages ($\pi_4 - \pi_{35}$ and $\pi_{41} - \pi_{62}$, respectively). Then, the average values of WIX were computed only for stable CSs in each game Γ and in both stages (denoted as $\overline{WIX}^{STP}(\Gamma)$ and $\overline{WIX}^{STA}(\Gamma)$). These averages are defined as follows:

$$\overline{WIX}^{P/A} := \frac{1}{z}\left(\sum_{k\in\Pi^{MU(P/A)}} WIX(k)\right), \tag{7.8}$$

where $\Pi^{MU(P)} := \{\pi_4, ..., \pi_{35}\}$; $\Pi^{MU(A)} := \{\pi_{41}, ..., \pi_{62}\}$ and z is the cardinality of the sets $\Pi^{MU(P)}$ or $\Pi^{MU(A)}$, i.e. $z := |\Pi^{MU(P)}| = 32$ in the pre-accession stage and $z := |\Pi^{MU(A)}| = 22$ in the post-accession stage, and

$$\overline{WIX}^{STP/A}(\Gamma) := \frac{1}{z}\left(\sum_{k\in\bar{\Gamma}^{STP/A}} WIX(k)\right), \tag{7.9}$$

where $\bar{\Gamma}^{STP/A} :=$ {all stable CSs for game Γ in all scenarios/shocks}[20] either in the pre- or post-accession stage and z is the cardinality of sets $\bar{\Gamma}^{STP}$ or $\bar{\Gamma}^{STA}$, i.e. $z = |\bar{\Gamma}^{STP}|$ or $z = |\bar{\Gamma}^{STA}|$. Note that $\overline{WIX}^{P/A}$ can be interpreted as the expected WIX throughout all scenarios and shocks and $\overline{WIX}^{STP/A}(\Gamma)$ as the expected WIX of the coalition formation mechanism Γ.

Table 7.13 Effectiveness of simultaneous coalition formation mechanisms

Index	$\overline{WIX}^{P}$	$\overline{WIX}^{A}$	$\overline{std(WIX)^{P}}$	$\overline{std(WIX)^{A}}$
	6.1105%	6.4666%	2.9731%	2.6050%
Index	$\overline{WIX}^{STP}$	$\overline{WIX}^{STA}$	$\overline{std(WIX)^{STP}}$	$\overline{std(WIX)^{STA}}$
OMG	–	–	–	–
$ROMG$	9.8153%	9.1567%	0.0423%	1.1981%
$EMG(\Delta)$	9.5712%	10.1547%	0.0752%	1.2704%
$EMG(\Gamma)$	7.9452%	9.3584%	1.1729%	0.5136%

The average values of WIX obtained in stable CSs in (all the games throughout all the scenarios/shocks), i.e. $\overline{WIX}^{STP}$ for the pre-accession stage and $\overline{WIX}^{STA}$ for the post-accession stage, are above the average values of WIX for all the CSs (throughout all the scenarios/shocks), i.e. $\overline{WIX}^{P}$ and $\overline{WIX}^{A}$, respectively. This suggests that our simultaneous coalition formation mechanisms are not effective from the social point of view in the considered setting, as (on average) they result in higher losses than the expected total loss of players. The question arises why we compare the expected loss from coalition formation mechanisms with the average loss throughout all CSs, and not with the average loss obtained in the non-cooperative regimes. It could be argued that if coalition formation mechanisms are not present players play non-cooperatively. However, we assume that if no (institutionalized) mechanism is present, then players are still able to pursue cooperative strategies informally. Hence, in our approach the non-cooperative regime is not the natural benchmark for comparison of effectiveness of coalition formation mechanisms. NC does not have to be an equilibrium even when no mechanism is present.

Average values are informative but they do not show what is the dispersion of WIX between different CSs. A higher dispersion of welfare indices for stable CSs than for all CSs would mean that, in addition to lower averages, coordination mechanisms may result in substantially worse (or substantially better) outcomes than no coordination. For risk-averse players such a volatility would be undesirable. The dispersion of WIX is measured by a simple standard deviation formula in the following way. First, the standard deviation of WIX over all CSs in each of the 9 combinations of a scenario/shock is computed. Then, the average value of the standard deviations of WIX for the whole game is calculated ($\overline{std(WIX)^{P}}$ and $\overline{std(WIX)^{A}}$ in the pre- and post-accession

[20]Note that certain CSs in this set may be repeated.

stages, respectively). A similar method is used to compute the standard deviation of WIX for stable CSs (i.e. $\overline{std(WIX)^{STP}(\Gamma)}$ and $\overline{std(WIX)^{STA}(\Gamma)}$), where, of course, only stable CSs are taken into account. Note that in many cases $std((WIX)^{STP}(\Gamma))$ for a particular scenario/shock and coalition formation mechanism Γ equals zero. This is caused by the fact that in many cases only one CS is stable, i.e. the NC regime (see Tables 7.11 and 7.12). Table 7.13 shows that, on average, the dispersion of losses between stable CSs is (much) lower than between all the CSs in a given scenario/shock combination. Hence, we may conclude that, although coalition formation mechanisms are on average less effective from the social point of view than no-institutionalized negotiations, they provide the players as a whole with a less volatile loss.

Effectiveness of the different coalition formation mechanisms gives mixed results. In the pre-accession stage we see that the higher the degree of unanimity in the coalition formation mechanism is, the better is the expected outcome of simultaneous negotiations from the social point of view. This result follows basic intuition that the outcome which is obtained due to consent of all the players involved should be more closer to the optimum (in fact, this was one of the observations from Chapter 6 concerning the (also unanimous) SNG, see Section 6.4). However, in the post-accession stage, $\overline{WIX}^A$ for the EMG(Δ) is the highest and $\overline{WIX}^A$ for the EMG(Γ) is still higher than $\overline{WIX}^A$ for the ROMG. To investigate this issue further a larger game should be constructed with a higher number of fiscal players (e.g. $n_f \geqq 6$). It is possible, that the EMG(Γ) becomes more effective than the ROMG and the EMG(Δ) when the number of players involved in the game increases.

7.5.6 Effects of accession

To obtain further insights on the effects of different scenarios we use some simple statistical methods. It is interesting to see what are for a particular player the average (optimal) losses over all CSs. More formally, the average value $\overline{\hat{J}_i}$ is defined as follows. For $\Pi^{MU} := \{\pi_4, \pi_2, ..., \pi_{35}\}$ in the pre-accession stage $\overline{\hat{J}_i} := \frac{1}{32}\sum_{s=4}^{35} \hat{J}_i(\pi_s)$ and for $\Pi^{MU} := \{\pi_{41}, \pi_2, ..., \pi_{62}\}$ in the post-accession stage $\overline{\hat{J}_i} := \frac{1}{22}\sum_{s=41}^{62} \hat{J}_i(\pi_s)$ where $\hat{J}_i(\pi_s)$ is an optimal loss of a player i in CS π_s. We compute $\overline{\hat{J}_i}$ for every player $i = C1, C2, ..., CB5$ in every shock/scenario combination in the pre-accession and post-accession stage. These results are reported in Table 7.14:

Table 7.14 - Average value of losses in pre- and post-accession cases

Sc:	Structural Symmetry ($sc_1^{P/A}$)			Structural Asymmetry ($sc_2^{P/A}$)			Structural and bargaining power asymmetry ($sc_3^{P/A}$)		
PRE-ACCESSION STAGE									
Pl.\S.	s_{0S}^P	s_{0A}^P	s_{0E}^P	s_{0S}^P	s_{0A}^P	s_{0E}^P	s_{0S}^P	s_{0A}^P	s_{0E}^P
C1	0.2466	0.1694	0.1553	0.2479	0.0899	0.2660	0.2475	0.0830	0.2670
C2	0.2466	0.1694	0.1553	0.2471	0.0698	0.2124	0.2474	0.0704	0.2254
CB	0.4888	0.1121	0.0849	0.4893	0.0594	0.1351	0.4894	0.0562	0.1429
C3	0.2468	2.7953	0.1528	0.2474	2.9271	0.2099	0.2475	2.9306	0.2211
CB3	0.4885	2.3880	0.0828	0.4891	2.5570	0.1260	0.4891	2.5689	0.1287
C4	0.2468	0.1600	0.1528	0.2458	0.0640	0.2170	0.2456	0.0516	0.1937
CB4	0.4885	0.1097	0.0828	0.2453	0.0765	0.1629	0.2454	0.0782	0.2005
C5	0.2484	0.1272	2.0009	0.2494	0.0615	1.9389	0.2495	0.0605	1.9230
CB5	0.4873	0.1106	1.7837	0.4877	0.0580	1.6183	0.4878	0.0573	1.5951
POST-ACCESSION STAGE									
Pl.\S.	s_{0S}^A	s_{0A}^A	s_{0E}^A	s_{0S}^A	s_{0A}^A	s_{0E}^A	s_{0S}^A	s_{0A}^A	s_{0E}^A
C1	0.2464	0.9575	0.1591	0.2478	0.6197	0.2735	0.2474	0.5483	0.2746
C2	0.2464	0.9575	0.1591	0.2471	0.4900	0.2187	0.2473	0.4563	0.2316
C3	0.2464	6.8494	0.1591	0.2471	7.3495	0.2187	0.2473	7.4667	0.2316
CB	0.4893	0.1116	0.0827	0.4895	0.0729	0.1304	0.4896	0.0670	0.1368
C4	0.2466	0.1826	0.1522	0.2458	0.0921	0.2179	0.2456	0.0598	0.1947
CB4	0.4889	0.1188	0.0814	0.2453	0.0975	0.1588	0.2454	0.0872	0.1955
C5	0.2484	0.1267	2.0030	0.2495	0.0635	1.9408	0.2495	0.0596	1.9253
CB5	0.4876	0.1180	1.8015	0.4877	0.0711	1.6370	0.4878	0.0639	1.6150

Since Table 7.14 reports average (optimal) losses it shows at hand many characteristics of our model. First of all, they provide a picture of different shocks and scenarios' effects on players' losses. Obviously, in (sc_1^P, s_{0S}^P) losses of $C1$ and $C2$ and $C3$ and $C4$ are symmetric since economic spillovers and resulting economic externalities influence them symmetrically. Naturally, this symmetry breaks up under the asymmetric shocks s_{0S}^P and s_{0E}^P and in the asymmetric scenarios sc_2^P and sc_3^P. The same holds in the post-accession stage.

Comparing $sc_2^{P/A}$ to $sc_1^{P/A}$ and $sc_3^{P/A}$ to $sc_2^{P/A}$ we see that structural asymmetries have a larger impact on players' losses than bargaining power asymmetries. This was also our conclusion from Chapter 6. The adjustment process after a shock is mainly driven by economic spillovers since both monetary and fiscal authorities have only limited influence on economic systems. When a shock occurs they can only partially control economies. Hence, even an almost complete lack of bargaining power in any coalition is not likely to increase losses substantially as, to a large extent, the economic system returns to balance by itself.

The average losses for (sc_1^P, s_{0S}^P) can be also compared with losses obtained in the non-cooperative regime π_4 in sc_1^P (Table 7.2). This shows that on average all the fiscal players lose from coordination compared to the non-cooperative regime. From this, it could be argued, that if it is completely unclear which CS will be actually played after the coordination process, then all the fiscal players would not enter to any negotiations at all. They would prefer to play non-cooperatively since the expected loss from coordination is higher. However, this argument does not hold for any other combination of scenarios and shocks, i.e. expected loss from coordination for some players is lower than the (optimal) loss in the non-cooperative regime. The conclusion is that under these conditions players would support the existence of some coordination mechanism as their expected loss from any form of cooperation is lower than from a non-cooperative playing.[21]

To analyze the effects of accession we will compute the difference between post- and pre-accession losses for each player, i.e.: $\Delta \pounds_i = \hat{J}_i^{(A)} - \hat{J}_i^{(P)}$. Hence, the upper part of Table 7.15 is obtained by subtracting the upper part from the lower part of Table 7.14 after deleting $CB3$.

Table 7.15 Accession effects

Sc:	Structural Symmetry ($sc_1^{P/A}$)			Structural Asymmetry ($sc_2^{P/A}$)			Structural and bargaining power asymmetry ($sc_3^{P/A}$)		
Pl.\S.	$s_{0S}^{P/A}$	$s_{0A}^{P/A}$	$s_{0E}^{P/A}$	$s_{0S}^{P/A}$	$s_{0A}^{P/A}$	$s_{0E}^{P/A}$	$s_{0S}^{P/A}$	$s_{0A}^{P/A}$	$s_{0E}^{P/A}$
C1	-0.0002	**0.7881**	**0.0038**	-0.0001	**0.5298**	**0.0075**	-0.0001	**0.4653**	**0.0076**
C2	-0.0002	**0.7881**	**0.0038**	**0.0000**	**0.4202**	**0.0063**	-0.0002	**0.3859**	**0.0061**
C3	-0.0004	**4.0541**	**0.0062**	-0.0004	**4.4224**	**0.0088**	-0.0002	**4.5361**	**0.0104**
CB	**0.0005**	-0.0005	-0.0021	**0.0002**	**0.0135**	-0.0047	**0.0002**	**0.0109**	-0.0061
C4	-0.0002	**0.0226**	-0.0006	**0.0000**	**0.0281**	**0.0008**	**0.0000**	**0.0082**	**0.0010**
CB4	**0.0003**	**0.0090**	-0.0014	**0.0000**	**0.0210**	-0.0041	**0.0000**	**0.0089**	-0.0050
C5	**0.0001**	-0.0005	**0.0021**	**0.0000**	**0.0020**	**0.0019**	**0.0000**	-0.0009	**0.0022**
CB5	**0.0003**	**0.0074**	**0.0178**	**0.0000**	**0.0131**	**0.0187**	**0.0000**	**0.0066**	**0.0199**
Pl.\S.	$s_{0S}^{P/A}$	$s_{0A}^{P/A}$	$s_{0E}^{P/A}$	$s_{0S}^{P/A}$	$s_{0A}^{P/A}$	$s_{0E}^{P/A}$	$s_{0S}^{P/A}$	$s_{0A}^{P/A}$	$s_{0E}^{P/A}$
C1	-0.9447	**318.6935**	-38.9715	-1.1057	**268.0334**	-41.1210	-0.4596	**363.7363**	-45.9721
C2	-0.9447	**318.6935**	-38.9715	-0.3059	**290.7028**	-47.3543	-0.9331	**317.0422**	-46.0456
C3	-1.3493	**107.1257**	-40.6423	-1.5312	**101.9906**	-49.5838	-1.5048	**126.4361**	-48.3950
CB	-0.8734	-48.4791	-60.8350	-1.0685	-57.7988	-59.5872	-1.1717	-45.8547	-66.3998
C4	-1.4535	-43.0445	-28.0726	-0.5290	-46.4178	-19.1622	-0.4256	-52.2334	-43.0154
CB4	-1.1415	-74.5119	-53.9182	-2.5047	-85.7951	-56.4075	-2.5258	-76.7464	-65.7843
C5	-0.5273	-21.4326	-4.3745	-0.3959	-35.3513	-5.6319	-0.4160	-24.1123	-5.5649
CB5	-1.1415	-49.1089	-15.4125	-1.3110	-64.2081	-17.7996	-1.3695	-60.0355	-22.3932
Pl.\S.	$s_{0S}^{P/A}$	$s_{0A}^{P/A}$	$s_{0E}^{P/A}$	$s_{0S}^{P/A}$	$s_{0A}^{P/A}$	$s_{0E}^{P/A}$	$s_{0S}^{P/A}$	$s_{0A}^{P/A}$	$s_{0E}^{P/A}$
WMU	-0.03	173.43	2.14	-0.02	171.19	2.17	-0.02	171.90	2.11

Positive values in the upper part of Table 7.15 mean that for a particular player the accession is not (on average!) profitable. Hence, it comes out that on average accession is rather not profitable for the fiscal insiders under asymmetric

[21] Of course, players can block an existence of a coordination mechanism hoping that they will (possibly) coordinate informally in a subgroup and free ride, when other players will pursue non-cooperative strategies. Such a situation is, in a way, contradictory to our assumption of perfect information, since due to spillovers/externalities every form of cooperation would be immediately noticed by other players.

shocks. Only in the case of a symmetric shock for sc_1 and sc_3 they both gain on average. In all combinations of scenarios and asymmetric shocks they lose. Moreover, note that these average losses from enlargement are in general much higher than feasible profits. The accession country $C3$ gains from entering the MU only in the case of a symmetric shock, however, in all the three scenarios. The enlargement is on average profitable for all three directly involved fiscal players together only in (sc_1, s_{OS}) and (sc_3, s_{OS}). This suggests that actually, when structural/shock asymmetries are present, it would be very difficult in our model to reach an agreement on an MU enlargement, since, usually, such a decision typically has to be taken under unanimity.

Note that by far the highest increase in the average loss is faced by countries of the enlarged monetary union in the case of an asymmetric price shock. This happens with no exception for all 3 scenarios and certainly calls for further investigation. Therefore, we compute for each player (except $CB3$) the difference between the minimal losses in the post-accession stage (π_{42} to π_{59}) and maximal losses in the pre-accession stage (π_4 to π_{35}). More formally, we use the following formula to obtain the values in the middle part of Table 7.15:

$$\triangle\hat{\mathcal{L}}_i = \frac{\hat{J}_i^{\min(A)} - \hat{J}_i^{\max(P)}}{\hat{J}_i^{\max(P)}} \times 100$$

where $\hat{J}_i^{\min(A)} = \min_{\pi_{41-62}} \hat{J}_i$ and $\hat{J}_i^{\max(P)} = \max_{\pi_{4-35}} \hat{J}_i$. Note that $\hat{J}_i$ is the ith policymaker' optimal loss in a particular coalition structure. $\triangle\hat{\mathcal{L}}_i$ is in percentages and is computed for all three scenarios and shocks. All the negative numbers tell that there exists a post-accession CS in which the loss for the particular player is lower than the maximum of all losses that this player may incur in the pre-accession CSs. More formally: $\hat{J}_i^{\min(A)} < \hat{J}_i^{\max(P)}$. The result is ambiguous in these cases and requires further investigation. The only conclusion that can be drawn, is the following: for these types of shocks and scenarios we cannot exclude the possibility that gains from enlargement can be found when particular CSs before and after accession are considered.

However, in the case of an asymmetric price shock that hits accession country $C3$, in all three scenarios, all countries of the enlarged monetary union, have increased losses in every possible coalition structure. So, always: $\hat{J}_i^{\min(A)} > \hat{J}_i^{\max(P)}$ for $i = C1, C2, C3$. The enlargement cannot be profitable for any of the fiscal players in the case of an asymmetric price shock. Even, in the presence of a very effective coordination scheme, there is no CS that could assure gains for $C1, C2$ and $C3$ after enlargement. It suggests the very important conclusion, that when there is a high risk of an asymmetric price shock in the accession country, the enlargement is unprofitable. Moreover, no coordination mechanism can make it profitable. This result obtained here using a framework with an extensive game-theoretic background is in line with results of the basic OCA analysis which lacks any game-theoretic considerations.

The question arises what the effect of enlargement will be on the total loss of the enlarged monetary union, defined as: $J_{MU} \equiv J_{C1} + J_{C2} + J_{C3} + J_{CB}$. The last line of Table 7.15 presents the percentage change in the average value of J_{MU} with regard to the. pre-accession stage. J_{MU} is positive in six cases, and negative in 3 cases. Moreover, increases of average losses are in general much higher than decreases; hence, we may conclude that the enlargement is rather not profitable also from the point of view of the MU joint welfare.

7.6 Conclusion

We find that the net effects of accession depend in particular on three factors: (i) the regime of policy coordination in place before and after accession; (ii) the type of macroeconomic shock and its degree of symmetry across countries; (iii) the degree of symmetry between countries in economic structure, sizes of countries and their policy preferences.

The main insights from our analyses can be summarized as follows: (i) Enlargement is likely to be unprofitable with increasing asymmetries in economic structures and economic shocks. (ii) Our findings stress the importance of an asymmetric shock. In our setting and in all the examples it emerges that if an asymmetric price shock occurs in the accession country it is never profitable to enlarge the monetary union. What is more, the differences in losses between the pre-accession stage and the post-accession stage are so high that it will be difficult to design a transfer system to compensate for a worse situation of some countries. (iii) Policy coordination can to a certain extent diminish losses of players and make accession more viable in the case of certain shocks. Therefore appropriately designed coordination mechanisms are likely to play a very important role in the enlargement process.

More in detail, we find that in our setting that countries are more likely to create partial, full fiscal or grand fiscal coalitions than full MU/national coalitions with their central banks. Hence, similarly to Chapter 4, our present analysis suggests that full MU cooperation may be rather unsustainable and policymakers should look for institutional settings which support fiscal coordination. However, in general, there are relatively little stable CSs. In fact, for many combinations of scenarios/shocks none of the simultaneous coalition formation mechanisms (the OMG, the ROMG and both versions of the EMG) results in non-trivial stable CSs. Moreover, they turn out to be rather inefficient from the social point of view.

Several further issues call for further research. First of all an effort could be made in the direction of less myopic games, in which players forecast possible responses of other players to their own actions. Secondly, different types of shocks could be studied to further strengthen the obtained results. For example, it seems interesting to evaluate the effects of an exchange rate shock that hits the monetary union as a whole.[22] If such a shock happens, is $C3$ better off in the pre-accession stage than in the post-accession stage? If, in such a case, being in a monetary union is more profitable, the issue of accession will be concerned with

[22] Such a shock will be studied in the next chapter.

a trade-off between the vulnerability to asymmetric price shocks and asymmetric exchange rate shocks.

7.7 Appendix A

Defining vectors and matrices $\iota_{n_f x1} := \begin{bmatrix} 1 \\ 1 \\ 1 \\ ... \\ 1 \end{bmatrix}$, $\hat{I} := \begin{bmatrix} \iota_k & 0_{k\times 1} & ... & 0_{0_{k\times 1}} \\ 0 & 1 & ... & 0 \\ ... & ... & ... & ... \\ 0 & 0 & ... & 1 \end{bmatrix}_{n_f \times (n_f - k+1)}$,

$$\eta := \begin{bmatrix} \eta_1 & 0 & ... & 0 \\ 0 & \eta_2 & ... & 0 \\ ... & ... & ... & ... \\ 0 & 0 & ... & \eta_{n_f} \end{bmatrix}, \gamma := \begin{bmatrix} \gamma_1 & 0 & ... & 0 \\ 0 & \gamma_2 & ... & 0 \\ ... & ... & ... & ... \\ 0 & 0 & ... & \gamma_{n_f} \end{bmatrix},$$

$$\rho := \begin{bmatrix} 0 & \rho_{12} & ... & \rho_{1n_f} \\ \rho_{21} & 0 & ... & \rho_{2n_f} \\ ... & ... & ... & ... \\ \rho_{n_f 1} & \rho_{n_f 2} & ... & 0 \end{bmatrix}, \zeta := \begin{bmatrix} \zeta_1 & 0 & ... & 0 \\ 0 & \zeta_2 & ... & 0 \\ ... & ... & ... & ... \\ 0 & 0 & ... & \zeta_{n_f} \end{bmatrix},$$

$$\varsigma := \begin{bmatrix} 0 & \varsigma_{12} & ... & \varsigma_{1n_f} \\ \varsigma_{21} & 0 & ... & \varsigma_{2n_f} \\ ... & ... & ... & ... \\ \varsigma_{n_f 1} & \varsigma_{n_f 2} & ... & 0 \end{bmatrix}, \delta := \begin{bmatrix} -\sum\limits_{i\in n_f/1} \delta_{1i} & \delta_{12} & ... & \delta_{1n_f} \\ \delta_{21} & -\sum\limits_{i\in n_f/2} \delta_{2i} & ... & \delta_{2n_f} \\ ... & ... & ... & ... \\ \delta_{n_f 1} & \delta_{n_f 2} & ... & -\sum\limits_{i\in n_f/n_f} \delta_{n_f i} \end{bmatrix},$$

$$\kappa := \begin{bmatrix} \sum\limits_{i\in n_f/1} \varsigma_{1i} & -\varsigma_{12} & ... & -\varsigma_{1n_f} \\ -\varsigma_{21} & \sum\limits_{i\in n_f/2} \varsigma_{2i} & ... & -\varsigma_{2n_f} \\ ... & ... & ... & ... \\ -\varsigma_{n_f 1} & -\varsigma_{n_f 2} & ... & \sum\limits_{i\in n_f/n_f} \varsigma_{n_f n_f} \end{bmatrix}, \hat{\nu} := \left[-1\iota_{(n_f-k+1)} + I_{(n_f-k+1)}\right],$$

$\hat{\gamma} := \gamma\hat{I}$, $\hat{\kappa} := \kappa\hat{I}$, $\hat{\delta} := \delta\hat{I}$, and $i(t) := \left[i_U^{1,...,k}(t), i_{CB(k+1)}^{k+1}(t), i_{CB(k+2)}^{k+2}(t), ... i_{CBn_f}^{n_f}(t)\right]$ (as a vector of interest rates of each central bank[23]) the structural form of the model can be rewritten as:

$$\begin{aligned} y(t) &= -\hat{\gamma} i(t) + \eta f(t) + \gamma \dot{p}(t) + \delta p(t) + \rho y(t) + \hat{\delta} e(t) \\ \dot{p}(t) &= \zeta y(t) + \varsigma \dot{p}(t) + \hat{\kappa} i(t), p(0) = p_0 \\ \dot{e}(t) &= i(t) - \iota_{(n_f-k+1)} i_E^{1,...,k}(t), e(0) = e_0. \end{aligned}$$

Note that an exchange-rate derivative is defined as a deviation of country j's interest rate from the first country's interest rate.

Rearranging we obtain:

[23]Note that this formulation of the vector $i(t)$ presents a situation where k countries form a monetary union with a central bank denoted as CB, whereas other $n-k$ countries have own interest rates managed by central banks denoted as CBi, $(i = n-k+1, n-k+2, ..., n)$, respectively.

$$\begin{bmatrix} y(t) \\ \dot{p}(t) \\ \dot{e}(t) \end{bmatrix} = \begin{bmatrix} W^{-1} & 0 \\ 0 & I \end{bmatrix} \begin{bmatrix} \delta & \hat{\delta} & \eta & -\hat{\gamma} \\ 0 & 0 & 0 & \hat{\kappa} \\ 0 & 0 & 0 & \hat{\nu} \end{bmatrix} \begin{bmatrix} p(t) \\ e(t) \\ f(t) \\ i(t) \end{bmatrix}$$

where $W = \begin{bmatrix} I-\rho & -\gamma \\ -\zeta & I-\varsigma \end{bmatrix}$ and [0] are matrices of the appropriate size.
Rearranging:

$$\begin{bmatrix} y(t) \\ \dot{p}(t) \\ \dot{e}(t) \end{bmatrix} = \underbrace{\begin{bmatrix} W^{-1}\begin{bmatrix} \delta \\ 0 \end{bmatrix} & W^{-1}\begin{bmatrix} \hat{\delta} \\ 0 \end{bmatrix} & W^{-1}\begin{bmatrix} \eta \\ 0 \end{bmatrix} & W^{-1}\begin{bmatrix} -\hat{\gamma} \\ \hat{\kappa} \end{bmatrix} \\ 0 & 0 & 0 & \hat{\nu} \end{bmatrix}}_{L\ matrix} \begin{bmatrix} p(t) \\ e(t) \\ f(t) \\ i(t) \end{bmatrix}$$

we can rewrite the reduced form equations for real outputs as:

$$\begin{cases} y_1(t) =: L_1 z(t) \\ \dots \\ y_{n_f}(t) =: L_{n_f} z(t) \\ \dot{p}_1(t) =: L_{n_f+1} z(t) \\ \dots \\ \dot{p}_{n_f}(t) =: L_{2n_f} z(t) \end{cases}$$

where L_i is the ith row of matrix L and

$$z^T(t) := \Big[p_1(t), p_2(t), \dots p_{n_f}(t), e_{11}(t), e_{(k+1)1}(t), \dots, e_{n_f 1}(t),\ f_1(t),\ f_2(t), \dots f_{n_f}(t), \\ i_U^{1,\dots,k}(t), i_{CB(k+1)}^{k+1}(t), \dots i_{CBn_f}^{n_f}(t) \Big].$$

Thus, government j's loss function becomes:

$$\begin{aligned} J_j(t_0) &= \frac{1}{2}\int_{t_0}^{\infty} \left\{ \alpha_j \left(\dot{p}_j(t) - p_j(t)\right)^2 + \beta_j y_j^2(t) + \chi_j f_j^2(t) \right\} e^{-\theta(t-t_0)} dt \\ &= \frac{1}{2}\int_{t_0}^{\infty} \{ z^T(t)(\alpha_j \left(L_{n_f+j}^T - \varpi e_i^T\right)\left(L_{n_f+j} - \varpi e_i\right) \\ &\quad + \beta_j L_j^T L_j + \chi_j e_{2n_f+j}^T e_{2n_f+j}) z(t) \} e^{-\theta(t-t_0)} dt \\ &= \frac{1}{2}\int_{t_0}^{\infty} \{ z^T(t) M_j z(t) \} e^{-\theta(t-t_0)} dt, \qquad M_j \in \mathbb{R}^{(4n_f-k+1)\times(4n_f-k+1)} \end{aligned}$$

where $e_i \in \mathbb{R}^{4n_f-2k+2}$ is a vector with all entries equal to zero, except for entry i that is equal to one.

Similarly, we can rewrite the CB's loss function as:

$$J_U(t_0) =$$

$$= \frac{1}{2}\int_{t_0}^{\infty} z^T(t)\left\{ \begin{array}{c} \alpha_U^M \left(\sum_{i\in n_f}\left(L_{n_f+i} - \varpi e_i^T\right)\right)^T \left(\sum_{i\in n_f}\left(L_{n_f+i} - \varpi e_i\right)\right) + \\ +\beta_U^M \left(\sum_{i\in n_f} L_i\right)^T \left(\sum_{i\in n_f} L_i\right) + \chi_U^M e_{3n_f+m}^T e_{3n_f+m} \end{array} \right\} z(t)\} e^{-\theta(t-t_0)} dt$$

$$= \frac{1}{2}\int_{t_0}^{\infty} \{z^T(t) M_U z(t)\} e^{-\theta(t-t_0)} dt \qquad M_U \in \mathbb{R}^{(4n_f-k+1)\times(4n_f-k+1)}$$

Finally we can rewrite the mth national central bank's loss function as:

$$J_{Cm}(t_0) = \frac{1}{2}\int_{t_0}^{\infty} \left\{\alpha_{Cm}^M \dot{p}_j^2(t) + \beta_{Cm}^M y_j^2(t) + \chi_{Cm}^M e_{3n_f-k+1+m}^T e_{3n_f-k+1+m}\right\} e^{-\theta(t-t_0)} dt =$$

$$= \frac{1}{2}\int_{t_0}^{\infty} z^T(t)\left\{\alpha_{Cm}^M L_{n_f+j}^T L_{n_f+j} + \beta_{Cm}^M L_j^T L_j + \chi_{Cm}^M e_{3n_f-k+1+m}^T e_{3n_f-k+1+m}\right\} z(t)\} e^{-\theta}$$

$$= \frac{1}{2}\int_{t_0}^{\infty} \{z^T(t) M_{Cm} z(t)\} e^{-\theta(t-t_0)} dt \qquad M_{Cm} \in \mathbb{R}^{(4n_f-k+1)\times(4n_f-k+1)}$$

where $m = n_f - k + 1, n_f - k + 2, ..., n_f$ and j is a corresponding country.

The basic algorithm to derive the game solutions

Similar to the computations in Chapter 2 and the Appendix in Chapter 6 the algorithm is described by the following 5 steps.

1. Factorize matrices M_i for any country or any central bank ($i = 1, 2, ..., n_f, n_f + 1, ..., w + 1$), where $w = 2n_f - 2k + 1$ as
$M_j =$

$$\begin{pmatrix} Q_j & S_{1j} & S_{2j} & S_{3j} & \cdots & S_{wj} & S_{wj} & S_{(w+1)j} \\ S_{1j}^T & R_{1j} & P_{11[j]} & P_{12[j]} & \cdots & P_{1(w-1)[j]} & P_{1w[j]} & P_{1(w+1)[j]} \\ S_{2j}^T & P_{11[j]}^T & R_{2j} & P_{22[j]} & \cdots & P_{2(w-1)[j]} & P_{2w[j]} & P_{2(w+1)[j]} \\ S_{3j}^T & P_{12[j]}^T & P_{22[j]}^T & R_{3j} & \cdots & P_{3(w-1)[j]} & P_{3w[j]} & P_{3(w+1)[j]} \\ \cdots & \cdots & \cdots & \cdots & \cdots & \cdots & \cdots & \cdots \\ S_{(w-1)j}^T & P_{1(w-1)[j]}^T & P_{2(w-1)[j]}^T & P_{3(w-1)[j]}^T & \cdots & R_{(w-1)j} & P_{ww[j]} & P_{w(w+1)[j]} \\ S_{wj}^T & P_{1w[j]}^T & P_{2w[j]}^T & P_{3w[j]}^T & \cdots & P_{w(w)[j]}^T & R_{wj} & P_{(w+1)(w+1)[j]} \\ S_{(w+1)j}^T & P_{1(w+1)[j]}^T & P_{2(w+1)[j]}^T & P_{3(w+1)[j]}^T & \cdots & P_{w(w+1)[j]}^T & P_{(w+1)(w+1)[j]}^T & R_{(w+1)j} \end{pmatrix}$$

for $i \in \{1, 2, ..., w+1\}$, where $Q_i \in \mathbb{R}^{(2n_f-k+1)\times(2n_f-k+1)}$, $S_{ij} \in \mathbb{R}^{(2n_f-k+1)\times 1}$, and R_{ij} for $j \in \{1, 2, ..., w+1\}$ and the other coefficients are scalars.

2. Compute the following matrices:

$$G := \begin{pmatrix} R_{11} & P_{n_f n_f[1]} & \dots & P_{(w+1)2[1]} & P_{(w+1)1[1]} \\ P^T_{(w+1)(w+1)[2]} & R_{22} & \dots & P_{w2[2]} & P_{w1[2]} \\ \dots & \dots & \dots & \dots & \dots \\ P^T_{(w+1)2[w]} & P^T_{w2[w]} & \dots & R_{ww} & P_{11[w]} \\ P^T_{(w+1)1[w+1]} & P^T_{w1[w+1]} & \dots & P^T_{11[w+1]} & R_{(w+1)(w+1)} \end{pmatrix}$$

$$H_1 := \begin{pmatrix} -A & 0 & 0 & 0 & \dots & 0 \\ Q_1 & A^T & 0 & 0 & \dots & 0 \\ Q_2 & 0 & A^T & 0 & \dots & 0 \\ \dots & \dots & \dots & \dots & \dots & \dots \\ Q_p & 0 & 0 & A^T & \dots & 0 \\ Q_{p+1} & 0 & 0 & 0 & \dots & A^T \end{pmatrix}$$

$$H_2 := \begin{pmatrix} B_1 & B_2 & \dots & B_w & M \\ -S_{11} & -S_{21} & \dots & -S_{w1} & -S_{(w+1)1} \\ -S_{12} & -S_{22} & \dots & -S_{w2} & -S_{(w+1)2} \\ \dots & \dots & \dots & \dots & \dots \\ -S_{1w} & -S_{2w} & \dots & -S_{ww} & -S_{(w+1)w} \\ -S_{1(w+1)} & -S_{2(w+1)} & \dots & -S_{w(w+1)} & -S_{(w+1)(w+1)} \end{pmatrix}$$

$$H_3 := \begin{pmatrix} S^T_{11} & B^T_1 & 0 & \dots & 0 & 0 \\ S^T_{22} & 0 & B^T_2 & \dots & 0 & 0 \\ \dots & \dots & \dots & \dots & \dots & \dots \\ S^T_{ww} & 0 & 0 & \dots & B^T_w & 0 \\ S^T_{(w+1)(w+1)} & 0 & 0 & \dots & O & M^T \end{pmatrix}$$

where B_i is the ith column of matrix B, we can define the following matrix:

$$H := H_1 + H_2 G^{-1} H_3$$

4. After computing the eigenstructure of H, take $2n_f - k + 1$ positive eigenvalues and the corresponding eigenvectors v_i to write the following expression:[24]

[24]Notice that matrix H coincides up to a minus sign with the corresponding matrix in Chapter 2. Therefore we consider here the positive instead of negative eigenvalues of H. If matrix H has more than $2n - k + 1$ positive eigenvalues multiple equilibria arise, whereas if this matrix has less than $2n - k + 1$ positive eigenvalues no equilibrium exists (for more details see Engwerda (2005a)).

$$\begin{pmatrix} y \\ Y_1 \\ Y_2 \\ \dots \\ Y_w \\ Y_{w+1} \end{pmatrix} := \begin{pmatrix} v_1 & v_2 & \dots & v_{2n_f-k+1} \end{pmatrix} := V \in \mathbb{R}^{(2n_f-k+1)(n_f+2)\times n_f}$$

from which we can derive the optimal controls:

$$\begin{pmatrix} f_1(t) \\ f_2(t) \\ \dots \\ f_{n_f}(t) \\ i_U(t) \\ i_{C1}(t) \\ \dots \\ i_{C(n_f-k)}(t) \end{pmatrix} = -G^{-1} \begin{pmatrix} S_{11}^T + B_1^T K_1 \\ S_{22}^T + B_2^T K_2 \\ \dots \\ S_{pp}^T + B_p^T K_p \\ S_{pp}^T + M_{p+1}^T K_{p+1} \end{pmatrix} \begin{bmatrix} p \\ e \end{bmatrix} =: F \begin{bmatrix} p \\ e \end{bmatrix}$$

where $K_i := Y_i y^{-1}$ for $i \in \{1, 2, ..., w+1\}$.

5. Assume: $q = \begin{bmatrix} p \\ e \end{bmatrix}$. Rewrite the cost functions of the policymakers[25] and the dynamics of the model as $J_i(t) = \frac{1}{2}\int_0^\infty q^T \left[(I, F^T)\, M_i \begin{pmatrix} I \\ F \end{pmatrix} \right] q(t)\, dt$ and $\dot{q}(t) = (A + (Bn_f)\, F)\, q(t) =: A_{CL}\, q(t)$, respectively. The problem is then solved by considering:

$$J_i = q_0^T y_i q_0$$

where y_i solves the following Lyapunov equation (for $i \in \{1, 2, ..., 2n_f - k + 1\}$):

$$A_{CL}^T y_i + y_i A_{CL} + \frac{1}{2}(I, F^T)\, M_i \begin{pmatrix} I \\ F \end{pmatrix} = 0.$$

Cooperative solutions are achieved by using the same algorithm considering joint losses minimization and the factorizing M_is in a similar way.

[25] See also note the Appendix in Chapter 6.

7.8 Appendix B

Table 7.B.1 Definition of asymmetric bargaining power, pre-accession stage

π_1	1	1	1	1	1	1	1	1	1
π_2	2/3	1/3	1	1	1	1	1	1	1
π_3	4/9	2/9	1/3	1	1	1	1	1	1
π_4	1	1	1	1	1	1	1	1/2	1/2
π_5	1	1	1	1/2	1/2	1	1	1/2	1/2
π_6	1	1	1	1	1	3/4	1/4	1/2	1/2
π_7	1	1	1	1/2	1/2	3/4	1/4	1/2	1/2
π_8	1	1	1	1/3	2/3	1	1	1/2	1/2
π_9	4/9	2/9	1/3	1	1	1	1	1/2	1/2
π_{10}	4/9	2/9	1/3	1/2	1/2	1	1	1/2	1/2
π_{11}	4/9	2/9	1/3	1	1	3/4	1/4	1/2	1/2
π_{12}	4/9	2/9	1/3	1/2	1/2	3/4	1/4	1/2	1/2
π_{13}	4/9	2/9	1/3	1/3	2/3	1	1	1/2	1/2
π_{14}	2/3	1/3	1	1	1	1	1	1/2	1/2
π_{15}	2/3	1/3	1	1/2	1/2	1	1	1/2	1/2
π_{16}	2/3	1/3	1	1	1	3/4	1/4	1/2	1/2
π_{17}	2/3	1/3	1	1/2	1/2	3/4	1/4	1/2	1/2
π_{18}	2/3	1/3	1	1/3	2/3	1	1	1/2	1/2
π_{19}	1/2	1/4	1/4	1	1	1	1	1/2	1/2
π_{20}	1/2	1/4	1/4	1	1	3/4	1/4	1/2	1/2
π_{21}	2/3	1/3	1	1	1	1	1	1/2	1/2
π_{22}	2/3	1/3	1	1	1	3/4	1/4	1/2	1/2
π_{23}	1/2	1/2	1	1	1	1	1	1/2	1/2
π_{24}	1/2	1/2	1	1	1	3/4	1/4	1/2	1/2
π_{25}	2/5	1/5	2/5	1	1	1	1	1/2	1/2
π_{26}	2/5	1/5	2/5	1	1/2	1/2	1	1/2	1/2
π_{27}	1/2	1/2	1	1	1	1	1	1/2	1/2
π_{28}	1/2	1/2	1	1	1/2	1/2	1	1/2	1/2
π_{29}	1/3	2/3	1	1	1	1	1	1/2	1/2
π_{30}	1/3	2/3	1	1	1/2	1/2	1	1/2	1/2
π_{31}	1/3	1/6	1/6	1/3	1	1	1	1/2	1/2
π_{32}	1/2	1/2	1/2	1/2	1	1	1	1/2	1/2
π_{33}	2/5	1/5	2/5	1	1	1	1	1/2	1/2
π_{34}	1/4	1/4	1/2	1	1	1	1	1/2	1/2
π_{35}	2/3	1/3	1/3	2/3	1	1	1	1/2	1/2
π_{36}	1/4	1/8	1/8	1/4	1/4	1	1	1	1
π_{37}	12/79	6/79	9/79	6/79	6/79	12/79	4/79	12/79	12/79

Table 7.B.2 Definition of asymmetric bargaining power, post-accession stage

π_{38}	1	1	1	1	1	1	1	1
π_{39}	2/3	1/3	1	1	1	1	1	1
π_{40}	3/8	3/16	3/16	1/4	1	1	1	1
π_{41}	1	1	1	1	1	1	1/2	1/2
π_{42}	1	1	1	1	3/4	1/4	1/2	1/2
π_{43}	3/8	3/16	3/16	1/4	1	1	1/2	1/2
π_{44}	3/8	3/16	3/16	1/4	3/4	1/4	1/2	1/2
π_{45}	1/2	1/4	1/4	1	1	1	1/2	1/2
π_{46}	1/2	1/4	1/4	1	3/4	1/4	1/2	1/2
π_{47}	2/3	1/3	1	1	1	1	1/2	1/2
π_{48}	2/3	1/3	1	1	3/4	1/4	1/2	1/2
π_{49}	1	1/2	1/2	1	1	1	1/2	1/2
π_{50}	1	1/2	1/2	1	3/4	1/4	1/2	1/2
π_{51}	2/3	1/3	1	1	1	1	1/2	1/2
π_{52}	2/3	1/3	1	1	3/4	1/4	1/2	1/2
π_{53}	1/2	1/2	1	1	1	1	1/2	1/2
π_{54}	1	1/3	2/3	1	1	1	1/2	1/2
π_{55}	1	1	1/3	2/3	1	1	1/2	1/2
π_{56}	2/3	1/3	1/3	2/3	1	1	1/2	1/2
π_{57}	2/3	1/3	1/3	2/3	1	1	1/2	1/2
π_{58}	1/2	1/2	1/2	1/2	1	1	1/2	1/2
π_{59}	2/5	1/5	2/5	1	1	1	1/2	1/2
π_{60}	2/5	1/5	2/5	1	1	1	1/2	1/2
π_{61}	1/4	1/4	1/2	1	1	1	1/2	1/2
π_{62}	1/3	1/6	1/6	1/3	1	1	1/2	1/2
π_{63}	1/4	1/8	1/8	1/4	1/4	1	1	1
π_{64}	1/6	1/12	1/12	1/9	1/6	1/18	1/6	1/6

7.9 Appendix C

Table 7.C.1 - Optimal losses for $(sc_1^P,\ s_{0S}^P)$ multiplied by 10

	π_1	π_2	π_3	π_4	π_5	π_6	π_7	π_8	π_9	π_{10}
C1	2.46207	2.46233	2.48693	2.46118	2.46471	2.46471	2.47458	2.46060	2.48220	2.47958
C2	2.46207	2.46233	2.48693	2.46118	2.46471	2.46471	2.47458	2.46060	2.48220	2.47958
CB	4.92611	4.91515	4.87089	4.90548	4.88948	4.88948	4.88050	4.90008	4.86797	4.88093
C3	2.46206	2.46046	2.46473	2.46024	2.48397	2.46178	2.47896	2.46021	2.47406	2.47861
CB3	4.92610	4.91862	4.88887	4.90512	4.87011	4.88865	4.86270	4.89679	4.88285	4.87943
C4	2.46206	2.46046	2.46473	2.46024	2.46178	2.48397	2.47896	2.46021	2.47406	2.49238
CB4	4.92610	4.91862	4.88887	4.90512	4.88865	4.87011	4.86270	4.89679	4.88285	4.89134
C5	2.46206	2.46046	2.46473	2.49041	2.48397	2.48397	2.47896	2.48810	2.48020	2.47861
CB5	4.92610	4.91862	4.88887	4.88493	4.87011	4.87011	4.86270	4.87978	4.86735	4.87943
WIX	-	-	-	14.77%	11.39%	11.39%	8.34%	10.34%	10.31%	7.49%
CFI	4.46%	4.75%	31.20%	0.00%	3.16%	3.16%	7.18%	4.87%	17.73%	23.51%

	π_{11}	π_{12}	π_{13}	π_{14}	π_{15}	π_{16}	π_{17}	π_{18}	π_{19}	π_{20}
C1	2.47958	2.48004	2.48140	2.46129	2.46480	2.46480	2.47471	2.46068	2.46153	2.46529
C2	2.47958	2.48004	2.48140	2.46129	2.46480	2.46480	2.47471	2.46068	2.46153	2.46529
CB	4.88093	4.92068	4.86717	4.89770	4.88479	4.88479	4.87852	4.89311	4.88708	4.87816
C3	2.49238	2.48074	2.47418	2.45939	2.48252	2.46152	2.47825	2.45935	2.45986	2.46163
CB3	4.89134	4.91778	4.88077	4.89994	4.86742	4.88568	4.86174	4.89239	4.88670	4.87747
C4	2.47861	2.48074	2.47418	2.45939	2.46152	2.48252	2.47825	2.45935	2.45809	2.47996
CB4	4.87943	4.91778	4.88077	4.89994	4.88568	4.86742	4.86174	4.89239	4.89133	4.86275
C5	2.47861	2.48074	2.47944	2.48822	2.48252	2.48252	2.47825	2.48613	2.48448	2.47996
CB5	4.87943	4.91778	4.86650	4.88006	4.86742	4.86742	4.86174	4.87553	4.87201	4.86275
WIX	7.49%	5.11%	5.86%	11.34%	8.05%	8.05%	5.06%	7.13%	5.84%	2.74%
CFI	23.51%	30.69%	18.18%	3.94%	6.75%	6.75%	9.82%	6.66%	8.41%	10.74%

	π_{21}	π_{22}	π_{23}	π_{24}	π_{25}	π_{26}	π_{27}	π_{28}	π_{29}	π_{20}
C1	2.46173	2.46523	2.46019	2.46437	2.46153	2.46529	2.46173	2.46523	2.46019	2.46437
C2	2.46019	2.46437	2.46173	2.46523	2.46153	2.46529	2.46019	2.46437	2.46173	2.46523
CB	4.89885	4.88534	4.89885	4.88534	4.88708	4.87816	4.89885	4.88534	4.89885	4.88534
C3	2.46014	2.46167	2.46014	2.46167	2.45809	2.47996	2.45938	2.48243	2.45938	2.48243
CB3	4.89720	4.88374	4.89720	4.88374	4.89133	4.86275	4.89983	4.86723	4.89983	4.86723
C4	2.45938	2.48243	2.45938	2.48243	2.45986	2.46163	2.46014	2.46167	2.46014	2.46167
CB4	4.89983	4.86723	4.89983	4.86723	4.88670	4.87747	4.89720	4.88374	4.89720	4.88374
C5	2.48818	2.48243	2.48818	2.48243	2.48448	2.47996	2.48818	2.48243	2.48818	2.48243
CB5	4.87996	4.86723	4.87996	4.86723	4.87201	4.86275	4.87996	4.86723	4.87996	4.86723
WIX	10.83%	7.54%	10.83%	7.54%	5.84%	2.74%	10.83%	7.54%	10.83%	7.54%
CFI	4.13%	6.68%	4.13%	6.68%	8.41%	10.74%	4.13%	6.68%	4.13%	6.68%

	π_{31}	π_{32}	π_{33}	π_{34}	π_{35}	π_{36}	π_{37}
C1	2.46170	2.46074	2.46239	2.45903	2.46074	2.46075	2.49812
C2	2.46170	2.46074	2.45903	2.46239	2.46074	2.46075	2.49812
CB	4.87609	4.89292	4.88919	4.88919	4.89292	4.87083	4.77473
C3	2.45936	2.45928	2.45991	2.45991	2.45928	2.45902	2.49342
CB3	4.87558	4.89259	4.88641	4.88641	4.89259	4.87041	4.76837
C4	2.45936	2.45928	2.45991	2.45991	2.45928	2.45902	2.49342
CB4	4.87558	4.89259	4.88641	4.88641	4.89259	4.87041	4.76837
C5	2.48005	2.48613	2.48441	2.48441	2.48613	2.45902	2.49342
CB5	4.86297	4.87553	4.87184	4.87184	4.87553	4.87041	4.76837
WIX	0.00%	7.12%	4.95%	4.95%	7.12%	-	-
CFI	12.87%	6.67%	9.16%	9.16%	6.67%	6.50%	50.72%

Table 7.C.2 - Optimal losses for $(sc_1^A,\ s_{0S}^A)$ multiplied by 10

	π_{38}	π_{39}	π_{40}	π_{41}	π_{42}	π_{43}	π_{44}	π_{45}	π_{46}
C1	2.46207	2.46242	2.48564	2.46105	2.46458	2.48263	2.48274	2.46121	2.46501
C2	2.46207	2.46242	2.48564	2.46105	2.46458	2.48263	2.48274	2.46121	2.46501
C3	2.46207	2.46019	2.48564	2.46105	2.46458	2.48263	2.48274	2.46121	2.46501
CB	4.92613	4.91676	4.86414	4.90616	4.88974	4.88012	4.92311	4.88888	4.87945
C4	2.46204	2.46022	2.47501	2.45903	2.48298	2.49455	2.48020	2.45616	2.47925
CB4	4.92611	4.91890	4.88010	4.90533	4.86884	4.89142	4.92173	4.89206	4.86165
C5	2.46204	2.46022	2.47501	2.49004	2.48298	2.47728	2.48020	2.48423	2.47925
CB5	4.92611	4.91890	4.88010	4.88500	4.86884	4.88019	4.92173	4.87245	4.86165
WIX	-	-	-	14.24%	10.91%	4.02%	0.00%	7.57%	4.56%
CFI	5.47%	6.39%	48.75%	0.00%	3.13%	35.16%	40.83%	6.07%	8.84%

	π_{47}	π_{48}	π_{49}	π_{50}	π_{51}	π_{52}	π_{53}	π_{54}	π_{55}
C1	2.46134	2.46485	2.46001	2.46423	2.46134	2.46485	2.46178	2.46020	2.46020
C2	2.46134	2.46485	2.46134	2.46485	2.46001	2.46423	2.46020	2.46178	2.46020
C3	2.46001	2.46423	2.46134	2.46485	2.46134	2.46485	2.46020	2.46020	2.46178
CB	4.89956	4.88581	4.89956	4.88581	4.89956	4.88581	4.89998	4.89998	4.89998
C4	2.45792	2.48157	2.45792	2.48157	2.45792	2.48157	2.45865	2.45865	2.45865
CB4	4.90027	4.86610	4.90027	4.86610	4.90027	4.86610	4.89741	4.89741	4.89741
C5	2.48786	2.48157	2.48786	2.48157	2.48786	2.48157	2.48772	2.48772	2.48772
CB5	4.88021	4.86610	4.88021	4.86610	4.88021	4.86610	4.87990	4.87990	4.87990
WIX	11.29%	8.07%	11.29%	8.07%	11.29%	8.07%	10.54%	10.54%	10.54%
CFI	3.13%	6.09%	3.13%	6.09%	3.13%	6.09%	3.88%	3.88%	3.88%

	π_{56}	π_{57}	π_{58}	π_{59}	π_{60}	π_{61}	π_{62}	π_{63}	π_{64}
C1	2.46050	2.46050	2.46076	2.46188	2.46188	2.45875	2.46147	2.46064	2.48331
C2	2.46050	2.46076	2.46050	2.46188	2.45875	2.46188	2.46147	2.46064	2.48331
C3	2.46076	2.46050	2.46050	2.45875	2.46188	2.46188	2.46147	2.46064	2.48331
CB	4.89403	4.89403	4.89403	4.88962	4.88962	4.88962	4.87771	4.87236	4.79249
C4	2.45757	2.45757	2.45757	2.45783	2.45783	2.45783	2.45660	2.45695	2.48102
CB4	4.89298	4.89298	4.89298	4.88715	4.88715	4.88715	4.87647	4.87132	4.78536
C5	2.48573	2.48573	2.48573	2.48401	2.48401	2.48401	2.47968	2.45695	2.48102
CB5	4.87562	4.87562	4.87562	4.87194	4.87194	4.87194	4.86300	4.87132	4.78536
WIX	7.78%	7.78%	7.78%	6.23%	6.23%	6.23%	2.54%	-	-
CFI	5.66%	5.66%	5.66%	7.47%	7.47%	7.47%	10.24%	5.43%	74.03%

Chapter 8

World-wide Regional Policy Coordination

8.1 Introduction

In Chapter 7, the open MU was studied and it was analyzed how the interactions with countries that are outside the MU imply additional spillovers and coordination issues. Moreover, the possibility that countries enter the MU was investigated, resulting in a number of new interesting insights. In this chapter the analysis takes a final step by considering the setting of multiple economic and currency unions.

The Bretton-Woods monetary system, briefly discussed in Chapter 1, was the most important form of international monetary policy coordination after World War II. Since then, commitment to macroeconomic cooperation among G-7 countries has been relatively weak (see Currie (1993)). However, in an increasingly integrated and globalized world, the importance of macroeconomic spillovers and resulting externalities has significantly increased. In particular, contagion effects can provoke regional crises with high costs in terms of welfare. Consequently, a higher degree of integration and globalization, has also broadened the scope for international policy coordination. In the context of our model, several additional interesting questions can be asked concerning international macroeconomic policy coordination, e.g. what are the scope and effects of coordination of policies in the form of global or regional arrangements like e.g. the EU, NAFTA, ASEAN, MERCOSUR, etc.? Does the need for coordination apply mainly to monetary policy coordination or does it also arise in case of fiscal policy? How are the benefits of international economic policy coordination related to the degree of symmetry of shocks, i.e. whether shocks are global, regional or country-specific? Answers to these questions may also vary under different assumptions about the degree of symmetry of countries in economic structures, sizes policy preferences and bargaining power.

An aspect that also deserves our attention is the possibility of coalition formation in the form of blocks of countries. In general, a block is understood as a group of countries that decide to coordinate policies such as trade, environmental, monetary, fiscal and regulatory policies. In this chapter, we consider that actual interactions often take place in international negotiations between blocks of countries. In this way, more insights can be obtained on the likely future talks which revolve around the stabilization of exchange rates and trade issues among blocks like the E(M)U, NAFTA, ASEAN, MERCOSUR, among others.

From the international macroeconomic point of view, crucial variables to stabilize are exchange rates, since these determine a substantial share of the spillovers and resulting externalities between different currency blocks. Since the case where all central banks would collapse in a unique international institution and a world currency would be created is quite far from the present day situation, these aspects of international coordination and exchange rate management are highly topical. For example, the recent swings of the US$ have shown that exchange rates may have major implications and it could well be argued that policy coordination needs to be given serious attention since the alternative of a completely non-cooperative international policy framework is likely to be highly disruptive.

Problems of enforcement arise particularly in the area of international policy coordination due to the lack of a supranational authority and free-riding incentives. Consequently, even in the presence of significant spillovers/externalities and a clear room for international coordination of macroeconomic policies, the actual implementation may fail because some countries may defect and it is notoriously difficult to impose sanctions in a context of sovereign states.

Regional blocks may internally coordinate their macroeconomic policies to internalize the externalities inside blocks. However, externally, they still face the question whether or not to coordinate macroeconomic policies with other blocks.

In this chapter we emphasize that, in the case of an MU that interacts with the Rest of the World (ROW), internal coordination issues, as analyzed in the previous chapters, remain important. In other words, internal coordination issues continue to matter but are possibly complicated further by external coordination of the MU. In principle, if shocks are restrained to the MU and international interactions limited, internal coordination is the most appropriate tool. If, however, shocks are of an external origin and the MU is strongly integrated with the ROW, internal policy coordination alone is not enough/inadequate and external coordination arrangements are needed. International monetary policy coordination is often more important than international fiscal policy coordination since it has a direct impact on a very important source of international spillovers, the exchange rates. Here, coordination helps to provide a well-considered adjustment of exchange rates, whereas uncoordinated policies are an invitation for disruptive exchange rate adjustments that are inducing large spillovers and resulting externalities.

To focus our analysis more precisely we propose six research questions. We consider them to be relevant in a world-wide context:

1. Should each of the two monetary blocks (MUs) coordinate their respective fiscal and/or fiscal and monetary policies internally?
2. Should agents of the monetary blocks (MUs) coordinate their respective fiscal and/or fiscal and monetary policies?
3. Is the grand fiscal coordination regime profitable for countries?
4. Should monetary players coordinate their policies at the international (global) level (Bretton Woods)?
5. Is the coordination mentioned in question 4 profitable if fiscal players also coordinate globally?
6. Should all the players coordinate their policies as a world coalition?

In our analysis we will try to suggest answers to all these questions; however, for the reason of brevity, we cannot pursue a full analysis of all the cases which are in the scope of our interest. Instead, we will indicate the most interesting outcomes of simulations and their interpretations. In general, we may attempt to answer the above questions in two ways:

- *normative way* - focussing on the global profitability of a given cooperation arrangement, i.e. the answer to a particular question is affirmative if a regime is advantageous from the social (global) point of view;
- *positive way* - focussing on the actual feasibility of a given regime.

After a general analysis of the simulation outcomes, the normative answers will be obtained from the analysis of welfare indices, whereas the positive ones by methods of endogenous coalition formation.

The chapter is structured as follows: Section 8.2 provides general assumptions about the setting, the model and its parameterization. The numerical simulation analysis in Section 8.3 aims to deliver more insights about the interaction between MU and non-MU countries and the role of various asymmetries. Finally, Section 8.4 summarizes the main conclusions derived from the analysis.

8.2 Model of international economy

We consider the setting developed in Chapter 7, where it is assumed that N players interact. They can be divided in two groups: a group F of n_f countries, governed by a fiscal authority j ($j \in F$) and n_b central banks b ($b \in B$). The underlying economic multi-MU model was already presented in Section 7.2. We are interested in potential losses of individual countries from different shocks. We focus on the impact of symmetric and asymmetric price and exchange rate shocks, making a distinction between whether they hit all countries, one or more members of an MU or an outside country.

8.2.1 A setting for two MUs

Our numerical analysis considers 6 countries: $C1$ and $C2$ are assumed to be the members of MU($CB1$) and $C3$ and $C4$ of MU($CB2$); $C5$ and $C6$ keep an independent currency. Therefore, the world economy consists of 6 fiscal authorities Cj for $j = \{1, ..., 6\}$ and 4 monetary authorities CBk for $k = \{1, 2, 3, 4\}$.

To keep our setting of 10 players tractable, we consider only a reduced set Π^R of feasible CSs. Out of all possible CSs, we focus on 19 CSs that appear to be the most interesting ones to analyze. The exact definition of Π^R is presented in Table 8.1.

Table 8.1 The reduced set Π^R of feasible CSs

π_1	C1 C2 CB1 C3 C4 CB2 C5 CB3 C6 CB4
π_2	(C1,C2) CB1 C3 C4 CB2 C5 CB3 C6 CB4
π_3	C1 C2 CB1 (C3,C4) CB2 C5 CB3 C6 CB4
π_4	(C1,C2,C5) CB1 C3 C4 CB2 CB3 C6 CB4
π_5	(C1,C2,CB1) C3 C4 CB2 C5 CB3 C6 CB4
π_6	C1 C2 CB1 (C3,C4,CB2) C5 CB3 C6 CB4
π_7	(C1,C2) CB1 (C3,C4) CB2 C5 CB3 C6 CB4
π_8	(C1,C2,CB1) (C3,C4,CB2) C5 CB3 C6 CB4
π_9	(C1,C2,C3,C4) CB1 CB2 C5 CB3 C6 CB4
π_{10}	(C1,C2,CB1,C3,C4,CB2) C5 CB3 C6 CB4
π_{11}	C1 C2 CB1 C3 C4 CB2 (C5,CB3) C6 CB4
π_{12}	(C1,C2,CB1) C3 C4 CB2 (C5,CB3) C6 CB4
π_{13}	C1 C2 CB1 (C3,C4,CB2) (C5,CB3) C6 CB4
π_{14}	(C1,C2,CB1) (C3,C4,CB2) (C5,CB3) C6 CB4
π_{15}	(C1,C2,C3,C4,C5) CB1 CB2 CB3 C6 CB4
π_{16}	(C1,C2,C3,C4,C5,C6) CB1 CB2 CB3 CB4
π_{17}	C1 C2 C3 C4 C5 C6 (CB1,CB2,CB3,CB4)
π_{18}	(C1,C2,C3,C4,C5,C6) (CB1,CB2,CB3,CB4)
π_{19}	(C1,C2,CB1,C3,C4,CB2,C5,CB3,C6,CB4)

Policy regimes in Table 8.1 range from the fully non-cooperative CS, π_1, to world-wide full cooperation, π_{19}. CSs π_2 and π_3 are the *intra*-MU fiscal coordination cases, a topic studied in detail in Chapter 3. CSs π_5 and π_6 are the cases of *intra*-MU monetary and fiscal coordination, which was introduced in Chapter 4. CS π_7 implies internal fiscal coordination in each of both MUs, whereas CS π_8 implies internal full coordination. CS π_9 is a regime of fiscal coordination between both MUs, whereas CS π_{10} is a regime of fiscal and monetary coordination between both MUs. CS π_{14} is the regime of full internal coordination in both MUs and between $C5$ and its central bank. CSs π_{11}, π_{12} and π_{13} are partial arrangements of π_{14}. In π_{15}, the first five countries cooperate. Full fiscal coordination (grand fiscal coalition) takes place in π_{16} and full monetary coordination in π_{17}. CS π_{18} implies full fiscal and full monetary coordination. These assumptions appear e.g. to be consistent with the G-3 meetings of Euroland, the US and Japan and with the Bretton-Woods system, respectively, where for clarity MU($CB1$) can be interpreted as the EMU, MU($CB2$) as another (potential) MU in the world, $C5$ as the USA and $C6$ as the ROW (with, principally, Japan).

Regarding our six questions in the introductory section, we may now relate each of them to one or more specific CS(s). The first question on internal coordination in two monetary blocks concerns (among others) CSs π_7 and π_8, whereas the second question on coordination between two monetary blocks concerns CSs π_9 and π_{10}. The grand fiscal coalition (question 3) emerges in π_{16}. In this CS all the CBs play non-cooperatively. The Bretton-Woods type of arrangement, in which all the CBs coordinate their policies (question 4), is represented by π_{17}. To answer question 5 on simultaneous coordination between fiscal players and between CBs, CS π_{18} should be studied. Finally, CS π_{19} provide insights on the effects of world-wide policy coordination.

Note that, in contrast to Chapter 7, Π^R in Table 8.1 is not the MU-reduced set of CSs, i.e. Π^R does not meet the conditions of Definition 5.19. For instance, in this setting we assume that CBs may cooperate with each other in a monetary coalition. Hence, we cannot utilize here the OMG(MU), the ROMG(MU) and the EMG(Δ, MU) concepts of Subsection 5.4.2 in Chapter 5. However, Π^R does have the independence property (see Definition 5.3) and, therefore, a (slightly modified) concept of the EMG(Γ) can be applied (see Algorithm 5.7 in the Appendix of Chapter 5). To correctly define the EMG(Γ) for this setting, we have to modify the players' strategy spaces in Definition 5.17. More in detail, each player's strategy set should contain only those messages that correspond to (possibly trivial) coalitions in Table 8.1 in which a given player participates. For instance, $C5$'s strategy space should be (re-)defined as follows: $\Sigma_{C5} := \{C^1_{C5} := (C5),\ C^2_{C5} := (C1,\ C2,\ C5),\ C^3_{C5} := (C5,\ CB3),\ C^4_{C5} := (C1,\ C2,\ C3,\ C4,\ C5),\ C^5_{C5} := (C1,\ C2,\ C3,\ C4,\ C5,\ C6),\ C^6_{C5} := (C1,\ C2,\ CB1,\ C3,\ C4,\ CB2,\ C5,\ CB3,\ C6,\ CB4)\}$. The EMG($\Gamma$), defined in this way, will be denoted as the EMG*(Γ).

8.2.2 Parameterization

We follow the lines of Chapters 6 and 7 in the parameterization of our model. In the symmetric scenario, we assume that all direct price, output and competitiveness spillovers are equal to 0.08. In this way, the total value of direct (structural) spillovers, experienced by each country from the 5 other countries, is 0.4 as it is also the case in the two previous chapters.

Similarly to Chapter 7, we consider 3 scenarios:

1. The benchmark scenario with a symmetric economic structure (sc_1) - all countries are assumed to be symmetric in the structural and preference parameters and sizes. As in all the previous cases, fiscal players' preferences are asymmetric w.r.t. CBs' preferences. The following set of parameters underlies this baseline case: $\gamma_{j^b} = 0.2$, $\eta_{j^b} = 0.75$, $\rho_{j^b\ell} = 0.08$, $\delta_{j^b\ell} = 0.08$,

$\zeta_{j^b} = 0.25$, $\varsigma_{j^b\ell} = 0.08$, $\alpha_{j^b} = 0.2$, $\beta_{j^b} = 0.4$, $\chi_{j^b} = \chi_U^M = \chi_{j^b}^M = 0.4$, $\alpha_U^M = \alpha_{j^b}^M = 0.4$, $\beta_U^M = \beta_{j^b}^M = 0.2$, $\omega_{j^b} = 0.5$, $\theta = 0.10$.

2. An asymmetric structural scenario (sc_2) - in this example, we consider a situation where the countries are marked by asymmetries in the economic structure. In particular, we assume that $C1$ is twice as big as $C2$, MU ($CB1$) is twice as big as MU($CB2$), and $C5$ and $C6$ are equally big as MU($CB1$). Since $C3$ and $C4$ are relatively smaller countries, they are more sensitive to output, price and competitiveness spillovers from $C1$, $C2, C5$ and $C6$. Hence, we assume the following numerical values for parameter matrices defined in Appendix A of Chapter 7:[1]

$$\rho := \varsigma := \begin{bmatrix} 0 & 4/85 & 3/85 & 3/85 & 12/85 & 12/85 \\ 8/95 & 0 & 3/95 & 3/95 & 12/95 & 12/95 \\ 5/61 & 3/73 & 0 & 2/65 & 8/65 & 8/65 \\ 5/61 & 3/73 & 2/65 & 0 & 8/65 & 8/65 \\ 8/75 & 4/75 & 1/25 & 1/25 & 0 & 4/25 \\ 8/75 & 4/75 & 1/25 & 1/25 & 4/25 & 0 \end{bmatrix} \text{ and}$$

$$\delta := \begin{bmatrix} -4/10 & 4/85 & 3/85 & 3/85 & 12/85 & 12/85 \\ 8/95 & -4/10 & 3/95 & 3/95 & 12/95 & 12/95 \\ 5/61 & 3/73 & -4/10 & 2/65 & 8/65 & 8/65 \\ 5/61 & 3/73 & 2/65 & -4/10 & 8/65 & 8/65 \\ 8/75 & 4/75 & 1/25 & 1/25 & -4/10 & 4/25 \\ 8/75 & 4/75 & 1/25 & 1/25 & 4/25 & -4/10 \end{bmatrix}.$$

Since $C2$ is half of $C1$, $CB1$ is more concerned with the economic performance in $C1$ than in $C2$, implying that countries' weights in $CB1$'s loss function are asymmetric: $\omega_1 = 2/3$ and $\omega_2 = 1/3$ (see also Section 7.2).

3. An asymmetric structural scenario with asymmetric bargaining power (sc_3), where we add asymmetric bargaining power τ to the previous scenario. More specifically, $C1$ is assumed to have a twice as high bargaining power as $C2$; in the full MU coalitions, the CB is assumed to possess the average fiscal players' power; moreover, the MU($CB2$) is assumed to have only half of MU($CB1$)'s power, $C5$ is twice as powerful as $CB3$ and $C6$ is three times more powerful than $CB4$. Table 8.A.1 in the Appendix presents the exact definition of τ.

Note that sc_3 is (much) more realistic than sc_2, because it takes into account that larger countries have a larger bargaining power.

8.2.3 Shocks

Six different types of shocks are analyzed:

[1] Note that, as in Chapters 6 and 7, all rows of the off-diagonal elements of spillover matrices ρ, δ and ς add to 0.4.

1. a symmetric negative supply (price) shock:[2] $s_{0SP} := [0.01;\ 0.01;\ 0.01;\ 0.01;\ 0.01;\ 0.01;\ 0;\ 0;\ 0]^T$;
2. an asymmetric negative supply shock that hits only country $C5$: $s_{0AP(C5)} := [0;\ 0;\ 0;\ 0;\ 0.01;\ 0;\ 0;\ 0;\ 0]^T$;
3. an asymmetric negative supply shock that hits only country $C1$: $s_{0AP(C1)} := [0.01;\ 0;\ 0;\ 0;\ 0;\ 0;\ 0;\ 0;\ 0]^T$;
4. an asymmetric negative supply shock that hits both members of MU($CB1$) = $MU1$ in equal size: $s_{0AP(MU1)} := [0.01;\ 0.01;\ 0;\ 0;\ 0;\ 0;\ 0;\ 0;\ 0]^T$;
5. an asymmetric exchange rate shock that hits only $C5$'s currency: $s_{0AE(C5)} := [0;\ 0;\ 0;\ 0;\ 0;\ 0;\ 0;\ 0.01;\ 0]^T$; and, finally,
6. an asymmetric exchange rate shock that hits MU($CB2$) = $MU2$'s currency: $s_{0AE(MU2)} := [0;\ 0;\ 0;\ 0;\ 0;\ 0;\ 0.01;\ 0;\ 0]^T$.

8.3 Results of numerical simulations

As in previous chapters, we focus our discussion on the impact of different shocks on the symmetric scenario sc_1, while the numerical simulations for both asymmetric scenarios sc_2 and sc_3, characterized by the structural asymmetry of the model and structural and bargaining power asymmetry, respectively, will be analyzed more briefly. All the tables with (optimal) losses for these 2 asymmetric scenarios, each under 6 different shocks, can be found in Appendix A.

8.3.1 Symmetric scenario sc_1

Symmetric price shock s_{0SP}

For the symmetric price shock, s_{0SP}, we compare the model results with the relevant cases in Chapters 6 and 7, i.e. (sc_1, p_{0S}) and $(sc_1^P, s_{0S}^P)/(sc_1^A, s_{0S}^A)$, respectively. This comparison is feasible since it is assumed that the sum of the direct spillovers is equal (to 0.4) over these chapters. First, consider the non-cooperative regime π.[1] Losses in the second column of Table 8.2 are very similar to those in the second column of Tables 6.2 and 7.2. In two open economy settings (Tables 7.2 and 8.2) we may compare CS π_2 in which two countries of the first MU create a fiscal coalition. Both tables show that in such a regime cooperating players lose and all the other fiscal players gain. Also further comparison of corresponding CSs is possible, for instance, π_5 from Table 8.2 with π_3 from Table 7.2 and with π_{40} from Table 7.6. The similar patterns of losses obtained in all these cases are the argument in favour of the robustness of our results.

[2]Note that in this setting, there are 3 nominal exchange rates w.r.t. MU($CB1$)'s anchor currency.

Table 8.2 Optimal losses for (sc_1, s_{0SP})[3]

	π_1	π_2	π_3	π_4	π_5	π_6	π_7	π_8	π_9	π_{10}
C1	0.2462	0.2462	0.2461	0.2462	0.2481	0.2463	0.2461	0.2476	0.2461	0.2495
C2	0.2462	0.2462	0.2461	0.2462	0.2481	0.2463	0.2461	0.2476	0.2461	0.2495
CB1	0.4930	0.4921	0.4924	0.4909	0.4881	0.4899	0.4916	0.4875	0.4896	0.4845
C3	0.2462	0.2461	0.2462	0.2459	0.2463	0.2481	0.2461	0.2476	0.2461	0.2495
C4	0.2462	0.2461	0.2462	0.2459	0.2463	0.2481	0.2461	0.2476	0.2461	0.2495
CB2	0.4930	0.4924	0.4921	0.4915	0.4899	0.4881	0.4916	0.4875	0.4896	0.4845
C5	0.2462	0.2461	0.2461	0.2462	0.2462	0.2462	0.2460	0.2479	0.2456	0.2475
CB3	0.4930	0.4924	0.4924	0.4909	0.4898	0.4898	0.4919	0.4887	0.4903	0.4865
C6	0.2462	0.2461	0.2461	0.2459	0.2462	0.2462	0.2460	0.2479	0.2456	0.2475
CB4	0.4930	0.4924	0.4924	0.4915	0.4898	0.4898	0.4919	0.4887	0.4903	0.4865
WIX	1.33%	1.24%	1.24%	1.09%	1.02%	1.02%	1.16%	1.02%	0.92%	0.91%
CFI	0.00%	0.09%	0.09%	0.23%	0.53%	0.53%	0.17%	0.83%	0.40%	1.33%

	π_{11}	π_{12}	π_{13}	π_{14}	π_{15}	π_{16}	π_{17}	π_{18}	π_{19}
C1	0.2460	0.2477	0.2469	0.2475	0.2460	0.2459	0.2462	0.2458	0.2486
C2	0.2460	0.2477	0.2469	0.2475	0.2460	0.2459	0.2462	0.2458	0.2486
CB1	0.4913	0.4872	0.4889	0.4888	0.4883	0.4871	0.4929	0.4879	0.4784
C3	0.2460	0.2469	0.2477	0.2475	0.2460	0.2459	0.2462	0.2458	0.2486
C4	0.2460	0.2469	0.2477	0.2475	0.2460	0.2459	0.2462	0.2458	0.2486
CB2	0.4913	0.4889	0.4872	0.4888	0.4883	0.4871	0.4929	0.4879	0.4784
C5	0.2485	0.2477	0.2477	0.2476	0.2460	0.2458	0.2462	0.2454	0.2485
CB3	0.4893	0.4871	0.4871	0.4886	0.4883	0.4871	0.4929	0.4877	0.4779
C6	0.2460	0.2466	0.2466	0.2495	0.2454	0.2458	0.2462	0.2454	0.2485
CB4	0.4913	0.4888	0.4888	0.4896	0.4891	0.4871	0.4929	0.4877	0.4779
WIX	1.11%	0.93%	0.93%	1.14%	0.75%	0.58%	1.32%	0.62%	0.00%
CFI	0.35%	0.76%	0.76%	0.76%	0.57%	0.74%	0.01%	0.70%	2.13%

The symmetry of losses in π_1 is broken up in π_2 and other CSs when some players coordinate their policies. The internal (fiscal or full) coordination in both MUs leads to effects, being different from those in the case where internal coordination takes place in only one MU. The internal fiscal coordination in both MUs, π_7, is profitable w.r.t. π_1 for all the players involved. Considering π_8 vs. π_7 and π_1, it is clear that none of the fiscal players would prefer full MU coalitions over full MU fiscal coalitions. Consequently, for (sc_1, p_{0S}) the answer to question 1 is, in the framework of our model, positive w.r.t. π_7 and negative w.r.t. π_8. Similarly, there seems to be a positive answer to the first part of question 2 since all the players in both MUs prefer regime π_9 to π_1. However, this is not the case for π_{10}; hence, the answer to the second part of question 2 is negative. The grand fiscal coalition (regime π_{16}) is also profitable w.r.t. π_1 for all the fiscal players, which suggests that the answer to question 3 for a symmetric model and shock is positive.

In general, for (sc_1, s_{0SP}) there are relatively many CSs in Table 8.2 which are profitable for players in non-trivial coalitions, a phenomenon on which we will come back later.

[3] For tables with greater precision see www.ua.ac.be/joseph.plasmans.

Comparing losses of CSs π_{17}, π_{18} and π_{19} helps us to answer questions 4, 5 and 6 about world-wide policy regimes. It appears that for countries of MUs, separate fiscal and monetary coordination π_{18} is the most preferable arrangement of these three (and in fact in general in (sc_1, s_{0SP})), whereas the CBs obtain minimal losses under full international coordination π_{19}. This can be explained by the fact that CBs have a more limited influence on economies than fiscal authorities (parameters γ_{j^b} and $\delta_{j^b\ell}$ compared with η_{j^b} in the model in Section 7.2); hence, stabilization of output is more effective than stabilization of prices. This causes higher CBs' losses in regime π_{18} due to asymmetric policy preferences between CBs and fiscal players. When all the players coordinate in order to minimize joint profit, fiscal players put more attention on price stabilization at the expense of output stabilization, which results in higher fiscal players' losses and lower monetary authorities' losses. As expected, π_{19} is the most profitable CS from the social point of view (i.e. social optimum). Overall, the Bretton-Woods type of the regime, π_{17}, seems to be unstable, since fiscal players would prefer to start fiscal cooperation, π_{18}. However, this CS is also not stable, since monetary authorities would dismantle cooperation in order to create π_{16}. The creation of π_{19} would be blocked by fiscal players. Hence, the above analysis suggests negative answers to questions 4, 5 and 6.

Overall, the above findings resemble outcomes of previous chapters: symmetric price shocks are conducive to policy coordination between fiscal players (e.g. π_{16}) but benefits are fairly limited, which is visible in the relatively small volatility of the welfare index.

Asymmetric price shock $s_{0AP(C5)}$

The resulting losses for an asymmetric negative supply shock to country C5, $s_{0AP(C5)}$, are given in Table 8.3. This table can be compared to Table 7.3, where also a country which is outside an MU is hit by an asymmetric shock. In both cases, the shock imposes the highest losses on the countries that are hit by the shocks, i.e. on $C5$ in Table 8.3 and $C3$ in Table 7.3, respectively. The shock to $C5$ causes spillovers to the rest of the countries. Note that, in spite of the assumed symmetry concerning (the sum of) direct (structural) spillover parameters in sc_1, players' losses in Table 8.3 are in general different from those in Table 7.3. This can be explained by two facts. First, in the present setting, there is one more fiscal player so that the distribution of spillovers is somewhat different. More in detail, the share of spillovers from $C5$ in total spillovers experienced by any other country, i.e. $0.08/0.4 = 0.2$, is different from the share of spillovers induced by $C3$ in Chapter 7, i.e. $0.1/0.4 = 0.25$. Second, there are now two MUs instead of one, and, since MUs absorb spillovers in ways different from outsiders, the distribution of losses must differ w.r.t. Table 7.3. However, the general observations from both cases remain valid. In the case of an asymmetric shock that hits a country outside an MU, outsiders (which are not directly hit by a shock as $C6$) are better off than insiders in the non-cooperative regime (compare situations of $C4$ in Table 7.3 with $C6$ in Table 8.3). This effect may be explained by the fact that in the process of spillovers' absorption, outsiders may utilize the exchange rate mechanism more efficiently.

Table 8.3 Optimal losses for $(sc_1, s_{0AP(C5)})$

	π_1	π_2	π_3	π_4	π_5	π_6	π_7	π_8	π_9	π_{10}
C1	0.1129	0.1149	0.1095	0.1219	0.0658	0.1257	0.1114	0.0643	0.1132	0.0818
C2	0.1129	0.1149	0.1095	0.1219	0.0658	0.1257	0.1114	0.0643	0.1132	0.0818
CB1	0.0641	0.0570	0.0618	0.0953	0.0986	0.0748	0.0549	0.1293	0.0416	0.0791
C3	0.1129	0.1095	0.1149	0.1232	0.1257	0.0658	0.1114	0.0643	0.1132	0.0818
C4	0.1129	0.1095	0.1149	0.1232	0.1257	0.0658	0.1114	0.0643	0.1132	0.0818
CB2	0.0641	0.0618	0.0570	0.0713	0.0748	0.0986	0.0549	0.1293	0.0416	0.0791
C5	3.0993	3.1162	3.1162	3.0028	3.0609	3.0609	3.1326	3.0093	3.1863	3.1061
CB3	2.4620	2.4757	2.4757	2.4908	2.4175	2.4175	2.4889	2.3552	2.5327	2.4371
C6	0.1082	0.1050	0.1050	0.1176	0.1176	0.1176	0.1019	0.1365	0.0924	0.1109
CB4	0.0645	0.0621	0.0621	0.0717	0.0753	0.0753	0.0599	0.0989	0.0529	0.0749
WIX	14.96%	15.19%	15.19%	15.43%	13.39%	13.39%	15.41%	11.35%	16.53%	13.15%
CFI	0.00%	0.89%	0.89%	3.47%	4.25%	4.25%	1.51%	9.25%	3.66%	3.15%
	π_{11}	π_{12}	π_{13}	π_{14}	π_{15}	π_{16}	π_{17}	π_{18}	π_{19}	
C1	0.1101	0.0759	0.1163	0.0722	0.1138	0.1096	0.0970	0.0956	0.0619	
C2	0.1101	0.0759	0.1163	0.0722	0.1138	0.1096	0.0970	0.0956	0.0619	
CB1	0.0618	0.0838	0.0655	0.1011	0.0793	0.0710	0.0788	0.0865	0.1523	
C3	0.1101	0.1163	0.0759	0.0722	0.1138	0.1096	0.0970	0.0956	0.0619	
C4	0.1101	0.1163	0.0759	0.0722	0.1138	0.1096	0.0970	0.0956	0.0619	
CB2	0.0618	0.0655	0.0838	0.1011	0.0793	0.0710	0.0788	0.0865	0.1523	
C5	2.4213	2.4306	2.4306	2.4402	2.9915	3.0068	2.9961	2.9049	2.1508	
CB3	2.6081	2.5543	2.5543	2.4769	2.5647	2.6080	2.4213	2.5572	2.5849	
C6	0.1084	0.1126	0.1126	0.1232	0.1135	0.1049	0.1044	0.1023	0.0818	
CB4	0.0620	0.0658	0.0658	0.0778	0.0688	0.0712	0.0769	0.0849	0.1227	
WIX	4.94%	3.73%	3.73%	2.12%	15.66%	16.00%	11.87%	12.97%	0.00%	
CFI	13.35%	13.76%	13.76%	14.87%	4.02%	4.36%	4.01%	6.81%	24.33%	

Overall, $C5$ is in the best situation when it participates in the grand coalition π_{19}. If this country plays non-cooperatively, it incurs the highest losses, whereas different forms of cooperation with $CB3$ are relatively profitable for $C5$; however, they considerably increase losses of this CB. This suggests that in cooperative arrangements, the country hit by an asymmetric shock is able to stabilize output at the expense of prices, which feature higher volatility.

In general, members of MUs do not profit from fiscal coordination in the framework of a union (regimes π_2 and π_3), unless both MUs simultaneously exhibit internal fiscal coordination (regime π_7). Countries of an MU, which create a full MU coalition with the corresponding CB considerably gain, whereas players of the other MU lose (π_5 and π_6), however their CBs lose. If both MUs opt for full MU coalitions (π_8), all involved fiscal players are better off w.r.t. all the previous arrangements. However, π_8 is not advantageous for $CB1$ or $CB2$ and this CS is unstable. More specifically, full fiscal coordination in both MUs at the same time, regime π_7, seems to be unstable as either $C1$ and $C2$ or $C3$ and $C4$ want to deviate (to π_3 or π_2). This observation suggests negative answers to questions 1 and 2.

Welfare effects of cooperative arrangements are quite different under an asymmetric shock compared to the situation under the symmetric shock analyzed before. For instance, the regime of world-wide fiscal coordination π_{16} is scoring poorly compared to (sc_1, p_{0SP}), where it was the second best outcome from the social point of view. Clearly, this regime is not effective in addressing the problems of an asymmetric price shock, which is also visible in welfare effects of other CSs, which consist of fiscal coalitions (π_2, π_3,.etc). Apart from the full macroeconomic coordination regime, π_{19}, the comparatively effective regimes are π_{11}, π_{12}, π_{13} and π_{14}, in which full national cooperation between $C5$ and $CB3$ occurs. Most of these welfare gains come from the internalized economic externalities of both players; however, in most cases a fiscal player gains whereas the CB loses. Again, we may argue that in case of an asymmetric price shock national coordination helps fiscal players to stabilize output but this at the expense of prices, which become more volatile.

It is interesting to compare in case of an asymmetric shock a country with an independent CB to a country within an MU. Such a situation is considered next.

Asymmetric price shock to a country of an MU $s_{0AP(C1)}$

The losses resulting from an asymmetric negative price shock to $s_{0AP(C1)}$ are given in Table 8.4. Similar to the previous case, i.e. $s_{0AP(C5)}$, the shock-receiving country, $C1$, experiences the highest losses throughout all the CSs. This country is now the source of strong spillover effects to its MU($CB1$) partner $C2$. Note that, as we already saw for the case (sc_1, p_{0A}) in Section 6.3.1 of Chapter 6, country $C2$, due to its competitiveness advantage, experiences an increase of output (in contrast to $C1$). From $C2$'s perspective, the losses are generally one third of $C1$'s losses, but increase considerably in π_5, π_8, π_{10}, π_{12}, π_{14} and π_{19}, where it is exposed to even higher spillovers due to the joint policy design. Compared to the previous case, where the same shock hits $C5$, we see that it clearly matters to $C2$ whether the shock hits an outside country or a member of its own MU, even if the countries are symmetric in all other respects. Hence, similarly to Chapter 7, it comes out that the exchange rate is a very important instrument to stabilize the economy in the case of an asymmetric shock.

Table 8.4 Optimal losses for $(sc_1, s_{0AP(C1)})$

	π_1	π_2	π_3	π_4	π_5	π_6	π_7	π_8	π_9	π_{10}
C1	5.7482	5.6576	5.7755	5.6067	4.7106	5.6225	5.6860	4.6945	5.5881	4.6114
C2	1.3829	1.3875	1.3706	1.3955	1.9452	1.4685	1.3752	1.9723	1.3944	1.9920
CB1	0.4454	0.4124	0.4511	0.4200	0.5732	0.4289	0.4178	0.5451	0.4336	0.5429
C3	0.1161	0.1238	0.1183	0.1271	0.1014	0.0659	0.1262	0.0727	0.1213	0.0572
C4	0.1161	0.1238	0.1183	0.1271	0.1014	0.0659	0.1262	0.0727	0.1213	0.0572
CB2	0.0668	0.0722	0.0593	0.0746	0.0571	0.1041	0.0642	0.0754	0.0914	0.1262
C5	0.1107	0.1177	0.1074	0.1199	0.1005	0.1213	0.1142	0.1037	0.1199	0.1134
CB3	0.0671	0.0726	0.0646	0.0998	0.0572	0.0795	0.0699	0.0599	0.0744	0.0677
C6	0.1107	0.1177	0.1074	0.1207	0.1005	0.1213	0.1142	0.1037	0.1199	0.1134
CB4	0.0671	0.0726	0.0646	0.0750	0.0572	0.0795	0.0699	0.0599	0.0744	0.0677
WIX	7.26%	6.30%	7.33%	6.41%	1.70%	6.30%	6.38%	1.12%	6.05%	0.98%
CFI	0.00%	2.11%	0.84%	3.27%	21.95%	5.00%	1.61%	22.68%	3.05%	24.63%

	π_{11}	π_{12}	π_{13}	π_{14}	π_{15}	π_{16}	π_{17}	π_{18}	π_{19}
C1	5.7222	4.7132	5.5818	4.6936	5.5950	5.6206	5.5630	5.4447	4.5355
C2	1.4034	1.9503	1.5014	1.9815	1.3865	1.3732	1.4808	1.4673	2.0413
CB1	0.4424	0.5682	0.4251	0.5374	0.4493	0.4669	0.4617	0.4848	0.6286
C3	0.1181	0.1008	0.0644	0.0704	0.1172	0.1128	0.1101	0.1069	0.0567
C4	0.1181	0.1008	0.0644	0.0704	0.1172	0.1128	0.1101	0.1069	0.0567
CB2	0.0688	0.0565	0.1111	0.0777	0.0830	0.0743	0.0623	0.0683	0.0838
C5	0.0810	0.0866	0.0808	0.0833	0.1116	0.1076	0.1064	0.1032	0.0704
CB3	0.0752	0.0566	0.0948	0.0640	0.0832	0.0745	0.0626	0.0685	0.0654
C6	0.1118	0.0995	0.1249	0.1041	0.1166	0.1076	0.1064	0.1032	0.0704
CB4	0.0692	0.0567	0.0848	0.0613	0.0719	0.0745	0.0626	0.0685	0.0654
WIX	6.98%	1.50%	5.98%	0.91%	5.96%	5.87%	5.89%	4.54%	0.00%
CFI	1.17%	22.14%	6.59%	22.97%	2.51%	2.36%	4.05%	5.65%	27.63%

Asymmetric price shock to an MU $s_{0AP(MU1)}$

The resulting losses of a negative supply shock, that hits both $C1$ and $C2$ equally, are reported in Table 8.5. $C1$ and $C2$ feature the highest losses as countries which are hit by the asymmetric shock. Consequently, their CB also experiences the highest loss among all the CBs. Fiscal coordination between members of both MUs also increases losses of $C1$ and $C2$ and, moreover, is not advantageous for $C3$ and $C4$ (regime π_7). Their efforts are set off by $CB1$, which cares more about stability of prices than about stability of output. Hence, $C1$ and $C2$ would like to create a full MU($CB1$) coalition because in the regimes π_5, π_8 and π_{10} they experience substantially lower losses than in the regimes π_1, π_2 and π_7. However, the full MU coalitions are very disadvantageous for $CB1$ and it is not likely that any of such CSs emerges. In general, comparing all the regimes in which $C1$ and $C2$ cooperate with $CB1$ with other regimes, it is clear that there are strong opposite interests between these countries on the one side and their CB on the other side. Whenever full MU($CB1$) emerges fiscal players are much better off and $CB1$ is comparatively much worse off. Internal fiscal coordination in the MU($CB1$), e.g. π_2 and π_7, is not able to stabilize output more efficiently and reduce fiscal players' losses. This analysis suggests that the answer to questions 1 and 2 is negative.

It is interesting to compare $(sc_1, s_{0AP(MU1)})$ with the previous case $(sc_1, s_{0AP(C1)})$. Note that, on average, countries of an MU are better off when they are hit by a symmetric shock than by an asymmetric one. The reason is that in the former case there is a lack of competitiveness spillovers between MU($CB1$) countries, which adjust their prices in exactly the same manner. This is not the case in $(sc_1, s_{0AP(C1)})$, where $C2$ experiences opposite movements of the output gap and price. Note also that the situation of $CB1$ is completely different in both of these cases. In $(sc_1, s_{0AP(C1)})$, the bank features comparatively very low losses because the very low aggregates of prices and output gaps of $C1$ and $C2$ are moving with opposite signs. This is not the case for $(sc_1, s_{0AP(MU1)})$, where both countries are hit by the same shock. In fact, results obtained in $(sc_1, s_{0AP(MU1)})$ may be compared with those of Chapter 6 to some extent. It is because in the global context, $s_{0AP(MU1)}$ is an asymmetric price shock, whereas in the context of the first MU it is a symmetric one. Finally, $C1$ and $C2$ gain mostly by participating in the grand international coordination π_{19} and the same is the case for all other fiscal players. However, $CB1$ experiences the highest losses in this regime and also for other CBs this CS is suboptimal.

Table 8.5 Optimal losses for $(sc_1, s_{0AP(MU1)})$

	π_1	π_2	π_3	π_4	π_5	π_6	π_7	π_8	π_9	π_{10}
C1	2.1569	2.1924	2.1869	2.1066	1.4136	2.0766	2.2244	1.4358	2.0670	1.3090
C2	2.1569	2.1924	2.1869	2.1066	1.4136	2.0766	2.2244	1.4358	2.0670	1.3090
CB1	1.7816	1.6498	1.8046	1.6802	2.2929	1.7157	1.6714	2.1807	1.7347	2.1716
C3	0.4647	0.4953	0.4733	0.5086	0.4058	0.2636	0.5051	0.2910	0.4853	0.2290
C4	0.4647	0.4953	0.4733	0.5086	0.4058	0.2636	0.5051	0.2910	0.4853	0.2290
CB2	0.2672	0.2888	0.2373	0.2984	0.2287	0.4166	0.2568	0.3019	0.3657	0.5049
C5	0.4430	0.4711	0.4296	0.4796	0.4022	0.4854	0.4569	0.4149	0.4797	0.4538
CB3	0.2687	0.2905	0.2586	0.3995	0.2291	0.3182	0.2796	0.2399	0.2976	0.2711
C6	0.4430	0.4711	0.4296	0.4831	0.4022	0.4854	0.4569	0.4149	0.4797	0.4538
CB4	0.2687	0.2905	0.2586	0.3001	0.2291	0.3182	0.2796	0.2399	0.2976	0.2711
WIX	26.27%	28.04%	26.61%	28.53%	7.55%	21.99%	28.37%	4.98%	26.91%	4.35%
CFI	0.00%	4.42%	2.03%	6.42%	26.56%	11.04%	4.43%	26.82%	5.71%	32.37%

	π_{11}	π_{12}	π_{13}	π_{14}	π_{15}	π_{16}	π_{17}	π_{18}	π_{19}
C1	2.1457	1.4291	2.0610	1.4524	2.0652	2.0898	1.9824	1.9260	1.2556
C2	2.1457	1.4291	2.0610	1.4524	2.0652	2.0898	1.9824	1.9260	1.2556
CB1	1.7698	2.2728	1.7007	2.1497	1.7972	1.8677	1.8470	1.9392	2.5147
C3	0.4727	0.4032	0.2579	0.2816	0.4690	0.4515	0.4405	0.4279	0.2270
C4	0.4727	0.4032	0.2579	0.2816	0.4690	0.4515	0.4405	0.4279	0.2270
CB2	0.2754	0.2262	0.4446	0.3111	0.3320	0.2973	0.2495	0.2734	0.3353
C5	0.3243	0.3467	0.3232	0.3333	0.4465	0.4304	0.4256	0.4129	0.2816
CB3	0.3010	0.2266	0.3792	0.2562	0.3330	0.2982	0.2507	0.2741	0.2618
C6	0.4474	0.3980	0.4997	0.4167	0.4667	0.4304	0.4256	0.4129	0.2816
CB4	0.2771	0.2269	0.3395	0.2452	0.2878	0.2982	0.2507	0.2741	0.2618
WIX	25.06%	6.66%	20.61%	4.03%	26.51%	26.12%	20.18%	20.17%	0.00%
CFI	2.55%	26.80%	14.02%	27.07%	4.39%	4.14%	6.33%	8.84%	39.19%

Asymmetric exchange rate shock $s_{0AE(C5)}$

For an exchange rate shock to $C5$'s currency, the resulting losses are given in Table 8.6. In the case of shocks to the exchange rate, international monetary policy coordination, π_{17}, is expected to be an appropriate stabilization instrument since it can directly address the root of the problems. However, from the global point of view this regime scores poorly, since $WIX(\pi_{17}) = 15.38\%$. Neither monetary nor fiscal players obtain the lowest losses. The explanation of this fact should be found in the behaviour of fiscal players in this regime. Full monetary cooperation is able to internalize economic externalities from monetary policies but is not able to internalize externalities from fiscal policies which are set in a non-cooperative manner. In π_{18} the situation of all, now cooperating, fiscal players is, in fact, better as they may internalize externalities from fiscal policies. Moreover, the increased losses of CBs in π_{18} compared to π_{17} suggest that cooperating fiscal players are able to stabilize output gaps at the expense of prices, when CBs cooperate. The same observation holds for the social optimum CS π_{19}, which is the most favorable CS for fiscal players, whereas it is the worst solution for almost all the CBs (with the exception of $CB5$ which loses most in π_{11}). Note however, that fiscal players themselves are not able to gain much from fiscal cooperation without any form of cooperation of central bank, e.g. π_2 or π_{16}. Hence, in the case of exchange rate shock we face similar effects as in the previous one of a negative price shock $s_{0AP(MU1)}$ - there are strongly opposite interests between these countries on the one side and their CBs on the other side. Fiscal players gain from cooperation of CBs and CBs (if they do not cooperate) gain from cooperation of fiscal players. Therefore, it is not surprising that the second-best socially optimal regime is π_{14} - separate full coordination in both MUs and between $C5$ and $CB3$, i.e., $\pi_{14}^{SOP} = [C1C2CB1|\ C3C4CB2|\ C5CB3|\ C6|CB4]$. This result could be directly compared with Table 7.4 but we have to keep in mind that in the computations of WIX reported in Chapter 7 both $C5$ and $CB5$ were not taken into account and this welfare index was only computed for $\pi_4 - \pi_{35}$. Hence, the optimal regime in Table 7.4 is π_{31}, which is of different form than π_{14} in the present setting. However, when we recompute the welfare index WIX for Table 7.4 considering all 9 players from Chapter 7's pre-accession stage, it comes out that $\pi_{12}^{SOP} = [C1C2CB|\ C3CB3|\ C4CB4|\ C5CB5]$ becomes the second-best socially optimal regime. A similar result is obtained in the post-accession stage if we compute WIX for all 8 players, i.e. $\pi_{44}^{SOP} = [C1C2C3CB|\ C4CB4|\ C5CB5]$. Thus, we may conclude that from the social point of view, the second-best arrangement in the case of the exchange rate shock is full coordination between fiscal players and their respective central banks. Note that from the political point of view it is much easier to create a regime in which players cooperate in the framework of own monetary arrangements (i.e. π_{14}) than a regime of full international cooperation (i.e. π_{19}).

Table 8.6 Optimal losses for $(sc_1, s_{0AE(C5)})$

	π_1	π_2	π_3	π_4	π_5	π_6	π_7	π_8	π_9	π_{10}
C1	0.1131	0.1151	0.1096	0.1213	0.0653	0.1261	0.1116	0.0639	0.1134	0.0816
C2	0.1131	0.1151	0.1096	0.1213	0.0653	0.1261	0.1116	0.0639	0.1134	0.0816
CB1	0.0647	0.0574	0.0623	0.0946	0.0998	0.0759	0.0553	0.1316	0.0419	0.0804
C3	0.1131	0.1096	0.1151	0.1230	0.1261	0.0653	0.1116	0.0639	0.1134	0.0816
C4	0.1131	0.1096	0.1151	0.1230	0.1261	0.0653	0.1116	0.0639	0.1134	0.0816
CB2	0.0647	0.0623	0.0574	0.0715	0.0759	0.0998	0.0553	0.1316	0.0419	0.0804
C5	2.7573	2.7739	2.7739	2.6641	2.7154	2.7154	2.7900	2.6586	2.8428	2.7567
CB3	1.6830	1.6956	1.6956	1.7149	1.6354	1.6354	1.7077	1.5693	1.7482	1.6492
C6	0.1082	0.1049	0.1049	0.1172	0.1179	0.1179	0.1019	0.1372	0.0923	0.1112
CB4	0.0650	0.0626	0.0626	0.0719	0.0764	0.0764	0.0603	0.1010	0.0532	0.0761
WIX	19.45%	19.69%	19.69%	20.08%	17.34%	17.34%	19.94%	14.61%	21.25%	16.80%
CFI	0.00%	1.07%	1.07%	4.12%	5.36%	5.36%	1.79%	11.70%	4.33%	3.96%

	π_{11}	π_{12}	π_{13}	π_{14}	π_{15}	π_{16}	π_{17}	π_{18}	π_{19}
C1	0.1085	0.0752	0.1144	0.0716	0.1134	0.1093	0.0967	0.0947	0.0594
C2	0.1085	0.0752	0.1144	0.0716	0.1134	0.1093	0.0967	0.0947	0.0594
CB1	0.0605	0.0817	0.0637	0.0980	0.0785	0.0701	0.0801	0.0868	0.1509
C3	0.1085	0.1144	0.0752	0.0716	0.1134	0.1093	0.0967	0.0947	0.0594
C4	0.1085	0.1144	0.0752	0.0716	0.1134	0.1093	0.0967	0.0947	0.0594
CB2	0.0605	0.0637	0.0817	0.0980	0.0785	0.0701	0.0801	0.0868	0.1509
C5	2.0134	2.0212	2.0212	2.0289	2.6543	2.6699	2.6491	2.5637	1.7732
CB3	1.8874	1.8316	1.8316	1.7514	1.7868	1.8280	1.6399	1.7725	1.8365
C6	0.1070	0.1110	0.1110	0.1212	0.1129	0.1046	0.1043	0.1017	0.0796
CB4	0.0607	0.0641	0.0641	0.0752	0.0686	0.0703	0.0781	0.0851	0.1208
WIX	6.30%	4.67%	4.67%	2.52%	20.32%	20.71%	15.38%	16.69%	0.00%
CFI	18.87%	18.96%	18.96%	20.26%	4.69%	5.15%	5.09%	8.23%	30.97%

Asymmetric exchange rate shock $s_{0AE(MU2)}$

For an exchange rate shock to the currency of $MU(CB2)$ the resulting losses are given in Table 8.7. We may expect similar findings as in the case of the previous shock $s_{0AE(C5)}$. Indeed, in $(sc_1, s_{0AE(MU2)})$ the second-best socially optimal CS is again π_{14}, which confirms previous results. It is interesting to compare the distribution of losses among players under the asymmetric exchange rate shocks $(sc_1, s_{0AE(MU2)})$ and $(sc_1, s_{0AE(C5)})$. The main observation is that the shock to the MU($CB2$)'s currency induces (around four times) higher spillovers and economic externalities than the shock to a single economy's currency. The intuition behind this result is straightforward. In the former case, spillovers originate in two economies, whereas in the latter case only in one. Since players are symmetric, there are two times more spillovers in the world if a currency of an MU is subject to an asymmetric shock. Moreover, since loss functions are quadratic, fiscal players' losses are about four times higher in $(sc_1, s_{0AE(MU2)})$ than in $(sc_1, s_{0AE(C5)})$.

Table 8.7 Optimal losses for $(sc_1, s_{0AE(MU2)})$

	π_1	π_2	π_3	π_4	π_5	π_6	π_7	π_8	π_9	π_{10}
C1	0.4658	0.4746	0.4957	0.4743	0.2618	0.3999	0.5056	0.2886	0.4840	0.2240
C2	0.4658	0.4746	0.4957	0.4743	0.2618	0.3999	0.5056	0.2886	0.4840	0.2240
CB1	0.2700	0.2399	0.2911	0.2077	0.4227	0.2235	0.2589	0.2933	0.3635	0.4853
C3	1.8365	1.8660	1.8703	1.9185	1.7485	1.0467	1.9017	1.0660	1.7507	0.9556
C4	1.8365	1.8660	1.8703	1.9185	1.7485	1.0467	1.9017	1.0660	1.7507	0.9556
CB2	1.0575	1.0782	0.9393	1.1150	0.9863	1.6437	0.9586	1.5269	1.0241	1.5138
C5	0.4433	0.4298	0.4707	0.4556	0.4868	0.3968	0.4565	0.4084	0.4781	0.4445
CB3	0.2716	0.2611	0.2927	0.2083	0.3235	0.2240	0.2816	0.2327	0.2983	0.2602
C6	0.4433	0.4298	0.4707	0.4067	0.4868	0.3968	0.4565	0.4084	0.4781	0.4445
CB4	0.2716	0.2611	0.2927	0.2435	0.3235	0.2240	0.2816	0.2327	0.2983	0.2602
WIX	34.32%	34.67%	36.65%	35.43%	28.64%	9.51%	37.00%	6.04%	35.20%	5.24%
CFI	0.00%	2.38%	4.94%	5.99%	13.57%	34.40%	4.98%	34.44%	6.22%	39.97%

	π_{11}	π_{12}	π_{13}	π_{14}	π_{15}	π_{16}	π_{17}	π_{18}	π_{19}
C1	0.4742	0.2562	0.3970	0.2793	0.4680	0.4507	0.4411	0.4254	0.2225
C2	0.4742	0.2562	0.3970	0.2793	0.4680	0.4507	0.4411	0.4254	0.2225
CB1	0.2790	0.4521	0.2207	0.3013	0.3293	0.2944	0.2509	0.2709	0.3318
C3	1.8225	1.7294	1.0608	1.0807	1.7504	1.7756	1.6547	1.6072	0.9127
C4	1.8225	1.7294	1.0608	1.0807	1.7504	1.7756	1.6547	1.6072	0.9127
CB2	1.0429	0.9684	1.6214	1.4928	1.0835	1.1496	1.1231	1.2170	1.8083
C5	0.3224	0.3215	0.3436	0.3303	0.4451	0.4293	0.4255	0.4111	0.2776
CB3	0.3052	0.3868	0.2204	0.2469	0.3303	0.2953	0.2521	0.2717	0.2575
C6	0.4481	0.5017	0.3923	0.4097	0.4645	0.4293	0.4255	0.4111	0.2776
CB4	0.2806	0.3462	0.2213	0.2369	0.2877	0.2953	0.2521	0.2717	0.2575
WIX	32.68%	26.77%	8.29%	4.69%	34.60%	34.03%	26.28%	26.24%	0.00%
CFI	3.22%	17.31%	34.70%	34.74%	4.89%	4.67%	7.77%	10.38%	47.63%

8.3.2 Asymmetric scenario sc_2

In the previous chapters, we have always analyzed not just symmetric scenarios but also cases where countries in an MU (and outside the MU in Chapter 7) differ in their economic structures, preferences and/or size viz. bargaining power in cooperative arrangements. This last setting is clearly most realistic when considering the real world. This holds even more in a global economy context. For the reason of brevity, a detailed study of the asymmetric scenarios sc_2 and sc_3 is left to the reader. We just mention a few (though important) characteristics.

Optimal losses for six shocks in the structural asymmetric scenario sc_2 are presented in Tables 8.A.2-8.A.7 of the Appendix. In general, we observe similar effects of structural asymmetries as in the previous chapters. First of all, asymmetries in the model in general tend to increase losses, since spillovers do not set off each other any more. Note that the importance of spillovers and economic externalities from some countries has considerably changed. Now, the shock in relatively more closed (but big) economies as $C5$ or $C1$ may have much more impact than in the baseline. Moreover, note that both (symmetric) fiscal players' losses of MU($CB2$) coincide.

The case of a specific price shock to $C1$, i.e. $(sc_2, s_{0AP(C1)})$, is presented in Table 8.A.4. Country $C1$ is now in a better situation than in the baseline, whereas $C2$ is always worse off. It is caused by the fact that $C1$ acquires less spillovers from $C2$, hence the anti-symmetric difference between output gaps and prices of both countries is lower in $(sc_2, s_{0AP(C1)})$ than in $(sc_1, s_{0AP(C1)})$.

Regarding the asymmetric exchange rate shock cases, i.e. $(sc_2, s_{0AE(C5)})$ and $(sc_2, s_{0AE(MU2)})$ in Tables 8.A.6-7, it is interesting to compare both of them to the baseline. Note that we assumed that $C3$ and $C4$ are exactly half of MU($CB1$) and $C5$ and $C6$. Hence, we may expect that all countries will experience an increase of losses in $(sc_2, s_{0AE(C5)})$ w.r.t. $(sc_1, s_{0AE(C5)})$, since the importance of $C5$'s spillovers and economic externalities have grown. Regarding the last shock, there should be a quantitative difference between $(sc_2, s_{0AE(MU2)})$ and $(sc_1, s_{0AE(MU2)})$, since almost all other MUs/countries are comparatively more closed w.r.t. $C3$ and $C4$. Indeed, both suppositions are confirmed in Tables 8.A. 6-7 spillover effects are higher than in the symmetric model.

8.3.3 Asymmetric scenario sc_3

To the previous case we add an asymmetric bargaining power division, which exactly corresponds to our assumptions concerning different sizes (openness) of countries. As mentioned before, this scenario seems to be more realistic than the previous asymmetric scenario, since large countries are assumed to have large bargaining power. Optimal losses are reported in Tables 8.A.8-13 in the Appendix. In general, the differences in losses are as expected. Country $C1$ uses its relatively large bargaining power in all coalitions with $C2$ to diminish its losses in comparison with $C2$ and other players. The same can be said for $C5$ w.r.t. $CB3$ and $C6$ w.r.t. $CB4$.

8.3.4 Normative analysis - social optima

The normative analysis will be done using the concept of social optimum.[4] Social-optimum CSs for the three scenarios under all 6 price and exchange rate shocks are given in Table 8.8.

Table 8.8 Social optimum CSs

π^{SOP}	sc_1	sc_2	sc_3
s_{0SP}	π_{19}	π_{19}	π_{19}
$s_{0AP(C5)}$	π_{19}	π_{19}	π_{14}
$s_{0AP(C1)}$	π_{19}	π_{19}	π_{18}
$s_{0AP(MU1)}$	π_{19}	π_{19}	π_{19}
$s_{0AE(C5)}$	π_{19}	π_{19}	π_{14}
$s_{0AE(MU2)}$	π_{19}	π_{19}	π_{19}

As expected from Theorem 5.3 in Chapter 5, the full macroeconomic coordination regime, π_{19}, is a social optimum if players have symmetric bargaining

[4]See Section 5.6 in Chapter 5.

power in different cooperative arrangements. Hence, π_{19} is a social optimum for any shock in sc_1 and sc_2 (first two columns of Table 8.8) and normative analysis is trivial in these cases. However, the introduction of bargaining power asymmetry in sc_3 changes the socially-optimal CS in three cases: $s_{0AP(C5)}$, $s_{0AP(C1)}$ and $s_{0AE(C5)}$. In fact, this scenario is the most interesting to analyze from the policy recommendation point of view since it is the closest to reality. On the other hand two kinds of asymmetries which are present in sc_3 make this setting difficult to interpret, but at this point it should be stressed again that different CSs from π_{19}, which emerge as a social optimum in sc_3, are solely due to asymmetries in bargaining power and not to structural or shock asymmetries.

Looking at Table 8.8 from the broader perspective we see another characteristic of social optimum CSs. In all of them, i.e. π_{14}, π_{18}, and π_{19} all monetary players are involved in cooperation.

Concluding, we may say that, when bargaining powers are symmetric, it is optimal from a social point of view to play in a full macroeconomic coordination regime, π_{19}. This conclusion directly follows from Theorem 5.3. However, when bargaining power are asymmetric (which occur often in a real world) asymmetric shocks are likely to produce different social optima than world-wide full cooperation. It is worth to notice that under a symmetric negative price (supply) shock π_{19} is still a social optimum in sc_3. The intuition behind this result is straightforward. If shocks are global (symmetric), only global forms of coordination, in spite of bargaining power asymmetries, are likely to produce the socially optimal outcome, since, only then, the full scale of economic externalities can be addressed. Finally, it comes out that the involvement of central banks in cooperative arrangements seems to be indispensable to achieve socially optimal outcome.

Since the normative analysis based on the social optimum CSs is rather trivial we may investigate which are the second-best CSs from the social point of view. Such CSs are presented in Table 8.9.

Table 8.9 Second-best CSs from the social point of view

$\pi^{second\ best\ SOP}$	sc_1	sc_2	sc_3
s_{0SP}	π_{16}	π_{16}	π_{16}
$s_{0AP(C5)}$	π_{14}	π_{14}	π_{18}
$s_{0AP(C1)}$	π_{14}	π_{10}	π_{17}
$s_{0AP(MU1)}$	π_{14}	π_{10}	π_{14}
$s_{0AE(C5)}$	π_{14}	π_{10}	π_{18}
$s_{0AE(MU2)}$	π_{14}	π_{10}	π_{10}

The first general observation is that second-best socially optimal CSs are characterized by a high degree of cooperation between players. It is clear that the gain in total welfare is caused by internalization of economic externalities. More in detail, CS $\pi_{14} := [\,C1C2CB1\,|C3C4CB2\,|C5CB3\,|C6\,|CB4]$ is the second best social choice for all the asymmetric shocks in sc_1. This CS is characterized by the highest number of full MU/national cooperation arrangements and requires considerable involvement of the CBs. In this CS economic externalities from, otherwise conflictive, monetary and fiscal policies, are internalized. This relatively good performance of the full MU/national arrangements means that (some) players take advantage of exchange rate mechanisms. In other words, CBs and fiscal players internalize economic externalities on the MU/national level and, at the same time, successfully improve their overall situation by using the exchange rate mechanism. Of course, this outcome does not have to be optimal from the individual point of view.

When structural asymmetries come into play in sc_2, for four shocks out of six, CS $\pi_{10} := [\,C1C2CB1\ |C3C4CB2\ |C5|CB3\ |C6\ |CB4]$ is the second best social choice. This CS is similar to π_{14} and we may expect that it can be explained using a similar intuition. In the most asymmetric scenario sc_3 the results are again mixed and a general picture can be hardly drawn. Any specific conclusions from this the-most-down-to-earth example have to be drawn for every case separately.

For the symmetric price shock s_{0SP} CS $\pi_{16} := [C1C2C3C4C5C6\ |CB1\ |CB2\ |CB3\ |CB4]$ is the second best socially optimal outcome in every scenario. This result is also found in Chapter 7.[5] Hence, in case of a symmetric price shock either full international coordination should be supported by a social planner or full fiscal coordination if the former regime is not feasible.

Regarding our six questions posed at the beginning of this chapter, the above normative analysis based on the social optimum suggests the following answers.

Question 1: The internal coordination of fiscal and/or fiscal and monetary policies in each of the two monetary blocks (MUs) separately (as in π_7 and π_8) does not seem to be optimal (or almost optimal) from the social point of view in any combination of shocks/scenarios;

Question 2: Full coordination of fiscal and monetary policies between two MUs (π_{10}) is desirable from the world-wide point of view when structural and shock asymmetries are present but players are characterized by equal bargaining power;

Question 3: Full fiscal coordination regime (π_{16}) is advisable in the case of a symmetric price shock (if full international coordination is not feasible);

Question 4: World-wide coordination of monetary policies (Bretton Woods, as in π_{17}) is second best optimal in the case of an asymmetric price shock, which occurs in one country of an MU; However this is the only case in which π_{17} performs well; hence, this result should be interpreted with caution;

Question 5: World-wide separate coordination of fiscal and monetary policies performs reasonably well from a social welfare perspective;

Question 6: World-wide coordination between all the players in a game is a social optimum in the scenarios of symmetric bargaining powers. In the case of a symmetric price shock it is always a social optimum.

[5]See Tables 7.2, 7.6, 7.C1, and 7.C.2 for a symmetric price shock in Chapter 7.

In general, in the presence of asymmetric price and exchange rate shocks, the above social-optimum results advocate a strong need for coordination of monetary and fiscal policies on the MU/national level.

8.3.5 Positive analysis - stable coalition structures in the EMG*(Γ)

Our analysis in the previous subsection was conducted from the point of view of global rationality. However, one of the main assumptions of economics is that agents are self-oriented. While officially they may recognize the need for coordination, in reality they may try to free-ride. Hence, we also need a positive analysis, which provides at least some hints which cooperative arrangements actually might be stable. As mentioned in the beginning, we will utilize the EMG*(Γ). Table 8.10 presents the stable CSs obtained for all scenarios and under all shocks.

Table 8.10 Stable CSs in the EMG*(Γ)

EMG*(Γ)	sc_1	sc_2	sc_3
s_{0SP}	$\frac{1,2,3,4}{7,9,15,16,17}$	$1, 3$	$1, 2, 3, 9$
$s_{0AP(C5)}$	$1, 16$	$1, 4, 15, 16$	$1, 16$
$s_{0AP(C1)}$	$1, 16$	$1, 9, 15, 16$	1
$s_{0AP(MU1)}$	$1, 16$	1	$1, 16$
$s_{0AE(C5)}$	$1, 16$	$1, 4, 15, 16$	$1, 16$
$s_{0AE(MU2)}$	$1, 16$	1	$1, 16$

The most important observations from Table 8.9 are the following:

1. Comparing to the EMG(Γ) results in Chapter 7 (see Tables 7.11 and 7.12), there are relatively more stable CSs;

2. Most of the stable CSs occur for the symmetric price shock s_{0SP} (in sc_1 and sc_3);

3. In the fully symmetric case (sc_1, s_{0SP}) all 9 (on 19) types of stable CSs appear:

   $\pi_1 := [C1|C2|CB1|C3|C4|CB2|C5|CB3|C6|CB4]$

   $\pi_2 := [C1C2|CB1|C3|C4|CB2|C5|CB3|C6|CB4]$

   $\pi_3 := [C1|C2|CB1|C3C4|CB2|C5|CB3|C6|CB4]$

   $\pi_4 := [C1C2C5|CB1|C3|C4|CB2|CB3|C6|CB4]$

   $\pi_7 := [C1C2|CB1|C3C4|CB2|C5|CB3|C6|CB4]$

   $\pi_9 := [C1C2C3C4|CB1|CB2|C5|CB3|C6|CB4]$

   $\pi_{15} := [C1C2C3C4C5|CB1|CB2|CB3|C6|CB4]$

   $\pi_{16} := [C1C2C3C4C5C6|CB1|CB2|CB3|CB4]$

   $\pi_{17} := [C1|C2|C3|C4|C5|C6|CB1CB2CB3CB4]$

Except for the fully non-cooperative regime π_1, almost all these stable CSs consist of only partial or full fiscal coalitions, i.e: ($C1$, $C2$), ($C3$, $C4$), ($C1$, $C2$, $C5$), ($C1$, $C2$, $C3$, $C4$), ($C1$, $C2$, $C3$, $C4$, $C5$), ($C1$, $C2$, $C3$, $C4$, $C5$, $C6$) or two fiscal coalitions at the same time: ($C1$, $C2$), ($C3$, $C4$) as in π_7. The only stable CS, where fiscal cooperation does not emerge, is π_{17}, which is the full monetary cooperation regime. Since in Chapter 7 we did not consider CBs' cooperation, these results strengthen our findings there: fiscal players prefer rather fiscal coalitions over cooperation with the monetary authorities.

4. The grand fiscal coordination regime π_{16} occurs in 13 out of the 18 entries in Table 8.10. It means that this CS is very often profitable for all the fiscal players in the game compared to the non-cooperative regime π_1. Hence, from a world perspective but taking individual rationality into account, there seems to be a large need for an institution that coordinates fiscal policies. This institution should possess supranational characteristics. The G-7 seems to be a pre-configuration of such an institution. Moreover, this finding positively answers question 3, i.e. in most of the cases, the grand fiscal cooperation between all the countries is preferred (over the non-cooperative regime).

5. Note that the stable CSs in scenario sc_3 with structural and bargaining power asymmetries are very similar to the stable CSs in scenario sc_1. In fact, the former CSs form a subset of the latter CSs for each of the shocks (even often the same). The explanation is that sc_2 is the least realistic of all three scenarios, since it does not recognize the different bargaining power for countries which are considerably different in size. On the contrary, even the symmetric scenario sc_1 takes account of this issue, because it attributes to each (symmetric) country (or block of countries) the same bargaining power.[6]

6. The grand monetary cooperation regime π_{17} is stable only for a symmetric price shock s_{0SP} in the symmetric scenario. In this case of a kind of a new oil shock, the Bretton-Woods type of monetary arrangement seems to be advisable. Hence, for a symmetric price shock in the symmetric setting, the answer to question 5 is positive. For other shocks, some of the CBs prefer the non-cooperative regime π_1 to π_{17}.

Overall, it is clear that the positive analysis produces different outcomes than the normative one. In fact, no socially-optimal CS is stable in the EMG*(Γ). This can be checked by comparing every entry of Table 8.8 with the corresponding entry of Table 8.10. Moreover, even the second best socially optimal CSs from Table 8.9 are not stable in the EMG*(Γ), except for π_{16} in (sc_1, s_{0S}). This result is not surprising. On the one hand, the normative analysis suggests that CBs should be an important part of the cooperative arrangements (see

[6]If MU($CB1$) is interpreted as a representation of the EMU, this MU is supposed to be divided into two equal blocks of countries in the symmetric scenario sc_1.

Table 8.8). On the other hand, the positive analysis points out that CSs in which fiscal players cooperate with a corresponding CB are hardly feasible. Hence, the main conclusion is that both normative and positive analyses advocate for national/regional/international cooperation but, taking into account the international context of the analysis, especially the sovereign nature of the states, we may argue that, even in the supportive-to-all-kinds-of-cooperation institutional setting, fiscal arrangements are much more likely to emerge.

8.4 Conclusion

The process of increasing globalization and the rapid growing economic integration inside economic blocks have significantly increased the importance of international macroeconomic spillovers and, through policy formulation, also international macroeconomic externalities. The possibility to internalize these (increased) externalities has therefore also broadened the scope for macroeconomic policy coordination among nations. In the presence of important global and/or regional shocks, it is expected that countries will actively seek for arrangements of international economic policy coordination, be it global or in the form of regional arrangements like e.g. the EU, NAFTA, ASEAN, MERCOSUR. This chapter analyzed issues of international policy coordination in the framework of our multi-country dynamic model.

Most results are in line with findings of the two previous chapters, although the issues which we have analyzed in this chapter have a broader perspective. In Chapter 7, we focussed on effects of the accession of one country to an MU, whereas in this chapter we studied perspectives of (possibly global) cooperation in the presence of (possibly many) MUs. In this extended setting, we investigated more different types of (asymmetric) shocks and additional cooperative regimes, principally between monetary authorities; the latter regimes were not analyzed in Chapter 7.

In general, different regimes of international macroeconomic coordination may be evaluated, either in a normative or in a positive way. Our normative analysis studies which arrangements are the best from the global welfare point of view, whereas our positive analysis tries to indicate which coalition structures might be actually stable, even when none of them is optimal for the world as a whole.

The main conclusions can be summarized as follows:

1. As in Chapter 7, we find that fiscal players prefer fiscal coalitions rather than cooperation with the monetary authorities;

2. Since the grand fiscal coordination regime is often profitable for fiscal players, there seems to be a large need for a world-wide institution that coordinates fiscal policies. The G-7 may be perceived as a pre-configuration of such an arrangement;

3. The grand monetary cooperation regime appears to be stable under a symmetric price shock and in the symmetric setting. In this case of a kind of a new oil shock, the Bretton-Woods type of monetary arrangement seems to be advisable. It should be mentioned that world-wide cooperation still would be better in the case of a symmetric price shock from the point of view of the global welfare; however, this regime would not be sustainable without a form of a (utility) transfer system;

4. The normative analysis shows that from the global welfare point of view, there is a strong need for coordination of monetary and/or fiscal policies either on the global or on the MU/national level.

The most important insight is that both kinds of analysis suggest that national/regional/international cooperation should be supported, although they substantially differ in specific recommendations. Due to the sovereign nature of the states, we expect that fiscal arrangements are much more likely to emerge.

8.5 Appendix

Table.8.A.1 Definition of asymmetric bargaining power

π_1	1	1	1	1	1	1	1	1	1	1
π_2	2/3	1/3	1	1	1	1	1	1	1	1
π_3	1	1	1	1/2	1/2	1	1	1	1	1
π_4	1/3	1/6	1/2	1	1	1	1	1	1	1
π_5	4/9	2/9	1/3	1	1	1	1	1	1	1
π_6	1	1	1	1/3	1/3	1/3	1	1	1	1
π_7	2/3	1/3	1	1/2	1/2	1	1	1	1	1
π_8	4/9	2/9	1/3	1/3	1/3	1/3	1	1	1	1
π_9	4/9	2/9	1/6	1/6	1	1	1	1	1	1
π_{10}	8/27	4/27	2/9	1/9	1/9	1/9	1	1	1	1
π_{11}	1	1	1	1	1	1	2/3	1/3	1	1
π_{12}	4/9	2/9	1/3	1	1	1	2/3	1/3	1	1
π_{13}	1	1	1	1/3	1/3	1/3	2/3	1/3	1	1
π_{14}	4/9	2/9	1/3	1/3	1/3	1/3	2/3	1/3	1	1
π_{15}	4/15	2/15	1/10	1/10	2/5	1	1	1	1	1
π_{16}	4/21	2/21	1/14	1/14	2/7	2/7	1	1	1	1
π_{17}	1	1	1	1	1	1	2/7	1/7	2/7	2/7
π_{18}	4/21	2/21	1/14	1/14	2/7	2/7	2/7	1/7	2/7	2/7
π_{19}	8/63	4/63	2/21	1/21	1/21	1/21	4/21	2/21	3/14	1/14

Table 8.A.2 Optimal losses for (sc_2, s_{0SP})

	π_1	π_2	π_3	π_4	π_5	π_6	π_7	π_8	π_9	π_{10}
C1	0.2462	0.2463	0.2462	0.2462	0.2494	0.2463	0.2463	0.2492	0.2466	0.2554
C2	0.2462	0.2461	0.2461	0.2459	0.2466	0.2462	0.2461	0.2465	0.2460	0.2479
CB1	0.4925	0.4918	0.4924	0.4900	0.4880	0.4915	0.4917	0.4877	0.4903	0.4851
C3	0.2463	0.2462	0.2463	0.2460	0.2465	0.2468	0.2462	0.2464	0.2461	0.2471
C4	0.2463	0.2462	0.2463	0.2460	0.2465	0.2468	0.2462	0.2464	0.2461	0.2471
CB2	0.4927	0.4923	0.4925	0.4908	0.4900	0.4904	0.4920	0.4884	0.4908	0.4863
C5	0.2461	0.2460	0.2461	0.2464	0.2461	0.2461	0.2460	0.2466	0.2458	0.2467
CB3	0.4923	0.4918	0.4922	0.4896	0.4896	0.4913	0.4917	0.4892	0.4908	0.4875
C6	0.2461	0.2460	0.2461	0.2457	0.2461	0.2461	0.2460	0.2466	0.2458	0.2467
CB4	0.4923	0.4918	0.4922	0.4903	0.4896	0.4913	0.4917	0.4892	0.4908	0.4875
W1X	1.49%	1.41%	1.47%	1.19%	1.23%	1.36%	1.40%	1.17%	1.25%	1.20%
CFI	0.00%	0.08%	0.02%	0.31%	0.48%	0.19%	0.10%	0.57%	0.25%	1.08%

	π_{11}	π_{12}	π_{13}	π_{14}	π_{15}	π_{16}	π_{17}	π_{18}	π_{19}
C1	0.2462	0.2485	0.2467	0.2486	0.2464	0.2461	0.2461	0.2459	0.2488
C2	0.2461	0.2460	0.2465	0.2462	0.2457	0.2454	0.2461	0.2452	0.2445
CB1	0.4895	0.4869	0.4890	0.4879	0.4883	0.4865	0.4926	0.4872	0.4762
C3	0.2463	0.2476	0.2462	0.2461	0.2458	0.2456	0.2462	0.2449	0.2423
C4	0.2463	0.2476	0.2462	0.2461	0.2458	0.2456	0.2462	0.2449	0.2423
CB2	0.4897	0.4883	0.4881	0.4886	0.4888	0.4871	0.4928	0.4876	0.4766
C5	0.2502	0.2493	0.2499	0.2493	0.2469	0.2465	0.2462	0.2462	0.2558
CB3	0.4872	0.4863	0.4868	0.4873	0.4877	0.4859	0.4924	0.4866	0.4771
C6	0.2459	0.2470	0.2463	0.2484	0.2454	0.2465	0.2462	0.2462	0.2558
CB4	0.4893	0.4881	0.4888	0.4890	0.4888	0.4859	0.4924	0.4866	0.4771
W1X	1.18%	1.15%	1.12%	1.21%	0.97%	0.72%	1.49%	0.73%	0.00%
CFI	0.54%	0.85%	0.64%	0.73%	0.56%	0.80%	0.03%	0.76%	2.74%

Table 8.A.3 Optimal losses for $(sc_2, s_{0AP(C5)})$

	π_1	π_2	π_3	π_4	π_5	π_6	π_7	π_8	π_9	π_{10}
C1	0.3244	0.3340	0.3222	0.3024	0.1975	0.3391	0.3318	0.1951	0.3611	0.2467
C2	0.2817	0.2832	0.2798	0.2627	0.1545	0.2936	0.2813	0.1520	0.2849	0.1759
CB1	0.1767	0.1582	0.1752	0.2030	0.2683	0.1883	0.1570	0.2992	0.1260	0.2311
C3	0.2703	0.2633	0.2729	0.2625	0.2916	0.1511	0.2659	0.1433	0.2621	0.1562
C4	0.2703	0.2633	0.2729	0.2625	0.2916	0.1511	0.2659	0.1433	0.2621	0.1562
CB2	0.1680	0.1626	0.1601	0.1627	0.1929	0.2503	0.1550	0.3028	0.1332	0.2496
C5	2.8176	2.8424	2.8240	2.7148	2.7592	2.7847	2.8486	2.7206	2.9026	2.7903
CB3	2.1347	2.1531	2.1394	2.2886	2.0792	2.1050	2.1577	2.0440	2.1980	2.0912
C6	0.3610	0.3520	0.3587	0.3508	0.3887	0.3748	0.3498	0.4126	0.3309	0.3807
CB4	0.1954	0.1894	0.1939	0.1894	0.2224	0.2077	0.1879	0.2465	0.1753	0.2235
WIX	17.26%	17.28%	17.24%	17.24%	14.67%	14.67%	17.27%	11.55%	17.86%	12.25%
CFI	0.00%	1.53%	0.48%	5.16%	8.31%	6.39%	1.74%	15.15%	4.86%	9.52%

	π_{11}	π_{12}	π_{13}	π_{14}	π_{15}	π_{16}	π_{17}	π_{18}	π_{19}
C1	0.3173	0.2259	0.3258	0.2213	0.2764	0.2676	0.3015	0.2447	0.1681
C2	0.2778	0.1783	0.2847	0.1741	0.2423	0.2318	0.2618	0.2117	0.1402
CB1	0.1698	0.2328	0.1747	0.2530	0.1598	0.1389	0.1773	0.1478	0.2479
C3	0.2686	0.2799	0.1770	0.1662	0.2347	0.2227	0.2600	0.2148	0.1375
C4	0.2686	0.2799	0.1770	0.1662	0.2347	0.2227	0.2600	0.2148	0.1375
CB2	0.1603	0.1716	0.2211	0.2543	0.1470	0.1318	0.1676	0.1388	0.2382
C5	2.2749	2.2864	2.2767	2.2889	2.7576	2.8014	2.6589	2.6615	1.8875
CB3	2.2460	2.1689	2.2057	2.1179	2.4650	2.5616	2.1575	2.5450	2.5543
C6	0.3596	0.3742	0.3674	0.3900	0.3171	0.2989	0.3379	0.2758	0.2371
CB4	0.1893	0.2004	0.1942	0.2143	0.1675	0.1553	0.1961	0.1647	0.2216
WIX	9.42%	7.18%	7.28%	4.63%	17.29%	17.80%	13.55%	14.23%	0.00%
CFI	9.86%	12.35%	12.37%	16.78%	9.41%	11.73%	3.85%	14.30%	31.49%

Table 8.A.4 Optimal losses for $(sc_2, s_{0AP(C1)})$

	π_1	π_2	π_3	π_4	π_5	π_6	π_7	π_8	π_9	π_{10}
C1	4.5458	4.4486	4.5520	4.3898	4.1919	4.4939	4.4543	4.1817	4.4499	4.1135
C2	2.1467	2.1489	2.1429	2.1522	2.2489	2.1938	2.1456	2.2649	2.1311	2.2797
CB1	0.8693	0.9290	0.8714	0.9441	0.9322	0.8559	0.9309	0.9147	0.9761	0.9538
C3	0.1353	0.1298	0.1368	0.1384	0.1278	0.0734	0.1311	0.0778	0.1251	0.0662
C4	0.1353	0.1298	0.1368	0.1384	0.1278	0.0734	0.1311	0.0778	0.1251	0.0662
CB2	0.0867	0.0788	0.0827	0.0828	0.0845	0.1296	0.0751	0.1191	0.0800	0.1381
C5	0.1804	0.1736	0.1792	0.1828	0.1700	0.1879	0.1725	0.1757	0.1672	0.1723
CB3	0.1004	0.0923	0.0996	0.1279	0.0978	0.1073	0.0916	0.1038	0.0878	0.1017
C6	0.1804	0.1736	0.1792	0.1852	0.1700	0.1879	0.1725	0.1757	0.1672	0.1723
CB4	0.1004	0.0923	0.0996	0.0972	0.0978	0.1073	0.0916	0.1038	0.0878	0.1017
WIX	4.99%	3.95%	4.98%	4.47%	2.12%	4.12%	3.94%	1.45%	3.96%	1.09%
CFI	0.00%	2.45%	0.27%	3.35%	6.63%	3.63%	2.45%	8.15%	3.50%	10.12%

	π_{11}	π_{12}	π_{13}	π_{14}	π_{15}	π_{16}	π_{17}	π_{18}	π_{19}
C1	4.5043	4.1944	4.4428	4.1810	4.4562	4.5098	4.3629	4.3897	3.9293
C2	2.1947	2.2630	2.2533	2.2830	2.1071	2.0662	2.2772	2.1490	2.4088
CB1	0.8600	0.9191	0.8450	0.9001	1.0049	1.0429	0.8885	1.0280	1.0661
C3	0.1387	0.1296	0.0695	0.0729	0.1258	0.1198	0.1302	0.1127	0.0677
C4	0.1387	0.1296	0.0695	0.0729	0.1258	0.1198	0.1302	0.1127	0.0677
CB2	0.0921	0.0897	0.1423	0.1319	0.0749	0.0669	0.0832	0.0711	0.1032
C5	0.1362	0.1369	0.1366	0.1359	0.1680	0.1646	0.1713	0.1496	0.1239
CB3	0.1134	0.1066	0.1257	0.1189	0.0960	0.0808	0.0969	0.0857	0.0936
C6	0.1846	0.1720	0.1951	0.1808	0.1677	0.1646	0.1713	0.1496	0.1239
CB4	0.1061	0.1028	0.1163	0.1130	0.0863	0.0808	0.0969	0.0857	0.0936
WIX	4.84%	2.05%	3.94%	1.39%	4.15%	4.19%	4.10%	3.17%	0.00%
CFI	2.10%	6.99%	6.14%	9.17%	4.00%	4.85%	4.38%	5.53%	15.96%

Table 8.A.5 Optimal losses for $(sc_2, s_{0AP(MU1)})$

	π_1	π_2	π_3	π_4	π_5	π_6	π_7	π_8	π_9	π_{10}
C1	2.4382	2.5064	2.4444	2.2841	1.6517	2.4021	2.5131	1.6598	2.4182	1.5641
C2	2.1585	2.1688	2.1640	2.0133	1.3496	2.1295	2.1746	1.3574	2.1384	1.3230
CB1	1.9039	1.7689	1.9086	1.7370	2.4446	1.8745	1.7734	2.3985	1.8675	2.4607
C3	0.3112	0.3318	0.3146	0.3815	0.2789	0.1669	0.3355	0.1952	0.3155	0.1649
C4	0.3112	0.3318	0.3146	0.3815	0.2789	0.1669	0.3355	0.1952	0.3155	0.1649
CB2	0.2016	0.2186	0.1923	0.2587	0.1693	0.3017	0.2086	0.2225	0.2447	0.2911
C5	0.4141	0.4407	0.4113	0.5276	0.3727	0.4318	0.4378	0.3781	0.4285	0.3750
CB3	0.2328	0.2517	0.2309	0.4486	0.2010	0.2494	0.2496	0.2030	0.2433	0.2027
C6	0.4141	0.4407	0.4113	0.5052	0.3727	0.4318	0.4378	0.3781	0.4285	0.3750
CB4	0.2328	0.2517	0.2309	0.2964	0.2010	0.2494	0.2496	0.2030	0.2433	0.2027
WIX	24.97%	26.32%	25.04%	28.10%	6.15%	21.87%	26.38%	4.27%	25.34%	3.31%
CFI	0.00%	4.21%	0.49%	13.32%	27.61%	6.40%	4.16%	28.53%	2.07%	32.34%

	π_{11}	π_{12}	π_{13}	π_{14}	π_{15}	π_{16}	π_{17}	π_{18}	π_{19}
C1	2.4193	1.6804	2.3792	1.6890	2.3059	2.2913	2.2722	2.1370	1.4257
C2	2.1450	1.3739	2.1126	1.3823	2.0577	2.0512	2.0122	1.9128	1.2579
CB1	1.8834	2.4135	1.8509	2.3598	1.8805	1.9364	1.9550	2.0040	2.6038
C3	0.3196	0.2743	0.1582	0.1827	0.3360	0.3328	0.3001	0.3191	0.1607
C4	0.3196	0.2743	0.1582	0.1827	0.3360	0.3328	0.3001	0.3191	0.1607
CB2	0.2151	0.1671	0.3324	0.2294	0.2499	0.2358	0.1904	0.2160	0.2623
C5	0.3103	0.3294	0.3114	0.3251	0.4285	0.4163	0.3963	0.3998	0.2524
CB3	0.2643	0.1958	0.2938	0.2055	0.3447	0.3045	0.2212	0.2806	0.2601
C6	0.4245	0.3663	0.4492	0.3755	0.4566	0.4163	0.3963	0.3998	0.2524
CB4	0.2471	0.1970	0.2717	0.2032	0.2621	0.3045	0.2212	0.2806	0.2601
WIX	23.96%	5.45%	20.61%	3.47%	25.55%	25.03%	19.85%	19.91%	0.00%
CFI	2.82%	27.45%	9.66%	28.43%	6.41%	5.94%	5.29%	9.30%	38.90%

Table 8.A.6 Optimal losses for $(sc_2, s_{0AE(C5)})$

	π_1	π_2	π_3	π_4	π_5	π_6	π_7	π_8	π_9	π_{10}
C1	0.3243	0.3341	0.3222	0.3017	0.1962	0.3393	0.3319	0.1938	0.3614	0.2455
C2	0.2816	0.2831	0.2797	0.2625	0.1534	0.2937	0.2812	0.1509	0.2849	0.1749
CB1	0.1777	0.1591	0.1762	0.2020	0.2707	0.1898	0.1578	0.3024	0.1267	0.2338
C3	0.2700	0.2631	0.2727	0.2618	0.2919	0.1499	0.2657	0.1423	0.2619	0.1552
C4	0.2700	0.2631	0.2727	0.2618	0.2919	0.1499	0.2657	0.1423	0.2619	0.1552
CB2	0.1690	0.1635	0.1611	0.1630	0.1950	0.2520	0.1559	0.3060	0.1339	0.2522
C5	2.4787	2.5029	2.4849	2.3795	2.4151	2.4434	2.5090	2.3734	2.5619	2.4428
CB3	1.3868	1.4036	1.3911	1.5363	1.3266	1.3551	1.4078	1.2890	1.4446	1.3339
C6	0.3607	0.3516	0.3583	0.3498	0.3889	0.3746	0.3494	0.4132	0.3304	0.3811
CB4	0.1964	0.1902	0.1948	0.1896	0.2245	0.2092	0.1887	0.2495	0.1759	0.2259
WIX	22.00%	21.98%	21.96%	21.85%	18.68%	18.73%	21.95%	14.73%	22.58%	15.51%
CFI	0.00%	1.78%	0.56%	6.00%	10.13%	7.71%	2.03%	18.38%	5.65%	11.72%

	π_{11}	π_{12}	π_{13}	π_{14}	π_{15}	π_{16}	π_{17}	π_{18}	π_{19}
C1	0.3117	0.2237	0.3198	0.2191	0.2765	0.2675	0.3007	0.2435	0.1653
C2	0.2728	0.1765	0.2792	0.1724	0.2422	0.2313	0.2610	0.2102	0.1366
CB1	0.1648	0.2248	0.1690	0.2434	0.1587	0.1375	0.1785	0.1477	0.2450
C3	0.2639	0.2744	0.1754	0.1647	0.2343	0.2219	0.2597	0.2139	0.1348
C4	0.2639	0.2744	0.1754	0.1647	0.2343	0.2219	0.2597	0.2139	0.1348
CB2	0.1554	0.1651	0.2140	0.2445	0.1465	0.1309	0.1688	0.1390	0.2348
C5	1.8652	1.8746	1.8662	1.8760	2.4221	2.4674	2.3143	2.3231	1.5244
CB3	1.5716	1.4906	1.5297	1.4368	1.7031	1.7957	1.4074	1.7746	1.8215
C6	0.3537	0.3673	0.3611	0.3823	0.3160	0.2994	0.3361	0.2747	0.2335
CB4	0.1841	0.1935	0.1883	0.2059	0.1674	0.1534	0.1974	0.1641	0.2180
WIX	11.52%	8.58%	8.86%	5.38%	21.70%	22.24%	17.22%	17.65%	0.00%
CFI	14.84%	16.62%	17.14%	21.13%	10.93%	13.63%	4.67%	16.67%	37.96%

Table 8.A.7 Optimal losses for $(sc_2, s_{0AE(MU2)})$

	π_1	π_2	π_3	π_4	π_5	π_6	π_7	π_8	π_9	π_{10}
C1	0.0988	0.1020	0.1027	0.0993	0.0574	0.0823	0.1060	0.0647	0.1797	0.0812
C2	0.0859	0.0865	0.0893	0.0811	0.0449	0.0725	0.0899	0.0514	0.1147	0.0505
CB1	0.0568	0.0509	0.0595	0.0416	0.0873	0.0461	0.0534	0.0562	0.1278	0.1651
C3	2.5513	2.5635	2.5777	2.6078	2.5183	1.3958	2.5904	1.4091	2.4502	1.3464
C4	2.5513	2.5635	2.5777	2.6078	2.5183	1.3958	2.5904	1.4091	2.4502	1.3464
CB2	1.6218	1.6319	1.5464	1.6675	1.5828	2.4221	1.5563	2.3777	1.5041	2.2490
C5	0.1091	0.1062	0.1132	0.1192	0.1188	0.0941	0.1102	0.0948	0.1393	0.1237
CB3	0.0624	0.0604	0.0654	0.0430	0.0725	0.0516	0.0632	0.0511	0.0839	0.0675
C6	0.1091	0.1062	0.1132	0.0963	0.1188	0.0941	0.1102	0.0948	0.1393	0.1237
CB4	0.0624	0.0604	0.0654	0.0535	0.0725	0.0516	0.0632	0.0511	0.0839	0.0675
WIX	34.38%	34.79%	34.41%	36.37%	32.22%	4.91%	34.83%	4.06%	33.72%	3.35%
CFI	0.00%	0.74%	2.09%	3.15%	3.52%	43.83%	2.22%	43.24%	8.26%	44.30%

	π_{11}	π_{12}	π_{13}	π_{14}	π_{15}	π_{16}	π_{17}	π_{18}	π_{19}
C1	0.1024	0.0553	0.0803	0.0609	0.1706	0.1639	0.0877	0.1558	0.0597
C2	0.0887	0.0430	0.0707	0.0482	0.1291	0.1353	0.0758	0.1283	0.0503
CB1	0.0607	0.0987	0.0445	0.0572	0.1347	0.1305	0.0689	0.1315	0.1490
C3	2.5420	2.5021	1.4107	1.4239	2.3405	2.2949	2.4576	2.2092	1.2772
C4	2.5420	2.5021	1.4107	1.4239	2.3405	2.2949	2.4576	2.2092	1.2772
CB2	1.6054	1.5584	2.4077	2.3541	1.4575	1.4532	1.5868	1.4599	2.1780
C5	0.0813	0.0817	0.0854	0.0822	0.2063	0.1828	0.0977	0.1742	0.0795
CB3	0.0711	0.0890	0.0485	0.0511	0.1731	0.1612	0.0751	0.1620	0.1443
C6	0.1120	0.1260	0.0915	0.0939	0.1671	0.1828	0.0977	0.1742	0.0795
CB4	0.0665	0.0817	0.0497	0.0508	0.1031	0.1612	0.0751	0.1620	0.1443
WIX	33.70%	31.24%	4.79%	3.81%	32.79%	31.65%	30.17%	28.08%	0.00%
CFI	1.21%	5.20%	43.52%	42.80%	14.85%	16.62%	4.16%	18.47%	47.81%

Table 8.A.8 Optimal losses for (sc_3, s_{0SP})

	π_1	π_2	π_3	π_4	π_5	π_6	π_7	π_8	π_9	π_{10}
C1	0.2462	0.2462	0.2462	0.2463	0.2477	0.2463	0.2462	0.2476	0.2461	0.2486
C2	0.2462	0.2462	0.2461	0.2464	0.2483	0.2462	0.2462	0.2481	0.2462	0.2495
CB1	0.4925	0.4919	0.4924	0.4900	0.4884	0.4915	0.4918	0.4880	0.4908	0.4862
C3	0.2463	0.2462	0.2463	0.2460	0.2465	0.2468	0.2462	0.2464	0.2463	0.2497
C4	0.2463	0.2462	0.2463	0.2460	0.2465	0.2468	0.2462	0.2464	0.2463	0.2497
CB2	0.4927	0.4923	0.4925	0.4910	0.4902	0.4904	0.4921	0.4886	0.4907	0.4860
C5	0.2461	0.2460	0.2461	0.2460	0.2461	0.2461	0.2460	0.2466	0.2458	0.2467
CB3	0.4923	0.4919	0.4922	0.4902	0.4898	0.4913	0.4918	0.4893	0.4910	0.4879
C6	0.2461	0.2460	0.2461	0.2457	0.2461	0.2461	0.2460	0.2466	0.2458	0.2467
CB4	0.4923	0.4919	0.4922	0.4906	0.4898	0.4913	0.4918	0.4893	0.4910	0.4879
WIX	1.07%	1.01%	1.05%	0.81%	0.85%	0.95%	0.99%	0.77%	0.86%	0.83%
CFI	0.00%	0.06%	0.02%	0.27%	0.45%	0.19%	0.08%	0.55%	0.20%	1.03%

	π_{11}	π_{12}	π_{13}	π_{14}	π_{15}	π_{16}	π_{17}	π_{18}	π_{19}
C1	0.2463	0.2474	0.2468	0.2475	0.2461	0.2461	0.2462	0.2458	0.2481
C2	0.2463	0.2480	0.2466	0.2481	0.2463	0.2463	0.2461	0.2460	0.2489
CB1	0.4908	0.4879	0.4901	0.4886	0.4888	0.4868	0.4926	0.4877	0.4806
C3	0.2465	0.2476	0.2466	0.2465	0.2465	0.2465	0.2461	0.2460	0.2496
C4	0.2465	0.2476	0.2466	0.2465	0.2465	0.2465	0.2461	0.2460	0.2496
CB2	0.4910	0.4893	0.4891	0.4891	0.4886	0.4867	0.4928	0.4875	0.4806
C5	0.2475	0.2471	0.2474	0.2472	0.2458	0.2457	0.2462	0.2455	0.2466
CB3	0.4894	0.4881	0.4887	0.4888	0.4889	0.4870	0.4924	0.4878	0.4804
C6	0.2461	0.2471	0.2464	0.2483	0.2455	0.2457	0.2462	0.2455	0.2456
CB4	0.4906	0.4891	0.4899	0.4897	0.4894	0.4870	0.4924	0.4878	0.4805
WIX	0.89%	0.84%	0.81%	0.87%	0.64%	0.40%	1.07%	0.44%	0.00%
CFI	0.29%	0.67%	0.44%	0.59%	0.45%	0.69%	0.03%	0.62%	1.74%

Table 8.A.9 Optimal losses for $(sc_3, s_{0AP(C5)})$

	π_1	π_2	π_3	π_4	π_5	π_6	π_7	π_8	π_9	π_{10}
C1	0.3244	0.3272	0.3222	0.3490	0.1854	0.3391	0.3251	0.1829	0.3238	0.1976
C2	0.2817	0.2898	0.2798	0.3156	0.1639	0.2936	0.2879	0.1611	0.2887	0.1764
CB1	0.1767	0.1610	0.1752	0.2687	0.2741	0.1883	0.1597	0.3055	0.1415	0.2597
C3	0.2703	0.2643	0.2729	0.2906	0.2935	0.1511	0.2670	0.1440	0.2834	0.1816
C4	0.2703	0.2643	0.2729	0.2906	0.2935	0.1511	0.2670	0.1440	0.2834	0.1816
CB2	0.1680	0.1634	0.1601	0.1845	0.1942	0.2503	0.1557	0.3051	0.1243	0.2350
C5	2.8176	2.8387	2.8240	2.6647	2.7533	2.7847	2.8449	2.7145	2.8879	2.7717
CB3	2.1347	2.1504	2.1394	2.1587	2.0756	2.1050	2.1550	2.0403	2.1874	2.0791
C6	0.3610	0.3534	0.3587	0.3875	0.3911	0.3748	0.3511	0.4153	0.3360	0.3886
CB4	0.1954	0.1903	0.1939	0.2138	0.2238	0.2077	0.1888	0.2483	0.1786	0.2289
WIX	13.99%	14.03%	13.97%	16.00%	11.52%	11.47%	14.02%	8.47%	14.56%	9.10%
CFI	0.00%	1.32%	0.48%	6.13%	8.70%	6.39%	1.53%	15.50%	3.96%	10.32%

	π_{11}	π_{12}	π_{13}	π_{14}	π_{15}	π_{16}	π_{17}	π_{18}	π_{19}
C1	0.2664	0.1998	0.2689	0.1944	0.3384	0.3143	0.2972	0.2900	0.1628
C2	0.2341	0.1787	0.2360	0.1735	0.3023	0.2767	0.2578	0.2550	0.1413
CB1	0.1444	0.1810	0.1440	0.1901	0.2519	0.2077	0.1837	0.2126	0.3123
C3	0.2277	0.2308	0.1690	0.1580	0.2928	0.2682	0.2555	0.2554	0.1409
C4	0.2277	0.2308	0.1690	0.1580	0.2928	0.2682	0.2555	0.2554	0.1409
CB2	0.1351	0.1361	0.1704	0.1854	0.2354	0.1905	0.1739	0.1948	0.2897
C5	1.7604	1.7854	1.7714	1.7982	2.6384	2.6489	2.6705	2.5135	1.5947
CB3	2.9434	2.8580	2.9004	2.8012	2.1919	2.3007	2.1392	2.3024	2.8194
C6	0.3055	0.3096	0.3074	0.3164	0.3869	0.3404	0.3335	0.3167	0.1626
CB4	0.1621	0.1616	0.1613	0.1659	0.2137	0.2385	0.2028	0.2435	0.3997
WIX	4.33%	2.13%	2.55%	0.00%	16.34%	14.87%	10.23%	11.37%	0.38%
CFI	31.58%	31.19%	31.98%	32.19%	7.18%	6.73%	4.00%	10.25%	44.69%

Table 8.A.10 Optimal losses for $(sc_3, s_{0AP(C1)})$

	π_1	π_2	π_3	π_4	π_5	π_6	π_7	π_8	π_9	π_{10}
C1	4.5458	4.4748	4.5520	4.3751	3.2008	4.4939	4.4811	3.1984	4.4097	3.1663
C2	2.1467	2.1837	2.1429	2.1954	3.2959	2.1938	2.1801	3.3088	2.1990	3.3050
CB1	0.8693	0.8435	0.8714	0.8726	1.2361	0.8559	0.8455	1.2166	0.8501	1.1911
C3	0.1353	0.1396	0.1368	0.1456	0.1161	0.0734	0.1411	0.0856	0.1558	0.0781
C4	0.1353	0.1396	0.1368	0.1456	0.1161	0.0734	0.1411	0.0856	0.1558	0.0781
CB2	0.0867	0.0893	0.0827	0.0943	0.0692	0.1296	0.0851	0.0878	0.1323	0.1651
C5	0.1804	0.1860	0.1792	0.1811	0.1557	0.1879	0.1848	0.1569	0.1927	0.1657
CB3	0.1004	0.1034	0.0996	0.1430	0.0833	0.1073	0.1026	0.0827	0.1084	0.0874
C6	0.1804	0.1860	0.1792	0.1937	0.1557	0.1879	0.1848	0.1569	0.1927	0.1657
CB4	0.1004	0.1034	0.0996	0.1090	0.0833	0.1073	0.1026	0.0827	0.1084	0.0874
WIX	1.51%	1.13%	1.50%	1.20%	1.88%	0.67%	1.13%	1.28%	1.80%	1.62%
CFI	0.00%	1.91%	0.27%	3.73%	35.38%	3.63%	1.75%	35.84%	3.95%	36.65%

	π_{11}	π_{12}	π_{13}	π_{14}	π_{15}	π_{16}	π_{17}	π_{18}	π_{19}
C1	4.4297	3.1891	4.3611	3.1841	4.3640	4.3929	4.3762	4.2327	3.0137
C2	2.2448	3.3242	2.3127	3.3431	2.1933	2.1674	2.2701	2.2882	3.4352
CB1	0.8398	1.1941	0.8239	1.1677	0.8918	0.9465	0.8802	0.9558	1.1868
C3	0.1505	0.1204	0.0720	0.0820	0.1408	0.1317	0.1304	0.1268	0.0689
C4	0.1505	0.1204	0.0720	0.0820	0.1408	0.1317	0.1304	0.1268	0.0689
CB2	0.1017	0.0704	0.1602	0.0965	0.1111	0.0891	0.0857	0.0881	0.1426
C5	0.1005	0.1158	0.0984	0.1124	0.1770	0.1669	0.1687	0.1563	0.0888
CB3	0.1628	0.1116	0.1807	0.1159	0.1348	0.1129	0.1000	0.1119	0.1709
C6	0.2002	0.1615	0.2133	0.1652	0.1915	0.1669	0.1687	0.1563	0.0794
CB4	0.1170	0.0841	0.1301	0.0857	0.1078	0.1129	0.1000	0.1119	0.1946
WIX	1.71%	1.64%	0.83%	0.96%	1.17%	0.77%	0.67%	0.00%	1.14%
CFI	5.52%	35.56%	9.68%	36.39%	4.04%	3.68%	4.00%	7.44%	43.44%

Table 8.A.11 Optimal losses for $(sc_3, s_{0AP(MU1)})$

	π_1	π_2	π_3	π_4	π_5	π_6	π_7	π_8	π_9	π_{10}
C1	2.4382	2.4585	2.4444	2.3340	1.5612	2.4021	2.4651	1.5694	2.3826	1.5166
C2	2.1585	2.2154	2.1640	2.0929	1.4219	2.1295	2.2213	1.4303	2.1413	1.3782
CB1	1.9039	1.7888	1.9086	1.8599	2.4858	1.8745	1.7934	2.4396	1.8085	2.4051
C3	0.3112	0.3287	0.3146	0.3401	0.2748	0.1669	0.3323	0.1933	0.3564	0.1736
C4	0.3112	0.3287	0.3146	0.3401	0.2748	0.1669	0.3323	0.1933	0.3564	0.1736
CB2	0.2016	0.2160	0.1923	0.2253	0.1667	0.3017	0.2061	0.2184	0.3053	0.3852
C5	0.4141	0.4367	0.4113	0.4192	0.3672	0.4318	0.4338	0.3722	0.4501	0.3926
CB3	0.2328	0.2488	0.2309	0.3314	0.1981	0.2494	0.2467	0.1998	0.2586	0.2126
C6	0.4141	0.4367	0.4113	0.4515	0.3672	0.4318	0.4338	0.3722	0.4501	0.3926
CB4	0.2328	0.2488	0.2309	0.2592	0.1981	0.2494	0.2467	0.1998	0.2586	0.2126
WIX	23.19%	24.46%	23.25%	23.69%	4.57%	20.12%	24.52%	2.75%	25.33%	3.52%
CFI	0.00%	3.70%	0.49%	5.37%	28.62%	6.40%	3.64%	29.41%	5.64%	31.85%

	π_{11}	π_{12}	π_{13}	π_{14}	π_{15}	π_{16}	π_{17}	π_{18}	π_{19}
C1	2.3505	1.5685	2.3083	1.5784	2.3234	2.3562	2.2873	2.2154	1.3906
C2	2.0867	1.4306	2.0524	1.4407	2.0813	2.1098	2.0260	1.9840	1.2518
CB1	1.8389	2.3855	1.8044	2.3247	1.9063	2.0316	1.9366	2.0637	2.5114
C3	0.3468	0.2888	0.1637	0.1851	0.3266	0.3084	0.3033	0.3005	0.1687
C4	0.3468	0.2888	0.1637	0.1851	0.3266	0.3084	0.3033	0.3005	0.1687
CB2	0.2378	0.1759	0.3744	0.2493	0.2548	0.2028	0.1959	0.1955	0.3049
C5	0.2284	0.2617	0.2237	0.2539	0.4102	0.3880	0.3899	0.3660	0.2113
CB3	0.3783	0.2762	0.4208	0.2931	0.3107	0.2585	0.2281	0.2512	0.3749
C6	0.4605	0.3857	0.4914	0.3983	0.4442	0.3880	0.3899	0.3660	0.1874
CB4	0.2726	0.2067	0.3041	0.2164	0.2543	0.2585	0.2281	0.2512	0.4264
WIX	22.17%	3.89%	18.74%	1.84%	23.47%	23.07%	18.47%	18.55%	0.00%
CFI	8.69%	27.85%	15.44%	29.60%	4.78%	4.28%	4.59%	8.33%	43.11%

Table 8.A.12 Optimal losses for $(sc_3, s_{0AE(C5)})$

	π_1	π_2	π_3	π_4	π_5	π_6	π_7	π_8	π_9	π_{10}
C1	0.3243	0.3272	0.3222	0.3466	0.1842	0.3393	0.3251	0.1817	0.3238	0.1964
C2	0.2816	0.2898	0.2797	0.3126	0.1627	0.2937	0.2878	0.1599	0.2887	0.1753
CB1	0.1777	0.1619	0.1762	0.2660	0.2764	0.1898	0.1605	0.3087	0.1423	0.2624
C3	0.2700	0.2641	0.2727	0.2895	0.2937	0.1499	0.2667	0.1430	0.2834	0.1806
C4	0.2700	0.2641	0.2727	0.2895	0.2937	0.1499	0.2667	0.1430	0.2834	0.1806
CB2	0.1690	0.1643	0.1611	0.1845	0.1962	0.2520	0.1566	0.3083	0.1250	0.2377
C5	2.4787	2.4993	2.4849	2.3322	2.4092	2.4434	2.5054	2.3673	2.5475	2.4245
CB3	1.3868	1.4011	1.3911	1.4165	1.3233	1.3551	1.4053	1.2855	1.4348	1.3225
C6	0.3607	0.3529	0.3583	0.3859	0.3913	0.3746	0.3507	0.4159	0.3355	0.3890
CB4	0.1964	0.1911	0.1948	0.2137	0.2259	0.2092	0.1896	0.2512	0.1793	0.2314
WIX	17.49%	17.50%	17.46%	19.91%	14.34%	14.34%	17.47%	10.52%	18.05%	11.24%
CFI	0.00%	1.55%	0.56%	7.01%	10.57%	7.71%	1.78%	18.79%	4.61%	12.65%

	π_{11}	π_{12}	π_{13}	π_{14}	π_{15}	π_{16}	π_{17}	π_{18}	π_{19}
C1	0.2633	0.1985	0.2656	0.1930	0.3363	0.3130	0.2962	0.2874	0.1584
C2	0.2312	0.1774	0.2330	0.1723	0.2998	0.2753	0.2568	0.2524	0.1371
CB1	0.1419	0.1770	0.1412	0.1853	0.2489	0.2046	0.1853	0.2115	0.3104
C3	0.2250	0.2278	0.1678	0.1570	0.2906	0.2670	0.2551	0.2534	0.1367
C4	0.2250	0.2278	0.1678	0.1570	0.2906	0.2670	0.2551	0.2534	0.1367
CB2	0.1327	0.1329	0.1669	0.1806	0.2323	0.1874	0.1755	0.1936	0.2880
C5	1.3778	1.4008	1.3878	1.4123	2.3079	2.3199	2.3262	2.1806	1.2350
CB3	2.2495	2.1617	2.2054	2.1032	1.4498	1.5537	1.3886	1.5490	2.0829
C6	0.3021	0.3058	0.3039	0.3122	0.3849	0.3386	0.3316	0.3132	0.1584
CB4	0.1596	0.1583	0.1584	0.1618	0.2129	0.2355	0.2045	0.2424	0.3976
WIX	5.43%	2.65%	3.24%	0.00%	20.25%	18.42%	12.72%	13.95%	0.13%
CFI	39.43%	38.83%	39.81%	39.76%	8.12%	7.71%	4.87%	12.03%	53.62%

Table 8.A.13 Optimal losses for $(sc_4, s_{0AE(MU2)})$

	π_1	π_2	π_3	π_4	π_5	π_6	π_7	π_8	π_9	π_{10}
C1	0.0988	0.0998	0.1027	0.1031	0.0538	0.0823	0.1037	0.0610	0.1062	0.0508
C2	0.0859	0.0886	0.0893	0.0933	0.0476	0.0725	0.0921	0.0547	0.0951	0.0446
CB1	0.0568	0.0518	0.0595	0.0400	0.0890	0.0461	0.0543	0.0575	0.0831	0.1022
C3	2.5513	2.5617	2.5777	2.6002	2.5154	1.3958	2.5885	1.4077	2.5047	1.3572
C4	2.5513	2.5617	2.5777	2.6002	2.5154	1.3958	2.5885	1.4077	2.5047	1.3572
CB2	1.6218	1.6304	1.5464	1.6614	1.5809	2.4221	1.5548	2.3754	1.5811	2.3534
C5	0.1091	0.1067	0.1132	0.1074	0.1196	0.0941	0.1107	0.0953	0.1209	0.1065
CB3	0.0624	0.0607	0.0654	0.0492	0.0730	0.0516	0.0635	0.0514	0.0708	0.0576
C6	0.1091	0.1067	0.1132	0.0980	0.1196	0.0941	0.1107	0.0953	0.1209	0.1065
CB4	0.0624	0.0607	0.0654	0.0546	0.0730	0.0516	0.0635	0.0514	0.0708	0.0576
WIX	32.28%	32.64%	32.31%	34.07%	30.08%	3.27%	32.67%	2.39%	31.37%	1.24%
CFI	0.00%	0.63%	2.09%	2.73%	3.70%	43.83%	2.19%	43.24%	2.97%	44.73%

	π_{11}	π_{12}	π_{13}	π_{14}	π_{15}	π_{16}	π_{17}	π_{18}	π_{19}
C1	0.1117	0.0541	0.0857	0.0590	0.1017	0.0971	0.0961	0.0942	0.0531
C2	0.0965	0.0475	0.0752	0.0527	0.0896	0.0857	0.0837	0.0832	0.0467
CB1	0.0671	0.1148	0.0469	0.0645	0.0697	0.0557	0.0555	0.0544	0.0851
C3	2.5071	2.4597	1.4021	1.4151	2.4902	2.5150	2.4389	2.4076	1.2981
C4	2.5071	2.4597	1.4021	1.4151	2.4902	2.5150	2.4389	2.4076	1.2981
CB2	1.5783	1.5235	2.3712	2.3063	1.6475	1.7235	1.6435	1.7429	2.4287
C5	0.0597	0.0573	0.0697	0.0654	0.1088	0.1036	0.1060	0.1005	0.0576
CB3	0.1012	0.1279	0.0686	0.0748	0.0796	0.0653	0.0611	0.0639	0.0970
C6	0.1215	0.1403	0.0973	0.1018	0.1175	0.1036	0.1060	0.1005	0.0506
CB4	0.0733	0.0936	0.0523	0.0552	0.0682	0.0653	0.0611	0.0639	0.1102
WIX	30.74%	28.11%	2.64%	1.53%	31.45%	32.66%	28.34%	28.84%	0.00%
CFI	3.79%	8.24%	43.08%	42.53%	2.72%	2.66%	3.58%	6.00%	49.51%

Chapter 9

Concluding Remarks

International macroeconomic policy coordination is an important, but complex topic. The practice of international policy coordination has not been without disappointments, fuelling the arguments of sceptics to propagate a *laissez-faire* approach instead. A *laissez-faire* approach, however, ignores that in an increasingly integrated and global world economy, there are significant positive and negative externalities. Economic externalities create the scope and scale for coordinated policies in order to outperform upon a setting with non-cooperative policies. Or putting it in a more negative manner: in case of non-cooperative policies, policymakers -purposely or not- impose with their policies externalities upon each other, since their individual policy decisions do not take account of the consequences for other policymakers. In other words a non-cooperative setting is unlikely to deliver optimal outcomes.

This book has focussed on international macroeconomic policy coordination in the presence of (a) monetary union(s) between otherwise sovereign countries. Inspired by the recent creation of the euro area, we presented a framework in which many of the aspects of a monetary union could be analyzed. In this framework, there was ample room for both economic components (especially in the form of the theory of macroeconomic stabilization in dynamic, open economies and the 'optimal currency area' theory playing an important role) and more institutional and game-theoretic aspects (this concerns the institutional design of monetary and fiscal policies in a monetary union and the strategic interactions between policymakers in a monetary union and in international policy coordination in general).

This combination of economic theory, institutions and game theory in a dynamic analysis of monetary unions and international policy coordination in a broader sense, proved very useful. It confirmed existing insights and also provided new ones. E.g. that the basic insights of the 'optimal currency area' theory also apply to our broader analysis with a dynamic model and strategically behaving policymakers. In other words, the amount of integration, the similarity of macroeconomic shocks and economic structures play an important role in our analysis. To this, we added insights that the institutional design and aspects of policymakers' strategic behaviour also matter a great deal for the final outcomes produced by monetary unions and international policy coordination.

Most studies of monetary unions, like the euro area, take a comparative static perspective. Clearly, a dynamic perspective is more relevant; in reality macroeconomic adjustment, macroeconomic policies and policy coordination are essentially taking place as dynamic processes. A static analysis ignores the dynamics and is essentially like looking at pictures: it is interesting to consider a situation at a certain point in time and to understand how things seen are related, but it is even more interesting to know the dynamic processes that produced the situation and how the situation is likely to develop from this specific point in time. In that sense, a dynamic analysis as developed in this book is essentially like watching a film and be able to follow and understand the dynamics that occur.

Our analysis took a dynamic two-country monetary union model as a starting point. In Chapter 3, we focussed on fiscal policy in a symmetric monetary union with a passive monetary authority and without interactions with non-monetary union countries. In this manner, we analyzed in detail the effects of fiscal policy coordination, fiscal stringency requirements and a fiscal transfer system in a monetary union. In principle, fiscal coordination arises as something beneficial in a monetary union: it enables to internalize the economic externalities from individual policies. This is in general welfare improving for the participants.

Fiscal stringency requirements (like the Stability and Growth Pact for the EMU countries) limit the flexibility of individual countries to deal with macroeconomic shocks. This may imply efficiency losses, as the countries will remain with less ability to stabilize their economies in case of being hit by a shock. On the other hand, if fiscal flexibility is reduced, countries are likely to decrease the use of control instruments (fiscal policies) in a monetary union when they play non-cooperatively. In other words, the effect is similar to some form of cooperation, because excessive fiscal policies are reduced and externalities decreased. In fact, in the framework of this basic model, we showed that if the amount of fiscal stringency is increased, the cooperative fiscal policy arrangement and the non-cooperative case become similar to each other. Moreover, we showed that a fiscal transfer system increases the internal stability of the economy; hence, welfare costs may be considerably reduced. So, when national fiscal policies are restricted, such a transfer system can be considered as a potentially powerful stabilization instrument in the presence of business cycle divergences.

The introduction of active monetary policy in Chapter 4 produced several effects. In this setting not only the coordination of fiscal policies is relevant, but also the coordination of monetary and fiscal policies. Assuming that the common central bank is concerned with variables at the aggregate level, it is clear that the individual fiscal authorities have a less strong (bargaining) position compared to a situation with national central banks. This has therefore implications for both the fiscal and monetary policies. A number of institutional aspects of monetary policy, such as the institutional preferences *viz.* the independence of the central bank, are also shown to determine adjustments in a monetary union. More in detail, we showed that fiscal cooperation is often advantageous for the fiscal players, provided that they are not very asymmetric in preferences, structural characteristics and bargaining strength. The non-cooperative regime is most likely to be the outcome when countries are comparatively more asymmetric. Cases where the central bank cooperates with one government against the other, generally produces suboptimal monetary and fiscal stabilization policies and are unlikely to be feasible in practice. These results suggest that a central bank has a rationale to pursue independent monetary policy. In other words, the institutional setting should guarantee a high degree of independence of the monetary authority. On the other hand, governments may pursue a design based on fiscal cooperation, which leave them independent in interacting their policies with the monetary policy of a central bank.

Even though the basic insights gained so far generalize also to a multi-country monetary union, the amount of interactions is richer with more countries. Policy coordination is also more complex in the multi-country setting due to the possibility of coalition formation: subgroups of countries may find it optimal to coordinate their fiscal policies and act as a block against other (groups of) countries. To address this complexity, we develop a framework, where countries decide to engage in policy coordination based on the principles of the 'endogenous coalition formation' theory. This provides a consistent approach towards coalition formation in a large set of players. It allows to determine under which circumstances which coalitions may arise. Moreover, coalition formation games can be interpreted as models of different institutional settings of macroeconomic policy coordination. By examination of welfare effects of these mechanisms, we could evaluate their effectiveness from the point of view of all the players in the game or a monetary union, in particular.

In the two-country monetary union of Chapter 4, the cooperative arrangements are clear but limited: apart from fiscal coordination and full monetary and fiscal policy coordination, there are two additional -but less likely- arrangements, where each of the fiscal players coordinates with the common central bank. For a richer setting, we considered in Chapter 6 a monetary union with a large number of countries. This clearly adds more realism to our analysis if one considers, for example, that the euro area currently consists of twelve members with new members joining in the foreseeable future. We find that in the case of a common shock and symmetric countries, fiscal coordination is better for fiscal players than full coordination (with the central bank). This result is consistent with our findings in Chapter 4. However, full fiscal coordination is hardly sustainable due to the existence of free-riding incentives of individual fiscal players, who prefer to leave this coalition and play non-cooperatively. This conclusion could not be obtained in the two-country model of Chapter 4; hence, our example in Chapter 6 shows that issues of international coordination should be considered in a multi-country setting.

In general, structural and bargaining power asymmetries tend to reduce the scope for cooperation. However, this effect does not always occur when asymmetry of shocks is considered. For a country-specific shock, it appears that full policy coordination may be sustainable. In addition, in the case of an anti-symmetric shock, only the cooperation of affected countries is needed and full or fiscal cooperation is not associated with any extra gains in the policymakers' welfare. An interesting result comes from the analysis of an asymmetric structural model with asymmetric bargaining power. First of all, asymmetry of the model (hence, real economic conditions) seems to be more important than asymmetry of (political) power. Since, players have only limited influence on the economies, mainly model asymmetries drive the stabilization process, whereas bargaining power seems to be less weighty. Consequently, it came out from the analysis in Chapter 6 that advantageous bargaining power enhances the effects of structural asymmetries in our model.

Chapter 7 analyzed the decision of countries to participate (or not) in monetary unions. It was shown that the accession to a monetary union raises several additional interesting and important questions. For example, what are the consequences for the accession countries and is the accession beneficial for the acceding countries and the current monetary authorities? How does the accession of new members affect the monetary policy of the common central bank? How does the accession affect the coordination of fiscal policies? Is there any effect of accession on the interaction between the monetary union and the rest of the world? We showed that these questions can be answered in our analysis as they are essentially questions concerning the optimal currency area problem and concerning institutional arrangements in a monetary union. Our findings stress the importance of an asymmetric price shock. In the framework of our model, it is never profitable to enlarge a monetary union when asymmetries in initial price shocks may be present. What is more, the differences in losses between the pre-accession stage and the post-accession stage are so high that it seems to be difficult to design a transfer system to compensate for a worse situation of some countries. However, for symmetric price and exchange rate shocks outside a monetary union, our findings are not straightforward. Even if some players are worse off due to accession, there exist cooperation regimes that may improve their situation.

The last chapter of the book focussed on the interactions in a global context. Now, in an open-economy setting, a monetary union is connected with other economies through several channels. Of crucial importance is the introduction of exchange rates: in a global economy, exchange rate adjustments are an important source of linkages between countries and thereby of spillovers. In principle, non-coordination cannot produce optimal outcomes from a global-economy perspective. The question is how international policy coordination should take form and be enforced at the international level.

Given that exchange rates are directly observable, it is of no surprise that many initiatives of international macroeconomic policy coordination have attached a crucial importance to exchange rate targets. This also suggests that in a global perspective, the gains from coordination could be even larger than inside a monetary union. Unfortunately, on a global base, cooperation is often much less enforceable than at the level of a monetary union, where the participating countries are also tied in a number of other institutional arrangements.

Most results of Chapter 8 are in line with findings of the two previous chapters. We evaluated various regimes of international macroeconomic coordination in a normative as well as in a positive way. Our normative approach studies which arrangements are the best from the global welfare point of view, whereas our positive analysis searches for those coalition structures that might be actually stable, even when none of them is optimal for the world as a whole. The main conclusions of Chapter 8 are as follows: (i) similarly to Chapter 7, fiscal players prefer rather fiscal coalitions over cooperation with the monetary authorities; (ii) the grand fiscal coordination regime is often profitable for fiscal players; G-7 is a step towards such an institutional arrangement; (iii) the grand monetary cooperation regime appears to be stable in the symmetric setting under a symmetric price shock.

From the analysis in Chapters 6, 7 and 8 we may derive some conclusions about coalition formation games. More in detail, in Chapters 6 and 7 we compared four simultaneous coalition formation games: the open-membership game, the restricted open-membership game and two versions of the exclusive-membership game. We attempted to answer the question which coalition formation mechanism is efficient from the social point of view and defined the (degree of) effectiveness as the average (expected) difference of the coordination mechanism's outcome from the social optimum. In addition to the results mentioned above, we found that in the settings considered our coalition formation mechanisms turn out to be rather inefficient from the social point of view.

Even though this book provides a number of interesting insights into policy-making in a monetary union and in international policy coordination in general, there remain several aspects that would require further analysis. At the macroeconomic side, a more detailed modelling of the economies could be desirable. Recent developments in the New Open Economy Macroeconomics (NOEM) have produced richer macroeconomic models, involving rational expectations in discrete time. Such an approach would allow for a sound empirical analysis (of e.g. international spillovers and externalities) which is lacking in our approach which can be interpreted as a naive and most elementary form of NOEM modelling. With a NOEM model, it is likely that (some of) our insights will need to be partly modified and additional insights are likely to appear. Moreover, regarding the linear-quadratic games, the study of a feedback instead of an open-loop information structure seems to be a very promising extension of our model. There are many possible directions to extend our coalition formation analysis. First of all, different equilibrium concepts could be studied in which, for example, a deviation of a group of players (and not only one of them) is considered. Moreover, also less myopic approaches in simultaneous games could be utilized in considering stability of a coalition structure (i.e. farsighted stability concepts). Finally, the study of different modifications of the concept of sequential negotiation games appears to be a very promising task. The first immediate extension of the analysis presented in this book could be an examination of different rules of order and their impact on final outcomes. Moreover, an interesting observation is that from the welfare point of view, the sequential unanimous-agreement coordination mechanism (the sequential negotiation game) is very often more effective than simultaneous exclusive-membership games; hence, we believe that this issue should be investigated further.

References

Aarle, B. van, L. Bovenberg and M. Raith (1995),"Monetary and fiscal policy interaction and government debt stabilization", *Journal of Economics*, Vol. 62, pp. 111-140.

Aarle, B. van, L. Bovenberg and M. Raith (1997), "Is there a tragedy of a common central bank?", *Journal of Economic Dynamics and Control*, Vol. 21, No. 2-3, pp. 417-447.

Aarle, B. van, G. Di Bartolomeo, J. Engwerda and J. Plasmans (2002b), "Coalitions and dynamic interactions between fiscal and monetary authorities in the EMU", *Ifo Studien*, Vol. 48, No. 2, pp. 207-229.

Aarle, B. van, G. Di Bartolomeo, J. Engwerda and J. Plasmans (2004), "Policymakers' Coalitions and Stabilization Policies in the EMU", *Journal of Economics*, Vol. 82, No. 1, pp. 1-24.

Aarle, B. van, J.C. Engwerda, J. Plasmans and A. Weeren, (2001), "Macroeconomic policy interaction under EMU: A dynamic game approach", *Open Economies Review*, Vol.12, pp.29-60.

Aarle, B. van, J.C. Engwerda and J. Plasmans (2002a), "Monetary and fiscal policy interaction in the EMU: A dynamic game approach", *Annals of Operations Research*, Vol. 109, pp. 229-264.

Aarle, B. van, H. Garretsen and N. Gobbin (2003), "Fiscal policy transmission in the Euro area: Evidence from a structural VAR Analysis", *Journal of Economics and Business*, Vol. 55, pp. 609–638.

Acocella, N. and G. Di Bartolomeo (2001), "Wage and public expenditure setting in a monetary union", Working Paper No. 42., Department of Public Economics, University of Rome 'La Sapienza', Rome.

Acocella, N. and G. Di Bartolomeo (2004), "Is a conservative central banker a (perfect) substitute for wage coordination?", *Empirica*, Vol. 31, pp. 281-294.

Alesina, A. and V. Grilli (1992), "The European Central Bank: Reshaping monetary politics in Europe" in Canzoneri M., V. Grilli, and P. Masson (eds.), *Establishing a Central Bank. Issues in Europe and Lessons from the US*, Cambridge University Press, Cambridge.

Alesina, A. and R. Perotti (2004), "The European Union: A Politically Incorrect View", NBER Working Paper No. 10342, Washington DC.

Angeloni, I., A. Kashyap, B. Mojon and D. Terlizzese (2002), "Monetary transmission in the Euro-area: Where do we stand?", ECB Working Paper No. 114, Frankfurt.

Artis, M. and W. Zhang (1997), "International business cycles and the ERM: Is there a European business cycle?", *International Journal of Finance and Economics*, Vol. 2, pp 1-16.

Aspremont, C.A. d', A. Jacquemin, J.J. Gabszewicz and J. Weymark (1983) "On the stability of collusive price leadership", *Canadian Journal of Economics*, Vol. 16, pp. 17-25.

Aumann, R.J. (1990), "Nash Equilibria Are Not Self-Enforcing," in J.J. Gabszewicz, J.-F. Richard and L.A. Wolsey (eds.), *Economic Decision Making: Games, Econometrics and Optimisation*, Elsevier, Amsterdam.

Aumann, R. J. and J. Drèze (1974), "Cooperative Games with Coalition Structures", *International Journal of Game Theory,* Vol. 3, pp. 217–237.

Barro, R.J. and H.I. Grossman (1971), "A general disequilibrium model of income and employment", *American Economic Review*, Vol. 61, pp. 82-93.

Başar T. and G.J.Olsder (1999), *Dynamic Noncooperative Game Theory*, SIAM, Philadelphia.

Bayoumi, T., and B. Eichengreen (1993), "Shocking aspects of European monetary integration" in F. Torres and F. Giavazzi (eds.), *Adjustment and growth in the EMU*, Cambridge University Press, Cambridge.

Bayoumi, T. and P. Masson (1995), "Fiscal flows in the United States and Canada: Lessons for monetary union in Europe", *European Economic Review*, Vol.39, No. 2, pp. 253-274.

Bayoumi, T., and E. Prassad (1995), "Currency unions, economic fluctuations and adjustment: Some empirical evidence", CEPR Discussion Paper No.1172, London.

Beetsma, R.M.W.J. and A.L. Bovenberg (1998), "Monetary union without fiscal coordination may discipline policymakers?", *Journal of International Economics*, Vol. 45, pp. 239-258.

Beetsma, R., X. Debrun and F. Klaassen (2001), "Is fiscal policy coordination in EMU desirable?", *Swedish Economic Policy Review*, Vol. 8, pp. 57-98.

Beetsma, R. and H. Uhlig (1999), "An analysis of the Stability and Growth Pact", *Economic Journal*, Vol. 109, pp. 546-571.

Bindseil, U. (2001), "A coalition-form analysis of the 'one country - one vote' rule in the governing council of the European Central Bank", *International Economic Journal*, Vol.15, No.1, pp.141-164.

Bindseil, U. and C. Hantke (1997), "The power distribution in decision making among EU member states", *European Journal of Political Economy*, Vol. 13, No. 1, pp.171-85.

Bini Smaghi, L. and C. Casini (2000), "Monetary and fiscal policy cooperation: Institutions and procedures in EMU", *Journal of Common Market Studies*, Vol. 38, pp. 375-391.

Bittanti S. (1991), "Count Riccati and the early days of the Riccati equation" in S. Bittanti, A.J. Laub and J.C. Willems (eds.), *The Riccati equation*, Springer-Verlag, Berlin, pp.1-10.

Bittanti S., A.J. Laub and J.C. Willems (eds.), (1991), *The Riccati equation*, Springer-Verlag, Berlin.

Bohn, F. (2004), "Monetary Union and the Interest-Exchange Rate Trade-off", *Open Economies Review*, Vol. 15, pp. 111-141.

Bloch, F. (1996), "Sequential formation of coalitions in games with externalities and fixed payoff division", *Games and Economic Behavior*, Vol. 14, pp. 90-123.

Bloch, F. (1997), "Non-cooperative models of coalition formation in games with spillovers" in C. Carraro and D. Siniscalco (eds.), *New directions in the economic theory of the environment*, Cambridge University Press, Cambridge.

Boone, L. and M. Maurel (1999), "Economic convergence of the CEECs with the EU", *CEPR Discussion Paper* No. 2018, London.

Bordo M. and L. Jonung (2003), "The future of EMU: What does the history of monetary unions tell us?" in F. Capie and G. Wood (eds.), *Monetary Unions. Theory, History, Public Choice*, Routledge, London.

Breuss, F. and A. Weber (2001), "Economic policy coordination in the EMU: Implications for the Stability and Growth Pact" in A. Hughes Hallett, P. Mooslechner and M. Schuerz (eds.), *Challenges for economic policy coordination within European Monetary Union*, Kluwer Academic Publishers, Dordrecht, pp.143-167.

Buti, M., S. Eijffinger and D. Franco (2003), "Revisiting the Stability and Growth Pact: Grand redesign or internal adjustment?", European Commission Economic Papers, No.180, Brussels.

Buti, M. and G.Guidice (2002) "Maastricht's Fiscal Rules at Ten: An Assessment" *Journal of Common Market Studies*, Vol. 40, No.5, pp 823-848.

Buti, M., W. Roeger and J. in 't Veld (2001), "Stabilizing output and inflation: Policy conflicts and co-operation under a Stability Pact", *Journal of Common Market Studies*, Vol. 39, No. 5, pp. 801-828.

Buti, M. and A. Sapir (eds.), (1998), *Economic Policy in EMU: A Study by the European Commission Services,* Oxford University Press, Oxford.

Cadha J. and Ch. Nolan (2002), "Inflation and Price Level Targeting in a New Keynesian Model", *Manchester School*, Blackwell Publishing, Vol. 70(4), pp. 570-595.

Canzoneri M., R. Cumby and B. Diba (2004), "The Need for International Policy Coordination: What's Old, What's New, What's Yet to Come?", NBER Working Paper No. 8765, Washington, forthcoming in the *Journal of International Economics.*

Canzoneri, M. and B. Diba (1999), "The Stability and Growth Pact: A delicate balance or an albatross?", *Empirica*, Vol. 26, pp. 241-258.

Canzoneri, M. B. and D. W. Henderson (1988), "Is Sovereign Policymaking Bad?", *Carnegie-Rochester Series on Public Policy*, Vol. 28, pp. 93-140.

Carraro, C. (1997), "Modelling International Policy Games: Lessons from European Monetary Coordination", *Empirica*, Vol. 24, pp. 163-177.

Carraro, C. (1999), *The Structure of International Agreements on Climate Change*, Kluwer, Dordrecht.

Carraro, C. and F. Giavazzi (1991), "Can International Policy Co-ordination really be Counterproductive?" in C. Carraro, D. Laussel, M. Salmon and A. Soubeyran (eds.), *International Economic Policy Coordination*, Blackwell, Oxford, pp. 184–198.

Carraro, C. and C. Marchiori (2003), "Stable Coalitions" in C. Carraro (ed.), *The Endogenous Formation of Economic Coalitions*, E. Elgar, Cheltenham.

Carraro C. and D. Siniscalco (1998), "International environmental agreements: Incentives and political economy", *European Economic Review*, Vol. 42, pp. 561-572.

Casella, A. (1999), "Tradable Deficit Permits: Efficient Implications of the Stability Pact in the European Monetary Union", *Economic Policy*, No. 29, pp. 323-347.

Christodoulakis, N., S. Dimelis and T. Kollintzas (1995), "Comparisons of business cycles in the EC: Ideosyncracies and regularities", *Economica*, Vol. 62, pp. 1-27.

Clarida, R., J. Galí and M. Gertler (1999), "The Science of Monetary Policy: A New Keynesian Perspective", *Journal of Economic Literature*, Vol. 37, No. 4, pp. 1661-1707.

Comtet, L. (1974), *Advanced Combinatorics*, Kluwer, Dordrecht.

Cooper, R. (1985), "Economic Interdependence and Coordination of Economic Policies", in R. Jones and P. Kenen (eds.), *Handbook of International Economics*, Vol. 2, North Holland, Amsterdam.

Corsetti, G. and P. Pesenti (2001), "International Dimensions of Optimal Monetary Policy", FRB of New York Staff Report No. 124, NewYork.

Cukierman, A. (1992), *Central bank strategy, credibility and interdependence*, MIT Press, Cambridge (MA).

Currie, D. (1993), "International Cooperation in Monetary Policy: Has it a Future?", *Economic Journal*, Vol. 103, No. 416, pp. 178-187.

Dalsgaard, T. and A. de Serres (2000), "Estimating prudent budgetary margins for EU Countries. A simulated SVAR Model approach", *OECD Economic Studies*, Vol. 30, pp. 115-147.

Decressin, J. and A. Fatás (1995), "Regional labour market dynamics in Europe", *European Economic Review*, Vol. 39, pp. 1627-1655.

De Grauwe, P. (2000), "Monetary policies in the presence of asymmetries", CEPR Discussion Paper No. 2393, London.

De Grauwe, P. (2003), *Economics of monetary union*, Oxford University Press, Oxford.

De Haan, J. (1997), "The European Central Bank: Independence, Accountability and Strategy", *Public Choice*, Vol. 93, pp. 395-426.

Di Bartolomeo, G., J. Engwerda, J. Plasmans, and B. van Aarle (2003), "Macroeconomic stabilisation policies in the EMU: Spillovers, asymmetries, and institutions", *Research Paper* 2003/019, Faculty of Applied Economics UFSIA-RUCA, University of Antwerp, Antwerp.

Di Bartolomeo, G., J.C. Engwerda, J.E.J. Plasmans and B. van Aarle (2004), "Staying together or breaking apart: Policy-makers' endogenous coalitions formation in the European Economic and Monetary Union", *Computers and Operations Research,* preprint and forthcoming.

Di Nardo, J. and M.P. Moore (1999), "The Phillips Curve is Back? Using Panel Data to Analyze the Relationship Between Unemployment and Inflation in an Open Economy", NBER Working Paper No. 7328, Washington DC.

Dixit, A. (2003), "Symbiosis of monetary and fiscal policies in a monetary union. A repeated game model of monetary union", *Journal of International Economics*, vol 60, pp. 235-247.

Dornbusch, R. and Y.C. Park (1998), "Flexibility or nominal anchors", in Collignon, S., J. Pisani-Ferry and Y.C. Park (eds.), *Exchange Rate Policies in Emerging Asian Countries*, Routledge, London.

Ecchia, G. and M. Mariotti (1998), "Coalition formation in international environmental agreements and the role of institutions", *European Economic Review*, Vol. 42, pp. 573-582.

Ehrmann, M. (2000), "Comparing monetary policy transmissions across European countries", *Weltwirtschaftliches Archiv*, Vol. 136, No. 1, pp. 58-83.

Eichengreen, B. (1994), *International Monetary Arrangements for the 21st Century*, The Brookings Institution, Washington DC.

Eichengreen, B. (1998), "Does Mercosur need a single currency?," NBER Working Paper No. 6821, Washington DC.

Eichengreen, B. and A.M. Taylor (2003), "The monetary consequences of a free trade area of the Americas," NBER Working Paper No. 9666, Washington DC.

Engwerda, J.C. (1998a), "On the open-loop Nash equilibrium in LQ-games", *Journal of Economic Dynamics and Control*, Vol.22, pp.729-762.

Engwerda, J. (1998b), "Computational aspects of the open-loop Nash equilibrium in linear quadratic games", *Journal of Economic Dynamics and Control*, Vol. 22, pp. 1487-1506.

Engwerda, J.C. (2005a), *Linear Quadratic Dynamic Optimization and Differential Games*, Wiley, Chichester.

Engwerda, J.C. (2005b), "Uniqueness conditions for the infinite-planning horizon open-loop linear quadratic differential game", CentER Discussion Paper No.32, Tilburg University, Tilburg.

Engwerda, J.C., B. van Aarle and J. Plasmans (1999), "The (in)finite horizon open-loop Nash LQ game: An application to the EMU", *Annals of Operations Research*, Vol. 88, pp. 251-273.

Engwerda, J., B. van Aarle and J. Plasmans (2002), "Cooperative and non-cooperative fiscal stabilisation policies in the EMU", *Journal of Economic Dynamics and Control*, Vol. 26, pp. 451-481.

Engwerda, J.C., J. Plasmans, B. van Aarle and T. Michalak (2005), "Macroeconomic policy coordination in the EMU: Effects of Accession", Working Paper, Faculty of Economics, University of Antwerp, Antwerp.

European Commission (2001), "Public finances in EMU - 2001", European Economy Reports and Studies, No. 3, Brussels.

European Economic Advisory Group at CESifo (2004), *Report on the European Economy 2004*, CESifo, Munich.

European Parliament (1999), "EMU and enlargement: A review of policy issues", Working Paper 12/99, Directorate-General for Research, Brussels.

Eyckmans, J. and M. Finus (2003), "Coalition Formation in a Global Warming Game: How the Design of Protocols Affects the Success of Environmental Treaty-Making", Diskussionsbeiträge No. 342, Fachbereich Wirtschaftswissenschaft, University of Hagen, Hagen.

Favero, C., X. Freixas, T. Persson, and C. Wyplosz (2000), *One money, Many countries, Monitoring the European Central Bank 2*, CEPR, London.

Feldstein, M.S. (1988), "Distinguished Lecture on Economics in Government: Thinking about International Economic Coordination", *Journal of Economic Perspectives*, Vol. 2, No. 2, pp. 3-13.

Fidrmuc, J. and I. Korhonen (2003), "Similarity of supply and demand shocks between the euro area and the CEECs", *Economic Systems*, Vol. 27, No. 3, pp. 313-334

Finus, M. (2001), *Game Theory and International Environmental Cooperation*, E. Elgar, Cheltenham.

Finus, M. (2003), "New Developments in Coalition Theory: An Application to the Case of Global Pollution" in L. Marsiliani, M. Rauscher and C. Withagen (eds.), *Environmental policy in an international perspective*, Kluwer, Dordrecht.

Finus, M. and B. Rundshagen (2001), "Endogenous Coalition Formation in Global Pollution Control", Fondazione Eni Enrico Mattei, Working Paper 2001.43, Milan.

Finus, M. and B. Rundshagen (2003), "How the Rules of Coalition Formation Affect Stability of International Environmental Agreements", Fondazione Eni Enrico Mattei, Working Paper 2003.62, Milan.

Frankel, J. (1988), "Obstacles to international macroeconomic policy coordination". International Monetary Fund Working Paper 87/28, Wasgington DC.

Frankel, J.A. (1990), "Obstacles to Coordination, and a Consideration of Two Proposals to Overcome Them: International Nominal Targeting (INT) and the Hosomi Fund" in W. Branson, J. Frenkel and M. Goldstein (eds.), *International Policy Coordination and Exchange Rate Fluctuations*, University of Chicago Press, Chicago,

Frankel, J. and K. Rockett (1988), "International Macroeconomic Policy Coordination When Policymakers Do Not Agree on the True Model", *American Economic Review*, Vol. 78, pp. 318-340.

Frankel, J. and A. Rose (1997),"Is EMU more justifiable ex-post than ex-ante?", *European Economic Review*, Vol. 41, pp. 753-760.

Fratianni, M. and A. Hauskrecht (2002), "A centralized monetary union for MERCOSUR: Lessons from EMU", Paper prepared for the Conference on "Euro and Dollarization: Forms of Monetary Union in Integrated Regions", Fordham University, New York.

Garcia, S. and A. Verdelhan (2001), "The Euro zone's policy-mix. An evaluation of the impact of monetary and fiscal shocks", *Economie et Prévision*, Vol. 148, pp. 23-40.

Ghosh, A.R. and P.R. Masson (1987), "International Policy Coordination in a World with Model Uncertainty", IMF Working Paper WP/87/81, Washington DC.

Ghosh, A.R. and P.R. Masson (1991), "Model Uncertainty, Learning, and the Gains from Coordination", *American Economic Review*, Vol. 81, pp. 465–479.

Ghosh, A.R. and P.R. Masson (1994), *Economic Cooperation in an Uncertain World*, Blackwell, Oxford.

Goodfriend, M. and R. King (1997), "The New Neoclassical Synthesis and the Role of Monetary Policy" in *NBER Macroeconomics Annual*, MIT Press, Boston, pp. 231-283.

Hagen, J. von, and G. Hammond (1995), "Regional insurance against asymmetric shocks. An empirical study for the European Community", CEPR Discussion Paper No.1170, London.

Hagen, J. von, A. Hughes Hallett and R. Strauch (2001), "Budgetary Consolidation in EMU", Economic Papers No. 148, European Commission, Brussels.

Hagen, J. von and S. Lutz (1996), "Fiscal and Monetary Policies on the Way to EMU", *Open Economies Review*, Vol. 7, pp. 299-325.

Hagen, J. von. and R. Suppel (1994), "Central bank constitutions for federal monetary unions", *European Economic Review*, Vol. 38, pp. 774-782.

Gros, D. and C. Hefeker (2000), "One size must fit all national divergences in a monetary union", CESifo Working Paper No. 326, Munich.

Hart, S. and M. Kurz (1983), "Endogenous Formation of Coalitions", *Econometrica*, Vol. 51, pp. 1047-1064.

Hooper, P., K. Johnson and J. Marquez (1998), "Trade elasticities for G-7 countries", International Finance Discussion Paper No. 609, Board of Governors of the Federal Reserve System, Washington DC.

Horn, R.A. and C.A. Johnson (1985), *Matrix Analysis*, Cambridge University Press, Cambridge.

Hosli, M. (1996), "Coalitions and power: Effects of qualified majority voting in the Council of the European Union", *Journal of Common Market Studies*, Vol. 34, No. 2, pp. 255-273

Hughes Hallett, A. and Y. Ma (1996), "Changing partners: The importance of coordinating fiscal and monetary policies within a monetary union", *The Manchester School*, Vol. 64, pp. 115-134.

Hughes Hallett, A.J. and P. McAdam (1997), "Fiscal Deficit Reductions in Line With the Maastricht Criteria for Monetary Union: An Empirical Analysis" in J. Frieder, D. Gros, E. Jones (eds.), *Towards European Monetary Union: Problems and Prospects*, Cambridge University Press, Cambridge.

Hughes Hallett, A. and N. Viegi (2003), "On the need for Inter-institutional Coordination in EMU: A re-evaluation of the theory of optimal currency areas" in F. Breuss, G. Fink and S. Griller (eds.), Institutional, Legal and Economic Aspects of the EMU, Springer, Berlin, pp. 117-141.

Isaacs, R. (1954-1955), "Differential games I,II,III,IV", Research Memorandum RM-1391. RM-1399, RM-1411, RM-1486, RAND Corporation, Santa Monica.

Issing, O. (1999), "The Eurosystem: transparent and accountable, or Willem in Euroland", *Journal of Common Market Studies*, Vol. 37, pp. 503-521.

Italianer, A. (1999), "The Euro and internal economic policy coordination", *Empirica*, Vol. 26, No. 3, pp. 201-216.

Italianer, A., and M. van Heukelen (1993), "Proposals for Community stabilization mechanisms: Some historical applications", *European Economy*, Reports and Studies No. 5, "The Economics of Community Public Finance", pp. 495-510.

Krichel, T., P. Levine and J. Pearlman (1996), "Fiscal policy coordination under EMU: Credible inflation targets or monetised debt?", *Weltwirtschaftliches Archiv*, Vol. 123, pp. 28-54.

Lambertini, L. and R. Rovelli (2003), "Monetary and fiscal policy coordination and macroeconomic stabilization. A theoretical analysis", Working Paper No. 464, Dipartimento di Scienze Economiche-Università di Bologna, Bologna.

Laxton, D., P. Isard, H. Faruqee, E. Prasad and B. Turtleboom (1998), "MULTIMOD Mark III - The Core Dynamic and Steady-State Models", IMF Occasional Paper No. 164, Wasgington DC.

Lancaster, P. and M. Tismenetsky (1985), *The Theory of Matrices*, Academic Press, London.

Lancaster, P. and L.Rodman (1995), *Algebraic Riccati Equations*, Clarendon Press, Oxford.

Laruelle, A. and M. Widgrén (1996), "Is the allocation of voting power among the EU states fair?", CEPR Discussion Paper No.1402, London.

Laub, A.J. (1991), "Invariant subspace methods for the numerical solution of Riccati equations", in Bittanti S., A.J.Laub and J.C. Willems (eds.),, *The Riccati equation*, Springer, Berlin, pp.163-199.

Lay, D.C. (2003), *Linear Algebra and its Applications*, Pearson, New York.

Levine, P. and A. Brociner (1994), "Fiscal policy coordination and EMU: a dynamic game approach", *Journal of Economic Dynamics and Control*, Vol. 18, pp. 699-729.

Levinsky, R. and P. Silarsky (1998), "Voting power and coalition formation: The case of the Council of the EU", *East European Series*, No.56, Institute for Advanced Studies, Vienna.

Malinvaud, E. (1977), *The Theory of Unemployment Reconsidered*, Basil Blackwell, Oxford.

Masson, P. (1992), "Portfolio Preference Uncertainty and Gains from Policy Coordination", *IMF Staff Papers*, Vol. 39, No. 1, Washington DC.

McKibbin, W. (1997), "Empirical Evidence on International Economic Policy Coordination" in M. Fratianni, D. Salvatore and J. von Hagen (eds.), *Handbook of Comparative Economic Policies*, Vol. 5, Macroeconomic Policies in Open Economies, Greenwood Press, Westport.

McKinnon, R.I. (1963), "Optimum currency areas", *American Economic Review*, Vol. 53, pp. 717-725.

Meersman, H. and J. Plasmans (1983), "De Theorie van de Werkloosheid" in A. Devreker (ed.), *Werkgelegenheid voor de Jaren Tachtig*, Vereniging voor Economie, Gent, pp. 279-327.

Mélitz, J. (2000), "Some Cross-country Evidence about Fiscal Policy Behaviour and Consequences for EMU" in European Commission (ed.), *European Economy*, Reports and Studies No. 2, Public Debt and Fiscal Policy in EMU, pp. 3-21.

Meyer L.H, D.M. Doyle, J.E. Gagnon and D.W. Henderson (2002), "International coordination of macroeconomic policies: Still alive in the New Millennium?", International Finance Discussion Paper No. 723, Board of Governors of the Federal Reserve System, Washington DC.

Michalak, T., J. Plasmans and J. Engwerda (2005), "Endogenous coalition formation in a monetary union", *mimeo*, University of Antwerp.

Monticelli, C. and O. Tristani (1999), "What does the single monetary policy do? A SVAR benchmark for the European Central Bank", ECB Working Paper Series, No.2, Frankfurt.

Mundell, R.A. (1961), "A theory of optimum currency areas", *American Economic Review*, Vol. 51, pp. 657-665.

Muscatelli, A., P. Tirelli and C. Trecroci (2002), "Monetary and fiscal policy interactions over the cycle: Some empirical evidence", in R. Beetsma, C. Favero, A. Missale, V.A. Muscatelli, P. Natale and P. Tirelli (eds.), *Fiscal policies, monetary policies and labour markets. Key aspects of European macroeconomic policies after monetary uniÞcation*, Cambridge University Press, Cambridge.

Nash, J.F. (1950), "Equilibrium points in N-person games", in *Proceedings of the National Academy of Sciences of the United States of America*, Vol. 36, pp. 48-49.

Nash, J.F. (1951), "Non-cooperative games", *Annals of Mathematics*, Vol. 54, pp.286-295.

Neck, R. and E.J.Dockner (1995), "Commitment and coordination in a dynamic-game model of international economic policy-making", *Open Economies Review*, Vol. 6, pp. 5-28.

Neck, R.,G. Haber and W. McKibbin (2002a), "Monetary and fiscal policy-makers in the European Economic and Monetary Union: Allies or adversaries?", *Empirica,* Vol. 29, pp. 225-233.

Neck, R., G. Haber and W.J. McKibbin (2002b), "Global Implications of Monetary and Fiscal Policy Rules in the EMU", *Open Economies Review* 13, pp. 363-379.

Oates, W. (1972), *Fiscal Federalism*, Harcour Brace Jovanovich, New York.

Obstfeld, M. and K. Rogoff (2002), "Global Implications of Self-Oriented National Monetary Rules", *Quarterly Journal of Economics,* Vol. 117, pp. 503-535.

Peersman, G. (2004), "The transmission of monetary policy in the Euro area: Are the effects different across countries?", *Oxford Bulletin of Economics and Statistics,* Vol. 66, pp. 285-308.

Plasmans, J. (1984), "Comment on 'Investment, Output and Labour Constraints, and Financial Constraints: The Estimation of a Model with Several Regimes", *Recherches Economiques de Louvain*, Vol. 50, No. 1-2, pp. 53-57.

Plasmans, J., G. Di Bartolomeo, B.Merlevede and B. van Aarle (2004), "Monetary policy regimes with hybrid output gaps and inflation rates with an application to EU-accession countries" in S. Késenne and C. Reyns (eds.), *Kwantitatief bekeken, Liber Amicorum Prof. dr. Robert Van Straelen*, Garant, Antwerpen, pp. 95-136.

Plasmans, J. and V. Somers (1983), "A Maximum Likelihood Estimation Method for a Three Market Disequilibrium Model", FEW-Research Memorandum, No. 126, Tilburg University.

Ploeg, F. van der (1991), "Macroeconomic policy coordination issues during the various phases of economic and monetary integration in Europe", *European Economy*, Special Edition No.1, "The Economics of EMU, background studies for One Market, One Money", pp. 136-164.

Ploeg, F. van der (2005), "Back to Keynes?", CESifo Working Paper No. 1424, Munich.

Ray, D. and R. Vohra (1997), "Equilibrium binding agreements", *Journal of Economic Theory*, Vol. 73, pp. 30-78.

Ray, D. and R. Vohra (1999). "A theory of endogenous coalition structures", *Games and Economic Behavior*, Vol. 26, pp. 286-336.

Razin, A. and C.W. Yuen (2001), "The 'New Keynesian' Phillips curve: Closed economy vs. open economies", NBER Working Paper No. 8313, Washington DC.

Riccati, J.F. (1724), "Animadversationes in aequationes differentiales secundi gradus", *Actorum Eruditorum quae Lipsae publicantur*, Supplementa 8, pp. 66-73.

Rogoff, K.S. (1985), "Can International Monetary Policy Coordination Be Counterproductive?", *Journal of International Economics*, Vol. 18, pp. 199-217.

Rossiter, A. and K. Tang (2004), "Fiscal policy coordination within a monetary union in the presence of risk premia", in The Ninth Australasian Macroeconomics Workshop, Australian National University, Canberra.

Rundshagen, B. (2002), "On the Formalization of the Open Membership in Coalition Formation Games", Working Paper No. 318, University of Hagen, Hagen.

Sargent, T. and N. Wallace (1981), "Some unpleasant monetarist arithmetic", *Federal Reserve Bank of Minneapolis Quarterly Review*, Vol. 5, pp. 1-17.

Shenoy, P. (1979), "On coalition formation: a game-theoretical approach", *International Journal of Game Theory*, Vol. 8, pp. 133-164.

Smets, F. (2000), "What horizon for price stability", ECB Working Paper No. 24, Frankfurt.

Sutter, M. (1998), "Voting and voting power in the stability pact", Working Paper, University of Innsbruck, Innsbruck.

Starr, A.W. and Y.C. Ho (1969a), "Nonzero-sum differential games", *Journal of Optimization Theory and Applications*, Vol.3, pp.184-206.

Starr, A.W. and Y.C. Ho (1969b), "Further properties of nonzero-sum differential games", *Journal of Optimization Theory and Applications*, Vol.3, pp.207-219.

Tijs, S. (2004), *Introduction to Game Theory*, Hindustan, New Delhi.

Turnovsky, S., T. Başar and V. d'Orey (1988), "Dynamic strategic monetary policies and coordination in interdependent economies", *American Economic Review*, Vol. 78, pp. 341-361.

Vanhoose, D. (2004), "The New Open Economy Macroeconomics: A critical appraisal", *Open Economies Review*, Vol. 15, pp. 193-215.

Weber, A. (1991), "EMU and asymmetries and adjustment problems in the EMS. Some empirical evidence", *European Economy*, Special Edition No.1, "The Economics of EMU, background studies for One Market, One Money", pp. 187-207.

Wehinger, G. (2000), "Causes of Inflation in Europe, the United States and Japan: Some Lessons for Maintaining Price Stability in the EMU from a Structural VAR Approach", *Empirica*, Vol. 27, pp. 83-107.

Widgrén, M. (1994), "Voting power in the EC decision making and the consequences of two different enlargements", *European Economic Review*, Vol. 38, pp. 1153-70.

Woodford, A. (2003)), *Interest and Prices - Foundations of a Theory of Monetary Policy*, Princeton University Press, Princeton.

Wyplosz, C., (1999), "Economic Policy Coordination in EMU: Strategies and Institutions", ZEI Policy Paper B11, Rheinische Friedrich-Wilhelms-Universität, Bonn.

Yergin, D. and J. Stanislaw (1998), *The Commanding Heights,* Simon & Schuster, New York.

Yi, S. (1996), "Endogenous formation of customs unions under imperfect competition: open regionalism is good", *Journal of International Economics,* Vol. 41, pp. 151-75.

Yi, S. (1997), "Stable coalition structures with externalities", *Games and Economic Behaviour,* Vol. 20, pp. 201-37.

Yi, S. and H. Shin (1995), "Endogenous formation of coalition in oligopoly", Department of Economics Working Paper No. 2, Dartmouth College, Hanover (NH).

Zhou, K., J.C. Doyle, and K. Glover (1996), *Robust and Optimal Control,* Prentice Hall, New York.

Index

(New-) Keynesian dynamic open-economy macroeconomic models, vii, 307

Accession to a monetary union, 236
AFTA, 34
Algebraic Riccati equation
  stabilizing solution, 51, 70
ASEAN, 30, 33–36, 273, 294
ASEAN Free Trade Area, *see* AFTA
ASEAN+3, 34
Association of South East Asian Nations, *see* ASEAN

Bank jurisdictional set, 164, 166, 167, 169, 174, 175, 179, 180, 191–193, 195, 254
Basis, 42
Bretton Woods, 1, 10, 16, 17, 30, 273, 275, 277, 281, 291, 293, 295

CFI, 190, 202, 214, 241, 244
Characteristic polynomial, 44
Chicago School, 1
Class of coalition formation games, 153
  class of exclusive-membership games (delta version), 160
  class of exclusive-membership games (gamma version), 161
  class of exclusive-membership games for MU, delta version, 169
  class of exclusive-membership games for MU, gamma version, 169
  class of open-membership games, 156
  class of open-membership games for MU, 166
  class of restricted open-membership games, 158
  class of restricted open-membership games for MU, 167
Coalition, 146
  non-trivial coalition, 147
  trivial coalition, 147
Coalition form, 119
  externally supported, 119
  internally supported, 119
  sustainable, 119
Coalition formation game, 152
  multiple-agreement, 153
  multiple-agreement, simultaneous, 156
    exclusive-membership game (delta version), 160
    exclusive-membership game (gamma version), 161
    exclusive-membership game for MU, delta version, 168
    exclusive-membership game for MU, gamma version, 169
    open-membership game, 156
    open-membership game for MU, 165
    restricted open-membership game, 158
    restricted open-membership game for MU, 167
  sequential, 153
  simultaneous, 153
  single-agreement, 153, 154
Coalition formation index, *see* CFI
Coalition function, 152–154, 156–158,

160–164, 166–169, 174
Coalition structure, 146
external stability, 154
internal stability, 154
number of coalition structures, 146
social optimum, 189
stability of , 154
stable, 151
support set, 171
Coalition-Structure Deviation Set, 176
Coalition-Structure Full Deviation Set, 176
Commitment, 9, 23
Council of Economics and Finance Ministers of the EU countries, *see* ECOFIN
Credibility, 9

Determinant, 43
Deviation, 162, 171–178
full, *see* Full deviation
Deviation set, 172–174, 178
Dimension, 42
Discretionary coordination, 5
Distinction assumptions, 154, 157, 206
size, 157
SNG, *see* Sequential Negotiation Game
status quo, 158
Dominated strategy, 60

ECB, 2, 19–23, 25, 27, 28, 32, 86, 111, 112, 116, 135, 231, 235, 236
ECOFIN, 22, 91, 185, 187
Economic and Monetary Union, *see* EMU
EEC, 16–18
EFTS, 95–97, 102–104
Eigenspace, 44
Eigenvalue, 43
Eigenvector, 43
algebraic multiplicity, 45
geometric multiplicity, 45
EMS, 10, 18, 19
EMU, vii, ix, 2, 10, 11, 16, 19–24, 28–30, 33, 35, 38, 88, 95, 96, 99, 103, 111–113, 146, 159, 186, 188, 230, 231, 234, 235, 277, 304
Endogenous Coalition Formation, 145
ERM, 18, 231
European Central Bank, *see* ECB, 19
European Economic Community, *see* EEC
European fiscal transfer system, *see* EFTS
European monetary integration processes, 16
European Monetary System, *see* EMS, 18
Exchange Rate Mechanism (in the EU), *see* ERM
Externalities
from coalition formation, 145, 150, 151, 191, 202, 211, 246, 247, 250
mixed externality game, 152
negative externality game, 151
positive externality game, 151

Folk theorem, 9
Full deviation, 172, 173, 176
Full deviation set, 172, 173, 175

G-3, 279
G-5, 31
G-7, 2, 9, 29–32, 36, 39, 273, 293, 294, 307
G-8, 31
GATT, 186
General Agreement of Trade and Tariff, *see* GATT
Graph subspace, 51

Hamada's diagram, 6
Hamiltonian matrix, 51

IMF, 30, 31, 34

Independence property, 148, 165, 196, 277
Independent coalition structure, 148, 178, 196
International Monetary Fund, *see* IMF
Issue linkage, 9

Jordan-canonical form, 47

Kronecker Delta, 42

Length (Euclidean), 42
Library Group, 31, 32
Linear (in)dependent, 42
Linear combination, 42
Linear quadratic control problem
 Coopertive game
  theorem, 62
 infinite-planning horizon, 54
  theorems, 55
Linear subspace, 42
Linear System, 53
Louvre Accord, 32

Matrix
 full row (column) rank, 43
 identity, 43
 image, range, 43
 inverse, 43
 negative (semi-) definite, 49
 nonsingular, invertible, 43
 null space, kernel, 43
 positive (semi-) definite, 49
 rank, 43
 spectrum, 44
 square, 43
 transposition, 42
Mercado Común del Sur, *see* MERCOSUR
MERCOSUR, 30, 33, 35, 36, 275, 296

NAFTA, 30, 33, 35, 36, 273, 294
Nash Equilibrium, 154
New-Keynesian
 macroeconomic paradigm, 1
 models, 2
noncooperative Nash equilibrium, 68
 open-loop, 69
North American Free Trade Area, *see* NAFTA
Numerical algorithm for
 open-loop algebraic Riccati equation, 70
 Pareto frontier, 63
 regulator algebraic Riccati equation, 55

OCA, 11–14, 16, 37, 215, 229–231, 234, 248, 253, 261
OECD, 30, 31
Open-loop linear quadratic differential game, 67
 infinite-planning horizon theorem, 70
Optimal Currency Areas theory, *see* OCA
Organization of Economic Cooperation and Development, *see* OECD
Orthogonal vectors, 42
Orthonormal vectors, 42

Pareto, 61
 efficient, 61
 frontier, 61
 solution, 61
Payoff vector, 150
Per-membership partition function, 148, 150–153, 155, 157, 170, 173, 189, 202, 205
Permutation matrix, 78
Plaza Agreement, 32
Prisoners' dilemma, 2, 4, 7, 8

Rule of uncertainty, 10
Rules of coalition formation, 154

Sequential negotiation game, *see* SNG
 (SNG) strategy of the player, 182
 history of the game, 182
Sequential Negotiation Game Equilibrium, *see* SNGE

Set of feasible coalition structures
 full, 147
 MU-reduced, 165
 reduced, 147
SGP, 2, 10, 19, 20, 22–26, 28, 29, 85, 88, 103, 111, 113, 185, 231, 234, 235, 237
Shock, 3, 21, 22, 149
 anti-symmetric, 4
  price, 202, 211–213
 asymmetric, 2, 4, 23, 210
  exchange rate, 241, 254, 256, 263, 275, 279, 286, 287
  price, 200, 207, 209, 213, 220–222, 252, 255, 256, 261–263, 275, 279, 281–285, 291, 292, 306
 country-specific, *see* asymmetric
 demand, 25
 idiosyncratic, *see* asymmetric
 oil, 17
 symmetric, 2, 4, 12, 14, 21, 23, 26, 28, 197, 200, 247, 283, 306
  price, 200, 205, 207–209, 211–215, 238, 244, 245, 247, 252–255, 261, 275, 279–281, 285, 290–293, 295, 307
 technological, 2
 to preferences, 13
SNG, 180, 188, 189, 205, 207–209, 211, 217, 219
 distinction assumptions, 185, 209, 211
  SNG-rank assumption, 185
  SNG-size assumption, 185
 game tree, 180, 184, 206
 history of the game, 182–185
 threat point, 219, 222
SNGE, 183
Span, 42
Spillovers, 3, 15
 competitiveness, 15
 government debt, 15
 interest rate, 15
 output, 15
 price, 15
 via the external exchange rate, 15
Stability and Growth Pact, *see* SGP
Stabilizable, 53
Stabilizing solution ARE, 51, 70
 strongly stabilizing solution, 51, 70
Stable, Hurwitz, 53
Subspace, 42
 graph, 51
 invariant, 47
 orthogonal complement, 42

Two-stage game, 149

Undominated strategy, 60

Welfare index, 190
Werner plan, 17
World Bank, 30
World Trade Organization, 30
WTO, *see* World Trade Organization, 186

MIX
Papier aus verantwortungsvollen Quellen
Paper from responsible sources
FSC® C105338

If you have any concerns about our products,
you can contact us on
ProductSafety@springernature.com

In case Publisher is established outside the EU,
the EU authorized representative is:
Springer Nature Customer Service Center GmbH
Europaplatz 3, 69115 Heidelberg, Germany

Printed by Libri Plureos GmbH
in Hamburg, Germany